The Dictionary

of World Pottery

and Porcelain

By LOUISE ADE BOGER

Furniture Past and Present

The Complete Guide to Furniture Styles

WITH H. BATTERSON BOGER

*The Dictionary of Antiques and
the Decorative Arts*

The Dictionary
OF
World Pottery
AND
Porcelain

BY LOUISE ADE BOGER

CHARLES SCRIBNER'S SONS · NEW YORK

A-5.71 [H]

PRINTED IN THE UNITED STATES OF AMERICA
Library of Congress Catalog Card Number 72-123829
ISBN 0-684-14962-1
1 3 5 7 9 11 13 15 17 19 H/C 20 18 16 14 12 10 8 6 4 2

ACKNOWLEDGMENTS

First, I wish to acknowledge with deep appreciation the many excellent books without which this dictionary could not have been compiled. Our present knowledge of ceramics is predicated on the pioneer research and scrupulous scholarship of these works, which it has been my sincere aim to present accurately and clearly.

My warm thanks for the permissions given to reproduce each photograph, the source of which appears in the accompanying caption. To encounter the courtesy and cooperation of museums, collectors and other sources is always a rewarding experience. I particularly wish to thank the two sources who supplied by far the majority of the photographs: first, The Metropolitan Museum of Art, Mr. John Goldsmith Phillips, Chairman of the Board of Western European Arts, the reference library, the photograph library and catalogue departments, for the many facilities readily accorded; and second, Mr. Hanns Weinberg, Chairman of the Board, The Antiques Company of New York, Inc., The Antique Porcelain Company, who was exceedingly generous and helpful in providing all but several of the colored illustrations.

My deep appreciation to Charles Scribner's Sons for the untiring interest they have given to every detail associated with the production of this book. In particular, I am indebted to my editor, Elinor Parker, whose knowledge and enthusiasm have greatly helped in its preparation.

Finally, my gratitude to my late husband and best friend, Hermon Batterson Boger, who more than three decades ago remarked to me, "Why don't you write a dictionary on antiques, you're not busy," and together we did.   LOUISE ADE BOGER

New York
December 15, 1970

FOREWORD

Out of the earth with understanding
The potter makes everything

(Inscribed on a Pennsylvania-German plate dated 1847)
E. A. Barber: TULIP WARE

This book in dictionary form gives an account of the meaning and significance of the names and terms most frequently encountered in the study of pottery and porcelain over a span of almost 7000 years.

The Dictionary of Antiques and the Decorative Arts supplied the material on ceramics as the original basis of the present work, here adapted to the concept of a dictionary on a single subject, whose purpose is to provide readily accessible, clear and accurate information, in this case on the earliest handicraft of which continuous knowledge exists. I hope *The Dictionary of World Pottery and Porcelain* will share the good fortune of its predecessor.

The vast literature on the subject has been selected and edited to make a comprehensive but concise guide that will be useful to the collector and student as well as the general reader.

The photographs were chosen to promote a fuller understanding and appreciation of the potter's art. The black and white photographs, with notes, serve as a sufficient outline of most of the historical and aesthetic aspects of ceramic art as it developed slowly from prehistoric times to the present. They record the diversity of this subject, mirroring the character and taste of different civilizations, the periods and styles, the materials and techniques, the forms and patterns, and the potters associated with them. The color photographs serve to illustrate qualities that can be made clear in no other manner.

It is hoped that every user of this book will gain much from reading its pages and from the wide scope of its illustrations.

CONTENTS

ILLUSTRATIONS IN COLOR

*Numbers in parentheses at the end of paragraphs refer to
the photographs following page 383.*

A

A R In German ceramics; the cipher (for Augustus Rex)of King Augustus II of Poland "The Strong," reigned 1697–1704, 1709–1733, Elector of Saxony from 1694, and of King Augustus III, reigned 1733–1763, added on Meissen porcelain originally intended for the royal palaces or as royal gifts. However, as the mark was underglaze, before the overglaze enameled decoration was applied, it cannot always indicate that the piece was so used. The mark was more widely used on porcelain dating from around 1725 to 1730 and like the crossed swords of Meissen it sometimes appears in the decoration. See *Meissen.*

Abaquesne, Masséot (d. c. 1564) Probably the first great French master of majolica in the Italian style, working at Rouen from 1526 to 1557. His son Laurent continued his manufactory until around the end of the 16th century. (235)

Absolon, William An independent decorator or enameler working at Yarmouth, England, in the early 19th century. He painted flowers, monograms, shields and crude landscapes on cream-colored earthenware and porcelain obtained from Wedgwood, Shorthose, Leeds, Davenport and elsewhere.

Abstract Pottery A new movement evident in the United States since the later 1950's. In general, abstract pottery, though not intended for practical use, is to be described in such terms rather than ceramic sculpture, since it has visibly or by implication an interior as well as an exterior form. An important figure in this movement has been Peter Voulkos of California. See *Rhodes, D.; Voulkos, P.* (560-562)

Abtsbessingen In German ceramics; a faïence manufactory is believed to have been in existence at Abtsbessingen, Thuringia, from around 1739, founded by the brother of the Prince of Schwarzburg; however, the earliest records are from 1753. The faïence produced here ranks among the best faïence of Germany. The wares are sometimes marked with a pitchfork taken from the Schwarzburg coat-of-arms, together with the painters' initials. Included among their productions were vases, tureens, carefully modeled flowers for table decoration, boxes in the form of pug dogs and cylindrical tankards. The painted decoration was in blue and in other high temperature colors. Enamel colors painted over the glaze in the style of porcelain were also used. The motifs for the painted decoration were in the Baroque and subsequent Rococo styles. Favorite Chinese subjects such as pavilions and Chinese flowers were also found.

Accouchement Set In ceramics; a five, or occasionally nine, piece service designed to fit together in the form of a vase or urn, made in Italy during the Renaissance, and in succeeding years, as a gift for a lady during her confinement. It comprised a broth bowl on the rim of which is placed the plate for bread to serve as a cover; on this an inverted drinking cup which is surmounted by a covered standing salt or salt cellar. As a rule the set was elaborately decorated and seemingly intended for commemoration as much as for utilitarian purposes. This type of set was extensively made in Europe; some were often much more simple.

Acier, Michel-Victor (1736-1795) French modeler working as chief modeler at Meissen 1764 to 1781. His most typical figures, in the sentimental moralizing style, include such groups as The Happy Parents, 1755, and The Broken Bridge, 1777. See *Louis XVI; Kaendler, J. J.; Meissen.*

AUGUSTUS REX
1697-1704; 1709-1763

ABTSBESSINGEN
1739 ON

Adam, Robert (1728-1792) and his brothers, John, James and William, English architects and designers. Robert Adam went to Italy in 1754 and, during the course of his itinerary, he visited the ruins of Diocletian's palace at Spalatro. In 1764 he published a splendid work entitled THE RUINS OF THE PALACE OF DIOCLETIAN. Much of his subsequent work reflected the influence of these studies and was to a large extent based upon them. In 1773, Robert and his brother, James, began publishing WORKS IN ARCHITECTURE which contained designs of many of their more celebrated works and was instrumental in popularizing the Adam style of ornament. Robert Adam was able through his extraordinary ability to mold and adapt classic ornament in such a manner as to create a new treatment for classic ornament which was distinctive for its elegance and grace and for its refined and finished detail. The style of ornament used by Robert Adam was exceedingly rich in variety and was essentially borrowed from the ornament of the ancient Romans. Included among the favorite motifs were festoons of husks, drapery swags, a radiating design resembling a fan, the anthemion or honeysuckle, medallions, rosettes, delicate acanthus scrolling, trophies of armor, vases and urns of classical form, arabesques, the lyre motif, wheat sheafs, garlands, husk chains, classical figure subjects, masks and animal motifs such as the ram's head. See *Classic Revival; Louis XVI; Kauffmann, Angelica; Pergolesi, Michele Angelo; Engraved Designs.*

Adam Style circa 1760-1765 to 1792. See *Adam, Robert.*

Adamantine China See *Wheeling Pottery Company.*

Adams, William and Sons (Ltd.) In English ceramics; a well-known family of Staffordshire potters; earlier titles include W. Adams, W. Adams and Company, W. Adams and Sons; active since 1769 at Tunstall and Stoke. It is generally believed that the first member of this family mentioned specifically as a potter is William Adams (1550-1617) of Burslem. From 1787 onward William Adams (1746-1805) of Greengates, Tunstall, made fine quality jasper ware and cream-colored earthenware. He was succeeded by his son Benjamin who operated the pottery until 1820. Another branch was William Adams (1748-1831) of the Brick House, Burslem and Cobridge, who was a general potter. A third branch was William Adams (1772-1829) of Stoke. He made large quantities of blue transfer-printed wares for the American market in the early 19th century. William Adams (1798-1865) of Greenfield, Tunstall, son of the last named, made similar wares. Late in the 19th century descendants of this Adams acquired the Greengates pottery, which together with other kilns are still worked by them. The name Adams and W. Adams is included in a number of marks of varying design.

Adelberg, Louise See *Rörstrand.*

Aelmis See *Rotterdam.*

Aesthetic Movement In England the *l'art pour l'art* movement was much in evidence in decorative art from the 1870's until the trial of Oscar Wilde, the leading aesthete, in 1895, which resulted in his banishment. The aesthetes were enchanted by the artistic charm of Japan, the medievalism of Morris and Rossetti, the ideals of Ruskin, the elegance of Wilde and the free treatment of artistic ways of expression followed by Whistler. The symbols of the movement—the lily (purity), peacock (beauty) and sunflower (constancy)—were much in evidence. Other manifestations associated with the movement include "blue and white" (Nanking ware) introduced from Paris to London by Whistler. The force of the movement did much to promote a general interest in art and design.

Afghanistan See *Islamic Pottery.*

ADAMS
ENGLAND

ADAMS, W. & SONS
1891 ON

Africa In art; the term *African art* refers to the regions south of the Sahara; the north is a separate area which belongs to the Arabic East. Pottery has long occupied an outstanding position in the traditional cultures of the peoples of Africa. An estimation of its true role and importance must take into consideration the level of these cultures which are essentially simple and are connected with a subsistence economy. Except in relatively rare cases pottery in Africa serves a definite utilitarian purpose. The variety of uses to which fired clay is adapted are considerable. They include ritual objects for ceremonial uses, molds for beads and bracelets, pipes and pipe bowls, sinkers for fishing nets, tuyeres in smithing, spindle whorls, drums, whistles and children's dolls and animal toys. Its most important use, however, is for vessels, namely pots for cooking and jars for water. Owing to the absence from much of Africa of the potter's wheel, most of its peoples rely on simple hand methods, the most common of which are modeling from the lump or from a "saucer" of clay; true coiling; modeling from a "quoit," or, for larger vessels, from a number of quoits placed one upon the other. Molding either around another pot or inside a basket, and building with flattened slabs of clay are two other methods also employed. The body of the vessel is shaped with the simplest of tools. A slip is generally applied. Any artistry finds expression either in the form these utilitarian articles take, such as the mouth of a vessel shaped to resemble an animal's face, or in the decoration, which is generally incised or painted with simple geometrical patterns. Occasionally additional clay is applied as a decorative embellishment. Pottery produced by the Mangbetu, south of the Uele River near Bomokandi, is unique in Africa; the upper portion of the water and wine jugs consists of a female human head with a carefully carved headdress, which, made in a naturalistic style, gives the racial characteristics a portrait-like quality. The face is ornamented with a decorative design composed of rows of dots or lines. The making of pottery is mainly a woman's craft. This is appropriate, for the chief use of pottery is in the domestic field. See *Oceania; Pre-Columbian Pottery.*

Agano In Japanese ceramics; sometime after 1602 the Korean potter Chon Hae in the service of the Hosokawa clan began producing at Agano, in present Fukuoka Prefecture, a Karatsu-type ware known today as Agano ware. In 1632 when the Hosokawa clan moved to a new fief in Kumamoto, Chon Hae accompanied them. He began a new kiln enterprise in an area called Yatsushiro. Chon was almost ninety years old when he died in 1654. His new kilns continued to produce what is known today as Yatsushiro ware until well into the 19th century. Though Agano and Yatsushiro are of the Karatsu type, Japanese connoisseurs today regard the wares produced at these two different kiln sites operated by Chon Hae as two different wares. See *Karatsu.*

Agate Ware In English ceramics; the practice of mixing clays of two or more colors to produce an agate or marbled ware had its origin in antiquity. The solid agate ware made in Staffordshire around the second quarter of the 18th century was produced by mixing white, brown and blue stained clays. A little later the process was adopted by Wedgwood and he produced a material closely resembling natural agate which he made into vases and other similar objects. See *Marbled Ware; Staffordshire.* (390, 391)

Aghkand See *Islamic Pottery, Medieval.*

Ahrenfeldt, Charles (1807-1893) Born in Germany, he started a decorating workshop at Limoges in the 1880's, where he began to produce porcelain in 1894. About the same time he started a porcelain manufactory at Carlsbad-Altrohlau. Both Limoges and Altrohlau were very active

AHRENFELDT, CHARLES
1894 ON

ceramic centers, focusing their attention especially on porcelain wares for the export market. The business was carried on by his son, Charles J. Ahrenfeldt (b. 1856). Among the marks were the initials CA in monogram.

Akae See *Gosu-Akae.*

Akahada See *Kyo.*

Akaji Kinga In Japanese ceramics; the Japanese term given to a style of brocade pattern executed in gold on a red ground, introduced on Kutani porcelain around 1840 by Iida Hachiroemon. See *Kutani.*

Akashi See *Kyo.*

Alabastron In Greek antiquities; a flask for scented oils widely used by women. It had a flat lip rim, narrow neck and an elongated body which was round on the bottom. It was thrown on the wheel as a complete piece. Two lugs were placed high on the body and were used to attach a cord for suspension.

Alafia In Spanish ceramics; an Arabic term meaning pardon, benediction, blessing and the like. Bands of alafia (that is, stylized Arabic inscriptions) are frequently found as part of the decoration on Hispano-Moresque tin-glazed earthenware.

Albany Slip In American ceramics; a rich, dark brown clay, found near Albany, New York, used sometimes as a glaze and after c. 1800 as a lining for salt-glazed stoneware vessels. See *Bennington.*

Albarello In ceramics; an Italian word for a variety of drug or apothecary jar. The form was practically cylindrical. Generally the center was slightly more narrow than the top and lower portions of the body. It had a wide round mouth and foot rim. Sometimes slight characteristic variations occurred in the form. The albarello form was found in Persian and in Meso-

potamian wares from the 12th century, in Hispano-Moresque wares from the 15th century and in the Italian Renaissance majolica wares. The albarello form was also used in other continental wares. One explanation for the derivation of the word is that the name is an Italian corruption of the Persian *el barani,* or a vase for drugs. It is also said that because of its supposed resemblance to a section of bamboo in which drugs were exported from the Orient, it was given the Italian name of albarello or little tree. See *Pharmacy Vase.* (169, 218, 228, 230, 235)

Albertolli, Giocondo (1742-1839) Italian designer of ornament and famous master of the Neo-Classicists in Italy. His decorative designs in the style of the antique were instrumental in developing and diffusing the Neo-Classic art in Italy. He was a director of the Academy of Milan, founded in 1775. See *Engraved Designs.*

Albissola See *Savona.*

Alcock, Samuel and Company In English ceramics; operated a pottery at Cobridge from around 1828-1853; also the Hill Pottery at Burslem, from around 1830-1859; both were in the Staffordshire district. They produced porcelains, earthenwares, parian, ironstone and the like. Among their wares are two early unglazed porcelain busts dated October 31, 1828. They also made transfer-printed earthenwares, molded parian jugs in blue and white, and the widely popular relief-decorated white stoneware jugs. Many classical subjects were copied by this firm and were found painted on porcelain and earthenware vases. They also produced many fine parian articles including a parian figure of the Duke of Wellington modeled by G. Abbott around 1852. Many different printed, painted or impressed marks were used by this firm and incorporate either the initials or name. See *Relief-Decorated Wares.*

Alcora In ceramics; a pottery manufactory

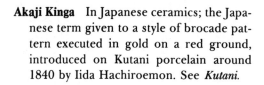

ALCOCK, SAMUEL & CO.
C. 1830 ON

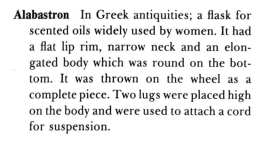

ALABASTRON

founded in Alcora, Valencia, Spain, about 1726 by the Count of Aranda (d. 1749). It was a leading manufactory for faïence in Spain during the 18th century, and the faïence produced there during the lifetime of its founder may be regarded as some of the finest of its kind made in Europe. Its production can be classified in three groups: the tin-glazed faïence from c. 1726-c. 1785, the porcelain first made around 1776 and the cream-colored earthenware made from around 1777. Of these three the faïence was the most important. Especially distinctive was the pictorial painting which was an original feature of Alcora faïence. Good figure modeling in the cream-colored ware is also worth noting. Other earthenware was an imitation of Wedgwood jasper ware and pottery in the English style, and displayed little originality. The manufactory mark of A was used after 1784. See *Soliva, Miguel; Caussada, Jacinto; Aranda, Count of; Faïence Fine.* (291)

Aldegrever, Heinrich (1502-1558) German painter and engraver. See *Engraved Designs.*

Aldgate See *Lambeth.*

Aldin, Cecil Charles Windsor See *Buffalo Pottery.*

Alexandra Porcelain Works See *Turn.*

Alhambra Vase In Spanish ceramics; a celebrated Hispano-Moresque, large pear-shaped vase, with two wing-handles, of tin-glazed earthenware, painted with arabesque foliage, interlacements, and inscriptions in pale blue and golden luster, dating from around 1380-1400, and now kept at the Alhambra Palace, Granada. Several other vases of the same type were formerly there, but they have disappeared. "Alhambra" vases were made at or near Granada or Malaga.

Alkaline Glaze See *Glaze.*

Alkaline-Glazed Pottery See *Glazed Quartz Frit Ware; Roman Pottery.*

Alicatados In Spanish ceramics; a Spanish term meaning cutwork, given to a mosaic tilework made in the Near East, and also made in Spain from around the 14th century. See *Seville; Tiles.*

Alla Castellana Ware In Italian ceramics; a lead-glazed earthenware with sgraffiato decoration. This type of ware was made in Italy from the early Renaissance in the 14th century onward at many important pottery centers. However, the majority of centers producing this ware have not been conclusively identified, with the exception of Bologna and Pavia. It appears that Città di Castello near Perugia and neighboring La Fratta were important centers for producing lead-glazed earthenware with sgraffiato decoration.

Alla Porcellana In Italian ceramics; a contemporary term given to a kind of Italian majolica decoration characterized by foliage in the manner of 15th century Chinese blue and white porcelain or its Islamic derivatives.

Aller Vale Art Potteries In English ceramics; flourished near Newton Abbot, Devon, from 1887-1901. Subsequently the Royal Aller Vale and Watcombe Pottery Company. The Aller Vale wares achieved the distinction of being described and illustrated in the catalogue of Liberty's, the quintessence of fashion in London at the end of the 19th century. See *Linthorpe Pottery.*

Alluaud A prominent family of pottery-owners at Limoges, France. The first Alluaud served as director of the royal factory at Limoges from 1788 to 1793. See *Limoges; Haviland, Charles Field; Bordeaux,* in French porcelain.

Almanac Ware See *Punch'ong.*

Aloncle, François (b. 1734) A painter at

ALBARELLO

ALCORA
1784 ON

N

ALTHALDENSLEBEN
1810 ON

ALTROHLAU

HASSLACHER, BENEDICT
1811-1823

NOWOTNY, AUGUST
1823-1884

ALTROHLAU

ZDEKAUER, MORITZ
1884 ON

MANKA, FRANZ
1833 ON

VICTORIA, A. G.
1918 ON

OSCAR & EDGAR GUTHERZ
1899 ON

Sèvres, 1758-1781, specializing in birds, animals and emblems.

Alpine Pink In English ceramics; self-colored pink translucent bone china introduced in 1936 at Josiah Wedgwood and made in the traditional Wedgwood shapes.

Altar Cup In Chinese ceramics; a white porcelain cup of refined quality having the Chinese character t'an (altar) engraved inside the bowl. It is generally believed that they were first made in the Hsüan Tê period, 1426-1435, of the Ming dynasty. See *Ming*.

Altenburg In German ceramics; an earthenware manufactory was started at Altenburg, Thuringia, Germany, in 1794 by the brothers Döll. It was continued from 1806 by Heinrich Mühlberg. An impressed A is believed to have been used as a mark.

Althaldensleben In German ceramics; a manufactory making cream-colored earthenware and porcelain was started at Althaldensleben, Hanover, Germany, by Gottlob Nathusius in 1810. The mark of the factory was his name or the initial N.

Altrohlau In Bohemian ceramics; a number of factories making china wares for daily use were located at Altrohlau which is near Carlsbad, Austria. An important factory making cream-colored earthenware was started here in 1811 with Benedict Hasslacher as proprietor. H and BH in monogram were among the accepted marks until 1823, when it was taken over by August Nowotny. Until 1884 the mark was AN or his full name. Mortiz Zdekauer became the proprietor and his distinguishing initials MZ are found in marks of different design. The name of the firm is now Altrohlauer Porzellanfabriken A.G. At some time porcelain was added to the production and, judging by the extant quantity in the United States bearing the distinguishing initials MZ, became a popular export product. In 1909 the factory was bought by

C. M. Hutschenreuther of Hohenberg. See *Hutschenreuther, C.M.* In 1833 Franz Manka, whose mark includes his initials in monogram, began to make porcelain. In 1883 the firm Victoria A.G. started in business; included in their production program were souvenirs, as well as tablewares and tea and coffee services. In 1899 a factory was started by Oscar and Edgar Gutherz whose initials O & EG were included in the mark. After the First World War this part of Austria became part of the new country called Czechoslovakia. See *Ahrenfeldt, Charles; Czechoslovakia*.

Altrohlauer Porzellanfabriken A.G. See *Altrohlau*.

Altwasser In German ceramics; a porcelain factory was started at Altwasser, Silesia, in 1845 by C. Tielsch and Company. Their wares received honorable mention at the Great Exhibition, London, 1851, and later in the 19th century became a popular export product to the United States. The distinguishing initials C.T. are found in several marks of varying design. In 1918 the factory was purchased by C. M. Hutschenreuther of Hohenberg. See *Hutschenreuther, C. M.*

Aluminia In Danish ceramics; a ceramic factory founded at Copenhagen in 1863 as a private enterprise. In 1882 Aluminia and the Royal Copenhagen Porcelain Manufactory merged and in 1884 the latter was moved to its present site where the Aluminia factory was already built. Up to about 1900 Aluminia's production was mainly cheap earthenware for daily use. In 1902 when Frederik Dalgas became the new director he decided to do what his predecessor Philip Schou had done so successfully for the porcelain by stressing the importance of artistic influence. He employed two artists, particularly Harald Slott-Møller and Christian Joachim, who agreed with him that earthenware should look like itself and nothing else; that is, not serve as a cheap substitute for porcelain.

The soundness of this new approach was proved at the World Fair at St. Louis, in 1904, where an entirely original collection of bowls, vases and the like was shown decorated in rich underglaze colors in browns, yellows, blues, greens and purples, which attracted international attention. The sharp line once drawn between earthenware and porcelain no longer exists. Ceramists or artists simply chose the material which brings out best their aesthetic aims. Nils Thorsson, who served his apprenticeship under Christian Joachim, and is now leader of the earthenware factory, has brought the decorative technique of stencil color-spraying to perfection, achieving excellent artistic effects. Since 1968 Royal Copenhagen faïence bears a capital A mark crossed horizontally with the characteristic three waves. Apparently Royal Copenhagen gives the name faïence to earthenware possessing artistic merit, and not necessarily a tin-glazed ware.

Amberg In German ceramics; a faïence pottery was founded at Amberg, Bavaria, Germany, in 1759 by Simon Hetzendörfer. The pottery began to manufacture cream-colored earthenware and porcelain in 1790. The manufactory was in existence until 1910. Much of the production was limited to useful wares in plain white or crudely painted in blue. The mark on the faïence was AB in monogram. The cream-colored ware was marked with the name of the town Amberg impressed.

Ame-Gusuri In Japanese ceramics; the Japanese term, literally caramel glaze, given to a dark brown glaze introduced in the early 14th century on vessels made at the Seto kilns.

American Craftsmen's Council Established by Mrs. Vanderbilt Webb in 1943, it has been chiefly responsible for the renaissance of craftsmanship in America. The Council, following the trail blazed by William Morris, has enforced, within the new order of things, a respect for the hand-made product and has secured the recognition of the individual artist-craftsman. See *Arts and Crafts Movement.*

American Porcelain Manufacturing Company In American ceramics; started at Gloucester, New Jersey; produced soft paste porcelain from 1854 to 1857. The Gloucester China Company established in 1857 was a continuation; no decorating was done and all ware was sold in the white. Closed in 1860.

American Pottery Company In American ceramics; in 1833 David Henderson organized the American Pottery Manufacturing Company at Jersey City, New Jersey, which was a continuation of the D. and J. Henderson pottery already established here. Two new printed pottery marks were adopted, one in the form of a flag, the other elaborate and elliptical. For about the next seven years they chiefly made earthenware with a buff- or cream-colored body of fine quality. In 1839-1840 for the first time in America the English method of transfer printing was successfully adopted by these works. About this time the designer and modeler Daniel Greatbach was employed here where he designed a number of relief-decorated items including the well-known Rockingham hound-handle pitcher. In 1840 the company was reorganized and its name was changed to the American Pottery Company. The new name appeared in the impressed marks. In 1845 the business passed into new hands, and the name Jersey City Pottery Company was adopted. All lines were discontinued except for common white earthenware which was made until 1854 when the company was dissolved. Next it was purchased by a company consisting of Rouse, Turner, Duncan and Henry. Shortly after, the last two withdrew and the company was reorganized once again under the title of Rouse and Turner. Wares of a high quality were produced, but they were made for the trade to

ALTWASSER
TIELSCH, C. AND COMPANY
C. 1850 ON

ALUMINIA
FAIENCE 1968 ON

AMBERG
1759 ON

A.P.M. Cᵉ

AMERICAN PORCELAIN
MANUFACTURING COMPANY
1854-1857

AMERICAN POTTERY
COMPANY
c. 1833-1840

AMERICAN POTTERY
MANUFACTURING COMPANY
1840-1845

be decorated and sold. The wares were never marked, except for white ware to be decorated, on which they placed the British Royal Arms with a lion and unicorn, and beneath the distinguishing initials R. and T. In brief, after 1845 little or nothing made at the Jersey City Pottery possessed interest for collectors. In 1892 when the pottery passed into other hands, the old buildings which had stood for almost seventy-five years were torn down, bringing to an end one of the oldest ceramic landmarks in the United States. See *Jersey Porcelain and Earthenware Company; Greatbach, D.; Relief-Decorated Wares.* (435, 436)

American Pottery Manufacturing Company
See *American Pottery Company.*

Amol   See *Islamic Pottery, Medieval.*

Amphora   In Greek antiquities; the amphora, a vase with two sturdy vertical handles, extending from the neck to the shoulder, was a popular shape for the storage of wine. It was also used as a container for olive oil, honey or water. There are two principal types; namely, the amphora with the neck and body forming a continuous curve, and the amphora with the neck set off from the body by a definite change in contour, the so-called neck-amphora. Amphorae varied in size. The panathenaic amphora, which was extremely large, was filled with oil and presented to victors at the Panathenaic games, part of a festival held every four years in Athens in honor of the Goddess Athena. The decoration followed a fixed pattern; with Athena on one side and on the other the contest for which the prize was given, such as a race or other games. It bears an inscription: I am [a prize] from the games at Athens.

Amphora Porcelain Factory   See *Turn.*

Amstel   In Dutch ceramics; see *Weesp.*

AMPHORA

PANATHENAIC AMPHORA

Amsterdam   In Dutch ceramics; it is certain that some of the early majolica made in the Netherlands was produced here, perhaps as early as 1557, and the manufacture of tiles continued to exist throughout the 17th and 18th centuries, but the Amsterdam production can seldom be identified. Adriaen Jansz Bogaert, probably a member of the Antwerp family of majolica potters, is mentioned in 1587. The Old Prince or De Oude Prins was Amsterdam's most important tile factory. It was active from 1649 to 1802. The ware was very well known and tiles were exported abroad. See *Old Prince, The; Netherlandish Majolica; Antwerp; Dutch Tiles; Tiles.*

An-hua   In Chinese ceramics; a Chinese term meaning "secret decoration," faintly engraved, or painted in white slip on white porcelain which can be seen only when the piece is held to the light. See *Ming.*

Anasazi   In pre-Columbian Southwestern United States ceramics; early representatives of the Anasazi were living in the Southwest of the United States at the beginning of the Christian era, but they made no pottery and are named Basketmakers after their fine baskets, the majority of which were made by the coiling method. Eventually they began to mold vessels of clay mixed with vegetable fibers in baskets and dry them in the sun. This phase lasting until about 700 A.D. is called the Modified Basketmaker period. Subsequent developments are divided for convenience into the following periods: Developmental Pueblo, 700 to 1050; Great Pueblo, 1050 to 1300; Regressive Pueblo, 1300 to 1700. These are followed by Historic Pueblo which lasts until the present day. The first pottery was plain grey ware fired in a reducing atmosphere and shaped like gourds or baskets, and occasionally bowls had designs like those on baskets, painted in black on the inside. The earliest pots were built up from rings and later from continuous coils of clay which were obliterated by scraping while still wet. In the Developmental Pueblo period the most typical type is a black and white pottery in which the pottery is decorated in black over a white slip. Many kinds of black-on-white pottery were made in the Developmental and Great Pueblo periods. The shapes are relatively few and simple, comprising open bowls, bowls with constricted mouths known as seed jars, ladles, mugs and jugs or pitchers. Essentially the designs are simple; they are either hatched, longitudinally or diagonally, or blacked in, and consist chiefly of triangles, rectangles, zigzag bands, frets, spirals and the like. Apart from the black-on-white wares, black-on-red wares with similar designs were made. Polychrome wares were introduced in the Great Pueblo period. These can be made by the addition of white to the black-on-red ware. Notable innovations and great changes mark the Regressive Pueblo period. Black-on-white wares were no longer made; polychrome wares were remarkably developed. In addition to the geometrical designs, stylized life forms, such as birds, feathers, animals and masked human figures, were much used. Yellow and red backgrounds predominate due to the use of iron-bearing clays and an oxidizing atmosphere in firing. Bowls and jars were by far the most common forms. Since the Great Pueblo period, the region was divided into a number of areas, the pottery of each having distinctive features. For example, an important area is named after the settlement of Hopi in northeast Arizona, where a black-on-yellow ware was developed by the addition of red into the striking Sikyatki polychrome. The deliberate use of glaze containing lead or copper for ornamental purposes, but never for waterproofing, was introduced during the Regressive Pueblo period. Cremation and jars to contain the cremated ashes also date from this time. See *Southwestern United States Pottery.*

Anatolia   See *Near East,* in prehistoric ceramics; *Islamic Pottery.*

Ancient American Pottery   See *Pre-Columbian Pottery.*

Andean   In pre-Columbian South American ceramics; the central Andean region was the scene of the highest development not only in civilization in general but also of the potter's art in South America. Here are found examples of the most advanced processes of manufacture and almost every decorative technique used by South American potters. Utilitarian pottery was first known about 1200 B.C. and comprised egg-shaped jars with rounded bottoms. About 800 B.C. a more advanced people appeared, whose complex culture named Chavín or Cupisnique must have been developed elsewhere. The Chavín people introduced some very notable decorated pottery which was used solely for ceremonial purposes, especially for burial with the dead. The whistle jar and the vessel with a stirrup-shaped handle serving as a spout are common in this area. The body of the vessel takes many forms; objects represented include animals or their heads, fruits and vegetables, sea shells and rarely human figures or houses, molded in the round or less frequently in low relief. In time the technical processes were improved, resulting in well-fired vessels, and more decorative techniques were introduced including coarse brush painting and later negative or resist painting in which the design appears in the color of the body of the pot against a black background. The distinctive Recuay style was centered in the highland area of the Santa River valley of central Peru and is currently thought to date from 300 B.C. to A.D. 700. Here is found a great variety of vessel forms of white clay with positive decoration in red and overall negative designs in black. Some vessels are simple in shape, but complex forms are also characteristic and many include groups of small figures—men, llamas and buildings—representing a scene. In the south coastal region a distinctive pottery style is found in association with the early occupation of the Paracas Peninsula known as Paracas Cavernas. The forms include bowls and jars and modeled life forms. Many are decorated with incised lines enclosing areas of bright color, yellow, green and red with a predominantly black background. This Paracas Cavernas pottery forecasts features of south coast pottery which were to develop more strongly later; namely the manner of depicting life forms which is usually inferior to that of the north coast and the use of many colors in contrast to the two or three colors which were used in the north at the same time. The highest point of technological development appears to have been reached in the last few centuries B.C. or the beginning of the Christian era when a considerable region, now called Mochica, flourished in a group of north coastal valleys centering in that of the Chicama River, while smaller groups of people, probably related to one another, lived in the south, in the Nazca valley and close to the Paracas Peninsula. Mochica and Nazca peoples are notable for their pottery and Paracas people for their textiles. The third is the Tiahuanaco style which marks the highest development of pottery in its respective area. The conquest of most of the coast by the bearers of the Huari or Tiahuanaco culture marks the end of Mochica and Nazca culture. This conquest probably dates from around the end of the first millennium A.D. and is marked by the introduction of a widespread pottery style known as Coast Tiahuanaco or Epigonal. This style is found throughout the coast except in the extreme north, and from the coast it appears to have spread into the northern highlands. It differs from the pottery found at Tiahuanaco itself, but is decorated with Tiahuanaco motifs, including pumas and condors, which may have

party eyes (eyes divided vertically into black and white halves; "party" is the heraldic term), and figures with bird masks shown in profile. According to southern tradition the designs are brightly painted in polychrome. Finally three states emerged on the coast—north, center and south; the most significant was Chimu in the north which roughly covered the same area as the Mochica and may be considered its successor. Each area had its typical pottery style, but that of Chimu alone had recognizable qualities in common with its pre-Tiahuanaco predecessor. The chief focus of the pottery style of the central state was the Chancay Valley and it is known as Chancay Black-on-White, or White style. The pottery of the vicinity of Ica is typical of the southern state. It is a hard, burnished, buff, orange or red ware, chiefly decorated with textile-inspired patterns in black, white and red. The rise of the Incas and their conquest by the Spaniards brings this period to an end. See *Mochica; Nazca; Tiahuanaco; Chimu; South American Pottery; Whistling Jar; Stirrup Vessel.* (15-20)

Andokides See *Red-Figure Ware.*

Andreoli, Maestro Giorgio (d. ·c.1553) Majolica potter and master of ruby and gold luster-painting at Gubbio. See *Gubbio.*

Andries, Guido See *Antwerp.*

Angoulême In French ceramics; a faïence manufactory was started at Angoulême, Charente, in 1748 and remained active until late in the 19th century. As a rule the wares were unmarked, but rare pieces bear the name of the town in full. The wares were in imitation of those made at Rouen and Moustiers.

Angoulême Porcelain See *Rue de Bondy.*

Annam See *Indo-China.*

Ansbach In German pottery; a manufactory for producing faïence was started around

1708-1710 at Ansbach, Bavaria, Germany, with the support of the Margrave Frederick William of Brandenburg, by Mathias Bauer (d. 1725), manager. After 1747 it was under the management of the Popp family. It changed ownership in 1807 and closed in 1839. Ansbach faïence was not regularly marked. The mark was often signed by the chief painter, sometimes with the date and the name of the town being added. After 1769 the mark A.P. was sometimes used. The mark, On, which stands for Onolzbach, another name for the town, was occasionally found. Much of the early ware reflected the influence of Delft and Hanau and was painted in a clear full blue. The finest work was done from about 1729 to 1757. This ware was in imitation of the Japanese brocaded Imari pattern or imitated the Chinese Famille Verte coloring and design. Included among their wares were cylindrical tankards, enormous vases and faïence figures. Some of the finest German faïence was produced at this factory. After 1769, when the manufactory was entirely owned by the Popp family the wares were relatively unimportant. See *Löwenfinck, A.F.von; Popp.* (288)

Ansbach In German porcelain; around 1758 porcelain was produced in the faïence manufactory at Ansbach with the support of the Margrave Earl Alexander (d. 1791) and managed by Johann Friedrich Kaendler. In 1762 the porcelain kiln was moved to the Margrave's hunting castle at Bruckberg. It flourished until 1791, and in 1806 it ceased to operate as a state concern but survived privately until 1860. The mark was an A with or without an eagle of Brandenburg and the shield of arms of Ansbach in underglaze blue. On figures the shield mark was impressed. Much of the ware was not marked. Their finest productive period was from around 1767 to 1785. This porcelain ranks with the finest German porcelain. Many Ansbach figures were notable for their singular delicacy. Decorative and useful wares were distinc-

tive for their finely molded designs and painted decoration.

Anstett, François-Antoine I (1732-1783) Painter and potter working at Strasbourg, Niderviller, 1754-1779, and potter at Haguenau. The factory at Haguenau was carried on by his widow and sons.

Antimony See *Colors; Yellow.*

Antiques Law Effective February 1, 1967. By Public Law 89-651, objects 100 years old are designated as "antiques." The law affects objects arriving in the United States from abroad and frees them from duty. It supersedes the earlier rule setting 1830 as the date before which an object became "antique." The 1967 law relieves importers of customs duty on glass, porcelain, silver plate, tables, case furniture and chairs.

Antonibon, Giovanni Battista See *Nove.*

Antwerp In Netherlandish ceramics; the first and principal center producing pottery of the majolica type in the Netherlands until the second half of the 16th century when persecutions and the war with Spain which began in 1568 severely injured the prosperity of Antwerp and caused many craftsmen to migrate to Haarlem, Amsterdam and Delft. It is recorded that in 1512 Guido Andries (d. c.1541), a potter from Castel Durante, started a pottery at Antwerp which was carried on by his sons who died in the 1570's. One son started the first recorded pottery in Holland at Middelburg in 1564. Another son or grandson moved to Norwich and then to Lambeth, launching English delftware on its career. Another important family was named Floris; members of this family later worked in Spain. Jan Boghaert (or van den Bogaert) was active from 1552 to 1561, and his son of the same name is noted in 1575. Also recorded is Barnaert Vierleger (or Fierleger) and his son Hans Barnaert who moved to Haarlem around

ANSBACH

A. P

FAIENCE 1769 ON

PORCELAIN C. 1758 ON

1598. In the course of the century a number of styles were created differing from the Italian. A most distinctive and striking Antwerp variety is marked by the use in the designs of strapwork, volutes and scrolled devices imitating ironwork (ferronnerie) in the style of the designer Cornelis Bos and Cornelis Floris, both of Antwerp, Pieter Coecke of Aelst and Hans Vredeman de Vries of Leeuwarden. See *Netherlandish Majolica; Janson, Jacob; Amsterdam; Faïence; Engraved Designs.*

Ao-Bizen In Japanese ceramics; the name given to an unusual variety of Bizen ware made from a greyish-green clay which was greatly admired during the Edo period, 1615-1868. See *Bizen.*

Ao-Kutani See *Kutani.*

Apfelstädt, Johann Adam See *Schwerin.*

Apocryphal Mark A false mark copied from a legitimate mark of an earlier period, as frequently found on Chinese porcelains, where the names of earlier reigns famous for porcelain were generally used. It appears clear, however, that the name chosen did not necessarily bear any relation to the type of ware to which it was to be added. For example, the names of Hsüan Te, Ch'êng Hua and Chia Ching are common on K'ang Hsi porcelain of many kinds that were new in that reign. However, this centuries-old practice of both the Chinese and Japanese of copying their classical wares and adding the marks of earlier periods is not always inspired by honest piety. See *False or Fake Marks; Mark,* in ceramics.

Apostle Jug See *Minister Jug.*

Apostle Tankard See *Kreussen.*

Apple Green In Chinese ceramics; a green transparent enamel, varying from a light to a dark emerald green, distinctive for its luster, iridescence and brilliance, applied over a greyish or brownish crackled white glaze. It has shining white flakes, called by the French *ailes de mouches,* or fly's wings, which were caused by the internal breaking of the enamel over the crackle. Apple green wares, which are principally small pieces, were first made during the K'ang Hsi reign, 1662-1722. See *Ch'ing.*

Aprey A French faïence manufactory was founded in 1744 by Jacques Lallemant de Villehaut, Baron d'Aprey, and his brother, Joseph. The finest period of production was from around 1769 to 1792. Its best work was a type of painted colored enamel decoration in the style of Strasbourg. The manufactory closed for a period during the French Revolution and reopened in 1806. It operated under various changes of management until 1885. The accepted mark is AP or APR in a monogram, although it was not always used. Their finest work ranks with the best of French faïence decorated in painted enamels. It was known above all for its painted decorations of birds and flowers and for its grounds of striped pink ribbons copied from Louis XVI silks.

Apt In French ceramics; an important center for pottery making. The earliest pottery was established at Le Castelet near Apt in 1728 by César Moulin, and it remained in the Moulin family until 1852. Other pottery factories were founded in and around Apt. The finest Apt wares are of excellent quality and are distinctive for their finished workmanship and graceful forms. An early type was a yellow ware, the forms for which were molded after silver objects such as écuelles or porringers and ewers. Especially characteristic was a fine yellow and brown marbled pottery made into useful wares and figures. This marbled pottery was decorated with applied leaves and flowers and scrollwork in white or a light-colored clay. See *Faïence Fine.*

Apulian Pottery In ancient Greek ceramics; in the 5th century B.C. the Greek colonies in Southern Italy witnessed the rise of a group of artists whose pottery reveals

APREY
C. 1744 ON

their Athenian training. Noteworthy of these local styles are the red-figure vases found at Apulia.

Arabesque In ornament; a word simply meaning Arabian applied to a particular form of decorative design displaying a fantastic or intricate interweaving or interlacing of lines. It is applied to the grotesque decoration derived from Roman mural paintings and stucco work of the early Roman Empire and not to any form derived from Arabian or Moorish work. The term is more or less restricted to the varieties of Italian Renaissance decorations which are a development derived from Greco-Roman grotesque designs revealed in ancient excavated buildings. With this in mind it seems that grotesque is a more appropriate name for these decorations than arabesque. A marked feature in this later Renaissance decoration is a floriated or foliated standard branching out with graceful and symmetrical intertwining lines of scrollwork, branches and leaves enriched with animals, birds, humans and fanciful figures. The arabesques of the Renaissance are elaborate and extravagant in their design with naturalistic and grotesque human and animal figures as well as trophies, armor and vases within the scrollwork. The arabesques in the Loggia of the Vatican executed by Raphael are said to have been inspired by those found in the ancient buildings of Rome and Pompeii. Later arabesques by such French designers of ornament as Bérain, Audran and Pierre Le Pautre are remarkable for their varied and fanciful composition. See *Grotesque; Raphaelesque; Bérain, Jean.* (233, 234, 239)

Arabesque A dinner service. See *St. Petersburg; Pompeian Taste.*

Arabia In Finnish ceramics; the industrial ceramic production of Finland is mainly concentrated in one great factory near Helsinki known as Arabia, started in 1874 as a subsidiary of the Swedish firm Rörs-

trand. Apart from porcelain it also produces earthenware and tiles. Imitative earlier styles were followed until around 1900 when the well-known Finnish "Romantic" painter Kallela (in Swedish, Gallen) provided designs. In 1916 Arabia was released from Rörstrand. From the 1920's under the leadership of Swedish-born Thure Öberg, who was art director from around 1900 to 1931 and of artist-designers such as Greta-Lisa Jaderholm-Snellman, works of importance were produced. Finnish-born Kurt Ekholm, talented designer and potter, succeeded Öberg as art director. Shortly after the Second World War in 1948 a separate design-planning studio was started under Kaj Frank, who was formerly known as a glass and textile designer. In the same year Frank designed the revolutionary "Kilta" service introduced on the market in 1953, which set a precedent for many others in Finland and elsewhere. "Kilta" is a range of oven-proof earthenware vessels in several plain colors, a multi-purpose service, which combines the functions of cooking, serving and use at the table. This has been followed at the Arabia factory, for example, by the deep brown "Liekki" heat-resisting ware designed in 1957 by Ulla Procopé which is designed in such a manner that the pieces can be stacked and that the lids of cooking vessels can be used as serving dishes. Such wares represent a new approach to functionalism, and when well designed can be pleasing. In recent years since the 1940's Arabia has produced important ceramic pieces made by a number of Finnish sculptors, all of whom studied at the School for Arts and Crafts at Helsinki. Among these may be included Austrian-born Friedl Holger-Kjellberg who came to Arabia in the mid-1920's; Birger Kaipiainen, Kyllikki Salmenhaara, Michael Schilkin and Rut Bryk whose unique ceramic plaques with their narrative content and beautiful glazes have won world acclaim. Arabia is a subdivision of the Wärtsilä group, the oldest art industry

ARABESQUE

ARABIA
PRESENT

in the country, founded in 1793. (503, 508, 510)

Aranda, Don Buenaventura Pedro, Count of (d. 1749) Founder of the Alcora faïence factory in Alcora, Spain. Under his son, Don Pedro Pablo (d. 1798) the famous tenth count, the factory was constantly experimenting to improve the quality of their faïence, and to investigate new methods of making porcelain and cream-colored earthenware.

Arbeid, Dan English artist-potter; active at the Abbey Art Center, New Barnet, Hertfordshire, since 1956 producing studio-type stonewares. His vases are frequently formed by coiling, a process often used to achieve a more personal interpretation of shape than is possible by throwing on the wheel. See *Leach, B.* (557)

Arcanist In ceramics; a workman claiming knowledge of the secret of porcelain making and other important pottery methods, especially in the 18th century. Although some arcanists did possess valuable knowledge many were imposters. The strict measures enforced at Meissen to prevent a leakage of Böttger's secret for making porcelain proved an incentive for many runaway workmen. See *Ringler, J. J.*

Ardus In French ceramics; a faïence manufactory was started at Ardus, in Quercy, Tarn-et-Garonne, around 1739 by François Duval, Baron de Lamothe (d. 1744) under the management of Denis Molinié. After 1744 it was leased by various persons and remained in existence until 1876. The early wares, 1739-1752, are in the Moustiers-Bérain manner and of good quality.

Argentina (northwest) and Chile (northern) In pre-Columbian South American ceramics; both regions were incorporated in the Inca Empire. Of the indigenous pottery styles, the best are connected with the name of the Diaguite, a tribe or group of tribes who were living in a large part of both areas when the Spanish arrived. Though it is doubtful that the Diaguite made all of the pottery ascribed to them, they are reliably associated with a distinctive group of styles in Chile. In one type, the vessels are decorated in red, white, and a color which is more often grey than black. Geometrical motifs prevail, and are occasionally interrupted by a highly conventionalized face, with some details indicated in relief. In northwest Argentina the most familiar and distinctive pottery is the Santa Maria urn decorated in black on a·yellow or white slip. In general the designs appear to represent a highly stylized human figure clad in elaborate textiles. These urns come from the central part of the area, while in the south is the Belen urn, with characteristically black-on-red painted decoration, the designs being much less complex than those on the Santa Maria urns. See *South American Pottery.*

Arikawa Modern Japanese artist-potter; working near Tajimi in the Gifu Prefecture. He typifies that group of Japanese artist-potters who have made it their life work to revive and continue some of the traditional Japanese pottery styles. Arikawa is identified with the Shino style. His tea bowls made by methods and materials used in the area for several hundred years are highly prized by collectors. See *Seto; Rosanjin, Kitaoji.*

Arita In all her ceramic wares Japan owed her technical knowledge entirely to one or other of her two neighbors, Korea and China. In the early part of the 17th century the southern island of Kyushu witnessed a great and fairly sudden emergence of beautifully decorated enameled porcelains. Essentially it could happen suddenly as the techniques were available in the Ming and Ch'ing porcelains imported from China. A Korean potter named Yi, called Sampei, who is found in the records

ARNHEIM
1755-1773

with a variety of given names, is credited with the discovery of clay deposits suitable for fine porcelain at Izumiyama near the village of Arita in the province of Hizen in 1616. Yi was one of the many experienced Korean potters taken captive during Hideyoshi's invasion of Korea in 1592 and brought to Japan two years later. Yi's discovery eventually led to the production of several different kinds of porcelain wares in this area, known today under a variety of names: Imari, Kakiemon and Nabeshima. Throughout the 17th and 18th centuries porcelain was costly in Japan and its use was limited to the aristocracy and the rich merchant class. Except for a brief period when Japan was able to enter the export market due to a shortage of Chinese porcelain wares, the industrialization of ceramics in Japan did not occur until after the Meiji Restoration, 1868, when clan control was abolished. The bulk of the Japanese porcelains exported came from the Hizen kilns. It is generally accepted that the first considerable export of Japanese porcelains for the Asian and European (Dutch) market occurred around 1658-1659. By 1750 the great days of export were over. From 1804 onward the quality of Arita wares declined. In 1829 a great fire destroyed almost the whole of Arita and a great tidal wave damaged the coasts of Kyushu. From 1850 onward attempts were made to resume the industry. The surface texture of Japanese porcelain compares to that of "muslin" and this is true for the ordinary run of Arita wares. The finest of Kakiemon wares are of a fine milk-white dense texture with a rather greasy sheen. See *Imari; Kakiemon; Nabeshima; Japanese Porcelain Motifs; Shonsui; Blue and White,* in Japanese ceramics; *Celadon,* in Japanese ceramics; *Hizen.*

Arkhangel'skoe See *Iusupov, Prince Nikolai Borisovich.*

Armenian Bole See *Turkish Pottery.*

Armorial Ware As the name indicates, this ware is decorated with a coat-of-arms. From the time of the Renaissance onward, coats-of-arms were widely used on European wares. In Chinese ceramics; a kind of export porcelain made and decorated in China with the crests of European and American families. These arms are generally in the colors called for in the original arms, but in the early period of the late 17th and early 18th century the arms are often all in underglaze blue. Occasionally the arms are found executed en grisaille and then the direction of the hatching (horizontal lines for blue, vertical lines for red, dots for gold) will indicate the various colors of the arms. It would be well to mention that a coat-of-arms belongs to a specific individual and not to a family, while the crest is used by all the members of the family. A full coat-of-arms includes the crest which rests on a bar or wreath of the two major colors of the arms, which in turn is above a helmet. Beneath is the shield, and if the arms carry them, a motto and figures, often animals, on each side of the shield which are called supporters. The form of the arms and the surrounding decoration varies from large arms with profuse decoration or mantling, in the first part of the 18th century, to a plain spade-like shield without any decoration at the end of the century. The various styles of the arms, starting with those of profuse decoration, are known as Early English, Jacobean, Chippendale, Festoon, Spade and Plain Armorial by bookplate collectors and their dates definitely defined. See *Chinese Lowestoft.* (114, 217, 219, 220, 224, 271, 273)

Arnheim or **Arnhem** In Dutch ceramics; a faïence manufactory was founded at Arnheim in 1755 by Johannes van Kerckhoff. The wares were largely in the manner of Delft. Around 1756 it was taken over by J. Hanau, and it ceased to operate in 1773. Especially characteristic was painted decoration in deep blue or manganese of good quality. The accepted mark is a cock.

Arnoux, Léon (1816-1902) See *Minton.*

Arras In French ceramics; a French soft paste porcelain manufactory was founded in 1770 at Arras, Pas de Calais, by Joseph François Boussemaert of Lille. About a year later it was taken over by four ladies, Demoiselles Delemer, dealers in faïence. It ceased to operate in 1790. The wares were patently made in rivalry with the wares of Tournay. Tablewares alone were made here. The accepted mark was AR.

ARRAS
1770-1790

Arretine See *Roman Pottery.*

Art Deco An assertively modern style which became dominant in Europe and America in the 1920's and 1930's. The name Art Deco was the subtitle of the catalogue of the great exhibition Arts Décoratifs held at Paris in 1925. There are many other names for this style: Modernistic, Art Moderne, Functional, La Mode 1925, Les Années 25, to mention a few. It drew inspiration from various sources, including the more severe aspect of Art Nouveau (Secession); Cubism; the Russian Ballet; ancient Egyptian art; the design of Aztec temples and the Bauhaus. It was a classical style as it observed symmetry rather than asymmetry, and the rectilinear rather than the curvilinear. Its ultimate aim was to end the conflict between art and industry. The influence of Art Deco was widely disseminated in metal work, glass, cabinetwork, silver, textiles and ceramics.

Art Moderne A style brought into existence by the Paris Exposition of 1925. See *Art Deco.*

ARRETINE CUP

Art Nouveau A significant movement possessing the desire to break with the past, to start anew. It flourished between 1895 and 1905, and was in full bloom around 1900. It possessed the merit, as did the English Arts and Crafts Movement, of reviving handicraft; it was the 19th century's final reaction against the machine. Art Nouveau, acclaimed as New Art, was never free from the bondage of the historical past. It reveals features from earlier traditional styles, especially the Gothic, Rococo and Baroque. Each in its own way contributed to mold Art Nouveau—the first in theory and to some extent in ornament, especially the Flamboyant Gothic with its flame-like and leaf-like tracery; the second with its application of asymmetry; and the third with its plastic conception of form. It also found inspiration in the highly linear and colorful art of Japan. In part it was an inspired return to nature; sensuous undulating lines studied from the movement of growth are a striking feature. The sinuous whiplash curve became Art Nouveau's typical contour, embracing the arts of decoration with forms reminiscent of plants and flowers. Art Nouveau at its best, rich in linear rhythm, reveals a harmony of line which is noteworthy in the history of decorative art. This New Art may be placed midway between Historicism and the Modern Movement. It was more concerned with decoration than with form, which explains its sudden demise as the rumblings from the Modern Movement with its emphasis on form, which was slowly evolving in Germany and Austria, kept increasing in intensity. In ceramics; Art Nouveau, a markedly linear style, was chiefly expressed in the decoration. It was, however, associated with a vogue for tall, slender forms and in its mature development it also affected details of shaping. Essentially Art Nouveau was more often found in the works of artist-potters or of small art-potteries than in the products of the great factories. See *Rozenberg; Zsolnay; Japanism; Bracquemond, F.; Gallé, Emile; Solon, L. V.; Jugendstil; Léonard, A.; Modern Movement; Secession; Maison de l'Art Nouveau.* In American ceramics; around 1900 the influence of the French-inspired Art Nouveau became evident. Among the most important potters working in the new style were Grueby, van Briggle, Tiffany and the group of decorators working for the Rookwood and Newcomb potteries. Characteristic of Art Nouveau in America was the appearance of a number of large commercial art-potteries, especially the Zanesville, Ohio, potteries of J. B. Owens, S. A. Weller and Roseville which quickly exploited the original ideas of the American artist-potters and of the international style of this time. See *Grueby, William H.; Briggle, Artus van; Tiffany, Louis C.; Weller, S. A.; Owens, J. B.; Roseville; Rookwood; Newcomb; Pewabic Pottery.*

Art Pottery In its widest meaning, the phrase *art pottery* might be interpreted to apply to all creative, decorative wares; but in the later Victorian era, when it was most widespread, the phrase carried with it the implication of pottery which was intentionally creative or artistic. In this context art pottery was apt to reflect the intellectual, "aesthetic" approach of the period and to interpret in a more or less popular sense the ideals of the Arts and Crafts Movement. See *Artist-Potter; Studio-Pottery; Doultons Lambeth School of Art.*

Art Workers' Guild In English arts and crafts; founded in 1884. Walter Crane and Lewis F. Day were its leading originators. See *Arts and Crafts Movement.*

Arts and Crafts An inclusive title for the arts of decoration and handicraft; that is, all those that contribute to the making of the house beautiful. The title is also identified with the movement usually understood as the English revival of the decorative arts, which began about 1875. During the 1880's England built up an artistic vitality which affected all Europe. This was the decade when the English guilds for arts and crafts were founded and produced some of their best work. See *Arts and Crafts Movement.*

Arts and Crafts Exhibition Society See *Arts and Crafts Movement.*

Arts and Crafts Movement The title, originating in England, came into general use when the Arts and Crafts Exhibition Society was founded in 1888 with the aid of William Morris. The Arts and Crafts Movement was, in the words of Morris, "to help the conscious cultivation of art and to interest the public in it." It brought a revival of artistic craftsmanship. Between 1880 and 1890 five societies for the promotion of artistic craftsmanship were started: Century Guild, 1882; Art Workers Guild, 1884; Home Arts and Industries Assocation, 1884; Ashbee's Guild and School of Handicraft, 1888; Arts and Crafts Exhibition Society, 1888. England was the home of the Arts and Crafts Movement which made important contributions not only to the theory of handicrafts but, also, finally, to the concept of industrial design. See *Morris, William; Design and Industries Association; Arts and Crafts; Craft Centre of Great Britain; Council of Industrial Design; American Craftsmen's Council; Associated Artists.*

Artel In modern Bohemian ceramics; the spirit of Austrian design in the early years of the 20th century was evident at Prague in an organization under the name Artel, formed in 1908 by a group of architects, artists and designers to produce well-designed articles in various media. In the ensuing years the products of its workshops included ceramics designed by such architects as Vlastislav Hofman and Pavel Janák, whose geometrical forms conveyed an emphatic Cubist approach. See *Secession.* (225)

Artificial Porcelain See *Soft Paste.*

Artigas, Joan Gardy See *Artigas, J. L.*

Artigas, José Llorens Spanish Catalan artist-potter; working in Paris from the end of the First World War for a long period. In the 1920's he began to produce ceramics for the painter Raoul Dufy, and later for Pierre Albert Marquet. Since 1944 he has

ARYBALLOS

ARZBERG

HUTSCHENREUTHER, C. M.
1918 ON

SCHUMAN, CARL
1881 ON

ASKOS

produced distinguished pottery, tilework and ceramic sculpture in collaboration with his old friend and fellow Catalan the painter Joan Miró. In 1954 he left Barcelona and settled at Gallifa with his son Joan Gardy Artigas, who is also a ceramist. Artigas is a potter of considerable importance in his own right, producing stoneware which depends entirely upon the beauty of exactly controlled glazes and a Mediterranean intuitive sense of form. Artigas would have nothing to do with such conveniences as electric or gas ovens, nor did he approve of commercially prepared glazes and clays. The technique of high-fired pottery was dear to him. Tradition, and perhaps the very nature of the method, compelled him to construct his own kiln, to choose his own wood and to supervise the firing very closely. In a like manner, preparation of the clays and sandstones, and mixing and applying the glazes, require exacting care. Owing to his approach he is able to enrich his art continually. He can assert his personality so strongly because he is involved personally in every stage of preparation and execution. See *Gauguin, Paul; Miró, Joan; Leach, B.* (541)

Artist-Craftsman See *Artist-Potter.*

Artist-Potter Properly a potter who designs as well as makes his own pots in order to establish his complete responsibility for the object produced. The conception of an artist-potter may vary from the studio-potter to the artist-craftsman or designer-craftsman who produces designs for industrial wares but also produces his own studio work. See *Leach, B.; Deck, T.; Artigas, J. L.; Binns, C. F.; Gustavsberg; Studio-Potter.*

Aryballos In Greek antiquities; a small container filled with olive oil, carried by athletes, provided with one or two handles for attaching a thong to loop over the wrist or to hang on the wall. As a rule aryballoi are globular in shape with either a cup-shaped lip rim (generally with two handles) or a wide disc-shaped lip rim (generally with one handle). Occasionally the bottom of the body of the aryballoi was formed flat, so it would not turn over when it was set down.

Arzberg In German ceramics; a porcelain factory was started at Arzberg, Bavaria, in 1834 by von Acker, making fine dinner services, wares for daily use and hotel wares. In 1918 it was purchased by C. M. Hutschenreuther of Hohenberg. See *Hutschenreuther, C. M.* The still-existing Schumann porcelain factory at Arzberg, Bavaria, was started in 1881 by Carl Schumann. The wares are of notably fine quality. The distinguishing initials C S or Schumann are found in several marks of differing design. The modern style of table service has been firmly established at this factory since the Second World War.

Aschach In German ceramics; a pottery making cream-colored and other earthenwares in the English style was worked at Aschach in northern Bavaria by Wilhelm Sattler and his son from 1829 to 1860. The impressed marks were W S & S and Aschach.

Ashbee, Charles Robert (1863-1942) English architect, designer and writer; in 1888 he founded in the East End of London the Guild and School of Handicraft, with himself as chief designer. In 1902 Ashbee moved to Chipping Campden, in the Cotswolds, in his attempt to revive handicraft far from the center of modern living. Here he started the School of Arts and Crafts, which lasted from 1904 to 1914. The Guild itself functioned until 1908. See *Arts and Crafts Movement.*

Ashikaga The Ashikaga period in Japan, A.D. 1333-1573. See *Japanese Periods.*

Askos In ancient ceramics; a small vase or jar used as an oil vessel. (67)

Associated Artists In American decorative

arts; the Louis C. Tiffany Company, Associated Artists, formed in 1879, followed the trail blazed by William Morris and his followers. It was launched as a guiding hand to improve taste in the decorative arts and to restore an interest in them. The group comprised Candace Wheeler (1827-1923); John La Farge (1835-1910); Lockwood de Forest (1850-1932); Samuel Coleman and Louis C. Tiffany (1848-1933). They decorated interiors for many private homes and public buildings, including the White House, in 1882-1883. See *Arts and Crafts Movement; Tiffany, L. C.*

Astbury, John (1686-1743) In English ceramics; John Astbury and his son Thomas, who began producing wares around 1725, and other members of the same family were potters in Shelton and in other parts of Staffordshire in the 18th century. The name *Astbury* is generally applied to a type of earthenware covered with a lead glaze of yellowish tone. The color of the body varied from a red which became dark brown under the glaze, to a chamois color. The ware was decorated with applied reliefs, generally made of a white pipe clay, which were stamped, molded or modeled by hand. Birds, coats-of-arms, lions, vine leaves and grapes were included among the motifs. The reliefs were usually in white on a dark-colored ground; however, the color scheme was sometimes reversed. Occasionally a piece of Astbury ware was made in an almost white clay and can be considered among the earliest examples of cream-colored earthenware. However, the characteristic Astbury earthenware still consisted in part of colored clays. Some early pieces of Astbury ware date from around 1730 and some late pieces around 1745; its characteristic production flourished around 1739. The wares associated with the Astbury name were never marked. See *Portobello; Staffordshire.* (385, 386, 388)

Astbury, Thomas See *Astbury, John.*

Asuka The Asuka period in Japan, A.D. 538-645. See *Japanese Periods.*

Atkinson and Company See *Southwick Pottery.*

Atri See *Castelli.*

Attic See *Greece.*

Aubergine In Chinese ceramics; a pure purple enamel or glaze derived from manganese. It is generally accepted that the color aubergine was first used on porcelains made during the Ming dynasty, 1368-1644.

Audran, Claude (1658-1734) One of the foremost French decorative artists of his time. He is noted for his designs and compositions of figures, flowers, leaves, arabesques, grotesques and attributes which contributed in a large part to the creation of the Rococo style of ornament of the 18th century. The decorative designs of Watteau and Gillot were undoubtedly inspired to some extent by the work of Audran as well as by Bérain. See *Rococo; Engraved Designs.*

Augarten Porcelain Manufactory A 20th century Viennese firm. See *Vienna; Secession.* (499, 501)

Augustus Rex See *A R.*

Auliczek, Dominicus (1734-1804) Sculptor of Bohemian birth; modeler at Nymphenburg, 1753-1797; succeeded F. A. Bustelli as master modeler in 1764 and was in charge of the factory until 1793. His severe but accomplished work in the Louis XVI style is in marked contrast to that of Bustelli. Some single figures of birds, dogs and monkeys and groups of animals, such as lions or wolves attacking horses or stags, are notable essays in the style of Oudry and are perhaps his most interesting work for the factory. His son, Dominicus II, was also a painter and an assistant to his father at Nymphenburg, 1794-1797, and was again working there in 1808. He is

AUDRAN, DECORATIVE DESIGN

believed to have been the owner of a porcelain factory at Regensburg around 1830.

Ault, William English potter and proprietor. In 1887 he established the Ault Pottery, a small art pottery, at Swadlincote in southern Derbyshire where he produced earthenwares. Much of the style and emphasis of Ault's pottery was reminiscent of Linthorpe ware; in the years around 1892 to 1896 Christopher Dresser produced a series of pottery designs for William Ault. In 1923 it became Ault and Tunnicliffe, Ltd., and subsequently in 1937 to the present day Ault Potteries Ltd. See *Linthorpe Pottery; Tooth, Henry.*

Ault and Tunnicliffe Ltd. See *Ault, William.*

Ault Potteries, Ltd. See *Ault, William.*

Aumund In German ceramics; a faïence manufactory was founded at Aumund near Vegesack, Bremen, in Hanover, in 1751. It was in operation only until 1761. Included among its wares were tureens in the Rococo style and cylindrical tankards painted in blue or in high temperature polychrome. The wares were essentially without distinction. The marks were the initials of the various owners: MTT; D & WT and AvE.

Austin, Jesse See *Pot Lids.*

Australia See *Oceania.*

Austria, Czechoslovakia and Hungary In ceramics; the early Hafner wares of Austria are closely related to those of Germany, especially Salzburg. The faïence of the former Austrian Empire comprises for the greater part peasant pottery of remarkably vigorous design. Habaner ware or peasant majolica of Moravia and Hungary is another distinctive variety. The only Hungarian factory making faïence patronized by the aristocracy was Holitsch. In the early 19th century a considerable number of potteries making cream-col-

ored earthenwares were active in Bohemia, at Kaschau and Prague. In the 18th century the only porcelain manufactory of any significance was that of Vienna, which was in decline in the second quarter of the 19th century and finally closed in 1864. Bohemia, now the metropolitan area of Czechoslovakia, was in the 19th century the leading ceramic-producing region of the Austro-Hungarian Empire. In the early part of the 19th century a number of small porcelain manufactories were started at Schlaggenwald and elsewhere in Bohemia. In the latter part of the 19th century manufactories at Altrohlau, which is near Carlsbad, Bohemia, produced china for everyday use, much of which was for the export market. The early 20th century was a period of great activity in the Austro-Hungarian Empire. Around 1900 the Art Nouveau style was strongly manifested in the work of the Zsolnay firm of Pécs in Hungary, while in Austria the Secession movement proved an important stimulus to Austrian ceramics. In later years the influence of Austria in industrial ceramics stemmed chiefly from the Augarten porcelain factory of Vienna, started in 1922. See *Vienna; Altrohlau; Holitsch; Pirkenhammer; Schlaggenwald; Prague; Hafner; Zsolnay; Czechoslovakia; Secession; Wiener Keramik; Artel; Turn; Hungary,* in contemporary ceramics; *Herend; Habaner Ware.*

Austrian Art Nouveau See *Secession.*

Austrian Werkbund See *Deutscher Werkbund; Oesterreichischer Werkbund.*

Autio, Rudy (b. 1926) American potter-sculptor and teacher; concerned with architectural ceramics; working at Missoula, Montana. His work is representative of a movement toward abstract pottery that has been evident in the United States since the later 1950's. The prominent leader in this group has been Peter Voulkos of California. See *Voulkos, P.*

Avelli, Francesco Xanto Of Rovigo, gener-

AULT POTTERY
1887 ON; 1937 ON

AULT AND
TUNNICLIFFE LTD.
1923-1937

AUMUND
1757-1761

ally known as Xanto, painter at Urbino about 1530–1540. A master with a recognizable character, his compositions, like those of Pellipario and other *stile bello* (or istoriato style) artists, were often inspired by engravings, particularly those of the school of Raphael. See *Urbino*. (232)

Avignon   In French ceramics; a class of distinctive pottery vessels in elaborate forms covered with light or dark brown glazes was produced here late in the 16th century. Of particular interest were some color-glazed ewers or jugs with extravagant applied decoration in green and yellow glazes on an aubergine ground. (200)

Avisseau, Jean Charles   (1796-1861) French artist-potter of Tours, who is believed to be the first potter to revive the work associated with the 16th century potter Bernard Palissy. He began to make Palissy wares in the early 1840's. He also made wares in the Henri Deux manner. He was followed by his son, Edouard, and his nephew, Landais. See *Saint-Porchaire*.

Avon   In French ceramics; lead-glazed wares in the style of Bernard Palissy were made at Avon and at neighboring Fontainebleau in the 16th and 17th centuries. Well-known as a class of figures and groups. (207-209)

Awaji   See *Kyo; Kochi; Shuhei, Ogata; Mimpei, Kaja*.

Awata   In Japanese ceramics; the history of ware made in the Awata district in Kyoto is essentially one of individual studio potters. The celebrated potter Ninsei and many of his followers, including several members of the Dohachi family, worked at Awata and elsewhere. See *Ninsei; Dohachi, Ninami; Bunzo, Hozan; Eisen, Okuda*.

Aynsley, John and Sons (Ltd.)   In English ceramics; John Aynsley established himself as a master potter in 1775 at Lane End (name changed to Longton around 1848) in the Staffordshire district. In those early days he specialized in the manufacture of beer and cider mugs, decorating them in color from his own engravings with illustrations of sporting, political and humorous events. As the custom of tea drinking grew in England, Aynsley began to produce tea services. The pottery prospered. John Aynsley was succeeded by his eldest son, James, and later by his grandson, John. During the latter's lifetime the factory was built on its present site and the company went to the forefront of the manufacture of fine bone china, a position it has occupied ever since. Today the company specializes in the manufacture of dinner and tea services. The bulk of their production is exported.

Aztec   In pre-Columbian Central American ceramics; although black-on-orange pottery was found long before the rise of the Aztecs, 1325-1521, this ware is usually known as Aztec as later examples are very common in Tenochtitlan (Mexico City) founded in 1325. It is yellowish or orange in color, unpolished, well fired and relatively thin, enriched with painted decoration in the form of very thin-lined geometrical or concentric patterns. In the late Aztec phase, 1400-1521, naturalistic bird, animal and floral designs executed in very thin black lines embellished with thicker areas of red prevailed. The forms comprised the usual range of plates and bowls with or without tripod supports. See *Central American Pottery; Mixteca Puebla Pottery*. (14)

Azulejos   In Spanish interior decoration and ceramics; the term *azulejos*, which is the Spanish and Portuguese name for tiles, is derived from the Spanish *azul* meaning blue; however, the word was probably adopted at a later date because the early tiles were in polychrome. It is generally accepted that polychrome pottery tiles as a wall decoration originated in the Near East in the 9th century and were later made in Spain around the 14th century. These

AWAJI PLATE

AYNSLEY, JOHN & SONS
1891 ON

polychrome pottery tiles were used in Spanish interior decoration for dadoes and frequently for the facings of doorways, windows and window seats. They were also used to line the interior of niches, and for the enrichment of stairs, generally only the risers but occasionally for the treads as well. The fashionable Dutch monochrome tiles in blue and white or in manganese purple and white were made during the 17th and 18th centuries in Spain; however, the traditional polychrome tiles continued to be made in the regional districts where the latest fashions were of little concern to the inhabitants. See *Seville; Tiles.*

B

Bachelier, Jean-Jacques (1724-1805) Art director at Vincennes and Sèvres, 1751 to 1793. About 1751-1753 Bachelier introduced unglazed porcelain, called biscuit, as a material for figure modeling and thus initiated a European porcelain fashion. He was largely responsible for the invention of the distinctive Vincennes and Sèvres styles of painting. The high standards of Sèvres productions during the first forty years of the manufactory's existence were no doubt due mainly to Bachelier's ability. He called in the best artists of the day, Jean-Baptiste Oudry, François Boucher and others, to design models especially for Sèvres, such as Boucher's Children (Les Enfants de Boucher). See *Blondeau.*

Bacile Amatori In Italian ceramics; emblematic love-gifts in majolica. A well-known Castel Durante type of dish painted with portraits, generally of ladies and helmeted warriors, was perhaps an invention of Nicola Pellipario.

Bacini In ceramics; the Italian term for painted and glazed earthenware plaques that were set into the walls of churches in different Italian cities as ornaments to the architecture. They were made in Italy, Spain, and more often in the Near East. Early majolica plaques served a similar decorative purpose.

Backstamp In English ceramics; the use of a backstamp is a feature of great interest associated with transfer-printed pottery. It is the small printed device on the underside of a piece of pottery which gives much information. The device is invariably decorative and charming, but with character and quality. It will probably give the name of the fanciful scene—Passion Flower, Venice, Aladdin, Siam, Toyoda or countless others—the maker's trade name for the body such as opaque porcelain, new stone or granite ware, and the distinguishing initials or the name of the maker. See *Transfer Printed Ware; Flow Blue.*

Badarian See *Near East,* in prehistoric ceramics.

Baden-Baden In German ceramics; after earlier and ineffectual attempts, a faïence and porcelain manufactory was established here in 1770 by Zacharias Pfalzer with private financial aid. It was active until 1778. All types of porcelain including busts and figures were made and were simply decorated with flowers of different colors. It was marked with the Baden coat-of-arms under an Electoral Hat. Glazed earthenware or faïence fine was also made and was decorated like the porcelain. Another and very active manufactory was founded in 1795. It made glazed earthenware or faïence fine in the English style. All types of wares were made including stoves. Relief decoration was especially characteristic and popular. The mark was AA impressed.

Badorf In German ceramics; a well-fired unglazed earthenware, comprising useful pots and storage jars, occasionally enriched with horizontal grooves and bands, was made at the village of Badorf, near Bonn, from around 720 to 860. This new type of unglazed pottery supplanted the post-Roman wares of western Central Europe with their typical shapes. These vessels showed an appreciable tendency toward squatter, more or less rounded shapes. A continuation of provincial Roman tradition is seen in some of the decoration, such as rouletted raised bands on the Badorf storage jars. The other two groups in this class of unglazed wares are Mayener and Pingsdorf. Badorf wares were exported down the Rhine to England and

FAENZA BACINI

BACKSTAMP
1842-1844

BADEN-BADEN
1770-1778

23

the Baltic regions. See *Mayener Ware; Pingsdorf.*

Baggs, Arthur   See *Binns, Charles F.*

Baignol   See *Limoges.*

Balzar-Kopp, Elfriede   German artist-potter; first became prominent in the 1920's. He produced elegant stoneware and also purely sculptural works.

BANKO

Bamboo Ware   In English ceramics; a dark shade of cane ware made to imitate bamboo. It was introduced by Wedgwood in 1770. See *Cane Ware.*

Bampi, Richard   (d. 1966) German artist-potter; first became prominent in the mid-1920's; worked for a short time at the Bauhaus; also influenced by Max Laüger. At one time interested in majolica, he concentrated on stoneware from the late 1930's onward.

Banded Hedge   See *Japanese Porcelain Motifs; Kakiemon.*

Banko   (1736-1795) Japanese amateur potter of Kuwana in the province of Ise, who copied Raku, Ninsei and Kenzan. He also decorated porcelain in the style of the Late Ming red and green enameled export wares, the so-called Swatow wares. Banko's seal and his favorite types of wares have been widely imitated. See *Ninsei; Kyo; Swatow; Gosu-Akae.*

BARANOVKA
C. 1801 ON

Baranovka   In Polish ceramics; a porcelain factory was started at Baranovka, Volhynia, Poland, by Michael Mezer (d. c. 1825), and his brother in 1801. It is believed that production ceased in 1895. The wares of the Empire period rivaled in style of decoration and quality those of the Russian Imperial manufactory. Among the marks were Baranovka and an Imperial double eagle.

Barbeaux   In ceramics; a French term meaning cornflowers given to a conventional decoration of sprigs of cornflowers widely used in French and English ceramics. It is reputed to have been designed in 1782 by Hettlinger of Sèvres for Marie Antoinette. However, it was commonly used on a number of French porcelains produced during the late 18th century and early 19th century.

Barber's Basin   In ceramics; an oval shallow pottery basin of the 18th century having the center portion of one side cut out in a semicircular manner so that it could be held against the front of a person's neck. It is also made in other materials such as pewter. (253, 426)

Barberini Vase   See *Portland Vase.*

Barbotine   In ceramics; the French term for slip. Designs drawn by means of a slip of creamy consistency (of white pipe-clay) freely trailed on in the manner of icing-sugar on a cake. This style of slip decoration is usually referred to as barbotine. This technique required the utmost sureness of touch and permitted no hesitations or afterthoughts. See *Slipware; Roman Pottery; Castor Ware; Slip; Pastillage.*

Barcelona   See *Catalonia.*

Barlaston Period   1940-. See *Wedgwood, J.*

Barlow, Hannah, Florence and Arthur   See *Doulton, Lambeth and Burslem.*

Baroque   A French word meaning whimsical or irregularly shaped as applied to the arts, apparently taken from the Italian word *barocco* meaning a misshapen pearl. The word did not obtain any wide usage until around the middle of the 19th century when it was derisively used to describe a later phase of Renaissance art. It is commonly considered that Michelangelo led architecture and the decorative arts into the ways of the Baroque. It first became evident in Italy during the latter part of the 16th century, with Rome, which is called the Baroque city, being the fountainhead of Baroque art. The Italian architect and sculptor Bernini is often regarded as the creator of the Roman Baroque. In Italy Baroque art was purely a continuation of the art of the late 16th century and reached its culmination around the middle of the 17th century. This later phase of Renaissance art was in reaction against the classical purity and pedantic perfection of the High Renaissance. Baroque art is characterized by a dynamic sense of movement, a dramatic planning and bold contrast, and very often massive forms. As a rule it has an air of splendid vitality and stateliness which offsets to a great extent its violation of High Renaissance design and ornament. Some Baroque art with grossly exaggerated and unsuitable ornament can best be described as a lapse in discretion. The classic ornament was of a sculpturesque and florid character and its plastic possibilities were completely exploited. Cartouches, large foliated scrolls, C-scrolls and S-scrolls, volutes, heraldic devices, banderoles, grotesques, human figures, and strapwork in intricate designs were all included among the favorite Baroque motifs. The Baroque style was known in France as the Louis XIV style where it was developed under the patronage of Louis XIV, 1643-1715. It was supplanted by the Rococo style of ornament which differs from the Baroque in its lightness and its avoidance of the characteristic symmetry of the latter. In ceramics; in the latter part of the 17th century Baroque began to make itself felt with the adoption of the designs of Jean Bérain, Daniel Marot and of the Augsburg and Nuremberg school of engravers. The Louis XIV style in France and the Laub-und-Bandelwerk of Germany are aspects of the Baroque of particular significance for ceramic art. Various types of the Baroque in ceramic decoration are seen in certain examples of early Rouen faïence, Saint-Cloud porcelain, Castelli and late Venice majolica, early Doccia porcelain, Bayreuth faïence, Vienna and Meissen porcelain. In figure modeling the work of the Meissen artists Johann Kirchner and Johann Kaendler belongs essentially to the Baroque. See *Rococo; Bérain, Jean, the Elder; Marot, Daniel; Laub-und-Bandelwerk; Meissen; Rubens, Peter Paul; Louis XIV; Michelangelo; Chinoiserie; Bernini, G. L.; Engraved Designs; Ferronnerie; Lambrequin; Style Rayonnant.*

Barr, Flight and Barr   See *Worcester.*

Bartmann Jug or **Bartmannkrüge**   In German ceramics; a Rhenish salt-glazed stoneware jug having a bearded mask molded on the front. It was first made toward the end of the 15th century onward throughout the 17th century. Toward the end of the 16th century it was given the name of *bellarmine* because of the supposed resemblance of the bearded mask to the face of Cardinal Bellarmino who was intensely disliked in the Protestant countries. The English name of *greybeard* was also given to the globular Bartmann jug. See *Rhenish Stoneware; Frechen.* (192)

Barum Ware   See *Brannam, C. H.*

Basalt or **Black Basaltes**   In English ceramics; the term *black basaltes* was the name given by Wedgwood to his black stoneware introduced around 1769. It was the first ornamental ware developed by Wedgwood. Essentially it was a refinement of a ware previously made in Staffordshire around 1740. The stoneware is a dense fine-grained material and is extremely hard. The black color is derived from iron and manganese. After its improvement by Wedgwood it was made by many contemporary potters in Staffordshire as well as in other places in England. It was also made on the Continent. Wedgwood used black basaltes for both ornamental and useful wares. A large number of relief plaques, vases, busts, medallions, portraits and small intaglios were made in black basaltes. It formed also the ground on which Wedgwood made classical encaustic paintings with a special palette of enamel colors

JEAN LE PAUTRE, BAROQUE DESIGN

that gave a mat surface though unglazed when fired, and resulted in a similar effect to that of the early Greek and Etruscan vases. Relief decoration of black basaltes started in the jasper period of 1774 and has been carried on ever since, using models created by Flaxman, Hackwood, Stubbs and others. See *Wedgwood, Josiah.* (421, 507)

Base Ring Ware See *Near East,* in prehistoric ceramics.

Bat Printing In English ceramics; a variety of transfer-printed decoration in which the impressions of the stipple engravings were taken on soft, flexible glue sheets or bats instead of the earlier method of taking the line engravings on thin sheets of paper. In this bat printing method the impressions are taken in oil and the transferred design is later dusted with enamel pigment. This method was introduced in England toward the end of the 18th century. See *Transfer-Printed Wares.*

Batavian Ware In Chinese ceramics; a porcelain ware made during the K'ang Hsi period called Tzu Chin or lustrous brown. It derived its name from the trading station in Java of the Dutch East India Company who imported this ware into Europe. See *Tzu Chin.*

Batenin, Sergei (d. 1814) In Russian ceramics; founded the small but important Batenin porcelain manufactory at St. Petersburg in 1812. It was carried on by his sons Peter (d. 1829) and Filipp (d. 1832). It is generally accepted that operations ceased in 1839 as a result of a fire. They specialized in vases and tea services. Their best wares possess a naïve charm of a distinctly Russian provincial flavor. Among the marks were S.B.; B; SFMB (St. Petersburg Factory of the Merchant Batenin). See *Russia.*

Batkin, Walker and Broadhurst In English ceramics; Staffordshire potters working at

Church Street, Lane End, 1840-1845, producing earthenwares, stonewares and the like. The distinguishing inititals B W & B are found on several printed marks of differing design; the name of the individual pattern is often included.

Bauhaus In Weimar, 1919, a new school and workshop, the Staatliches Bauhaus, was opened under the directorship of Walter Gropius to teach experimental methods of designing for the machine. It was also established at Dessau and Berlin. The school's chief workshop at Dessau, designed by Gropius, was one of the important buildings of the 1920's. Closed by the National Socialists in 1933, the Bauhaus was pre-eminent in establishing internationally a style of design related to the requirements of machine production. Its theories are often summarized in the slogan of functionalism: form should follow function, creation for use. In ceramics; the effect of Gropius' teachings was worked out and transmitted to the world through the work of several artists connected with the school; in particular, Gerhard Marcks, Theodor Bogler, Otto Lindig and Marguerite Wildenhain. Such work was not only significant for its own time, but it also established the standards for important designs made after the Second World War. See *Weimar School for Arts and Crafts; Modern Movement; De Stijl; Gropius, W.; Zeisel, Eva; Lindig, Otto.*

Baumann, Hans Theo See *Rosenthal.*

Bauscher Brothers See *Hutschenreuther, Lorenz; Weiden.*

Baxter, Thomas (1782-1821) Son of an independent porcelain painter who had a workshop in London. At first Thomas II also worked independently in London, then for Flight and Barr at Worcester, later for Swansea and finally returning to Worcester. He painted in numerous styles—birds, flowers, shells, landscapes and figures in a classical or romantic manner.

БАТ.Е
НАСА-БАТЕН.

BATENIN, SERGEI
1812-C. 1839

Bayer, Johann Christoph (1738-1812) Nuremberg artist living at Copenhagen from 1768 where he decorated the famous Flora Danica porcelain service. See *Flora Danica*.

Bayreuth In German ceramics; one of the most outstanding German manufactories of the late Baroque era was started at Bayreuth, Bavaria, around 1713-1714. It produced beautiful faïence and a fine brown glazed ware with gilt, silver and engraved decoration. It closed in 1852. Its finest work was from around 1728 to 1745. One variety of faïence was painted in a pale mist-like tone of blue. Another variety of faïence consisted of fine pieces painted with coats-of-arms enclosed in rich Baroque strapwork borders. A third type of faïence comprised fine distinctive work of several well-known artists. After 1728 the ware was frequently marked. The mark consisted of the initials of the place and the owners, together with the painter's marks. They produced fine brown and yellow glazed ware. The Bayreuth brown glazed ware was not a stoneware but a reddish earthenware covered with a manganese brown or red glaze. The yellow glazed ware was practically the same except that it was lighter in body and was covered with a buff or pale yellow glaze. The typical decoration for this brown and yellow ware is in fired-on gold and silver and is often beautifully painted. Engraved decoration was also done. Porcelain was also produced at Bayreuth; however, not very much is known about the porcelain production. It apparently was first made around 1745-1748 and at later intervals.

Beaker Folk A people of the Bronze Age, c. 2000 B.C., widely spread over Europe and the British Isles, who are associated with a distinct type of prehistoric pottery known as bell-beakers. These are drinking cups, 7-8 inches high, varying in color from light brown to bright red and profusely decorated with intricate incised geometrical designs. (80)

Bear Jug In English ceramics; a stoneware vessel in the form of a sitting bear, frequently hugging a small dog. The head of the bear was detachable and formed a cup. The jug is identified with the wares made at Staffordshire and Nottingham during the 18th century. Essentially it was a rather awkward and clumsy jug.

Beautiful Style See *Stile Bello*.

Beauvais In French ceramics; toward the end of the Middle Ages Beauvais potters were the first in France to make hard non-porous pottery or stoneware. An extant stoneware dish with a blue-tinted glaze over low relief decoration dates from 1497-1521. The fine quality of these grès azures de Beauvais (blue stonewares of Beauvais) was widely acknowledged. See *Berry*. (198)

Beek, Jan Bontjes van German artist-potter of Dutch birth; a potter of remarkable sensitivity; since the mid-1920's he has been an important figure in German artist-pottery. His work in stoneware with fine glaze effects, both before and after the Second World War, has been pleasing and influential.

Behrens, Peter (1868-1940) German architect, painter and graphic artist; one of the leading artists in the Munich School. He first worked as a designer of glassware, jewelry, porcelain and furniture in 1898. He was an original member of the artist colony of Mathildenhöhe from 1899 to 1903. His first building was his own house in the artist colony, 1901, for which he also designed the interior decoration and furniture. Here his style began to turn away from Jugend's linear rhythm to the more simple and geometrical. This is apparent in a porcelain dinner service of advanced modern design with straight-sided dishes which Behrens designed and was made by Bauscher Brothers of Weiden, Oberpfalz, Germany, around 1901. See *Jugendstil; Munich School; Mathildenhöhe; Weiden*.

BAYREUTH
C. 1713-C. 1727

BEAR JUG, STAFFORDSHIRE

Belen Urn See *Argentina and Chile.*

Belfast See *Ireland.*

Belgium A country in northwest Europe, formerly part of the Low Countries or Netherlands; the name only came into general use with the foundation of the modern kingdom in 1830. See *Netherlandish.*

Bell A foremost family of American potters who worked throughout the 19th century in a hundred-mile stretch of the Shenandoah Valley, just south of Pennsylvania. The first was Peter Bell who from 1800 to 1845 made earthenware utensils at Hagerstown, Maryland, and Winchester, Virginia. His oldest son John Bell worked at Waynesboro, Pennsylvania, and in turn was followed by five sons who carried on the pottery until about 1900.

BELL, J. AND M. P.
AND COMPANY
C. 1881-1928

Bell, J. and M. P. and Company (Ltd.) In Scottish ceramics; operated the Glasgow Pottery, Dobbies Loan, Glasgow, Scotland, 1842-1928, producing earthenwares, parian and the like. The distinguishing initials J. B. or J. & M. P. B & Co. are found on several marks of differing design. A bell or eagle often occurs in these marks.

Bell Krater See *Krater.*

Bellarmine In German ceramics; see *Bartmann Jug.*

BELLEEK POTTERY
1863-1891

Belle Vue Pottery See *Hull.*

Belleek In Irish ceramics; the Belleek factory in County Fermanagh, Northern Ireland, was established around 1863 after earlier successful experiments were made with the local clay. The factory was managed by David McBirney and Robert Williams Armstrong under the name McBirney and Company. The wares, including figures, were first introduced at the Dublin Exhibition of 1865. The factory used a parian-like body with a characteristic iridescent pearl-like glaze. Skilled

BELLE VUE POTTERY
C. 1826-1841

workmen from Staffordshire were employed and the range of objects quickly grew and included the now traditional Belleek marine form objects and openwork baskets. The standard mark is printed and includes a central tower, a dog and a harp above the word Belleek. As a rule the wares are very thinly potted or cast and are as a result very light. The factory has changed ownership several times. At the present time Belleek includes in its production many designs of the 1865-1875 period, as they continue to win new admirers each year. In American ceramics; perhaps the most typical American porcelain of the later 19th century was Belleek or "eggshell" china. Ott and Brewer made ivory porcelain in Trenton in 1876 for the Centennial Exhibition held in Philadelphia. It was decorated to look like Belleek and was greatly admired. In 1883 Ott and Brewer brought the Bromleys from Ireland who knew how to make Belleek. From 1883 to 1892 Ott and Brewer made this new type of especially thin porcelain with a pearl-like glaze. Belleek became popular almost overnight and was soon produced by other Trenton firms, particularly the Willets Manufactory Company, the Ceramic Art Company (renamed Lenox in 1906) who produced a shell-shaped dish in 1887 and the swan dish in 1890, and the Columbian Art Pottery. A considerable amount of Belleek was made by Knowles, Taylor and Knowles of East Liverpool in the 1880's, who soon afterward developed a similar ware known as Lotus ware, perhaps America's finest porcelain at that time. See *Luster; Brianchon, J. J.; Parian.* (456-459, 478)

Bellevue A French faïence manufactory was founded at Bellevue around 1755 by Lefrançois. In 1771 the ownership passed to François Boyer and Charles Bayard who received permission to use Manufacture Royale. It is generally accepted that their most important wares were figures and groups in a chalk-like biscuit. Terra-cotta painted garden figures and wares for daily use in faïence and faïence fine were also made. Some of the excellent faïence fine tableware was distinctive for its charming decoration of landscapes painted in black or brown monochrome. The characteristic 18th century mark on biscuit figures was Bellevue Ban de Toul, incised. The mark Bellevue, impressed, was common on the excellent faïence fine tableware. Potteries are still active at Bellevue.

Belvedere See *Warsaw.*

Benckertt, Hermann Hausmaler, originally of Sweden; painter in Schwarzlot (black enamel) in a style derived from Johann Schäper, working at Nuremberg and perhaps also at Regensburg, around 1670-1680. See *Schäper, Johann; Schwarzlot.*

Benckgraff, Johann Porcelain arcanist. See *Ringler, J. J.*

Benedetto, Maestro Painter of Italian majolica first recorded at Siena in 1509.

Bengtson, Hertha See *Rörstrand.*

Bennett, Edwin In 1846 English-born Edwin Bennett started a pottery at Baltimore. In 1848 he was joined by his brother William who withdrew in 1856. During this period the mark was E & W Bennett, Canton Ave., Baltimore, Md. Afterward the distinguishing initials E B alone or in marks of varying design were commonly found. The pottery used some hard sage-green and blue-colored bodies for relief-decorated jugs and pitchers in the English manner, notably a "marine" jug ornamented with relief designs of fishes. It also used much earthenware with the deep brown Rockingham glaze for objects of ths type, such as the well-known teapot with a relief decoration of Rebekah at the Well. This teapot was modeled by Charles Coxon, a competent designer who was with Bennett for about twelve years until 1863, when he started Coxon and Company at Trenton,

N. J. Copies of the flint enamel and other wares of Bennington were also produced. Victorian majolica with colored glazes appears to have been made by Bennett as early as 1853. It included the well-known large fish pitchers with a light blue glaze and molded designs of fish, lobsters and shells. Vases with grapevine designs and lizard handles, pitchers, coffee pots and other pieces with blue, brown and olive mottled glazes were produced at this pottery. Later Bennett introduced white ware or white granite and in 1870 he issued a transfer-printed platter depicting Pickett's Charge at Gettysburg. In the course of time semi-porcelain and Hotel China were included in the production. See *Majolica; Bennett, Edwin, Pottery Company; Relief-Decorated Wares.* (437)

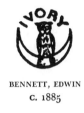

BENNETT, EDWIN
c. 1885

Bennett, Edwin, Pottery Company In American ceramics; organized in Baltimore, 1890. The printed mark adopted for all their semi-porcelain wares was a globe, pierced through the United States by a sword, on the guard of which appear initials of the company, EBPC. The motto. forming part of the mark is "Bona Fama Est Melior Zona Aurea." Closed in 1900. (437)

Bennington In American ceramics; two well-known potteries flourished at Bennington, Vermont, during the mid-19th century, producing wares in more than a dozen different types of pottery and porcelain, using a variety of colored glazes. Nothing could be more erroneous than to associate only brown Rockingham glaze with the production of these potteries. In fact this very variety was their most important influence on American ceramics manufacture. The first and longest-lived pottery was started at Bennington by Captain John Norton in 1793. He and his descendants produced little else but stonewares, the simple utilitarian wares required by the community, such as jugs, preserve and butter pots and crocks and churns, until

BENNETT, EDWIN, POTTERY
COMPANY
1890 ON

1894 when the Norton pottery closed. The early pieces of stoneware made at Bennington sometimes had a solid, shiny glaze, sometimes a lead glaze and even a glaze made of very thin clay, locally called Albany slip, being solid dark brown in color. Soon afterward salt-glazed stoneware was introduced. Other production at the Norton pottery was limited to a small quantity and was made chiefly in Rockingham glaze. In 1823 Captain Norton turned the pottery over to his two sons, Luman, the first born, and John, Jr. Subsequently, the latter withdrew; Luman's son Julius became manager and in 1841 Luman retired. By this time Luman had acquired a son-in-law who was concerned with making more decorative, more artistic wares. Late in 1844 Julius Norton and his brother-in-law, Christopher Webber Fenton, formed a partnership which lasted only until 1847. Fenton persuaded Norton to add to the homely stoneware items other articles made in a mottled glazed ware called Rockingham (since it was an imitation of the brown glaze made at the Rockingham kiln at Swinton, England) and in yellow and white glazed ware. By 1847 Bennington had two potteries since Fenton had started his own pottery in the north wing of the Norton pottery works, where he continued his experiments in the new parian wares popular in England. In 1848 he moved his pottery to another building and acquired two partners, Lyman and Park. Under the name of Lyman, Fenton and Park they advertised white flint and white earthen crockery ware. In the following year, 1849, Park withdrew and the pottery was known as Lyman, Fenton & Company. Many pieces bear the mark of this partnership. During the eleven-year period of the Fenton-directed pottery from 1847 to 1858, when it finally closed owing to financial difficulties, the pottery produced a greater variety of wares than was produced at any other pottery in the United States. This remarkably rich variety of ceramic wares included many dis-

tinctive vases and pitchers with applied-relief decoration and figures made in parian and in blue and white porcelain. An English designer and modeler, Daniel Greatbach, was responsible for many of the unusual animal designs and Toby forms, most of which were made in Rockingham and in a ware known as flint enamel, the latter being patented by Fenton in 1849. In this method various metallic oxides (copper-green, cobalt-blue and others) in powder form were sprinkled on the previously glazed piece and then fired in the kiln. In this manner the powdered oxides melted and fused together with the Rockingham glaze, forming brilliant streaks or spots of color—green, orange, yellow and blue. In the 1850's, the most important production of Staffordshire-style jugs and related wares made in the United States came from the Fenton factory. Perhaps the rarest kind of pottery made by Fenton is his little-known scroddled ware. Also in the 1850's several changes occurred in the name of the Fenton pottery. For a while it was managed by Oliver A. Gager, though Fenton kept an interest. In 1850 a new pottery was built with three large kilns. In 1853 samples under the name of the United States Pottery Company were exhibited at the Crystal Palace Exhibition, New York. The pottery was later officially incorporated under this name. In 1870, twelve years after its closing, the pottery was finally torn down. Included among the Norton Pottery marks are: L. Norton & Company, Bennington, Vt. (1822-1828), L. Norton, Bennington, Vt. (1828-1833), L. Norton & Son, Bennington, Vt. (1833-1840), Julius Norton, Bennington, Vt. (1841-1845), Norton and Fenton, Bennington, Vt. (1845-1847), Julius Norton, Bennington, Vt. (1847-1850), J. & E. Norton, Bennington, Vt. (1850-1859), J. Norton & Co., Bennington, Vt. (1859-1861), E. & L. P. Norton, Bennington, Vt. (1861-1881), E. Norton, Bennington, Vt.(1881-1883), Edward Norton & Co., Bennington, Vt. (1883-1894). Of all

BENNINGTON

NORTON AND FENTON
1845-1847

FENTON'S WORKS
1847-1848

LYMAN, FENTON AND
COMPANY
1849-1858

the Norton marks the E. & L. P. Norton, Bennington, Vt. is the most common. Only about one-fifth of the wares made at Fenton's pottery bear one of the ten known marks. Included among these marks are: Norton and Fenton, Bennington, Vt., 1845–1847, appears on stoneware and Rockingham; Fenton's Works, Bennington, Vermont, 1847–1848, appears mainly on porcelain and parian; Fenton's Enamel Patented 1849, Lyman, Fenton & Co., Bennington, Vt., 1849–1858, a most common mark appearing on flint enamel and frequently also on Rockingham; U.S.P. "ribbon mark," 1852-1858, appears mainly on porcelain and parian; United States Pottery Co., Bennington, Vt., "lozenge or medallion mark," 1852–53–1858, appears mainly on parian and smear-glazed porcelain; United States Pottery Co., Bennington, Vt., "oval mark," 1853–1858, appears mainly on scroddled ware. See *Hound-Handle Pitcher; Flint Enamel Ware; Rockingham; Parian; Book Flask; Swiss Lady; Yellow Ware; Paul and Virginia; Relief-Decorated Wares.* (438-443)

Bennington Hound-Handle Pitcher See *Hound-Handle Pitcher.*

Bennington Poodle In American ceramics; probably the best-known animal made at the Fenton-directed pottery at Bennington, Vermont, is the distinctive so-called Bennington poodle. It was made in a variety of glazes, colors and materials—Rockingham, flint enamel, parian, granite ware and yellow ware. Fundamentally it is always of the same design; that is, a standing poodle with a basket of fruit in its mouth. The shaggy mane is applied. Called cole-slaw decoration by the Staffordshire potters for many years, it was made by pushing moist clay through a screen directly onto the dog or other animal to be so decorated.

Bentley, Thomas See *Wedgwood, Josiah.*

Bérain, Jean, the Elder (1638-1711) Belgian-born painter, designer and engraver of ornament living at the Louvre from 1677. His published designs greatly influenced contemporary decorative art. He was particularly gifted in assimilating the works of those who preceded him and in adapting those works to the prevailing Louis XIV style. He revived the grotesques of the Renaissance and imparted to them a light fantasy that made them truly French, and also extremely popular. His brother, Claude Bérain, was also an engraver and executed a number of plates of ornament, which included various kinds of grotesques. His son Jean Bérain the Younger (1678-1726) carried on the work of his gifted father. He is probably best known as an engraver. His style was remarkably similar to that of his father's. See *Baroque; Watteau, Antoine; Chinoiserie; Engraved Designs; Lambrequin.* (269, 272, 276, 300)

Bérain, Jean, the Younger See *Bérain, Jean, the Elder.*

Béranger, Antoine (b. 1785) Painter at Sèvres working 1807-1846. He was among those painters hired to celebrate Napoleon's victories in porcelain.

Berettino or **bianco sopra azzurro.** In Italian ceramics; an Italian term applied to decorative designs executed in opaque white on a light or dark blue tin-glaze ground. This style of decoration was used in Faenza, Venice, and other leading Italian majolica centers from the early 16th century.

Berlin In German ceramics; a porcelain manufactory was started in 1751 by Wilhelm Kaspar Wegely with the permission of Frederick the Great. It closed in 1757. The factory mark was a W in underglaze blue. In 1761, Johann Ernst Gotzkowsky bought the manufactory. The porcelain was marked with a G in underglaze blue. In 1763 Frederick the Great (d. 1786) became the owner. It was called the Royal Berlin Porcelain Manufactory and it is still in op-

BENNINGTON

UNITED STATES POTTERY COMPANY

1852-1858

1852-53—1858

1853-1858

eration. It is regarded as one of the seven outstanding German porcelain manufactories of the 18th century. The mark was a scepter in various forms. Its finest period was from 1761 to 1786. Table services made for the King and his friends were its outstanding productions, the finest being made prior to 1770 and featuring an entire new series of designs in the Rococo style. Vases in the Rococo taste with profusely applied modeled flowers also were made. Underglaze blue porcelain was also made for daily use. The artistic merit of the porcelain was lost when the Neo-Classic style was adopted around 1780. Figure modeling practiced at Berlin was often very charming and distinctively painted in the Meissen style during its early and best period. Outstanding among the 19th century productions were the lithophanes or panels made from around 1830. The manufactory has remained State property. Until the First World War it was known as the Koenigliche Porzellan Manufactur and since then as the Staatliche Porzellan Manufactur. The ORB in use from 1832 onward is the mark added at the time of decoration. It appears above the initials KPM. The Prussian eagle with the letters KPM was first introduced about 1823 and is used as either a decoration or factory mark. A modern form of the scepter mark dates from 1870 onward. See *Meyer, F. E.; Riese, J. C. F.; Scheurich, P.; Pfeiffer, M. A.* (473, 500, 526)

BERLIN

1763-1770

1832 ON

1870 ON

Berlin   In German ceramics; four potteries making faïence were active in and near Berlin in the 17th and 18th century. A Dutch potter, Pieter van der Lee, started a pottery in 1679 which remained active until late in the 18th century. Another Dutch potter, Cornelius Funcke, started a flourishing pottery in 1699 which closed in the late 1750's. Karl Friedrich Lüdicke (d. 1797) started a pottery in 1756 which ceased to operate in 1779 or later. A pottery was started at Potsdam by C. F. Rewend, making wares in the Dutch Delft manner. An extant vase is marked Potsdam 1740.

Bernardaud, L. & Cie.   In French ceramics; started a porcelain factory at Limoges in 1863 for making tablewares for daily use. The mark was B & Cie.

Bernini, Giovanni Lorenzo (1598-1680) Celebrated Italian architect and sculptor. The art of Rome during the 17th century is closely connected with his work. Bernini's most famous work is the great colonnade of St. Peter's. He was greatly favored by the court at Rome, and he is generally regarded as the artistic dictator of Italian decorative art for the 17th century. See *Baroque.*

Berry or **Berri**   In French ceramics; an early pottery center still active today is located in Berry, a former province which was absorbed in 1790 in the departments of Cher and Indre. A hard, grey salt-glazed ware was made there in the 16th century which ranks as stoneware. The majority of extant examples of Berry stoneware belong to the end of the 18th and to the 19th century, an era when the potters of the Talbot dynasty at La Borne, Cher, became celebrated for their stonewares and everyday pottery. See *Beauvais.*

Berthevin, Pierre   Of French origin. Modeler at Mennecy; working at Copenhagen 1765; director at Marieberg 1766-1769. Here he made a creamy soft-paste porcelain not unlike that at Mennecy and decorated chiefly in the Mennecy manner of flower painting in soft warm colors. The shape most favored was the typical French ice cream cup with cover. From 1769 to 1770 Berthevin was at Frankenthal and from 1770 to 1772 was manager at Mosbach and in 1774 was made director at Sèvres of the "manufacture de poteries pour les colonies."

Besnard, Jean   (b. 1889) French artist-potter; member of the committee of Society of Decorative Artists. His stonewares exhibited at the Salon des Tuileries and Salon d'Automne between the years 1927-1937, were notable for their vigorous creativity combined with thorough technical knowledge.

Beyer, Johann Christian Wilhelm (1725-1806) German architect, painter and sculptor. From 1759 in the service of the Duke of Württemberg; modeler for Ludwigsburg, c. 1761-1767; in Vienna from 1768 onward where he was made court sculptor and was in contact with the Vienna porcelain manufactory. His figures are notable for the graceful blending of the Rococo and Neo-Classical styles.

Beyer, Paul (d. 1946) French artist-potter; showed stonewares at the Salon d'Automne between 1921 and 1937. He was chiefly responsible for reviving the use of salt-glazed stoneware among the artist-potters of France. He frequently made up figures from thrown units, permitting the ridges left by the throwing to make clear their origin.

Beyer and Bock See *Volkstedt-Rudolstadt.*

Beyerlé, Jean-Louis, Baron de See *Niderviller; Strasbourg.*

Bianco In Italian ceramics; the majolica potter's term for white tin-glaze.

Bianco sopra Azzurro In Italian ceramics; see *Berettino.*

Bianco sopra Bianco In ceramics; an Italian term for a decorative design executed in opaque white on a very pale bluish or greyish white ground. It was much used on Italian majolica made from the early 16th century at Faenza, Castel Durante, and other leading ceramic centers. During the 18th century a similar decoration was used at English Delftware manufactories and at certain Continental manufactories such as Nevers, Marieberg and Rörstrand.

Bibelot The French term *bibelot* is given to a small curio; a small object of virtu. The term is frequently used in the plural, *bibelots,* when it is applied to such articles placed on an étagère or what-not, or on a chimney piece.

Biedermeier In Germany and elsewhere in Central Europe the term *Biedermeier* is frequently used in ceramics to describe the aftermath of the decorative principles of the First French Empire style, 1804-1814, which had been followed in the first several decades of the 19th century. The first notable change came with the appearance of the Revived Rococo, which in certain areas was followed by a revived interest in chinoiserie. See *Revived Rococo.*

Bigot, Alexandre (1862-1927) French artist-potter; became concerned with pottery in the 1890's. He is identified with the remarkable flowering of art pottery in France centered in Paris in the decades around 1900. (493, 514)

Billingsley, William (1758-1828) Flower-painter and porcelain maker. After serving an apprenticeship at Derby in 1775, he decorated wares at several potteries around England. In 1808 he was at Worcester; in 1813 he started a porcelain factory at Nantgarw, and in 1819 he accepted an invitation from John Rose and went to Coalport. His flower painting is in a soft naturalistic style, especially roses, with the highlights wiped out of the overglaze enamel colors. This manner of painting flowers was widely imitated at other English factories.

Billington, Dora M. English 20th century artist-potter, writer and teacher; comes from a family who have been potters for the last three generations. Her hand-thrown pots are notable for their simplicity and purity of form. She is the author of THE ART OF THE POTTER, 1937.

B & C°
LIMOGES
(FRANCE)
BERNARDAUD, L. & CIE.
1891 ON

BILLINGTON, DORA
1920 ON

Bindesbøll, Thorvald (1846-1908) Danish architect, graphic artist and designer, distinguished in the development of modern Danish arts and crafts. It may be said that in Denmark the use of ceramics as a medium of expression for the individual artist was initiated by his activities in the 1880's. The material he used was earthenware, and his intention was purely decorative. Of interest is a glazed pottery plate with incised abstract decoration signed and dated Th. B. 1893. He was equally interested in other decorative arts, notably silverwork. (488)

Bing, Samuel (or **Siegfried**) See *Maison de l'Art Nouveau.*

BING AND GRØNDAHL
1853 ON

Bing and Grøndahl In Danish ceramics; a porcelain factory founded in 1853 by Harold Bing at Copenhagen, which rapidly attained a fine reputation for its wares, eventually rivaling the productions of the Royal Copenhagen Porcelain Manufactory. Their wares first attracted attention at the Paris Exhibition of 1900, notably those designed and made by Kai Nielsen (1882–1924), modeler of figures, and Jean Gauguin, modeler and potter, a son of Paul Gauguin. Thorwaldsen busts and statues were made in the 19th century. In 1888 the firm's art director, Pietro Krohn, designed the "Heron" table service which is notable for its crowded but asymmetrical and severe patterns. Most of the other work of this Danish firm tended to follow in the steps of Royal Copenhagen. F. A. Hallin, who was probably the best known of the artists, had been a pupil of Arnold Krog. In the 1930's and 1940's it was one of the two large porcelain firms, Royal Copenhagen being the other, which developed a perfect glazing technique for stoneware that benefited the Danish stoneware production as a whole. From the 1930's onward stoneware mostly replaced porcelain as the material used for figure-making, as in the work of Mogens Bøggild and Jean Gau-

guin, whose figure sculpture is notable for its vitality and imagination. (534, 536-538, 547)

Bingham, Edward and his son Edward W. English potters operating the Hedingham Art Pottery, Castle Hedingham, Essex, 1864-1901. Subsequently the Essex Art Pottery. (484)

Binns, Charles Fergus (1857-1934) American, English-born, educator, technologist and potter; the most influential figure in American ceramics during the first quarter of the 20th century. In 1900 he was made the first director of the New York School of Clay Working at Alfred University, which later became the New York State College of Ceramics. During the 35 years he directed this pioneer school of ceramics it became the leading institution for ceramic education and research in the U.S. His book THE POTTER'S CRAFT, 1922, was for many years the standard work in the field. He worked exclusively in high-fired stoneware, fired in a coal-burning kiln which he constructed at Alfred. Many important ceramists and educators were his students, including Charles E. Cox, Arthur Baggs, John F. McMahon, Marion L. Fosdick and Charles Harder. This group spread the idea of the individual potter, in complete command of both process and design. Binns' pieces were severely simple; he turned to China, especially the Ch'ing dynasty, for his inspiration, rather than to Art Nouveau.

Bird Tureen In ceramics; tureens in the form of a duck, goose or other birds were fashionable during the Rococo style and were made in faïence at such manufactories as Strasbourg and in porcelain at Meissen and Chelsea. (281, 311)

Biscuit In ceramics; the name applied to porcelain and pottery which has been fired once but not glazed, especially to the former. It is also called bisque.

Biscuit Figure In European ceramics; biscuit or unglazed porcelain figures were first made around 1751 at Vincennes and Sèvres. They became very fashionable and were made at many French porcelain manufactories during the latter part of the 18th century. They were also made in Germany. The principal manufactory for biscuit figures in England was Derby. Biscuit figures of soft paste or pâte tendre in distinction to biscuit figures of hard paste porcelain had a remarkable smoothness to the touch and a warm soft tone which gave them much of their charm. It is generally agreed that the soft paste biscuit figures of Sèvres and Vincennes were the most appealing in respect to the beauty of the material. The finest Derby soft paste biscuit figures date from about 1790. See *Bachelier, Jean-Jacques.* (354-355)

Biscuit Ware See *Nicaragua, Costa Rica and Panama.*

Bishop Bowl In Danish ceramics; a popular form of pottery or porcelain bowl during the middle of the 18th century was called a bishop bowl. It was in the shape of a bishop's mitre and was often decorated with a drinking party scene. The term *bishop* has been applied in England since early in the 18th century to a sweet drink, of various formulas, the principal ingredients being wine, oranges or lemons and sugar; or mulled and spiced port. See *Schleswig.* (297)

Bisque In ceramics; see *Biscuit.*

Bizen In Japanese ceramics; the old province of Bizen, now in present Okayama Prefecture, was a leading center for the production of Sue wares and is one of the traditional sites of the Six Old Kilns period. In contrast to the Seto potters who desired to produce wares more or less resembling Sung wares, Bizen potters were more influenced by local materials

and local demands, such as a need for durable, relatively plain, containers for agricultural products and particularly for seed storage. The methods of oxidation firing also gained in popularity with the Bizen potters. The Bizen kilns continued to produce notable wares long after the Six Old Kilns era, to which the connoisseurs ascribe Old Bizen. Much of the 16th century or later ware is just as interesting in its own right as any other. From this time onward the aesthetic ideals of the tea cult became increasingly important in the output of the Bizen kilns, as they did in virtually all kinds of Japanese wares. Bizen potters made a great variety of objects designed for auxiliary use in the tea ceremony, as they felt that the clay available to them was not suitable for tea bowls. Bizen ware is always distinctive for its high-fired clay body. The smoother Bizen wares show the influence of Chinese Yi-hsing stoneware. Traditionally characteristic is the unglazed high-fired Bizen ware, its reddish-brown body at times resembling bronze both to the eye and touch. In the 17th and 18th centuries the production included delightful figure subjects representing mythological personages, gods, animals, birds, and fish. The plastic character of the fine clay used is believed to account for the quality of the numerous excellent figures. Bizen continued to be an important pottery center down to relatively modern times. See *Six Old Kilns; Hidasuki; Ao-Bizen; Imbe.* (138)

Bjorquist, Karin See *Gustavsberg.*

Black In ceramics; black glazes and enamels are generally made from iron and manganese occasionally mixed with cobalt. See *Basalt Ware; Colors; Jasper Ware; Monochrome Painting; Colored Grounds; Schwarzlot; Manganese.*

Black Basaltes or **Black Basalt** In English ceramics; see *Basalt.*

Black-Figure Ware See *Greece.*

Black Gold Ware In Chinese ceramics; see *Mirror Black.*

Black Lead See *Graphite.*

Black-on-Orange See *Aztec.*

Black Porcelaine In English ceramics; the name given by Wedgwood to his black basalt which he regarded to be of such hardness as to be worthy of the implied comparison. See *Basalt.*

Blanc de Chine In Chinese ceramics; a beautiful white Chinese porcelain ware that is generally best known under its French name of *Blanc de Chine.* It was first made in the Ming period at Tê-Hua in Ch'üan-Chou in the province of Fukien. It is made into such articles as bowls, incense pots and religious figures. The beautifully modeled figures are generally considered to be its finest work. The Chinese goddess, Kwan Yin, was an especially favorite subject. The glaze in Blanc de Chine is united with the body in such a manner that it is difficult to perceive where the one stops and the other starts. The finest Blanc de Chine was made during the Ming dynasty. The glaze was thick and lustrous and had a rich warm glow. The later glazes have a tendency to be glassy and the glaze is dead white and cold. The Chinese term is *Chien Yao* and also *Pai Tz'u.* See *Fukien.* (108)

Blanc Fixe In ceramics; a French term meaning opaque white. See *Bianco sopra Azzurro; Bianco sopra Bianco.* (243)

Bleu Celeste In French ceramics; a turquoise ground color prepared by Jean Hellot and appearing on Sèvres in 1752. See *Sèvres.*

Bleu-de-Nevers See *Nevers.*

Bleu-de-Roi In French ceramics; the blue enamel color employed on Sèvres porcelain. It was invented at Sèvres prior to 1760 by Jean Hellot and supplanted the former underglaze gros bleu. This bleu-de-roi was the first of the family of enamel ground colors employed on porcelains. See *Sèvres.*

Bleu Persan In French ceramics; a name given by a director of the Sèvres porcelain manufactory to the deep blue-ground faïence of Nevers because he thought it was of Persian origin. The color was imitated at Rouen, Delft, Lambeth and other manufactories. The color was probably originally inspired by 17th century Chinese porcelain. See *Nevers.* (240, 243)

Blind-Earl's Pattern In English ceramics; a pattern comprising rose leaves and birds executed in relief found on Worcester porcelain from around 1760. It was later named after the Earl of Coventry who became blind in 1780. (372)

Blondeau Modeler at Vincennes-Sèvres. His principal works were the eight Enfants d'après Boucher modeled in 1752-1753. Some figures of animals after Oudry, 1752-1756, have been ascribed to Blondeau. See *Bachelier, J. J.*

Bloor, Robert Proprietor of the Derby porcelain manufactory, 1811-1848. See *Derby.*

Bloor Derby See *Derby.*

Blue In ceramics; a pure blue color is derived from cobalt, a pottery pigment known to the ancient Egyptians. Cobalt is mainly found in connection with nickel, iron and arsenic and the purity of the blue produced depends to a great extent on the degree of refinement to which the mineral has been processed. It can be employed as a substance for coloring glazes and tin-enamels of every kind, for painting directly on the body of the ware before coating it with a clear lead or feldspathic glaze, or on the unfired white surface of a tin-enamel or slip. With an admixture of oxide of lead or some other kind of flux or glass it becomes a muffle-color which may be added over all such glazes and enamels. Mixed with clay slip it was applied to the surface of stoneware about to be salt-glazed or it could be employed to stain clays for marbled wares. In lead glazes used on white pottery and porcelain it was common practice to add a minute quantity of cobalt to counteract a yellowish tone owing to the accidental presence of iron. When cobalt-blue is fired on pottery or porcelain without being protected by a glaze, it produces an almost black color. See *Monochrome Painting; Blue and White; Colors; Colored Grounds; Jasper Ware.*

Blue and White In Japanese ceramics; according to tradition the earliest Japanese underglaze blue and white porcelain was made in the Arita area soon after 1616, and showed very strong Korean influence. Many of these early wares were similar to Korean blue and white wares of the Yi Dynasty, 1576-1614. After a short time, probably from around 1640, the influence of imported late Ming blue and white, in particular Wan Li, prevailed. In the 18th century Japanese indigenous designs or Chinese motifs completely Japanized supplanted all others. Counted among the kilns making blue and white porcelain are those at Arita, Nagasaki and Kyoto, Nabeshima, Kakiemon and Hirado. The skillful application of underglaze blue is no easy task. In broad terms, it is the same as working with a brush entirely saturated with ink on a piece of blotting paper. The unfired porcelain body is very porous and absorbent and the work can be done only with the quickest, most deft touch. To execute the elaborate uniform decorations on large pieces of porcelain demanded almost incredible resources of skill and patience on the part of the decorator. On matched pieces, such as the sets of Nabeshima bowls for formal dining of five, ten, or twenty, the decorator had the task of duplicating the impossible that many times. To meet this necessity of uniformity, a decoration transfer technique was developed in which the design was first executed on tracing paper in charcoal which would provide as many as twenty or more impressions when carefully rubbed off against the unfired body. These outline impressions were filled in with underglaze blue guaranteeing remarkable uniformity. However, the work of finishing off these underglaze details remained as difficult as ever. See *Hirado; Nabeshima; Kakiemon; Shonsui; Arita; Sometsuke; Underglaze Blue.* (140, 150, 153)

Blue and White Ch'ing In Chinese ceramics; the Chinese technique in the production of blue and white on porcelain is unrivaled. The porcelain body of the Chinese ware to which underglaze blue is applied is only dried, while in other countries it is hardened in a kiln. The blue is mixed with water and painted on with a brush. Then the glaze is applied and the piece is placed in the kiln to be fired. The K'ang Hsi blue and white ware which is held in such high esteem is executed with the finest technical workmanship. The body of this ware is white and has a fine texture. It is finely potted. The blue pigment is carefully prepared and the glaze is made as clear as possible. The blue in the inferior pieces is not so fine. It is duller and generally reflects a trace of red or deep violet-blue tint. The painted decoration is first outlined faintly, and then is carefully filled in, in varying tones, which at times resemble marbling and ice crackling. Sometimes the design is in reserve on a blue ground. Blue and white wares were also produced in the Yung Chêng period, the Ch'ien Lung, and the later eras, but the work was progressively inferior to the K'ang Hsi wares. See *Prunus; Ch'ing; Blue and White Ming; Chinese Soft Paste; Nanking Ware.* (110)

Blue and White Ming In Chinese ceramics; the blue which was skillfully used by the Chinese in underglaze blue decoration was obtained from the cobaltiferous ore of manganese. Although this mineral was ob-

BLUE AND WHITE VASE, MING

tainable in certain sections of China it had been imported from the Near East since the time of the T'ang period. During the Ming dynasty the best quality of cobalt was imported from the Near East. The characteristic Chinese blue and white was porcelain. The designs were painted on the unglazed body which was then covered with a glaze and fired. Although Chinese records substantiate that underglaze blue decoration was used during the Sung dynasty, it did not become fashionable until the Ming dynasty. The Sung dynasty favored monochrome glazes. It is generally accepted that blue and white porcelain wares were produced from the beginning of the Ming dynasty, although Chinese records fail to make mention of them before the reign of Yung Lo, 1403-1424. During the Ming dynasty the finest blue and white was made from the imported blue known as Mohammedan blue. Supplies of Mohammedan blue were available during the Hsüan Te reign,1426-1435, Chêng Tê reign, 1506-1521 and Chia Ching reign, 1522-1566. It is generally believed that the supplies of Mohammedan blue were very low during the Ch'êng Hua reign, 1465-1487, and during the Wan Li reign, 1573-1619. See *Ming; Blue and White Ch'ing; Mohammedan Blue.* (99, 102, 104)

Blue-Dash Charger   In English ceramics; the name generally given to the faïence dishes painted in majolica colors made during the 17th and 18th centuries at Lambeth and Bristol. These dishes are generally characterized by a border of slanting lines or dashes in blue. (258, 259)

Bocage   In ceramics; a French term meaning little wood, used to describe a background of modeled leaves and flowers forming a part of a ceramic figure or group. Perhaps the most extravagant bocages are found on Chelsea figures and groups of the gold-anchor period, around 1760-1770. (366)

Boch, William, and Brother   In American ceramics; a family of German potters who started a factory around 1850 at Greenpoint, Brooklyn, N.Y., for the manufacture of porcelain hardware such as door knobs and door plates. The firm prospered and subsequently at various times they opened several factories; for a time their name was connected with the Union Porcelain Works. See *Union Porcelain Works.*

Böck, Joseph   See *Vienna.*

Bodenbach   In German ceramics; a pottery was started by Schiller and Gerbing at Bodenbach, Bohemia, where in the second quarter of the 19th century they made in quantity a curious type of red, green and other colored ware with a varnished wax-like surface in forms somewhat in the manner of Wedgwood's stoneware. Later they separated as W. Schiller and Sons, and F. Gerbing. The impressed marks were S & G; F G; W S & S; Wedgwood.

Body   In ceramics; the clay or mixture of clays and other materials used for making any ceramic article; the body as distinct from the glaze. The porcelain body is often described as the paste (French *pâte*). The word *body* is also used to describe the principal part of an article, as for example the body of a jug in distinction to its handle and pouring spout.

Body Mark   The name of the body such as semi-porcelain, majolica or bone china. See *Mark,* in ceramics; *Backstamp.*

Boehm, Edward Marshall (1912-1969) American ceramist-sculptor whose lifelike porcelain birds are world famous; started a studio pottery in 1949 at Trenton; later, his workshop was at Washington Crossing, also in New Jersey. Although he executed works of farm animals, religious subjects, ornamental figures and bowls, he was most celebrated for his creation of birds, notable for their realistic, delicate and detailed execution.

Bogaert, Adriaen Jansz   See *Amsterdam.*

BOCAGE BACKGROUND, CHELSEA-DERBY GROUP

Bøggild, Mogens See *Bing and Grøndahl.*

Boghaert or **van den Bogaert, Jan** See *Antwerp.*

Bogler, Theodor See *Bauhaus.*

Bohemia See *Austria, Czechoslovakia and Hungary; Czechoslovakia.*

Boizot, Louis-Simon (1743-1809) Sculptor; succeeded E. M. Falconet as model master at Sèvres, 1774-1802. He assumed charge of the modeling department just about the same time that hard paste began to be used for figures. Among his numerous works are the coronation group of Louis XVI and Marie Antoinette (L'Autel Royale), 1775, an equestrian figure of Frederick the Great, 1781, and figures and groups in the Classical taste, frequently very large and executed in hard paste, and his famous girandole of Zephyr and Flora.

Bolsward See *Friesland.*

Bonbonnière A small decorative box used to hold sweetmeats or comfits derived from the French word *bonbon* meaning sweetmeat.

Bone Ash In ceramics; calcined bones, crushed and ground to a powder, used as an ingredient in bone china to give it whiteness and translucence.

Bone China or **Bone Porcelain** In English ceramics; a ware having as an ingredient in its porcelain composition the ash of calcined bones, which is pure white in color. A patent for using bone ash was taken out by Thomas Frye of Bow in 1748, which date marks its first known actual use. Later bone ash was combined in England to form a hybrid paste containing china clay and stone. This hybrid bone ash paste was covered with a lead glaze and was introduced by Spode at Stoke-on-Trent and by Barr at Worcester late in the 18th century. This became the standard English body during the 19th century and is still being used at the present time. Bone china is softer than hard paste. It is more durable and less expensive to make than soft paste. Sweden was the only continental country to use bone china, probably due to the strong influence of English earthenware in that country. Of the two great Swedish factories in the second half of the 19th century, Gustavsberg began to make bone china in the early 1860's while Rörstrand introduced it around 1856-1857. See *Soft Paste; Porcelain.*

Bongard, Hermann See *Figgio.*

Bonn See *Poppelsdorf.*

Bonnin and Morris In American ceramics; a porcelain factory started late in 1769 at Philadelphia by an artisan Gousse Bonnin and a Philadelphia entrepreneur George Morris. The factory operated until 1772. Extant identified pieces are all blue and white and relate to the blue and white wares made at Bow, Worcester, Lowestoft and Longton Hall in England. See *Tucker.*

Book Flask or **Book Bottle** In American ceramics; a popular humorous pottery article made at Bennington, Vermont, 1849-1858, in the form of a book, usually with a flint enamel glaze. Originally made to hold liquor, probably rum, it was also used with either hot sand or hot water as a hand warmer. See *Bennington.*

Boote, T. and R. (Ltd.) In English ceramics; operated the Waterloo Pottery and other addresses at Burslem in the Staffordshire district from 1842, producing earthenwares, parian wares, tiles and the like. In 1906 the Waterloo Pottery was closed and the firm has subsequently concentrated on the making of tiles. In the 1840's Boote registered several scenes for the widely popular relief-decorated white stoneware jugs. Also in 1847 Boote registered a "new shape for jugs;" it was straight-sided in shape, tapering slightly inward toward the rim. T. & R. B. and T. & R. Boote are incor-

BOOTE, T AND R (LTD.)
1891-1906

porated in several marks of varying design. See *Relief-Decorated Wares.*

Booth, Thomas and Son   English potters who operated the Church Bank Pottery at Tunstall in the Staffordshire district from 1872 to 1876, where they produced earthenwares. Subsequently T. G. Booth, 1876-1883; T. G. & F. Booth, 1883-1891; Booths Ltd., 1891-1948; Booths & Colcloughs Ltd., 1948-1954; retitled Ridgway Potteries Ltd. 1955. Around the late 19th and beginning of the 20th century Booths made reproductions of early Worcester porcelains in opaque earthenware or semi-porcelain. The distinguishing initials T. B. & S. are found in marks of differing design.

Booths and Colcloughs Ltd   See *Booth, Thomas and Son; Colclough, H. J.*

Booths Ltd.   See *Booth, Thomas and Son*

BOOTHS LTD.
C. 1906 ON

Bordeaux   In French ceramics; a faïence manufactory was started at Bordeaux by Jacques Fautier and Jacques Hustin in 1711 and was in operation until 1783. No factory mark was used. To a large extent the finest production of this manufactory was adapted versions of the faïence made at Moustiers, Nevers and Rouen. The greater part of the wares produced here was without distinction and consisted chiefly of dishes and plates painted in a simple manner.

Bordeaux   A French porcelain manufactory was founded by Pierre Verneuilh in 1781 at Bordeaux. In 1787, it passed to the ownership of Alluaud and Vanier. The accepted marks are: two V's joined as a W; AV in monogram in circle, the upper part of which was enclosed in a semi-circle with the inscription "Bordeaux." It made a fine-quality ware for table service. The decorative motifs employed included foliage festoons in the style of Louis XVI, and strewn flowers, such as yellow daisies, cornflowers and pan-

sies. The wares closely resembled those of Paris.

Bornholm Island   In Danish ceramics; a flourishing factory producing cream-colored earthenwares was active here in the late 18th and early 19th century operated by Johann Spietz whose name was used sometimes as a mark. The island, which belongs to Denmark, is a source of kaolin used at Royal Copenhagen.

Borrmann, Johann Balthasar   (1725-1784) A porcelain painter working at Meissen and Berlin, 1763-1779. He specialized in landscapes and figures.

Bott, Thomas   (1829-1870) English painter and designer working at Worcester where he was instrumental in raising its reputation. He was responsible for the so-called Limoges enamels developed during the Kerr and Binns period, 1852-1862. His son, Thomas John Bott (1854-1932) was employed at the Worcester porcelain factory for some years where he painted in the manner popularized by his father. See *Worcester.*

Bottengruber or **Pottengruber, Ignaz**   German water-colorist and miniature painter; a famous porcelain Hausmaler working at Breslau and Vienna around 1720 to 1730 or later. Bottengruber's painting, rich in fantasy and vitality, ranks with the best in the history of porcelain.

Böttger, Johann Friedrich   (1682-1719) Celebrated German alchemist and ceramic technician. In 1708 he started the Dresden faïence manufactory. He invented and perfected in 1708-1709 a fine red stoneware which was hard enough to be polished on the lapidary's wheel. It resembled the Chinese buccaro ware of Yi-hsing. The ware is known by his name. In 1708 he made the first true or hard paste porcelain in Europe and in 1709 he produced a suitable glaze for it. In 1710 the Elector of Saxony established the Meissen manufactory and appointed Böttger as manager. See *Meissen; Porcelain; Buccaro.* (301-303)

Boucher, François (1703-1770) A celebrated French painter and decorative designer. He was a principal exponent of the Rococo style and a prolific inventor of decorative fantasies in the Rococo manner. He also invented numerous fantastic chinoiseries which are closely related to the Rococo style and were a favorite decoration on porcelains. His designs were adapted for popular use through the works of contemporary engravers. See *Rococo; Louis XV; Engraved Designs; Bachelier, J. J.* (354, 366)

Bouffioulx In Netherlandish ceramics; much stoneware in imitation of the Rhenish stoneware was made at Bouffioulx and at Châtelet, Namur, Dinant and other places in the Walloon country from the late 16th century onward. Among the earlier wares, dull brown in glaze, were globular Bartmann jugs and a curious form of flattened circular pilgrim bottle with relief decoration. Later types attributed to the region include grey jugs and tankards of blue and purple coloring with cut decoration which were close copies of Westerwald wares.

Boulevard Poissonnière See *Honorè, F-M; Petite Rue Saint-Gilles.*

Boullemier, Anton or **Antonin** (c. 1840-1900) German-born designer and painter who settled in England in 1872 and was engaged by Mintons. He excelled in delicate, charming figure compositions, often of cupid subjects in the French style. His work graced many of Mintons' most important commissions and he also painted portraits and miniatures. He broke his contract with Mintons and started his own studio at Stoke-on-Trent where he decorated for other houses as well as Mintons. He exhibited at the Royal Academy exhibitions of 1881 and 1882.

Boumeester, Cornelis See *Rotterdam.*

Bourg-la-Reine In French ceramics; see *Mennecy.*

Bow In English ceramics; it is generally believed that the Bow manufactory in east London was established in 1744 by Thomas Frye and Edward Heylyn. Some of the best English porcelain in a rather unsophisticated style was produced here around 1750 and 1760 and later. Frye was manager until 1759. Weatherby (d. 1762) and John Crowther became the owners; the latter declared bankruptcy in 1763. It is assumed that the manufactory was aided by William Duesbury who transferred the models and molds to Derby around 1775-1776. There was no factory mark on the early wares. From around 1760-1765 an anchor and a dagger in red is rather common on wares assumed to have been made at Bow. The wares believed to have been made before 1750 have little artistic merit. For the next ten years a soft paste porcelain, of varying quality, apparently having bone ash as an ingredient, was made. The best material was similar to Mennecy porcelain. The figures as well as the useful wares were chiefly copied from Meissen. Vases in the Rococo style with applied leaves and flowers and with Rococo masks were most charming. Underglaze blue painting was practiced but it was without distinction. Figures of birds were notable for their fine coloring. The later productions, which were frequently marked with the anchor and dagger, reveal quite a decline in quality. The material was full of imperfections and of a dull tone. The figures, which were poorly painted, occasionally revealed good modeling. The figures, vases, and tablewares were mostly copied from other English factories as well as these factories' marks. See *Bone China.* (376)

Bowl In Chinese ceramics; in useful wares the bowl or wan is found in numerous sizes and shapes. Undoubtedly the most common is the small rice bowl or kung

⚓ †

BOW
1760 ON

wan. A shallower form of bowl, called t'ang wan, was used for soup. The tea bowl or ch'a wan was furnished with a cover. When drinking tea, one tilted the cover slightly to form a narrow opening in order to keep the tea leaves in the bowl. After the introduction of the teapot, which apparently was not before the Ming dynasty, the tea cup or ch'a pei without a cover or handle was generally used. It seems that vessels with spouts and handles before the Ming dynasty were used as wine pots or for other liquids. A tiny bowl is the customary form for a wine cup, although goblets with deep bowls and with shallow or tazza-shaped bowls resting on tall stems were also used. Ceremonial wine cups used for weddings and libations were similar in shape to the bronze ritual vessels. See *Cup Stand.*

Bracquemond, Félix (1833-1914) French painter and etcher who from the 1860's devoted himself mainly to pottery. His designs are an important early manifestation of the new Japanese influence on ceramics and reveal a remarkably sensitive response to the essential spirit of Japanese art. After having worked at Sèvres for a short time around 1870 he accepted the position of art director of the Paris atelier of the firm of Charles Haviland of Limoges, a post he held for many years. As early as 1867 Bracquemond used in his decoration on pottery plates plant-like motifs which approximate those of Art Nouveau. See *Japanism.*

Braden, Nora English artist-potter; outstanding pupil of Bernard Leach at his St. Ives pottery, around 1924-1928. She and another outstanding pupil of Leach, Katherine Pleydell-Bouverie, worked together at Coleshill, Wiltshire, from around 1928 to 1936. Her studio-type pottery was strongly formed and sometimes decorated with brushwork. NB in monogram was her customary mark. See *Leach, B.*

Brameld See *Rockingham.*

BRADEN, NORA
1924-1936

VAN BRIGGLE POTTERY CO.

BRISTOL
PORCELAIN C. 1773-1781

Brannam, C. H. Ltd. In English ceramics; the Litchdon pottery, a small art pottery, was started at Barnstaple, Devon, in 1879 by Charles H. Brannam, whose father Thomas Brannam was a potter at Barnstaple for many years and exhibited at the Great Exhibition, London, 1851. The ware was called Barum after the Roman name for that town. It achieved the distinction of being described and illustrated in the catalogues of Liberty's, the quintessence of fashion in London at the end of the century. See *Linthorpe Pottery.*

Braque, Georges (1882-1963) French painter who became interested in the decoration of pottery at the incentive of José Llorens Artigas. See *Artigas, J.L.*

Bretby Art Pottery See *Tooth and Company (Ltd.).*

Brezova See *Pirkenhammer.*

Brianchon, Jules Joseph In French ceramics; Brianchon, a partner in the ceramic firm of Gillet and Brianchòn, Rue de Lafayette, Paris, received a patent in 1857 for an improvement involving ceramic substances by applying a glaze with colored and variegated reflections; a pearl-like luster. He also took out a patent in England. Wares with a mother-of-pearl luster were popular in the latter part of the 19th century. Irish Belleek is typical of this taste. After the patent expired in England, the process was used at Worcester. In America, Knowles, Taylor and Knowles successfully manufactured this ware. See *Luster.*

Bric-à-brac A French term reputed to be formed from the French phrase *de bric et de broc* meaning by hook or by crook. The term is collectively given to old curiosities possessing an artistic quality, such as various antiquarian odds and ends as porcelain, plate, glass and similar articles.

Briggle, Artus van (d. 1904) American artist-potter; spent three years studying in Paris in the 1890's. Originally he was a decorator at Rookwood, where he is said to have been interested in the mat glaze developed at Rookwood in the late 1890's. In 1901 he moved to Colorado Springs, Colorado, where he started a pottery. His modeled pottery finished with distinctive soft mat glazes can be regarded as an integrated expression of the Art Nouveau style. See *Art Nouveau.* (520, 521)

Brinjal Bowl   See *Three-Color Ware.*

Brislington   See *Bristol,* in English pottery.

Bristol   In English porcelain; a soft paste porcelain manufactory was founded around 1750 at Lowdin's glass house and was transferred to Worcester in 1752. In 1770 a hard paste porcelain manufactory was established at Bristol by William Cookworthy, with Richard Champion as manager. It was a continuation of the previous porcelain manufactory at Plymouth. It was purchased by Richard Champion in 1773. Due to financial embarrassment Champion sold his patent for making hard paste porcelain to a group of Staffordshire potters, who continued the manufacture of simply decorated wares at New Hall. The mark while Cookworthy owned the factory was the same as the Plymouth mark, the alchemist's sign for tin; later a cross in blue enamel or gold and a capital B in blue were the marks commonly found on tableware. Figures and vases were not so often marked. The porcelain, like that of Plymouth, was technically imperfect and was often somewhat misshapen. Undoubtedly the best work was the productions by Champion. Many of these pieces were obviously for presentation. In his work the style of Sèvres predominated. Figure modeling closely imitated Sèvres and Derby figures. Large vases, generally of hexagonal form, decorated with applied flowers were also made. The designs for fine tableware were in the Sèvres style. See *Cookworthy, W.*

Bristol   In English pottery; it is generally believed that pottery was probably produced here from medieval times. However, the chief claim to fame for Bristol pottery is due to the tin-glazed earthenware produced here during the second half of the 17th century and the 18th century. Several potteries were in operation at Bristol as well as at neighboring Brislington and Wincanton. Edward Ward started a pottery at Water Lane or Temple Back, Bristol, in 1683, which was operated by his family until 1741. It continued to operate at Temple Back under different proprietors until 1884, when new premises were taken, and is still in existence at Fishponds just outside the city of Bristol. No regular factory mark was used on Bristol pottery. It is practically impossible to separate the wares of the Bristol and Brislington potteries, which are in turn very often hard to separate from those of Lambeth of the earlier period and of Liverpool of the later period. The early tin-glazed wares which were made until around 1720 were of the majolica types. After 1720 they were largely supplanted by wares which imitated Chinese porcelains and Dutch Delft. The forms were similar to the Delft wares. Tiles were also made. Punch bowls painted with ships were made around the middle of the 18th century at Bristol and also at Liverpool. The wares produced at Wincanton were essentially similar to those of Bristol. Toward the last quarter of the 18th century the production of faïence types was largely succeeded by cream-colored earthenware. Brown stoneware with Bristol glaze was made in the 19th century. (255, 258, 259)

British Royal Arms   The British Royal Arms and many close copies occur in the printed or impressed marks of many 19th and 20th century British manufactures. It should be mentioned that foreign firms also copied these arms; for example, some 19th century American potteries made use of them. The basic form of the mark can be a guide to dating, for all arms engraved after the

BRISTOL TIN-GLAZED
EARTHENWARE PLATE

BRITISH ROYAL ARMS

PRE-1837

POST-1837

accession of Queen Victoria in 1837 will have the simple quartered shield; but the pre-1837 arms have an extra shield in the center of the quartered shield. The small inescutcheon or extra shield during the period from 1801 to 1814 had a cap over the top, and this was supplanted by a crown from 1814 to 1837.

BROUWERS AARDEWERK
C. 1901 ON

Brocade Patterns   In Japanese ceramics; designs taken from textiles. Especially noteworthy are the colorful Imari brocaded wares decorated in Nishiki (enameled polychrome) fashion. These so-called brocade patterns were freely adapted, especially at the English porcelain manufactories of Worcester and Derby where they became widely popular. See *Imari; Chinese Imari; Nishiki; Some Nishiki; Japanese Porcelain Motifs.* (142, 143, 371)

BROWNFIELD, WILLIAM
1850-1871

Bromley, William, Sr.   English-born modeler working for Ott and Brewer around 1883-1892. Surviving examples of his work include a grey Belleek woven basket decorated with a rim of modeled flowers in color, and an oval Belleek picture frame decorated with lilies-of-the-valley in a high relief. See *Belleek.*

Brongniart, Alexandre   (1770-1847) In 1800 he was appointed by Napoleon Bonaparte as director of the Sèvres porcelain factory, a position which he held until his death.

Bronze Doré   See *Metal Mounts on Ceramics.*

BROWN-WESTHEAD, MOORE
AND COMPANY
C. 1895-1904

Broome, Isaac   American sculptor and modeler; noteworthy are the sculptures and relief decorations he modeled for Ott and Brewer of Trenton: parian busts of Lincoln and Cleopatra; a parian "Baseball Vase" made for the Philadelphia Centennial Exhibition of 1876, and a grey biscuit tea service with a George and Martha Washington motif in slight relief, also made for the Centennial Exhibition. One of his last pieces was a parian bust of John A. Roebling made by Lenox of New Jersey around 1909. (446)

Brouwer, William Coenraad   (1877-1933) Dutch sculptor and potter; in 1901 established a pottery manufactory in Leiderdorp which in time became a successful business, producing countless decorative terra-cotta sculptures for buildings in Holland, including the Peace Palace in the Hague. Marks include Brouwers Aardewerk, meaning pottery, literally "earthwork."

Brown   In ceramics; brown colors, particularly those tending to red or yellow, are mainly prepared from iron compounds, but also a range of different browns as well as purples can be prepared from manganese. A high temperature brown prepared from iron, known as dead-leaf or café-au-lait, was widely popular on Chinese porcelain but was relatively little employed in Europe except for Meissen where it was called Capuziner Braun. However, it occurred as a café-au-lait tin-glaze ground on some faïence, while a chocolate-brown enamel ground was occasionally used on porcelain. The tortoiseshell-brown high-temperature glaze (fond écaille) on Sèvres was prepared from iron and manganese, while the tortoiseshell lead glaze of the so-called Astbury-Whieldon ware was derived only from manganese. Also due to manganese alone was the Rockingham brown glaze of Swinton. A notable class but quite distinct are the rich browns resulting from a wash of iron-bearing clay on German salt-glazed stonewares. See *Colors; Colored Grounds; Clays; Manganese.*

Brownfield, William   English potter who operated a pottery at Cobridge in the Staffordshire district from 1850 to 1891. He produced earthenwares and from 1871 porcelains of excellent quality. The marks include W. B., Brownfield, and W B & S or W B & Sons after 1871. In 1890 a cooperative company was formed entitled Brownfield's Guild Pottery, producing china and earthenwares; it ceased to operate in 1898.

Brown Porcelain or **Brown China** See *Red Porcelain.*

Brown Ware See *Yellow Ware.*

Brown-Westhead, Moore and Company In English ceramics; this firm of Staffordshire potters succeeded John Ridgway at Cauldon Place, Hanley, in 1855. Like the Ridgways they were appointed Potters to the Queen and their decorative porcelain and pottery, including elaborately designed vases, well-modeled animal figures, colossal candelabra and brackets and dessert services decorated with designs from La Fontaine's fables, were shown at the international exhibitions. Anton Boullemier decorated for this firm which subsequently became Cauldon Ltd. in 1904.

Bruhl, Count Heinrich (1700-1763) Chief minister and favorite of Augustus III, King of Poland and Elector of Saxony. He was administrator of the Meissen porcelain manufactory, 1733 to 1763. See *Swan Service.*

Brunswick In German ceramics; the Old or Ducal faïence manufactory was started by Duke Anton Ulrich of Brunswick with Johann Philipp Frantz as manager in 1707. In 1710 it was leased to Heinrich Christoph von Horn who took Werner von Hantelmann as a partner in 1711. This partnership continued until 1749 and the mark used was VH in a monogram. From 1749 to 1756 the proprietors were Reichard and Behling and the mark was B & R or R & B. Duke Karl bought the manufactory in 1756 and leased it to Rabe (d. 1803) who bought it in 1776. It ceased to operate in 1807. The mark used was B; the mark R & C is also recorded. The early productions were painted blue and were obviously in imitation of the Dutch. Around the middle of the 18th century the wares began to show some inventiveness and freshness in their style. Rococo molded vases and ewers were often distinctive for their delicate coloring and touch. A certain paleness in

the color was especially typical. The successive contemporary vogues for faïence figures, tureens in the form of birds and vegetables, pierced baskets and classical vases were all followed at Brunswick. Another faïence manufactory was founded at Brunswick, in 1745, by Rudolph Anton Chely and his sons, Christoph and Georg Heinrich. Included among their productions were vases of Chinese form painted with landscapes in the Delft style, tureens in forms of birds and figures of peasants. The mark was a monogram of crossed C's. It closed in 1757.

Brush Bath See *Writing Equipage.*

Brush Jar In Chinese ceramics; a deep cylindrical porcelain jar used by the Chinese to hold their writing brushes. See *Writing Equipage.*

Brussels In the 17th century several small faïence factories made inferior copies of Dutch Delft at Brussels. In 1705 a new factory producing wares of importance was started here by Corneille Mombaers and Thierry Witsenburg. Tureens and other vessels in forms of ducks, cabbages, melons and fish were typical and displayed considerable originality. In 1751 another faïence factory was begun by Jacques Artoisenet and in the ensuing decade was united with the Mombaers factory. It closed about 1825. A third factory was active from around 1802 to 1866. In time cream-colored earthenware supplanted the faïence. The wares of the three factories were unmarked. A porcelain factory, named the Manufacture de Montplaisir, was started by J. S. Vaume, and was active from 1786 to 1790. The name of the manager was Biourge; the mark was a B with or without a crown. The wares were in imitation of the contemporary Paris porcelain, the decoration being in sepia and green monochrome with sprigs and festoons in polychrome. Two other porcelain factories were also active in the closing decade of the 18th century. (293)

BRUNSWICK

C. 1711-1749

1745 ON

BRUSH JAR, CH'ING

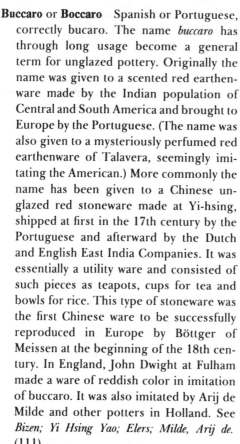

BUCCARO TEAPOT, MING

BUDAPEST
FISHER, EMIL
C. 1870 ON

BUEN RETIRO

1760-1804

1804-1808

Bryk, Rut Finnish artist-potter. Started her ceramic experiments at Arabia in 1924. Her decorative wall plaques have brought her world renown. See *Arabia*.

Buccaro or **Boccaro** Spanish or Portuguese, correctly bucaro. The name *buccaro* has through long usage become a general term for unglazed pottery. Originally the name was given to a scented red earthenware made by the Indian population of Central and South America and brought to Europe by the Portuguese. (The name was also given to a mysteriously perfumed red earthenware of Talavera, seemingly imitating the American.) More commonly the name has been given to a Chinese unglazed red stoneware made at Yi-hsing, shipped at first in the 17th century by the Portuguese and afterward by the Dutch and English East India Companies. It was essentially a utility ware and consisted of such pieces as teapots, cups for tea and bowls for rice. This type of stoneware was the first Chinese ware to be successfully reproduced in Europe by Böttger of Meissen at the beginning of the 18th century. In England, John Dwight at Fulham made a ware of reddish color in imitation of buccaro. It was also imitated by Arij de Milde and other potters in Holland. See *Bizen; Yi Hsing Yao; Elers; Milde, Arij de.* (111)

Bucchero, Etruscan In ancient ceramics; bucchero (or grey ware) had been popular for a long time in Aeolis when Etruscan bucchero first emerged. Apparently there was no direct connection in shape and decoration, nor yet in technique. In Etruria the development of the bucchero technique can be traced from traditional Italian wares; the clay is refined and the reduction in firing, previously probably accidental, is finally deliberate and complete. In this manner the good examples are fired throughout to a dark grey with a shiny black surface, but the color varies to a light and occasionally yellowish grey.

The earliest distinctly bucchero pottery of Etruria is found in the second quarter of the 7th century. In the first phase, which covers the middle years of the 7th century, the technique is frequently excellent, the shapes well conceived and executed, the decoration, where desired, depends on simple ornaments boldly incised or neatly pricked out. By 600 B.C. increasing Greek influence had modified the forms, which were more refined and less bold; decoration had dwindled to groups of bands lightly incised; the technical quality is still good but frequently less stimulating. In the next phase refinement yields to awkward ostentation and by the middle of the 6th century it was evident that the style and technique were rapidly declining. Among the common shapes are amphora, oinochoë, kantharos and kyathos. Decoration, at least until the late phase, is subordinate to the form and is frequently omitted. In general the models for bucchero decoration, incised or relief, are Greek and probably from painted pottery; occasionally, perhaps regularly, the incised lines were filled with white or red paint. There was also in Etruria a small amount of colored bucchero, that is, bucchero with decoration painted in white and purple, and occasionally blue over the dark ground. Bucchero is common throughout Etruscan Italy and was most likely made in many places; there was some export. (65)

Buchwald, Johann Repairer and arcanist at Höchst, 1748; Fulda, 1748; Holitsch, 1754. Worked successively at the Swedish factories of Stralsund, Rörstrand and Marieberg, 1755-1758; then in Schleswig-Holstein at Eckernförde, c. 1761-1768, Kiel, c. 1768-1772, and Stockelsdorf, 1772-1785 or later. His son Johann Heinrich was painter and potter at Rheinsberg, 1795-1798, at Neustadt-Eberswalde, 1799, and later at Stockelsdorf. See *Leihamer, J.* (296)

Budapest In Hungarian ceramics; a porcelain factory was started here by Emil V. Fischer in 1866 producing useful and ornamental wares.

Buddha   In Chinese art; see *Chinese Gods.*

Buen Retiro   In Spanish ceramics; the principal porcelain manufactory of Spain founded by Charles III (d. 1788) King of Naples, who, in 1759, inherited the crown of Spain and who transported with him the ceramic artists and workers from Capo di Monte. The wares began to decline after 1780 and it ceased to operate after 1808. La Moncloa, 1817-1850, was to some extent a continuation. The manufactory was established in the gardens of the royal palace of Buen Retiro, near Madrid. The mark of a fleur-de-lis, generally in blue or gold, was almost always used on the wares produced until 1804. After 1804 a crowned M was used, which was afterwards used at La Moncloa. The finest and most typical Buen Retiro porcelain was made from about 1765 to 1780 and differed in certain details from the Louis XVI style. It was as carefully finished as Sèvres, by which it was much influenced, and it was made of a beautiful soft paste material having a wax-like texture. Figures were the chief production and they merit high praise. The painted decoration at its best was remarkable for its fineness. Vases, tableware, bowls, jugs, mirror frames and other similar objects were all produced here and showed distinction and refinement. During the last two decades of the 18th century classical biscuit figures and biscuit vases with low relief decoration were characteristic productions. See *Capo di Monte.* (340-342)

Buffalo Pottery   In American ceramics; owes its existence to a cake of soap, Sweet Home Soap, made by the John D. Larkin Company of Buffalo. Giving premiums for the purchase of its soap helped make Larkin a household word and eventually the need for more and better premiums resulted in the Buffalo Pottery started in 1903 by John Larkin to produce ceramic wares for that purpose. Originally the production went entirely to Larkin, but eventually outside firms and organizations ordered articles made for their specific needs. In its most flourishing period Buffalo Pottery made not only Larkin premiums and mail-order merchandise for Larkin but advertising and commemorative items for others and commercial tableware as well. The most famous of all Buffalo wares are the distinctive and colorful Deldare and Emerald Deldare pieces. Buffalo Pottery wares can be readily identified since most of them are clearly marked and dated. From the beginning until complete mechanization was adopted in the 1940's almost all Buffalo Pottery bore the date of manufacture. In 1915 they introduced vitrified china which was marked Buffalo China instead of Buffalo Pottery as stamped on their semi-vitreous wares. In 1956 the name of the company was changed to Buffalo China Inc.; at present the firm is producing hotel and institutional wares. In 1905 Buffalo Pottery introduced its Blue Willow ware, and in 1908, seeking to produce an artistic quality ware, it introduced Deldare ware with its distinctive olive-green body color. The transfer-printed and hand-decorated Fallowfield Hunt scenes appearing on Deldare ware dated 1908 and 1909 were reproduced from colored scenes drawn by the English artist, Cecil Charles Windsor Aldin (1870-1935). Much of the Emerald Deldare ware (introduced in 1911 and virtually every piece is dated 1911) was decorated with Dr. Syntax scenes with borders showing Art Nouveau influence. Earlier Dr. Syntax scenes in blue have the characteristic Clews floral borders.

Bulb Bowl   In Chinese ceramics; a shallow bowl-shaped vessel of varying form, averaging around 9½ inches in diameter, principally used as a stand or saucer for a flower pot and often used individually as a bulb bowl. It is sometimes called a flower

BUFFALO POTTERY

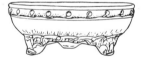

BULB BOWL, SUNG

1879 ON

pot stand. It was mounted on three or four feet which were very often engraved in the form of cloud scrolls. The Chün yao bulb bowl was without decoration except for the bowl with a plain round body which had two bands of raised studs or bosses. Chün yao bulb bowls corresponded in shape to the flower pots which they held, and both were remarkable for the elegant simplicity of their forms and for the indescribable beauty of their glazes. It is generally believed that bulb bowls were very frequently used separately, like the vessels of similar form made in celadon and Ming monochromes. See *Chün Yao.*

Bulidon, Henri Modeler at Chantilly, 1737, and at Vincennes and Sèvres, 1745-1759.

Bunzlau In German ceramics; a distinctive variety of salt-glazed stoneware, having a peculiar bright and rich rust-brown and coffee-brown color, was made at Bunzlau, Silesia, or in that vicinity chiefly during the 18th and 19th centuries. It had a fine grey-brown body and it is believed that its color was due to a wash of a ferruginous material. Its principal wares were pear-shaped tankards and coffee pots, which were sometimes spirally reeded. Decorative motifs when used consisted of applied reliefs of yellowish clay of formal leaves and flowers and coats-of-arms. Sometimes the reliefs were painted in enamel colors of red, blue and black with touches of gilding. The manufactory has been active until modern times. No mark was found on the 18th century pieces.

Bunzo, Hozan (d. c. 1720) Japanese studio-potter, whose art name was Yasabei. He specialized in decorating faïence in under-glaze blue, especially with landscape and in imitating Delft. He was a teacher of Moku-bei and Dohachi. It is said that the Bunzo family came from Omi in the mid-17th century and that pottery bearing the mark of Hozan surpassed all other Awata pottery in originality and beauty. They were among the many imitators of Ninsei. This

family is reputed to have created the curious arabesque pattern of thick enamels in blue with ground colors of white or yellow, on an unglazed surface.

Burgauté In Chinese ceramics; a term given to porcelain covered with black lacquer and inlaid with mother-of-pearl. Early specimens of this work were found in the Ming dynasty; however, the majority were in the Ch'ing dynasty. It is also called *lac-burgauté.*

Burgess and Campbell In American ceramics; started a pottery at Trenton, New Jersey in 1879, and were active until around 1900. Included in their production was white granite and white earthenware.

Burgess and Leigh (Ltd.) In English ceramics; operated the Hill Pottery, c. 1867-1889 and Middleport Pottery c. 1889, at Burslem in the Staffordshire district where they produced earthenwares. Burleigh ware occurs in their printed marks from the 1930's. The distinguishing initials B & L or Burgess and Leigh are found on several printed or impressed marks of differing design.

Burslem Period 1759-1769. See *Wedgwood, Josiah.*

Burton, William and Joseph English ceramists. See *Pilkington's Tile and Pottery Company.*

Bussi See *Castelli.*

Bustelli, Franz Anton (1723-1763) Born at Locarno, Switzerland; he is perhaps the most talented genius of all modelers for porcelain figures. He worked for Nymphenburg from 1754 to 1763 where he created a series of figures from Italian Comedy, allegorical putti, Chinese boys, shepherds, hawkers, beggars, lovers, cavaliers and ladies, dogs and other animals which for creative fantasy, rhythmical flowing lines, masterly composition and simplification of form have few equals in European ceramics. (321-323)

Buthaud, René (b. 1886) French painter and ceramist; his stonewares exhibited at the Salon d'Automne in the 1920's were notable for their vigorous creativity combined with thorough technical knowledge. He was noted for his pottery with theatrical human figures and reclining nudes. (530)

Butler, Frank See *Doulton, Lambeth and Burslem.*

Byzantine The art of the Eastern Roman Empire. It is a mixed art and is composed of Greco-Roman and Oriental elements. An important stimulus was given to the development of Byzantine art in A.D. 330 when the Emperor Constantine made the ancient city of Byzantium the new capital of the Roman Empire and moved his court and government to Constantinople, which was the new name for Byzantium. Christianity had also been established as the state religion. The final division of the Roman Empire into Eastern and Western became permanent in A.D. 395. The influence of Byzantine art, except for the interruption caused by iconoclasm, persisted until 1453 when the Moslems conquered Constantinople. While the West was in chaos, Greco-Roman civilization blended with Oriental influence was sustained by Byzantine art. The 6th century was a glorious period in Byzantine art. It rose to a new period of great splendor under the Macedonian emperors, 867-1056. After this time a general deterioration became increasingly evident. The influence of Byzantine art spread throughout Europe. It was one of the principal elements in Romanesque art which attained its highest development in Europe in the 12th century. See *Romanesque.*

Byzantine In ceramics; some interesting varieties of pottery classed as Byzantine have been found in the territory of the old eastern Roman Empire, which covers a wide area of Eastern Europe, and in time the entire period of the Eastern Empire from the foundation of Constantinople in 324 to its conquest by the Turks in 1453. Undoubtedly the finest wares belong to medieval times and include green and yellow glazed pottery with sgraffiato and incised decoration. They date from the 10th to the 13th centuries. On the incised wares geometrical, radiating and small symmetrical foliate motifs predominated. Other wares displayed impressed designs or were painted in yellow, brown, green, blue, red and manganese in the same motifs found on the incised wares. Probably dating from the 15th century are some interesting peasant wares with marbled slip decoration in green and brown, and some types associated with the Greek Islands showing strong Turkish and Spanish influence. (181-185)

BYZANTINE BOWL WITH
SGRAFFIATO DECORATION

C

C. T. The distinguishing initials appearing in a popular 19th century porcelain mark of varying design. See *Altwasser*.

Cabaret A French term meaning tea or coffee service. The name is usually given to a matched set, generally made of silver or porcelain, comprising a teapot or coffee pot, sugar bowl, creamer, cups and saucers and tray, for one or two persons. Sometimes the silver spoons, knives and forks are included. During the 18th century finely worked traveling cabarets in fitted cases were very fashionable.

Cachepot In French ceramics; a French term for an ornamental container to hold a flower pot. Especially notable were the fine porcelain cachepots made at Vincennes and Sèvres. (343)

CADOGAN TEAPOT

Cadogan Teapot In English ceramics; a variety of teapot or hot water pot having the form of a Chinese peach-shaped wine pot, filled through a hole in the base. It derived its name from the Hon. Mrs. Cadogan who had brought the original Chinese wine pot to England. It is believed that it was first made as a coffee pot at Swinton early in the 19th century and was later made by several Staffordshire potters.

Caen In French ceramics; a French porcelain manufactory that operated during the late 18th century. The accepted mark is Caen in red. Included among the wares were coffee pots, milk jugs, cups and bowls decorated with landscapes in black enclosed in small squares and suspended from wreaths and festoons painted in green and gold. Some of the wares were sent to Paris to be decorated in the style of Sèvres.

Caffaggiolo In Italian ceramics; during the first three decades of the 16th century some of the most beautiful of all Italian majolica was made at Caffaggiolo, near Florence. It is believed that the manufactory was under the patronage of the Medici family. Among the marks are SPR in monogram; a trident. Many pieces have no mark at all. Although Caffaggiolo majolica was influenced by the work at Faenza it revealed much originality in its design. An unusual dark cherry red was almost peculiar to this manufactory. A deep strong dark blue heavily laid on with a coarse brush was much used as a background. The green was clear and transparent and the orange and lemon yellows were excellent. The finest painting was from around 1508 to 1525. Attributed to Caffaggiolo are plates and dishes and large jugs.

Caille, Pierre Belgian artist-potter and teacher who first became prominent for his ceramics in the 1940's. Originally producing faïence, his later work includes stoneware. He has made figures and ornamental panels as well as pottery decorated in a modern manner.

Cailloutages In ceramics; the French term for cream-colored earthenware. It was so called because calcined flints were included among its ingredients.

Caillouté In French ceramics; a decorative marbled colored ground used on Sèvres porcelain, marked with a pebble-shaped network.

Callot Figure In ceramics; a grotesque figure of a dwarf made of porcelain. It was so called because it was copied after engravings or drawings by the French designer Jacques Callot (1593-1635) or after the work of other engravers executed in a Callotesque manner. Callot figures were made at Meissen, Vienna and Chelsea. (304)

Caltagirone See *Sicily*.

Calyx Krater See *Krater*.

Camaieu In ceramics; a French term used to describe painting in different tones of the same color.

Cambrian Pottery See *Swansea*.

Cameo Engraved relief work done on hard stones or gems. The work is in direct contrast to that of intaglio. The material selected for this type of engraving usually has layers of different colors; in this manner the figure is cut in relief in one layer, while another layer of a different color serves as a background. In ceramics; noteworthy are the cameos in jasper and other bodies with the ornament in relief in one color on a ground of a different color made by Wedgwood. See *Intaglio*. (423, 424)

Cameo China See *Wheeling Pottery Company*.

Candaliere In Italian ceramics; the Italian contemporary term, meaning candle stick, for a favorite decoration employed on Renaissance Italian majolica. It consisted of a symmetrically arranged design centering a vertical motif which was generally a candelabrum of fantastic form.

Cane Ware In English ceramics; a buff or cane-colored stoneware made by Wedgwood and other contemporary Staffordshire potters which was occasionally enriched with enamel decoration. Essentially it was a refinement of the ordinary iron-bearing buff body which, in 1770, Wedgwood made into a new and lighter body and called cane. Chocolate-colored stonewares were also made. See *Wedgwood, Josiah; Bamboo Ware; Colored Bodies*.

Canopic Jar In Etruscan ceramics; a kind of pottery cinerary urn placed in Etruscan tombs, so called from its resemblance to the jars made extensively at Canopus, Egypt, in which the Egyptians placed the

viscera of a corpse and buried it with the mummy. In the early Etruscan examples dating from the 8th century B.C. the cover of the jar was in the form of a human head and finally, in the most developed type of the 5th century B.C., the jar was given a primitive human figure, the handles being in the form of human arms.

Cantagalli In Italian ceramics; perhaps the most celebrated of the potteries devoted to the imitation of Italian majolica wares of the 16th century was started at Florence by Ulysse Cantagalli in 1878. See *Majolica*.

Canton In Chinese ceramics; from as early as the 12th century stoneware articles, and possibly porcelain, were produced and exported by the many kilns in the province of Kuangtung, of which the city of Canton, the chief commercial center and port on the Pearl River, is the capital. With the rapid growth of the East India trade which followed upon the reopening of the port of Canton in 1699 vast quantities of blue-and-white, Famille Verte porcelain, followed in the 1720's by Famille Rose wares and others were shipped from the ports of the Canton estuary (among them Hong Kong) where orders were taken from the European traders. Though all this porcelain ware itself was of Ching-tê-Chên manufacture, the decoration of much of it was done at Canton. Frequently the finest examples of this Canton-painted porcelain are of eggshell thinness and being colored on the reverse with rose-pink or crimson enamel are known as "ruby back" porcelain. The majority of them date from the middle decades of the 19th century. See *Famille Rose; Ching-tê-Chên*. In America the name *Canton ware* is commonly reserved for a type of lowly Chinese blue and white export porcelain. It was not made at Canton but at potteries near Canton as well as at Ching-tê-Chên to the north, although much of the painting was done at the port of Canton where families, including the children, did the work. American trade

CANTON CHINA CANISTER

with China began in 1785, and almost immediately Chinese porcelain tableware was imported directly from Canton, the first port visited. Therefore the term *Canton Ware* became common when speaking of this tableware. It was brought continuously to America in ships' cargoes until the Communist regime. It was heavy, which made it useful as ballast, and it was cheap, so it could be sold at home for common dishes. The charm of Canton is the endless variation of the design. In the pattern there are always willow trees, a tea house, bridge, a flight of birds and a landscape. Canton made before 1890 is better quality than later ware; even before that date deterioration had begun when the great demand was to meet orders sent out from America and England. Though the Chinese knew the method of transfer printing, they continued to decorate their ware by hand, hence the variation of pattern and color.

CAPO DI MONTE

1743-1759

1771 ON

1771 ON

Capo di Monte In Italian ceramics; a porcelain manufactory was founded in the royal palace of Capo di Monte by King Charles III of Naples. It was active from 1743 to 1759, when Charles III inherited the Spanish throne and took with him the ceramic workers and established a new factory at Buen Retiro, near Madrid. Ferdinand IV reopened it in 1771 and at the same time removed it to the royal Villa di Portici. He transferred the works again in 1773 to the royal palace at Naples where it flourished until 1806. From 1807 to 1834 the factory and materials changed hands several times. The production of this last period had little artistic importance. Eventually the molds and models were acquired by the Doccia manufactory. The porcelain from 1743 to 1759 was often not marked; however, a fleur-de-lis impressed was commonly found on figures. During the second period the marks were a crowned N and FR or RF in monogram. The material for Capo di Monte porcelain was a creamy white color. Especially fine and

ranking with the best made in Europe were some beautifully modeled figures marked with a fleur-de-lis and made of a slightly yellowish soft paste porcelain. Figures from the Italian Comedy were much favored. The majority of wares such as tableware and vases decorated in low relief and enameled in harsh colors and very often marked with a crowned N are later Doccia reproductions and were made of a greyish paste. Classical figures in glazed or unglazed porcelain were made from around 1785 and figures of Neapolitan folk types appeared around 1800. In the final period, 1807-1834, biscuit and white glazed figures in the style of the Empire were typical. The porcelain material after 1771 was generally of a pleasing ivory tone and the texture had much charm. See *Gricci, G.; Verdone, G.; Falcone, A.; Celebrano, C.; Schepers, L. O.; Naples; Buen Retiro.* (339)

Carbonnel, Guidette French designer, specializing in sculptured pottery for decorative purposes and in earthenware with a tin glaze such as tiles with incised designs for the tops or support-ends of tables; working since the Second World War. Member of the Salon d'Automne.

Cardew, Michael English artist-potter; was a pupil of Bernard Leach at St. Ives, 1923-1926. Here he studied to produce a well-conceived, simple and artistic type of ware that would attract by its appearance, could be acquired by the public at a reasonable cost, and would fulfill its purpose as a household necessity for daily use. The result was his slipware and galena-glazed pottery, for which he is well known. At his small pottery near Winchcombe in the Cotswolds he produced lead-glazed pottery for cottage and kitchen use, including among other things casseroles, bowls, beer and cider jugs and mugs, all having a racily native character. His large cider jars are his triumph. Cardew succeeded in reviving lead-glazed earthenware in the English style. In 1942 he took over from

Harry Davis the pottery school connected with the Achimota College in West Africa. After the craft part was closed he set up his own workshop and kiln at Vumé on the Volta River, some one hundred miles away. There Cardew made stoneware, some of which is among the most beautiful to come from the hands of modern potters. (539)

Carlsbad   See *Austria, Czechoslovakia and Hungary; Altrohlau.*

Carlstadt, Jakob and Cornelius   Modelers at Kelsterbach from 1763 probably until 1766. Jakob, who was at Höchst before 1771, returned to Kelsterbach. They made some interesting porcelain figures.

Carp Pattern   The name given to an Ansbach faïence pattern. (288)

Carpet Bowls   In ceramics; pottery balls of solid clay were made in England and Scotland for use in a game called carpet bowls. They were probably made during the first half of the 19th century. It was a favorite winter game played with six pairs of heavy pottery balls. The balls were decorated with bands of various colors and the jack was a white ball.

Carquois, à la   In French ceramics; a characteristic polychrome Rococo painted decoration used on Rouen faïence from around the middle of the 18th century that was imitated elsewhere. The motifs included bows and arrows, flowers, quivers and other similar subjects. See *Rouen.*

Carr, James   English potter working in the United States at Jersey City Pottery. From about 1852 to 1853 he operated the Congress Pottery at South Amboy, New Jersey, in partnership with Daniel Greatbach. Aroung 1853–1855, Carr started the New York City Pottery in partnership with Morrison. See *New York City Pottery.*

Carrara   In English ceramics; a dense white stoneware with only a slight glaze which gave its surface a texture suggestive of marble, introduced at Doultons of Lambeth in the 1880's. It was decorated with colored patterns, often with a lustered effect.

Carriès, Jean   (d. 1894) French sculptor who in the 1880's became interested in the glazing techniques of the Far East. Before his early death he employed this new medium for sculpture and for making vessels.

Cartlidge, Charles   (d. 1860) Of Staffordshire origin, Charles Cartlidge, who had been an agent for the Staffordshire Ridgway Potteries in the United States, established a factory in 1848 at Greenpoint, Brooklyn, N.Y., where he and his partner Henry Q. Ferguson made porcelain buttons, doorknobs, doorplates and other china hardware, candlesticks, portrait busts in biscuit and cameos or plaques. His brother-in-law, Josiah Jones, is believed to have been responsible for making the molds for much of the work. Elijah Tatler is credited with most of the painted decoration. The factory closed in 1856 but the works was carried on under the name Union Porcelain Works. See *Union Porcelain Works; Jones, Josiah.*

Cartouche   In ornament; a French term given to a decorative motif having the shape of a scroll of paper. It was especially used as a tablet in the form of a partly unrolled scroll of oval form on which could be placed a heraldic device or some inscription. The cartouche was a favorite motif in the Baroque and Rococo styles of ornament. (274)

Cascabel   See *Central American Pottery.*

Cash Pattern   In Chinese ceramics; a Chinese round copper coin or disc having a square hole in the center. It is a symbol of prosperity and is used in decoration either singly or worked into a diaper pattern.

CARDEW, MICHAEL
C. 1926 ON

Cassel In German ceramics; there were four potteries in existence at Cassel, Hesse-Nassau, during the 18th century. A faïence manufactory from 1680 to 1786-1788; a porcelain manufactory 1766 to 1788; the Steitz vase and earthenware factory, 1771 to 1862 or later; and Le Fort's, later Hillebrecht's, earthenware factory, 1772 to 1805. All these factories were either owned or patronized by the Landgrave of Hesse-Cassel at some time or other. Of these four the most important was the one established in 1771 making marbled and agate ware and glazed earthenware. The faïence wares, 1680 to 1786, had little artistic merit. They were largely blue and white and at first were strongly influenced by the wares of Delft. The mark HL in monogram was sometimes used. The porcelain wares, 1766 to 1788, were chiefly blue and white wares for daily use. The mark is the lion of Hesse with a double tail, or HC. The porcelain material was imperfect. Earthenware in the English style, 1771 to 1862, included marbled and agate ware and glazed earthenware, especially vases and figures. Vases modeled in the Neo-Classic style in imitation of Wedgwood vases were especially outstanding. The mark Steitzische Vasenfabrik in Cassel was sometimes found on the vases. Another mark after 1788 was the Hessian lion impressed, but it is very seldom found. Useful wares were also made.

CASSEL

PORCELAIN 1766-1788

Castel Durante In Italian ceramics; the majolica made at Castel Durante, renamed Urbania in 1635, near Urbino, during the first three decades of the 16th century ranks among the world's most beautiful painted pottery. Its productions, like those of Tuscany and Faenza, had a great formative influence on the majolica styles adopted in Italy. Its painted decorations are especially associated with two great artists, Giovanni Maria and Nicola Pellipario, who later was at Urbino. Included among the characteristic decorative manner of Castel Durante as found on dishes

and plates were borders of foliage and central medallions; fantastic subjects with cupids, grotesques and demons occasionally arranged symmetrically or *a candaliere*; bound and blindfolded figures; white ribbon streamers on a blue ground; borders composed of grotesques, cupids, masks, foliations and trophies. Bianco sopra bianco, particularly for inner borders, was a feature of Castel Durante. The so-called *a trofei* decoration was much favored. It is generally believed that the full istoriato manner known as the Urbino style was the invention of Pellipario while still working at Castel Durante. Another familiar type of dish was the so-called bacile amatori, which was usually painted with portraits of ladies or helmeted warriors. Pellipario's best painting was remarkable for its beauty of color, for its delicate and sensitive drawing and for its skillful composition. He is generally regarded as the greatest of all majolica painters. The majolica workshops at Castel Durante flourished during the 16th century; however, in the succeeding century the work was very inferior. See *Istoriato; Pellipario, Nicola; Maria, Giovanni.* (231)

Castelli In Italian ceramics; a leading center for majolica during the 17th and 18th centuries. The productions of the neighboring centers at Naples, Atri, Teramo and Bussi are generally included in the majolica of Castelli. Their productions were almost completely decorative works and were representative of the final revival of the art of Italian majolica. Especially characteristic are borders of putti or cupids among flowers and foliage, and pictorial panels of landscapes or of three-quarter length mythological subjects notable for their charming composition and delicate painting. Gilding was often used. Much of the fame of Castelli rests on the work of Carlo Antonio Grue (1655-1723). After 1750 the quality of the painting declined. The potteries survived into the 19th century; however, the

Terracotta Kneeling Madonna, by Mateo Civitali, c. 1490. *Collection: John T. Dorrance, Esq.*

Meissen Boettger Bowl, c. 1715. *The Antique Company of New York, Inc.; The Antique Porcelain Company.*

Meissen Tureen from the "Red Dragon" Service, made for Augustus II, King of Poland, Elector of Saxony, c. 1730. *The Antique Company of New York, Inc.; The Antique Porcelain Company.*

Capo di Monte Topographical Dish, Group of Dottore and Harlequin quarrelling while separated by Columbine and Bonbonniere, c. 1745–50. *The Antique Company of New York, Inc.; The Antique Porcelain Company.*

LEFT: Meissen Tureen, "Yellow Lion" Service in the Kakiemon style, c. 1728. RIGHT: Meissen Tureen in the Kakiemon style, c. 1728. *The Antique Company of New York, Inc.; The Antique Porcelain Company.*

Imari Plate decorated with peony basket and floral motif in underglaze blue and overglaze enamels. Edo Period, 1700. *Smithsonian
Institution, Freer Gallery of Art.*

Kakiemon Jar decorated with floral medallions and arabesques in overglaze
enamels. Edo Period, 17th century. *Smithsonian Institution, Freer Gallery of Art.*

Kutani Plate with quail on a rock and peonies. Edo Period, probably fourth quarter of the 17th century. *Seattle Art Museum.*

Meissen Chinoiserie Tankard, decoration ascribed to Christian Friedrich Herold and Johann Gregor Herold, before 1730. *Collection: Mr. and Mrs. Howard B. Noonan.*

Nymphenburg Food Warmer (Réchaud), c. 1755–60. *The Antique Company of New York, Inc.; The Antique Porcelain Company.*

Meissen Ewer and Basin, by Adam Friedrich von Loewenfinck, c. 1735. *The Antique Company of New York,*
Inc.; The Antique Porcelain Company.

Worcester (Dr. Wall) Plate, c. 1765. Coffee Pot, Tea Pot and Cream Jug, decorated by James Giles, c. 1765. *The*
Antique Company of New York, Inc.; The Antique Porcelain Company.

Vincennes Chocolate Cup with Lid and Stand, before 1755. *Collection: The Walters Art Gallery, Baltimore.*

St. Cloud Pair of Cachepots, c. 1730, and Miniature Chinoiserie Group, c. 1720. *The Antique Company of New York, Inc.; The Antique Porcelain Company.*

Worcester (Dr. Wall) Tea and Coffee Service. *Collection: Mr. and Mrs. Paul Mellon.*

work had little artistic merit. See *Italian Majolica*.

Castleford In English ceramics; a pottery was founded around 1790 by David Dunderdale at Castleford, Yorkshire, England, for making cream-colored earthenware similar to that made at Leeds. The pottery also made black basaltes and other characteristic Leeds and Staffordshire wares. White or cream-colored half-glossy stoneware with relief molded patterns frequently outlined in bright blue is a typical Castleford variety of about 1815, but it was also made at Leeds and at other potteries.

Castleton China Company See *Zeisel, Eva.*

Castor Ware In English ceramics; a pottery industry favored by the presence of excellent local clay and stimulated by economic conditions developed rapidly in the vicinity of modern Castor near Peterborough, in Northamptonshire. Beginning probably in the second century A.D. and flourishing in the third century, it apparently lasted into the early fifth century. These dark-surfaced wares were ornamented by means of trailed slip (barbotine) either in the form of scrolled ornament or of figures or animal subjects. Both kinds of decoration reveal the spirit of pre-Roman Celtic art modified by Roman influences. The indebtedness of these wares to the Gaulish barbotine-decorated red-gloss wares can be readily detected, but the Castor potters seem to revel in the emancipation from molded decoration which the Gaulish potters had only tentatively started. See *Roman Pottery; Barbotine.*

Catalonia In Spanish ceramics. It appears that pottery was made in several centers in this province from the 15th century onward, chiefly in imitation of Valencian. Perhaps at Barcelona the blue and white tiles of Valencia were imitated in the late 15th and 16th century.

Caughley In English ceramics; a manufactory was founded at Caughley, in Shropshire, shortly after 1750. Thomas Turner became the proprietor in 1772, and porcelain of the Worcester type began to be made. In 1799 it was purchased by John Rose of the Coalport manufactory. He produced biscuit ware at Caughley which he had glazed and finished at his Coalport manufactory. It closed in 1814. Caughley porcelain was of undistinguished quality and it chiefly imitated Worcester. A principal decoration was transfer printing in underglaze blue; however, painting in colors was also found. The familiar name for the wares was Salopian from the old Anglo-Saxon name for that part of the country. Much of the Salopian as well as early Coalport ware which it closely resembles was decorated in London. A bright hard quality of gilding was often added to the Salopian ware decorated in London. Among the marks were S in blue, C in blue or gold and Salopian in blue.

Cauldon Ltd. In English ceramics; a Staffordshire pottery, 1905-1920, located at Cauldon Place, Shelton, Hanley. They made china and earthenwares; formerly Brown-Westhead, Moore and Company and subsequently Cauldon Potteries Ltd., 1920-1962. See *Ridgway.*

Cauldon Potteries Ltd. See *Cauldon Ltd.*

Cauliflower Ware In English ceramics; a cream-colored ware modeled and colored in imitation of a cauliflower, developed in 1759 when Josiah Wedgwood was in partnership with Whieldon. (397)

Caussada, Jacinto And his sons, Jacinto and José, painters at the Alcora manufactory in Spain. José was working at Talavera, 1743-1750.

Cavetto A term applied to the center portion of a dish, saucer or plate.

CAUGHLEY

C. 1775-1790

CAULDON LTD.
1905-1920

CAULDON POTTERIES LTD
1950-1962

Caylus, Anne Claude Philippe, Comte de (1692-1765) French archaeologist and man of letters. He was an enthusiastic admirer of Greco-Roman art and he devoted much of his time to the study and collection of antiquities. He traveled extensively in Italy, Greece, the Near East, England and Germany. Among his antiquarian works is the RECUEIL D'ANTIQUITÉS published over a period of years beginning in 1752. This publication along with numerous others appearing around and after 1750 hastened the development of the Classic movement in France and the final abandonment of the Rococo style. He was also an excellent engraver, and he made many engraved copies of the paintings of the greater masters. See *Classic Revival; Engraved Designs; Cries of Paris.*

Cazin, Jean-Charles (1840-1901) French painter who, while teaching in London in the early 1870's, became involved in the early history of artist-pottery in England where he made stoneware decorated in relief in the Japanese manner.

CAZIN, C.
c. 1871-1874

Celadon In Chinese ceramics; a classic Chinese ware with a beautiful translucent green glaze having a velvet-like texture. The color of the green, which was developed to imitate jade, varies. The body varied from grey to white and burnt yellowish to reddish brown where exposed. The best-known kilns were at Lung-ch'üan in Chekiang which were famed for their celadon during the Sung dynasty. The characteristic Sung Lung-ch'üan celadon has a body that approaches a white porcelain in character, but its main glory rests in the radiant, light bluish-green glaze, obscured in depth and lustrous and smooth to the touch, which covers the strong clean contours of the ware like clinging velvet. Much of the existing ware is in the form of thick and heavy bowls, plates and jars. The decoration was carved with a knife, etched with a fine point or molded in low relief and was generally under the glaze. It is recorded that in the early Ming dynasty the Lung-ch'üan kilns were moved to nearby Ch'ü-chou Fu. However, this is not to be interpreted that celadon was no longer made at Lung-ch'üan or that it was not made prior to early Ming at Ch'ü-chou Fu. This celadon is known as Ch'ü-chou ware. Spotted celadon, or Chinese, Pao-pie, or Japanese, Tobi Seiji, is so called because it had spots of reddish brown which were caused by iron that turned reddish brown in firing. There were also celadon kilns in northern provinces, such as the kilns in Honan, near the capital Kai-Feng Fu which wàs the eastern capital under Northern Sung before A.D. 1127. An important kiln for celadon was at Ch'ên-liu which is southeast of Kai-Feng Fu. This is called Tung Yao or Eastern ware. They made a light and dark shade of celadon that was imitated during the Yung Chêng period at the Imperial manufactory. The name *celadon* is also given to early green Korean wares and to good imitations of Chinese celadon made in Japan. Green porcelain is called Ch'ing Tz'u in China and Seiji in Japan. It is said that this distinctive green was called celadon, which is a French word, after a character named Celadon in D'Urfé's romance of ASTRÉE. See *Korea; Porcelain; Sung; Yüeh Yao.* (96, 119, 123, 124, 244)

Celadon In Japanese ceramics; Japanese celadons were copied from Sung wares but they are generally clearer and more luminous in color because of their white body, with the muslin-like surface quality frequently seen on Japanese porcelain. Celadon porcelain was made at Arita, Hirado, Nabeshima and at Sanda in the province of Settsu where according to tradition it was first made around 1806 by Kanda Sobei. Sanda celadons are considered among the finest in Japan. Kyoto studio potters such as Mokubei also made celadon wares. See *Owari Celadon.*

Celebrano, Camillo Italian modeler at Capo di Monte in the early 19th century.

Central American Pottery In pre-Columbian ceramics; the three main periods of historical developments in Central America before the Spanish conquest are also used to designate their arts: Formative, 1500 B.C.-A.D. 300; Classic, A.D. 300-980; Post Classic, 980-1521. At the beginning simple utilitarian forms prevailed, such as plates, bowls, and storage jars. In the later phase of the Formative period the basic forms were given various kinds of supports. Of these the tripod support, which lent itself to a variety of forms, is perhaps the most typical feature of Central American pottery. The simple solid cone was later made hollow, and in some areas, especially on the Gulf coast, it evolved into a swollen mammiform shape. At times the hollow feet had small clay pellets inside which rattled when moved. These are known as cascabel feet. From the earliest times little effigy figures were modeled by hand, perhaps for use as votive offerings. Later, these representations were combined with vessel forms, such as a vase in the form of a fish. Included among the various decorative techniques were painting with a slip, which was sometimes scraped away to produce a design; incising, and negative or resist painting in which a resist substance is used to produce a design. Polychrome pottery in which only two colors were used, the natural clay surface providing the third color, was introduced late in the Formative period. In the succeeding Classic period the most important of the large regions in central Mexico were Teotihuacan, Monte Alban, the home of the Zapotecs in Oaxaca, and Cholula. To the southeast in Chiapas, Yucatan, Guatemala and Honduras was the Maya culture. On the Gulf coast the Olmecs continued and other groups such as the Huaxtec and Totonac were developing. In western Mexico the traditions of the Formative period were continued and certain rather specialized wares were introduced. It is convenient to date the end of the Classic period and the beginning of the Post Classic period with the destruction of Teotihuacan and the founding in 980 of Tula, the chief city of the Toltecs whose influence spread far and wide. The last phase of the Post Classic begins in 1325, the year Tenochtitlan (Mexico City) was founded. Gradually the Aztecs became the dominant power, which was to last until their final overthrow by Cortez in 1521. Pottery in this period is highly varied both in shape and style of decoration, as all the local styles were brought to Tenochtitlan by processes of war and trade. See *Pre-Columbian Pottery; Teotihuacan; Maya; Zapotec; Colima; Toltec; Aztec; Mixteca Puebla Pottery; Huaxtec; Totonac; Nicaragua, Costa Rica and Panama; Cholula; Olmec; Vera Cruz; Remajodas; Tarascan; Oaxaca; Puebla.* (6-14)

Century Guild In English arts and crafts; the Century Guild was formed in 1882 by Arthur Mackmurdo and Selwyn Image. Its aim was "to render all branches of art the sphere no longer of the tradesman, but of the artist. It would restore building, decoration, glass-painting, pottery, wood-carving and metal to their right place beside painting and sculpture." Mackmurdo started HOBBY HORSE, the Guild's magazine, in 1884. See *Arts and Crafts Movement.*

Century Vase In American ceramics; designed by Karl Müller and exhibited at the Philadelphia Centennial of 1876. The porcelain vase commemorates events in American history in six biscuit panels, while painted vignettes show the contemporary machines that were forging her progress. The relief profile of George Washington and the gilded eagle above establish the patriotic tone. Modeled heads of North American animals such as the walrus, bighorn sheep and bison (the latter serving as handles) ornament the vase. It bears the mark on the underside Century Vase Exhibited at Centennial Exhibition at

Philadelphia Manufactured 1876 By Union Porcelain Works Greenpoint, and UPW with an eagle's head with S in its beak. See *Union Porcelain Works.* (453)

Ceramic, Ceramics Derived from the Greek meaning earthenware. Ger. keramik; Fr. ceramique; It. ceramica. (*Ceramic* and *ceramics* do not appear in English as technical terms until the middle of the 19th century.) The potter's art; pottery, of or pertaining to pottery; the study of the art of pottery.

CERAMIC ART COMPANY
C. 1890-1906

Ceramic Art Company In American ceramics; established in 1889 at Trenton, New Jersey, by Jonathan Coxon Sr. and Walter Scott Lenox, who had learned the process of manufacturing Belleek when employed at Ott and Brewer. The factory excelled in Belleek, and the swan dish made around 1890 was one of its celebrated pieces. In 1906 the company was renamed Lenox Inc. The Belleek swan dish is still being made by Lenox. Characteristic marks include The Ceramic Art Co. Trenton, N.J. enclosed within a wreath, and CAC enclosed within a circle with a painter's pallette and brushes above to the left and the word Belleek printed in red below this stamp over the glaze. See *Belleek; Lenox Company.* (457)

BELLEEK SWAN DISH

Ceramic Plaques as Furniture Decoration In ceramics; the practice of decorating furniture with porcelain plaques was a marked feature of the French Louis XVI style, 1760-1790. Plaques of Sèvres porcelain were used at least as early as 1760. Under the First French Empire, 1804-1814, this taste is shown in a singular manner in the five still-existing large guéridon tables made of bronze mounted in Sèvres. In one model, the Table des Maréchaux (Table of the Marshals) dated 1810, the circular top made of a single piece of porcelain was taken from a design by Charles Percier, 1764-1838, French architect, and was painted by Jean-Baptiste Isabey with portraits as detailed as miniatures. It centers

Napoleon surrounded by thirteen golden rays each having the name of one of his famous victories. Between the rays are thirteen medallions with portrait busts of eleven marshals of the Empire and two great dignitaries. The top rests on a porcelain column depicting allegorical figures, mounted on a bronze base. The taste for porcelain to adorn furniture continued to a greater or less extent in France throughout the 19th century. In England, Wedgwood plaques in the Classical taste were occasionally found on late 18th century cabinetwork designed in the Neo-Classical style. It also occurred in some 19th century furniture. Notable are the two drawing room chairs exhibited at the Great Exhibition, held in London, 1851, the back of each being set with a large oval porcelain plaque, one with the portrait of Queen Victoria and the other with that of Prince Albert. See *Jasper Ware.* (360)

Ceramist A ceramic artist; one skilled in making ceramics.

Ch'a Hu In Chinese ceramics; the Chinese term given to a teapot.

Cha-Jin or **Tea Master** See *Rikyu, Sen-no.*

Cha-no-yu or **Japanese Tea Ceremony** In Japanese ceramics; the pottery vessels used in the tea ceremony embodied an ideal of simple austerity and humility. All were required to be beautiful, yet as simple and unpretentious and free from display and triviality as the conversation and. demeanor of the participants. The vessels comprised small jars for holding the powdered tea and bowls for infusing and drinking it, a vessel for water, a fire pot for burning charcoal, incense boxes and incense burners, a vase for a flowering spray, bottles for saké and dishes for cakes and sweetmeats. See *Iga; Rikyu, Sen-no; Six Old Kilns; Mino; Takatori; Satsuma; Hagi; Raku; Karatsu.*

Ch'a-yeh Mo In Chinese ceramics; the Chinese term for tea-dust glaze. See *Tea Dust.*

Chaffers, Richard (1731-1765) Potter working at Liverpool. See *Liverpool.*

Chalkware In American ceramics; the name is generally given to mantel or chimney ornaments made of plaster of Paris in imitation of the more costly ceramic figures so fashionable in the late 18th and 19th centuries. It appears that they were first imported from Europe and subsequently made in America. In 1768 Henry Christian Geyer of Boston advertised plaster of Paris figures of American manufacture. Early in the 19th century peddlers were selling chalkware portrait busts and figures on the streets of London, Philadelphia and New York. No doubt most of the trade in chalkware was carried on by Italians in America and abroad. The process of manufacture was relatively simple. The mold in two or more parts was also made of plaster of Paris and after the parts were joined together the plaster, of the consistency of pancake batter, was poured into the mold and swirled quickly around on the oiled inner surface until it had hardened in a thin layer. Occasionally after being finished the figure was filled with a cheaper type of plaster to give it weight as it was so light. Chalkware was invariably unglazed. The early figures were sized and colored with oil paints; at a later time water colors were used. The coloring was always applied by hand. Practically every object came in pairs, each facing in opposite directions. Especially favored were all kinds of animals and birds, fruit occasionally arranged in pyramid manner on the top of a vase, portrait busts of popular heroes and cottages occasionally provided with a candleholder inside. Undoubtedly Staffordshire chimney ornaments were the principal source of inspiration for the chalkware designs.

Chamberlain, Robert A former apprentice and potter at Worcester; he left the Worcester manufactory around 1783-1786 and founded a rival firm in the same city which was at first a decorating establishment only. By around 1791 Chamberlain started to manufacture his own porcelain. Marks were rarely used before 1795 but when they are found they appear as Chamberlains or Chamberlains Worcester Warranted. As the Chamberlain Works gained prestige, so the range of their products expanded and was no longer confined to useful tablewares. Richly decorated ornate vases painted by accomplished artists became a feature of their manufacture. Among the painters were Humphrey and Walter Chamberlain. In 1840 the two rival firms, that of Flight, Barr and Barr and that of Chamberlain were combined and new workshops were built at the Chamberlain site. Perhaps the absence of rivalry between the two firms resulted in a general decline in the standards of workmanship as well as a dearth of new ideas. The only innovation that was to become a traditional style` in the Worcester factories throughout the Victorian period was a series of double-walled objects introduced around 1845; the outer wall was pierced with geometrical designs, giving a "honeycomb" effect. In 1852 when the business of the Chamberlain Company was terminated, W. H. Kerr and R. W. Binns formed a new company in which the old spirit was recovered and the name of Worcester porcelain re-established. Binns, the art director, infused new ideas and directed the training of new young talent. In 1862 when Kerr retired and returned to his native Ireland, Binns formed a new joint stock company under the still-existing title of the Worcester Royal Porcelain Company. See *Worcester.* (476)

Chamberlains or **Chamberlains Worcester Warranted** See *Chamberlain, Robert.*

Chamberlains
Worcester
& 63. Piccadilly.
London
CHAMBERLAIN'S
C. 1814-1816

Champlevé Pottery See *Teotihuacan; Islamic Pottery, Medieval.*

Chanak Kale See *Islamic Pottery, Later.*

Chancay Black-on-White See *Andean.*

Chanou A family of potters working at Vincennes, Sèvres and other kilns in France in the 18th century. Chanou the Elder (b. 1724) was working as a modeler at the Rue de la Ville-l'Evêque at Paris and at Vincennes and Sèvres, 1745-1768. Chanou the Younger was a modeler at Vincennes and Sèvres, working there 1746-1779 and 1785-1792, and later. Several members of the second generation were repairers at Sèvres in the late 18th and early 19th century. Dame (mother) Chanou was a painter at Sèvres, in the late 18th century, specializing in flowers.

Chantilly In French ceramics; a famous soft paste porcelain manufactory was founded at Chantilly by Louis-Henri de Bourbon, Prince de Condé, in 1725 under the direction of Ciquaire Cirou (d. 1751). It was in existence until about 1800, and after this date several independent manufactories were established making hard paste porcelain and earthenware. The finer Chantilly was made under Cirou's management and its distinctive glaze was made white and opaque with tin-ashes as in faïence. This early glaze with its milky whiteness and smoothness was unsurpassed in the history of porcelain. The glaze after 1750 during the second period was the usual lead glaze of a slightly yellowish warm tone; however, it was still of fine quality. The accepted mark is a hunting horn; red enamel in the earlier period and underglaze blue in the later period. Especially characteristic of Chantilly were the delicate painted designs inspired by the Japanese Kakiemon porcelain which were in vogue from around 1725 to 1740. The painted colors were remarkable for their soft brilliance. Figure modeling of the early period was in the Japanese French

CHANTILLY
1725 ON

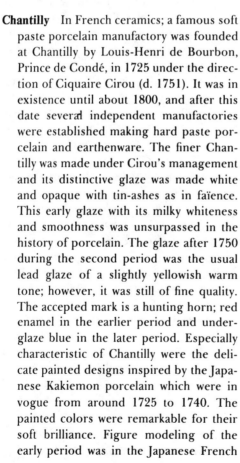

CHANTILLY PLATE

CHAPLET, ERNEST
AFTER 1860

taste and revealed an individual charm. The influence of Vincennes was apparent after the middle of the 18th century. During the later period quantities of simple and very often graceful tableware were produced. The plates were principally decorated in underglaze blue with slight floral patterns. During the last quarter of the 18th century there was evident an increasing amount of formalism in the designs which to a large extent detracted from their artistic interest. See *Faïence Fine.* (345, 346)

Chaplet, Ernest (1835-1909) French potter noted for his stoneware and porcelains. He started a school, L'Art du Feu; among the pupils was Auguste Delaherche. While the work of Théodore Deck may be regarded as the starting point of French artist-pottery, it was Chaplet who contributed the most to developing the cult of glaze techniques among a considerable group of French potters in the later years of the 19th century. In the 1870's Chaplet was interested in developing the barbotine technique of decoration, a process that involved painting in colored slips rather than in the style of oil painting. In the 1880's his stoneware began to arouse interest, which he pursued first with the support of Haviland and later in his own studio at Choisy-le-Roi. He spent the remaining years of his life working with porcelain which he covered with flambé glazes frequently as perfected as any from the Far East. See *Gauguin, P.* (490)

Charger A large flat dish or plate for carrying a large joint of meat to the table by the servant who, in medieval times in England, was also called a charger. See *Blue-Dash Charger.*

Charles X King of France, 1824-1830. See *Louis Philippe.*

Chatironné   See *Fleurs Chatironnées.*

Chavín   See *Andean.*

Chelsea   In English ceramics; the foremost English porcelain manufactory. It was established prior to 1745 at Chelsea, London, and was in existence until 1784. The early pieces marked with a triangle were generally in white and the forms were frequently taken from silver. It is assumed that Charles Gouyn was the manager during the "triangle" period. The next manager was Nicholas Sprimont. The manufactory seems to have been owned by Sir Everard Fawkener, secretary to the Duke of Cumberland who was a patron of the factory. Its first period was from around 1749 to the death of Fawkener in 1758. The manufactory seems then to have been closed for a couple of years. The mark for this period at first was a raised anchor or an anchor in relief and later a red anchor painted on the surface. The material for this period was a soft paste of exceptionally fine quality and the glaze which was slightly opaque was a cool white tone. The styles at first were influenced by Meissen; the Japanese brocaded Imari pattern and the Kakiemon designs were favored and borrowed from Meissen. The forms were in the Rococo taste. It is generally accepted that the Chelsea figures of this period are the finest ever made in England and rank among the best in European porcelain. Most of the figures were in the contemporary Meissen style and were simply and boldly modeled. Beautifully modeled figures of birds in natural colors were outstanding. Especially charming were the scent bottles, snuff boxes and other small objects, usually known as Chelsea toys and generally in the form of miniature figures. After Fawkener's death, Sprimont seems to have become proprietor as well as manager. The anchor mark was generally in gold. There was a noticeable change in the wares. Bone ash was included in the material and the glaze was more glassy. The general influence was Sèvres. Gilding was more profusely used and the decoration became more elaborate. Sprimont sold the manufactory to James Cox in 1769, who resold it in 1770 to William Duesbury and John Heath of Derby. The Chelsea factory was principally used by them for making tableware until it closed in 1784. The productions of this period, 1770-1784, are commonly called Chelsea-Derby and essentially follow the style of the Derby manufactory. See *Sprimont, N; Willems, J.; Donaldson, J.* (362-369)

Chelsea and Dedham   In American ceramics; an art pottery started in 1866 by Alexander W. Robertson at Chelsea, Massachusetts, called the Chelsea Keramic Art Works. Two years later Hugh Cornwall Robertson, apparently a younger brother, became a partner, and in 1872 James Robertson (d. 1880) a practical potter of wide and varied experience in Scotland, England, New Jersey and New York joined his sons, when work of a more ambitious character was undertaken. They made a variety of wares from reproductions of Greek vases and plaques with illustrations of La Fontaine's Fables to experiments with Sang de Boeuf. Around 1877 they introduced Chelsea faïence known as Bourg-la-Reine of Chelsea, produced by painting on the surface of the vessel with colored clays and covering with a transparent glaze. Imitations of Japanese crackle ware with underglaze blue decoration were also made. Hugh Robertson, who had been conducting experiments for many years, was instrumental in initiating these art wares. In 1884 Alexander Robertson retired, and in 1888 the pottery closed for lack of funds. In 1891, however, a company was incorporated under the name of Chelsea Pottery, U.S., of which Hugh Robertson was appointed manager. On account of certain disadvantages of the location, the kilns were abandoned; in 1896-1897 a new pottery was established at Dedham, Massachusetts, called the Dedham Pottery.

CHELSEA PATCH BOX

CHELSEA

TRIANGLE C. 1745-50

RAISED ANCHOR C. 1749-52

RED ANCHOR C. 1752-56

GOLD ANCHOR C. 1756-69

CHELSEA AND DEDHAM

CHELSEA KERAMIC
ART WORKS
1866

CHELSEA KERAMIC
ART WORKS
ROBERTSON & SONS
1875-1888

CHELSEA POTTERY, U.S.
1891-C. 1896

DEDHAM POTTERY
C. 1896

Here the grey crackle ware perfected at Chelsea won wide public acclaim. Made by hand, the porcelain body was decorated in underglaze blue designs, covered with a soft grey crackled glaze. In the beginning the forms included vases, fruit and salad plates, but as the demand increased more pieces were added. The patterns for plates included flowers and foliage, animals and such others as lobsters, crabs, butterflies and dolphins. Probably the most popular pattern is the rabbit, while the elephant is one of the most rare. The familiar mark is a conventionalized rabbit with Dedham Pottery above. (454)

Chelsea-Derby See *Chelsea; Derby.*

Chelsea Keramic Art Works See *Chelsea and Dedham.*

Chelsea Pottery, U.S. See *Chelsea and Dedham.*

Chelsea Toys See *Chelsea.*

Chely, Rudolph Anton See *Brunswick.*

Chên In Chinese ceramics; the name given to a headrest or pillow to be filled with hot or cold water or with scented petals or leaves.

Chenavard, Aimé French designer of ornament; wielded great influence. In 1830 he was appointed art director of Sèvres; in 1833 he published his NOUVEAU RECUEIL D'ORNEMENTS. He is reputed to have plundered the ornamental repertoire of all countries and all ages for motifs which he crammed into his chaotic and overcharged designs. Chenavard's pupils and others continued in the same tradition. Gothic, Louis XV, long-forgotten Assyrian, Chinese, Egyptian and Greek ornaments were included among the many sources explored for "new" motifs. See *Historicism; Victorian; Engraved Designs.*

Ch'êng Hua The Ch'êng Hua reign of the Ming dynasty in China; 1465-1487. See *Chinese Dynasties.*

Chêng Tê The Chêng Tê reign of the Ming dynasty in China; 1506-1521. See *Chinese Dynasties.*

Chêng T'ung The Chêng T'ung reign of the Ming dynasty in China; 1436-1449. See *Chinese Dynasties.*

Chesapeake Pottery In American ceramics; started in 1880-1881 at Baltimore, Maryland, by three English potters, John Tunstall, Henry Brougham and Isaac Brougham. They made Rockingham and yellow ware. In 1882 it was purchased by D. F. Haynes and Company and in 1887 the Chesapeake Pottery was organized. In 1885 parian wares were made here. These include heads, flowers and medallions of Thorwaldsen's Seasons, as well as original plaques with relief designs of heads of cattle modeled by the sculptor James Priestman, which were highly regarded. In 1890 the pottery became Haynes, Bennett and Company and in 1895, D. F. Haynes and Son. Victorian majolica with colored glazes was made here and is called Clifton Ware and bears the mark Clifton Decor B on crossed crescents with the monogram D.F.H.

Chi Chou Yao See *Kian Temmoku.*

Chi Hung In Chinese ceramics; the name given to the brilliant red derived from copper. This sacrificial red is particularly identified with the reigns of Hsüan Tê and Ch'êng Hua during the Ming dynasty. During the K'ang Hsi reign of the Ch'ing dynasty an attempt was made to reproduce this Ming red. The attempt was not successful but the misfiring did result in the magnificent monochromes called Peachbloom and Lang Yao or Sang de Boeuf. See *Ming; Underglaze Red.*

Ch'i-Lin In Chinese art; a fabulous or mythical animal subject extensively used in painting, sculpture and ceramics. It has a dual nature and is both male and female. It is generally portrayed as having a head

CHESAPEAKE POTTERY
1882-1885

that resembles the head of a dragon, the body of a deer with slender legs and horse's hoofs, a curly and bushy tail like a lion's, and shoulders with flames. It is regarded as the noblest form of animal creation and it is reputed to live for one thousand years. It is symbolic of perfection and happiness and its appearance portends a virtuous ruler. It is also called a kylin. See *Chinese Animal Figures.*

Chia Ching The Chia Ching reign of the Ming dynasty in China; 1522-1566. See *Chinese Dynasties.*

Chia Ch'ing The Chia Ch'ing reign of the Ch'ing dynasty in China; 1796-1820. See *Chinese Dynasties.*

Chiang T'ai See *Chinese Soft Paste.*

Chiang Tou Hung Bean red. See *Peach-bloom.*

Chiapas See *Central American Pottery.*

Chibcha Ware See *Ecuador and Colombia.*

Chicago Terra Cotta Company In American ceramics; established in 1858 by J. M. Blashfield. In 1870 James Taylor was brought over from England to become superintendent. By the introduction of English methods, the factory soon made better work than had been produced up to this time in the United States.

Chicaneau, Pierre (d. before 1678) He and his family were potters and porcelain-makers at Saint-Cloud; he is credited with the establishment of the porcelain factory at Saint-Cloud, the first important porcelain factory in France. It is believed that he must have known a formula for making porcelain which was improved upon by his widow (who married Henri-Charles Trou in 1679), and his children, Pierre II, Jean, Jean-Baptiste and Geneviève who joined in a patent of 1693. Pierre II was the manager of Saint-Cloud until his death in 1710. In the same years his widow Marie Moreau and her cousin by marriage, L. D. François

Chicaneau, together established the branch factory in Paris at the Rue de la Ville-l'Evêque, which appears to have been independent in 1722. L. D. François Chicaneau was alone in operating it, 1731-1743. One grandchild of Pierre I, Marie-Anne Chicaneau (who was admitted to the Saint-Cloud porcelain secret in 1741), married François Hébert, a potter at the Rue de la Roquette (Faubourg Saint-Antoine) factory in Paris and another married Denis Jacquemart, potter of the Rue Saint-Denis also in Paris. See *Rue de la Roquette; Saint-Cloud.* (300)

Chicanel See *Maya.*

Ch'ien Lung The Ch'ien Lung reign of the Ch'ing dynasty in China; 1736-1795. See *Chinese Dynasties.*

Chien Wên The Chien Wên reign of the Ming dynasty in China; 1399-1402. See *Chinese Dynasties.*

Chien Yao In Chinese ceramics; the Chien ware, which was first made during the Sung dynasty, was so named because it was made in the province of Fukien, first at Chien-an and then at Chien-yang. It consists almost entirely of tea bowls. The characteristic Chien yao tea bowl is conical in shape and has a coarse reddish-black stoneware body. The glaze is blue-black streaked or mottled with a lustrous brown. Sometimes the brown is the strong color and the mottlings and streaks are in black. Especially fine is the Chien yao bowl with a shining black glaze having fine radial rust-colored streaks that resemble the fur of a hare or the markings of a partridge. See *Temmoku; Kian Temmoku; Honan Temmoku.* The term *Chien yao* is also the Chinese term for Blanc de Chine. See *Blanc de Chine.* (97)

Chikusen A Japanese family of studio potters associated with the Kyoto circle of potters; they made excellent underglaze blue and white porcelain in the Chinese

CHIA CHING DOUBLE-GOURD VASE

taste, especially copies of Shonsui wares. Miura Chikuzen, the fourth generation to operate the family kiln, enjoys a fine reputation for his underglaze blue and white imitating Chinese Ming and Ch'ing wares. See *Kyo.*

Chimu In pre-Columbian Andean pottery; the pottery is almost always of a single color, either grey to black or red, and polished, the black being produced by firing in a reducing atmosphere combined with smoking. Painted vases are rare; when they are found they are usually decorated in red on a white slip. The modeling tradition of the Mochica was revived by the Chimu, but though a wide variety of forms were made, they were artistically inferior to the work of the earlier period. Among the conspicuous forms were the vessel with a stirrup spout and the double vase which may be a whistling jar. See *Andean.*

Ch'in Early period in Chinese art history, c. 221-206 B.C. See *Chinese Dynasties.*

China See *Porcelain.*

China In Far Eastern ceramics; to a great extent the history of Far Eastern ceramics is dominated by China, who furnished a source of-cultural dynamism for the entire area. For this reason the potters in such neighboring lands as Korea, Indo-China and Japan were deeply influenced by the ceramic art of China, both in technique and in design. In all these countries, the interaction was a fruitful one, for it brought a new richness to their native traditional skills. Clarity and refinement, a smooth perfection, are the classic qualities of the Chinese style in ceramic art, to which must be added a further elusive quality more consciously sought after in Far Eastern than in Western art generally, the nature of which embodies a freedom and directness, a complete disregard of mere smoothness and facility and mechanical perfection of finish. No particular superiority in technique is to be noted in the wares of the archaic periods in China.

The new impetus became evident in the centuries immediately preceding the Christian era, when by acquiring a mastery of high-temperature kiln-firing methods, the Chinese potter learned to make vitrifiable stonewares and to cover them with very durable glazes, a necessary step toward the later making of porcelain. In the following centuries the potter's skill in potting, glazing and firing became so improved that his wares became increasingly appropriate for refined usage. By the time of the T'ang dynasty, 618-908, his wares began to vie with the precious metals and jades. In the opinion of many connoisseurs the acme of the potter's art was achieved in the Sung dynasty, 960-1279. However, China's greatest single contribution to the advancement of ceramic art was a more purely technical accomplishment, namely the invention of white translucent porcelain. Though such a ware was already being made by the 9th century, it did not begin to acquire its modern role until the 14th century when techniques of painting in colors were developed. From this role other kinds of pottery were increasingly excluded. The wares of the ensuing Ming, 1368-1644, and Ch'ing, 1644-1912, dynasties are essentially based on this comparatively standard material. From the time porcelain of this kind first reached the Western world, European potters were inspired to create their own porcelain art. This, however, represents only a late phase of China's influence on the ceramic art of the world, which had been nurtured by export wares increasing consistently in quantity since the 9th or 10th century onward. Thus their imprint is seen on the pottery of the Islamic Near East, while medieval fragments of Chinese pottery confirm the vast sea trade which reached to Japan, Indo-China and the entire southeast Asian archipelago, and then westward to India and the Arab lands, even down the east coast of Africa as far as Zanzibar. See *Shang; Han; T'ang; Sung; Ming; Ch'ing.*

China Clay In ceramics; the English term for kaolin. See *Kaolin; Clay.*

China Stone In ceramics; the English term for petuntse. See *Petuntse.*

China-Trade Porcelain See *Chinese Lowestoft.*

Chiné In English ceramics; the name given at Doultons of Lambeth to a ware decorated, often attractively, by the impress of lace on its surface, introduced in the late 19th century.

Chinese and Japanese Influences Since the 16th century the influence of Chinese porcelain has been evident in European ceramic art, and its history is mainly a record of repeated endeavors to copy it both in material and in decoration. The desire to emulate the whiteness of Chinese porcelain resulted in tin-glazed faïence long before Böttger in 1709 finally succeeded in producing a genuine white-bodied porcelain. See *Islamic Pottery.* From the vast trade opened up by the Dutch East India Company, founded in 1609, stemmed the Dutch faïence industry which toward the middle of the 17th century found its incentive in the increased importation and popularity of Chinese porcelain. To this class belongs the imitation, mainly in Holland, Germany and France, of the paneled blue and white of the reign of Wan Li, 1573-1619. In the ever-increasing trade that grew up at the end of the 17th and beginning of the 18th century the English and French East India Companies, established in 1600 and 1664, respectively, played a dominant part bringing Japanese Arita wares as well as K'ang Hsi and later porcelains from China. Included among the very many varieties of Far Eastern painted decoration imitated in Europe at this time are the familiar blue and white of K'ang Hsi, and later the Famille Verte and Famille Rose, the slightly painted Japanese Kakiemon wares and Imari brocaded patterns, both made in the Japanese province of Arita. Apart from the painted porcelain, there was the Chinese Blanc de Chine made at Tê-hua and the buccaro, or imported red stoneware of Yi-hsing. Distinct from the direct influence of imported wares was the more diffused interest in the Far East to which can be attributed that remarkable phenomenon of fantastic European Chinoiserie. See *Chinoiserie; Japanism; Glaze,* in modern Western ceramics.

Chinese Animal Figures In Chinese art; a variety of animal subjects were extensively used by the Chinese in painting, sculpture, textiles and ceramics. The animal subjects to a large extent represent mythical creatures; however, some were also borrowed from the animal kingdom. Among the animal motifs which played an important part in Chinese culture and art are the following: Dog of Fo; Ch'i-Lin; Fêng Huang; Lung; Lu; Hu; Ho; T'u and Fu. See *Chinese Gods; Chinese Symbols and Emblems; Chinese Four Season Flowers.*

Chinese Blue and White See *Blue and White Ch'ing; Blue and White Ming.*

Chinese Dynasties and Reigns In Chinese art; the art work of China is designated by the dates of the dynasties and the reigns of the monarchs in each dynasty. The following is a chronological list of the dynasties and the reigns.

Hsia	? 1989-? 1523 B.C.
Shang or Yin	? 1523-? 1028 B.C.
Chou	? 1122-c. 256 B.C.
Warring States	c. 403-221 B.C.
Ch'in	c. 221-206 B.C.
Han	206 B.C.-A.D. 220
Six Dynasties	c. 222-589
Northern Wei	386-535
Liang	502-556
Sui	c. 581-618
T'ang	618-906
Five Dynasties	907-960
Sung	960-1279

Northern Sung		960-1127
Southern Sung		1127-1279
Yüan		1280-1368
Ming		1368-1644
Hung Wu	1368-1398	
Chien Wên	1399-1402	
Yung Lo	1403-1424	
Hung Hsi	1425	
Hsüan Tê	1426-1435	
Chêng T'ung	1436-1449	
Ching T'ai	1450-1457	
T'ien Shun	1457-1464	
Ch'êng Hua	1465-1487	
Hung Chih	1488-1505	
Chêng Tê	1506-1521	
Chia Ching	1522-1566	
Lung Ch'ing	1567-1572	
Wan Li	1573-1619	
T'ai Ch'ang	1620	
T'ien Ch'i	1621-1627	
Ch'ung Chêng	1628-1643	
Ch'ing		1644-1912
Shun Chih	1644-1661	
K'ang Hsi	1662-1722	
Yung Chêng	1723-1735	
Ch'ien Lung	1736-1795	
Chia Ch'ing	1796-1820	
Tao Kuang	1821-1850	
Hsien Fêng	1851-1861	
T'ung Chih	1862-1873	
Kuang Hsü	1874-1908	
Hsüan T'ung	1909-1912	
Chinese Republic		1912-

See *Chinese Porcelain Marks*.

GALLIPOT WITH LOTUS
DECORATION, MING

CHINESE PLATE WITH PEONY
MOTIF

Chinese Export Porcelain See *Chinese Lowestoft*.

Chinese Four Season Flowers In Chinese art; the Chinese artist revealed great talent in floral painting. Some of the finest porcelain designs are of flowers. Flowers treated in a conventional manner occur in scrolls and in continuous running designs; especially favored were the lotus and peony scrolls. However, the majority of floral designs are treated in a naturalistic manner and are admirable for their flowing and graceful qualities. Each flower is easily recognizable, but without a copied or studied character. The Chinese were great lovers of flowers and had a special flower for each month and one for each season. The peony was for spring, the lotus for summer, the chrysanthemum for fall and the plum blossom, or prunus, for winter. See *Chinese Gods; Chinese Animal Figures; Chinese Symbols and Emblems.*

Chinese Gods In Chinese art; there are four kinds of subjects recognized in Chinese art. They are figures; nature which includes birds, animals and flowers; landscapes; and miscellaneous subjects. The motifs borrowed from these four categories are endless. The figure subjects are deities and deified mortals borrowed from the three religions, namely Confucianism, Taoism and Buddhism. Taoism, which has the strongest hold on the Chinese imagination, has furnished the largest number of motifs for decorative art. Included among the favorite figure subjects are the following: Confucius, Buddha, K'uei Hsing, Kuan Ti, Kuan Yü, Shou Lao, Lu-hsing, Fu-hsing, Hsi Wang Mu, Kuan Yin, Pu-Tai Ho-Shang and the Eight Taoist Immortals or Pa Hsien. See *Chinese Animal Figures; Chinese Symbols and Emblems; Chinese Four Season Flowers.* (105, 108, 362)

Chinese Imari In Chinese ceramics; Chinese porcelain decorated with underglaze blue and overglaze colored enamels in the Japanese Imari style. It was made during the reign of K'ang Hsi, 1662-1722, and it is generally accepted that Japanese models continued to be used during the succeeding reign of Yung Chêng, 1723-1735. They copied the Kakiemon style and the characteristic old Imari wares. Especially characteristic of the old Imari was the porcelain with masses of a dark cloudy blue with a soft Indian red and gilding; these colors being supplemented by touches of green, aubergine and yellow enamels and a brownish black. The designs, which consisted of asymmetrical panels and mixed brocade patterns, had a bold decorative effect due to the prominence of the blue, red and gold. See *Imari; Kakiemon.*

Chinese Lowestoft In Chinese ceramics; a hard paste porcelain ware made in China and imported by the European countries from the early 1700's to 1835. It was known as Company Porcelain; it was also called East India porcelain because of the trading companies that handled it. It acquired the name *Lowestoft* in error as it was thought to have been made at a little factory at Lowestoft, England. It was an "export" quality ware and has only a historical value. It is generally agreed that much of this porcelain was manufactured at Ching-tê-Chên and was sent to Canton to be decorated. The ware was decorated in accordance with the merchant's taste. The final destination of the ware in Europe such as France, England and Portugal was often revealed in the taste of its decoration. A great many dinner and tea services were ordered with the coats of arms of the purchaser. It is also called Chinese Export Porcelain and Oriental Lowestoft. While technically Canton, Nanking and Rose Medallion can be classified as Chinese Export Porcelain, they are not called Oriental or Chinese Lowestoft, but rather retain their individual names based on the style of decoration. Chinese Lowestoft bears no factory or other marks. It was imported into the United States, directly from China, from 1784 when the *Empress of China* sailed from New York, to around 1835, when the market for porcelain was taken over to a great extent by the English manufacturers. The factories at Ching-tê-Chên continued to produce porcelain of an increasingly inferior quality until 1856 when they were destroyed during the Tai Ping revolution. See *Armorial Ware; Jesuit Ware.* (114-118)

Chinese Porcelain Marks Essentially marks are an unprofitable study for one interested in the art of the Chinese potter; attention to them should follow and not precede a study of shapes, designs, and physical characteristics of the ware. Marks, though sometimes used before, began to be regularly added to Chinese porcelains in the early part of the Ming period. From that time onward they were generally painted in underglaze blue, frequently enclosed in a double circle; but toward the end of the reign of K'ang Hsi, 1662-1722, colors and sometimes gold began to be used as well as the underglaze blue. Seal marks were frequently used in red in a square panel, which was occasionally, particularly in the reign of Ch'ien Lung, 1736-1795, and later, reserved on a turquoise-green ground. The Chinese have two methods of indicating a date. First by a nien hao, or name given to the reign or part of the reign of an emperor; second, by reference to a "cycle" of sixty years. A reign name is selected after the emperor has ascended the throne, and dates from the beginning of the first new year after his accession. Like the name of the dynasty, it is an epithet of good fortune selected from some classical text. Thus the reign name K'ang Hsi means Joys of Peace; the name of the Manchu dynasty Ch'ing means Pure. Reign names and dynastic names are the names of periods; thus a piece of porcelain is spoken of as belonging to a period rather than to a reign. The "six character" mark is generally written in two columns, composed as follows: two characters signifying the name of the dynasty prefaced by the word great (ta); two the reign name, and two more meaning period (nien) and make (chih). In the "four character" mark the name of the dynasty or in rare cases the reign-name is omitted. It is stated in the T'ao Lu that in 1677 an edict was issued prohibiting the use on porcelain of the reign-name of K'ang Hsi, lest the ware be broken and the Imperial name be profaned on the rubbish pile. This may explain the relative infrequency of the K'ang Hsi mark and for the use alone of the empty double circle that should have con-

EIGHT PRECIOUS OBJECTS
OR PA PAO

CH'ING

SHUN CHIH
1644-1661

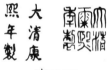

K'ANG HSI
1662-1722

YUNG CHING
1723-1735

CH'IEN LUNG
1736-1795

tained it. Reign-marks are by no means to be taken as a direct indication of the date of manufacture. Even wares made for Imperial use were not always, though generally, supplied with the proper reign-name of the period. The names of earlier reigns famous for porcelain were commonly used; but it appears clear that the name selected did not necessarily bear any relation to the type of ware to which it was to be added. For instance, the names of Hsüan Tê, 1426-1435, Ch'êng Hua, 1465-1487, and Chia Ching, 1522-1566, are common on K'ang Hsi porcelain of many kinds that were new in that reign. Dates named on the cycle system, by which time is reckoned in periods, beginning with the year 2637 B.C., are much rarer and less easy to read. A cycle is composed of sixty years. As no indication is, as a rule, given of the particular cycle intended, these marks are of no use in determining the date of manufacture, unless a reign-name is given when the year may be determined without difficulty. The name *hall mark* is given to a class of marks in which occur such words as t'ang (hall), chu (retreat) or chai (study). They are numerous but often of uncertain significance. Though some of the marks indicate the Imperial or other residence for which the wares were intended, it is certain that some of the marks represent studio or factory marks. Thus it is generally impossible to distinguish a potter's mark from a hall mark. Actual potters' signatures in the Western sense are rare. Signatures and seal-marks in the field of the decoration on a piece may on rare examples be those of the artist whose work has been reproduced. Other inscriptions in the field may be poems or descriptive matter and rarely furnish any indication of date or origin.

Chinese Soft Paste   In Chinese ceramics; a kind of fine white porcelain called Chiang t'ai (paste-bodied) and called in Europe by the unfortunate name of soft paste. It is opaque, but extremely fine-grained with an undulating surface and slight crazing. It is compounded with a special clay that is described by the Chinese as Hua Shih or soapy rock. It seems to be a kind of pegmatite which makes the body of the ware especially receptive to painted designs executed in underglaze blue. The Chinese used their finest quality of cobalt blue on this ware as well as the most skillful brush work. It generally had a crackled glaze. This so-called soft paste blue and white ware was first made during the K'ang Hsi reign and in the succeeding reigns of Yung Chêng and Ch'ien Lung during the Gh'ing dynasty. Especially typical of the ware are small pieces such as snuff bottles, incense bottles and objects essential for writing. See *Ch'ing; Blue and White Ch'ing.*

Chinese Symbols and Emblems   In Chinese art; a great diversity of emblematical devices and symbols were often employed in Chinese art. A popular set was the Eight Precious Objects or Pa Pao. They are the pearl or chu that grants every wish, a copper coin or ch'ien for wealth, the lozenge or hua, the open lozenge or fang shêng symbol of victory, musical stone or ch'ing, a pair of books or shu, a pair of horn-like objects or chüeh, and a leaf of artemisia or ai yeh, a plant of good omen. Another favorite set was the Eight Happy Omens or Pa Chi Hsiang which were among the signs on Buddha's feet. They are the wheel or lun, knot of longevity or ch'ang, canopy or kai, umbrella of state or san, lotus or hua, twin fishes or yü, shell or lo and vase or p'ing. The eight attributes of the Eight Taoist Immortals were also much favored. See *Chinese Gods; Eight Taoist Immortals; Hundred Antiques; Eight Trigrams.*

Ch'ing   In Chinese ceramics; a Chinese color word. It is generally described as the color of nature. It was used in early Chinese records in a comprehensive and vague manner. It was applied to the sea green in celadon, to the pale shades displayed in the Sung glazes and to certain other colors and neutral tints. See *Celadon.*

Ch'ing   The Ch'ing dynasty of China, 1644-1912. The art of this period is referred to as Ch'ing. In Chinese ceramics; the splendid porcelains which are associated with the Ch'ing dynasty were not made during the early years of this period due to unsettled domestic conditions and spasmodic fighting. The Imperial manufactory at Ching-tê-Chên was destroyed during the rebellion of 1673. In 1680, after the rebellion was practically over, the Emperor ordered the rebuilding of the Imperial manufactory at Ching-tê-Chên, and a glorious age of Chinese porcelains which was to last almost one hundred years began. The great emperors K'ang Hsi, 1662-1722, Yung Chêng, 1723-1735, and Ch'ien Lung, 1736-1795, were all patrons of the arts. Essentially the period marked a renaissance in ceramics. There were several new developments in Ch'ing; however, the basic principles had already been established during the Ming dynasty. The processes are chiefly those of the preceding dynasty. The monochromes during the Ch'ing dynasty were widely diversified and numerous, and are representative of some of the most refined porcelain of this period. The Ch'ing monochromes were chiefly developments of Ming monochromes, imitations of Sung glazes and numerous innovations. The success of the Imperial manufactory is attributed to three remarkably talented superintendents. Ts'ang Ying-Hsüan was appointed in 1680 to reorganize the Imperial manufactory. He was followed in the Yung Chêng period by Nien Hsi-Yao. T'ang Ying, who was appointed to assist Nien Hsi-Yao in 1728 and who later succeeded to the position which he held until 1749, is generally considered to be the greatest of the three. Although the influence of the work of these three was felt for many years, the absence of inspired leadership gradually became apparent in subsequent production. The

final blow occurred during the T'ai P'ing rebellion, 1850-1875, when the Imperial manufactory was razed. See *Chinese Dynasties; Sung; Ming; Peach-bloom; Mirror Black; Sang de Boeuf; Clair de Lune; Flambé; Powder Blue; Apple Green; Imperial Yellow; Famille Verte; Blue and White Ch'ing; Three Color Ware; Chinese Soft Paste; Ching-tê-Chên; China,* in Far Eastern ceramics; *Chinese Porcelain Marks.* (106-113)

Ch'ing Ho Hsien   In Chinese ceramics; wares of the Tz'u Chou type were made at this site during the Sung dynasty. See *Tz'u Chou.*

Ch'ing-pai   In Chinese ceramics; the Chinese name given to a slight bluish- or greenish-white glaze. The name is given to a class of pure white porcelain with a faintly bluish-green glaze, the so-called Ch'ing-pai wares made in the province of Kiangsi in the Ching-tê-Chên region during the Southern Sung period. They are delicately and translucently potted in shapes of notable merit. After the fall of the Sung dynasty in 1279 vast quantities of Ch'ing-pai ware were exported to southeast Asia and to Japan. It came from lesser kilns where somewhat coarser wares were produced. See *Sung.*

Ching T'ai   The Ching T'ai reign of the Ming dynasty of China, 1450-1456. See *Chinese Dynasties.*

Ching-tê-Chên   A renowned ceramic center, active by the 10th century if not earlier, in China, usually considered to be the greatest pottery center in the world. It was located east of the large Po Yang lake in the northern Kiangsi province. In 1369, Hung Wu (1368-1398) who was the founder of the Ming dynasty, rebuilt the various kilns already located there and made it the Imperial manufactory. The colored and painted porcelains of the great Ming dynasty were developed there. In the succeeding Ch'ing dynasty a veritable renaissance in Chinese porcelains was

CHIA CHING
1796-1820

TAO KUANG
1821-1850

HSIEN FENG
1851-1861

T'UNG CHIH
1862-1874

KUANG HSU
1875-1908

achieved at Ching-tê-Chên. This great ceramic center had about three thousand kilns. The many hundreds of private manufactories located there followed the work of the Imperial potteries. See *Ming; Ch'ing*.

Chinoiserie In ornament; a French word meaning Chinese art is particularly applied to European decorative designs which depict an imaginary world of pseudo-Chinese figures and scenes, popular as a decoration on ceramics as well as on silver, furniture, lacquered woodwork, textiles and the like, in the late 17th and 18th centuries. In addition to the influence of imported Chinese wares in Europe, there were certain travel books, especially those published by the Dutch about the third quarter of the 17th century, which played an important part in developing an interest in Chinese art. Essentially chinoiseries fall into two distinct groups. The earlier, dating from around the end of the 17th century and first three or four decades of the 18th century, mirrors the influence of numerous engravings published by Peter Schenck of Amsterdam and several German houses including J. C. Weigel of Nuremberg, Joseph Friedrich Leopold, Jeremias Wolff and Martin Engelbrecht of Augsburg. The engravings of Elias Baeck, published by both Wolff and Leopold, were especially popular, and were adapted at Meissen and Vienna. It seems that Herold at Meissen created original chinoiseries for painting in polychrome. Japanese Kakiemon furnished the inspiration for the chinoiseries of Löwenfinck. At Delft pseudo-Chinese figures appear in rich Baroque compositions seemingly taken from designs of Daniel Marot. The fanciful reliefs on certain Staffordshire salt-glazed ware, around 1740-1760, have been traced by woodcuts in the EMBASSY TO THE GRAND TARTAR CHAM (Nieuhof) published in 1669 by J. Ogilby. The familiar decoration of grotesques often mingled with Chinese figures found on Moustiers and Alcora

CHINOISERIE BY PILLEMENT

may be credited to Joseph Olerys. The later group or Rococo phase was mainly due to the French school of decorative designers under the aegis of Boucher, though it was in other countries that the subjects were most frequently copied on ceramic wares. The delightful porcelain figures of Saint-Cloud, Chantilly and Mennecy were generally either adaptations from Chinese and Japanese models or original creations of the potters. It was not until relatively late in the century that gilt Chinese figures were painted on dark lacquer grounds on Sèvres and Vienna porcelain. Watteau, Pillement and Boucher were the leading designers in this style, while Peyrotte and Huquier were noteworthy among the engravers. Apart from the French sources, the German factories were inspired by the engravings of chinoiseries made by J. E. Nilson and G. B. Göz. The designs of Pillement were included with others in the collections brought out in England by Robert Sayer and found favor at Chelsea, Lowestoft and Worcester; the two latter-mentioned frequently used them on transfer-printed wares. A still later group of chinoiseries may be seen in the English Regency work and in the Revived Rococo. In the case of the former, notable is the decoration of the Brighton Pavilion. See *Chinese and Japanese Influences; Revived Rococo; Engraved Designs*. (279, 303, 305, 332-334, 343)

Chiriqui See *Nicaragua, Costa Rica and Panama*.

Chojiro, Sasaki See *Raku*.

Cholula See *Mixteca Puebla Pottery; Teotihuacan*.

Chou Early period in Chinese art history, ?1122 - c. 256 B.C. See *Chinese Dynasties*.

Chow, Fong (b. 1923) American, born in China, artist-potter; came to the United States in 1943 and studied art, concentrating on ceramics. He designed for Glidden Pottery from 1954 to 1957 and was appointed assistant curator of Far Eastern art at the Metropolitan Museum of Art in 1958. Chow has strong admiration for the work of the potter Shoji Hamada. He believes that simplicity is not poverty of expression but the discarding of the non-essential. This is evident in his pottery.

Choy, Katherine Pao Yu (1929-1958) American, born in Hong Kong, artist-potter; in 1952 became assistant professor of art and head of the ceramic department at Newcomb College, New Orleans. While here, until her untimely death, she was very productive in the creation of her own unique pieces of pottery.

Christoffersen, Helge See *Royal Copenhagen.*

Chrysanthemum See *Chinese Four Season Flowers; Japanese Porcelain Motifs; Kiku-no-go-mon.*

Chrysanthemum Vase In Chinese ceramics; a vase with a long slender neck on an ovoid-shaped body having reeding around the lower portion resembling the petals of a chrysanthemum. In particular, one of the seven classic shapes of the Chinese Peachbloom wares.

Ch'ü Chou See *Celadon.*

Chü-Lü Hsien In Chinese ceramics; wares of the Tz'u Chou type were made at this site during the Sung dynasty. See *Tz'u Chou.*

Chün Yao In Chinese ceramics; a large group of wares first made in the early part of the Sung dynasty in Honan province at Chün Chou or Chün T'ai. The ware was strong and durable, and was chiefly composed of bulb bowls, deep flower pots with plates, bowls and other similar useful pieces. Each piece of first quality generally had a Chinese numeral from 1 to 10 carved on the base. It had a hard glaze that was very thick and highly opalescent and that

often flowed sluggishly. The colors were rich and variegated. The characteristic Chün glaze had a foundation of lavender-grey or blue-grey usually with a faint flush of red detected somewhere in the glaze. Sometimes this pale lavender flecked with greyish-white had a large splotch or splotches of dappled dark purple. In other bowls the red in the glaze suffused into a lilac-purple which sometimes shaded on to crimson. Sometimes the red almost dominated the grey on the outside of the bowl, while the inside was a lavender grey. Occasionally the grey formed an opaque greenish-grey layer over the lavender; this layer as a rule occurred inside the bowl and was often broken by Y-shaped or irregular lines which the Chinese called earthworm marks. The red and purple glazes were full of bubbles, which in bursting gave the surface a pitted appearance. These pin holes, which the Chinese called ant tracks, explained to a large extent the characteristic dappling and fine streaking. Often added to this blend of colors was an interesting brownish tint. This occurred at the edge of the rim and other similar projecting parts where the glaze was thin and was almost transparent and colorless. The crackle, which occasionally occurred, is generally regarded to be accidental. The body of the ware varied widely in texture and in quality. The ware having the incised numerals had a fine greyish white porcelaneous body. The glaze flowed with relative smoothness. Another ware, which was always without numerals, usually had a coarse-grained buff-grey porcelaneous body. The glaze flowed unevenly and ended above the base, which was rough and unglazed, in a wavy roll or in heavy drops. Between these two Chün wares was another ware which has sometimes arbitrarily been called Kuan Chün, or Kuan ware of the Chün type. It is also regarded as a finer ware of the second category. It was without numerals, and was characterized by thinner potting and by a controlled glaze. Soft-Chün, which the Chinese called

CHRYSANTHEMUM VASE

CHUN YAO FLOWER POT

Ma-Chün, was a beautiful ware. It had a buff earthy-looking body and a thick opaque glaze. The glaze was finely crazed, and was more waxy than the characteristic Chün glaze. As a rule the color was pale lavender-blue and occasionally peacock blue, and generally there was a splash or two of crimson. (95)

Ch'ung Chêng   The Ch'ung Chêng reign of the Ming dynasty in China; 1628-1643. See *Chinese Dynasties.*

Cinquecento   An Italian term referring to the 16th century. It is particularly applied to the 16th century as a period, representing the highest development of Italian Renaissance art. It follows the quattrocento period.

Cistercian Ware   In English ceramics; a variety of English red ware having almost the hardness of stoneware made during the 16th century and found around the Cistercian abbeys. Some of the pottery bears dates prior to 1540 when the monasteries were dissolved. The ware has a black or dark brown glaze and occasionally has an applied white clay or a trailed white slip decoration.

Città di Castello   See *Alla Castellana Ware.*

Clair de Lune   In Chinese ceramics; Clair de Lune or moon white is the name given to a Chinese ware having a beautiful glaze of the palest blue. It was first made during the K'ang Hsi reign at Ching-tê-Chên. It was made in the same forms as Peach-bloom with an additional few forms of its own. It is sometimes faintly tinged with lavender. The glaze is without crackle. (107)

Clanta   See *Tooth and Company.*

Clark, Kenneth   English, born in New Zealand, artist-potter and lecturer; in 1953 he set up his own studio which he shares with his wife, Ann Wynn Reeves, artist-potter and painter. See *Reeves, Ann Wynn.*

Classic Period   See *Pre-Columbian Pottery.*

Classic Revival   Or Neo-Classic. The term is applied to the style of classic ornament which derived its inspiration from a revived interest in Greek and Roman art. It is generally accepted that the excavations begun at Pompeii and Herculaneum in 1738 resulted in discoveries of antique art that aroused a new interest in it. Publications on antiquities by Comte de Caylus and Sir William Hamilton and the archaeological researches by Johann Winkelmann and his eulogies on antique art were all important factors. The Adam brothers and Giovanni Piranesi were also noteworthy figures in this renewed revival of interest in antique culture. However, the success of the movement was undoubtedly largely due to a reaction against the Rococo, for France had begun to tire of her Rococo style around the middle of the 18th century. By a concurrence rather difficult to explain the Classic Revival was joined with a sentimental mode, seen in the art of Greuze and Angelica Kauffmann and such books as Goethe's SORROWS OF WERTHER, 1775. The light and graceful Louis XVI style is the early phase of the Neo-Classic and the pompous Empire style is the later phase. The so-called Zopf (pigtail) style is a German variant of the Louis XVI style and is characterized by the wide popularity of silhouette portraits and the solemn rendering of figures in the costume of the era. During the Louis XVI style the classic ornament was borrowed from the Renaissance and antique art, and was interpreted in the lighter form of the 18th century. Gradually as antique art was better understood the taste for the antique became more exacting and its closer imitation was sought, which finally resulted in the Empire style. In England the principal genius of the Neo-Classic was Robert Adam. He is regarded as virtually the creator of a style which is known by his name. In ceramics; the movement was fostered by the potter Josiah Wedgwood. Apart from Wedgwood the Sèvres, Fürstenberg and Berlin porcelain manufactories had in different ways the strongest influence on the styles adopted in the ceramic art of the period. See *Adam, Robert; Louis XVI; Empire; David, Jacques Louis; Albertolli, Giocondo; Hamilton, Sir William; Caylus, Comte de; Piranesi, Giovanni; Rococo; Kauffmann, Angelica; Engraved Designs.*

Clay In ceramics; a stiff viscous earth found in many varieties. It consists mainly of hydrated aluminum silicates and is derived mostly from the decomposition of feldspathic rocks. Clays differ in plasticity. Red-burning clays which contain iron are generally more plastic than the white-burning pipe clays. Clays may be fusible from the presence of an alkaline flux such as lime or some other kind of material such as iron which acts in the same manner. Clays may be refractory or comparatively infusible, a property increased by the addition of silica, such as sand, flint or quartz. The water found in their composition varies, making them liable to shrink and become deformed in the kiln. This tendency is lessened by adding pulverized potsherds (fragments of pottery or fired clay from which the water has already been removed). As a rule, very plastic clays, called in English fat clays, shrink more than the dry or lean clays which ordinarily contain free silica. Kaolin or china-clay, a decomposition substance of the feldspar of granite, is the most important potter's clay. See *Kaolin.*

Clay, Preparation of In ceramics; after being dug from the ground, clay, which occasionally requires to be weathered before use, is mixed with water and permitted to stand in order that the coarser particles may sink and the finer can be strained off (levigation); the water then is generally driven off by heat. It is necessary for the clay to be thoroughly mixed and before throwing it must be cut and beaten to get rid of air bubbles (wedging).

Clementson, Joseph English Staffordshire potter operating the Phoenix Works at Shelton, Hanley, from around 1839 to 1864, producing earthenwares. A familiar transfer-printed pattern, Nestor's Sacrifice, was registered by Clementson in 1849.

Clerici, Felice See *Milan.*

Clérissy, Pierre and Joseph Sons of Antoine Clérissy (d. 1679). About 1679 Pierre (d. 1728) became the proprietor of the principal faïence manufactory at Moustiers where he produced wares of artistic importance. About that time he engaged François, Gaspard and Jean-Baptiste Viry, members of a talented family of faïence-painters. Also about that time Joseph Clérissy (d. 1684) took over a faïence manufactory at Saint-Jean-du-Désert, a suburb of Marseilles. His widow married François Viry, a faïence-painter working at this manufactory, and his son, Antoine, successfully operated the business from 1694 to 1733. See *Moustiers; Marseilles; Viry.*

Clews, James and Ralph Staffordshire potters operating the Cobridge Works, Cobridge, 1818-1834. They were well known for the good quality of their blue transfer-printed earthenwares, most of which were made for the American market. Like other Staffordshire potters who catered to the important American market, Clews made numerous American views taken from contemporary topographical prints. Sometimes the prints were taken from paintings with a story interest as in Clews' interesting series, Dr. Syntax, Don Quixote, and Wilkie. See *Indiana Pottery Company.*

Clifton Art Pottery See *Lonhuda Pottery.*

Clifton Ware See *Chesapeake Pottery.*

Clignancourt In French ceramics; a porcelain manufactory founded at Clignancourt, Paris, in 1771 by Pierre Deruelle,

CLEWS, JAMES AND RALPH
C. 1818-1834

CLIGNANCOURT

1771-1775

1775 ON

under the patronage of Louis-Stanislas-Xavier, known as Monsieur, Comte de Provence, brother of Louis XV. It remained in existence until at least 1798. The porcelain was of a fine quality. Included among the accepted marks are a windmill; crowned M; M; LSX in a monogram.

Clodion, Claude-Michel (1738-1814) French sculptor. He is particularly noted for his finely modeled terra-cotta statuettes of mythological figures as well as for his decorative friezes of cupids, nymphs and similar subjects. The early pieces were made at Nancy and the later pieces in biscuit were produced at Sèvres.

Cloisonné Pottery See *Teotihuacan.*

Clough, Alfred (Ltd.) In English ceramics; Staffordshire potters who operated the St. Louis Works, Longton, c. 1913-1961, when the firm continued as Clough's Royal Art Pottery. See *Smith, Sampson (Ltd.).*

Clough's Royal Art Pottery See *Clough, Alfred (Ltd).*

Coachman Bottle See *Toby Jug.*

Coalbrookdale See *Coalport.*

Coalport Often known as Coalbrookdale. In English ceramics; a porcelain manufactory was founded at Coalport, Shropshire, by John Rose around 1796. It absorbed the factory at Caughley in 1799 and it acquired molds and material from Nantgarw and Swansea around 1822-1823. It is not possible to distinguish the early Coalport porcelain from that of Caughley. A large part of it was sent in white to London to be decorated. At the beginning of the Victorian period the Coalport factory had already established itself as the leading producer of floral encrusted porcelain which is generally known as Coalbrookdale. This style, with its pronounced Rococo feeling, was to continue for many years and influenced the entire range of the factory's output. Vases, baskets and jugs profusely adorned with applied naturalistic floral encrustation were made in great quantities. The factory was outstanding for its interpretation of the Revived Rococo style. John Rose died in 1841 and was succeeded by his nephew, W. F. Rose. By 1850 the Coalport factory was completely committed to its revival of Sèvres porcelain and in some instances the copies were so successful that they were sold as real Sèvres and bore the factory's mark. For the second half of the 19th century the emphasis at Coalport was mainly on the imitation of continental 18th century styles. Late 19th century Coalport wares essentially followed the styles for which the factory had already a reputation. Probably the best known of the everyday porcelain production at Coalport was the Indian Tree pattern which they had originated about 1801. About 1885 Coalport was taken over by Peter Schuyler Bruff whose son, Charles Bruff, revitalized Coalport and enjoyed further success by thoroughly exploiting the North American market which is still today its largest market. In 1923 the Bruff family sold the business to Cauldon Potteries Ltd. of Shelton, Stoke-on-Trent. In 1926 Coalport was transferred to the Cauldon Works. In 1936 both Coalport and Cauldon were moved from Shelton to the Crescent Potteries of George Jones & Sons Ltd. in Stoke. In 1958 Coalport changed ownership again when it was taken over by E. Brain and Company Ltd., an old family business, whose Foley China Works had been started in 1850. Many patterns in production in the 1960's date back to 1830 or even earlier. Among the many new designs and patterns probably the most successful is Revelry, an Adamesque design of cupids against a background panel of dusty blue surrounded by delicate grey tracery. The marks include Coalbrookdale, Coalport, J. R. & Co., replicas of the crossed swords of Meissen, the gold anchor of Chelsea and the like. Around 1960

COALPORT

Dale

1810-1825

JOHN ROSE & Cⁱᵉ
COLE BROOK DALE
1850.

COALPORT
ENGLAND
AD1750

1891 ON

BONE CHINA
COALPORT
MADE IN ENGLAND
EST.1750

1960 ON

the firm, Coalport China, Ltd., reintroduced the floral encrusted "Coalbrookdale" wares, bearing the mark Coalbrookdale/By Coalport/Made in England. See *Billingsley, W.; Jones, George.* (474)

Coast Tiahuanaco   See *Andean.*

Cobalt   See *Colors; Blue.*

Cochin, Charles-Nicholas, the Younger (1715-1790) Noted French designer, engraver and writer on art. He was appointed First Painter to the French court in 1755. Although his decorative designs were often executed in the Rococo style, he was a strenuous opponent of that style of art. Some of his work resembled the compositions of Boucher. He possessed a remarkable facility as a draftsman. A number of his engravings were adapted by the porcelain-painters. See *Engraved Designs.*

Coclé   See *Nicaragua, Costa Rica and Panama.*

Coiling   A technique of early origin, one of the more primitive processes employed before the introduction of the potter's wheel. In this process a pot or vessel is made by building up with coils or rolls of clay. This method is frequently used by 20th century artist-potters to achieve a more personal interpretation of shape than is possible by throwing on the potter's wheel. (557)

Coin Bank   A popular form of folk pottery. (434)

Colclough, H. J.   Staffordshire potter operating the Vale Works at Longton, 1897-1937, producing china and earthenware. Subsequently Colclough China Ltd., 1937-1948, and Booths and Colcloughs Ltd., 1948-1954; the latter retitled Ridgway Potteries, Ltd. from 1955.

Cold Colors or **Cold Painted**   A term used in ceramics and glass for unfired colors. It is generally believed that much of this form of painting has been lost by repeated cleaning or rubbing, while colors transmuted by heat or fire are in effect imperishable. See *Unfired Colors.*

Cole, Sir Henry   (1808-1882) English author; played an important role in shaping the new course of English decorative arts. He was a prime mover in the Great Exhibition of 1851; he was chiefly responsible for the success of the South Kensington Museum, the ancestor of the Victoria and Albert Museum, and was in effect its first director. In 1846 he received a prize from the Society of Arts for an earthenware tea service made by Mintons which led to the beginning of Felix Summerly's Art Manufactures. See *Summerly's Art Manufactures; Great Exhibition of 1851.*

Cole-Slaw   In ceramics; the name given by the Staffordshire potters to the shaggy mane made by pushing moist clay through a screen directly onto the dog or other animal to be so decorated. See *Bennington Poodle.* (439)

Coleman, William Stephen   (1829-1904) See *Minton.*

Colenbrander, Theodorus A. C.   (1841-1930) Dutch pottery and textile designer; one of the leaders of the modern decorative art movement in Holland. By the mid-1880's he had originated his distinctive Javanese batik-inspired style, which appeared in patterns at the Rozenburg pottery. See *Rozenburg.*

Colima   In pre-Columbian Central American ceramics; in the extreme west of Mexico the well-known culture of Colima had its roots in the Formative period. The pottery of Colima differs from that of Teotihuacan in the valley of Mexico and the Maya in the light-hearted manner in which the potters depicted, almost caricatured, warriors and religious dignitaries. Especially remarkable for this same quality are the delightful

ENGLAND

COLCLOUGH
1908-1928

effigies of the little fat dogs of the region. See *Central American Pottery*. (10, 11)

Collaert, Adriaen (1560-1618) Flemish engraver. See *Engraved Designs*.

Cologne In German ceramics; the great production of Rhenish stoneware at Cologne and nearby Frechen had its origin in medieval times. The typical brown ware was made at least as early as the 15th century; however, it did not achieve artistic importance until around 1525 and it showed evidence of decline around 1600, when the potteries for making salt-glazed stoneware were transferred to Frechen. The material for the stoneware was grey and the color of the surface, which was achieved by a wash of ferruginous clay, varied in tone from a chestnut brown to a dull yellow. The color was invariably more or less speckled. After 1600 the coloring generally had irregular patches of blue. There were three principal manufactories in Cologne. The most active pottery was in the Maximinenstrasse. It produced pear-shaped jugs and the so-called Bartmann jugs with a bearded mask on the neck. A very fine variety of jugs was decorated with applied oak leaves on scrolled stems. The best production was from around 1520 to 1550. A smaller manufactory was in the Komödienstrasse. A third and rather important manufactory was in the Eigelstein, producing the characteristic stoneware jugs. See *Frechen*. (192)

Colombia See *Ecuador and Colombia*.

Colonna, Edward French decorative artist; designer of pottery, textiles and furniture. A foremost representative of Art Nouveau. (494, 514)

Colored Bodies In European ceramics; apart from the red and brown colored bodies produced naturally from iron-bearing clay, colored bodies were relatively little used until the 18th century when the discovery of white-bodied wares had clarified the process of producing them by adding the ordinary coloring oxides. The great pioneer in this medium was Josiah Wedgwood. See *Basalt; Jasper Ware; Cane Ware; Pâte-sur-Pâte; Wedgwood, Josiah*.

Colored Grounds; Ground Colors In European ceramics; though it may be said that colored grounds in pottery date from primitive times when clay slips were used, the coloring of glazes or tin enamels to produce a ground appropriate for fine painting is a relatively recent development, probably having its beginnings in the Near East in medieval times. Among the immediate predecessors of the European types may be mentioned the Persian and Syrian wares of the 13th to 15th century painted in luster over a blue glaze. The first purely European example using a colored ground is the Italian blue-ground majolica with opaque white decoration (bianco sopra azzuro) introduced at Faenza in the late 15th century, for which there is no actual prototype. Wares with a blue ground and decorated in opaque white first date in China from the reign of Chia Ching, 1522-1566. From the second half of the 17th century onward, Chinese prototypes were the vogue, and the black grounds of Delft faïence were no doubt copied from examples of the reign of K'ang Hsi, 1662-1722. Undoubtedly Chinese powder blue inspired the sprinkled blue and manganese grounds of some faïence made in Holland and elsewhere. The typical 18th century porcelain decoration in panels reserved on a colored enamel ground was originally suggested by porcelain wares of the reigns of K'ang Hsi, 1662-1722, and Yung Chêng, 1723-1735. Superb classical paneled porcelains date at Meissen from around 1725-1745. A clear canary-yellow of the muffle-kiln was one of the first ground colors made at Meissen and it possessed the same refinement as those that followed it—the pale blue, deep lilac or pale violet, purple, apple-green, grey-green, brick-red, and above all the turquoise or sea-green. In time the supremacy of Meissen was challenged by Vincennes and Sèvres, whose soft, readily fusible glazes gave the colors a depth which was impossible to achieve on hard paste. The early gros-bleu of about 1749 and those that followed it, the bleu-de-roi, jaune-jonquille, rose-pink (rose Pompadour), apple-green (or pea-green), bleu-celeste (or turquoise) and the rare lilac (a lilac-pink as related to the rose pink) afforded a notable range of colors which every rival factory attempted, generally in vain, to imitate, in the third quarter of the 18th century. As a rule the ground-colors used for paneled decoration on porcelain were enamels; the main exceptions being the gros-bleu of Vincennes and the mazarine-blue of Chelsea, which were practically colored lead-glazes, stained by taking up dark cobalt-blue put under them, and the fond écaille (or tortoiseshell brown) of Sèvres and similar brown colors used elsewhere which were high-temperature hard-paste glazes apparently deriving their color from manganese and iron. During the 19th century, owing to scientific research, new and less costly ground colors were introduced. For example, a green enamel and a dull raspberry-pink or maroon were obtained from chromium and supplanted copper-green and rose-pink (purple of Cassius) respectively. In more recent times handsome underglaze greys and blacks have been extracted from iridium and titanium. See *Purple of Cassius; Colored Bodies; Colors; Herold, J. G.*

Colors Ceramic colors require the action of the fire for their transmutation. Red has occasionally been described as the basic color of all pottery as red remains the normal color of all baked clay, due to traces of iron which almost all contain. Notwithstanding that grey is the color of the body of some high-fired stonewares as well as primitive wares, red is the natural color of the commonest clays when fired. Red is the color of the earliest Egyptian ware, of the typical Greek pottery, of the Roman red-gloss, of Chinese buccaro and Böttger's stoneware. Covered with a lead glaze, which is itself stained deep yellow with iron, it produces the warm brown color well known in many kinds of primitive glazed earthenware and peasant pottery. The color of ceramic glazes owes its character to a different action of the fire, fusing the ingredients to a glassy state, thus protecting and enriching the tones produced by the oxides employed. Certain colors are essentially peculiar to glazed pottery, for instance, the copper-reds, copper-greens and manganese purples. Different glazes impart a distinct quality to the colors used with them. For example, much lead in a glaze imparts a deep, velvet-like glow to the rich brown obtained from manganese to the very different browns given from iron. The alkaline glazes incline to give a greater brilliance and clearness; in them copper develops a characteristic turquoise and manganese an amethyst or violet. The high-fired feldspathic glazes, which produce a more limited range of colors, include the soft greyish celadons, opalescent bluish-greens and browns and blacks of unrivaled beauty, as occur in the early Chinese stonewares. These are all made from the iron-bearing earth. Glazes and enamels vary widely in the completeness of their vitrification, translucency and transparency, and the special aesthetic quality of their colors mainly relies on this. Impurities in ingredients and imperfect firing may give the glaze something of a beauty more satisfying than the more "pure" glazes. Apart from the completely uncharacteristic and rare unfired, the so-called cold colors, the pigments employed for ceramic decoration always comprise inorganic materials, occasionally simply clays and ochres rich in metallic oxides but more frequently the refined oxides or other compounds obtained from the minerals in which they are found. They may be divided into two classes; namely, high temperature (grand feu) colors and muffle-kiln (feu de mouffle) colors. Also with the former may be included those capable of being used to give color to glazes. The high temperature colors are: iron-browns; iron-red; manganese and cobalt; copper; antimony.

1. Iron is the most common "impurity" in clays. Its presence in the body gives a yellowish tone to lead glazes. Clay rich in iron, which by itself fixes to a dark red, has been extensively employed in peasant pottery as a means of deliberately giving glazes a brown or deep yellow color. The accidental presence of iron in the lead ore (galena) employed for primitive lead glazes gave the latter a more or less pronounced yellowish tone. Natural clays rich in iron were applied as a surface wash on the stonewares of the Rhineland and elsewhere to give a light or dark brown color to a grey stoneware. At the very high temperature of the porcelain kiln, iron produces the "dead leaf" and coffee-brown and the celadon green glazes of Chinese porcelain reproduced to a slight degree at Meissen and Sèvres.

2. Iron-red, a red pigment, difficult to manage as a grand feu color, and thus more generally a muffle color, was extracted from a red earth known as bole and from calcined sulphate of iron. It was frequently absent from the grand feu palette because of its difficult quality and was occasionally supplanted on faïence by an unfired lacquered red.

3. A relatively common mineral giving dark purplish and brownish colors is the impure ore of manganese. When it is mixed with a material rich in iron it produces a fine black, for example Wedgwood's black basaltes. Soft purples and browns are obtained from a purified manganese oxide. Cobalt is generally found in association with iron and nickel, and the cobalt oxide extracted from the ore produces a color which is a pure blue or tends to violet with absence or presence of traces of these other metals. Cobalt-blue

remains unchanged at a grand feu temperature and is available both for painting and glazes on faïence and earthenware. It is the main underglaze color for decorating porcelain; however, on soft paste porcelains a manganese-purple is sometimes used.

4. The use of copper to obtain a blue or turquoise color in an alkaline glaze or tin glaze is of early origin. When lead is present the color tends to green and in an ordinary medium-fired lead glaze copper produces a variety of shades of leaf or emerald green. At the temperature of the porcelain kiln, under different conditions, reds and lavenders are obtainable from copper, but until the 19th century these colors were not used in Europe. Copper-red is one of the colors available for underglaze painting on porcelain, but is extremely difficult, and though freely used (like the related red glazes) in China, it was not until recent times understood in Europe.

5. Antimoniate of lead will produce a fine clear yellow in a moderately high temperature necessary for faïence, but it will not survive the high temperature of the porcelain kiln. It is the coloring agent employed for the yellow enamel ground on some faïence made at Moustiers and elsewhere in southern France, and with ochres or clays rich in iron gives yellow and orange pigments for painting. Antimony will not produce a translucent yellow as it is an opaque color and lacks the property of dissolving in the glaze. In summary, there are four principal high-temperature colors that are available for painting on tin-glazed wares; namely, cobalt-blue, copper-green, manganese-purple and antimony-yellow and orange. A soft green was also made by mixing antimony-yellow with cobalt. The high-temperature palette also offered iron-red, but few faïence potteries were able to master it. Blue was the main high-temperature underglaze color for porcelain, copper-red, iron-green and brown were essentially unknown and unused.

A wider variety of colors is accessible for painting in enamels or overglaze colors fired at a relatively low temperature in a muffle-kiln. These need to be richly fluxed with lead or lead-glass in order to increase their fusibility, and the varying proportion of these ingredients produces a variety of tones. Also available is a rose-pink obtained from gold (purple of Cassius) and opaque whites extracted from tin, arsenic and zinc and which when mixed with the metallic oxides produce an extended variety of colors. Though the technique of painting in muffle-colors was known in ancient Roman times and was employed on Islamic pottery at least as early as the 13th century, it was first adopted as a method of decorating European pottery in the 17th century. From around 1622 it was used by Kreussen potters on stoneware, and on faïence from around 1660 by German Hausmalerei. Painting in muffle-colors has furnished the principal decoration on European porcelain since the earliest Meissen, and on the faïence inspired by it from around 1750 onward. See *Colored Grounds; Colored Bodies; Monochrome Painting; Purple of Cassius; Black; White; Red; Purple; Manganese; Brown; Blue; Turquoise; Yellow and Orange; Green; Rose-Pink; Glazes; Enamel; Ground Colors.*

Columbian Art Pottery In American ceramics; established by Morris and Willmore at Trenton, New Jersey, for the manufacture of table and toilet wares in a Belleek body, in 1893, the year of the World's Columbian Exposition at Chicago, hence the name. Among their accepted marks is the name of the company. See *Belleek.*

Columbian Pottery In American ceramics; a pottery was started at Philadelphia in 1808 by Alexander Trotter, proprietor, making cream-colored earthenware in the English style. In the same year examples from his pottery were exhibited at Peale's museum. Mr. Trotter retired from business around 1813. At the present time no extant examples are known.

Combed Ware In English ceramics; a method of marbling in which colored clay slips were combed on the surface to produce a marbled effect. Simple forms of combing were characteristic of peasant pottery. *Welsh ware* was an early English term for combed slip ware. From the late 17th century in England feathered patterns were made by combining white and brown slips and then later covering the combed surface with a yellow glaze. The technique is known as combing. See *Marbled Ware; Slipware.* (389)

Combing See *Combed Ware.*

Comedy Figures See *Italian Comedy Subjects.*

Commemoratives A class of transfer-printed wares. See *Historical Blue.*

Company Porcelain A name given to Chinese Export Ware. See *Chinese Lowestoft.*

Compendiario See *Faenza.*

Confucius (551-478 B.C.) The great Chinese philosopher and teacher. His Chinese name is Kung-Fu-Tse. See *Chinese Gods.*

Cook Pottery Company In American ceramics; succeeded Ott and Brewer of Trenton, New Jersey. They produced porcelain and earthenwares. It is said that the best imitations of Delft faïence made in the United States came from the Cook Pottery. The mark on this faîence ware was also copied from the familiar mark of the Porcelain Bottle, an important Delft pottery. See *Ott and Brewer.*

Cookworthy, William (1705-1780) A Devon apothecary. Discoverer of the materials of true hard-paste porcelain in England. As early as 1745 Cookworthy was cognizant of the nature of the china-clay and china-stone which are the essential ingredients

COLUMBIAN ART POTTERY
1893 ON

COOK POTTERY
1895 ON

of true porcelain. He found them in Cornwall at least by 1758. After a period of experiment he took out a patent in 1768. Cookworthy remained director of the successive Plymouth and Bristol porcelain factories from 1768-1773. See *Plymouth; Bristol.*

Copeland, W. T. (and Sons Ltd.) In English ceramics; have operated the Spode Works at Stoke-on-Trent from 1847 to the present day producing porcelain, parian and earthenwares. At the Great Exhibition held in London in 1851 Copeland made a great display of Copeland parian or statuary porcelain as it was known at Copelands, based on designs and originals by the best-known sculptors of the day. Copeland did not to any great extent try to copy the Sèvres styles so popular at Coalport and Mintons. They did however follow the lead started at Worcester in Japanese styles during the 1870's and 1880's. Copeland made countless thousands of parian figures, but their production of porcelain figures was essentially non-existent. The artists responsible for decorating Copeland porcelains such as Hürten, flower painter, Daniel Lucas, Jr., landscape painter and James Weaver, bird painter, enjoyed a reputation equal to the excellent quality of the porcelain and the glaze itself. Apart from porcelain they also produced transfer-printed wares, Victorian majolica with colorful glazes and painted tiles, mostly earthenwares, for interior decoration. The marks include Spode; Spode's New Stone; Copeland, Late Spode; Copeland and Garrett; Copeland; while the reuse of the old Spode name dates from around the late 1930's. The firm W. T. Copeland and Sons, Ltd. still continues to manufacture on the site in Stoke-on-Trent where it was originally founded. The wares which have played an important part in the company's history continue to be its main activities today—fine bone china, earthenware and fine stone. The last is a unique specialist body produced in reproduc-

tion 18th century shapes and patterns. The principal decorations of the Company tend to be highly traditional. The most famous include Spode's Tower and Camilla patterns. See *Parian; Stone-China; Bone China.*

Summary of Spode: a pottery was started at Stoke-on-Trent, Staffordshire, around 1770 by Josiah Spode (1773-1797) who had previously worked for Thomas Whieldon. His son, Josiah Spode II (1754-1827) carried on the business. He introduced porcelain around 1800 and stone-china around 1805. The porcelain was a hybrid bone-ash paste. He is generally given credit for establishing the standard composition for English bone china or bone porcelain. The porcelain made under Josiah Spode II was technically of fine quality; however, the painted decoration and the forms were often ostentatious. Especially typical were ornately gilded vases with colored grounds. Some wares with simplified Japanese designs were generally more pleasing. William Taylor Copeland, who had become a partner in 1813, succeeded to the business in 1833. Josiah Spode III having died in 1829. The firm was Copeland and Garrett from 1833 to 1847, and then Copeland, late Spode or W. T. Copeland until 1867, when it became W. T. Copeland and Sons. See *Bone China; Stone-China; Copeland and Garrett.*

Copeland and Garrett In English ceramics; operated the Spode Works, Stoke-on-Trent, from 1833 to 1847. It was formerly Spode and subsequently W. T. Copeland (and Sons Ltd.). See *Spode; Copeland, W. T. (and Sons, Ltd.).*

Copenhagen In Danish ceramics; see *Kastrup; Store Kongensgade; Osterbro; Royal Copenhagen; Fournier, Louis.*

Coper, Hans English artist-potter, born in Germany; active at Digswell House, Welwyn Garden City, Hertfordshire, from 1947; formerly at Albion Mews, London, where he worked for a time with Lucie Rie.

COPELAND
COPELAND
1851-1885
COPELAND
SPODE
ENGLAND
New Stone
20TH CENTURY

COPELAND AND GARRETT
1833-1847

COPER, HANS
1947 ON

His delight in large, vigorous forms is evident in his sculpturesque, studio-type stonewares. Since 1947 his mark is HC, impressed or incised, in seal form. See *Leach, B.*

Coperta In ceramics; an Italian term meaning covering, given to a clear lead glaze occasionally applied over the tin glaze of Italian majolica at a second firing to obtain greater gloss and depth to the colors. See *Kwaart.*

Copper See *Colors; Green; Red; Turquoise.*

Coquillage In ornament; the term, which means a shellfish, is derived from the French word *coquille* meaning a shell and is applied to a Rococo motif of shell form. See *Rococo.*

Cord Impression See *Jomon.*

Corea See *Korea.*

Corinth See *Greece.*

Cornaille, Antoine-Toussaint (b. 1734) Porcelain painter at Chantilly, Vincennes and Sèvres, 1755-1799. One of the chief flower painters working in the mature Sèvres style.

Corne, à la In French ceramics; a characteristic polychrome Rococo decoration used on Rouen faïence around the middle of the 18th century that was imitated elsewhere. The motifs included cornucopiae, butterflies, bees, flowers and other similar subjects. See *Rouen.* (275)

Cornflower In ceramics; see *Barbeaux.*

Cornucopia In ornament; a classic motif represented as a twisted horn filled to overflowing with fruits, flowers or vegetables. The term *cornucopia* means horn of plenty and it was used as a symbol of abundance. Also used in ceramics as a vase form. Parian porcelain vases made at Bennington are notable examples of this fashion. (275)

Costa Rica See *Nicaragua, Costa Rica and Panama.*

Costrel In English ceramics; a late Gothic variety of pilgrim's flask. It was generally in the form of a flattened elongated pear, having a tapering neck, with two or four loops attached to the shoulders or sides through which a cord was drawn. See *Pilgrim Flask.*

Council of Industrial Design Established in England in 1944 to bridge the gap between designer and industry, to encourage manufacturers to use the service of good designers and to educate the public taste so that their work will be appreciated. See *Design and Industries Association.*

Coupe In Chinese ceramics; a kind of jar or bowl to hold water for cleaning the brushes used in writing. The characteristic shape is of domical or beehive form with a small flaring mouth. The writer's coupe is a typical Peach-bloom form.

COUPE, K'ANG HSI

Cow-Creamer In English ceramics; a small vessel to hold cream made in the shape of a cow with its looped tail for a handle. The cream is poured through its mouth and is filled through an opening in the cow's back fitted with a cover, which is usually decorated with a band of minute flowers and a bee in full relief. It was introduced as a silver form during the reign of George II, 1727-1760, and became a characteristic form in English ceramics, in particular in Staffordshire ware. See *Silver-Forms.*

Coxon, Charles See *Bennett, Edwin; Rebekah at the Well Teapot.*

Coxon and Company See *Bennett, Edwin.*

Coyotlatelco See *Toltec.*

Cozzi, Geminiano See *Venice.*

Crab's Claw Crackle In ceramics; see *Crackle.*

Crabstock Ware In English ceramics; a variety of pottery, especially teapots, cream jugs and mugs having handles and spouts made to resemble wood with twigs and branches wrapped about them, mainly dating from about the 1750's. The body was generally decorated with small leaves, tendrils and delicate vines in applied relief. (386, 394, 411)

Crackle In ceramics; a glazed surface covered with a network of fine lines or cracks. It is generally agreed that crackle was originally accidental and later usually planned. Crackle was caused by the difference in the expansion and contraction of the body and the glaze under heat and cold. In Chinese ceramics; the name *crab's claw crackle* is given to a large crackle, and *fish roe* to a small and fine crackle. Often the two types were combined in one piece. See *Ko Yao; Kuan Yao; Sang de Boeuf; Sung.* (93)

Crailsheim In German ceramics; a faïence factory existed at Crailsheim, Württemberg, for an undetermined length of time, starting before 1749 and continuing into the 19th century. It was first owned by a family named Weiss. Georg Veit Weiss was the founder and his son(1714-1769) and grandson(1738-1800), both named Johann Georg Weiss, carried on the pottery. Essentially the wares showed little creativity and were of average quality. They were notable for their glowing high-temperature colors. No regular mark was employed.

Crane, Walter (1845-1915) English designer, painter, book illustrator and writer on art; the most popular of the disciples of William Morris. A promoter of the Art Workers' Guild, he was its first president. Many of Crane's wallpapers and ceramics from the 1870's and 1880's bear inscriptions. Crane worked for Wedgwood, Mintons and Pilkingtons, and as an independent designer. His personal mark

CRANE, WALTER
c. 1865-1915

on wares or patterns designed by him from around 1865 to 1915 was the initial C enclosing a crane. See *Arts and Crafts Movement.*

Crazing In ceramics; the accidental splits in a glaze consisting of a mesh of fine cracks. In Chinese porcelains the term *crackle* is generally used to describe a glaze characterized by a mesh of fine cracks; particularly when the crazing was deliberately planned. See *Crackle.*

Cream-Colored Earthenware In English ceramics; the English name applied to a fine lead-glazed ware originally and principally made in Staffordshire. It has a hard light-colored body that generally contains flint. From around 1760 it began to supplant Delft ware and tin-glazed faïence for tableware in the world's markets and is still the standard material. It was known by different names in various countries; in France it was called faïence fine, in Germany steingut and in Sweden flintporslin. Plain cream-colored earthenware was virtually the creation of Josiah Wedgwood, and after securing the patronage of Queen Charlotte about 1765 he named it the now familiar "Queen's Ware." Its qualities of thinness, durability and dense hardness were soon recognized, and Wedgwood's cream-colored earthenware was immediately imitated by innumerable potteries in the vicinity as well as by potteries at Leeds, Liverpool, Bristol, Swansea and elsewhere. It quickly secured a wide European market. Cream-colored earthenware was made into every kind of tableware. Wedgwood was constantly improving the utility of the forms such as the handles on teapots and cream jugs. The decoration was chiefly in imitation of silver and was largely confined to beaded and feather-edged borders and pierced openwork. See *Pearl*

Ware; Faïence; Faïence Fine; Queen's Ware. (388, 393-396, 401-406)

Creamware See *Cream-Colored Earthenware.*

Crefeld In German ceramics; lead-glazed red earthenware with frequently notably designed sgraffiato decoration in peasant style was produced in the 18th century at Schäphuysen near Crefeld and other villages, including Frechen and Xanten in the lower Rhenish district relatively near the Dutch border.

Creil In French ceramics; a manufactory was founded at Creil, Oise, about 1794. It produced faïence fine and other wares of the English type. It was joined to the manufactory of Montereau early in the 19th century and was active until 1895. Much of the Creil earthenware was decorated with transfer printing which was generally in black and rarely in underglaze blue. The subjects included transfer-printed views of Paris, portraits of celebrities, Italian and even English landscapes and country houses and villas, French chateaux, battle-scenes and historical subjects and fable subjects, particularly La Fontaine. The quality of the white earthenware was improved through the years. The mark Creil impressed was often used either with or without accompanying letters. Around the middle of the 19th century Leboeuf and Milliet were the proprietors. Hence the mark L M & Cie. See *Faïence Fine.*

Crete See *Minoan.*

Cries of Paris In German ceramics; the term *Cries of Paris* or *Cris de Paris* is given to a charming group or class of porcelain figures originally produced by Kaendler at Meissen in the 1740's. These figures of folk types were suggested from engravings by the Comte de Caylus published in 1737-1742. They portray such folk char-

acters as a bird-seller, hurdy-gurdy player, and other similar subjects. About 1753 other folk subjects were made after contemporary English engravings. See *Engraved Designs.*

Crinoline Group In German ceramics; the term *crinoline group* is applied to the small porcelain figures of ladies wearing wide spreading crinoline skirts. These figures which most frequently portray the ladies with their lovers first appeared in Meissen porcelain around 1737. They were modeled by Kaendler and his assistants after the works of such French artists as Watteau, Boucher and Lancret. Crinoline groups were also made by other factories such as Nymphenburg and Vienna.

Criseby In ceramics; see *Eckernförde.*

Crolius, William Stoneware potter working around 1730 in New York. Fifteen potters of the Crolius family worked in New York until around 1870 when Clarkson Crolius Jr., son of Clarkson Crolius(1773-1843) retired. An extant stoneware jug bears the inscription: New York Feb'y 17th, 1798/Flowered by Clarkson Crolius/Blue. See *Stoneware.*

Crouch Ware In English ceramics; the name given according to a doubtful tradition to a salt-glazed brownish or drab-colored stoneware, which derived its name from the use of a Derbyshire clay by that name, made in Staffordshire. It preceded Staffordshire white stoneware. This supposed Crouch ware is believed to have been made before 1714. The typical drab stoneware having a grey body and decorated with white reliefs, which is often identified as belonging to the Crouch ware class, is a Staffordshire ware of a later date. It is probable that this problematical Staffordshire pottery known as Crouch ware may be found among the wares classified as Fulham and Nottingham.

Crowan Pottery See *Davis, Harry.*

L.M & Cⁱᵉ
CREIL
1841 ON

Crown Derby See *Derby.*

Crowned Teapot, The See *Milde, Arij de.*

Crystalline Glaze This glazing technique introduced in the closing decades of the 19th century was the outcome of research and experiment which proved that porcelain hardened by firing to a degree which leaves it still porous, treated by saturation with certain metallic salts, and subjected to suitable atmospheric conditions before final firing, acquires a distinction of color and beauty of appearance not obtainable by superficial methods. During the process in which the porcelain is impregnated with its colors, and also during the process of firing, the various mineral salts which are absorbed by the paste crystallize and produce starry points, and luminous clouding seen in many specimens. Beyond determining the general scheme of color and design the final effects were not under the control of the operator. See *Glaze,* in modern Western ceramics; *Griemert, H; Sabrina.*

CUP STAND, SUNG

Cuccumos, Filippo In Italian ceramics; started a minor porcelain factory at Rome in 1761. It remained active until 1784.

Cuenca In Spanish ceramics; see *Seville.*

Cuerda Seca In Spanish ceramics; see *Seville.*

Culick, Jan Jansz See *Rose, The.*

Cup Stand In Chinese ceramics; a small circular stand of varying form characterized by a hollow ring in which the base of the tea bowl or wine cup was inserted. The cup stand is of early origin and fine Chün yao and Northern Sung celadon cup stands are found in private collections of Chinese porcelains. Chinese cups were later furnished with straight edged trays, and they served the same purpose as a saucer, since saucers in the European style were not used. See *Bowl.* (91)

Cupisnique See *Andean.*

Curio A well-known abbreviation of the word *curiosity* given to an object of art possessing the value of a rarity or curiosity. The term is especially applied to an object of this type having its origin in the Far East, such as an article from China and Japan.

Curnock, Percy See *Doulton, Lambeth and Burslem.*

Curtis, John American potter producing creamware and earthenware of good quality at his pottery in Philadelphia from around 1790-1811.

Cuvilliés, François de (1695-1768) A well-known designer of ornament working in the Rococo style, born at Hainaut. He received his training in France, although he worked entirely abroad. From 1725 he had the title of architect to the Court of Bavaria and held posts of increasing importance under the successive Electors until his death. He derived the inspiration for his ornament chiefly from the designs of Meissonnier, Pineau and Lajoue, although he did not slavishly copy their work. His drawings were executed with much facility. The Rococo art at Würzburg, Nymphenburg and elsewhere in Bavaria from around 1730 onwards was largely inspired by Cuvilliés. See *Rococo; Engraved Designs.*

Cybis Porcelains In American ceramics; a firm started by Polish-born Boleslaw Cybis and his wife Marja, around 1942 at Trenton, New Jersey, where they specialize in a wide range of porcelain sculptures.

Cyfflé, Paul Louis See *Lunéville.*

Cyprus In ancient ceramics; the potters of Cyprus have long been known for their individualism and exuberance. They created some of the most pleasing painted pottery of the ancient world. (44-48)

Czechoslovakia In ceramics; when the Austro-Hungarian Empire was broken up in 1918 at the end of the First World War, Bohemia, Slovakia and Silesia, previously part of the Austro-Hungarian Empire, were extracted to form an independent republic given the name of Czechoslovakia. For this reason any pottery or porcelain mark that includes the name of Czechoslovakia invariably shows that the article was made after 1918. Bohemia, which is now the metropolitan area of Czechoslovakia, was in the 19th century the chief ceramic-producing area in the Austro-Hungarian Empire. See *Austria, Czechoslovakia and Hungary.*

D

Dagoty, P. L. French potter who was a partner of F. M. Honoré until about 1822. See *Honoré, F. M.; Petite Rue Saint-Gilles.*

Dakatsu Gusuri See *Karatsu.*

Dale, John English potter working at Burslem in the Staffordshire district where he made earthenware figures of the Walton type, bearing his name, J. Dale, late 18th and early 19th century. See *Walton, John.*

Dalpayrat, Adrien-Pierre (b. 1844) French artist-potter. Dalpayrat was concerned with the elaboration of glaze effects on stoneware and porcelain. His sense of form is perhaps best seen in the Art Nouveau era, at the end of the 19th century, when he used slightly asymmetrical shapes. (492)

Daly, Matthew E. See *Rookwood Pottery.*

Damascus Ware See *Islamic Pottery, Later.*

Damm In German ceramics; a factory for both white and cream-colored earthenware in the English style (steingut, as it was called in Germany) was started at Damm, near Aschaffenburg, in 1827 by Anna Maria Müller. It was continued by her son Daniel Ernst Müller who in 1830 bought the old molds of Höchst figures and groups, of which three hundred and sixty favorite models were made here. It is for these well-made reproductions that this factory is chiefly known. In 1886-1887 the molds and materials were sold to the Mehlem factory at Poppelsdorf near Bonn. Both Damm and Mehlem used the six-spoked wheel of Höchst to mark their wares. Sometimes the Damm mark was accompanied by a D. In 1903 the Höchst molds were sold to Dressel, Kister and Company of Passau, which produced

DAMM
1830 ON

Höchst models both in faïence and porcelain from this time onward.

Dammouse, Albert (1848-1926) A French sculptor and glass artist who in the 1870's became interested in porcelain and later became known for his stoneware. His chief concern was with the elaboration of glaze effects on porcelain and stoneware. Working at Sèvres, he continued stylistically Bracquemond's interpretation of Japanese aesthetics in art. See *Japanism.*

Dannhauser, Leopold (d. 1786) Modeler at the Vienna porcelain manufactory from c. 1762 to 1786.

Dannhöfer, Joseph Philipp (1712-1790) Ceramic painter at Vienna, Bayreuth, 1737-1744, Abtsbessingen, 1744-1747, Fulda, Poppelsdorf, 1758, and Ludwigsburg, 1762-1790. His name is especially connected with the Baroque and chinoiserie decoration of early Vienna. Notable are his charming landscapes in overglaze enamels framed with leaf-and-strapwork or Laub-und-Bandelwerk.

Dart, Jacques See *Miklashevskii, Andrei.*

Date Mark A mark bearing a date, letter, figure or arbitrary device representing a date, such as the chronological marks of Sèvres, Worcester, Rookwood and many others. See *Mark,* in ceramics.

Davenport In English ceramics; John Davenport and his successors were potters at Longport, Staffordshire, from 1793 to 1887. They made cream-colored and blue-printed earthenware and porcelain. The wares were technically of good quality. They sometimes used an excellent dark blue ground color. The Davenport manufactory was one of the chief makers of porcelain in Staffordshire. Fine porcelain dessert services were a specialty of this pottery and they were frequently decorated with landscapes. A great quantity of tea sets were made in the 1880's when they specialized in colorful Japan patterns in the Derby manner of the early part of the 19th century. Included among the marks were Davenport with an anchor and Davenport over Longport. See *Staffordshire.*

David, Jacques Louis (1748-1825) French painter. David completely dominated the art of his time. He was the principal exponent of a more intense Classic Revival which endeavored to recapture the spirit of the antique through its closer imitation. See *Denon, Baron; Empire; Louis XVI; Watteau, Antoine; Classic Revival; Engraved Designs.*

Davis, Harry English artist-potter. Trained as a potter at Poole, he worked for a time with Bernard Leach, running the Leach pottery at St. Ives when Bernard Leach went to Japan for a year in 1934. Later, he took charge of the pottery at Achimota College on the Gold Coast. After a few years in Patagonia, he converted in 1946 an old mill at Praze, near Camborne, Cornwall, into the highly efficient Crowan Pottery. He and his wife Mary developed in stoneware Leach's conception of handmade wares for daily use. In 1962 they emigrated to New Zealand where they continued potting. See *Cardew, M.; Leach, B.*

Dawson, John and Company In English ceramics; operated the South Hylton and Ford Potteries at Sunderland, Durham, from around 1799 to 1864, producing earthenwares. In 1837 the firm's name was Thomas Dawson and Company. Between the years 1800-1864 all marks include the name Dawson, South Hylton or Ford.

Day, Lewis Foreman (1845-1910) English designer, writer and lecturer. In 1870 he set up his own business and designed textiles, wallpapers, stained glass, embroidery, carpets, tiles, pottery and book covers. He was a founder member of the Arts and Crafts Exhibition Society, 1888. He wrote numerous books on ornament and design. See *Arts and Crafts Movement.*

De Distel In Dutch ceramics; an art pottery operating in Amsterdam, 1895-1923. See *Nienhuis, Bert.*

De Stijl One of the longest-lived and most influential groups of modern artists, originating in Holland during the First World War. From the start, it was marked by extraordinary collaboration on the part of painters and sculptors, architects and practical designers. Included among its leaders were the painter Piet Mondrian and the architect J. J. P. Oud; but its greatest influence was exerted mainly through the ideas and tireless propaganda of its founder, Theo van Doesburg, a man as versatile as a figure of the Renaissance. Three principles formed the essential basis of the work of De Stijl whether in painting, sculpture, architecture or the arts of decoration: namely, in form, the rectangle; in color the primary shades, blue, yellow and red; in composition, asymmetrical balance. From 1920 to 1925, the influence of De Stijl was notably expanded, first in Belgium, then in Germany, France, eastern Europe and even in Russia. The theories put forth by De Stijl artists and writers still furnish the essential formal aesthetic of a large part of modern architecture and much modern design.

Deck, Théodore (1823-1891) French artist-potter; generally regarded in the modern sense as the first of the artist potters. Early in his career he began to undertake research into the character of Persian and Turkish pottery of the 16th and 17th centuries, which enjoyed success at the Paris Exhibition of Arts and Industries in 1861. Later his research was directed to Chinese monochrome glazes. Much of Deck's early success was achieved in the production of pottery decorated with individually

DAVENPORT
C. 1795 ON

DE DISTEL
C. 1895 ON

painted scenes, mainly by painter friends. About 1880 he began to make porcelain and produced some excellent flambé glazes. In this, like other French artists, he was presumably inspired by the sight of Japanese glazed wares at the Paris Exhibition of 1878. Almost ten years later, in 1887, his book LA FAÏENCE was published in Paris. In the same year he was appointed art director at Sèvres (the first practical potter ever to attain that distinction), and introduced a new siliceous "soft paste" capable of rich coloring and a porcelaneous stoneware for architectural use which was perfected in the 1890's. The main feature of his work is its notable variety and perhaps for this reason he is now recognized more for the range of his technical innovations than for his individual ceramic style. See *Chaplet, E.; Gauguin, P.*

DELFT WIG STAND

Decoeur, Emile (b. 1876) French artist-potter; identified with the great period of French artist-pottery when stoneware and glazes of notable beauty were produced. He used mat glazes with remarkable sensitivity and his restrained surface decoration was always blended faultlessly to his stoneware forms. (528)

Décor Bois In ceramics; a style of painted decoration having a painted ground in imitation of grained wood. A decoration resembling a white sheet of paper or a card having a landscape painted in crimson, grey or black was made to appear as though attached to the ground. It is generally accepted that this style of decoration originated on Niderviller faïence around 1770. The style was extensively imitated at many ceramic manufactories, such as Frankenthal, Vienna, Nymphenburg and Nove.

Decorated Oribe See *Oribe.*

Decorator's Mark A name, letter, cypher or symbol, placed on the ware by the decorator or gilder. See *Mark*, in ceramics.

Dedham Pottery See *Chelsea and Dedham.*

Del Vecchio, Cherinto See *Naples.*

Delaherche, Auguste (b. 1857) One of the foremost French artist-potters of Art Nouveau; he was associated with S. Bing at various times. During his long career his work passed through many phases. Like Dammouse and Dalpayrat, he was concerned with the elaboration of glaze effects on stoneware or porcelain. His work displayed a notable strength of form. (491)

Deldare See *Buffalo Pottery.*

Delfshaven See *Dutch Tiles.*

Delft In Dutch ceramics; during the second quarter of the 17th century the town of Delft near Rotterdam assumed a leading position among the Dutch centers of faïence making, and became famous for its imitations of Chinese porcelains made in tin-glazed earthenware. Its finest period was from around 1640 to 1740. The material for Delft faïence was characterized by a whiteness and thinness of substance. Delft faïence in imitation of blue and white in the Chinese style bore the closest resemblance to the original of any of the European porcelain or faïence imitating Chinese prototypes. Perhaps the most typical early types of Delft blue and white faïence were in the designs of Wan Li (1573-1619) and in the transitional period from the end of Ming to the beginning of the reign of K'ang Hsi or from about 1644 to 1662. Practically every type of porcelain of the reign of K'ang Hsi, 1662-1722, was subsequently imitated. In another variety of Delft blue and white Dutch figures were occasionally intermingled with Chinese motifs and the forms were often adapted to the European taste. Another type of blue and white of much importance and dating from around 1650 was in the Dutch style of contemporary oil painting and was decorated only with European landscapes, figure and portrait subjects. Decorative designs in the Baroque taste were made from around 1675 and onward. A more common blue and white ware was made from 1750 to 1800 and later. Polychrome wares in the Chinese and Japanese style, particularly the Famille Verte porcelain of the reign of K'ang Hsi, and Japanese brocaded Imari ware, were closely imitated from early in the 18th century. At first only high-temperature colors were used on this faïence. They also made a polychrome ware with a black ground which may have been inspired by the Chinese Famille Noire. Other colored grounds were also used. As the 18th century advanced muffle colors and gold replaced the high-temperature colors on the more ambitious pieces. From late in the 17th century onward, polychrome wares in the Dutch style that were essentially original in design were made. Especially fine were the pieces with baskets and pots of flowers treated in a natural manner. Designs in the Baroque taste and in the Rococo taste subsequently followed; the latter being used until the 19th century, since the Neo-Classical style was never adopted. The Dutch were not skillful modelers, and as a result their figures and modeled wares, which they adopted from the Chinese and Meissen, were crude and were of little artistic importance. Delft faïence was often marked with the initials, the name or the mark of the owner. The owner's mark was usually the same as the sign of the factory such as The Three Bells; The Peacock; The White Star; The Golden Boat and The Ewer. Most of the names are old brewery names, as the rapid decline in the brewing trade made available suitable premises for the rapidly growing ceramic trade and the names were retained. See *Faïence; Two Little Ships, The; Greek A, The; Milde, Arij de; Young Moor's Head, The; Pietersz, Harman; Porcelain Bottle, The; Rose, The; Double Tankard, The; Metal Pot, The; Dutch Tiles; Arnheim; Kwaart; Old Moor's Head, The; Three Bells, The; Porcelain Claw, The; White Star, The; Hatchet, The.* (260-268, 294)

Delftware   In ceramics; the English name for tin-glazed earthenware. It is synonymous with faïence which is reserved for the later tin-glazed wares of the 17th century either in the more or less original styles made in France and in other countries or more often in the Dutch-Chinese or Delft tradition. See *Faïence; Delft.* (254-259)

Della Robbia   In ceramics; the tin-glazed terra-cotta made by a celebrated Florentine family of sculptors. It was made by Luca della Robbia (c. 1399-1482), his nephew Andrea (1435-1525), and the latter's sons, Giovanni (1469-c. 1529), and Girolamo (1488-1566). Essentially the work belongs to the art of sculpture or modeling rather than to ceramics. Luca della Robbia, who was a great sculptor in marble and bronze, made beautifully modeled terra-cotta reliefs on which he used colored glazes made with an admixture of tin ashes. The light blue and other tin glazes were often of remarkable beauty. It is erroneous to believe that Luca della Robbia invented the process or was the first to use opaque tin glazes. His reliefs were notable for his excellent knowledge of anatomy and for his fine modeling of hands. Especially striking are his colorful wreathed borders of fruits naturalistically represented, which were extensively imitated by followers belonging to his school. Andrea della Robbia did many beautiful reliefs of the Madonna and Child. His work is usually as highly regarded as that of Luca della Robbia. (223)

Della Robbia, Andrea   See *Della Robbia.*

Della Robbia, Luca   See *Della Robbia.*

Della Robbia Company, Ltd.   In English ceramics; an art pottery flourishing 1894-1906, founded by Harold Rathbone, a painter and pupil of Ford Madox Brown, at Birkenhead, Cheshire. It produced two kinds of ware: architectural "faïence" consisting chiefly of panels modeled with figure subjects in high relief, and hollow pottery wares. The latter, by far the more

DELLA ROBBIA PLAQUE

DELLA ROBBIA COMPANY LTD.
C. 1894-1901

DENVER CHINA AND
POTTERY COMPANY
C. 1900

interesting with their vivid coloring and unusual shapes, were almost always decorated with a combination of sgraffiato and painting. Included among the number of artists associated with this project was the Italian sculptor Carlo Manzoni.

Delpierre, Francine French artist-potter; working in the 20th century. In the years after the Second World War her style of stoneware reveals great accomplishment. Noteworthy are her stoneware vessels thinly coiled in delicate shapes.

Demi Grand Feu In ceramics; the French term for medium fired glazes. These glazes are applied to porcelain that has been biscuited or already fired in the porcelain kiln, since these glazes melt at a medium temperature and cannot stand the heat required to fire porcelain. After they are applied to the biscuited porcelain they are melted in a second temperate fire. These glazes are alkali lead silicates colored with metallic oxides. They melt at a temperature higher than is required to fire enamels. However, this term is seldom used in association with European ceramics. See *Glaze; Grand Feu.*

Denaura See *Lonhuda Pottery.*

Denon, Dominique Vivant, Baron de (1747-1825) French artist, architect and archaeologist. As a result of Napoleon's Egyptian campaign in 1798 and 1799 there was a vogue for Egyptian style of ornament. This was chiefly due to the archaeological studies done by Baron de Denon, who was a friend of David's. Napoleon invited him to accompany the military expedition to Egypt. In 1802 he published his most important work which was entitled VOYAGE DANS LA BASSE ET LA HAUTE EGYPTE; it was in two volumes and contained 141 plates. See *David, Jacques Louis; Empire; Engraved Designs.*

Denver China and Pottery Company See *Lonhuda Pottery.*

Derby In English ceramics; it seems that porcelain was made around 1745 at Cockpit Hill in Derby. In 1756 a porcelain manufactory was established in Nottingham Road with William Duesbury as manager, who soon became sole owner. It is believed that Duesbury purchased the Longton Hall works in 1760 and secured control of Bow in 1762. He bought the Chelsea manufactory in 1770 and continued to operate it in association with Derby until 1784, when he closed it. Duesbury's son succeeded his father upon the latter's death in 1786. In 1811 it was purchased by Robert Bloor and finally closed in 1848. The productions from 1786 to 1811 are generally known as Crown Derby and from 1811 to 1848 as Bloor-Derby due to the marks that were in general use. The early porcelain made at Derby was unmarked. After 1770 various marks were in regular use. A distinctive Derby mark is a crowned D with crossed batons and six dots between the D and the crown in blue, crimson or purple. An anchor traversing the D in red or gold is the usual Chelsea-Derby mark, 1770-1784. From about 1755 to 1770 figures were made in the Meissen style and the tablewares were in the style of the Chelsea wares marked with a red anchor and were often decorated with Meissen flowers. Painting in underglaze blue was relatively rare. During the Chelsea-Derby period, 1770-1784, the figure modeling as a rule revealed the influence of Sèvres, but the interpretation was in the Chelsea tradition for taste, and as a result the wares had a singular English charm and simplicity. The material was a pleasing, slightly warm white and the glaze was clear and brilliant but rather thick. The Crown Derby wares, 1784-1811, maintained the traditions of the Chelsea-Derby productions. The biscuit figures were of very good quality. The manufactory enjoyed a pre-eminent position in England during the last quarter of the 18th century. During the Bloor period, 1811 to 1848, a general artistic decline soon became evi-

DERBY

C. 1770-1784

C. 1782-1825

C. 1820-1840

C. 1861-1935

C. 1891 ON

dent that was to increase in the ensuing years. Robert Bloor, formerly a clerk and salesman at Derby, was forced to lower the standards of workmanship in order to pay the installments on the agreed purchase price. He concentrated on gaudy Japan patterns with their large areas of red, blue and gold—a work that could be produced cheaply and quickly by semi-skilled hands—and he flooded the market with "seconds." See *Duesbury, W.; Stephan, P.* After the original Derby factory closed in 1848 some of the former workmen banded together and making use of old models and using established patterns started a small factory in King Street, where they continued the Derby tradition. The wares produced at the Old Crown Derby China Works, as they named it, were well received. Marks of the period include the surnames of the original Derby potters who became managers: Locker, Stevenson, Sharp and Hancock(d. 1898). In 1876 a separate company was formed under the title of the Derby Crown Porcelain Company. Edward Phillips from Royal Worcester, together with his fellow directors in the new undertaking, tried from the beginning to exploit the large American market for fine decorative porcelains. The colorful traditional Derby "Japan" patterns were used and many new vase shapes were modeled. In 1890 the company was appointed "Manufacturers of Porcelain to Her Majesty," and given the privilege of using the title "The Royal Crown Derby Porcelain Company." This is a useful guide to dating later wares. An earthenware body was occasionally used for tablewares. In 1935 the King Street factory was purchased and merged with the Royal Crown Derby works which thus gained possession of the original Derby molds and patterns. In 1964 the Royal Crown Derby became part of a group of factories controlled by Allied English Potteries, Ltd., England's largest manufacturer of bone china and pottery tablewares. See *Stevenson and Hancock.* (377)

Derby Crown Porcelain Company   See *Derby.*

Deruta   In Italian ceramics; some of the world's most beautiful painted majolica, both polychrome and lustered, was made at Deruta, Umbria, from about 1490 to 1550. Potteries still exist at Deruta. It is generally accepted that potters were working there late in the 14th century and that majolica having artistic importance was made at Deruta from the latter part of the 15th century. A most important variety was the polychrome ware, 1500-1520, of the petal-back class, which was so called because of a distinctive imbricated floral pattern decorated on the backs of plates and dishes. The coloring was unrivaled and the figure painting was of the highest quality and was remarkable for its extreme delicacy and refinement. Luster painting was done at Deruta from about 1500. The golden yellow or mother-of-pearl and the ruby luster were of uncommon beauty. The ruby luster seems to have disappeared from Deruta around 1515; however, the golden yellow with its nacreous reflections was used for almost a half a century longer. A very familiar variety, which ranks among the masterpieces of majolica, had lustered and polychrome decoration and was made from about 1515 to 1540; the finest being made prior to 1530. The plates, which were often very large, were boldly painted with busts and figure subjects in a linear style and were often broadly outlined and shadowed in blue, having simple borders of star-rays, foliage or gadroons. Sometimes the designs were in relief. This style of painting characterized by its bold simplicity is closely associated with the familiar Deruta manner, which became well established on their wares, and is in direct contrast to the very sensitive painting on the so-called petal-back variety. See *Italian Majolica; Luster Decoration.*

Design and Industries Association   Established in England in 1915; it acknowledged

DERBY SUGAR BOWL WITH
IMARI PATTERN

the program developed by the Werkbund and stated in its JOURNAL, 1916, that it was "accepting the machine in its proper place, as a device to be guided and controlled, not merely boycotted." See *Arts and Crafts Movement; Deutscher Werkbund; Council of Industrial Design.*

Designer-Craftsman Used interchangeably with artist-craftsman. See *Artist-Potter.*

Deutsche Blumen In ceramics; a contemporary German name given to flowers painted in a natural manner. This style of flower painting was introduced at Meissen by Herold toward 1740. It rapidly became very fashionable and by the middle of the 18th century practically every existing porcelain factory was decorating its porcelain with the so-called Deutsche Blumen. They were especially fine on the earliest Vincennes and Chelsea porcelain. The Deutsche Blumen supplanted the earlier and stylized Indian or Oriental flowers. They remained in general favor until the rise to fashion of Sèvres when they were replaced by the more conventional French styles of flower painting. See *Engraved Designs; Fleurs de Strasbourg.* (336, 350)

DEUTSCHE BLUMEN ON
LUDWIGSBURG COFFEE POT

Deutsche Werkstätten In 1897 Obrist, Pankok, Paul and Riemerschmid founded the Münchener Vereinigte Werkstätten für Kunst in Handwerk. In 1898 a similar organization, the Dresdener Werkstätten für Handwerkskunst, was started in Dresden under the management of Karl Schmidt. Both organizations aimed to create a national German art, with no tinge of stylistic imitation and on a sound constructive basis through cooperation between artist and artisan. See *Deutscher Werkbund.*

Deutscher Werkbund Similar ideas to those held by the Deutsche Werkstätten guided the activities of the Deutscher Werkbund, established in 1907 to coalesce the various individual experiments into a world-wide recognized style. This association comprising manufacturers and designers was formed to promote high standards of craftsmanship and industrial design by encouraging a closer cooperation between architect, designer, manufacturer and workman. From the beginning this group felt no horror of the machine. The program developed by the Werkbund (the acceptance of the machine in its proper place) was adopted by other countries' associations: the Austrian Werkbund, 1910, the Swiss Werkbund, 1913, the English Design and Industries Association, 1915, etc. See *Deutsche Werkstätten.*

Devil's Work In Chinese ceramics; see *Kuei Kung; Ling Lung.*

Dewsbury, David See *Doulton, Lambeth and Burslem.*

Diaguite See *Argentina and Chile.*

Diato, Alberto Modern Italian artist-potter; using mainly the medium of brightly colored earthenware, he has produced both purely sculptural works and pottery vessels often modeled in strange or exaggerated forms.

Dijsselhof, Gerrit Willem (1866-1924) Dutch painter; leading designer in the sphere of decorative art in the 1890's; foremost among the artists inspired by Japanese design. The special batik-inspired Dutch Art Nouveau made its appearance in his work.

Dillwyn and Company See *Swansea.*

Dinos See *Lebes.*

Dipylon In ancient ceramics; pertaining to a style of Greek pottery found in Attic remains of about the 8th century B.C. originating in Athens near the gate called Dipylon, meaning double-gated. It belongs to the most developed period of the geometric style. Especially noteworthy are the colossal kraters made as a monument for a man's grave, depicting the funeral procession. (57)

Directoire The period in French history, 1793-1804, during the time of the Convention, 1792-1795, the Directory, 1795-1799, and the Consulate, 1799-1804.

Dixon and Company See *Sunderland Pottery.*

Doat, Taxile French artist-potter working at Sèvres around the closing decades of the 19th century. Noteworthy was his use of the pâte-sur-pâte decorative technique.

Doccia In Italian ceramics; a porcelain manufactory was founded in 1735-1737 by the Marquis Carlo Ginori and is still owned by the Ginori family. During the 19th century, the manufactory chiefly produced imitations of earlier wares, with the original marks often being added. The old Capo di Monte molds were bought by Doccia and they often copied Capo di Monte and sometimes marked it with a crowned N of Naples. It is sometimes difficult to distinguish Doccia porcelain from that of Venice and Capo di Monte. However, some original and distinctive work is ascribed to this factory. The designs and colors of their painted decoration showed the influence of Vienna, Meissen and Sèvres. No mark was used on the early wares from 1737 to 1757. The mark of the star was used during the late 18th and first half of the 19th centuries. It is generally found on very translucent porcelain painted with figures and landscapes, the latter being views of Florence of exceptional quality. A certain Nicola Letourneau of Nevers is recorded, after a stay in Faenza, to have settled in Doccia, in 1740, to work with the Ginori. Here in a manufactory best known for its porcelain he established the decorative style of the majolica department which enjoyed a much more considerable and continuous development in the 18th and 19th century than is generally believed. Here petit feu decoration on tin-glazed ware was produced side by side with grand feu ware. Late in the 19th century, in 1896, the Ginori porcelain factory was incorporated with the Società Ceramica Richard of Milan, giving rise to the present Richard-Ginori company. After the merger the production was dominated artistically by two facts: the adoption of the Art Nouveau style at the beginning of the 20th century and the renewed interest in the Neo-Classic style introduced by Gio Ponti and his group immediately after the First World War. The modern spirit has been elegantly expressed in the Donatella table service of porcelain decorated with grey and gilt bands designed about 1954 by Giovanni Gariboldi at the Richard-Ginori factory. (338, 505, 519, 527)

Dr. Wall or **Dr. John Wall** See *Worcester.*

Dog of Fo In Chinese art; a Chinese animal figure widely used in ceramics, sculpture and painting. He is a lion but is very gentle, and he is usually playing with a silk ball tied with a ribbon which he holds in his mouth. He is generally depicted in pairs, one playing with the ball and the other with a lion cub. The very large lion figures were placed as guardians at the entrance gate to a Buddhist temple; because of this duty they were called Dog of Fo or Buddha. The smaller lion figures were used as holders for incense sticks on the altars of Buddhist temples. See *Chinese Animal Figures.* (109)

Dohachi, Ninami (1783-1855) Kyoto studio-potter. Descendant of a hereditary line of Japanese potters, he is known for his bold overglaze decoration in the style of the Ogata Korin school of painting. Though he made imitations of Chinese porcelain wares, such as Shonsui underglaze blue and white, Kinran-de and Gosu-akae, he was much more famous for his Awata wares in the Ninsei style, for his excellent *raku chawan* (tea bowls), imitations of Koetsu tea bowls and copies of Kenzan. Though he was a student of Okuda Eisen, he is especially noteworthy because he specialized in producing traditional Kyo pottery wares in keeping with Japanese taste while his contemporaries were much

DOCCIA

LATE 18TH CENTURY

19TH CENTURY

Richard Ginori

PRESENT

DOHACHI

more interested in imitating Chinese porcelain wares. For example, after the death of Ninsei polychrome enameled wares were almost forgotten but Dohachi revived them. He kept making colored pieces for the powdered tea ceremony which had been supplanted by the more fashionable tea utensils for infused tea in the Mokubei style. His name is of course more closely associated with faïence than with porcelain. See *Ninsei; Mokubei, Aoki; Shonsui; Gosu-Akae; Kinran-de; Kyo; Shuhei, Ogata.* (151)

DON POTTERY
1820-1834

Don Pottery In English ceramics; the Don Pottery was started probably as early as 1790 at Swinton, Yorkshire. Around 1800 it was enlarged by John Green of Leeds, and in 1834 it was sold to Samuel Barker of the Mixborough Pottery. Included among the marks was "Don Pottery" impressed. Its principal productions were cream-colored earthenware and other wares in imitation of those made at Leeds.

Donaldson, John (1737-1810) English miniaturist and porcelain painter. Traditionally reputed to have worked for the Chelsea porcelain factory; signed specimens exist of his work at Worcester where he painted vases with mythological figure subjects, from around 1768 and later.

Donauwörth In German ceramics; the existence of a faïence manufactory at Donauwörth, Bavaria, is known only from an entry in local records and the record of Georg Friedrich Grebner departing from Oettingen-Schrattenhofen in 1740. An extant tankard signed by Grebner is inscribed Donauwörth 1741.

Donyu See *Raku.*

DOROTHEENTHAL
C. 1715 ON

Dordrecht In Dutch ceramics; a majolica pottery was started here in 1586. Two other potteries were also started here but none survived until the 18th century. The wares have not been identified.

Dorotheenthal In German ceramics; a faïence manufactory was founded at Dorotheenthal near Arnstadt, Thuringia, around 1715 by Augusta Dorothea, daughter of a Duke of Brunswick, with Johann Philipp Frantz apparently being the first manager. The factory closed prior to 1806. The mark occasionally used was AB in monogram in combination with painters' marks. Especially characteristic of their work is the painted decoration of Baroque scrollwork, or Laub-und-Bandelwerk, which they treated in a distinctive manner. Included among their wares were cylindrical tankards and two-handled vases and figures. They were painted in high-temperature colors of great brightness of tone and the designs were vigorously executed.

Douai In French ceramics; a manufactory for making faïence fine was founded at Douai, Nord, in 1781 by two Englishmen, Charles and James Leigh, and was in existence until 1820. The firm was known as Houzé de l'Aulnoit & Cie. Other potteries making similar wares were also active at Douai. The most common production of Douai was cream-colored earthenware similar to that of Leeds, England. Decorative motifs pierced in openwork, handles in the form of twisted stems, reliefs in biscuit and marbled wares were characteristic and were in imitation of English wares. During the period of the French Revolution snuff boxes, plates and similar pieces made of white or cream-colored earthenware were decorated with current patriotic emblems and mottoes. The wares were occasionally marked Leigh & Cie or Douai impressed. Other marks such as Martin Dammann and Halfort belonged to another pottery operating here.

Double Tankard, The or **De Dobbelde Schenckan** In Dutch ceramics; a pottery at Delft producing faïence from around 1659 to 1777 under various proprietors including Louwijs Fictoorsz or Vitorsz, a talented potter, who bought the pottery in 1688 and continued to operate it until his death in 1713. His polychrome pieces bear a marked resemblance to those of Lambertus van Eenhoorn. See *Eenhoorn, Wouter van; Delft; Faïence.* (262)

Doughty, Susan Dorothy (1892-1962) English ceramist-modeler whose work with birds and the exquisitely modeled flowers and plants with which they are usually identified has become a collector's item in the United States. She started producing her ceramic birds in 1935 for the Royal Worcester Porcelain Company. She made a specialty of American birds; in recent years she also brought out models for an English bird series. See *Worcester.* (546)

Doulton, Lambeth and Burslem In English ceramics; around 1815 John Doulton(1793-1873) with John Watts started a pottery at Lambeth, London S.E., known as Doulton and Watts which subsequently became Doulton & Co. (Ltd.), c. 1858-1956. It was known for many years for its stoneware and earthenware. The revival of decorative salt-glazed stoneware dates chiefly from the wares which Doulton exhibited at the South Kensington Exhibitions of 1871 and 1872. Under the aegis of Henry Doulton a notable decorative art department was developed as a result of his friendship with John Sparkes, the headmaster at the Lambeth School of Art. They conducted a novel experiment whereby a number of students were given free rein with the Lambeth pottery's salt-glazed stoneware. The result was shown at the Exhibition of 1871. This group of wares decorated and signed by students may be regarded as the first outstanding example of intellectual "art pottery" in England. Among the artists whose work developed in the studio were Hannah Barlow and her sister and brother, Florence and Arthur, George Tinworth, Emily Edwards and Frank Butler. Work of this kind was con-

tinued at the Doulton studio into the 20th century. In 1877 the Lambeth firm of Doulton took over a factory, formerly Pinder, Bourne and Company, at Burslem for the production of fine earthenware. The reputation of the factory in Burslem was established chiefly on the production of fine porcelains in the later years of the century, which became very popular, particularly in the North American markets. In 1901 King Edward VII conferred a double honor on the firm by the presentation of the Royal Warrant to its chairman and personally authorizing it to use the word "Royal" in describing its products. Among the leading artists working at Burslem were Percy Curnock (1885-1919); David Dewsbury (1889-1919); Charles Hart (1880-1927); Henry Mitchell (1893-1908); Walter Slater (1880-1910); and George White (1885-1912). These and other artists generally signed their work in full. Since October 1955 the Burslem firm has been retitled Doulton Fine China, Ltd. Production ceased at Lambeth in 1956. In 1968 Doulton Fine China Limited received the Royal Warrant appointing them suppliers of china to H. M. Queen Elizabeth II. See *Doultons Lambeth School of Art: Martin Brothers; Moore, Bernard.* (480, 481)

Doulton Fine China, Ltd. See *Doulton, Lambeth and Burslem.*

Doultons Lambeth School of Art In English ceramics; perhaps the first art-pottery made in England was the salt-glazed stoneware decorated in the Doulton factory at Lambeth in London from 1871 by students of the Lambeth School of Art. See *Doulton, Lambeth and Burslem; Carrara; Impasto; Silicon; Chiné.*

Drammen In Norwegian ceramics; a faïence factory was started here in 1757-1760 and continued until 1772. It mainly produced tableware coarsely painted in blue or manganese-purple.

Dreihausen In German ceramics; it is be-

Orange Blossom and Butterfly

by

DOUGHTY, DOROTHY
C. 1946

DOULTON

C. 1880-1891

1891 ON

C. 1902 ON

lieved some rare silver-mounted stone-ware drinking vessels with a decoration of masks in high relief were made at Dreihausen, a center of pottery making, southeast of Marburg, Hesse, in the first quarter of the 15th century. Six have survived, and judging from an engraved inscription on one of the mounts they were used to welcome guests and so were called Wilkomm (welcome). One of the cups has the hedgehog decoration on the bowl. These may be the earliest types of German stoneware with artistic pretension. See *Ring Jug*. (193)

Dresden In German ceramics; a faïence manufactory was founded in 1708 at Dresden, Saxony, by Johann Friedrich Böttger, a year before he discovered porcelain and the consequent establishment of the Meissen manufactory. The factory closed in 1784 after several changes in management. In 1710 Peter Eggebrecht (d. 1738) formerly of Berlin, became manager, and in 1712 was permitted to lease the factory. The only Dresden faïence of artistic importance was made from around 1710 to 1738. No mark was used for that period. From 1768 onwards the mark DH was used. Included among the early productions are vases, flower pots and figures; the latter being inspired by figures from the Italian Comedy and also from Chinese art. From about 1779 the forms became classical. A favorite painted decoration was medallion portrait heads in black silhouette or in grey monochrome on a light colored ground. An interesting and peculiar painted pattern consisted of a group of miscellaneous objects such as letters, scissors and other similar items arranged together; it was called quodlibetz or what you please. Blue and white porcelain for daily use was also made. The numerous figures were chiefly copies from other factories.

Dresden In ceramics; from the 18th century the term *Dresden china* has been a familiar name in England and America for Meissen porcelain. The mark of Dresden and D under a crown often occurs on 19th century porcelain executed in the Meissen style. A number of 19th century manufacturers and decorators worked at Dresden, which is near Meissen, in the Meissen manner, some of them using marks closely imitative of the crossed swords of Meissen. Included among the porcelain decorators working at Dresden were Donath, active 1872; Hamann, active 1866; K. R. Klemm, active 1869; A. Lamm, active 1887, and Meyers and Son, active late 19th century, who used a crossed swords mark bearing a strong resemblance to that of Meissen. See *Potschappel*.

Dresser, Christopher (1834-1904) English, born in Glasgow, designer and writer. His first book on design, THE ART OF DECORATIVE DESIGN, published in 1862, was followed by numerous others on botany, design and Japanese art, and a number of articles and lectures. Dresser visited Japan in 1876 as an official representative of the British government. He was a tireless worker and produced a great number of designs in practically all media—pottery, furniture, metalwork,—and in styles ranging from the purely functional to the most daring and unusual. See *Tooth, Henry*.

Dry Body A non-porous stoneware body which requires no glaze.

Dublin See *Ireland*.

Dubois, Vincent See *Rue de la Roquette*.

Duckworth, Ruth English artist-potter; active at Kew, Surrey, since 1956, producing studio-type pottery and sculpture. Notable are examples of her stoneware pots formed asymmetrically by coiling, with the surface only partially glazed. Ruth Duckworth, who has also worked in the United States, also makes purely sculptural works. A new movement toward abstract pottery which has been evident in the United

DUCKWORK, RUTH
1956 ON

States since the later 1950's is also reflected in some of her stoneware pots of the 1960's.

Duesbury, William (1725-1786) Proprietor of several English porcelain factories including Derby, 1756-1786. Bought the Chelsea factory in 1770; reputed to have obtained Longton Hall in 1760, and acquired control of Bow in 1762 or later. His son, William II (1763-1797) became proprietor of the Derby factory from 1786 until his death.

Dufy, Jean French designer; brother of the painter Raoul Dufy. At the Paris Exhibition of 1925 the Théodore Haviland factory of Limoges displayed an important work with decoration by Jean Dufy.

Dufy, Raoul (1877-1953) French painter; became interested in the decoration of pottery at the incentive of José Llorens Artigas.

Du Paquier, Claudius Innocentius See *Paquier, Claudius Innocentius du.*

Dunashov In Russian ceramics; an important porcelain manufactory was started at Turygino near Moscow by Dunashov in 1830. See *Russia.*

Dunderdale, David and Company See *Castleford.*

Dunn, Constance English artist-potter; a pupil of William Staite Murray, making a studio-type pottery. See *Murray, W.S.; Leach, B.*

Duplessis, Jean Claude (d.1774) An Italian sculptor, decorative designer and bronze founder working in Paris before 1742. In 1747 he was attached to the porcelain factory at Vincennes and continued his work when the latter was transferred to Sèvres. He provided both designs and mounts for porcelain. In addition to this work he was responsible for designing the mounts of the Bureau du Roi Louis XV, the most

celebrated piece of furniture in the world. In 1758 he was nominated Orfèvre du Roi. His son, Jean Claude Thomas Duplessis (d.1783) was also a sculptor and bronze founder, and flourished from 1761 onward. He is frequently confused with his father. See *Flowers Modeled in Porcelain.* (352, 358)

Durlach In German ceramics; a faïence manufactory was started at Durlach, Baden, in 1722 by Johann Heinrich Wachenfeld. A privilege was granted in 1723 by the Margrave of Baden. It closed in 1840 after having changed ownership several times. Its best and only distinctive work was from around 1775 to 1818. This group was composed of small pear-shaped jugs and coffee pots carefully painted with figure subjects taken from everyday life such as farm workers and craftsmen. The pieces were obviously meant for gifts and were almost always dated. They generally had rhymed inscriptions with the name of the recipient in black letters and were commonly decorated with borders of vine leaves. The manufactory enjoyed a large business but its other wares had little artistic merit. Toward the end of the 18th century they began to make a cream-colored earthenware which after 1818 was marked Durlach, impressed. The only 18th century marks ever found were those of the painters.

Dutch Refers to ceramic wares made in the North Netherlands, especially those made after the establishment of the Dutch Republic in 1609. See *Netherlandish.*

Dutch Tiles In Dutch ceramics; the most widespread and characteristic of the productions made at the Dutch faïence manufactories were tiles. Unlike their Italian prototypes which were mainly used for pavements, Dutch tin-glazed tiles were almost always wall tiles. Early tin-glazed tiles continued the tradition of Netherlandish majolica. Great centers of tile-making from the latter part of the 16th century

DUNASHOV
1830 ON

D. D. & Co.

DUNDERDALE, DAVID
AND COMPANY
1790 ON

onward were Haarlem, Amsterdam, Middelburg and especially Rotterdam which in the 17th century became the center of an enormous tile-making industry. In the 17th century Delfshaven and various centers in Friesland began to be important, and at Delft itself tiles were made by some potters who, however, were vessel-makers rather than tile-makers. In the case of the latter about the only other ware they made besides tiles were dishes. In the 17th century Chinese designs so common on Delft faïence are relatively rare on Dutch tiles. The typical motifs of the later 17th century tiles were mainly small figure subjects, often charmingly drawn, of soldiers, cavaliers and ladies, children at play, peasants, seascapes with ships, and small landscapes with or without figures, painted at first in blue only and toward 1700 frequently in manganese-purple. A tendency to abandon polychrome painting for blue or manganese-purple used alone dates from around 1625, the influence no doubt stemming from the Chinese blue and white.

DUX
1860 ON

After 1700 a decline in the popularity of Dutch faïence tiles became very marked. Nevertheless, the making of tiles continued in diminishing quantity until well into the 19th century and they are still being made. See *Tiles; Picture Tiles; Rotterdam; Amsterdam; Friesland; Faïence.*

Dux (Czech. Duchov) In Austrian ceramics; a porcelain factory was started at Dux, a town of Bohemia, by Ed. Eichler in 1860. Their products, especially portrait busts of charming young women and ornate vases, found favor in America. The factory prospered and in the 20th century became the Duxer Porzellanmanufaktur A.G. The distinguishing initial E appeared in several marks of varying design, one of which bore the inscription Royal Dux Bohemia.

Dwight, John (c. 1637-1703) English potter. He took out patents in 1671 and 1684 for the manufacture of stoneware at Fulham, Middlesex. See *Fulham; Buccaro.*

E

E-Karatsu In Japanese ceramics; a variety of Karatsu with painted decoration. See *Karatsu*.

E-Seto In Japanese ceramics; the name given to a variety of Seto ware with sketchily drawn designs, perhaps of reeds and grasses, executed in dark brown brush strokes under the glaze; made from around the late 16th century through the early part of the 17th century. See *Seto*.

Early Ming See *Ming*.

Earthenware In ceramics; the term is used in England for pottery which has a body that is not vitrified. Majolica, faïence, delftware and slipware are all varieties of earthenware. The term is synonymous with pottery. Earthenware is by far the largest and most common class of ceramics, and covers all natural clays or mixtures of natural clays which may fire red, buff, grey or yellowish according to certain impurities in the clay. See *Pottery*.

East India Porcelain See *Chinese Lowestoft*.

East Liverpool In American ceramics; East Liverpool, Ohio, became a great producing center of common white ware or granite ware; its development came a few years later than Trenton, and it is claimed that by around 1900 their production of white ware was equal to that of Trenton. The manufacture of white ware in East Liverpool is associated with Knowles, Taylor and Knowles, who began to manufacture white granite in 1872. White wares mainly comprise dinner services and pieces that have to withstand heat and daily usage. See *Taylor and Speeler; Knowles, Taylor and Knowles; Ironstone; Granite Ware; Trenton; Harker Pottery Company; Sterling China Company; East Liverpool Pottery Company; Laughlin, Homer, China Company; Taylor, Smith and Taylor*.

East Liverpool Pottery Company In American ceramics; this firm, located in East Liverpool, Ohio, manufactured "Waco" china and decorated wares, mainly in a white granite body. The first mark, a modification of the British Royal Arms, was found on souvenir china made for the Presidential campaign of 1896. Later marks had the name Waco in combination with the company's monogram.

Eberhard, Franz (1767-1836) Modeler at Nymphenburg, 1822 onward.

Eberlein, Johann Friedrich (d. 1749) Modeler at Meissen, 1735-1749, and assistant to Kaendler. Examples of his work show him hardly less able than Kaendler. See *Kaendler, J. J.* (314, 316, 319)

Echizen See *Six Old Kilns*.

Eckernförde A faïence manufactory was founded at Eckernförde, Schleswig, Germany, in 1765 and was a continuation of one founded at Criseby in 1759 by Johann Nicolaus Otte. The only work of artistic importance was some attractive Rococo faïence made from around 1761 to about 1768. Included among the productions were tureens in the form of vegetables and other types of vessels decorated with modeled and applied flowers and leaves. It is practically impossible to distinguish the wares made at Eckernförde from those made at Criseby. The marks used were the Scandinavian compound type and included the names or initials of the owner, the various painters and the town.

Eckhoff, Tias See *Porsgrund*.

Eckmann, Otto (1865-1902) German painter, graphic artist and designer; after 1894 he gave up painting and concentrated on decorative art. He belonged to the Munich School of Art Nouveau. He was an important early collector of Japanese woodblock prints; the influence of these is evident in the floral and plant fan-

EAST LIVERPOOL POTTERY CO.
1900 ON

ECKERNFÖRDE
1766

tasies he did for the magazines PAN and JUGEND. He was the leader of the German floral style. See *Jugendstil; Munich School; Art Nouveau.*

Ecuador and Colombia In pre-Columbian South American ceramics; the pre-Inca culture of Ecuador reveals far closer relationships with Colombia and parts of Central America than with Peru. Ecuador consists of three principal zones: the coast, the highlands and the Amazon forests. The most noteworthy pottery of the highlands was best developed in the province of Carchi in the extreme north of Ecuador and in the adjacent part of Colombia, to which has been given the name Tuncahuán. It is based on the same technique as that of Recuay in Peru, namely, simple red designs comprising, for instance, bands and discs on a buff slip with overall negative or resist decoration in black. The figure modeling of Recuay is lacking and it is generally accepted that Tuncahuán pottery is much later in date. In the coastal plain in the north lies the province of Esmeraldas, where clay figures have been found which cannot be overlooked. In their modeling they are somewhat reminiscent of the early cultures on the high plateau of Mexico. Most of the known ancient cultures of Colombia fall within the highland zone. The country must have been inhabited by a number of small tribes. Only in one region is there evidence of a larger organization. This area is around the modern towns of Bogotá and Tunjá in which dwelt the Chibchas, a group of isolated tribes. The pottery of the Chibchas is not distinguished by a high degree of artistic achievement. The body is white or buff, coarsely tempered, rough or imperfectly polished, and as a rule unpainted. Generally far better in quality than the Chibcha wares is the pottery made in the Quimbaya region which lies in and around the central part of the Cauca valley, an area also known for its metal work. See *South American Pottery.* (21)

Edge and Grocott English potters working at Tunstall in the Staffordshire district around 1830 producing earthenware figures of the Walton type, bearing the mark Edge and Grocott. The partnership apparently was of short duration, as both Daniel Edge and Samuel Grocott are listed separately in the Staffordshire directories. See *Walton, John.*

Edinburgh See *Portobello.*

Edmands and Company In American ceramics; working at Charlestown, Massachusetts, 1850-1868, producing stonewares such as jugs and crocks. (433)

Edo Period In Japanese historical periods; the Edo or Tokugawa period 1615-1868. The following are the names of the eras for the Edo period.

Early

Genwa	1615	Manji	1658
Kanei	1624	Kambun	1661
Shoho	1644	Empo	1673
Keian	1648	Tenwa	1681
Shoo	1652	Jōkyo	1684
Meireki	1655	Genroku	1688

Middle

Hōei	1704	Kanen	1748
Shotoku	1711	Horeki	1751
Kyoho	1716	Meiwa	1764
Gembun	1736	Anei	1772
Kampo	1741	Temmei	1781
Enkyo	1744	Kansei	1789

Late

Kyowa	1801	Manen	1860
Bunka	1804	Bunkyu	1861
Bunsei	1818	Genji	1864
Tempo	1830	Keio	1865
Koka	1844	Meiji	1868
Kaei	1848	Taisho	1912
Ansei	1854	Showa	1926

See *Japanese Periods.*

Edwardian Relating to Edward VII of England and his reign, 1901-1910.

Edwards, Emily See *Doulton, Lambeth and Burslem.*

Eenhoorn, Wouter van and his sons Samuel and Lambertus. See *Greek A, The; Metal Pot, The; Porcelain Bottle, The.*

Egg and Spinach Glaze In Chinese ceramics; see *Hu P'i; Three-Color Ware.*

Eggshell In Chinese ceramics; eggshell porcelain is called T'o T'ai or bodyless by the Chinese because of its extreme thinness. It was first made during the Ming dynasty, and as early as the reign of Yung Lo, 1403-1424, it was highly regarded. In some of the very rare examples the body material seems almost non-existent; it seems to consist of glaze only. In the fine white specimens the delicate decoration is traced on the body in a white slip and is scarcely visible except when held to the light. Other pieces have colored designs and some have a colored ground.

Egypt See *Near East,* in prehistoric ceramics; *Roman Pottery; Islamic Pottery; Glazed Quartz Frit Ware.*

Egyptian Black A contemporary term for the basalt type body. See *Basalt.*

Egyptian Detail In ornament; toward the end of the 18th century for a short space of time an attempt was made to introduce certain Egyptian ornamental features and symbolism in the arts of decoration. This fashion for Egyptian detail was established in France after Napoleon's Egyptian campaign in 1798, and it soon spread to England. See *Denon, Baron de; Engraved Designs.*

Egyptian Dynasties

First and Second	3400–2980 B.C.
Third	2980–2900 B.C.
Fourth	2900–2750 B.C.
Fifth	2750–2625 B.C.
Sixth	2625–2475 B.C.
Seventh and Eighth	2475–2445 B.C.
Ninth and Tenth	2445–2160 B.C.
Eleventh	2160–2000 B.C.
Twelfth	2000–1788 B.C.
Thirteenth to Seventeenth including the Hykos	1788–1580 B.C.
Eighteenth	1580–1350 B.C.
Nineteenth	1350–1205 B.C.
Interim	1205–1200 B.C.
Twentieth	1200–1090 B.C.
Twenty–first	1090– 945 B.C.
Twenty–second	945– 745 B.C.
Twenty–third	745– 718 B.C.
Twenty–fourth	718– 712 B.C.
Twenty–fifth	712– 663 B.C.
Twenty–sixth	663– 525 B.C.
Twenty–seventh (Persian)	525– 332 B.C.
Alexander the Great and the Ptolemies	332– 30 B.C.
became Roman province	30 B.C.

Ehder, Johann Gottlieb (1717-1750) Modeler at Meissen, 1739-1750. See *Kaendler, J. J.*

Eigelstein In German ceramics; see *Cologne.*

Eight Happy Omens or **Pa Chi Hsiang** See *Chinese Symbols and Emblems.*

Eight Precious Objects or **Pa Pao** See *Chinese Symbols and Emblems.*

Eight Taoist Immortals or **Pa Hsien** In Chinese art; Chung-li Ch'üan is represented as a fat man with a peach in one hand and a fan in the other with which he awakens the souls of the dead. Lü Tung-pin is depicted with a sword. He protects the world against evil. He is the patron of the barbers. Ts'ao Kuo-ch'iu carries a pair of castanets in his hand and is the patron of mummers and actors. Han Hsiang Tzu is represented as a young man playing a flute. He is the patron of musicians. Ho Hsien Ku is the patroness of housewives and is shown carrying a lotus. Chang Kuo Lao is the patron of artists and calligraphers. He is the god of literature and his attribute is a musical instrument composed of a drum and a pair of rods. Lan Ts'ai-ho is the patron of gardeners and florists and is seen carrying a hoe and a basket of flowers. Li T'ieh-kuai is portrayed as a lame beggar and has a pilgrim's gourd from which pour forth clouds and fanciful dreams. He is the patron of astrologers and musicians. These Eight Immortals are often seen in attendance on Shou Lao or are seen on the backs of mythical creatures crossing the sea to the Island of Everlasting Happiness. The eight attributes are among the favorite symbols employed in Chinese art. See *Chinese Gods; Chinese Symbols and Emblems.*

EIGHT TRIGRAMS OR PA KUA

Eight Trigrams or **Pa Kua**   In Chinese symbols; the pa kua or eight trigrams are represented by eight sets of straight lines. Each set consists of three parallel superimposed broken and unbroken straight lines. These eight trigrams are arranged symmetrically around a circular sign which is the symbol of Creation. This well-known disk-shaped symbol of Creation consists of two intertwining forms resembling commas which are the primary powers called yin and yang. The eight trigrams are said to have been evolved from markings on the shell of a tortoise by the mythological Emperor Fu Hsi (2852 B.C.). It is also said that eight trigrams were created from the two primary powers, the unbroken line (———) called yang or symbol of the male

source, and the broken line (— —) called yin or female source. Each one of the eight cabalistic signs is composed of a different combination of the broken and unbroken lines. Wên Wang (1231-1135 B.C.), father of Wu Wang the founder of the Chou dynasty, applied his vast knowledge to an exhaustive study of the trigrams and attached to each of them certain interpretations which constitute the most sacred and abstruse work of the Chinese classics known as the Canon of Changes. The Canon of Changes serves as the fundamental work for the knowledge of the principles that control or cause the power of foreseeing and foretelling future events by means of lines or figures, philosophical mysteries and the secrets of creation.

Eiraku (1795-1854)   Kyoto studio-potter whose real name was Zengoro Hozen; the eleventh in the Zengoro line of Japanese potters, he is outstanding for his mastery of the very graceful aspects of the Ninsei style. He was also adept in the imitation of Ming three-color ware, the so-called Japanese Kochi ware; Kinran-de porcelain and Shonsui underglaze blue and white. His fame spread rapidly; the Prince of Kei invited him to take charge of a private kiln in his own castle grounds at Wakayama. Here in 1827 he made a ware known as Oniwa or Kairaku-en, deriving its name from the garden. Essentially a two-color porcelain of purple and blue modeled after a class of Ming Three-Color ware (to which the Japanese had given the name of Kochi) in which the total impression given is dominated by a magnificent turquoise, dark purple and blue glazes. For his services he received from the Prince two seals, one of gold and one of silver; the former had upon it the characters Yeiraku (Eiraku) and the latter Kahei Shiriu. Eiraku is the Japanese pronunciation of the two Chinese characters which make up the name of the Ming Emperor Yung Lo whose mythical red and gold wares Eiraku is reputed to have skillfully reproduced. Eiraku's best work is considered to be his Kinran-de wares (the scarlet and gold brocade style) and his Akaji Kinga wares (gold designs on a red ground). His son Wazen, 1823-1896, who was the twelfth in the Zengoro line of Japanese potters, was also skilled in Kinran-de porcelains. See *Kochi; Kyo; Ninsei; Shonsui.* (152)

Eisen, Okuda (1753-1811) Kyoto studio-potter; it is generally accepted that Eisen introduced the production of fine enameled porcelain wares to the Ninsei or Kyo tradition of elaborately enameled earthenwares. Eisen is particularly remembered for his fine reproductions of Chinese enameled porcelains of the late Ming period. His most celebrated wares are those which the Japanese call Gosu-Akae. Pieces of this type have red and green enamels sometimes combined with underglaze blue. They are in effect Japanese imitations of the Ming enameled porcelain wares usually known in Europe as Swatow. Apart from his Gosu-Akae pieces, there are Kochi (three-colored ware in green, yellow and aubergine) and underglaze blue and white, but the number is small. He made a few pieces of pottery, but by far the majority of his extant pieces are in porcelain. It is generally believed that the oldest porcelain pieces at the Awata district in Kyoto were made by Eisen. The studio potters Mokubei and Dohachi both counted themselves as students of Eisen. His wares have been widely copied in Japan. See *Goso-Akae; Ninsei; Kyo.*

Ekholm, Kurt (b. 1907) Finnish designer and potter who received his training in Sweden. Appointed art director of the Finnish ceramic factory Arabia in 1931. At the present time he is principal of the School of Applied Art at Gothenburg, Sweden. See *Arabia.*

Elers In English ceramics; John Philip and David Elers, who were potters and originally silversmiths, came to England from Holland before 1686. According to evidence they made "brown mugs" and "red teapots" at Fulham for about three years prior to 1693. It seems that they moved to Staffordshire in 1693. By local tradition the Elers factory was at Bradwell Wood near Newcastle-under-Lyme. At the present time there is no authenticated specimen of their work. It is believed that they made a fine hard unglazed red stoneware in imitation of Chinese buccaro ware. Pieces of unglazed red stoneware attributed to them include small mugs, teapots, tea canisters, tea cups and other similar objects. They were delicately and thinly made and were often decorated with applied stamped reliefs. A plum blossom in the Chinese style was a favorite motif for the stamped reliefs. Numerous other pieces of unglazed Staffordshire red ware have been erroneously attributed to them. See *Fulham.* (199)

Elizabethan The term applied to the English style of Renaissance ornament during the reign of Queen Elizabeth I, 1558-1603. Irrespective of Flemish, French and German influences the Elizabethan style possessed a genuine national character.

Ellwangen In German ceramics; it is almost a certainty that porcelain was made at Ellwangen near Utzmemmingen, Württemberg, around 1759 by the widow of Arnold Friedrich Prahl who is believed to have successfully made a kind of soft paste. The widow's arcanist was J. J. Ringler.

Elton, Sir Edmund (d. 1920) English artist-potter; started to produce his Elton ware in 1879, at Clevedon Court, the family home in Somerset. His work was characteristic of late 19th century art pottery, although it was virtually made under studio conditions. Though he continued to work until 1920, his most usual style dates from

永 大
樂 日
造 本

GREAT JAPAN
EIRAKU MADE

ELLWANGEN
1760 ON

ELTON
1879-1920

EMPIRE DECORATIVE DESIGN

around the end of the 19th century and was characterized by asymmetrical relief patterns of flowers and foliage built up of colored slips with sgraffito outline. As a rule his ground colors were mottled shades of blue, perhaps combined with greens.

Emaux Ombrants In French ceramics; a French term meaning shading enamels applied to a process introduced around 1844 by Baron du Tremblay at his manufactory at Rubelles near Melun, which produced a monochrome picture formed by light and shade. In this method the design was impressed into the paste or body which was then covered with a translucent colored glaze; the deeper portions of the design appeared darker than those near the surface and more thinly covered. It was in effect a glazed version of a lithophane. Essentially it was a novelty and such success as it enjoyed was of short duration.

Emens See *Raeren; Mennicken.*

Emerald Deldare See *Buffalo Pottery.*

Empire The later phase of the Neo-Classic or Classic Revival style of ornament was largely created by two celebrated French architects, Percier and Fontaine. It is named after the period of the First French Empire, 1804 to 1814-1815, but survived for some years after, until the advent of the Neo-Gothic and Revived Rococo of the late 1820's. This later phase of the Classic Revival fostered the cult of antiquity. It was essentially an archaeological revival in which antique Greek and Roman as well as Etruscan and Egyptian forms were exactly copied. In 1785 Fontaine went to Rome to pursue his studies and he was accompanied by Percier. Upon their return they were engaged by Napoleon to remodel and redecorate the palace, Malmaison. Their designs established the official Empire style in Paris. Both Fontaine and Per-

cier were fervent disciples of antiquity and their strong attachment to antique culture dominated the style. The Empire style had an air of austere and imposing grandeur that was admirably suited to Napoleon and Imperial France. The style was cold, exact and formal and was characterized by elegant severity. Symmetry was a pronounced principle of the style. The classic ornament was principally borrowed from antique Greek and Roman art. Included among the favorite Empire motifs were stiff and formal acanthus foliage, tightly woven wreaths, Greek palm leaves, winged classical figures in flowing gowns, Olympian gods and goddesses, emblems of victory, eagles, swans, lions, chimeras, caryatids and terms, Egyptian lotus capitals, sphinxes, antique musical instruments and vessels such as lyres and kraters, winged trumpets, flaming torches, thunderbolts and stars. In ceramic art the most notable examples of the Empire style are the porcelains of Sèvres, Vienna and Russia under Alexander I. Regrettably, an entire loss of feeling for porcelain characterizes the style, leading to elaborately pictorial art in the manner of oil painting entirely concealing the white glaze, and great areas of gilding simulating solid gold. See *Classic Revival; David, Jacques Louis; Denon, Baron; Fontaine, Pierre François Léonard; Louis Philippe.*

Enamel In ceramics; an enamel is a compound of glass tinted with mineral oxides to give various colors, such as copper for various shades of green, iron for yellow and manganese for a purplish brown. Vitreous enamels can stand only a relatively small amount of heat. Consequently they have to be applied on an already fired glaze or on an unglazed already fired body and fused or melted to it in another firing at a low temperature or petit feu in a muffle kiln. In order to obtain this low melting point a large amount of lead or other flux is added to make the enamels more fusible. Painting in enamels was found as early as the 13th century on the ceramic wares of China; however, the earliest pieces were simply done in red or green enamels. The so-called Rhages earthenware made by the Persians employed enamel colors during the 13th century or earlier. Although enamel decoration was first found on the European stoneware at Kreussen, Germany, around 1622, it was not until around 1660 that important specimens were made, when a full palette of enamel colors was used in decorating faïence in Germany. Hard paste porcelain with painted enamel decoration was first made at Meissen around 1710-1715. Enamel colors, which are available in a wide range, are also called overglaze colors, petit feu or muffle colors. See *Petit Feu.*

Encaustic Painting The term *encaustic,* which is derived from the Greek word meaning to burn in, is applied to the ancient methods of painting in heated wax, as practiced by the Greeks, Egyptians and Romans. By extension, although not entirely correct, the term is applied to all methods of painting in wax. Wedgwood gave the name to the copies of Greek vase-paintings produced in enamels on his black basalt wares. (421)

Encaustic Tile In ceramics; a tile with a pattern inlaid in clay of a color different from the ground, and burned in. Usually unglazed and used for floors.

Endell, August (1871-1925) German architect and designer; strongly influenced by Obrist in Munich, where he belonged to the Münchener Vereinigte Werkstätten. His ornament has an Obrist-like and Japan-inspired character. See *Munich School; Obrist, Hermann.*

Enghalskrug In German ceramics; a popular type of faïence jug with a long neck having a thick lip rim. It generally had a globular shaped body, which rested on a spreading circular foot, and a plaited rope handle. It was a popular 17th century form at Hanau and at the neighboring town of Frankfurt-on-Main. Sometimes it was mounted in pewter. (250)

Engine-Turned Decoration A method of decorating by means of a rose engine which is a machine or lathe attachment employed to produce an eccentric relative movement between the rotating mandrel and a cutting point so as to form on the work a variety of curved lines. Styles of this ornament appear on watch cases. In English ceramics; a lathe equipped with an eccentric motion was built for Josiah Wedgwood by Matthew Boulton about 1763. By means of this lathe, geometric, diced and fluted patterns were incised on the dried, leather-hard, unfired surfaces of vases, teapots and other such pieces. A pattern somewhat resembling basketwork was much favored. Engine turning as decoration is found principally on Staffordshire red wares, particularly Wedgwood's. See *Rosso Antico.*

English Faïence See *Lambeth; Bristol; Liverpool.*

ENGHALSKRUG, FRANKFURT-ON-MAIN

English Porcelain In ceramics; the porcelain made in England during the 18th century is distinctive for its variety of composition. The French form of soft paste porcelain was made at Chelsea, Derby and Longton Hall. Soapstone pastes were made at Worcester, Caughley and Liverpool. The manufactories at Plymouth and Bristol made a hard paste porcelain. For several decades after 1750 Derby was a most productive manufactory, and a large number of the existent English porcelain figures were made there. A soft paste was made at Nantgarw and Swansea from about 1813 to 1823. A type of porcelain was developed at Bow, around the middle of the 18th century, in which bone ash was used as an ingredient. This variety of hybrid porcelain, in which part of the kaolin was replaced by bone ash, became by the end of the 18th century and still remains the standard type for English porcelain. The production at Lowestoft resembles that of Bow inasmuch as it contained bone ash in its composition. See *Porcelain; Soft Paste; Bone China.*

English Soft Paste   In English ceramics; see *English Porcelain.*

Engobe   In ceramics; the French term for a mixture of clay, that is usually white, thinned with water and applied as a coating over the body of pottery to conceal its natural color which is generally reddish or buff. It was much used on peasant pottery to imitate the whiteness of porcelain and to provide a more appropriate ground for painted decoration. It also served as a preliminary for sgraffiato or incised decoration in which the design was scratched through to the original color of the body. See *Slip.*

DECORATIVE DESIGN BY
WATTEAU

Engraved Designs   The art of the potter was favorably affected by the rapid development of wood and copper engravings in the last quarter of the 15th century as it furnished him with easily adapted pictorial subjects as well as decorative designs. Such engravings became increasingly popular in the ensuing centuries, and not only painted decoration, but also reliefs, vase forms and figures modeled in the round can be traced in many cases to collections of engraved designs which the larger factories kept for reference. At first the Italian majolica painters in general were content to use details only, but by the second and third decades of the 16th century exact copies of engraved subjects became more customary. Undoubtedly the most popular sources at this time were the engravings of Raphael. In the second half of the 16th century the decorative designs of Raphael and his pupil Raphael dal Colle among the Loggia frescoes at the Vatican established the style of the grotesques so fashionable as a decoration at the Fontana factory and others at Urbino, the town where Raphael was born. In France the majolica painters freely used the designs in the so-called Fontainebleau style connected with Primaticcio and others, and in the Netherlands and Spain, those of Cornelis Floris, Pieter Coecke, Cornelis Bos and their followers are notable. The characteristic Ferronnerie style of ornament created by the engravers of Antwerp may be seen on the Netherlands majolica and also that of Spain. In many instances the reliefs on Rhenish stoneware were modeled after the design of such engravers as Virgil Solis, Heinrich Aldegrever, Cornelis Bos and Adriaen Collaert. In the last three decades of the 17th century the engraver's influence was markedly apparent in the rich and varied Baroque compositions painted on pottery. Hunting scenes in the manner of Antonio Tempesta made their appearance on Nevers and early Moustiers faïence. On Delft were found the decorative designs of Jean Le Pautre and Daniel Marot. On English Lambeth and Bristol delftware, prints from contemporary bibles and engraved portraits of Charles I were imitated. Jean Bérain and to a lesser degree Bernard Toro were formative influences on the later Moustiers. The familiar Laub-und-Bandelwerk style of interlacing scrollwork was chiefly the invention of Paul Decker, J. L. Eysler and other Baroque engravers, much of whose work was published by J. C. Weigel of Nuremberg in the early 18th century. The decorators at Vienna, Bayreuth, Dorotheenthal and many other factories all embraced this style. The etchings of Jacques Callot (1593-1635) also belong to this period. Some of Callot's designs were used as illustrations in Louis Riccoboni's HISTOIRE DU THEATRE ITALIEN published in Paris in

1728, from which many porcelain figures of the mid-18th century were borrowed. The Rococo style of ornament was chiefly the invention of two French designers, Gilles-Marie Oppenord and Juste-Aurèle Meissonnier. Apparently it was first used in ceramic art in Germany where Kaendler at Meissen adapted Meissonnier's designs for the celebrated Swan service, 1737-1741. The style was particularly suited for porcelain and rapidly came into vogue. Claude Gillot, Antoine Watteau, J. B. S. Chardin and particularly François Boucher were the most prolific creators, designing decorative fantasies as well as a new kind of chinoiserie and other figure compositions, all of which were adapted in painted decoration and porcelain figures through the work of such engravers as J. G. Huquier, N. Larmessin and others. Huquier also engraved groups of game in the manner of Oudry and fantastic Rococo compositions by Lajoue. The engraver Jean Pillement created a distinctive kind of chinoiserie that enjoyed a great vogue in England. Germany also had its share of decorative designers in the Rococo style, such as F. X. Habermann, J. W. Baumgartner, J. M. Hoppenhaupt, and particularly, but somewhat later, J. E. Nilson whose decorative compositions were very much used. The history-making Deutsche Blumen of Meissen was originally inspired by engravings published at Augsburg in 1737. Flowers were also copied from prints by Jean Vauquer, and Jean Baptiste Monnoyer, the leading French fleuriste of the 17th century. Prints also frequently inspired the porcelain figures of the Rococo period. In the Classic-Revival or Louis XVI period the famous illustrated works by Comte de Caylus, HERCULANEUM FRESCOES, 1752-1767, and Sir William Hamilton's books of GREEK VASES, 1766-1767, furnished decorative designs from the antique, while Michel Pergolesi, Giocondo Albertolli, Robert Adam and others provided original compositions in the same style. Prints after Greuze by Moreau the Younger, with paintings by Angelica Kauffmann and in Germany the engravings of Daniel Chodowiecki also furnished decorative compositions in the sentimental-Classical and so-called Zopf style. The fashion for Egyptian ornament was inevitable after Napoleon's campaign; accompanying the military staff was a staff of writers and archaeologists. Notable in this group was Dominique Vivant de Denon, whose important work LE VOYAGE DANS LA BASSE ET LA HAUTE EGYPTE, 1802, was most influential in propagating Egyptian ornament. Shortly after its publication, numerous Egyptian pieces appeared in collections of designs by Percier and Fontaine, who were Napoleon's architects and created to a great extent the Empire style, 1804-1814, the later phase of the Classic Revival. See *Historicism; Flora Danica; Chinoiserie; Chenavard, Aimé; Revived Rococo; Victorian; Style Étrusque, Le; Maîtres Ornemanistes.*

Engraving The art or process of producing marks or designs by incising or cutting into a surface of metal, stone or glass; the art of making pictures by printing from an engraved surface. Pictures are made by one of four varieties of engraving; namely, etching, line engraving, mezzotint and wood engraving. The term *engraving* also refers to the impression of the picture made from the engraved plate.

Enshu, Kobori See *Iga; Cha-no-yu; Rikyu, Senno.*

EPIAG In modern Bohemian ceramics; the distinguishing initials of Erste Böhmische Porzellan Industrie A. G., a combine that controls a group of Bohemian factories. These initials occur in a number of 20th century Bohemian factory marks.

Epigonal See *Andean.*

Erfurt In German ceramics; from 1717 to about 1792 a productive faïence manufac-

Made in Czechoslovakia

1918 ON

ERFURT
C. 1717-C. 1792

ture was carried on at Erfurt, Thuringia. The most activity and best work at the Erfurt factory owned by Johann Paul Stieglitz was from 1734 until about 1792. The factory mark, which was seldom used, was a wheel with six spokes taken from the arms of the Elector of Mayence. The wares were painted in the typical Thuringian high-temperature colors. Cylindrical tankards generally mounted in pewter were especially characteristic. They were decorated in a rough but effective manner with such motifs as figures, landscapes, flowers, animals and similar subjects. Dishes, bowls, jugs with narrow necks, and even some figures were included in their productions.

Escallier, Eléonore (1829-1888) French painter of fruits and flowers; working with Théodore Deck. She was especially concerned by the implications of Japanese design. See *Deck, Théodore.*

Escudella ab Orelles In Spanish ceramics; the name given to a type of small shallow pottery bowl with two and occasionally four flat, solid handles level with the rim, made at Valencia around the 15th and 16th centuries. It was so called because of the supposed resemblance of the form of each handle to the shape of an ear. (221)

Esmeraldas See *Ecuador and Colombia.*

Esser, Max See *Pfeiffer, M. A.*

Etruria Period 1769-1940. See *Wedgwood, J.*

Etrurian See *Etruscan; Victorian.*

Etruscan In English ceramics; the name popularly given to wares that set out to imitate in detail the admired red-figure pottery of classical antiquity. Wedgwood in his black basalt ware established the precedent which was followed by many other potters in the 19th century. The original antique ware was unglazed, and so

imitations of it necessarily belong to the class of unglazed wares. Wares of this kind were also calld Etrurian. See *Style Étrusque, Le; Victorian; Basalt.* (421, 471)

Etruscan In decorative art; Etruria, which was the name used by the Latins for the country of the Etruscans, flourished in the northwestern and central part of Italy before the rise of the Romans. The Etruscans, who were of foreign origin, settled here about 800 B.C. and their civilization attained its highest phase of development about 500 B.C. Etruscan art in its early stage was influenced by Egyptian and Near Eastern art, but its later and principal inspiration was drawn heavily from Grecian art. Essentially it was a hybrid art which never succeeded in completely assimilating the classic principles as perfected by the Greeks. Some of the best Etruscan work was achieved in bronze, such as decorative reliefs, figures of men and animals and mirrors. They also produced fine goldwork and jewelry, terra-cotta, pottery and the distinctive bucchero ware. (65-68)

Etruscan Majolica See *Griffin, Smith and Hill.*

Etui A French term meaning a small box or case. Etuis used for carrying toilet articles and other small personal utensils were mentioned in royal records in France from the 14th century. It was generally in the form of a small hollow cylinder or its variants, and was provided with a lid. It was a luxury article and for this reason whether the material was metal, enamel or porcelain the workmanship was of the highest quality.

Europe In prehistoric ceramics; the earliest appearance of pottery in prehistoric Europe coincides with the emergence of the Neolithic stage of culture. Most likely made almost entirely by women, prehistoric pots before the Iron Age were built up by hand and generally decorated with the simplest of techniques of incising and impressing. See *Near East, in prehistoric ceramics; Beaker Folk.* (79, 80)

European Soft Paste In ceramics; see *Soft Paste.*

Evans, David (b. 1795) English flower painter working at the Swansea porcelain factory from around 1814-1816; later at Worcester, Coalport, Mintons, Copelands and at the Alcock factory.

Evans, Etienne (b. 1733) Porcelain painter at Sèvres, 1752-1806, specializing in birds.

Ewer The name is given to a form of jug or pitcher having a wide spout and a handle. It was usually mounted on a stem and flaring foot or on three feet. Generally a deep circular dish or basin decorated in a similar manner was placed beneath the ewer. The ewer was chiefly used in early times to pour water over the hands after eating. The form and ornament of the elaborate Renaissance style ewer delighted the Victorians and countless adaptations of it appeared in 19th century ceramics.

Exekias See *Greece.*

RENAISSANCE EWER AND
DISH

F

Fabbri, Agenore Modern Italian artist-potter; using very largely the medium of brightly colored earthenware, he has produced both purely sculptural works and pottery vessels frequently modeled in strange or exaggerated forms.

Fabbrica di Santa Cristina See *Milan*.

Faber, Johann Ludwig German Hausmaler; glass and faïence painter working in Nuremberg around 1678-1693; follower of Johann Schäper. See *Schäper, Johann; Schwarzlot*.

Factory Mark The official trademark of a manufactory, such as the anchor of Chelsea or the crossed swords of Meissen. The factory mark may be unlettered or it may include the name or distinguishing initials of the manufacturer. See *Mark*, in ceramics; *Backstamp*.

FAENZA SPOUTED DRUG POT

Faenza In Italian ceramics; perhaps the leading productive center in Italy for majolica. From at least 1475 until the end of the 16th century its wares were equal in quality to those of any other Italian center producing majolica. Probably the majolica produced at Faenza from 1500 to 1530 may be regarded as the finest of all. Potteries still exist at Faenza. An early type of majolica painted chiefly in green and purple was made at Faenza during the late 14th and 15th centuries as well as at Orvieto and Tuscany. It is recorded that in 1454 a Faenza potter was commissioned to make a service of "white majolica" and it is clear that potteries were flourishing here at that date and that emigrant potters from the town helped to start potteries elsewhere. Extant 15th century specimens include plaques, tiles, vases, drug vases and globular jars with two handles in the form of winged dragons, drug pots and snake spouts and dishes and large plates.

The work is distinctive for the quality of coloring which is clear and strong, for the admirable figure drawing and for the excellent proportions of the forms. A purely decorative treatment of Renaissance motifs was traditional to Faenza work. Earliest specimens with a berettino ground, which was a favorite type at Faenza, were made late in the 15th century. The carefully and elaborately painted pieces which belong to the great period from 1500 to 1530 may be recognized as the work of one or other of about eight artists of the highest accomplishments. Large plates with panel painting in the true Faenza tradition with religious and sometimes mythological figures and subjects are among the most beautiful of all known majolica paintings. Majolica with fruit painting of a rich color was made at Faenza around the middle of the 16th century. It is probable that this style which is closely associated with Venice originated at Faenza. Before 1570, perhaps as early as the 1540's, an original and at times a very attractive style of painting showing the influence of the art of Parmigianino (1504-1540) painted in a limited range of color, cobalt-blue and yellow or cobalt-blue, yellow and orange, was introduced at Faenza, the so-called compendiario stylè. Though Faenza continued to produce majolica no new style of any significance was introduced after the end of the 16th century. A great quantity of its ware was probably left white and, being much exported as bianchi de Faenza or the white wares of Faenza, not only spread the fame of the town and gave the name Faïence to the tin-glazed earthenwares of other countries, but created a vogue for them. See *Istoriato; Ragnolis, Nicolaus de; Manara, Baldassare; Virgiliotto; Italian Majolica.* (224-227, 229, 230)

Faïence In ceramics; a French term derived

from the Italian town of Faenza which was a great center for Italian Renaissance majolica. This name is given on the continent of Europe to earthenware covered with a lead glaze which is made white and opaque by adding tin-ashes. The glaze is commonly called a tin glaze. All European faïence had its roots in Moorish Spain and Italy. In England the term *faïence* is increasingly being used and has the same meaning as *delftware*. A distinction recognized as a helpful practice is generally made between the earlier Italian Renaissance wares called majolica and the later faïence wares. The term *faïence* is usually restricted in meaning to the Dutch and other wares imitating the Chinese in the 17th century and to the later more or less original tin-glazed productions of Germany, France and other countries. This limitation marks the historical and artistic distinction between the two main classes of tin-glazed earthenware. The essential difference in making Italian majolica and Delft faïence was that the latter used a more refined clay which made possible a finer manipulation of the paste. After the article was shaped it was fired without glaze and then dipped in the tin glaze and dried. Until around 1675 the painting was generally done in the unfired tin glaze and then both were fired in the grand feu. Thus the colors were limited to the so-called high-temperature colors or those few colors that could stand the heat of the grand feu. In some of the finer Italian majolica and Delft faïence an additional lead glaze was applied over the tin-glazed decorated surface which imparted a higher gloss and enriched the colors. This final glaze was either fired by itself or in one single operation. In Spain during the 13th-17th centuries and in Italy in the 16th century, luster decoration was painted over the once-fired glaze and fixed in an additional firing under "reducing" kiln conditions. Due to the competition from porcelain, which began to develop late in the 18th century, with its overglaze painted enamel colors that per-

mitted a wider range of colors, the makers of faïence began to employ the enamel colors over the glaze and to fire them in the petit feu or at low temperature in a muffle kiln. This change from high temperature or true faïence colors fired with the tin-glazed ground to muffle colors added later over the glaze was not employed on the more common faïence wares. In Europe, as a whole, toward the close of the 18th century, the growing success of cheap cream-colored earthenware from England and the continental imitations of it (faïence fine) and the cheapening of porcelain on the other hand, gradually began to exert an economic pincer on faïence. Creamware was new and fashionable while porcelain had a snobbish appeal to those who wished to copy their betters. Then, too, faïence had a practical disadvantage as compared with creamware, being soft-bodied with a glaze which chipped easily. By 1800, the manufacture of faïence had practically ceased. See *Grand Feu; Petit Feu; Tin Glaze; Cream-Colored Earthenware; Marzacotto.*

Faïence Fine In European ceramics; a French term used to describe lead-glazed white or cream-colored earthenware of the English type. Probably the Pont-aux-Choux factory at Paris was the first to make creamware in France. In 1772 the factory advertised itself as Royal Manufactory of French earthenwares in imitation of English ones. Other early French factories were those of Monterau and Creil, both of whom became very well known for their transfer-printed earthenwares. The ink-black prints on a white ground were printed by the Paris firm of Stone, Cocquerel and Le Gros. The three Lorraine manufactories of Niderviller, Lunéville and Saint Clément by using a fine Lorraine clay (terre de Lorraine) were beginning to produce from around 1775 onward a hybrid ceramic material resembling the hard English creamware which was to launch a period of great popularity. At least by 1786 creamware was being made at Chantilly, while at Apt a yellowish creamware with combed slip decoration in imitation of English agate and marbled wares was made. The Italian factory, Le Nove, produced some fine creamware in the early years of the 19th century. Of the many other European factories making creamware mainly with border patterns imitating Wedgwood's Queen's ware, recognition should be given to the Holitsch factory in Hungary and the Rendsburg factory in Denmark. Both Alcora in Spain and Marieberg in Sweden produced quality creamware. In Holland an inferior creamware was made, but great quantities of English creamwares were imported in the "white" and decorated there. In a general sense, the French faïence fine revealed greater creativity than that made at the other European factories. See *Faïence; Cream-Colored Earthenware.*

FAÏENCE MANUFACTURING
COMPANY
1886 ON

Faïence Manufacturing Company In American ceramics; active at Greenpoint, New York, 1880-1892, producing art ware. Edward Lycett was director. His sons, Francis and Joseph, were both associated with the firm as modelers and decorators.

Faïence Parlante In French ceramics; a collective term for the different pieces made at Nevers and numerous other French manufactories having inscriptions in their decorative designs. The term *faïence patronymique* is applied to a variety having pictures of saints frequently bearing a date given as a presentation on birthdays, christenings and other similar events. The faïence patriotique or faïence populaire was chiefly characterized by emblems and was especially popular during the French Revolution.

Faïence Patriotique or **Populaire** See *Faïence Parlante.*

Faïence Patronymique See *Faïence Parlante.*

Falcone, Antonio Modeler at Capo di Monte, Naples, Italy, around the middle of the 18th century.

Falconet, Etienne-Maurice (1716-1791) A French sculptor; director of the modeling department at Sèvres from 1757 to 1766, when Catherine II invited him to Russia. The Cupid, 1758, and the companion Psyche, 1759, are among his most famous works in Sèvres biscuit. See *Boizot, Louis-Simon; Louis XVI.* (355)

False or **Fake Mark** See *Apocryphal Mark; Imitative Mark; Forged Mark; Skinning; Mark, in ceramics.*

Famille Jaune In Chinese ceramics; see *Famille Verte.*

Famille Noire In Chinese ceramics; the black ground or Famille Noire is derived from manganese. The black ground is made by overlaying a dull black pigment with a coating of transparent green enamel which results in the rich greenish black color which is so highly esteemed. See *Famille Verte; Famille Rose.* (106)

Famille Rose In Chinese ceramics; during the third decade of the 18th century the opaque colors of the rose family in which different shades of pink and carmine play a leading part largely supplanted in porcelain decoration the transparent Famille Verte enamels. Present evidence indicates that Famille Rose porcelains were in full production during the Yung Chêng reign, 1723-1735. See *Famille Verte.* (112)

Famille Verte In Chinese ceramics; the enameled polychrome porcelains in which green has a leading part, first made during the K'ang Hsi reign, 1662-1722. They are a development of the Wan Li five-color ware or wu ts'ai yao. Much of the Famille Verte is distinguished by an overglaze blue enamel; although some of the ware has an underglaze blue and some combine both the underglaze blue and the overglaze blue enamel. The Famille Verte colors are known to the Chinese as the ying ts'ai or hard colors in distinction to the Famille Rose known as juan ts'ai or soft colors. Famille Verte is further divided into Famille Jaune and Famille Noire depending on the color of the background. The polychrome enamels are either painted over the glaze or are enameled on the biscuit or unglazed porcelain. Some of the finest Ch'ing porcelains are enameled on the biscuit. In addition to a variety of greens the other transparent enamel colors are yellow, aubergine and violet blue. The red, which is half pigment and half enamel, is of a coral tone. A dry brown black pigment is also used. See *Famille Rose; Famille Noire; Five-Color Ware.* (109)

Fang Ku Yüeh Hsüan   See *Ku Yüeh Hsüan.*

Farrar, H. W.   See *Southern Porcelain Company.*

Fatimid Pottery   See *Islamic Pottery; Islamic Pottery, Early.*

Faubourg Saint-Antoine   See *Chicaneau, Pierre; Rue de la Roquette.*

Faubourg Saint-Denis   Or Faubourg Saint-Lazare. In French ceramics; a hard paste porcelain manufactory was established in Paris in 1771 by Pierre-Antoine Hannong who left before 1776. His porcelain was generally marked with a small H or crossed clay pipes. The mark CP was registered in 1779 showing the protection of Charles Philippe, Comte d'Artois, and was found until around 1793. Two new manufactories were active around 1798, apparently developing from the original. The early 19th century wares were often marked with the name *Schoelcher* who was one of the proprietors. The porcelain made by Hannong was extremely translucent and vitrified. The productions, which were principally tablewares, displayed the characteristic French refinement. The carefully painted decoration was similar in style to the contemporary styles in vogue

at the different Paris porcelain manufactories during the late 18th and early 19th centuries. See *Paris Porcelain.*

Faubourg Saint-Honoré   See *Rue de la Ville l'Evêque.*

Faubourg Saint-Lazare   In French ceramics; see *Faubourg Saint-Denis.*

Feathered Ware   In English ceramics; see *Combed Ware; Slipware.*

Feilner, Simon   (d. 1798) Porcelain painter and modeler at Höchst before 1753; master modeler at Fürstenberg 1753-1768. Shortly after 1770 he was working at Frankenthal where he was appointed director in 1775, a position he held until his death. At the first two manufactories his models include some outstanding Italian Comedy figures and Miners; apparently he was less active as a modeler at Frankenthal. (328)

Feldspar   In ceramics; a variety of crystalline rocks from which clays were formed by decomposition. It was used in the manufacturing of porcelain as fluxes or fusible ingredients.

Feldspathic Glaze   See *Glaze.*

Fên Ting   See *Ting Yao.*

Fêng-Huang   In Chinese art; an imaginary or mythical phoenix-like bird widely used in Chinese painting, textiles, sculpture and ceramics. It is commonly represented as having the head of a pheasant, the beak of a swallow, a long flexible neck, plumage of many brilliant colors and a flowing tail between an argus pheasant and a peacock, with long claws pointed backward as it flies. It has a dual nature, being both male and female. It was a special emblem of the Empress and was believed by the ancient Chinese to make its appearance when the country was ruled by a wise monarch. See *Chinese Animal Figures.*

FAUBOURG SAINT-DENIS

C. 1771 ON

CP
1779-1793

FENG-HUANG

Fenton, Christopher Webber American potter and pottery proprietor; inventor of flint enamel. See *Bennington*.

Fenton Stone Works See *Mason, Charles James and Company*.

Fenton's Works See *Bennington*.

Féraud, Jean-Gaspard See *Moustiers*.

Ferrat, Jean-Baptiste See *Moustiers*.

Ferronnerie In European ceramics; a French term given to a style or ornament having the appearance of wrought ironwork, consisting of scrolls and bands interpreted as pierced and as curling outward from the surface. It first appeared around the middle of the 16th century on majolica made in France and in the Netherlands. Occasionally the name is given to the scrolled designs found on some French faïence toward the end of the 17th and early 18th centuries. See *Engraved Designs*.

Fettling Finishing up a piece of ware in the clay state by touching up and removing traces of seams, cast lines and the like.

Feure, Georges de (1869-1928) French decorative artist, designer of interior decoration, pottery, textiles and furniture, a foremost representative of Art Nouveau. (516)

Fictoorsz or **Victorsz, Louwijs** See *Double Tankard, The*.

Figgio In Norwegian ceramics; a faïence factory started at Figgio near Stavanger in 1940, recently combined with the Stavanger Flint factory started in 1946. Ovenproof earthenware with polychrome decoration designed by Hermann Bongard has been an interesting production item of the Figgio faïence factory.

Figuline In ceramics; a term applied to the earthenware vessels made by the potter and also to the potter's clay of which these vessels are fabricated. The rustiques figulines made by Bernard Palissy (c. 1510-1590) at Saintes undoubtedly were the foundation upon which his reputation as a potter later depended. They were molded after nature and included such familiar objects as shells, leaves, fishes and lizards.

Fiji See *Oceania*.

Filippo, Stefano and **Piero di** Master painters, producing a series of majolica istoriato works of high quality at Caffaggiolo in the early 16th century. See *Istoriato*.

Finch, A. W. Of English parentage, he was born and educated in Belgium where he became associated with Henry van de Velde. In the late 1890's he went to Finland where in association with the Swede Louis Sparre, he started the short-lived Iris workshop in Porvoo (Borga) to make Sparre's furniture and Finch's pottery, which was practical in design and was decorated in a simple, linear Art Nouveau manner. As a teacher at the Central School of Arts and Crafts in Helsinki, Finch was to exert a strong influence upon the later ceramics of Finland.

Fine Orange See *Toltec*.

Finger Vase In ceramics; a variety of flower vase with five tubular holders set side by side in a fan-shaped arrangement. The form was introduced at Delft and was copied at other ceramic manufactories.

Fireclay Highly refractory clay.

Firing The process of transforming clay into porcelain or pottery by burning it in a special oven or kiln.

Fischer, Christian See *Pirkenhammer*.

Fischer, Emil v. See *Budapest*.

Fischer, V. T. See *Krog, A.*

Fischer and Mieg See *Pirkenhammer*.

Fischer and Reichenbach See *Pirkenhammer*.

Fish Roe Crackle See *Crackle*.

Fitzhugh Pattern A well-known Oriental Lowestoft pattern having a trellis work border with four split pomegranates showing the fruit inside and butterflies with wings spread. In the center of the piece appear four separate groups of flowers and emblems, martial and otherwise, surrounding a medallion or an oval monogram. Sets were made for the American market with a full-spread American eagle in the center, which was a striking combination. Of great interest was George Washington's Oriental Lowestoft dinner service decorated with the emblem of the Society of the Cincinnati and a Fitzhugh border in underglaze blue. The Fitzhugh pattern, which seems to have been used as early as the 1770's, is most frequently in underglaze blue; however, it also occurs in sepia, brown, bright green, orange and other colors. The name Fitzhugh is variously attributed to an American sea captain of that name who had a preference for this design and to the mispronunciation of the Chinese city of Foochow. See *Oriental Lowestoft*. (117, 118)

Five-Color Ware or **Wu Ts'ai** In Chinese ceramics; wu ts'ai, which is practically a Chinese way of saying polychrome, is most commonly applied to a decoration comprising designs painted in enamel colors. The design was outlined in a dull red or black pigment and the low-fired enamels were washed into the spaces. The method was well adapted for rendering pictorial designs. The use of enamels for brush painting on pottery was understood and practiced to a limited extent in the Sung dynasty, 960-1279. In the Ming dynasty, 1368-1644, in the Ch'eng Hua period, 1465-1487, enameled painting on porcelains was regarded as perfection. This particular class is known as tou-ts'ai or contrasted color. The enamels used on Ming porcelain are different shades of green, purplish brown or aubergine, yellow (generally rather muddy), a turquoise blue which seems to have been purely experimental for the beautiful violet blue enamel developed in the K'ang Hsi period, 1662-1722, of the succeeding Ch'ing dynasty which became an outstanding characteristic of the polychrome of that time, a composite black formed by a wash of green over a dry black pigment and a tomato red. They were made from a soft lead glaze tinted with metallic oxides; copper for green and turquoise, manganese for aubergine, and antimony for yellow. The dry black is a derivative of manganese and the tomato red of iron sulphate; both are more or less pigments and were principally used in outlining the design. The expression *five-color* is not to be taken too literally, as the colors used were not always five. These enamels are translucent and could be applied to glazed or unglazed porcelain, the latter being called biscuit. When they were applied over the glaze they acquired additional brilliance from the luster of the glaze, while the mat surface of biscuit gave them a softer quality. In the on-biscuit technique it was customary to cover practically the entire surface of the piece with enamels, while in the on-glaze method areas of white glaze could be effectively used to balance the colored decoration. Free painting on biscuit in low-fired enamels or medium-fired glazes does not seem to have been done much before the 16th century and most of the Ming examples date from the Chia Ching period, 1522-1566, and later. They are relatively very few compared with the great number made in the reign of K'ang Hsi, 1662-1722. Though in certain types the decoration was in enamels only, much of the Ming polychrome combines the overglaze enamels with underglaze blue. This color scheme was popular in the late Ming periods and is generally known by the name of Wan Li wu ts'ai or Wan Li polychrome since it is generally believed that the greatest quantity was made during the reign of Wan Li, 1573-1619. This class is also especially identified with the preceding reigns of Chêng Tê, 1506-1521, and Chia Ching, 1522-1566. See *Ming; Three-color Ware; Tou-Ts'ai.*

Five Dynasties See *Chinese Dynasties.*

Five Fabulous Creatures See *Japanese Porcelain Motifs.*

Flambé In Chinese ceramics; a copper-red glaze streaked with grey, purple, lavender and opalescent blue. It is generally believed that the glaze was intended to be Lang yao or Sang de Boeuf and that this transmutation in color was at first accidental. First made during the K'ang Hsi reign, the color was later purposely sought and mastered. Fine flambé red glazes were completely controlled in the following reign of Yung Chêng in the Ch'ing dynasty. See *Sang de Boeuf; Chi Hung.* (113)

Flamboyant The name given to the third and last phase of Gothic architecture in France. The term, which literally means flaming, was given to this Late Gothic style because of the resemblance of the flowing lines in window tracery to the curving lines of flames. See *Gothic.*

Flat-Back Figures In English ceramics; a remarkably naïve class of Staffordshire chimney-piece figures introduced around the mid-19th century that were especially popular in the 1850's and 1860's and continued to be made throughout the century. To spare the cost of casting they were simply pressed into molds and were colored, frequently very meagerly, by the use of overglaze or underglaze painting, but never by colored glazes. The range of subjects varied from contemporary celebrities to such popular themes as Uncle Tom's Cabin. They were produced in a number of small factories including some in Scotland, but the style of the more naïve figures is closely connected with the Sampson Smith pottery of Longton in Stafford-shire. The style of these figures is uniquely British and may be considered as a class of popular art in the field of ceramic figures. See *Smith, Sampson (Ltd.).*

Flaxman, John (1755-1826) English sculptor. He is particularly well known in the decorative arts for his designs in the Neo-Classic style which were used by craftsmen working in the different branches of the decorative arts. From 1775 to 1787 Flaxman was working at Josiah Wedgwood's pottery where he created decorative classical designs for earthenware pieces. Much of this work, which was executed in low relief, is noteworthy for the purity of its classic composition and for its delicate and refined workmanship. (423, 424)

Fleur-de-Lis In ornament; the French term for flower of the lily; the iris. The name was given to the floral design selected by Charles V of France, 1364-1380, as the royal emblem. The fleur-de-lis was a characteristic French Gothic motif.

Fleurs Chatironnées In ceramics; the French term given to a style of flower painting in enamel colors with outlines generally in black. See *Fleurs des Indes.*

Fleurs de Strasbourg In French ceramics; the great period of Strasbourg faïence dating from 1748-1749 was initiated by the advent of German porcelain painters of the famous Löwenfinck family who introduced the style of painting naturalistic German flowers, the Deutsche Blumen, which soon became the flowers of Strasbourg. (282)

Fleurs des Indes In ceramics; the French term for flowers of India given to flower painting of vaguely oriental character, essentially influenced by Kakiemon and Famille Rose styles and usually with black outlines or chatironné. See *Indian Flowers.*

Flight and Barr See *Worcester.*

Flight, Barr and Barr See *Worcester.*

Flint Pure silica, the natural stone. It is calcined in kilns and ground to a fine powder. Flint gives strength and solidity to the body and prevents warping.

Flint China See *Granite Ware; Ironstone China.*

Flint Enamel Ware In American ceramics; a special glazing process with more coloring, patented by C. W. Fenton at Bennington in 1849. Essentially it was a more sophisticated or elaborate form of the English Rockingham brown glaze and deliberately gave a mottled appearance with more coloring. See *Bennington.* (438)

Flintporslin In ceramics; a Swedish term for lead-glazed white or cream-colored earthenware in the English manner. See *Cream-Colored Earthenware.*

Flora Danica In Danish ceramics; the name given to a celebrated porcelain table service painted in enamel colors and gilt, ordered in 1789 by the Danish king, originally, it was thought, as a gift to Catherine II, Empress of Russia, who, however, died in 1796 before the service was completed. In 1802 the work was halted by Royal command, and the service which by this time comprised 1800 pieces was delivered to the Danish Royal Household. Today more than 1500 pieces still survive. This magnificent service made at the Royal Copenhagen Porcelain Manufactory was decorated by Johann Christoph Bayer (1738-1812), Nuremberg artist living at Copenhagen from 1768. Each piece is decorated with named plants copied from the colored plates in the great botanical work by G. C. Oeder, entitled FLORA OF THE DANISH KINGDOM. The Latin name of the plant appears on the back of each piece. (381)

Florence In Italian ceramics; See *Caffaggiolo; Tuscany; Medici Porcelain.*

Florida Porcelain See *La Moncloa.*

Floris See *Antwerp.*

Floris, Cornelis (1514-1575) Flemish sculptor, designer, engraver and architect. See *Engraved Designs.*

Flörsheim In German ceramics; a faïence factory still in existence was started at Flörsheim, near Frankfort-on-Main in 1765 by Georg Ludwig Müller. After changing hands several times, Machenhauer became proprietor in 1810. It was subsequently continued by his heirs. The customary factory mark was F. H. in monogram. The production varied from useful wares painted in peasant style in blue or high temperature colors to elaborate table center pieces. Painting in muffle colors in the Strasbourg style was occasionally done. Faïence fine was also made.

Flow Blue In English ceramics; transfer printing could be used on porcelain or pottery, over the glaze or under the glaze. The latter was favored because the glaze preserves the decoration from wear; however, it was difficult to avoid some slight blurring of the lines in a pattern when the glaze was fused over it. This slight blurring of line is a technical limitation, but it appears to add attraction and character to the traditional blue and white, and is now described in America as "flow blue." Blue was the color originally associated with the ware, because in the early stages blue derived from cobalt was the only color which would with certainty survive the temperature required to fuse the overlying glaze. Though the process of transfer printing had been practiced since the middle of the 18th century, the development of underglaze printing on pottery belongs mainly to the 19th century when it was made in Staffordshire by almost every pottery firm and by a number of firms elsewhere. In the second and third decades particularly, a considerable international trade was developed in this cheaply produced and attractive ware. Though blue continued to be by far the most popular

FLORSHEIM
C. 1765 ON

color, from the mid-1820's onward other colors were introduced for underglaze printing including black, red, purple, brown, yellow and varying shades of green. A development of the later 1840's was to use a number of colors in succession to produce a color print. The process used for the decoration of dinner services, however, proved too expensive for a popular market such as was being exploited by the monochrome prints. By the 1860's the popularity of monochrome printing on pottery was clearly declining. See *Transfer-Printed Wares; Backstamp*.

Flower Pot, The   See *Rotterdam*.

Flowers Modeled in Porcelain   In European ceramics; the widespread 18th century vogue for flowers naturalistically modeled in porcelain was initiated at Meissen toward 1740, with their use applied to or contained in vases. Especially outstanding are the guelder-rose vases or Schneeballenvasen (almost entirely covered with small flowers) among the earliest of which were those made for Louis XV of France, 1741-1742. As separate blossoms they came into vogue in the later 1740's and were imitated in fine soft paste at Vincennes-Sèvres. Tulips, daffodils, lilies and hyacinths, as well as the more usual rose, were made and were of full size and colored after nature. They were wired and mounted in gilt bronze. No doubt the most celebrated bouquet, of no less than four hundred and eighty separate flowers, was that sent in 1748-1749 by the Dauphiness Marie-Josèphe to her father the Elector of Saxony, apparently with the intention of showing him that Vincennes could compete successfully with Meissen. This bouquet mounted in gilt bronze by Duplessis with a glazed white vase and two glazed white groups belongs to the State Porcelain Collection at Dresden. (319, 320, 352)

Flux   In ceramics; an ingredient added to the silica and alumina in a pottery body,

glaze or muffle-color to increase its fusibility. The most common flux in glazes and muffle-colors is lead; but lime (calcium oxide or carbonate), soda, potash and borax have occasionally been used. The presence of the alkalis soda and potash, or of iron, lime or magnesia, helps the vitrification of a pottery body. Before the fusible feldspathic flux, petuntse (chinastone) used by the Chinese was discovered, Böttger in his earliest Meissen porcelain used calcareous fluxes, such as marble or alabaster.

Folk Pottery   A popular people's art, done by anonymous potters for the use of the ordinary people. See *Yanagi, Soetsu*.

Fomin   In Russian ceramics; a porcelain manufactory was started by T. Fomin around the first quarter of the 19th century in a village called Kuziaevo. The business was continued by his sons until 1883 when operations ceased. Faïence was also made; some of the wares were of good quality. Among the marks was the letter F. See *Russia*.

Fond Ecaille   In French ceramics; the French term given to a tortoiseshell brown high-temperature glaze used on hard paste porcelain made at Sèvres from about 1775.

Fondporzellan   In ceramics; the German term for porcelain with a colored ground. See *Colored Ground*.

Fontaine, Pierre François Léonard (1762-1853) French architect. The French Empire style was established in Paris by Fontaine and Percier, who were engaged by Napoleon during the Consulate, 1799-1804, to remodel and redecorate the palace, Malmaison. Included among their publications were: PALAIS, MAISONS, ET AUTRES EDIFICES DE ROME MODERNE, 1802; RECUEIL DE DECORATIONS INTERIEURES, 1812. Fontaine as architect to Napoleon I, Louis XVIII and Louis Philippe, was engaged in the principal architectural works erected in Paris during that long time. See

ΠЕΤΡΑ ФОМИНА

FOMIN
EARLY 19TH CENTURY ON

FONTANILLE AND MARRAUD
1925 ON

Empire; David, Jacques Louis; Engraved Designs. (360)

Fontana A surname taken by members of the Pellipario family of potters and painters, originally of Castel Durante and later of Urbino. See *Pellipario, Nicola.* (233, 234)

Fontana, Luci A leading modern Italian ceramic sculptor who became concerned with ceramics in the 1930's, working mainly in the medium of brightly colored earthenware.

Fontanille and Marraud In French ceramics; started Manufacture de Porcelaines Artistiques at Limoges in 1925, which was founded on two earlier Limoges porcelain works, Pillivuyt & Fils and Chauffriasse. The launching of this factory coincided with the Paris Exhibition of 1925. An accepted mark includes Porcelaines Artistiques and F M.

Food and Tea Warmer See *Veilleuse.*

Ford Pottery or **Low Ford** See *Dawson, John and Company.*

Forged Mark Factory marks are occasionally deliberately used by another factory for the purpose of marketing a ware as the product of the factory whose mark has been exactly copied. Probably the most widely forged of all marks are the crossed swords of Meissen and the crossed L's of Sèvres. It is probable that more than half the porcelain in private hands purporting to be Sèvres is partly or entirely false. Copies unquestionably made with fraudulent intention also occur in Chinese and Japanese wares. See *Mark, in ceramics; Apocryphal Mark; False or Fake Mark.*

Formative Period See *Pre-Columbian ceramics.*

Forsyth, Gordon M. See *Pilkington's Tile and Pottery Company.*

Foster, Herbert Wilson (1848-1929) English painter; he enjoyed a fine reputation as a figure artist specializing in portraits. He occasionally painted animal and bird subjects. Foster, who joined Mintons in 1872, was one of the several ceramic artists who exhibited at the Royal Academy Exhibitions.

Fouqué, Joseph In French ceramics; conducted a faïence factory at Moustiers in partnership with Jean-François Pelloquin and afterwards with the latter's son until 1783, when Fouqué obtained the Clérissy faïence factory which was one of the leading faïence factories at Moustiers. See *Moustiers.*

Fournier, Louis Modeler working at Vincennes-Sèvres, 1747-1749, Chantilly 1752-1756. Started a short-lived factory making soft paste porcelain at Copenhagen, 1759-1765. As a rule this porcelain bears the mark F5 for Frederick V, King of Denmark. Tablewares were the chief production, painted in soft enamel colors, occasionally in pink monochrome, with small sprays of flowers, cupids, and blue or pink scale pattern in the French manner.

François I King of France, 1515-1547. The name is given to one of the three principal styles of ornament of the French Renaissance. See *Henri II; Louis XIII.*

Franck, Kaj See *Arabia.*

Frankenthal In German ceramics; a porcelain manufactory regarded as one of the seven great 18th century German porcelain factories was established in 1755 by Paul-Antoine Hannong with a privilege from the Elector Palatine, Karl Theodor, at Frankenthal. It closed in 1799 after many changes in management, and the molds were removed to Grünstadt where they continued to be used during the 19th century; others found their way to Mannheim and Nymphenburg; they were used both for porcelain and pottery. The marks corresponded to the different periods in the history of the factory. From 1755 to 1759

FORSYTH, GORDON M.
1906 ON

FRANKENTHAL

1755-1759

1780-1793

the mark was PH and the lion or shield from the Elector's arms; from 1759 to 1762 IH incised or impressed, or JAH in blue with or without the lion; 1762 to 1793 the initials CT under an Electoral Hat in blue with the addition between 1770-1788, of a numeral for the year; and 1794 to 1799 the initials of the van Recums who were the last to operate the manufactory. Its finest period was from 1755 to 1775. The porcelain material was a hard paste of fine quality having a rather creamy white color. The glaze was thin and did not obscure the details of the modeling of figures which were the principal interest of the manufactory. The figures revealed exquisite workmanship, an admirable feeling for the plastic quality of a porcelain model and a lavish use of detail. As a rule the decorative pieces such as vases and also the tablewares were of fine quality. The flower and figure painting were notable; the latter was always a feature of Frankenthal decoration. The wares to a greater or less extent retained their highly individual character almost until 1780, after which the classical style as interpreted in Sèvres porcelain was the predominating influence. See *Lanz, J. W.; Hannong, P.A.; Lück, K. G.; Linck, F.K.; Feilner, S.; Melchior, J. P.; Ringler, J. J.; Riedel, G.F.* (324)

Frankfurt-on-Main In German ceramics; a faïence manufactory, one of the oldest and most important in Germany, was established here in 1666 by Johann Simonet under the patronage of Johann Christoph Fehr. It changed ownership several times and finally closed around 1772. The letter F was used enough to be generally accepted as a factory mark. The factory's chief claim to fame is due to the faïence made from around 1666 to 1723. The early ware was in imitation of Delft faïence and has often been commonly mistaken for Delft. The finer varieties were painted in blue or in blue and purple with designs derived from the blue and white Chinese late Ming. From these were eventually developed original and beautiful designs that generally can be distinguished by the presence of a motif of prickly lotus leaves. They made large dishes with wide flat rims and deep wells frequently painted with biblical or other figure subjects and jugs finely painted in purple occasionally with biblical subjects. Some of the most characteristic types were similar to those of the neighboring town of Hanau such as lobed and reeded dishes, armorial jugs and jugs with narrow necks or the so-called Enghalskrug. See *Delft; Enghalskrug.*

Frankfurt-on-Oder In German ceramics; a small faïence factory was started at Frankfurt-on-Oder, Brandenburg, in 1763 by Karl Heinrich. It closed between 1788-1798. They mainly made faïence cylindrical tankards painted in high temperature colors in the manner of Thuringia and Berlin. They were marked F over H.

Franklin Porcelain Company In American ceramics; active at Franklin, Ohio, in 1880. Their distinguishing initials F. P. Co. over F. were used as a mark.

Frechen In German ceramics; an important center for Rhenish stoneware. Late in the 16th century the potteries for making stoneware at Cologne were removed to nearby Frechen. Especially characteristic of their production from the late 16th century were globular Bartmann jugs decorated with the coats-of-arms of Cologne, Cleves, Amsterdam and other places. They continued to produce and export these Bartmann jugs throughout the 17th and into the 18th centuries. See *Cologne.*

Freiberg In German ceramics; a distinctive variety of grey stoneware jugs were made here in the latter part of the 17th century. They were decorated with bands or panels of carved ornament consisting of geometrical designs and rosettes enameled in white, black, light blue and red. They were often enriched with contemporary finely embossed pewter mounts. Due to the com-

FRANKENTHAL VASE

FRANKFURT-ON-MAIN
LATE 17TH CENTURY ON

F P C°
F

FRANKLIN PORCELAIN
COMPANY
1880

bination of black and white the misleading name of *mourning jug* or *Trauerkruge* was applied to these jugs. (196)

French Porcelain In French ceramics; the earliest porcelain made in France is composed of the unsurpassable soft pastes first made at Rouen around 1673 and at Saint-Cloud perhaps as early as 1677, and later at Chantilly and Mennecy and the earliest Vincennes, 1738-1753. Probably the finest and most finished soft paste porcelain was produced at Sèvres from 1753 to 1772. It is generally accepted that the productions of Saint-Cloud, Chantilly, Mennecy, Vincennes and early Sèvres rank among the finest porcelains ever produced. The Duc de Brancas made the first French hard paste porcelain in his laboratory at the Château de Lassay about 1763 to 1768. Sèvres first produced hard paste porcelain in 1768. After 1770 and onward the production of hard paste porcelain steadily increased. From about 1772 to 1800 both hard paste and soft paste porcelain were made concurrently in France. See *Soft Paste; Porcelain.*

Fresco Pottery See *Teotihuacan.*

Freytag, Daniel American potter working around 1810-1811 at Philadelphia where he produced a fine earthenware, the body resembling Queen's ware. In 1815 he appeared at Pittsburgh, also in Pennsylvania, where he apparently made a Queen's ware similar to the Philadelphia ware. His venture is one of the earliest in the production of fine earthenwares in America. There is no documented survival of his work.

Friberg, Berndt See *Gustavsberg.*

Friedberg In German ceramics; a faïence factory was started at Friedberg near Augsburg, Bavaria, in 1754 by Joseph Hackhl at the instance of Count Sigismund Haimhausen, patron of the Nymphenburg porcelain factory. It is reputed to have closed in 1768. The wares, like those of

nearby Göggingen, were of good quality and showed a preference for high-temperature colors, but displayed no outstanding creativity.

Friesland In Dutch ceramics; potteries producing faïence were located at several centers: Harlingen, Leeuwarden, Makkum and Bolsward. Faïence dishes painted in peasant style and tiles continued to be made at Friesland until the 19th century and later. See *Makkum; Harlingen; Dutch Tiles; Tiles.*

Frit In ceramics; the glassy ingredient of soft paste porcelain. Sometimes it is made of the separate ingredients of glass and sometimes it includes actual broken glass fused and powdered before it is mixed with the clay. See *Soft Paste.* Also used of any glassy material prepared for the potter. See *Glazed Quartz Frit Ware.*

Fritzsche, Georg Modeler at Meissen, 1712 to at least 1730. (302, 304)

Frog Mug A small English earthenware drinking mug, having a figure of a frog modeled on the inside. It was made in the 18th century at Sunderland, Leeds and other potteries.

Frog Service In English ceramics; an enormous dinner service of Queen's Ware comprising nine hundred and fifty-two pieces made by Josiah Wedgwood in 1773–1774 for Catherine II, Empress of Russia, each decorated with a different hand-painted view in purplish black monochrome of famous houses, castles and abbeys of England. There were one thousand two hundred and forty-four views painted on this service, the decorating being done at Chelsea, while the potting was carried out at Etruria. It was made for the palace of La Grenouillière near St. Petersburg and derives its name from a small green frog (grenouille) painted in a shield on the border of each piece. (401)

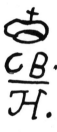

FRIEDBERG
1754-c. 1768

Fry, Laura A. American ceramist and decorator; one of Mary Louise McLaughlin's group. During her years at Rookwood she developed the airbrush method of spraying backgrounds. Later she was one of W. A. Long's decorators at the Lonhuda Pottery, whose ware closely resembled Rookwood's underglaze slip decoration. See *Lonhuda Pottery.*

TEN CONJOINED FUDDLING
CUPS, STAFFORDSHIRE

Fu In Chinese art; the Chinese bat which expresses happiness and good fortune was widely used as a decorative motif in Chinese ceramics, sculpture and painting. See *Chinese Animal Figures.*

Fu-hsing In Chinese art; a Taoist deity. See *Lu-hsing; Chinese Gods.*

Fu Lion In Chinese art; the lion or shih or shih tzu. See *Dog of Fo.*

Fuddling Cup A name given to an English earthenware puzzle cup. It consists of a group of cups, joined together in such a manner that when all the cups are filled, all the liquid can be drunk from any one of the cups. The word *fuddle* means to tipple, to booze, or to have a drinking bout. (254)

FULDA

FAIENCE C. 1741

PORCELAIN C. 1765-1788

Fujiwara Late Heian period in Japan, A.D. 897-1185. See *Japanese Periods.*

Fukien In Chinese ceramics; the province of Fukien has been renowned for its potteries from early days. See *Chien Yao; Blanc de Chine.*

Fuji-san or **Mt. Fuji** In Japanese ceramics; the name given by Koetsu to a Raku ware tea bowl which he made. It is one of Japan's two most celebrated tea bowls, the other being a Shino tea bowl. The latter has a typical opaque white Shino glaze with a design painted in iron-rust brown showing a bamboo trellis, in allusion to which the tea bowl's poetic name Un-no-hanagaki, literally The Flower Trellis of Utsugi Blossom, has been devised. The greyish-white glaze on the upper half of the Koetsu bowl suggests snow-capped

Mt. Fuji; the lower half the misty scenery at its foot. See *Raku.* (129, 133)

Fulda In German pottery; a faïence manufactory supported by the Prince-Bishop of Fulda was founded at Fulda, Hesse, in 1741 when the Meissen painter Adam Friedrich von Löwenfinck and his brother Karl Heinrich came from Bayreuth to Fulda. The manufactory achieved great distinction and closed in 1758 due to the troubles caused by the Seven Years War. The tin glaze was of a fine quality. The most typical decoration was in a Fulda-Chinese style and was painted in enamel colors and gold. It was distinctive for its fineness and brilliance. The Chinese Famille Verte porcelain was the principal inspiration for this decoration; however, the individual talent of the Fulda artists imbued it with some original quality. Painting in high temperature colors and painting in blue with manganese purple outlines was also done. Figure modeling was also practiced at Fulda. Factory marks were sometimes but not always used and included FD and Fuld with painters' marks. See *Löwenfinck, A.F. von.* (289)

Fulda In German porcelain; a porcelain manufactory of great distinction was founded at Fulda in 1765 under the patronage of the Prince-Bishop of Fulda at the request of Johann Philipp Schick, who also had a considerable share in the founding and directing of the Fulda faïence manufactory. It was active until 1790. The marks were in sequence a cross from the arms of the city; two F's in a monogram forming an H under an Electoral Hat and two crossed F's forming an A. The principal qualities identified with Fulda porcelain are the remarkable fineness and flawlessness both in the paste and in the glaze, and the extraordinarily careful and finished workmanship. The figures made at Fulda are among the most costly and highly prized of all German porcelain. The finer figures and groups seem to have been made from around 1768 to 1775 and are generally marked with a cross. They are distinctive for their delicate modeling and for their lightly painted fresh and clean harmonious colors. Shepherds and shepherdesses, figures from the Italian Comedy, elegantly dressed ladies and gentlemen and many others are among the exquisite and doll-like figures and groups. The tablewares revealed the same fine quality in material and in workmanship as the figures. The decoration, which showed little originality, included Meissen flowers, landscapes and monochrome, and en grisaille figure painting.

Fulham In English ceramics; stoneware has been manufactured at Fulham, Middlesex, from 1671 until the present time. The establishment of a pottery at Fulham was due to John Dwight (d. 1703) who took out a patent in 1671 and renewed it in 1684 for the manufacture of stoneware. Especially noteworthy is a distinctive series of figures made at Fulham. The Fulham pottery remained in the hands of Dwight's family until 1864, when it was bought by C. I. Bailey. The productions by Dwight fall into two principal types or groups. One group consists of a series of busts and statues fabricated in salt-glazed stoneware. The other group is composed of useful wares which vary from small mugs made in a fine translucent stoneware to rather coarse imitations of the Rhenish Bartmann or Bellarmine stoneware jugs. The figures which rank among the best contemporary plastic art were of a greyish white or buff-colored stoneware. Since his wares were always unmarked it is difficult to conjecture the extent of his manufacture of useful wares. In addition to the Bellarmines other authenticated pieces include small mugs some of which are a plain slightly brownish white and others are mottled with patches of brown and blue. After Dwight's death it seems that only ordinary wares were made at Fulham such as beer jugs and heavy cylindrical tankards with a drab colored body, the upper part being covered with an iron brown and salt-glazed and commonly decorated with clumsy applied reliefs. See *Elers.*

Fulper Pottery Founded in 1805 in Flemington, New Jersey, by the Fulper Brothers. They originally made drain tiles, using the rich local clay, and added mugs, bottles, jugs, churns and jars after 1860. J. M. Stangl was named ceramic engineer in 1910 and during World War I created the doll heads now valued by collectors. In 1926 Fulper took over the Anchor Pottery in nearby Trenton in addition to two Flemington plants, and when the larger of these was destroyed by fire in 1929 transferred all operations to Trenton. The smaller Flemington plant, its kilns still in place, is now used as a showroom. Stangl introduced a line of dinner ware in 1940 and, later, gift wares which are presently in active production and known as Stangl pottery.

Furnival, Jacob and Thomas Staffordshire potters producing earthenwares around 1843 at Shelton, Hanley. Subsequently Thomas Furnival and Company active at Hanley around 1844-1846; Thomas Furnival and Sons active at Elder Road, Cobridge, 1871-1890, when the name was changed to Furnivals. The present name Furnivals Ltd. has been used since 1913.

Fürstenberg In German ceramics; a porcelain manufactory regarded as one of the seven most important in Germany during the 18th century was established in 1747 by Duke Carl I of Brunswick. It was scarcely active before 1753 and enjoyed its most flourishing period between 1770 and 1814. It is still in existence. The mark of a cursive F in underglaze blue was generally used on all but the very early wares; after and around 1770 a running horse impressed was used on the biscuit busts. The productions of the early period, 1753 to 1768, were characterized by the skillful use of numerous relief patterns such as

FULDA GROUP

STONE CHINA
J & T F
FURNIVAL, JACOB AND
THOMAS
C. 1843

FURSTENBURG

1753-1768

19TH CENTURY

Rococo scrollwork. Of particular interest were some well-modeled porcelain figures. Clock cases, candlesticks and vases were all modeled in the most fantastic Rococo forms. Vases were always an important feature of Fürstenberg productions. The best work as an entirety was done from 1768 to 1795. The painting was frequently copied from engraved designs and was often done in monochrome. Landscapes, figure subjects, groups of birds and flowers were favorite motifs for the painted decoration. Figures were made in considerable numbers. A specialty were the carefully modeled biscuit medallions and busts of illustrious French and German contemporary persons and of scholars and poets from antiquity. The last period of artistic interest, about 1795 to 1814, and often referred to as the Classical period, was marked by a more exacting devotion to the antique. To the present the manufactory has continued to produce many of the old models. See *Feilner, S.* (327, 328)

FURSTENBERG VASE

G

G D A In French ceramics; the family of Gerard started a porcelain factory for the manufacture of tablewares at Limoges in 1798. The distinguishing initials G D A are identified with this factory. See *Haviland, Charles Field.*

Gabri See *Islamic Pottery, Medieval.*

Gádor, István (b. 1891) Hungarian sculptor and artist-potter; a true pioneer who may be said to have created the modern art of ceramics in Hungary. Throughout his work he has skillfully combined the gifts of the sculptor and of the ceramist. With his human and animal figures, produced on the potter's wheel, he has extended the technical frontiers of ceramics, and his large-scale sculptures bear witness to his talent for modeling. His work and that of the artist-potters Gorka and Kovács have one thing in common, namely a deeply felt Hungarian spirit, which, though the reaction of each of them is strongly individual, derives from their common heritage of Hungarian folk art. See *Gorka, Géza; Kovács, Margit.* (558)

Galena In ceramics; a natural sulphide of lead which is powdered and dusted on pottery before it is fired to make a lead-glaze. In the more primitive wares powdered galena was dusted on the pottery surface and in the firing combined with the silica present in the body to make a transparent glaze, as a rule stained yellow or brown by the iron in the galena or contained in the clay. Later a fluid lead glaze was developed.

Gallé, Emile (1846-1904) One of the most interesting of all Art Nouveau designers as well as France's outstanding naturalist. Though much better known for his glass and furniture he started a small pottery workshop at Nancy in 1874 together with his father. Regardless of the medium Gallé's decorative principles are entirely founded on a study of Nature. He permits flowers and leaves to keep their illusionistic effect; therefore as a rule his motifs are three-dimensional in effect even in the two-dimensional plane and often with the emphasis on the linear. In 1900 he wrote: "The shapes provided by plants are easily adapted to lines." See *Art Nouveau; Japanism.*

Gallipot In ceramics; the name given to a kind of jar that has a small mouth and a short neck. The elongated body is wider at the shoulders than at the base. The gallipot was a characteristic Chinese form. (100, 119, 120)

Gambone, Guido (b. 1909) Italian artist-potter; perhaps the most successful of Italian modern ceramists. Until around 1949 Gambone worked alone at Vietri, near Naples; in the early 1950's he started a workshop at Florence. His brightly colored earthenware vessels formed into fantastic and exaggerated shapes bearing little relation to practical use are unique. His pieces while unmistakably contemporary recall the vigor and fantasy of Etruscan figure pottery. He also produces purely sculptural works. See *Majolica.*

Garden Seat or **Barrel-Shaped Seat** The barrel-shaped garden seat or liang tun meaning cool seat, in the form of an ancient-drum, is of very early origin. It appears that barrel-shaped seats made of stone were placed around massive oblong stone altar tables from the early Sung dynasty and probably much earlier. Barrel-shaped seats made of porcelain were highly esteemed, for it is stated in the T'ao Shou, "We find that, when, during the Sung dynasty, the Minister of State, Wang Kuei, had audience of the Emperor in the Jui-chu

GAMBONE CERAMIC JAR

FRANCE

G D A

1891 ON

GADOR, ISTVAN

PRESENT

GARDEN SEAT, MING

Hall of the Palace, he was given a porcelain barrel-shaped seat painted purple and commanded to be seated." Porcelain barrel-shaped seats were chiefly decorated in polychrome enamels, in openwork designs filled in with color, and in underglaze blue and white. The latter is especially characteristic of the Wan Li reign.

GARDNER, FRANCIS
C. 1900 ON

Gardner, Francis (d. c. 1786) In Russian ceramics; started the Francis Gardner porcelain manufactory at Verbilki, near Moscow, in 1766. One of the privileges granted was to fix his name and over that the symbol of Moscow (St. George and the Dragon). The mark was first used in the succeeding century. Porcelains of the finest quality were made here; the decoration was rich and barbaric. In 1777 Catherine II, 1762-1796, commissioned the manufactory to make dinner services decorated with the ribbons, badges, and stars of the more important of the Imperial Orders: St. Alexander Nevskii, St. Andrew First Called, and St. George the Victorious. In 1783 Catherine II issued another commission for the service for the Order of St. Vladimir which was completed in 1785. Around 1770 porcelain figures mostly in the Meissen manner were added to the production program which up to that time consisted only of porcelain tablewares. In the 19th century these figures in glazed porcelain or biscuit became more intrinsically Russian, representing all classes, many in brilliantly colored native costumes and characteristic attitudes. The charm and vitality of these call forth the flavor of old Russia, as it is revealed in operas, novels and ballets. The Gardner manufactory led all others in the field of making figures which often approximated folk art. Among their marks was the letter G in the 18th and beginning of the 19th century. From 1847 to 1853 the manufactory which by that time was known as the Gardner Brothers concentrated on faïence of exceptional quality. It was sold in 1892 to Matvei Sidorovich Kuznetsov,

GARTER MARK

who owned the greatest combine of porcelain factories in Russia. See *Russia; Kuznetsov; Popov.*

Gariboldi, Giovanni   See *Doccia.*

Garniture-de-Cheminée   In ceramics; a term originally given to a mantel set of five porcelain vases comprising a pair of trumpet-shaped beakers and three baluster-shaped jars with hat covers such as were made in China for export to Europe late in the 17th and through the 18th century. The name was later applied not only to imitations and variations made at Delft and other faïence factories and at Meissen and other porcelain factories but also to silver interpretations, particularly Dutch and English.

Garrison Pottery   See *Sunderland Pottery.*

Garter Mark   In English ceramics; one of the basic mark forms used by the Staffordshire potters. The name or distinguishing initials of the proprietor of the pottery appeared in the garter, while the name of the pattern was inscribed within the circle. The mark is derived from the insignia of the Order of the Garter. See *Stafford Knot; Backstamp.*

Gaudy Dutch   In American ceramics; a popular name given to a colorfully decorated Staffordshire pottery made for the American trade, especially for the Pennsylvania Germans, which enjoyed wide popularity about 1810–1830. This white earthenware, comprising chiefly plates and tea wares, was made by a number of Staffordshire potters who painted the patterns (Butterfly, Urn, War Bonnet, Grape, Oyster, Strawflower, Single Rose, King's Rose and others) in almost frantic combinations of blue, bright yellow, green, red and other colors. (462, 463)

Gaudy Ironstone   In American ceramics; an English Staffordshire cottage type appearing in tea and dinner wares, having a dense and hard white earthenware body, dating from around 1850–1865. It occurred in a wide range of floral patterns generally with added detail in copper luster or gilding.

Gaudy Welsh In American ceramics; an English cottage ware; a translucent tea ware produced about 1830–1845 in the Swansea area. It occurred in a wide range of floral patterns generally with added detail in copper luster or gilding.

Gauguin, Jean (b. 1881) Son of Paul Gauguin. See *Bing and Grøndahl.*

Gauguin, Paul (1848-1903) French painter, sculptor, engraver and ceramist. Gauguin illustrates in paint the great interest easel painters have taken in ceramics, which undoubtedly influenced French art-pottery. Painters in France seem always to have been concerned with the performance of ceramic colors as compared with those on canvas. However, if the painter is to obtain the result he desires he will as a rule need a professional potter. Such excursions into ceramics by painters benefited Théodore Deck, Ernest Chaplet and other potters who produced ceramics for Gauguin, André Methey and others. See *Artigas, J. L.; Picasso, P.*

Gaulish Pottery See *Roman Pottery.*

Genre Pittoresque The French name generally given to the acceleration or second phase of the Rococo style marked by a deliberate use of asymmetry, to which Meissonnier was a chief contributer. See *Rococo; Louis XV.*

Geometric Style See *Greece*, in ancient ceramics.

Georgian Period In English history, 1714-1830; the reigns of George I, 1714-1727; George II, 1727-1760; George III, 1760-1820; George IV, 1820-1830. See *Regency.*

Gera In German ceramics; a porcelain manufactory was founded at Gera, Thuringia, in 1779 and was sold shortly afterwards to two members of the Greiner family, who owned the Volkstedt factory. The wares were marked with G, Gera or the crossed swords of Meissen. The useful wares made at Gera were imitated from the more ordinary types made at Meissen. They also made some presentation cups and saucers with carefully painted decoration consisting of views of Gera, inscriptions and mottoes and similar subjects. As a rule the figure modeling was of poor quality and roughly painted. Faïence was also made at Gera. A small manufactory was founded in 1752 that remained active at least until 1780. Some pieces still extant are marked with a G or Gera. The wares were painted in high-temperature colors in a clear white tin-glazed ground. Vases and cylindrical tankards were included in their productions.

German Flowers In French ceramics; see *Deutsche Blumen.*

German Porcelain In ceramics; soft paste porcelain was practically never made in Germany. Böttger of Meissen discovered the secret for making hard paste porcelain in 1708-1709, and the first hard paste porcelain in Europe was made in the royal Saxon factory at Meissen. The second manufactory for hard paste porcelain was established in Vienna in 1719. No other German manufactory was able to make true porcelain until after the second half of the 18th century when there were no less than twenty-three manufactories in Germany producing true porcelain in the Meissen manner. It was Vienna and not Meissen which was responsible for the "disastrous" spread of Böttger's secret chiefly through the arcanist J. J. Ringler. Practically all the German porcelain of artistic importance and originality was made from around 1750 to 1775 with the exception of Meissen and Vienna. Five of the principal manufactories, Höchst, Nymphenburg, Frankenthal, Ludwigsburg and Fürstenberg were essentially creations of the middle of the 18th century. The porcelain manufactory at Berlin, due to the sustained patronage of Frederick the Great, King of Prussia, enjoyed a predominance which lasted into the 19th century. Minor manufactories under princely patronage were located at Fulda, Ansbach, Ottweiler, Cassel, Baden-Baden, Kelsterbach, Pfalz-Zweibrücken and Kloster-Veilsdorf. A number of private manufactories were started around 1770 in the forest region of Thuringia. Their wares were made by a cheaper process and were coarse and had relatively little artistic merit. The exceptions were the productions of Gotha and Kloster-Veilsdorf, both in the Thuringian group. See *Ringler, J.J.; Riedel, G.F.*

German Stoneware   In ceramics; see *Rhenish Stoneware; Kreussen; Bunzlau; Freiberg; Böttger, Johann Friedrich; Stoneware.*

GIEN
1864 ON

Ghzel'   In Russian ceramics; Ghzel' district is the name given to an area about thirty miles from Moscow. Actually Ghzel' was one of no less than thirty villages in the region in which ceramics had been made in the 18th and 19th centuries. Pottery was made during the first half of the 18th century and faïence from around 1770 to 1815, when a kind of semi-faïence supplanted the faïence. The first kiln for porcelain making was started in the village of Volodino by Pavel Kulikov who originally made faïence. The area had a distinctly regional or provincial character. The majority of the kilns were owned by peasants and worked by peasants. Essentially, their wares were folk art, and rarely bore a maker's mark. See *Russia; Kiselev.*

Gien   In French ceramics; a pottery was established here by De Boulen in 1864 where imitations of 16th century Italian majolica were made as well as faïence fine for everyday use.

Gilding   In ceramics; the practice of decorating pottery and glass with gold was known in ancient times. In European ceramics gilding was probably first used around the middle of the 16th century; however, it was not until about one hundred years later that gilding was regularly used, when it was found on German faïence jugs richly decorated in gold. Four different methods were used for applying added decoration in gold to porcelain, stoneware and pottery before the 19th century. In an early method a gold sizing was painted on with a brush and while it was still tacky the gold leaf was applied. No firing was done. In this method the gilding easily wore off. In a second method known as lacquer gilding, the gold leaf was ground up with a lacquer varnish and applied with a brush. This gilding also wore off. The method apparently used in the 18th century for most of the fine porcelain gilding was done by grinding gold leaf in honey. The mixture was applied with a brush and secured by a light firing. This gilding was durable, soft and rich in tone and thick enough to permit chasing and tooling. In a fourth method introduced about 1780 an amalgam of gold and mercury was applied and the latter was evaporated in the muffle kiln. It resulted in a gold film that was burnished to a hard and brittle brightness. It was generally inferior to the earlier method. The commercial potter of the 19th century employed a liquid gold which did not require any burnishing and produced a thin film resembling luster painting. During the Middle Ages gilding was used in the Islamic East, as on the enameled wares of Rayy in Persia. In Chinese porcelain gilding was used during the Ming dynasty, 1368-1644, and in the subsequent Ch'ing dynasty, 1644-1912. The gilding on 18th century Chinese porcelain was very thin and had little brilliance. Gilding was also used on Japanese porcelains, as on the enameled Imari wares decorated in the brocade pattern. Gilding was regarded as indispensable on the finest European porcelain and its lavish use was a feature of the Baroque style.

It continued to play an important part during the following Rococo style both on porcelain and faïence. During the Empire period the practice of gilding large surfaces to simulate gold became the fashion, which is generally regarded with disfavor since the feeling for porcelain was lost in this practice.

Giles, James English enameler working independently in London around 1760-1780. Much of the decoration on Worcester and Bow porcelain was painted in his atelier in Berwick Street, Soho. He never signed his work. The painter O'-Neale may have been hired by him. See *O'Neale, J. H.* (376)

Gillet and Brianchon See *Brianchon, J. J.*

Gillot, Claude (1673-1722) French painter and decorative artist. See *Watteau, Antoine.*

Ginger Jar In Chinese ceramics; a porcelain jar having a wide mouth and a globular body tapering slightly toward the base and fitted with a cover. It is generally thought that these jars were filled with sweetmeats, ginger and tea and were given to relatives and friends during the Chinese New Year holiday as a present, with the jars being returned to the owners. Undoubtedly the most popular decoration for the ginger jar was the plum blossom, reserved in white on the ground, introduced in the K'ang Hsi period. See *Prunus.* (110)

Ginori, Marquis Carlo He and his descendants have owned potteries at Doccia, Italy, from 1737 to the present day. See *Doccia.*

Giustiniani, Nicola See *Naples.*

Glamorgan Pottery See *Swansea.*

Glasgow In Scottish ceramics; a pottery producing tin-glazed earthenware was started here in 1748, but in general the wares have not been identified. It appears that from after 1770 the production was cream-colored earthenware. See *Bell, J. and M. P.*

Glasgow Pottery See *Moses, John and Company.*

Glaze In ceramics; a substance containing sufficient silica and various fluxes which act upon the silica to cause the mixture to fuse and result in a "glassy" surface. It was originally applied to a surface with the intention of rendering it impervious to liquids, but usually also applied as a means of enhancement of color and to give an attractive brilliancy of surface. The five principal types of glazes are alkaline, lead, tin, salt and feldspathic. The alkaline siliceous glazes are of the nature of soda-glass and are essentially composed of sand fused with some form of soda. They were principally used on the wares of ancient Egypt and on the wares of Syria and Persia. They had a distinctive transparent quality and by adding copper to the glazes rich colors of blue or turquoise were obtained. The lead glazes consist of a silica, such as sand, which is fused with the aid of the natural sulphide of lead or with an oxide of the same metal. Sometimes potash was also used. Lead glazes were known to the ancient Romans and to the Chinese of the corresponding time. Lead glazes can be intentionally stained yellow or brown by the use of iron in some form, or green by the use of copper, blue by cobalt, purple and brown by manganese and black by manganese and iron. In contrast to the colored glazes is the refined and almost colorless lead glaze used on cream-colored earthenware. Lead glazes are the most extensively used of all the different kinds of glazes for ordinary glazing purposes. The white and opaque tin glazes are made by an admixture of ashes of tin to a lead glaze. Tin glazes, or tin enamel glazes, as they are sometimes called, are used on majolica and faïence. Lead glazes and tin glazes are the only glazes that can be used on soft paste porcelain. Salt glazes

GINGER JAR, K'ANG HSI

are produced on high-fired stoneware by throwing salt into the kiln when it has reached its highest temperature. They are thin and very hard. If coloring is desired, iron, cobalt or manganese is applied to the stoneware before it is fired. The feldspathic glazes are typically those associated with hard paste porcelain. They consist of fusible feldspathic rock or petuntse which is powdered and mixed with lime, sand, potash or quartz and other ingredients. They require a high temperature to fuse them and normally they are translucent and perfectly united with the hard paste material. They may be colored; cobalt gives blue, iron a range of greens and browns and copper gives lavender blues and reds. During modern times additional colored feldspathic glazes have been introduced. During the 19th century a leadless glaze was introduced for commercial pottery in which other fusible ingredients were used in place of lead in an otherwise lead glaze. This was done because of the injurious effect of lead upon the health of the potter. See *Colors.*

GLIENTZ
1753 ON

GOAT AND BEE JUG,
CHELSEA

Glaze   In modern Western ceramics; it is hardly wrong to say that modern ceramic art is first and foremost a glazing art. The use of elaborated glazes represent the influence of the Far East which in the latter part of the 19th century was affecting not only the great European ceramic factories but also the artist-potters and art-potteries. The Oriental glazes which European potters tried to produce included the Chinese monochrome glazes, such as celadon and Sang de Boeuf and the flambé glazes with variegated and splashed effects. No doubt the most typical of the period in Europe were the newly discovered crystalline glazes which embodied random groups of crystals formed naturally and often attractively within the smooth glazed surface. In America at the Rookwood Pottery of Cincinnati, a crystalline tiger-eye glaze was used in 1884. The crystalline glazes were a significant innovation at a

time when increasing attention was being given to the use of glaze effects as a sole means of decoration. In many instances even the form is determined by the possibilities the form itself gives for the glaze to flow properly and the decoration, as often as not, is only a vehicle for emphasizing the play of color in the glaze. This great interest in the color possibilities and textural effects of glazing as a means of artistic expression is related to the strong impression made by Japanese stoneware which became known in Europe at the close of the 19th century. See *Salto, Axel; Saxbo; Crystalline Glaze.*

Glazed Quartz Frit Ware   In ancient ceramics; a composite material having a powdered quartz body held together with a binding material so that it can be molded. The glaze is a soda-lime silicate, similar to modern glass, and relates to the composition of the body, so that when fired the two adhere. The coloring agent is mixed with it. The ware is commonly known as *faïence,* but since the name *faïence* is properly reserved for tin-glazed earthenware it seems that the term should be avoided as it gives a totally misleading idea of the composition of the body and glaze. Glaze quartz frit ware would be at least a more accurate term. See *Roman Pottery; Islamic Pottery, Medieval; Near East,* in prehistoric ceramics. (40-43, 75-78)

Glienitz   In German ceramics; a faïence factory started here in 1753 was owned by the Countess Anna von Gaschin. From around 1830 to 1870, when the factory produced cream-colored earthenware, it was owned by a family named Mittelstadt. The production under the Gaschin proprietorship was related to that of neighboring Proskau. Especially typical were the vases filled with modeled flowers painted in muffle-kiln colors. The flower painting was inspired by the Strasbourg style. Tureens in the form of vegetables, birds and the like were made. Among the accepted marks were G and G G.

Glier Tankard In German ceramics; a kind of Rhenish salt-glazed stoneware tankard bearing the name Hans Glier. (195)

Gloss In ceramics; a smooth glossy or shining surface given to a vessel or plate by surface-dressing of particular clays of small-particle size. See *Illite.*

Glost Fire A firing process through which ware passes to fuse the glaze; hence a glost kiln in which the glaze is fired on the ware.

Glost Kiln See *Glost Fire.*

Gloucester China Company See *American Porcelain Manufacturing Company.*

Glukhov Kaolin See *Miklashevskii, Andrei.*

Goat and Bee Jug In English ceramics; a cream jug introduced at Chelsea around 1745. The front of the jug was decorated with a reclining goat and bee modeled in relief. This curious shape of cream jug was also made in silver in the 18th century. (412)

Godwin, Thomas and Benjamin Operated the New Wharf and New Basin potteries at Burslem in the Staffordshire district from around 1809-1834, producing earthenwares, cream-colored wares and the like. Transfer-printed wares for the American market comprised a large part of their output. Subsequently became Thomas Godwin who operated the Canal Works, Navigation Road, Burslem, 1834–1854. The initials T. & B. G. and T. & B. Godwin occur in marks of varying design.

Göggingen In German ceramics; a faïence manufactory was established at Göggingen, near Augsburg, Bavaria, in 1748 by Georg Michael Hofmann with a privilege from the Landgrave of Hesse-Darmstadt. Although it operated for only six years it was very productive. The faïence ware was generally marked with the name of the town in full or abbreviated. Their productions covered a wide variety of articles, including figures modeled in a porcelain style, and stove tiles. The Enghalskrug, or a narrow-necked jug, made at Göggingen had a distinctive pear-shaped body and a long slender graceful neck. Wavy-edged plates and Rococo moldings were typical and the wares were especially thin and light. The painted decoration which reflected both European and Chinese influences was carefully executed and was done in either blue or in high temperature colors. Figure painting in blue or purple monochrome was sometimes found on jugs. See *Friedberg.*

Gold-Stone Glaze An aventurine glaze possessing an auriferous sheen. Called also Tiger-Eye Glaze. See *Tiger-Eye.*

Golden Horn See *Islamic Pottery, Later.* (175, 176)

Gombroon See *Islamic Pottery, Later.*

Göppingen In German ceramics; a faïence manufactory was established at Göppingen, Württemberg, by Andreas Pliederhäuser and Johann Michael Stiefvater in 1741. It was active until about 1778. The factory mark was a stag's horn from the arms of Württemberg. The faïence definitely identified as Göppingen work is of a rather poor quality with a greyish tin glaze and coarsely painted.

Gorka, Géza (b. 1894) Outstanding Hungarian artist-potter, whose work played a considerable part in raising contemporary Hungarian ceramics to its present level. His work represents a synthesis of forty years of experimenting both with different materials and with firing processes, in the course of which he became master of a wide range of glazing techniques and of a variety of form and decoration derived from the traditional work of the peasants and of the Habán school. In 1959 he received the title of Distinguished Artist of

GODWIN, THOMAS
c. 1834-1854

GOGGINGEN
1748 ON

GOPPINGEN
1741 ON

the Hungarian People's Republic. See *Gádor, István.*

Goss, William Henry   English potter; started the Falcon Pottery in 1858 at Stoke-on-Trent producing porcelains, parian and earthenwares. He was responsible for some fine Victorian "art productions." The wares greatly resembled in body and glaze those of Irish Belleek porcelain. From around 1934 the pottery was retitled Goss China Company, Ltd., when it was taken over by Cauldon Potteries, Ltd. Goss made popular souvenir china in so-called "ivory porcelain," bearing the arms of a town or county; shapes, besides tea table wares, included shoes, houses, bottles, vases, etc. A very thin china decorated with imitation emeralds, rubies or other "jewels" made from enamels, was known as "jewelled china."

GOSS, WILLIAM HENRY
C. 1862 ON

Gosu-Akae   In Japanese ceramics; the name given in Japan to the red and green family of enameled porcelain wares made at South China kilns in the late Ming period (the so-called Swatow wares) introduced into Japan in the early Yedo period by Nagasaki merchants. These wares have been imitated in Japan from the late 18th and early 19th century up to modern times. The earliest of these imitative wares always bear the name of the Kyoto potter Okuda Eisen, because he is regarded as the originator of Japanese Gosu-Akae. His important extant pieces are mainly plates, bowls and dishes decorated in red and green enamels sometimes combined with underglaze blue in the Swatow style. See *Swatow; Eisen, Okuda.*

GOTHA
C. 1830 ON

Gotha   In German ceramics; a porcelain manufactory was established at Gotha, Thuringia, in 1757 or later by Wilhelm von Rotberg, after earlier experiments by Nikolaus Paul. Prince Augustus of Gotha became the proprietor in 1802. The early mark was an R in underglaze blue or impressed; probably after 1783, R-g; probably after 1805, Gotha or G in blue or

enamel color. From around 1830 and later a rebus mark of a hen on a mountain peak, impressed, was used in association with the place name. The Gotha wares were essentially different from the other wares produced in the manufactories in Thuringia. The material was very fine, although slightly creamy colored, and the painted decoration was very carefully executed. It seems that the factory produced little until around 1775, at which time the classical style was adopted. Figure painting and floral sprig patterns were typical and were probably derived from Fürstenberg. Medallion heads, especially silhouettes, were carefully painted, sometimes on a gold ground. The influence of Fürstenberg was evident in the vase forms, classical figures and busts which were usually in biscuit.

Gothic   Around the middle of the 12th century in Ile-de-France, an old province in northern France with Paris as its capital, Gothic ornament began to evolve from the Romanesque. Except in Italy, it reigned unchallenged throughout the 15th century in all European countries, with national variations much stronger and more obvious than in the earlier Romanesque. Vertical line effects were a dominating feature of Gothic art except in Italy where more emphasis was placed on the horizontal effect. The great tracery windows first developed in Gothic architecture were such an important influence that the character of the stone framing was chiefly instrumental in the name of the different Gothic periods, such as Lancet, Rayonnant, Perpendicular and Flamboyant. With the exception of a few examples, the ornament in the Gothic style is always kept in strictest subordination to the form; it is particularly employed to supplement and complete the expression of the form in a harmonious manner. The principal ornament of Gothic is the leaf-molding, the plants being always selected from the native flora, the manner in which they are worked being in almost every instance an indication of the period

Gothic in the 13th century, the leaves were almost always more or less conventionalized with a slight naturalistic leaning. Later the leaves were produced with more force and energy, becoming finally in late Gothic much more naturalistic in their form. The figures of men and animals and birds made use of in the Gothic were treated in many instances in a humorous and exaggerated manner. In ceramics; especially noteworthy is the Gothic foliage, the typical coiled leaves on Italian, particularly Tuscan and Faenza, majolica of the 15th century continuing into the early part of the 16th century. See *Historicism; Renaissance; Orvieto.*

Gothic Revival or **Neo-Gothic** See *Louis Philippe; Historicism.*

Gotzkowsky, Johann Ernst (b. 1710) Prussian financier; porcelain manufacturer at Berlin, 1761-1763. Formerly a patron at Meissen, 1740-1750, he gave his name to a well-known border pattern of flowers in low relief known as Gotzkowsky Erhabene Blumen, 1744. It was extensively copied.

Gouda One of the great centers in Holland for the manufacture of tin-glazed tiles. Early faïence manufactories were active here under Willem Jansz from Rotterdam, 1621-c.1637; Hendrick Steenwijck and Jacob van der Togt, 1659-1667 or later. Several modern potteries are active here specializing in faïence for daily use and tea services and particularly tiles and tile pictures. They include the Zenith pottery established around 1749, which is managed by members of the Van 't Want family, and De Zuidhollandsche Platelbakkerij or the South Holland Pottery Manufactory, whose wares are of fine quality.

Graffiato In ceramics; see *Sgraffiato.*

Grain of Rice Pattern See *Rice Grain Pattern.*

Grainger Company In English ceramics; Thomas Grainger started a porcelain factory, the New China Works, in St. Martin's Street, Worcester, in 1800. In 1839 on the death of Thomas Grainger, his son George succeeded to the works. Generally the factory followed closely the styles popular at Chamberlain's Worcester, especially the "Japan" patterns, and at Royal Worcester. In 1851 Grainger introduced a semi-porcelain and also made a large quantity of parian, both useful and decorative figures and busts. In 1889 the Grainger factory was incorporated with the larger Royal Worcester, but continued in production until 1902, when it was closed. See *Chamberlain, R.; Worcester.*

Granada In Spanish ceramics; capital of the Moorish Kingdom of the same name founded in 1238 and celebrated as the site of the palace of the Alhambra, started before 1273. The Granada blue and white and blue and lustered tiles, occasionally decorated in relief, resemble in many respects those of Seville. Included among the motifs are interlacements, stylized plant-forms and birds. See *Hispano-Moresque.*

Granary Urn In Chinese ceramics; a kind of tomb pottery; a lead-glazed cylindrical vessel of the Han dynasty. As a rule it tapered slightly toward the base. It resembled a farmer's silo and had a top in the form of a tile roof with a hole in the center. (83)

Grand Feu In ceramics; the French term for the high-temperature kiln required to fire the body and glaze of porcelain, majolica, faïence and a few varieties of ware with a lead glaze. The temperature is generally from 1200° C. to 1400° C. The term *demi grand feu* is generally confined to Chinese ceramics, and is seldom used in European ceramics. See *Petit Feu; Colors.*

Granite Ware or **White Ware** In American ceramics; such names as Granite Ware, White Granite, Opaque Porcelain and Flint China were given to a heavy-grade ware

GOUDA

ZENITH
Aᵒ 1749
ZENITH POTTERY
19 CENTURY

ZUID HOLLANDISCHE
19TH CENTURY

GRAINGER COMPANY
C. 1850-1875

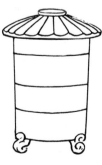

GRANARY URN, HAN

similar to ironstone that was a staple product of American potteries from around 1860 to 1900. Hotel China and Semi-Porcelain appeared around 1885. This is not to be confused with an earthenware made by Wedgwood with a greying or bluish mottled glaze in imitation of granite. See *Ironstone China.*

Grapen In German ceramics; a kind of unglazed earthenware cooking pot of tripod form, usually with a handle projecting on one side, but occasionally found with a loop handle, made all along the northern German seaboard from the 12th century onward. Later it became the standard product of the bronze-founders.

Graphite In ceramics; a form of carbon occasionally used as a surface-dressing on pottery. Also called plumbago or black lead.

Grassi, Anton (1755-1807) Pupil of J. C. W. Beyer and modeler at Vienna, 1778-1807. His work showed a preference for the Neo-Classical mode.

Greatbach, Daniel Modeler; member of a family of English potters, working for D. and J. Henderson at Jersey City, 1837, where he made the first of his hound-handle pitchers. From 1852 to 1854 he was in partnership with James Carr of Carr and Locker at South Amboy, New Jersey. Greatbach was the most famous of the Bennington designers and his hound-handle Rockingham pitcher is one of the best-known items of the Fenton-directed factory. Several of his other designs are identified with English originals. See *Hound-Handle Pitcher.* (439)

Greatbatch, Daniel Mentioned in Thomas Whieldon's notebook as father to William Greatbatch. Both were modelers of repute, and both were apparently employed by Whieldon as modelers. An extant tortoiseshell tea caddy bears the inscription Daniel Greatbatch, 1755.

Greatbatch, William (1735-1813) Staffordshire modeler and potter, closely associated with Josiah Wedgwood from around 1760. Served an apprenticeship with Whieldon and became one of his most noted modelers. In 1759 when Wedgwood terminated his partnership with Whieldon, Greatbatch also left Whieldon, and made an arrangement with Wedgwood to supply him with wares in the biscuit ready for glazing in color. First he was located at Lower Lane and later moved to Lane Delph. Wedgwood profited by the originality of Greatbatch wares. These included cauliflower, melon and pineapple wares, teapots in the form of various fruits, such as pears and apples, and molded wares with figures and scenes on them. Some interesting and frequently amusing prints were engraved by a William Greatbatch, and it is probable that the majority of pieces on which such prints occur were made by the modeler of that name. (397)

Great Exhibition of the Works of Industry of All Nations, 1851 The first international exhibition ever held; opened May 1, 1851, closed to the public October 11, 1851, final closing ceremony October 15, 1851. Built on a Hyde Park site, the Crystal Palace was the outstanding example of mid-19th century iron and glass architecture because of its great size (1851 feet long, much longer than Versailles) and the absence of any other material. The purpose of the Great Exhibition was to present a living picture of the point of development at which the whole of mankind had arrived and a new starting point from which all nations would be able to direct their further exertions. It was one of the few great undertakings in the 19th century that proved an unqualified success. In the decorative arts it was a stimulant to reform. See *Cole, Sir Henry; International Exhibitions of the Victorian Period.* (475)

Grebner, Georg Friedrich German painter working at Nuremberg 1717, 1720-1730, at Bayreuth 1731-1733 or later, at Oettingen-Schrattenhofen, 1738-1740, at Donauwörth, 1741. Probably Hausmaler. Many signed and dated works survive and show that Grebner worked in several styles. At Nuremberg he worked mainly in blue.

Greece In ancient ceramics; a disciplined austerity is a marked feature of all the finest Greek pottery, early and late. Greek vases or pots (essentially the terms have the same meaning as originally "vase" meant a useful pot) were primarily for use, domestic or ritual, and their shapes are constructed with a clean and vigorous precision of contour. The decoration, which is arranged in a band around the pot to confine or emphasize its structure, in appearance as well as in fact keeps to the plane of the surface. Of the decorative motifs the human figure, the subject which above all others interested the Greek artist, becomes the most outstanding; it is drawn with a precise economy of line, and though in time the roundness of the body is suggested, movement and grouping generally avoid the implication of depth. Greek pottery is wheel-made, painted, unglazed and relatively low-fired. Athens and Corinth dominate the history of Greek pottery. Historically, fine pottery made by the Greeks between 1000-400 B.C. falls into four main groups: Geometric, Orientalizing, Black-figure, and Red-figure. The wares of the first group were painted in black or brown monochrome with geometric decoration and were made from around 1000 to 700 B.C. Of the various geometric styles that of Athens is both the best known and the best. (In fact, apart from its eclipse by Corinth in the 7th century, Attic pottery set the pace until the 4th century.) Designs executed with ruler and compass were placed at strategic points on a pot and were organized in zones and panels according to principles which influenced the following generations. Somewhere before 750 B.C. figures of men and animals were introduced as the main theme in vase painting, and in time were reduced to canonical geometric form. Toward the end of the 8th century Greek art and pottery underwent profound modifications owing to trade contacts with Eygpt, Phoenicia, and the inland peoples of Asia. Carved ivory, textiles and metal objects appeared in Grecian cities, where their stylized ornament of human, animal and plant forms encouraged potters to give up the rigid symmetry and restrained emphasis of the geometric art, thus initiating the Orientalizing phase of the 7th century. About 700 B.C. or shortly after came the very important invention of the black-figure technique, in which black-painted silhouette figures on a clay ground are enriched with linear details of anatomy and drapery incised in the black before firing; white and purple (or purplish-red) may also be added in touches or for large areas of flesh or clothing. This technique became for almost two hundred years the medium of the progressive school of vase painting. Its two main branches are concerned, one with representations of animals, the other with scenes of human action, and though men and animals often appear on the same pot they rarely mix in the same field. Roughly the new scheme of animal friezes which constitutes the Orientalizing phase was the standard style of the 7th century when Corinth, the first Greek city to develop the style, took the lead in vase painting. She retained this lead into the 6th century when Athenian potters once again set the pace. The animal style based on the black-figure technique reached remarkable heights in the Corinthian vase painting in the second quarter of the 7th century, 675-650 B.C. It went out of favor in the 6th century and lingered on through the Classical, 480-400 B.C. The 6th century until about 530 B.C. witnessed the flourishing of the black-figure technique. By the 570's B.C. the character of the mature Attic black-figure style was becoming clear. It was a style that inherited the old Attic interest in human figures. Around the middle of the 6th century B.C. a generation of master painters culminating in Exekias brought the black-figure to its perfection. From about 530 to 400 B.C. Athenian pottery alone merits consideration, most of it being painted in the red-figure technique of figures reserved in a black-painted ground. It was the need for a medium more subtly expressive that around 530 B.C. created the red-figure technique and though the black-figure style continued into the 5th century until around 450 B.C., its artistic work was through. In the 4th century B.C. Attic red-figure ware declined in quality, quantity and variety. It enjoyed a limited popularity until around 320 B.C. when it was finally supplanted by the more popular wares enriched with decoration in relief by the use of models which had in their turn been impressed with stamps and roulettes. See *Red-Figure Ware; Roman Pottery; Near East; Europe.* (57-61)

THE GREEK A
1687-1701

Greek See *Style Étrusque, Le; Classic Revival.*

Greek A, The or **De Grieksche A** In Dutch ceramics; a faïence manufactory established at Delft in 1658 by Wouter van Eenhoorn who appointed his famous faïence-potter son, Samuel, as manager and later, in 1678, gave it to him. The SVE pieces are chiefly elaborate but accurate versions of Chinese scenes. He also made the so-called red teapots imitating Chinese buccaro ware. Upon his death in 1686 the pottery was sold to Adriaenus Koeks or Kocks whose initials AK became one of the most celebrated and most frequently forged of all Delft marks. Many of his pieces are in the Chinese K'ang Hsi style, 1662-1722. However, by the 1690's the influence of Daniel Marot became evident in his work. After Koek's death in 1701, his son Pieter Adriaenus (d. 1703) continued the pottery. His widow continued to operate the kiln and the initials PK and PAK appear on pieces after the death of these famous potters. Grieksche A wares en-

GREENWOOD ART POTTERY
AFTER 1868

joyed an enviable reputation and were exported to England, France, Austria and Italy. See *Buccaro; Delft; Faïence.* (260, 261, 267)

Greek Pottery Forms In Greek antiquities; see *Alabastron; Amphora; Aryballos; Dinos; Hydria; Kalpis Hydria; Kantharos; Kothon; Kotyle; Krater; Kyathos; Kylix; Lebes; Lebes Gamikos; Lekanis; Lekythos; Loutrophoros; Oinochoë; Pelike; Phiale; Pithos; Plemochoë; Psykter; Pyxis; Rhyton; Skyphos; Stamnos; Askos.*

Greek Revival or **Neo Grec** A renewed interest in Greek art flourishing in the second quarter of the 19th century chiefly in Germany, England and America. In effect, the period following the fall of the First French Empire, 1804-1814. In England the 1840's witnessed a renewed interest in imitation Greek wares which were commonly known at that time as Etruscan or Etrurian. See *Style Étrusque, Le; Empire; Classical Revival; Victorian; Louis XVI; Historicism.*

Green Frog Service See *Frog Service.*

Green, Guy A partner of John Sadler in the transfer-printing factory at Liverpool, 1756–1799. See *Sadler, John; Liverpool.*

Green In ceramics; prior to the 19th century green pigments for decorating pottery were most frequently derived from copper compounds. Copper-green ranks as a high-temperature color on majolica and faïence, while in porcelain painting it is always a muffle-color. In the 18th century at various places in Europe yellow and blue pigments were occasionally mixed to make a more soft and greyish green than was obtained by copper. Shortly after 1810 a green derived from chromium was introduced. Unlike the copper-green, the chrome-green could be used under the glaze on porcelain. In a class entirely distinct from these is the grey-green feldspathic glaze of Chinese celadon porcelain obtaining its color from iron. Essentially until modern times this was unknown on

European pottery. Copper was used to give a green color to lead glazes at least as early as ancient Roman times. See *Colors; Colored Grounds; Monochrome Painting; Jasper Ware.*

Green Oribe See *Oribe.*

Greenpoint See *Union Porcelain Works; Faïence Manufacturing Company.*

Greenwood Art Pottery Company In American ceramics; started in 1861 at Trenton, New Jersey, as Stephens, Tams and Company; in 1868 it was incorporated as the Greenwood Art Pottery Company. James Tams, president, came from Longton, Staffordshire, England, where he had learned all the branches of pottery. Until 1876 they produced stone china, then they specialized in a finer quality of white ware, the so-called Hotel China. Still later the firm made a porcelain art ware that was similar to the thinnest Royal Worcester, and was richly decorated in the Royal Worcester style.

Grenzau See *Westerwald.*

Grenzhausen In German ceramics; see *Westerwald.*

Grès The French term for stoneware. See *Stoneware.*

Grès de Flandre In ceramics; the name formerly given to the salt-glazed stoneware which is now recognized to have been made in the Rhineland, Germany. See *Steinzeug; Rhenish Stoneware.*

Greybeard In ceramics; the English name for the Bartmann or Bellarmine jug identified with Rhenish salt-glazed stoneware made during the late 16th century and the 17th century. The front of the jug was decorated with a molded bearded mask. The so-called greybeard jugs were made at Fulham, England.

Greuze, J. P. (1726-1805) See *Classic Revival; Engraved Designs.*

Gricci, Giuseppe (d. 1770) Modeler at Capo di Monte 1745-1759; at Buen Retiro 1759-1770, where he was also appointed art director. Succeeded by his sons Carlos (d. 1795) and Felipe (d. 1803). (341)

Griemert, Hubert German artist-potter, whose reputation dates from after the Second World War. He was particularly concerned with crystal glazes which to a greater or less extent have attracted many of the German potters.

Griffen, Smith and Hill In American ceramics; operated a pottery at Phoenixville, Pennsylvania; became widely known for their Etruscan majolica, 1879-1890. Among their popular patterns were the maple leaf, shell and seaweed, and cauliflower. The mark was an impressed monogram GSH, sometimes surrounded by a band with the words Etruscan Majolica. The monogram alone is also used and, sometimes, Etruscan Majolica impressed in a horizontal line. See *Majolica.*

Grisaille In painting, the term *grisaille,* which is derived from the French word *gris* meaning grey, is applied to a style of painting in various tints of grey used to depict solid bodies in relief. It appeared on many makes of porcelain in the late 18th century.

Gropius, Walter Adolf George (1883-1969) American, born in Germany, architect, writer and designer; a foremost pioneer of modern design. Essentially, the determination of the modern style in its synthesis of handicraft and engineering was brought about by Gropius.

Gros Bleu In French ceramics; an underglaze ground color of dark blue employed at Vincennes and Sèvres from around 1749 to 1760. The color, which was taken up by the glaze, was also copied at other manufactories, such as Chelsea, where it

GREYBEARD JUG

GRIFFEN, SMITH AND HILL
C. 1879-1890

was known as mazarine blue in order to distinguish it from the gros bleu and where it was employed from around 1758 to 1769.

Groszbreitenbach In German ceramics; a porcelain manufactory which is still operating was started at Groszbreitenbach, Thuringia, around 1778 by Anton Friedrich von Hopfgarten. As a rule it is very difficult to distinguish their productions and marks from those of Limbach. It is believed that the factory principally made blue and white wares. It seems that from around 1788 the trefoil mark of the Limbach pottery was also adopted as their mark.

Grotell, Maija American, born in Finland, artist-potter and teacher; came to the United States in 1927. She works chiefly in stoneware, understands good potting. Some of her pieces have considerable charm. (554)

Grotesque In ornament; a French term derived from the Italian applied to a distinctive form of decorative design employed in painting and in sculpture comprising representations of portions of human and animal figures fantastically portrayed and interwoven with foliage and flowers. This form of decorative design was found in the excavated ancient Greco-Roman buildings in Italy. This specialized meaning had its provenance in the statement that grotte was the popular name in Rome for these rooms in ancient buildings revealed by excavation and which contained these mural paintings that were characteristic examples of "grotesque." In a broad sense the term is applied to a form of design characterized by unnatural combinations or distortions that are extravagant or treated in a bizarre or fantastic manner. See *Arabesque; Raphaelesque.* (233, 234, 237, 239)

ITALIAN GROTESQUE

GRUEBY FAIENCE
C. 1900 ON

Ground Colors See *Colored Grounds.*

Grueby, William H. American artist-potter; in 1894 he began to produce bricks and tiles with a dull mat glaze that quickly became popular and had an almost immediate effect on the entire production of American pottery. In 1897 he began to make vases with the same mat glazes he used on his tiles at the Grueby Faïence Company at Boston, Massachusetts, thereby originating a distinctive group of American art-pottery wares. Apparently the general style was influenced by some works of the French potter, August Delaherche. The decoration comprised simple vertical leaf-like shapes, hand-modeled in slight relief, well integrated into the form of the vases, the entire surface covered with a mat glaze, generally green in color. The shapes were the work of George P. Kendrick. Like the pottery of Rookwood the faïence of Grueby was a notable success at the Paris Exhibition of 1900. He was one of the most important potters working in the French-inspired Art Nouveau. Tiffany was attracted by the superb quality of Grueby pottery and ordered Grueby bases for some of his lamps. In 1907 Grueby went out of business. See *Art Nouveau; Rookwood Pottery; Pewabic Pottery; Teco Pottery; Tiffany, Louis C.* (522)

Grueby Faïence Company See *Grueby, William H.*

Grünstadt In German ceramics; a still-existing factory was started in 1801 for making cream-colored earthenware in the English style, at Grünstadt, Rhineland, by Johann Van Recum (d. 1805) with the forms and materials removed from Frankenthal. It was sold in 1812 to Wilhelm and Bernard Bordollo, whose family remained owners until 1880 and whose name was until recently kept by the firm. The name or the initials GBD (Gebrüder Bordollo Grünstadt) occur in the marks.

Guatemala See *Maya.*

Gubbio In Italian ceramics; the acclaim given to the majolica made at Gubbio, which is in the Duchy of Urbino, principally rests upon the rare and breath-taking beauty of its ruby and gold luster decoration rather than upon its originality in designs. The best work was achieved during the first thirty years of the 16th century. Around 1495 Giorgio Andreoli, who generally signed his work as Maestro Giorgio, settled at Gubbio. Due to his renown for luster painting it is generally believed that in addition to original work that he lustered, he also added luster painting on other pieces made and painted elsewhere. The early pieces assigned to Maestro Giorgio have been the subject of much discussion. However, from 1519 majolica dishes having his factory mark in luster pigment are not uncommon. Dated specimens with his mark continue until 1541. Included among the finest and most original work of the potters at Gubbio are vases and dishes with gadrooning and embossed decoration artfully designed to permit the fullest play of light to the brilliant luster coloring. A characteristic and popular design at Gubbio consisted of a central panel, frequently square in shape, with a cupid or a bust surrounded by palmettes, grotesques or foliation. The influence of Castel Durante was evident in much of this work. See *Italian Majolica; Luster Decoration.* (231, 232)

Guelder Rose Vase See *Flowers Modeled in Porcelain.*

Guérin, William and Company See *Guérin-Pouyat-Elite (Ltd).*

Guérin-Pouyat-Elite (Ltd) In French ceramics; a still-existing porcelain factory at Limoges. The trade name Elite is included in some of their marks; other marks include the distinguishing initials W.G. (William Guérin & Cie) and J.P. (J. Pouyat).

Guild and School of Handicraft See *Ashbee, Charles; Arts and Crafts Movement.*

Guischard See *Magdeburg.*

Gulin In Russian ceramics; a porcelain factory was started by the peasant Vasili Gulin in the 1830's in the village of Friazevo. He was succeeded by several of his sons. In 1856 the factory was leased to the two Chernov brothers for one year, after which it ceased to operate. It was well known for its table and tea services and also for its figures. Included among the marks were VG and G. See *Russia.*

Gustavsberg In Swedish ceramics; a faïence factory was managed here by Henrik Sten of Marieberg, 1786-1797, during which time tablewares and ornamental pieces were made in the manner of Marieberg, of which the factory was essentially a continuation. The factory probably ceased to operate around 1822. In 1827 the still-flourishing Gustavsberg factory was established; their production was of the Staffordshire type, particularly cream-colored earthenware. In the early 1860's the factory started to make bone china and from the same time also used parian porcelain for figures and other ornamental pieces. The modern revival of Gustavsberg dates from around 1900 with the appointment of Wennerberg as art director, who was followed in 1917 by the distinguished craftsman Wilhelm Käge, often called the grand old man of Swedish ceramics. Käge was especially successful with functional tablewares of simple, pleasing forms which exemplify modern in the contemporary sense. Notable was his white porcelain "soft forms" service designed in 1940 for Gustavsberg. However, from the 1950's the most significant design has concerned tablewares of strictly functional design and composition, generally heat-proof and frequently in plain colors or else decorated with large, simple motifs. Such services or sets of vessels are characteristic of the industrial wares pro-

GUERIN-POUYAT
20TH CENTURY

LIMOGES
ELITE

FRANCE

LIMOGES
W.G.
& C?
FRANCE

LIMOGES
J.P.
L.
FRANCE

GUSTAVSBERG
C. 1910 ON

duced not only in the three great Swedish factories—Gustavsberg, Rörstrand and the Upsala-Ekeby combine, but also at the ceramic factories of Finland. At Gustavsberg such tableware has been designed by Stig Lindberg, who succeeded Wilhelm Käge, and Karin Bjorquist. Berndt Friberg has also made significant contributions. These artists have produced their own studio work as well as designs for industrial production. This approach illustrates the benefits stemming from an enlightened relationship between the artist-craftsman and industry in Sweden. (531)

Gutherz, Oscar and Edgar See *Altrohlau.*

Guzhev In Russian ceramics; about 1860 a factory for porcelain and faïence was started by N. A. Guzhev at Cherniatka, a village near Tver. In 1879 he sold the factory to S. I. Maslennikov. Under Guzhev the production was mainly figures and vases. See *Russia*.

H

Haarlem   In Dutch ceramics; an important early center for the manufacture of tin-glazed earthenware. Adriaen Bogaert, probably of Antwerp, started a majolica pottery here around 1572. Other potteries were soon founded. However, no pottery seems to have existed here after 1705. Apparently in the 17th century Chinese influences due chiefly to the importation of porcelain by the Dutch East India Company brought about a change in taste which before long put the Italian majolica type out of fashion. Haarlem and Middleburg yielded to Delft as the main center as it became famous, particularly for its fine imitations in faïence of Chinese porcelain. See *Netherlandish Majolica; Pietersz, Harman; Dutch Tiles.*

Habaner Ware   In ceramics; a distinctive and important variety of peasant majolica made in Moravia and on the borders of Hungary from the end of the 16th century onward. The earliest makers were German immigrants. Some of the earlier examples with their elaborate openwork borders strongly reflected the influence of Italian majolica. Especially characteristic of their productions are small globular jugs with short necks and dishes and plates with wide flat rims. The painting was executed in a remarkably vigorous and firm manner. According to some authorities the Habaner were a German-speaking sect of Anabaptists. Their religious beliefs forbade them from depicting human and animal figures. For this reason their earliest pottery was decorated only with flowers and plants. Toward the end of the 17th century when the Anabaptist movement was breaking up the potter's repertoire of motifs was less restricted. In the following century Habaner ware was absorbed in the folk pottery of Moravia and Slovakia. (251)

Habermann, Franz Xavier   (1721-1796) See *Rococo; Engraved Designs.*

Hachiroemon, Iida   See *Kutani.*

Hackwood, William   (d. 1839) Chief modeler for Josiah Wedgwood from 1769 to 1832. Though he was largely employed in adapting busts and reliefs from the antique he also executed considerable original work.

Hadley, James   (d. 1903) English designer and modeler working at the Worcester Royal Porcelain Company from about 1870 onward. He was mainly responsible for the Worcester "Japanese" work shown at the Vienna Exhibition of 1873, where Worcester tied with Mintons for the highest award. Notable, but less ambitious, is his charming series of children dressed in Kate Greenaway style costumes. These figures, often with baskets for use on the table, are delightful, and were produced in large quantities over many years. In 1875 Hadley established himself as an independent designer and modeler, but until 1894 his entire production was taken by Royal Worcester. In 1896 with the assistance of his three sons, he started manufacturing on his own account. His products were named Hadley Ware and chiefly consisted of ornamental vases with colored clay enrichments and painted with floral compositions. Many were of fine quality and are frequently painted in monochrome. In 1905 the business was taken over by Royal Worcester who continued to market wares in the Hadley tradition. See *Worcester.*

Hadley Ware   See *Hadley, James.*

Hafner   In German ceramics; a German term literally meaning stove-maker. The name was given to the potters, especially during the Renaissance, producing tile-work stoves, architectural ornaments and

HADLEY, JAMES
1897-1900

sometimes decorative objects and dishes from lead-glazed and other earthenware. The making of pottery stoves in Germany had its origin in Roman times and stove tiles were made at least from the middle of the 14th century. The principal type of late Gothic stove tiles were covered with a green glaze and were decorated in relief, sometimes with figure subjects. Around 1500 the green glaze was supplemented with additional colored glazes and with a white tin glaze or tin enamel glaze. Stove tiles were made throughout the 16th century in many places in Germany, Austria, Switzerland and the Tyrol. The most important center in Germany was Nuremberg. The tiles were notable for their rich and strong coloring and for their freely executed and forceful designs. The tiles were molded in relief and were sometimes further enriched with figures in the round and with foliage appliqués either modeled by hand or pressed in molds. The subjects were chiefly religious, historical or allegorical. The colored glazes were roughly separated by the reliefs. Especially noticeable and effective were the appliqués of rolls and strips of white clay. Pottery dishes and vessels made in this technique rank highly in 16th century German ceramic art. Especially remarkable were the jugs of the Nuremberg Hafner, Paul Preuning, active around 1550, and his followers employing this decorative technique. Perhaps the chief among the many Hafner potters at Nuremberg were Paul Preuning and Oscar Reinhart. In another distinctive type of tile stove introduced in. the last quarter of the 16th century the tiles with relief decoration and colored lead glazes were employed in combination with panels of majolica painted in colors, mainly blue and yellow, on a white tin-glazed ground. See *Vest, Georg, the Younger.* (210)

Hagi In Japanese ceramics; around 1600 two Korean potters named Yi Kyong and Yi Pyo-kwang started the Hagi kilns in pre-

sent Yamaguchi Prefecture, where Karatsu-type wares were produced. Hagi potters concentrated on tea ceremony utensils. A distinctive ware with a pinkish-grey crackled glaze was the typical production. See *Karatsu.* (135)

Hague, The In Dutch ceramics; a porcelain manufactory was started here around 1773 by Anton Leichner and was active until 1790. The mark, which was the emblem of the city, was a stork with a fish in its beak. It is thought that prior to 1776 the manufactory operated simply as a decorating establishment. The painted decoration was technically fine and showed finished workmanship; however, it was lacking in originality. Birds, flowers, cupids, and landscapes, sometimes with figure subjects, were characteristic motifs. The forms were in the early Neo-Classic style. Two faïence manufactories producing faïence in the Delft style were also operating at The Hague during the second half of the 16th century.

Haguenau In French ceramics; a branch manufactory of the Hannong factory at Strasbourg was active at Haguenau, Alsace, from 1724 to 1781. It seems probable that the wares may have been made here, since Haguenau was the source of the clay, and decorated at Strasbourg. Other minor faïence manufactories were active during the 18th century. Porcelain and cream-colored earthenware were also made at Haguenau; however, the reputation of Haguenau depends upon the branch Strasbourg factory. See *Hannong, Charles-François; Anstett, François-Antoine.*

Haile, Thomas Samuel (d. 1948) English artist-potter; working in stoneware. Though he found his expression in techniques relating to the early wares of China and Japan, he succeeded in infusing into his work an altogether modern spirit. He worked for a time in the United States, first in New York at the Henry Street Settlement House, then spent a year at Alfred

THE HAGUE
C. 1773 ON

HAILE, THOMAS SAMUEL
C. 1936-1948

and taught at the University of Michigan. He returned to England, where he met an untimely death. His influence in America has been considerable. See *Murray, William S.* (540)

Haji　See *Yayoi.*

Hakeme　In Korean ceramics; a class of Punch'ong wares known in Japan as Hakeme or brush-marked. It is decorated with brushed white slip by means of what has been called a miniature garden broom made of the grain ends of rice straw. In addition to the plain Hakeme, in another class the surface has been given an overall coating of white slip which is incised and cut away in broad areas down to the grey body to make a striking design in sgraffiato technique. The Japanese give the name *Hori Hakeme* or *Carved Hakeme* to this class. Carved Hakeme is among the more striking wares of the early Yi period. See *Punch'ŏng.*

Hald, Andreas　Repairer and modeler at Royal Copenhagen in the late 18th century. He is reputed to have been an artist of skill.

Hall, Ralph　English potter who operated a pottery at Tunstall in the Staffordshire district, 1822–1849. Formerly in partnership with John Hall at the Sytch Pottery, Burslem. He made earthenware figures painted in colors and with tree backgrounds in the manner of John Walton. Both Halls made transfer-printed wares for the American market. See *Walton, John.*

Hall Marks and **Potters' Marks**　In Chinese ceramics, the name is given to a variety of marks in which occur such words as t'ang (hall), chu (retreat), chai (study), t'ing (summer-house) and hsien (pavilion). Hall marks are numerous, but frequently of uncertain significance. They may sometimes indicate the place of manufacture, thus a studio or factory mark; in other instances they may indicate the residence or pavilion for which the wares were intended. Actual potters' signatures in the Western sense are rare; usually nothing is known of the artists so signing and the practice was in no manner characteristic. See *Chinese Porcelain Marks.*

Hamada, Shoji　(b. 1894) Japanese artist-potter; working exclusively in high-fired stonewares. He is perhaps the best-known of modern Japanese potters. He came to St. Ives with Bernard Leach in 1920, and he built his own kiln in the pottery village of Mashiko, Japan, in 1931. His pottery reflects the ease and complete mastery he brought to his work; with no waste of motion Hamada expresses everything simply, effortlessly. His work has had a strong influence on other Japanese potters as well as on the development of studio pottery in Europe and the United States. See *Mashiko; Leach, Bernard; Chow, Fong; Kawai, K.; Tomimoto, K.* (543)

Hamburg　In German ceramics; one of the earliest German faïence factories was active here for about forty years in the middle of the 17th century. Jugs are typical of their production program; frequently they bear the arms of Hamburg or of its citizens. Extant large jugs have quite a distinctive form. (246)

Hamilton, Sir William　(1730-1803) British diplomat and archaeologist. In 1764 he was appointed envoy to the court of Naples, which post he held until 1800. He was greatly interested in science and art, and was a notable collector. His collection of Greek vases and Etruscan and Roman antiquities which was published in books, 1766-1767, provided decorative designs from the antique and were instrumental in developing the Neo-Classic style, especially in England. See *Classic Revival; Engraved Designs.*

Hammond, Henry F.　English artist-potter; a pupil of William Staite Murray, making slipware as well as stoneware at the Oast

HAMMOND, HENRY F.
1934 ON

Pottery, Farnham, Surrey, 1934–1940, and 1946 onward. See *Murray, W. S.; Leach, B.*

Hampshire Pottery   In American ceramics; started in 1871 in Keene, New Hampshire, and run by Messrs. J. S. Taft and Company. They made ordinary ware and later Victorian majolica with colored glazes. They specialized in souvenir pieces for summer resorts, often using transfer-printed designs, frequently in black.

HAMPSHIRE POTTERY
C. 1871 ON

Han   The Han dynasty of China, 206 B.C. to A.D. 220, was a period of great development of the arts and a time when China was one of the greatest nations. In Chinese ceramics; the pottery of the Han period is represented in collections by mortuary wares that were undoubtedly made especially for burial purposes and are found in tombs. It was a burial custom of the Chinese to place in the tomb models of the things which surrounded them in life to accompany them to the spirit world. Models made of pottery were much used during the Han and T'ang periods. The pottery models included a vast number of objects such as farm buildings, grain towers, farm animals, their dwellings, utensils for cooking, food and drink, images of members of the family and servants. A great deal of the tomb pottery is an unglazed grey ware modeled after the bronze utility vessels. At times unfired designs are painted on the models or designs are stamped or molded. The glazed pottery is usually a red ware with a soft lead glaze which produces a reddish to a yellowish-brown tone. Occasionally the glaze was a green tint from copper oxide. The glaze is often mottled or streaked. Many pieces have a silvery or golden iridescence caused by being buried in the damp ground for so many centuries. Glazed Han ware is frequently decorated with relief appliqués which were stamped in molds and were fired on with a slip. Occasionally incised decoration was combined with the

HANAU
1740-1786

relief appliqués. See *China,* in Far Eastern ceramics; *Hill Jar; Granary Urn.* (81-84)

Hana Mishima   See *Punch'ŏng.*

Hanakago-de   See *Japanese Porcelain Motifs.*

Hanau   In German ceramics; a faïence manufactory was started at Hanau, near Frankfurt-on-Main, in 1611 by Jacobus van de Walle and Daniel Behaghel, from Holland. It was one of the earliest and most active German faïence manufactories. There was no factory mark until 1740; however, a repairer's mark of an incised crescent was often found on jugs. From 1740 to 1786 the mark was an HV and a monogram of crossed A's; the mark Hanau was often used in this period and also until 1806, when the factory closed. The early faïence was similar to Delft. The motifs used in the painted decoration were chiefly borrowed from the Chinese and Dutch until about the second quarter of the 18th century. Although manganese and other high temperature colors were sometimes used, most of the painted decoration was done in blue and often on a distinctive ground strewn with small groups of dots. Included among their productions were decorative pieces of Chinese forms such as double gourd vases, the so-called Enghalskrug or a jug with a narrow neck, lobed and radially ribbed dishes, inkstands, salt-cellars and similar pieces. Much of the Hanau ware both in form and in decoration was similar to that of Frankfurt-on-Main; however, the decoration on the Hanau ware was generally inferior. After 1725 the floral motifs reflected the influence of Meissen and were often done on the familiar Hanau dotted ground. From 1740 the manufactory began to show evidence of decline, and the wares were in the contemporary European taste.

Hancock, Robert   (1730-1771) English engraver for transfer-printing on porcelain.

One of the well-known pioneers in transfer-printing, his prints were first used around 1755. It appears that after his Worcester period in or before 1759 he sold engraved plates to various sources. See *Transfer-Printed Ware*. (374)

Handrest In Chinese writing accessories; the handrest or chên shou, meaning a pillow for the hand, is used by calligraphists as a support for the wrist while writing. The earliest handrest was made of bamboo which was cut in such a manner so that the one side placed on the paper was flat and the other side was slightly convex. Since Chinese script is written downwards the handrest also helped in alignment. Handrests were made of different materials such as porcelain, jade and ivory. See *Writing Equipage*.

Haniwa In Japanese ceramics; the name given to the striking unglazed red clay figures, "clay rings" or "clay circles," because it is believed that they were set in circles about the burial mounds in the Kofun or Tomb Mound period. They evolved from hollow pierced cylinders. As a rule Haniwa are either in the form of cylinders surmounted by men or women in various stations of life, or animal figures. These swiftly worked impressionistic sculptural studies in which the character of the subject is skillfully caught in look and gesture possess a singularly fascinating quality. See *Yayoi*. (128)

Hannong, Balthasar (1703-1753) Succeeded his father, Charles-François Hannong, at the Haguenau faïence manufactory in 1732 which he later sold to his brother Paul-Antoine Hannong in 1737. He returned to Haguenau where he is reputed to have worked as a painter, using the initials BH in monogram. See *Hannong, Charles-François; Strasbourg; Haguenau*.

Hannong, Charles-François Born at Maastricht, Holland, 1669, and died at Strasbourg, 1739. Founder of the Strasbourg

faïence manufactory in 1721, and a second manufactory at Haguenau, where he obtained his clay. The history of Strasbourg faïence is linked to the history of the Hannongs whose manufactory, the only one located here, was handed down from father to son for three generations. The great period of Strasbourg faïence started in 1748 and 1749 with the arrival of German porcelain painters of the celebrated Löwenfinck family. See *Strasbourg; Löwenfinck, A. F. von; Hannong, Paul-Antoine; Hannong, Pierre-Antoine; Hannong, Balthasar; Hannong, Joseph-Adam*.

Hannong, Joseph-Adam (b. 1734, d. early 19th century) Director of the porcelain and faïence manufactories at Frankenthal, 1757-1762, and at Strasbourg, 1762-1781. See *Strasbourg; Hannong, Charles-François*.

Hannong, Paul-Antoine (1700-1760) Potter at Strasbourg and Haguenau where he succeeded his father Charles-François Hannong at Strasbourg in 1730-1732 and at Haguenau in 1739. Also proprietor at Frankenthal, 1753-1759. At the time of his death in 1760 Strasbourg faïence had reached its artistic apogee. See *Strasbourg; Hannong, Charles-François; Hannong, Pierre-Antoine*.

Hannong, Pierre-Antoine (1739-c. 1794) Son of Paul-Antoine Hannong; manager at Strasbourg and Haguenau, 1760-1762; started a faïence manufactory at Haguenau in competition with his family in 1762. After starting several other faïence and porcelain manufactories, he was made a director at Sèvres in 1794.

Hard Paste In ceramics; another term for kaolinic and feldspathic porcelain. See *Porcelain*.

Harder, Charles See *Binns, Charles F.*

Hare's Fur In Chinese ceramics; see *Chien Yao*.

Harker Pottery Company In American

HARKER POTTERY COMPANY

c. 1890

PRESENT

ceramics; this still-existing pottery was established at East Liverpool, Ohio, by Benjamin Harker Sr. in 1840, when the manufacture of yellow and Rockingham wares was begun. From 1847 to 1850 or later, the firm was Harker, Taylor and Company, when they produced such Rockingham pieces as hunting and hound-handle pitchers. From 1885 white granite and semi-porcelain were the staples produced. In 1890 the Harker Pottery Company was incorporated. Among the marks is a bow and arrow with the name Harker or initials of the company, H.P., which was used for a number of years.

THE HATCHET
18TH CENTURY

Harlequin China In ceramics; the name given to a service or set, such as a set of cups, characterized by different colors, deriving its name from Harlequin, the performer in a pantomime who wears a particolored costume. References to harlequin china are found in English literature and the following is quoted from a book published in 1871, "she had six lovely little harlequin cups on a side-shelf in her china closet . . . rose, and brown, and gray, and vermilion, and green, and blue."

Harlingen In Dutch ceramics; faïence was made at Harlingen, in Friesland, Holland, in 1598. The chief productions of the potteries located here in the 17th and 18th centuries were tiles and blue and white dishes in peasant style. Among the several potteries active here at the end of the 17th century that of Theunis Clasen, after changing owners several times, was purchased in 1850 by Jan van Hulst and still is active under this name. See *Friesland.*

HAVILAND, CHARLES FIELD
C. 1870 ON

Hart, Charles See *Doulton, Lambeth and Burslem.*

Hartley, Greens and Company See *Leeds.*

Hasami In Japanese ceramics; an important center in the Nagasaki Prefecture for handcraft pottery. Since it was near Arita, in the Saga Prefecture, pottery-making

spread to Hasami. However, while Arita potters produced very colorful designs, the potters in Hasami produced mostly simple blue and white designs and their wares were limited to Japanese-style tea utensils. See *Japanese Contemporary Pottery; Arita.*

Hasslacher, Benedict   See *Altrohlau.*

Hatchet, The or **Het Bijltje**   In Dutch ceramics; a productive Delft faïence factory active from 1657 to 1802. See *Delft.*

Hauer, Bonaventura Gottlieb (1710-1782) Painter at Meissen from 1724 onward.

Hausmalerei In German ceramics; a German term, literally meaning home painting, given to the independent faïence and porcelain painters of Germany, whose painting included some of the best ceramic art work as well as some of the poorest. At first in the latter part of the 17th century the work was done by a few talented artist-enamelers who sometimes changed from enameling glass and metal to enameling the faïence then being made in Germany. These Hausmalerei also did some of the early enameled decoration on Meissen and Vienna porcelain. The porcelain manufactories soon regarded this practice with disfavor and did everything possible to check the work of these independent artist-enamelers. After the middle of the 18th century it had practically degenerated to hackpainting, although the practice was partially revived during the Empire style. The singular is Hausmaler. (248-250, 333, 334)

Haviland, Charles Field (b. 1842) Son of Robert Haviland (b. 1803) whose younger brother David Haviland (b. 1814) founded the porcelain firm of Haviland and Company at Limoges, France, in 1842. Ch. Field Haviland lived at Limoges from 1853, and until 1858 he worked at Haviland and Company. In the same year he married François Alluaud's granddaughter. (M. Alluaud was perhaps the most important china manufacturer at Limoges at the time, his factory having been started by his father in 1827.) About this time Ch. Field Haviland had his own factory. In 1870 he founded in New York the firm of Ch. Field Haviland, 49 Barclay Street. In 1876 he took over at Limoges the control of the Alluaud manufactory. In New York Ch. Field Haviland was associated with M. Abbott and at Limoges with Gerard, Dufraisseix and Morel. When Ch. Field Haviland retired in 1881 the firm became G D M and later G D A when Morel was replaced by Abbott. The trademark Ch. Field Haviland was used by G D A until 1942 when it was sold to the firm of Robert Haviland who is the grandson of Charles Field Haviland. The forms and patterns of G D A were always used by this firm. See *Haviland, David; Haviland, Théodore; G D A; Haviland, Robert; Haviland, Robert,* grandson of Charles Field Haviland.

Haviland, David (1814-1879) An American, living in 1839 in New York City where he was engaged in the retail china business. In 1842 he started Haviland and Company, a manufactory at Limoges, France, for the manufacture of French porcelain for the American market, which effectively contributed to the commercial success of Limoges. Among the artists working there from time to time were such well-known names as Bracquemond and Dammouse. Shortly after 1890, Théodore Haviland, son of David Haviland, built one of the largest and best-equipped factories at Limoges, and soon became a leader in the making of fine porcelain. At the Paris Exhibition of 1925 an important work was represented from the Théodore Haviland factory with decoration by Jean Dufy, the brother of the painter Raoul Dufy. In 1936 William Haviland, son of Théodore Haviland, started the production of American-made Haviland. At the present time the fourth generation of Havilands is managing the Theodore Haviland porcelain

factories at Limoges and in America. See *Limoges; Saint-Yrieix; Haviland, Charles Field.*

Haviland, Robert (b. 1803) Father of Charles Field Haviland. In 1824 he founded in Augusta, Georgia, the firm of R. B. Haviland and Company. In 1834 he arrived in Europe and in 1853 he was at Limoges. See *Haviland, Charles Field.*

Haviland, Robert Grandson of Charles Field Haviland. In 1924 he started his own porcelain factory, Robert Haviland and Company at Limoges, France. In the course of time the firm became Robert Haviland and Le Tanneur, and then Robert Haviland and C. Parlon which is the name of the firm at the present time. The trademark Ch. Field Haviland, which has been known all over the world for more than one hundred years and which was used by G D A, was purchased by Robert Haviland's firm in 1942. The firm was the recipient of a grand prize at the exhibitions held in Paris, 1925, Le Caire, 1929, Barcelona, 1929, and Paris, 1937. See *Haviland, Charles Field; Haviland, Robert.*

Haviland, Robert and Le Tanneur See *Haviland, Robert,* grandson of Charles Field Haviland; *Haviland, Charles Field.*

Haviland, Robert and Parlon, C. See *Haviland, Charles Field; Haviland, Robert,* grandson of Charles Field Haviland.

Haviland, Théodore (b. 1842) In French ceramics; founder of a still-existing hard paste porcelain factory at Limoges in 1892. See *Haviland, David; Haviland, Charles Field.*

Haviland and Company In French ceramics; a porcelain factory started at Limoges in 1797.

Hawthorn In Chinese ceramics; the name hawthorn or mayflower pattern is often erroneously applied to the prunus or plum blossom. See *Prunus; Ginger Jar.*

HAVILAND, ROBERT
1924 ON

HAVILAND, ROBERT AND
LE TANNEUR
C. 1924-1949

HAVILAND, ROBERT &
C. PARLON
PRESENT

HAVILAND, THEODORE
20TH CENTURY

HAVILAND AND COMPANY
AFTER 1797

Haynes, Bennett and Company See *Chesapeake Pottery.*

Haynes, D. F. and Son See *Chesapeake Pottery.*

Hébert, François See *Rue de la Roquette.*

Hedgehog In German ceramics; the name given to a rare type of stoneware jug dating from the end of the 16th century or perhaps earlier made at Waldenburg in Saxony. It is decorated with applied points of clay giving a prickly surface (hence so-called) with a crudely indicated bearded mask and a foot pierced in an openwork design of triangles. See *Waldenburg; Dreihausen.*

Heel, Johann (1637–1709) A well-known Nuremberg Hausmaler who was a follower of Schaper and precursor of Abraham Helmhack and Wolf Rössler (the monogrammist W. R.). He used the monogram I. H.

HERCULANEUM
C. 1833-1836

Heian A Japanese period; consisting of Jogan or Early Heian period A.D. 794-897 and the Fujiwara or Late Heian period A.D. 897-1185. See *Japanese Periods.*

Heider, Maximilian von German artist-potter working with his three sons at Schongau, Bavaria. Using luster glazes they produced individual work of considerable interest in the latter part of the 19th century.

Heinrich and Company See *Selb.*

Heintze, Johann Georg Painter at Meissen, 1720-1749. One of Johann Gregor Herold's earliest (and perhaps first) apprentices. In the course of a few years he became a painter of considerable ability; one of the most esteemed on Herold's staff. He may have been the creator of the Meissen style of landscape with harbor scenes and small figures.

Helladic In ancient Greek art; the name given to the early art on the Greek mainland to distinguish it from the later historical Hellenic or Greek art;

Early Helladic c.2700-c.2000 B.C.
Middle Helladic c.2000-c.1500 B.C.
Late Helladic c.1500-c.1100 B.C.

To the archaeologist this era is the Bronze Age; its successor is the age of Iron.

Hellot, Jean (1685-1766) Member of the Académie des Sciences; chemist at Vincennes and Sèvres where he supervised the processes of manufacture. He was joined in 1757 by Pierre-Joseph Macquer (1718-1784) who held the position as chief chemist at Sèvres from 1759 to 1783.

Helmet Ewer In French ceramics; a class of faïence ewers or jugs resembling an inverted helmet, resting on a spreading foot, dating from around the early 18th century. The form reproduces that of the silverware which faïence was to replace. The decoration, mainly in blue of elaborate lambrequins or Bérainesque grotesques, derives from the engraved designs from the end of the reign of Louis XIV. Probably the best examples of this class were made at Rouen and Moustiers. See *Silver Forms.* (269)

Helmhack, Abraham (1654–1724) One of the outstanding Nuremberg Hausmalerei painting on faïence, working from about 1675 to 1691. He especially favored biblical subjects in circular panels surrounded by a framework of somewhat naturalistic flowers and leaves painted in distinctive soft enamel colors dominated by pink, light green and blue. The painted decoration was found on the typical faïence jugs of both the Enghalskrug and pear-shaped types.

Hemphill See *Tucker.*

Henderson, D. and J. See *Jersey Porcelain and Earthenware Company; American Pottery Company.*

Henning, Gerhard See *Royal Copenhagen.*

Henri II King of France, 1547-1559. The name is given to one of the three principal styles of ornament of the French Renaissance.

Henri Deux Ware In French ceramics; see *Saint-Porchaire*.

Herculaneum In English ceramics; a manufactory was started near Liverpool on the right bank of the Mersey River by Richard Abbey, in 1793-1794. It was taken over in 1796 by Worthington, Humble and Holland, who called it Herculaneum. They made cream-colored earthenware, much of it being printed in blue or black, and other wares in the Staffordshire style. They also made an unimportant bone porcelain from about 1800 to 1841. The factory ceased to operate also in 1841. The mark was Herculaneum, impressed. Liver bird marks in different forms occurred around 1833–1836.

Herend In Hungarian ceramics; a porcelain manufactory was established by Maurice Fischer (1800-1880) with the patronage of Count Charles Esterházy at Herend, a town in the Bakony forest, about 1839. Its wares, which were usually of very fine quality, were copies of Oriental and 18th century European porcelains, especially those of Vienna, Berlin, Meissen, Sèvres and Capo di Monte. Herend porcelain became well known throughout Europe and at the International Exhibition in London in 1851 Queen Victoria ordered a dinner service which was decorated with a conventional design of flowers and butterflies in the Chinese manner. When the Vienna factory closed in 1864 Emperor Franz Joseph ordered that his favorite models and patterns be given to Herend for future use. In 1867 Fischer was made a member of the Magyar nobility with the title of Fischer of Farkasháza. Fischer retired in 1873 and gave the factory to his five sons who carried on for one year and became bankrupt in 1874. There were several changes in ownership until 1926 when the factory was

revived. Included among the marks is a version of the arms of Hungary.

Herold, Christian Friedrich (1700-1779) Perhaps a relative of Johann Gregor Herold, and one of the most outstanding painters at Meissen, 1725-1777. He was a versatile artist and specialized in chinoiseries, landscapes, and above all, harbor scenes. He was also an enameler at Berlin, probably before his arrival at Meissen.

Herold, Johann Gregor (1696-1775) Art director and to a major extent creator of the renown of the Meissen porcelain manufactory, 1720-1765. Early in his career at Meissen he invented a new range of enamel colors, including ground colors, 1726-1727, and developed and introduced several new kinds of decoration: in particular, chinoiseries and European landscapes perhaps as early as 1722; versions of the Oriental flower or Indianische Blumen about 1725; European landscapes with figures, notably harbor scenes, about 1730; German flowers naturalistically treated or Deutsche Blumen, and birds in more or less naturalistic style shortly after 1737. His influence diminished quickly after around 1745. At the beginning of the Seven Years War he fled to Frankfurt-on-Main, and returned in 1763. (305)

Herrebøe In Norwegian ceramics; a faïence manufactory was founded here in 1757 by Peter Hofnagel. It operated until 1770. No regular factory mark was used; sometimes the full name of the factory or an HB in monogram for Herre Bøe was used; however, much was unmarked. The painted decoration, which was almost always done in monochrome of blue or manganese purple, is a remarkable demonstration of the Rococo style. The motifs included Rococo Chinese subjects and characteristic Rococo motifs such as scrolls, foliage, shells and naturalistic flowers. The manner of painting, the selection of motifs and the twisting and wavy decoration in relief all contributed to give the finished work a

HEREND
C. 1875-1885

HERREBØE
C. 1757 ON

spirit of restlessness and rhythm which was most unusual. Included among their wares were wall fountains and lavabos, trays, tureens, bishop bowls and the customary tablewares.

HERREBOE BISHOP BOWL

Hess, Georg Friedrich (b. 1698) Potter, painter and probably modeler at Fulda, Höchst, 1746-1750, and again at Fulda, 1751-1757. His son Ignaz Hess was active as a painter at Fulda and Höchst, 1748-1758. Notable are his vases decorated with charming landscape panels. Another son, Johann Lorenz Hess, was a painter at Fulda, 1751-1757.

Hewelcke, Nathaniel F. See *Venice.*

Hidasuki In Japanese ceramics; the name, meaning cross-fire, given to a distinctive decorative technique interlacing bright-brownish red or scarlet lines, developed by Bizen potters. It is reputed originally to have been produced when fragments of straw accidentally became imbedded in the glaze and then caught fire in the kiln, causing this part of the surface to be fired at a higher temperature and thus leaving these unusual tapering lines in the glaze. To make Hidasuki ware each piece was partly wrapped in straw, dampened with salt water from the sea and placed in the kiln; in the firing the portions where this adhered became the intersecting lines in the design. Extant examples date from the late 16th century. Among these are a tea ceremony jar, tea caddy and a vessel intended for the storage of rice wine. See *Bizen.*

High Temperature Color or **Grand Feu Color** In ceramics; a term applied to the colors which can stand the heat of the high temperature kiln. See *Grand Feu; Petit Feu; Colors.*

Hikidashi-guro See *Seto Black.*

Hilgers or **Heilgers, Hans** German potter working at Siegburg about 1569 to 1595, who signed his work H.H. His most origi-

HILL JAR
HAN

nal work occurs in bold figure subjects on tall slender tankards of the Schnelle type, about 1570 to 1585. (190, 191)

Hill Jar In Chinese ceramics; a cylindrical lead-glazed pottery tomb vessel of the Han dynasty. It was always surmounted by a cover in the form of a conventionalized mountain with waves at its base; this represented the Taoist Heaven, the Islands of the Blest. The circular body which rested on three feet was usually enriched with a frieze molded in relief depicting exotic birds and animals against a hilly landscape. This so-called Hill Jar is also called a Po Shan Lu. There was also a hill censer of cup shape on a high foot standing in a circular tray, having a hill cover in the form of a conventionalized group of hills. (82)

Hine, Margaret See *Newland, William.*

Hirado In Japanese ceramics; the name given to the porcelain wares made at Mikawachi located in the village of Use in Nagasaki Ken several miles south of Arita in the province of Hizen, and shipped from the port of Hirado. Though the early history of these kilns is obscure they actually had a long history behind them and the earliest Mikawachi porcelain, a kind of rough blue and white, was made by Korean potters. In 1751 the kilns were taken under the patronage of Matsuura, Prince of Hirado, and from that time until 1843, when the patronage of the Matsuura family was withdrawn, made perhaps the finest Japanese porcelain of its time. Hirado owes its fame to these fine white, and blue and white wares which were invariably unmarked. Like the Nabeshima wares, the Hirado wares were normally restricted to the House of Matsuura. The two striking qualities of the perfected Hirado wares were the quality of the body, a fine-grained beautiful white porcelain material, and the texture of the underglaze blue decoration. Landscapes, trees and flowers, and figures were painted in miniature style in an exquisitely delicate, soft and clear, slightly

Chelsea Tureen, Mecklenburg-Strelitz Service, c. 1765. *Collection: The Campbell Museum.*

The "Swan" Service, made for Count Heinrich von Bruehl, modelled by Johann Joachim Kaendler, 1737–40. *Collection: The Honorable Nelson A. Rockefeller, Governor of the State of New York.*

Meissen Garniture, painted by Adam Friedrich von Loewenfinck, "AR" monogram, c. 1730. Meissen Pagodas, c. 1725. *The Antique Company of New York, Inc.; The Antique Porcelain Company.*

The "Swan" Service, made for Count von Bruehl, modelled by Johann Joachim Kaendler, 1737–40. *Collection: The Honorable Nelson A. Rockefeller, Governor of the State of New York.*

Meissen Garniture of Five Vases, "Augustus Rex" mark, c. 1725. *The Antique Company of New York, Inc.; The Antique Porcelain Company.*

Meissen Pair of Groups, one with Harlequin and Columbine, the other with Pantaloon and Columbine, modelled by Johann Joachim Kaendler, c. 1740. *Collection: William A. Coolidge, Esq.*

Meissen Candelabrum from the Royal Service of Augustus III with the Crests of Poland and Saxony, c. 1735. *The Antique Company of New York, Inc.; The Antique Porcelain Company.*

Chelsea, c. 1752–55. "Girl in a Swing" Figural Candlestick, c. 1745. *The Antique Company of New York, Inc.; The Antique Porcelain Company.*

Meissen Centerpiece, c. 1745. *The Antique Company of New York, Inc.; The Antique Porcelain Company.*

Louis XV Sèvres Pair of Pot-Pourri vases, c. 1760. From the Collection of the Marquise de Pompadour. *The Antique Company of New York, Inc.; The Antique Porcelain Company.*

Sèvres Bras-de-Cheminée, modelled by Jean-Claude Duplessis, from the Collection of the Marquise de Pompadour, 1757–61. *The Antique Company of New York, Inc.; The Antique Porcelain Company.*

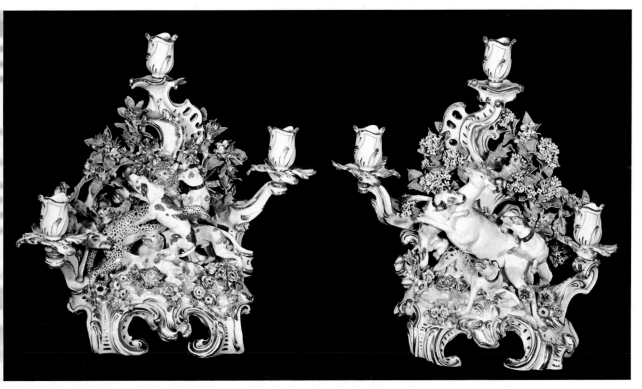

Chelsea Pair of Hunting Candelabra, c. 1760. *The Antique Company of New York, Inc.; The Antique Porcelain Company.*

Sèvres Service, 108 pieces, made for Marquis Sartine, Lieutenant-General of Police, 1773–74.
The Antique Company of New York, Inc.; The Antique Porcelain Company.

violet-toned blue. A deeper blue was employed as a ground color. No doubt the most favored and characteristic motif was that of Karo-Ko (Chinese boys at play). This design of three, four, or seven boys at play under a pine tree was frequently combined with a cord and tassel pattern border. Both the blue enamel and underglaze blue appear on Hirado wares, but the latter is more customary; it is frequently combined with a distinctive dark brown glaze. Relief decoration was much used; figures and objects were modeled in the round. Among the many small delightful products were water droppers, small incense burners, small brush rests and ink palettes. Celadon porcelain of equally perfect quality was made at Mikawachi. The later 19th century Hirado porcelain made for the open market and marked with the name is inferior. They also produced the distasteful egg shell porcelains. See *Japanese Porcelain Motifs; Arita; Blue and White*, in Japanese ceramics; *Hizen*. (150)

Hirasa or **Hirase** In Japanese ceramics; the Hirasa kiln located at Hirasa in Satsuma Province (present Kagoshima Prefecture) was started in 1776 for the manufacture of porcelain by potters brought from Arita. During the first part of the 19th century it was very active, but was soon abandoned. The wares were widely divergent.

Hispano-Moresque In Spanish ceramics; the lustered ware made in Spain by Moorish potters both before and after the termination of Moorish rule in 1492. The term may also be given to some of the non-lustered pottery made at Valencia, Granada and Seville. The origin of lustered pottery is not clear. It was found in the 9th century in Mesopotamia and almost as early in Egypt and Persia. It is generally believed that lustered wares were made in Spain by the end of the 14th century and that Malaga was an early productive center during the 15th century. The motifs for this ware were of Mohammedan inspiration

such as interlacements and a variety of geometrical designs. The development of Spanish lustered pottery subsequently centered around Valencia. The beautiful blue and white and lustered pottery of Valencia reflected a distinctive European quality and motifs such as flowers were increasingly used in the painted decoration. Valencian pottery exerted a strong influence on the ceramic styles of Italy, to which country large quantities were exported after the middle of the 15th century. It is reputed it became known as maiorca or maiolica because of the belief it was brought from Majorca. See *Luster Decoration; Valencia; Islamic Pottery.*

Historical Blue In American ceramics; the name given to transfer-printed Staffordshire pottery depicting American historical events, views of cities and towns, pictures of heroes and other notable persons, patriotic emblems such as the Eagle of the United States Seal, Arms of the States and the like. There was a total of about 800 subjects. The dark blue printed ware of the 1820's was supplanted in the 1830's and 1840's by light colors, that is a light blue or the familiar "pink" Staffordshire, black, sepia and green, and occasionally in two colors. The ware comprised tea services, dinner services, sets of plates, jugs and the like. Also called Old Blue. Of these so-called Anglo-American printed wares a much later class of blue-printed ware was the Commemoratives, made around 1900, of entirely new subjects produced to meet the wide demand for Historical Blue. Also included in the Anglo-American wares, though not fundamentally American, were the picture pot lids showing great English houses, scenes from literature and other similar subjects. See *Pot Lids; Transfer-Printed Wares.* (467, 468)

Historicism The excessive fondness for past styles or Historicism was the great weakness of the 19th century, as it stifles all attempts at original creation. From about 1820 to 1890 all the styles in Western Europe from Gothic to Louis XVI had been copied, transformed and recreated; and, in addition, toward the closing decades of the century, influences had been felt from other parts of the world. It may be said that the 19th century was a repository for the artistic ideas of all countries and all other centuries. In fact, this copying of other styles should be regarded as an independent expression of the age, as a typical stylistic phenomenon belonging to the realm of art history. The last three decades of Victoria's reign offered a melange of revivals, as virtually every historic period was explored for design inspiration. One of the most curious developments of the 1880's and 1890's was an interest in Orientalism of Near Eastern inspiration. Many potters turned to Persia and Islam for inspiration. See *Japanism; Revived Rococo; Louis Philippe; Chenavard, Aimé; Victorian.*

Hittite   See *Near East,* in prehistoric ceramics.

Hizen   In Japanese ceramics; a province famous in the ceramic history of Japan. See *Arita; Kakiemon; Imari; Nabeshima; Hirado.*

Ho or **Ho-Ho**   In Chinese art; a bird subject symbolic of longevity. It is represented as a form of phoenix, a crane, a heron or a stork. See *Chinese Animal Figures.*

Ho Chou   In Chinese ceramics; it is generally accepted that there were four potteries located in the Shansi province as early as the T'ang dynasty and that the one at Ho Chou produced the finest ware. It is assumed that during the Sung dynasty at Ho Chou a grey ware was made that was similar to a type of t'zu chou incised slip ware. It was washed in a white slip and had excellent free-flowing incised designs and was covered in a finely crackled yellow-green glaze.

HOCHST
C. 1763

Hob-in-the-Well   In English ceramics; a nickname at the Chelsea factory for the Imari scene of a boy breaking with a stone the fish bowl into which his companion had fallen. It was inspired by similarly decorated plates from Meissen which tell the same story. (364)

Höchst   In German ceramics; the town of Höchst, near Mayence, is known for its fine porcelain and also for some distinctive faïence made for a short time from around 1746 to 1757. The manufactory was established in 1746 with the support of the Elector of Mayence. From 1778 a rapid decline became evident and it finally closed in 1796. The factory mark for faïence was the mark of a wheel, generally with six spokes, taken from the arms of the Elector of Mayence. The influence of Meissen and Strasbourg was evident in the faïence wares, which were decorated only in enamel colors. It is doubtful if porcelain was made at Höchst before 1750. With the exception of the biscuit figures and reliefs which were not marked, the mark of the wheel was generally used. At first it was in red, some other enamel color or gold, and from about 1762 in underglaze blue. The Electoral Hat or crown over the wheel was probably used only from 1765 to 1774. An impressed or incised wheel was rarely found. Höchst is one of the seven important manufactories making porcelain during the 18th century in Germany. The glaze and the hard paste material were of a fine and distinctive quality. The tablewares reflected the influence of Meissen and Frankenthal and the painted decoration, which was done in delicate and clear enamel colors, was in accordance with the contemporary fashions, the Rococo motifs being later supplanted by the Neo-Classic motifs. The best known figures were made between 1767 and 1779 and were essentially German in style. However, some early figures inspired by Meissen models and in the style later developed at Frankenthal are praiseworthy.

See *Löwenfinck, A. F. von; Melchior, Johann Peter; Damm.* (325, 326)

Hoentschel, Georges French architect and artist-potter; became concerned with pottery in the 1890's and was active around 1900. He launched a kind of advanced Naturalism as a solution to the stylistic problems of the late 19th century. He is identified with the remarkable flowering of artist-pottery in France centered in Paris in the decades around 1900.

Hoffmann, Josef (1870-1955) Austrian architect, graphic artist and designer; played an important role in the founding of the Vienna Secession, 1897. His work on the whole stresses geometric forms. The simple geometric ornament, the square and the circle, which he and the architect Olbrich developed in the late 1890's, was sparingly employed and was subordinate to a strict ornamental order. Hoffmann favored the square motif, Olbrich the circle. The simpler relationships of flat surfaces preferred by Hoffmann showed the way to the next generation's stylistic ideals of undecorated geometric form. Due to the work of Hoffmann, Olbrich and others, Vienna quickly gained recognition as one of the most progressive centers of the new movement in Europe. Hoffmann founded with Moser and others the Wiener Werkstätte in 1903. See *Secession; Wiener Werkstätte; Klimt, Gustav; Vienna; Wiener Keramick.* (499)

Hofman, Vlastislav See *Secession; Artel.*

Hofnagel, Peter (1721-1776) Founder of the Norwegian factory at Herreboe and was a potter there, from 1757 to 1762, and at Østerbro, Copenhagen, from 1763 to 1765.

Hohenberg See *Hutschenreuther, C.M.*

Hohokam In pre-Columbian Southwestern United States ceramics; the Hohokam lived in the Gila and Salt valleys in Arizona in the United States from around the first century A.D. until around 1400; they may have been the ancestors of the modern Pima and Papago. They had many features in common with Mexico, among them the modeling of quantities of pottery figures, usually representing nude women, for religious purposes. Apart from the early ware with a grey background, the most characteristic Hohokam pottery is buff in color with red decoration, which is as typical of them as the black-on-white is of the Anasazi. It was apparently built up of broad bands of clay and finished by the paddle and anvil method, in which the walls of the vessel are thinned and shaped by beating them with a wood paddle against a mushroom-shaped anvil held against the inside. Bowls and jars are the most common forms; later, after 900, tripods, ladles and other forms were introduced. During the so-called Colonial period, 600-900, vessels were often painted with small birds or animals repeated over most of the surface, but occasionally divided into zones and bordered by bands of diagonal hatching. In the following Sedentary period, 900-1200, elaborate geometrical designs were made giving the effect of plaiting or weaving. In the 14th century the Anasazi people, called the Salado, invaded the Hohokam villages and brought with them their striking polychrome type comprising large jars covered with a red slip and painted with bold black and white designs on the outside, and simple bowls which usually have a plain red exterior and black designs on a white ground inside. See *Southwestern United States Pottery; Paddle and Anvil.*

Höhr In German ceramics; an important center during the 16th century for the production of German stoneware with a salt glaze. See *Westerwald.*

Holitsch In Hungarian ceramics; a faïence manufactory was established here in 1743 at the request of Francis of Lorraine, the consort of the Empress Maria Theresa,

HOLITSCH
C. 1745 ON

and was continued as an imperial project until 1827. The wares were principally inspired by French faïence and to a large extent were painted in enamel colors and closely imitated the Strasbourg styles. The wares were generally marked with an H. The motifs were also borrowed from the local peasant majolica. They also made wares in the Italian Castelli style which were painted in high temperature colors. After 1786 they principally made lead-glazed cream-colored and white earthenware in the English style bearing the mark of Holitsch, Holitsh or Holics, impressed. These wares until around 1810 were of admirable quality and workmanship, largely due to painters and workers brought here from the Vienna porcelain manufactory. See *Faïence Fine.*

Hölke, Friedrich and **List, J.G.** See *Pirkenhammer.*

Hollins, Samuel English potter working at Shelton, Staffordshire, during the last quarter of the 18th century. He principally made colored stoneware, such as red and green, in the Wedgwood style. His wares were of good quality. The pottery was carried on by his sons. The marks were S. Hollins and T. & J. Hollins, impressed.

Home Arts and Industries Association In English arts and crafts; particularly interested in rural crafts. Started in 1884, it established village classes in wood-carving, metalwork, weaving, pottery, needlework and the like. See *Arts and Crafts Movement.*

Honan Celadon In Chinese ceramics; see *Celadon.*

Honan Temmoku In Chinese ceramics; a tentative name, which through long usage is now generally given to a large variety of Chinese Sung black and tan glazed wares found in the province of Honan and in practically all the other provinces that made pottery with a dark brown glaze. The

Honan ware consists of vases, jars and bottles as well as tea bowls. The principal colors are black and tan with brown markings. The black glaze is thick and rich and glossy. Occasionally examples are found with a smooth reddish brown glaze with scarcely any black and the surface is more or less mat. Some Honan wares have a body of buff or buff-white, or of white or grey-white which is more or less porcelaneous. The rare oil spot temmoku generally belongs to this group. Occasionally a rare tea bowl is found that is covered with small silver spots which are actually a silver-like reflection caused by the metallic luster of the brown. This is referred to by the Chinese as the oil spot glaze. See *Temmoku; Kian Temmoku; Chien Yao.*

Honduras See *Central American Pottery.*

Honoré, François-Maurice (d. 1855) He and his sons were French porcelain manufacturers in Paris, Petite Rue Saint-Gilles and Boulevard Poissonière, and La Seynie. Until around 1822 Honoré had been in partnership with P. L. Dagoty. See *Petite Rue Saint-Gilles.*

Hookah See *Narghile.*

Hoppenhaupt, Johann Michael II (1709-d. after 1750) and **Johann Christian, the Younger** (d. between 1778 and 1786). See *Rococo; Engraved Designs.*

Hoppesteyn, Jacob and Rochus See *Young Moor's Head, The; Old Moor's Head, The.*

Hori Mishima See *Punch'ŏng*

Horn, Johann Christoph (b. 1698) Painter at Meissen from around 1720 to 1760, specializing in flowers.

Höroldt See *Herold, J.G.*

Horová, Julie Well-known Czechoslovakian artist-potter; trained partly in Paris and Prague; her pottery dating from the 1960's reflects her long, intimate experience with

Slovakian folk ceramics. In this respect her pottery has followed a similar course to the artist-pottery of Hungary, where the influence of folk art has been particularly strong.

Horse In Chinese art; the horse or ma is a favorite animal subject in Chinese ornamental design. The white horse or pai ma is one of the principal animals in Buddhist designs. The eight horses of the Emperor Mu Wang, 10th century B.C., which carried him to the palace of Hsi Wang Mu, the Queen Mother of the West, are associated with Taoist lore. They are generally seen at pasture gamboling about in playful frolic. There is also a dragon horse or lung ma connected with the Emperor Fu Hsi, 2852 B.C. Finally there are the sea horses who move rapidly over the waves in a flying gallop. See *Chinese Animal Figures.*

Horta, Victor (1861-1947) Belgian architect; the country's most important architect at the turn of the century. He was the first to achieve a fully developed mastery of Art Nouveau. It is generally accepted that Horta launched the new style in his house designed for Professor Tassel, No. 12 Rue de Turin in Brussels, completed in 1893. His dynamic and plastic forms were in part of Neo-Baroque inspiration. See *Art Nouveau.*

Høst, Marianne See *Krog, A.*

Hotei In Japanese art; one of the seven Japanese household gods of good fortune. He was the most popular one. See *Pu-Tai Ho-Shang; Chinese Gods.* (138)

Hotel China See *Semi-Porcelain; Ironstone China; Granite Ware.*

Houdon, Jean Antoine (1740–1828) Celebrated French sculptor. See *Sèvres.*

Hound-Handle Pitcher In ceramics; a stoneware pitcher having the handle modeled in the form of a fox, a dog, or a hound. It was originally made in Hungary and at a later date in England. They were first made in America during the second quarter of the 19th century. Of particular interest were those made at Bennington, Vermont. The glaze was a mottled Rockingham glaze of rich brown. The decoration was in relief and each side of the pitcher usually depicted a hunting scene or some animal of the chase. Only one hound design was made at Bennington, and it can easily be recognized by its four identifying features: the duck-billed hound has its head arched up over its paws, with sufficient space between the head and paws to insert a finger; it wears a chain collar with links; its ribs can be distinctly felt; a pointed mold mark down the stomach of the hound can also be felt. The Vance Faïence Company of Tiltonville, Ohio, organized in 1900, acquired the Bennington mold for the hound-handle pitcher. See *Bennington; Rockingham.* (441)

Hozan See *Bunzo, Hozan.*

Hozen, Eiraku or **Hozen, Zengoro** See *Eiraku.*

Hsi Wang Mu In Chinese art; a Taoist subject who was the goddess of long life. She is represented as a graceful slender young girl carrying a flower basket which at times was suspended on a cane over her shoulder. She is often seen under a peach tree in full blossom. See *Chinese Gods.*

Hsia Prehistoric period in Chinese art history, ?1989-?1523 B.C. See *Chinese Dynasties.*

Hsiang In Chinese art; the elephant or hsiang was a favorite animal subject. It was symbolic of strength and power. See *Chinese Animal Figures.*

Hsien Fêng The Hsien Fêng reign of the Ch'ing dynasty in China, 1851-1861. See *Chinese Dynasties.*

Hsien-Hung See *Underglaze Red.*

HOUND-HANDLE PITCHER, BENNINGTON

Hsiu Hua See *Ting Yao*.

Hsüan Tê The Hsuan Tê reign of the Ming dynasty in China; 1426–1435. See *Chinese Dynasties*.

Hsüan T'ung The Hsüan T'ung reign of the Ch'ing dynasty in China, 1909-1912. See *Chinese Dynasties*.

Hu In Chinese art; a Chinese animal figure extensively used in Chinese sculpture, painting and ceramics. It is a tiger, which in China is regarded as the king of all animals. His image served many purposes, such as calling the men to battle and watching over the graves of the dead. See *Chinese Animal Figures*.

Hu-lu P'ing In Chinese ceramics; the Chinese term for a double-gourd vase.

Hu P'i In Chinese ceramics; tiger skin or hu p'i is the name given to a variety of ware which combined several different colored glazes giving a splashed or spotted effect to this ware. This splashed effect was found on T'ang wares and later on K'ang Hsi wares; however, the glazes on the latter were thinner and the finished work was less effective.

Hua Hua See *Ting Yao*.

Huaxtec In pre-Columbian Central American ceramics; a pottery of the Huaxtecs in the Post Classic period, 980-1521, substantiates the belief that the state of Vera Cruz in eastern Mexico always seems to have had a rather independent approach to the making of pottery. This pottery is covered with a white slip enriched with conventional designs heavily painted in black. Noteworthy are the small effigy vases with a human form represented partly in relief and partly in black paint. The general impression of this ware is one of coarseness and unbalanced proportions. In striking contrast is the pottery of the Totonacs, also in the state of Vera Cruz. It is a well made, well fired ware with a sandy buff-colored paste ornamented with geometrical forms in white and brown or black, with the white prevailing. The usual impression is of broad horizontal bands of white interrupted at short intervals and accented by very thin bands of black or brown and varied by pleasant scrolls and curls. The paste recalls that of the Fine Orange ware. Quantities of this Totonac pottery made in the Post Classic period have been found on the Island of Sacrificios in the Gulf of Mexico. See *Central American Pottery*.

Hubble Bubble See *Narghile*.

Huber, Patriz (1878-1902) German architect and designer; one of the original seven artists invited to Mathildenhöhe.

Hubertusberg In German ceramics; a faïence factory started at Hubertusberg, Saxony, in 1770 by the arcanist Johann S. F. Tännich, apparently under the patronage of Count von Lindenau, who in 1774 assumed directorship. The competition of Meissen so hindered the growth of this faïence factory that it was ultimately offered by the Count as a gift to the Elector of Saxony. It came under the direction of Count Marcolini (d. 1814) who devoted its production to cream-colored earthenware in the English style which was flooding the markets of Saxony. It was carried on by the Saxon government from 1814-1835, and finally closed in 1848. Among the customary marks for the period 1815–1835 was K.S.ST.F. (Königliche Sächsische Steingut-Fabrik).

Huet, Christopher (d. 1759) French decorative painter and designer working in the Rococo style. His amusing singeries and delightful chinoiseries are remarkable for their airy and graceful delicacy. He undoubtedly belongs to the great line of decorative designers stemming from the work of Bérain and Audran.

K. S. St F
Hubertusberg

HUBERTUSBERG
1814-1835

Hull In English ceramics; a pottery was established in 1802 at Hull, Yorkshire, England, making earthenware in the Staffordshire style. From 1825 it was operated by William Bell, and the wares were frequently marked after that date with Belle Vue Pottery Hull, surrounding one or two bells.

Humpen In German ceramics; a name especially identified with a variety of German polychrome enameled glass drinking vessels made in the late 16th and 17th century, and also given to a stoneware tankard. The manner of painting and certain details of decoration found on examples of polychrome enameled stoneware humpen strongly indicate that the work was that of a glass painter. Its capacious size suggests that it was to be shared by several convivial drinkers. (197)

Hundred Antiques or **Pa Ku** In Chinese art; the term is applied to a comprehensive group of symbols and symbolical motifs which were often grouped together in panel decoration. A popular set of Pa Ku emblems is the Pa Pao or Eight Precious Objects. See *Chinese Symbols and Emblems.*

Hung Chih The Hung Chih reign of the Ming dynasty in China; 1488-1505. See *Chinese Dynasties.*

Hung Hsi The Hung Hsi reign of the Ming dynasty in China, 1425. See *Chinese Dynasties.*

Hung Wu The Hung Wu reign of the Ming dynasty in China; 1368-1398. See *Chinese Dynasties.*

Hungary See *Austria, Czechoslovakia and Hungary; Gádor, István; Gorka, Géza; Kovács, Margit.*

Hunger, Christoph Conrad Saxon gilder and enameler; one of the most notable porcelain arcanists of the 18th century. His pretension to a knowledge of porcelain manufacture is most likely without foundation, but his work as enameler is not without distinction. He was working at Meissen around 1715 with Böttger. Two years later he escaped to Vienna where the second European hard-paste porcelain factory was started in 1719 under the management of Du Paquier. With him was the Meissen kiln-master Samuel Stölzel. From 1719 to 1724 he was in Venice seemingly to assist the brothers Vezzi as porcelain makers. From that time onward he was at a number of ceramic centers from Rörstrand in Sweden to St. Petersburg in Russia.

Hürten, Charles Ferdinand (b. 1818) Of German origin, he became the leading flower painter at Copelands in 1859. His painted floral designs on porcelain were highly esteemed. He retired from Copelands in 1897. See *Copeland, W. T..*

Hutschenreuther, Carl Magnus (d. 1845) German porcelain painter from Wallendorf. Started a porcelain factory at Hohenberg, Bavaria, in 1814 which was carried on after his death by his widow Johanna Hutschenreuther and his two sons Christian and Lorenz. The latter started his own factory in 1857 at Selb. In 1860 Christian and his brother-in-law Philip Auvera took over the management. In 1877 Albert, the son of Christian, who was responsible for the fine cobalt decoration, became proprietor, and in 1904 the factory became a corporation. In 1909 they bought the porcelain factory of M. Zdekauer (M-Z) in Altrohlau near Carlsbad. In 1918 continuing their program of expansion they bought the porcelain factory of C. Tielsch and Company in Altwasser, Silèsia, and a porcelain factory in Arzberg, Bavaria, started by von Acker in 1839. Also after the First World War they established a factory, Zahnfabrik, in Radeberg near Dresden for hand painting on porcelain. Their losses were heavy in World War II. In 1960 they were operating three factories: Hohenberg, Arzberg and Zahnfabrik.

HUTSCHENREUTHER,
CARL MAGNUS
C. 1820 ON

Their products have always enjoyed a fine reputation. See *Hutschenreuther Company.*

Hutschenreuther, Lorenz (d. 1886) Son of Carl Magnus Hutschenreuther, started a porcelain factory at Selb, Bavaria, in 1857, which became incorporated in 1902. Initiating a program of expansion, the firm bought in 1917 the Paul Müller porcelain factory in Selb; in 1927 the Tirschenreuth porcelain factory at Tirschenreuth, Bavaria, by far their most important acquisition, and in the same year the Brothers Bauscher in Weiden, Oberpfalz, who specialized in hotel wares. At the present time the firm is one of the leading manufacturers in Germany. The fine china dinner services, porcelain figures and works of art produced by Lorenz Hutschenreuther have been designed, sculptured and modeled by leading artists of the past and present. See *Hutschenreuther Company.* (511, 548)

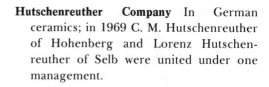

HUTSCHENREUTHER, LORENZ
C. 1860 ON

Hutschenreuther Company In German ceramics; in 1969 C. M. Hutschenreuther of Hohenberg and Lorenz Hutschenreuther of Selb were united under one management.

Hydria In Greek antiquities; a jar or vase for fetching and storing water provided with two small horizontal side handles used to lift the hydria and a larger vertical handle at the rear extending from the mouth to the shoulder of the body which was held while pouring. There are two distinct types. In one variety the neck is set off from the shoulder and the shoulder from the body. In the other variety called a Kalpis, the neck, shoulder and body form a continuous curve.

Hyksos See *Near East,* in prehistoric ceramics.

Hylton Pottery See *North Hylton Pottery.*

HYDRIA

KALPIS HYDRIA

I

Ice Cream Cup In ceramics; little "cre[am] cup" or "jelly pot" made for diffe[rent] kinds of sweets. Provided with a cov[er it] was a favorite 18th century French p[rod]uct. See *Berthevin, Pierre*. (379)

Ice Pail In French ceramics; ice pai[ls for] cooling drinks and foodstuffs were [much] in fashion in the closing decades [of the] 18th century. (359)

Iga In Japanese ceramics; the prod[ucts of] the Iga kilns have much in comm[on with] the Shigaraki kilns. Geographica[lly they] are close together (Iga is near [the town] Ueno in Mie Prefecture) and in [the early] part of their history they were two [parts of] the same administrative unit. Acco[rding to] tradition, in the mid-5th century [Korean] potters settled in the Iga area an[d it is a] certainty that this area was, as the [home of] the Six Old Kilns, a leading center [in the] production of Sue ware. Old Iga u[nder the] aegis of the Tsutsui family, 1585 t[o ...] was mainly made to the taste of the [famous] tea master Furuta Oribe (1544-1[...]). A second period of activity started [...] when the area was under the contro[l of the] Todo family. For several following years the output was chiefly under the tutelage of another tea master, Kobori Enshu (1579-1647). In 1700 Iga was administratively connected to Shigaraki, and from this time onward the two wares are even more difficult to distinguish from each other than in the preceding periods. Essentially it has the same dominantly reddish-brown body with fragments imbedded in it and the same light, transparent and at times almost glasslike glaze of a distinctive watery bluish-green tint where it has been permitted to gather in pools of some thickness. At times there are areas where the firing has oxidized the glaze completely, resulting in a murky grey-black. This is known as

[...] one of the most [...] in Iga ware. Both [...]lns continued their [...]ries. See *Shigaraki*; [...]*iagin*.

[...]urally occurring clay [...]e for the making of [...]*loss*.

[...]eramics; a porcelain [...]ted at Ilmenau, Thur[...] Christian Zacharias [...]y no mark was used [...] initial I was found; its [...] rare. From 1808 the [...]o have been N&R. The [...]re largely in imitation [...] the mark. Of particular [...] white biscuit medallion [...]ue ground in the style of [...] jasper ware, made from [...]808. Contemporary per[...] figures were the favorite [...]e medallions. It is still in

Image, Selwyn [...] (1849-1930) English designer and illustrator. One of the handful of enterprising men who started the Arts and Crafts Movement. See *Century Guild*.

Imari In Japanese ceramics; the village port within eight miles of the porcelain kilns at Arita in the province of Hizen, to which all porcelain was carried and then shipped to Nagasaki from where it was exported to other parts of Japan, China and Europe. Thus the name of the port of shipment became associated with this ware which otherwise would probably have been known as Arita. The term *Imari* not only survives in current use in Europe to describe a certain variety of Arita poly-

ILMENAU

i

1792-1808

1945 ON

chrome porcelain wares decorated for the main part in underglaze blue, iron-red and gold, but has now been usually adopted in Japan to cover all Arita wares with the exception of the Kakiemon, Nabeshima and Hirado wares. Imari wares are made in all three of the known porcelain techniques: underglaze blue and white, polychrome enameled or overglaze decorations in red, blue, green, yellow, purple and other colors; a combination of the two techniques, the *some nishiki* of Japanese collectors. In this ware the body was fired at a relatively high temperature, after which the resulting porcelain decorated with blue under the glaze was enameled or decorated with overglaze colors and fired a second time at a somewhat lower temperature. This complicated technique was learned from Chinese prototypes, especially K'ang Hsi, 1662-1722, and Yung Chêng, 1723-1735. The color schemes of Ko Imari (Old Imari) depend on a combination of underglaze blue, red enamel and gold, to which green, yellow, aubergine, blue and black enamel were added on the more interesting pieces. As the underglaze blue was often blurred in firing it was frequently lavishly covered with gold to hide the imperfections. The most common and characteristic export Imari together with the imitations the Chinese made of it was decorated only in iron-red enamel and underglaze blue with touches of gold. The designs of Nishiki show that they were taken from textiles. There were also the Occidental-inspired designs of Dutch sailing ships and figures of Dutch traders aimed to please the European market. The large Chinese character Ju (Longevity) appeared in so many designs that it became one of the marked features of Imari in Europe. Imari wares were produced chiefly for export. The kilns were operated as an economic enterprise and their products could not compete successfully with the uniformly high standard of excellence demanded from the Nabeshima kilns. Imari, like Japanese porcelain of the 18th

IMARI PLATE

century and earlier, seldom bears a mark of origin. See *Arita; Kakiemon; Blue and White,* in Japanese ceramics; *Japanese Porcelain Motifs; Nabeshima.* (141-143)

Imbe In Japanese ceramics; the name generally given to a very distinctive red, dark brown and slate-blue stoneware first made in the province of Bizen around the end of the 16th century by members of the clan or family of that name. It is clean and hard, at times almost metallic, with a faint gloss of the character of a salt glaze, produced (it is said) by throwing seaweed on the kiln-fire. The wares were made for the tea ceremony.

Imitative Mark Factory marks are sometimes suggested by the older marks of celebrated wares, such as the simulated Chinese marks used by the Elers Brothers of England and Böttger of Dresden. See *False or Fake Mark; Mark,* in ceramics.

Impasto In English ceramics; "impasto" ware was developed at Doultons of Lambeth in the late 1870's. In this technique the painting was carried out, not on the biscuit-fired body, but on the raw clay of the unfired vessel, and thickened color was used, which imparted a slight relief to the pattern. Impasto is closely related to Doultons faïence.

Impasto or **Impasto Italico** In ancient Etruscan ceramics; the name was given to a badly levigated volcanic clay from which were fashioned cinerary urns and other vessels from about the 9th to the 7th century B.C. or later. See *Canopic Jar.*

Imperial Ware In Chinese ceramics; see *Kuan Yao.*

Imperial Yellow In Chinese ceramics; a distinctive clear and strong yellow color that was obtained and mastered during the K'ang Hsi period. The usual tint was a full deep color like the yolk of an egg. It appeared darker when applied on unglazed porcelain and lighter when applied on a white glazed porcelain. Occasionally a delicate engraved design was worked under the yellow glaze. The Imperial ware had five-clawed dragons engraved under the glaze. This Imperial Yellow also included variations such as lemon, mustard and primrose.

Inca In pre-Columbian South American ceramics; the finest pottery of the Incas, who were originally a small tribe which settled in the highland valley at Cuzco about 1200, belongs to the period of their expansion in the 15th century. There are few shapes and these are most characteristic. Conspicuous among them is that now named after the Greek aryballus. Originally a water jar made to be carried on the back by means of a rope passing through the handles and over the nubbin, in the form of a stylized animal head, it is found in all sizes down to miniature. Standard forms also include plates with a bird-head handle and a pair of small projections representing the tail on the opposite side; jars and bowls with broad strap handles; a curious type of ceremonial drinking vessel, called in the Inca language *paccha*, which occasionally incorporates an aryballus. Inca ware is red in color, well made and polished, and is usually painted in polychrome. The prevailing colors are red, white and black; however, yellow and orange are occasionally added, especially in pottery made in the Titicaca area. Usually the decoration is geometrical in character. As the Inca Empire spread, their standard pottery forms were carried far and wide and not only were made in the local wares but also influenced local forms. See *South American Pottery.*

Incense Burning Accessories In Chinese ceramics; the equipage necessary for burning incense was regarded by the Chinese as an indispensable appointment in the library of a scholar. It comprised an incense box or hsiang ho, a vase or p'ing to hold the miniature tools, namely a poker, spade and a pair of tongs, and the urn or shao hsiang lu in which the incense was burned. It appears that the Chinese preferred a vase for the incense tools or chu p'ing which had a short neck and a narrow mouth and was heavy enough around the base to retain its balance. The incense burner was found in numerous forms, such as figures of animals and birds emitting the smoke through their nostrils and mouth or beak. However, the most common form was similar to the bronze tripod cauldron or ting with upright lobes on the rim. These accessories were also made in other fine materials such as lacquer and jade, while the tools were sometimes carved in jade, turquoise, lapis-lazuli or rock crystal.

Incising The decorative method of producing designs by cutting, carving or engraving into a surface of metal, wood, glass or pottery. In ceramics; designs secured by simple incising or cutting into the body itself are practically as old as the art of pottery itself. See *Sgraffiato.*

Indian Flowers or **Indianische Blumen** In ceramics; a kind of floral decoration used on porcelain in which the flowers were treated in a formal or stylized manner. The design was of Oriental origin and was chiefly inspired by the Japanese Kakiemon and the Chinese Famille Verte porcelain. It was introduced 1725-1730 by Herold of Meissen. It was also a popular decoration for the dresses of figures. The Indian flowers were sometimes done in monochrome, especially rose-pink or purple. However, they were more often done in polychrome, with an iron red as the predominating color. Indian flowers were imitated at the majority of porcelain manufactories. Later they were supplanted by the Deutsche Blumen, or flowers realistically treated. See *Deutsche Blumen.*

Indian Tree See *Coalport.*

INCENSE BURNER IN THE FORM OF A RABBIT

Indiana Pottery Company In American ceramics; established by the Staffordshire potter James Clews, with American capital, in 1837, at Troy, Indiana, on the Ohio River, for the manufacture of white ware. The local clay proved unsatisfactory for this finer ware. Clews suspended production in 1838 and returned to England. See *Clews, James and Ralph.*

Indianische Blumen   See *Indian Flowers.*

Indo-China In southeast Asian ceramics; buried wares excavated at Annam and Tonking, now in North Vietnam, dating from the Han dynasty, 206 B.C.-A.D. 220, substantiate early Chinese colonization. During the Sung dynasty, 960-1279, a native light grey stoneware appeared. Varieties of the period include Annamese wares with light celadon glazes applied over a white slip; brown glazes or simple brown painted designs. Popular Annamese forms include bowls, small jars and covered boxes. Under the Ming dynasty, 1368-1644, a rather coarse, almost porcelaneous ware painted in underglaze blue prevailed, and was chiefly derivative from Chinese Ming wares. Colored enamels were also employed. The wares were widely exported in southeast Asia. In the 13th century the Thai people of Siam (Thailand) who filtered slowly south from the Chinese border region had their major capital at Sukhothai. In the ensuing century farther to the north a substantial manufacture of pottery developed at Sawankhalok, much of which was exported throughout southeast Asia. It was a light grey stoneware, most frequently covered with celadon glazes, and showed strong Chinese influence. The varied celadon wares made at Sawankhalok and other lesser kilns during the 14th and early 15th centuries reveal in their forms a typically Siamese combination of strength and elegance. Another type made here, known by custom as Kaliang Ware, has a dark brown glaze and includes many small pieces such as votive figures of humans and animals. When Sawankhalok was abandoned in the mid-15th century the tradition of this pottery region was carried on for a century or more at other kilns in the north. (123-126)

Inglaze Colors painted on the unfired glaze, which becomes incorporated with the colored decoration when fired in the kiln.

Ingman, Elias Magnus (d. 1773) Ennobled Nordenstolpe. Potter at Rörstrand, 1753 onward, which under his general management and with Anders Fahlström as technical manager achieved its greatest success. His son was a potter at the rival faïence factory at Marieberg started in 1758, which he purchased in 1782 and managed until 1788 when it closed.

Intaglio The name given to a type of engraved, carved, or incised figure or design cut into a very hard material. The design or figure is below the surface of the material on which it is cut. It is exactly opposite to cameo or a design in relief. The term is especially applied to incised gems. See *Cameo; Relief Decoration; Jasper Ware.*

International Exhibitions of the Victorian Period International, as well as local and national, exhibitions with their heterogeneous assortment of ancient and modern "art treasures" were a popular form of Victorian entertainment. These exhibitions punctuated the second half of the 19th century and were in effect the tastemakers of that time.

1851   The Great Exhibition, London
1853   Dublin International Exhibition
1853   Exhibition of the Industry of All Nations, New York
1855   Paris Universal Exhibition
1862   London International Exhibition
1865   Dublin International Exhibition
1867   Paris Universal Exhibition
1871- South Kensington International
1874   Exhibitions
1873   Vienna Universal Exhibition
1876   Philadelphia Centennial Exhibition

1878 Paris Universal Exhibition
1887 Manchester, Royal Jubilee Exhibition
1893 Chicago World's Columbian Exhibition
1900 Paris Universal Exhibition
1900 Vienna Secession Exhibition
1901 Glasgow International Exhibition
See *Great Exhibition of the Works of Industry of All Nations, 1851.*

Iran See *Islamic Pottery.*

Ireland Delftware of slight significance was produced at Dublin, Belfast and Limerick, and was succeeded by cream-colored earthenware. It seems no porcelain was produced in Ireland in the 18th century. See *Belleek.*

Iridescence In glass and ceramics; the quality of showing a play of various and changing colors; the interchange and intermingling of colors as seen in mother-of-pearl, soap-bubbles, or a rainbow. In glass; much ancient Roman glass, as well as that of the countries of the Middle East, has a peculiar opalescence or iridescence due to its burial in damp soil. It is caused by a form of surface decay which is the result of being affected by dissolved carbonic acid in the soil moisture. Through the centuries this has drawn the alkali from the glass, leaving the surface in a disintegrated and laminated condition in which the light rays have been broken up in a prismatic manner. If a piece of this variety of ancient glass is immersed in water, which fills the minute spaces in the laminated surface, the iridescent coloring will disappear, but will reappear when it is again dry. In ceramics; the alkaline siliceous glazes on wares of ancient Egypt and the Middle East which have been buried for centuries are frequently found with the same iridescence. This was caused by the same conditions that affected the glass.

Iron See *Colors; Red; Brown; Green.*

Iron Red In Chinese ceramics; a red color made from iron oxide. It was neither an underglaze color nor a glaze color and had to be fired at a low temperature over a glaze. It was used in the so-called Five-Color Ming wares and in the Famille Verte wares of the K'ang Hsi dynasty. The Ming iron red was duller and darker. From the beginning of the Ch'ing dynasty the color became lighter as it became more refined. Iron red used as a monochrome was usually found on wares made after K'ang Hsi.

Ironstone China In English and American ceramics; a dense hard earthenware patented by Charles James Mason in 1813, which he introduced at his pottery at Lane Delph, Staffordshire. It was supposed to have pulverized slag of iron as an ingredient in its clay composition. Essentially it was similar to the stone china introduced by Spode around 1805. Similar white wares of heavy grade were a staple of American potters from around 1860 to 1900. It was given such names as White Granite, Opaque Porcelain and Flint China, the so-called Hotel China and Semi-Porcelain appearing about 1885. The body of ironstone was very suitable for dinner services and other articles which have to withstand heat and hard usage. See *Stone-China; Granite Ware; Semi-Porcelain.*

Isabey, Jean-Baptiste (1767-1855) Painter at Sèvres in the Empire period, working around 1807-1810. One of the painters employed to celebrate Napoleon's victories on porcelain. See *Ceramic Plaques as Furniture Decoration.*

Islamic Pottery In ceramics; Islam followed the ancient techniques of the Near East potters (glazed quartz fritwares, alkaline-glazed pottery, and lead-glazed wares) until about 800 A.D. when a new artistic awareness became apparent stemming from cultural contacts with T'ang China, 618-906. The history of Islamic pottery

ISLAMIC BOTTLE-FORM VASE

may be divided into three principal periods, each of which was initiated by successive waves of Chinese influence; the early period from the 9th to 11th century mirrored the influence of T'ang white porcelains and stonewares; the medieval period, 12th to 14th century, by Sung white wares, the later period, 15th to 19th century by Ming blue and white wares. See *Islamic Pottery, Early; Islamic Pottery, Medieval; Islamic Pottery, Later; Near East,* in prehistoric ceramics; *Roman Pottery; Medieval Near East Pottery.*

Islamic Pottery, Early 9th-11th century. It was in Mesopotamia, at Samarra, the capital of the Persian Abbasids, 836-883, that the earliest Chinese import wares (T'ang white porcelains, stonewares and splashed or mottled wares) and their local imitations were excavated. Chinese wares were also found side by side with local imitations at Susa and Kish. But the local wares soon ceased to be mere imitations. Though the Mesopotamian potters failed to discover the ingredients of true porcelain, they did in time achieve fine glazes which gave to the surface of their wares the semblance of Chinese stoneware and even porcelain. They also developed the technique of luster painting, a very important discovery, which remained their exclusive possession for centuries. Mesopotamian wares may be divided into two principal types: glazed and unglazed. The latter comprised bowls, vases and huge jars made of buff or whitish clay; the decorative motifs which included animals and birds, cable patterns and dots, were molded, incised, stamped on the body or in applied relief. These unglazed wares continued to be made and were found in every part of the Islamic world. The more ambitious glazed wares are of three types, two of which appear as copies of Chinese porcelains and stonewares. First are the lead-glazed splashed or mottled wares covered with a white slip over which was applied a colorless or yellowish transparent lead glaze. The ornament was applied under the glaze in green, yellow or manganese-purple. Often incised (sgraffiato) designs are found under the glaze. Relief decoration also appeared on some of this ware. (This type was known in Egypt many years before Islamic times.) The second variety of glazed wares is the opaque white tin-glazed painted pottery which was painted under the glaze with cobalt-blue, copper-green or antimony-yellow. As a rule the decoration was limited to floral patterns or Kufic inscriptions of which the most popular was the word Baraka (blessing). The third type is that with luster painting, a technique which probably originated in pre-Islamic Egypt where it is found on glass. In the luster process, metallic pigments are painted over a white opaque tin-glaze. The lustrous pigment was fixed on the glaze by a second firing under reducing conditions, after which a thin metallic film appears evenly over the surface producing glittering reflections. The process was applied on wall tiles as well as bowls, ewers and plates. At first the color range was wide but by the beginning of the 10th century it was restricted to brown or yellow monochrome. However, the designs had grown more complex. Around the same era that early Mesopotamian pottery was flourishing, an important variety of slip-painted pottery was being made in Iran and Afghanistan. Perhaps the most delightful among these slip-painted wares are those covered with white slip under transparent colorless glaze generally decorated in brown, tomato-red or manganese-purple. The most popular decoration was the Kufic script. In Egypt, Islamic pottery made notable progress under the Fatimid dynasty, 969-1171. Luster ware, in particular, was favored. Fantastic birds, beasts and human figures were widely popular motifs on Fatimid luster pottery. The Fatimids were overthrown by the Ayyubids who ruled over Egypt and Syria until 1250 when they were conquered by the Mamluks. (154-158)

Islamic Pottery, Later 15th-19th century. In the 15th century pottery making in Iran itself greatly declined. At the present time, knowledge of later Islamic pottery is extremely limited. It appears certain, however, that, under the influence of Chinese Ming porcelain, imitation of blue and white began in Iran, perhaps as early as the late 14th century. The earliest extant examples of Persian underglaze blue and white wares date from the 15th century and, according to contemporary accounts, were made in Meshhed and Kirman where kilns producing blue and white were still active until the 19th century. Blue-and-white first appeared at the same time or perhaps earlier in Syria than in Iran. By the 16th century, pottery making in Syria was overshadowed by the emergence of the Ottoman pottery of Isnik and by the so-called Kubachi wares perhaps originating in northwestern Iran. Until recently Ottoman-Turkish pottery was attributed to the island of Rhodes and Syria and was accordingly identified as Rhodian or Damascus ware. At the present time it is attributed entirely to Isnik (ancient Nicaea) in western Anatolia. Of the three principal types to be made there, the first to be ascribed as Isnik ware covers a period from 1490 to about 1700, which is now subdivided into three groups. Of these three groups Isnik III comprising "Rhodian" dates from 1555 to about 1700. The decline started at Isnik in the first half of the 17th century and by the end of the same century pottery making came to a halt at Isnik as the center of Turkish pottery-making shifted to Kütahya where in the 18th and 19th century the kilns chiefly made wares for Armenian and other Christian settlements in the Ottoman Empire. The material for Kütahya is a fine white earthenware on which are painted designs in blue, bluish-grey, yellow, green, and red on a white ground under a very fine, clear glaze. At the same time a less important pottery center was active in Chanak Kale in the Dardanelles. During the 19th century there were two attempts made in Turkey at Istanbul to make porcelain. Both enterprises were short-lived as they could not compete with the inexpensive European porcelains. The production of fine wares in Iran, apart from blue and white earthenware, was stagnant for about two hundred years until with the rise of a nationalist dynasty, the Safavids, at the beginning of the 16th century, there was a genuine revival in the arts of Iran, when several new pottery types were introduced and traditional techniques, such as luster-painting, were again introduced. Among these later wares are the so-called Kubachi wares, whose name is derived from that of a small town in Daghestan in the Caucasus, where most of the pottery was discovered, and the Gombroon wares, so-called from the port of Gombroon (modern Bender Abbas) in the Persian Gulf from where these wares were shipped to Europe and to the Far East. The actual origin of these two wares is not known. From the 16th to 18th century, a wide variety of monochrome glazed vessels was produced. Though the glazes are in many different colors—ranging from celadon through yellow and brown to vermilion and deep blue—they owe their origin to Chinese celadon. It appears that the chief center of production for these wares was Kirman. The Kajar dynasty came to the throne late in the 18th century. The 19th century eventually witnessed the complete decline of Islamic pottery-making, as the local wares could not compete with the mass-produced European wares. See *Turkish Pottery.* (170-180)

Islamic Pottery, Medieval 12th-14th century. Around the beginning of the 11th century new pottery centers were developed in the northern and northwestern mountainous areas of Iran, in the Caspian borderland, in Azerbaijan and Kurdistan. Pottery wares found in these regions are of particular interest as their decorative patterns executed in sgraffiato (incised) technique reveal strong Sassanian influence. They made three principal types of sgraffiato ware: simple sgraffiato, Champlevé and Aghkand. In the first type the simple designs are incised in the white slip and then glazed. It is also known as Amol ware, as it is attributed to Amol in Mazanderan. The Champlevé ware of the Garrus district of western Iran was long known as Gabri as it was thought to have been associated with Zoroastrian fire-worshippers who were called Gabri. In the Champlevé method large portions of the slip are cut away to form the design, exposing the general darker clay of the body. The glaze is colored in green or brown. These wares are decorated with naïvely drawn figures against a scroll background. In the Aghkand ware the designs are incised in lines into the slip, but, unlike the simple sgraffiato, they serve as dikes, in the same manner as cloisons, preventing the pigment from running over the designs. The colors are green, brown, and yellow. Under the Seljuq Turks from central Asia who overran Iran, Iraq, Syria and Asia Minor and thus built up an important empire in the middle of the 11th century, all the arts flourished. The Seljuq fine wares of Iran, 12th and 13th centuries, may be grouped into seven types. First, the white wares made from a composite paste of powdered quartz and alkaline frit, which were so perfect that the general effect was like porcelain. Occasionally these vessels were so thin that they seem almost translucent, an impression which was further accented by perforating the body with small holes and then filling them with a translucent glaze, creating an impression of glass. These white wares were chiefly decorated with incised floral designs. Seljuq white wares are the outstanding achievement of Persian pottery and their production is attributed to Rayy and Kashan, the two great Persian pottery centers. Next, the wares with colored monochrome glazes, by far the most numerous; a ware with carved decoration and

polychrome glazes known as Laqabi (painted) wares which is essentially a variant of the method used on Aghkand ware, in which the different glazes are applied directly on the ground and are separated by raised or incised lines; a ware with luster-painting; a silhouette-painted ware in which the potter after using a thick black slip carved out the decoration right down to the body and then covered the entire surface with either a turquoise or crackled ivory glaze; an underglaze painted ware with black, blue and turquoise pigment applied with a brush under a deep blue or turquoise blue transparent glaze; and finally an overglaze painted ware, of which there are two types, the so-called Mina'i (enamel) and Lajvardina wares. In the former the enamel colors, generally blue, green, red, black, brown, white and gold are painted over an opaque white or sometimes turquoise glaze and fixed by a second firing at a low temperature; in the latter which derives its name from the cobalt blue glaze which is applied as the ground the range of colors is restricted to black, red and white with the addition of leaf-gilding. Mina'i pottery is also decorated with a greater variety of motifs including human figures and inscriptions which are not found on Lajvardina wares. Mina'i pottery is closely related to miniature painting; some pieces display court scenes, scenes from Persian legends and hunting scenes. The best pieces were made at Rayy before the Mongols sacked the city in 1224; Kashan and Sava also contributed considerably to the Mina'i technique. The Seljuq pottery of Mesopotamia centered around Raqqa and Rusafa in the north. The two principal types produced here were underglaze-painted wares and luster-painted wares. The Seljuq pottery in Asia Minor revealed the same types of wares found in Iran and Mesopotamia. During the 13th and 14th century the production of Persian pottery, in particular the fine wares of Kashan, continued after the Mongol invasion. The Mamluks who checked and defeated the Mongols and reigned over Syria and Egypt from the middle of the 13th to the beginning of the 16th century, gave refuge to potters from Iran and Mesopotamia. It appears these refugee potters started kilns at Damascus, Cairo and many other places where they introduced some of their traditional techniques. Until around 1400 the most common Mamluk ware in Syria and Egypt was that painted in underglaze blue and black. Large and heavy bowls, jars and albarelli were decorated in this manner and were exported in great numbers to Europe, and were used for storing Oriental spices and medicine. The decoration was chiefly arranged in panels, and in Egypt, in accordance with Mamluk tradition, circular medallions enclosed heraldic devices. (159-169)

Isnik   See *Islamic Pottery, Later.*

Istoriato   In Italian ceramics; an Italian term, literally meaning storied, given to a style of pictorial painting on Italian majolica, generally occupying the entire surface of a plate or dish. The figure subjects were depicted against distant landscapes, with buildings and arcades in the foreground. This style of painting was developed and perfected by Nicola Pellipario, probably the greatest of all majolica painters. Istoriato painting is especially associated with the majolica made at Urbino where Nicola was working after 1528. However, he was working around 1515 at Castel Durante where he painted pieces in the istoriato manner. This style of painting, the stile bello or beautiful style, which matured and developed at Faenza and in the Duchy of Urbino during the first half of the 16th century, was adopted at most of the Italian majolica centers of the middle and latter part of the 16th century. Istoriato was also done at Lyons, France. (232, 238)

Italian Comedy Subjects   The name *commedia dell'arte* is given to the medieval Italian Comedy in which the main story or plot was well defined although the dialogue was impromptu and improvised by the actors. The characters of the Italian Comedy, wearing traditional costumes, were clearly identified as well as their plots and counterplots. The comedy includes such familiar names as Columbine, Harlequin, Cynthio, Pantalone and Isabella. The Italian Comedy became popular in France and other European countries around 1715 and its characters were portrayed in an endless series of charming porcelain figures. Superb modeling of these figures was produced at Nymphenburg, Höchst, Fürstenberg and Fulda. Perhaps the most notable series were those modeled by Bustelli at Nymphenburg. The influence of the Italian Comedy is reflected throughout European art and literature. The Italian Comedy was the inspiration for many designs by Antoine Watteau who introduced such characters as Gilles and the Troubadour from the contemporary French interpretation. See *Watteau, Antoine; Louis XV; Engraved Designs.* (315, 317, 321, 322, 331, 339)

Italian Majolica   In ceramics; the earliest decorated Italian pottery of any artistic interest was made toward the end of the 14th century. It was painted in copper green and manganese purple on a rather imperfect white ground most frequently obtained by the use of oxide of tin. This class of green and purple decorated ware, formerly known as mezzo-majolica, followed a widespread Mediterranean fashion, and the style is best exemplified in the superb 14th and 15th century Spanish wares of Paterna (Valencia) and Teruel. However, in forms and to a great extent in design, the Italian wares revealed the influence of native medieval traditions. The principal centers making this green and purple decorated majolica were Orvieto, perhaps the earliest, Siena and Florence in Tuscany, Faenza, Rome, Padua and others. Throughout the 15th century the green

PANTALONE,
NYMPHENBURG

and purple and the blue and white luster wares of Valencia, Spain, were very fashionable in Italy and influenced the work of the three great 15th century majolica centers, namely Tuscany, Faenza and Deruta. By the 16th century the vogue for majolica was firmly established. The art of majolica attained its acme of perfection between 1505 and 1525. The majolica was painted by a number of great individual artists whose paintings compare in beauty with the contemporary Italian masterpieces in oils. The fashionable and successive decorative styles in majolica were to a great extent employed at all the majolica manufactories. Each manufactory generally had its favorite type of decoration. The secret of metallic luster pigments which gave added beauty to the color was in the possession of several of the factories. From about 1500 onward a golden or a mother-of-pearl and a ruby luster were being used at Deruta; the ruby luster seems to have disappeared from Deruta about 1515 and was found at Gubbio where it is associated with the work of Maestro Giorgio Andreoli. Included among the leading 16th century majolica centers were Faenza, Castel Durante, Caffaggiolo, Deruta, Gubbio, Urbino and Venice. During the 17th and 18th centuries the majolica tradition was more or less maintained, particularly at Castelli. Included among the typical decorative majolica pieces were the bacili or large dishes, scudelle or dishes on a low foot, scannellati or gadrooned dishes modeled from examples in metal, albarelli or the more or less cylindrical pharmacy jars, spouted drug vases and confectionery vases and broth bowls. In addition many pieces were made for daily use, such as jugs and dishes. See *Majolica; Faïence: Istoriato; Orvieto; Faenza; Deruta; Castel Durante; Rome; Cantagalli; Caffaggiolo; Gubbio; Urbino; Venice; Padua; Mezza Majolica; Coperta.* (223-234)

Iusupov, Prince Nikolai Borisovich (1751-1831) Russian aristocrat and connoisseur. In 1792 he replaced Prince Viazemskii as director-general of the Imperial Porcelain manufactory near St. Petersburg where he remained until 1802. In 1814 he started a porcelain manufactory on his estate Arkhangel'skoe. The porcelains produced at the Iusupov manufactory clearly show the influence of aristocratic taste. They were not offered for sale but served as gifts to members of the Imperial family and to friends and members of the Iusupov family. Operations ceased when Prince Iusupov died. As a rule the wares bear the name Arkhangel'skoe or the French form, Archangelski. See *Russia.*

Архангельское

1827 Года.

IUSUPOV, PRINCE NIKOLAI
C. 1814 ON

J

Jackfield In English ceramics; a red earthenware with a black glaze was made at a pottery in Jackfield, Shropshire, managed by Maurice Thursfield from around 1750 to 1775. Jacobite emblems, mottoes and inscriptions were characteristic decoration, and were done in oil-gilding and unfired painting. It is occasionally referred to as shining black because of the typical brilliant gloss of its finish. A similar black ware, sometimes with applied reliefs, was made in Staffordshire before the Jackfield pottery was started. (386, 387)

Jaderholm-Snellman, Greta-Lisa See *Arabia.*

Jakobakrug or **Jakobakanne** In German ceramics; the name given to a new shape appearing in Siegburg stonewares from about 1400 onward. It is a tall jug of marked slenderness with a ring handle. It is seen as a wine jug next to drinking vessels in contemporary altar paintings of the Last Supper. See *Rhenish Stonewares.* (186)

Janák, Pavel See *Secession; Artel.*

Janson (or **Jansen**), **Jacob** An Antwerp potter who migrated to Norwich around 1567 and went on to London around 1570; started the Aldgate pottery in 1571. He and Jasper Andries, also an Antwerp potter, are recorded as having come to London from Norwich and settled at Aldgate. See *Antwerp; Lambeth.*

Japanese Contemporary Pottery Before the Meiji Restoration, 1868, Japanese pottery was made only for home consumption according to traditional Eastern methods of production. After the Restoration, manufacturers started to make export pottery to fill demands from the Western countries. German teachers contributed significantly to the introduction of Western methods of ceramics to Japan. In present-day Japan the two kinds of industry, traditional handcraft pottery (bowls, dishes, tea utensils and the like) and export industrialized pottery (Western style dinnerware) are proceeding each in its own way, without being mixed. Many pieces of Japanese handcrafted pottery are functional for the Western as well as for the Japanese manner of living and are suitable for quantity commercial production. Among the most important centers for handcrafted pottery are Seto, Tokoname, Mino, Yokkaichi, Shigaraki, Mashiko, Kyoto, Kutani, Tobe, Arita and Hasami. Export pottery is common to a greater or lesser extent to all these areas but it is not their specialty, with the exception of Yokkaichi. Most of the industrialized Western style dinnerware is made in or around Nagoya. Japanese pottery is produced mostly in the western half of Japan; Mashiko is one of the exceptions. See *Tokoname; Mino; Yokkaichi; Shigaraki; Mashiko; Kasaoka; Kyoto; Kutani; Tobe; Arita; Hasami; Noritake.*

Japanese Marks In Japanese ceramics; Japanese marks are very numerous and misleading. In addition to those formed on the same lines as the Chinese and often copied from them, a legion of artists' signatures and other names and words are found in the form of impressed seals. Such signatures are no more to be taken at their face value than Chinese reign names; but even in authentic examples they are difficult to interpret, because the potter may have used in addition to his family name one or more "art-names" comparable with the hall-names on Chinese porcelain, granted to him by a patron or adopted by him on starting a new workshop or a similar occasion. An artist-potter usually bequeathed the privilege of using his mark to his "sons" or pupils; for this reason the

JAPANESE PORCELAIN MARK
FUKU

identical mark may be found on the pottery made by several generations who worked in the same style. Place names and the names of princely patrons were also used and augment the already existing confusion. Japanese porcelain of the 18th century and earlier seldom bears a mark of origin, though Chinese marks, particularly Ming reign-names, were occasionally added. Cyclical dates, like the Chinese, were used at times, as well as the Japanese period-names. Most of the fine Kutani, Kakiemon, Nabeshima and Hirado porcelains bear no mark at all. Various forms of the word *fuku* (happiness) were typically added to early Kutani, but the full six, eight or ten character Kutani mark, including the name of a hall or potter, appears only on 19th century porcelain. In fact, practically all marks beginning Dai Nippon (Great Japan) indicate 19th or 20th century manufacture. Such marks, and some earlier ones, end with the same character as the Chinese Chih and Tsao which in Japanese are read Sei or Tsukuro (or 20). In brief, marks are an unprofitable study for one interested in the art of the Japanese potter; attention to them should follow and not precede a study of the shapes, designs, and physical characteristics of the ware.

Japanese Periods A chronology of Japanese art history. The dynastic and historical periods of Japan are referred to in the designation of their art in the same manner as the Chinese subjects. It should be noted that alternate names for some of the major periods are often used and that the precise dates for the major periods are much in dispute.

Archaeological eras	4000 BC-AD 538
Jomon	4000BC-c. 200 BC
Yayoi	c. 200 BC-c. AD 250
Kofun	c. AD 250-c. AD 538
Asuka	538-645
Nara or Tempyo	645-794
Heian	794-1185
Jogan (Early Heian)	794-897
Fujiwara (Late Heian)	897-1185
Kamakura	1185-1333
Muromachi or Ashikaga	1333-1573
Momoyama	1573-1615
Edo or Tokugawa	1615-1868
Modern	1868 onward
Meiji	1868
Taisho	1912
Showa	1926

See *Muromachi; Momoyama; Edo.*

Japanese Porcelain Motifs The designs for Imari decorated with underglaze blue and polychrome enamel show that they were taken from textiles. Perhaps the most common is the Hanakago-de or flower basket pattern, comprising a wicker basket with a high loop handle holding a profusion of flowers. The favorite pattern was the formalized treatment of the Kiku (chrysanthemum) which is featured as a conventionalized flower head of sixteen petals around a central calyx within a circle as one of the Imperial crests, the Kikumon. Later, the starlike treatment of this flower was widely popular on English Worcester. The Kirimon, also an Imperial crest, derived from the flower of the Kiri tree, is in the form of three spikes of blossom towering above a trefoil leaf. The chrysanthemum, frequently almost indistinguishable from the peony, and the plum were treated realistically and conventionally in many various ways, and were often presented in high relief. Included among other popular motifs were Shochikubai (pine, bamboo and plum); the five fabulous creatures: Ryu (dragon), Kirin (Japanese unicorn), Shihi (Buddhist lion), Minogame (water tortoise with the long hairy tail), Hoho (a form of phoenix). Though the original conception of these motifs is Chinese, they were completely Japanized. The tiger, crane and hare were other familiar motifs. The former was generally associated with bamboo and the banded hedge. This banded hedge along with the plum tree and birds is one of the most common motifs on Kakiemon wares which also depict in a highly creative manner flowering poppies in their designs. There is also the millet and quail pattern, and a wealth of designs borrowed from the Tosa and Kano schools of painting, from lacquer, embroidery and metal work. Ko-Kutani wares especially made use of elaborate combinations of lattice work, scale and diaper patterns. Less common are landscapes and human figures. Perhaps in some instances the flower and bud sprays and even landscapes appearing on Ko-Kutani wares derived from the work of the celebrated Kano artist Morikage. Nabeshima wares have their own intricate brocade and realistic flower designs, while Hirado wares favor boys playing under pine trees. In Japanese ceramic art as in their other arts there is the same sense of position and the use of unfilled spaces, the same command of asymmetric balance in the designs, and the same vitality in the brushwork. See *Arita; Hirado; Nabeshima; Imari; Kakiemon; Kutani; Shonsui.*

Japanese Tea Ceremony   See *Cha-no-yu.*

Japanism   In ceramics; European countries first became cognizant of the aesthetic effect of Japanese art in 1862 which marks the first time Japan participated in an International Exhibition, held that year in London. Within about a year the Japanese mania began and in the ensuing decade Japanese art had affected virtually all the arts of decoration. In the art of Japan which delights in all the subtleties of line, all the brilliant caprices of color and disdains symmetry, contemporary designers saw a chance to break the bonds of Historicism—the great weakness of the Victorian period—which could not fail to provoke weariness and revolt. They found in Japan a new unexplored world, an uncorrupted culture based on a different structure of thought. This revelation was to have far-reaching consequences. Japanese influence can now be seen in retrospect not only in the development of Art Nouveau

and the Modern styles of porcelain and pottery but also in the development of modern artist-pottery. In brief it implied an entire new approach to the problems of ceramics. It meant the freeing of decoration from border patterns and symmetrically arranged motifs; it meant freedom to leave a ground surface undecorated; it meant eventually the freeing of form from many conventions of classical origin. It became in effect the vehicle of revolt against the deeply ingrained classicism of European tradition. Designers such as Bracquemond and Dammouse of Sèvres and Krog of Copenhagen, whose work revealed important early manifestations of this new Japanese spirit, clearly illustrate in their interpretation that they looked to Japan for lessons but not for models. See *Bracquemond, F.; Dammouse, A.; Krog, A.; Glaze,* in modern Western ceramics.

Jaspée Ware   See *Palissy, B.*

Jasper Dip   See *Jasper Ware.*

Jasper Ware   In English ceramics; the name was given by Wedgwood to a hard, fine-grained stoneware which he perfected in 1775. It was obtained by adding sulphate of barium to a semi-porcelain clay. It was slightly translucent and pure white when fired. By mixing metallic oxides with the white body various colored bodies were obtained. A pale blue body is undoubtedly the best known. Later, after 1785, the color was applied only in surface washes and this ware is known as jasper dip. Included among the colors finally used were the familiar light blue or lavender, sage-green, olive green, pink-lilac, yellow and an intense black. Wedgwood's blue jasper ware with white reliefs was extensively imitated in other materials in England and on the Continent. A great diversity of articles was made from jasper ware, such as cameos and intaglios for seals, portrait-reliefs, beads and buttons, as well as vases, ewers, candlesticks and similar articles. Plaques of jasper ware were used by the cabinet-makers for the decoration of furniture. Jasper ware, one of the great achievements of the 18th century, was still being made in the 19th century. The design of this ware with its separately molded and applied-by-hand relief decoration was always predominantly of classical derivation. Perhaps the outstanding triumph in jasper was the copy of the Portland Vase. (423-425)

Jaune Jonquille In French ceramics; a yellow ground color prepared by Jean Hellot and appearing on Sèvres in 1753. See *Sèvres; Colored grounds.*

Jeanneney, Paul French artist-potter; identified with the notable flowering of artist-pottery in France centered in Paris in the decades around 1900. His stoneware is most reminiscent of the Far East.

Jersey City Pottery See *American Pottery Company.*

Jersey Porcelain and Earthenware Company In American ceramics; started at Jersey City, New Jersey, in 1825 for the manufacture of china and earthenwares. In 1826 at the annual exhibition of the Franklin Institute, Philadelphia, they were awarded a silver medal for their exhibit "the best china from American materials." It seems that the manufacture of porcelain was only carried on for about three years. The works were purchased by David Henderson and his brother about 1829. Their production comprised stone china, yellow ware and Rockingham bearing the mark D. & J. Henderson, Jersey City. In 1833 David Henderson organized the American Pottery Manufacturing Company "for the purpose of manufacturing the various kinds of pottery at the works already erected." See *American Pottery Company.*

Jesuit Ware In Chinese ceramics; the term is generally applied to a kind of Chinese porcelain whose decoration was thought to have been influenced by the Jesuit mis-

JERSEY PORCELAIN & EARTHENWARE CO. 1829 ON

JESUIT WARE BOWL

sionaries who were stationed at Ching-tê-Chên, from the early part of the 18th century until about 1745 when they were expelled. A number of decorations were taken from prints, books, and pictures which the Jesuits brought with them and include various religious subjects such as the Nativity, Baptism, Crucifixion, Resurrection, Rebecca at the Well, and others; allegorical and mythological subjects such as the Judgment of Paris and Juno and the Peacock. A number of the scenes were taken from well-known paintings by artists such as Lancret and Watteau. They are commonly executed en grisaille which may be touched with gold. There are also some fine examples in colored enamels, and some of the early pieces are entirely either in rust red and gold, or underglaze blue. Religious subjects in color are considered very rare. Most Jesuit type decoration dates from around 1730 to 1750. See *Chinese Lowestoft.*

Jever In German ceramics; a faïence factory was active at Jever, Oldenburg, from 1760 to 1776. It was founded by the arcanist Johann Friedrich Samuel Tännich who departed for Kiel in 1763. The best Jever faïence was made during those three years. It included tureens with rich plastic decoration and others in the form of swans, some openwork baskets and figures. The painting was in high-temperature colors without red. The marks included the name of the town, occasionally abbreviated.

Jeweled Decoration In French ceramics; the term is generally reserved for the unusual Sèvres decoration used from around 1781 and later. In this process drops of colored enamel were applied and fused over gold or silver. Although this process is supposed to have been introduced at Sèvres a similar process was in use earlier in the 18th century especially at the Saint-Cloud manufactory.

Jiggering The method of making plates by placing clay on a revolving mold or jigger.

A bat of clay is flattened on a revolving disc or spreader. Next, this clay is placed on a plaster mold which forms the front of the plate. As the mold revolves on the jigger the profile is brought down to scrape away the excess clay, leaving the exact thickness between the profile and mold for making the plate and at the same time forming back of the plate. See *Jollying*.

Jogan The name given to the early Heian period in Japan, A.D. 794-897. See *Japanese Periods*.

Jokei See *Raku*.

Jollying The method of making cups; the same as jiggering except in the reverse. The profile produces the inside of the cup and the mold forms the outside. See *Jiggering*.

Jomon The earliest prehistoric earthenwares found in Japan are called Jomon. The term, which means cord impressions, is a modern one, dating from the end of the 19th century, when the Japanese first became interested in modern archaeology. Jomon ware was made in vast quantities throughout Japan during the Japanese Neolithic Age, over a period of time usually estimated around two and three thousand years. Therefore it is scarcely surprising that the ware is found in a vast variety of styles and types. Viewed from the art of the potter, the interest centers in features that the Jomon wares have in common rather than in differences distinguishing the various types, and in the legacy of these wares to ensuing ages of Japanese ceramic art. Probably the most striking common feature is the clay, which is an almost unwashed clay, with the result that pieces of organic matter, pebbles and even shell fragments can be easily seen in many Jomon specimens. In a general sense the Japanese potter has been at his best through the ensuing centuries, when, as in this Jomon ware, he gave his material

full recognition and did not attempt entirely to transform it, to sacrifice it for an artistic creation. Briefly, the conflict was between medium and method, a problem which has never been divorced from ceramic art. In the Jomon wares, particularly the later more sophisticated decorated pieces, the contrast between the more or less unrefined clay and the elaborate handwork is probably their most delightful feature. Another outstanding characteristic is the fact that these vessels were all made by various hand-coiling methods rather than wheel thrown. The most striking Jomon shape, the kame or urn, owes its development to a technique through which a kneaded coil of clay was gradually and progressively built up to make the typical long, tapering cone shape of these vessels. After the lines between the layers had been smoothed away the surface was decorated with a wide variety of designs. These were sometimes impressed into the clay with cords, hence the name, but sharp instruments such as shells, stick ends, and a variety of spatula-like tools also seem to have been used. As the technique developed sureness, the Kame's sharp, pointlike base, practical for burying in the embers of a fire but in other aspects impractical, became flatter and flatter until finally it developed into a proper base. To make this, a more sophisticated technique must have been evolved in which a base piece was made first as a foundation on which to build up the coils forming the sides. In some examples the potter made no attempt to smooth away the evidence of the coiling technique by which such pre-wheel vessels were constructed; not only were the outer surfaces left untouched, but at times decoration was added to emphasize the coiled construction. Notable are the vessels with elaborate flaring tops and fancifully decorated rims. Among the interesting shapes are the spouted vessels or ewers probably used for holding and dispensing drinking water, suggesting they were less porous than most of the Jomon wares. See *Yayoi; Japanese Periods.* (127)

Jones, George Staffordshire potter working at Mintons until he started his own Trent Pottery in Stoke, 1861-1907. From 1873 "& Sons" was added to "George Jones." The Crescent Pottery, also in Stoke and owned by Jones, was active 1907-1957. In the early years Jones was much concerned with producing colorful majolica type earthenwares at a popular level. Porcelain was introduced in 1872. Pâte-sur-pâte decorated earthenware was also produced by this enterprising company from 1876-1886. Most of the wares are marked with the initials G.J. in monogram. See *Majolica; Coalport.*

JONES, GEORGE
C. 1861-1873

Jones, Josiah English-born modeler working in the Staffordshire region before settling in America where he achieved a fine reputation. He was the brother-in-law of Charles Cartlidge, who established a pottery at Greenpoint, Brooklyn, N.Y., and it is believed that he was responsible for making molds for much of the work. See *Union Porcelain Works; Cartlidge, Charles.*

Jones, Owen (d. 1874) English designer, writer and architect; published with Sir Matthew Digby Wyatt the monumental GRAMMAR OF ORNAMENT, 1856.

HEAD OF A JU-I SCEPTER

Joseph Jug In German ceramics; the name given to the well-known salt-glazed stoneware jugs made at Raeren. They were decorated with reliefs having as their subjects Joseph and his brothers. The original Joseph jug was made in 1587 by Jan Emens and was decorated with an arcaded frieze of reliefs depicting the story of Joseph.

Jouve, Georges French artist-potter; he may be regarded as belonging to that group of French artist-potters who in the years following the Second World War have tended to use their medium (stoneware and earthenware especially with a tin glaze) for figure making and for other purely decora-

tive purposes. In brief, his work was more that of a ceramic sculptor than of a potter of vessels.

Ju-i In Chinese art; the ju-i scepter with its fungus-shaped head and curved stem so often carried by divinities. Its meaning, ju-i (as you wish), suggested a power about fulfillment of wishes, and it is also an attribute of the god of longevity. The form of the ju-i head, which resembles somewhat the scroll of a Greek Ionic capital, is frequently represented in cloud scrolls. See *Ling Chih.* (105, 150)

Ju Ware In Chinese ceramics; probably the rarest of all Sung wares produced for a few years only to the order of the Northern Court at Ju Chou (modern Lin-ju Hsien) in Honan province in the early 12th century. It has a carefully prepared yellowish-buff porcelaneous stoneware body and a smooth dense glaze, sometimes but not always crackled, of light greenish-blue. Probably less than thirty examples of this famous Imperial ware survive outside of China. An inferior ware of the Ju type was made at T'ang Chou and T'êng Chou in Honan and at Yao Chou in Shensi. It is also called Ju Chou ware. See *Sung; Ying Ch'ing.* (92)

Juan Ts'ai In Chinese ceramics; the Chinese name given to soft enamels or the Famille Rose or Rose Family. See *Famille Rose.*

Jüchtzer, Christoph Gottfried (1752-1812) He was successively repairer, modeler and art director at Meissen, 1769-1812.

Jug A deep vessel for containing liquids, varying in shape and size, commonly having a cylindrical or swelling body or a body tapering toward the top, provided with a handle on one side and often having a pouring spout. Frequently the term is preceded by a descriptive word explaining its purpose or kind, such as wine, cream, milk, water or brown. The term is given in various localities with different extensions and limitations to vessels generally made of pottery, glass, metal and occasionally of leather and wood. Sometimes the jug, as in a hot water jug, is provided with a lid. See *Ewer; Toby Jug.*

Jugend See *Jugendstil.*

Jugendstil or **Jugend Style** A name Art Nouveau quickly acquired in Germany. It derived from JUGEND, a ribald and lively periodical first published in Munich in 1896, in which Otto Eckmann charmed his readers with Art Nouveau vignettes. The title, according to the editors, meant *youth.* The Jugend style had two principal centers, one in Munich and a second somewhat later at Mathildenhöhe in Darmstadt. See *Munich School; Mathildenhöhe; Art Nouveau; Maison de l'Art Nouveau; Deutsche Werkstätten.*

Jugtown In American ceramics; the earliest recorded pottery in North Carolina was that started by Peter Craven, a potter from Staffordshire, in the Steeds section of Moore County in 1750. There are no further records until 1861 when Doris Craven, the fourth in the Craven line, was still operating a little farm pottery near Steeds. In the meanwhile a Craven daughter married a Fox and later their son James Fox around the time of the Civil War with other members of his family joined the Cravens in the Jugtown pottery. Although Jugtown is nowhere and never existed the name grew after the Civil War from the output of "little brown" jugs made for the whiskey industry in North Carolina. Jugtown was a word of derision; any community making jugs was a jugtown. The adoption of Prohibition dealt a crippling blow to Jugtown. In 1917 the Craven family was still making some wares when the Carolinians Jacques and Juliana Busbee, both interested in the field of folk art, started a search for old potters who lived in the back country among the pines, still making traditional pottery. Around 1921 in order to have a greater control over the design and production of the pottery, Mr. Busbee decided to set up a kiln out in the pine woods about fifteen miles from Steeds and hire potters to work for him. It was the first pottery to bear the name Jugtown. The efforts of the Busbees to revive the old pottery industry have met with considerable success.

Jukushi A Japanese term meaning ripe persimmon, given to a famous Raku tea bowl made by Donyu. See *Raku.*

JU WARE EWER

K

K P M Koenigliche (Royal) Porzellan Manufactur; Krister Porzellan Manufactur. See *Berlin; Waldenburg.*

Kaendler, Johann Joachim (1706-1775) Modeler and sculptor. Modeler at Meissen, 1731-1775, master modeler from 1733 onward; creator of the European style of porcelain figure modeling. His first project was the large figures of animals and birds for the Japanese palace at Dresden. Audaciously Baroque, they were outstanding works of art. From around 1735 onward he was engaged with the forms and decoration of the great table services comprising several hundred pieces made for European royalty and aristocracy, such as the Swan Service for Count Brühl. In 1736 appeared the first of his small figures which rank as a creation of an entirely new type, and from 1737 onward figures from the Commedia dell'arte, the masquerade, mythology, contemporary life, groups of lovers, the crinoline groups, animals and birds were modeled in quick succession by Kaendler. The strength of movement and outline, the bold modeling with its deep hollows and pronounced projections for the play of light on the glaze in a deliberate Baroque manner reveal Kaendler's creative genius in the medium of porcelain sculpture to which he contributed so much. The use of strong coloring applied in large unbroken surfaces was equally characteristic and was probably developed by Kaendler; a strong red, a clear rich yellow and a fine black are particularly notable and sharply heightened the expressiveness. All have strong bases with a marked Baroque sentiment. Essentially Kaendler made few overtures to the Rococo. Kaendler's principal modeler assistant was Johann Friedrich Eberlein, 1735-1749. The staff was augmented in 1739 by Johann Gottlieb Ehder, in 1743

KAKIEMON PLATE

by Peter Reinicke and in 1749 by Friedrich Elias Meyer. With the outbreak of the Seven Years' War in 1756, the Kaendler style came to a sudden demise. A new era was ushered in with Rococo, which in turn yielded to the triumph of Neo-Classicism toward the close of the 18th century. New artists including Carl Christoph Punct, Michel-Victor Acier, Johann Carl Schönheit and Christoph Gottfried Jüchtzer explored these styles. (308-311, 313-317)

Käge, Wilhelm See *Gustavsberg.*

Kagemasa, Kato Shirozaemon See *Six Old Kilns.*

Kahla In German ceramics; see *Schönwald.*

Kähler In Danish ceramics; since the 1880's the Kählers, who it appears were always potters, have been in close contact with artists; the Naestved workshops are still the center for a number of artists.

Herman A. Kähler took over his father's pottery in 1872 and became well known for his luster-painted pottery. In the 20th century the work of two fine potters, Svend Hammershoj and Jens Thiirslund, came from the Kähler pottery. Stoneware jars and bowls designed by Nils J. Kähler (b. 1906) and glazed and fired by Herman A. Kähler (b. 1904) are commendable. (532)

Kaipiainen, Birger Finnish ceramic artist; worked in Arabia's art department as early as 1934. After spending some years at the Rörstrand factory in Sweden, returned to Arabia in 1958. Kaipiainen is before everything else a painter. Birds, swans, and decorative objects are his specialties. Faïence is his material, and color glazes and engraving the main decorating techniques. See *Arabia.*

Kairaku-en Ware See *Eiraku.*

Kajar See *Islamic Pottery, Later.*

Kakiemon In Japanese ceramics; traditionally the school of Kakiemon porcelain traces its beginnings to Kakiemon I (1596-1666) a potter who moved to Arita around 1615 and devoted himself particularly to discovering the secret of producing the red overglazes of late Ming porcelains. About 1640-1643 Kakiemon is believed to have successfully fired porcelain with the coveted red enameled decorations. His name derives from the incident, since the color desired was compared to that of a ripe persimmon (kaki). However, it was probably not until the lifetime of Kakiemon V (1660-1691) that the Kakiemon red was achieved, which is a little more in the proper relation to the chronology of its continental models. Regardless, the accepted Kakiemon enamel style is remarkable and unmistakable and for a time it was virtually the wonder of the world. In the Western world the name Kakiemon has been exclusively connected with a family of Japanese porcelains decorated in a certain range of enamels. A striking azure blue and a soft orange red which generally predominates are the two most typical features. A transparent primrose yellow is employed sparingly, as well as a blue and grass green. Occasionally aubergine and brown are introduced; gold is used, but it is frequently entirely absent. Underglaze blue occurs, but it is not characteristic; at times it is combined with blue enamel on the same piece. The colors are delicately applied and the decorations are sensitively drawn. The designs are never applied to the whole surface. From 1672 onward the so-called Kakiemon enamels were copied by other potters in Japan; they were also copied in China. Included among the favorite decorative motifs are the well-known tiger, bamboo and plum blossoms so much admired and frequently copied by Meissen; the millet and quail pattern which inspired the so-called partridge pattern of Bow and Chelsea, the squirrel and vine,

deer and maple, fox and grapes, the red dragon pattern of Meissen and the banded hedge called Wheat Sheaf in France. Of all the motifs the banded hedge might be chosen as the most distinctive. On plates and dishes Kakiemon used an iron glazing on the edge, which is called Kuchi Beni (mouth rouge). To most Japanese the golden age of Kakiemon covers the years from 1684 to 1704. One potter in the early Kakiemon line who was not in the direct Kakiemon succession was Shibuemon (d. 1716) thought to have been the younger brother of Kakiemon V and the tutor of Kakiemon VI. Underglaze blue and white wares are represented. Both Kakiemon IX (1776-1836) and Kakiemon X (1805-1860) are said to have concentrated on this family of Kakiemon wares. But it is the enameled wares which are the glory of the Kakiemon name. Not only were they exported to China where they were widely copied, but they were also shipped to Europe where they furnished the principal stimulus for the development of 18th century interest in porcelain. They were copied at Delft, Meissen, Saint-Cloud, Mennecy, Chantilly, Bow, Chelsea and Worcester. The hereditary house of Kakiemon is now in the twelfth generation, Kakiemon XII (b. 1879). See *Arita; Japanese Porcelain Motifs; Imari; Blue and White,* in Japanese ceramics. (144-146)

Kaliang Ware See *Indo-China.*

Kalpis See *Hydria.*

Kamakura The name given to the Japanese historical period A.D. 1185-1333. See *Japanese Periods.*

Kamares Style In ancient Cretan ceramics; Kamares, the Cretan term for bridges, has been given to a colorful ware excavated at the famous and almost inaccessible cave on Mount Ida. The vases were coated all over with black paint and the somewhat abstract and stylized imaginative decoration was painted a yellowish white. At the beginning of the Middle Minoan period, about 1900-1800 B.C., the vase shapes, the quality of clay, color and pattern were improved and refined to a degree which still wins high praise. They are outstanding examples of the potter's art at so early a date. See *Minoan*.

K'ang Hsi The K'ang Hsi reign of the Ch'ing dynasty in China, 1662-1722. See *Chinese Dynasties*.

Kanishebe Modern Japanese artist-potter; belongs to that group of famous potters who have directed their work along traditional paths. His work is identified with Bizen, one of the wares most highly prized by tea masters. He rediscovered the methods and materials which had been used to produce the great Bizen pots of the Monoyama period. His best pieces are scarcely distinguishable from Bizen masterpieces of the past. His work is highly respected by the Japanese. See *Rosanjin, Kitaoji*.

K'ANG HSI CLUB-SHAPED VASES

Kantharos In Greek antiquities; a type of drinking cup with a deep bowl generally mounted on a stemmed foot with two distinctive vertical loop handles attached to the bottom part of the bowl and to the rim and rising high above the rim. It may have been intended for use in tombs and was not a real drinking cup. See *Kylix*.

Kaolin or **China Clay** In ceramics; kaolin is a necessary ingredient in hard paste porcelain. The French word *kaolin* is derived from the Chinese word *Kao-ling* which is the name of a mountain northwest of the town of Ching-tê-Chên in north China where this material was originally obtained. Kaolin is a fine white clay which is the result of the decomposition of feldspar. See *Porcelain*.

KANTHAROS

Kaolin Ware See *Stone-China*.

Karatsu In Japanese ceramics; the name today is applied to a considerable variety of glazed pottery whose development can be traced to a greater or less extent to the introduction of ceramic techniques into Kyushu from Korea, which began to be produced at a great many kiln sites in Kyushu no earlier than about 1600. The name of the ware is derived from the village of Karatsu in present Saga Prefecture, on northern Kyushu. However, more than two hundred different kiln sites which produced these wares at one time or another are known, and throughout their long history these wares have usually been made not only in an area covering a great portion of modern Saga Prefecture but also in parts of Nagasaki Prefecture. It is believed that the ceramic tradition of the Karatsu wares, which was certainly begun by Korean potters, was done by the many Korean artisans taken captive during Hideyoshi's invasion of Korea in 1592 and 1596 who were brought back to Japan. Karatsu wares represent in the main the Japanized version of the skills of Korean potters. The majority of the production by far seems to have been focused on a variety of comparatively durable vessels for daily use and much less attention was given to utensils for the tea ceremony. However, this is not meant to imply that their tea utensils were not highly esteemed. Karatsu wares share in common the use of a heavy, rough clay and also the use of relatively dark glazes. The best Karatsu has an unassuming rusticity and a rather uninhibited quality combined with superb glazing techniques. The shapes are simple and characteristically beautiful in proportion and outline. Several principal varieties can be recognized including: a plain or almost plain ware; Mottled Karatsu in which several glazes were permitted to intermingle with planned decorative effects in mind; Decorated Karatsu, a painted ware remarkable for the superior decorative techniques which many of the extant examples show, and a great number of intermediate varieties. All seem to have been thrown on a foot-kicked wheel, a leading technological innovation from Korea which soon supplanted the hand-operated wheel used until this time. In spite of the well-established Korean derivation of all Karatsu wares, a particular type of this ware is singled out in Japan for the name *Korean Karatsu*. The term is generally reserved for examples in which the brownish-black glaze which covers the entire piece has been decorated in part with an opaque milk-white glaze. Other examples are covered roughly in halves with two sharply contrasting glazes. Much of the most interesting Karatsu is the Decorated Karatsu with powerful surface painting, generally in iron oxides, in which the painting seems to grow with perfect naturalness out of the form. Certain examples of Decorated Karatsu have a distinctive semi-opaque glaze resulting from a mixture of a silicate with a ferrous glaze termed by the Japanese as Dakatsu Gusuri (reptile finish). The nomenclature of Karatsu wares is somewhat complicated in the case of kilns operated, as a rule on a small scale, by important landed families in the Kyushu area. In most cases these kilns have carefully documented records even to the names of the Korean potters who began the work. Though they are simply further examples of Karatsu-type ware it is customary to label such wares with the name of the particular local kilns in which they are believed to have been produced. These include Satsuma, Takatori, Hagi, Agano and Yatsushiro. (134)

Karnes, Karen (b. 1925) American artist-potter; working at Stony Point, New York. She is chiefly concerned with wheel-thrown useful stonewares. She also produces hand-built larger architectural objects.

Karo-Ko See *Hirado*.

Kasaoka In Japanese ceramics; an important center in the Okayama Prefecture for handcrafted pottery. The origin of pottery in Kasaoka is very old, but the making of

it was not always successful. The present manufacturers built their kiln at Kasaoka in 1907 and called their wares Kibi Yaki; they make artistic traditional vases, plates and tea utensils. See *Japanese Contemporary Pottery*.

Kaschau See *Austria, Czechoslovakia and Hungary*.

Kashan See *Islamic Pottery, Medieval*.

Kastrup In Danish ceramics; a pottery manufactory was founded at Kastrup on the island of Amager around 1755 by Jacob Fortling (d. 1761). The best period was from around 1755 to 1762 and the mark was an F in manganese. The faïence was in the Strasbourg Rococo manner and was painted in muffle kiln colors. Figure modeling was also practiced. After several changes in ownership it closed in 1814. After 1772 commercial stoneware was made and cream-colored earthenware in the English style.

Kassel See *Cassel*.

Kast-stel A cupboard set. See *Rose, The*.

Kato, Hajime Modern Japanese artist-potter; belongs to that group of famous potters who have directed their work along traditional paths. A versatile potter, he works in different techniques and has achieved a mastery over them all. His son, Tatsumi, is also an artist-potter. See *Rosanjin, Kitaoji*.

Kauffmann, Angelica (1741-1807) A well-known painter and decorative artist born at Coire, Switzerland, and working in England from 1766 to 1781. She executed work for the Adam brothers, for whom she designed small-scale pictorial subjects to be used in the painted panel decoration for ceilings. Undoubtedly her work influenced the painted decoration in the Neo-Classic manner. Her manner of painting, like that of Greuze, displayed a certain sentimental mode associated with

KASTRUP
1755-1762

KELSTERBACH

FAIENCE C. 1789-1802

PORCELAIN 1789 ON

KEMP, DOROTHY
1939 ON

KENZAN

one phase of the Neo-Classic movement and seems to have resulted from an idealistic attempt to sentimentalize the ancient classic world. See *Classic Revival; Engraved Designs.*

Kawai, Kanjiro (b. 1890) Japanese artist-potter; his stoneware reveals great variety in shape and finish. Much of his work is hand-built rather than thrown. His son Hiroshi works with him. In Japan his work is highly prized. See *Hamada, S.*

Keiser or **Keyser, Albrecht Cornelisz** and his son Cornelis Albrechtsz. See *Two Little Ships, The.*

Kellinghusen In ceramics; a faïence manufactory was founded at Kellinghusen, Holstein, Germany, by Carsten Behrens around 1760 and was active until about 1826. At least three other local potteries were operating at Kellinghusen twenty years after Behrens started. They all used the same clay from Ovendorf which was very good. The wares were produced chiefly for a peasant market and were admirably designed and executed. The painted decoration which consisted largely of tulips and carnations was executed in a bold and vigorous manner, giving the wares a singular charm.

Kelsterbach In German ceramics; a faïence manufactory was founded in 1758 at Kelsterbach, Hesse-Darmstadt, by William Cron and Johann Christian Frede. In 1761 the Landgrave Ludwig VIII of Hesse-Darmstadt took over the manufactory and began to produce porcelain. When the Landgrave died in 1768, the manufacture of porcelain ceased and was not resumed until 1789. After 1802 the production was largely cream-colored earthenware in the English style. It closed around 1823. The mark was HD in monogram and was used from about 1766. On the faïence wares the HD was generally in manganese; on the porcelain in underglaze blue or impressed, and usually under a crown; on the

earthenware it was impressed. All varieties of porcelain and faïence wares were made from around 1761 to 1768. They were of fine quality but generally with little originality. However, some interesting porcelain figures of excellent workmanship were made during that period. The later wares were of little artistic importance. See *Siegfried, P.A.; Carlstadt, Jakob and Cornelius; Vogelmann, C.*

Kemp, Dorothy English artist-potter and teacher. Studied slipware with Bernard Leach at Shinner's Bridge, Dartington, and stoneware with him later at St. Ives during the Second World War. Her pronounced sense of form and vigorous style is apparent both in her stonewares and slipwares. Since 1939 she has been active at Felixstowe, Suffolk. Her mark is DK in monogram, incised or impressed.

Kendi In Korean ceramics; a kind of drinking vessel. (125)

Kenzan, Ogata (1664-1743) A Japanese potter, painter and calligrapher born in Kyoto; the younger brother of the renowned artist Ogata Korin (1658-1716). Owing in part to Ninsei's influence he became interested in ceramic art and in 1699 began to operate his own kiln at a site called Narutaki, northeast of Kyoto. To these years belongs his finest work, particularly a number of pieces made in collaboration with his artist brother. By 1712 his large inherited fortune was gone and he was forced to rent his own kilns, moving back to Kyoto where he earned his living by the mass production of inferior wares. At the age of nearly seventy Kenzan was rescued from this fate by a noble patron who called him to Edo (Tokyo) where in a glorious reburst of his earlier artistic talent he once more began to make fine wares. The great beauty of Kenzan's style is the emphasis he put upon decorative painting and calligraphy in both Chinese and indigenous Japanese styles. Indeed much of his work is almost more appreciated as painting than as ceramic art for in many pieces the pottery serves as little more than a base for the decoration. His decoration in overglaze iron-oxide executed in traditional Chinese ink style is outstanding for its artistic value, frequently with a calligraphic inscription perhaps describing the decoration. He principally made tea ceremony utensils. Kenzan often used Awata ware which he made in bold and original forms and decorated with irregular designs of great power and subtlety. Brown, black and white slips and "impure" greens and blackish blues of great richness were the principal materials with which he worked, touching in most bold and deft brushwork all kinds of designs, but mostly abstractions from landscapes and plant motifs. His "descendants" still use his name and a legion of followers use the same mark. See *Ninsei; Kyo.* (137)

Keramik   See *Ceramic.*

Kerr, W. H. and Company   See *Worcester.*

Kerr and Binns   See *Worcester.*

Key Fret   A repetitive pattern used universally. It was a favorite border pattern for Chinese porcelains. At times it was varied by the inclusion of the swastika, when it was known as the swastika fret.

Khrapunov-Novyi   In Russian ceramics; Nikita Semonovich Khrapunov, a peasant, started a porcelain manufactory before 1812 at Kuziaevo near Moscow which remained active until around the 1840's. Six Khrapunov brothers, probably the sons of Nikita, each had his own porcelain manufactory in the Ghzel' area near Myza. In the mid-1850's one of Nikita's grandsons, Iakov Gerasimovich, who had worked for a time with his grandfather, took over the Novyi manufactory at Kuziaevo which he had inherited through his wife. Under Iakov's sons this manufactory carried on to a greater or less extent the tradition of the

Novyi manufactory making both porcelain and faïence wares until 1918. The earlier and better wares bear as a mark variations of I.K.N. See *Russia; Novyi.*

Kian Temmoku   In Chinese ceramics; originally the name *kian* was an arbitrary name, which through usage is now given to a variety of Chinese ware that consists chiefly of tea bowls and occasionally vases. It is reputed that these bowls were found near the old Sung kilns at Yungo-ho Chên in the Chi Chou district in the department of Kian in south central Kiangsi province. If this location is correct this ware would be the Chi Chou ware mentioned in records and described as being brown, like that of Ting Chou, but thick and coarse. The Kian ware is quite different from the Chien ware. It is a close buff stoneware. The glaze is usually a lifeless black-brown with dabs of brown yellow which result in a tortoiseshell effect. The inside of the bowl is more richly colored. Later in the Sung period these bowls often had birds and foliage painted in a brown black on the mottled surface. The designs are often barely recognizable and seem more like an accident than a planned design. See *Chien Yao; Temmoku.*

Kiangnan Ting Ware   In Chinese ceramics; an arbitrary name given to a creamy white glazed ware made during the Ming dynasty that more or less resembled Ting yao. The provinces of Kiangsu and Anhwei which were formerly joined under the name of Kiangnan had a number of kilns that produced creamy white wares. It has never been established which one of the kilns made the so-called Kiangnan Ting ware. This ware has a light buff or grey stoneware body with a crackled cream-white glaze, which sometimes has a wrinkled or withered appearance. It has an unusual dull luster and the texture has often been compared to an ostrich egg shell. See *Ting Yao.*

Kibi Yaki   See *Kasaoka.*

KHRAPUNOV
C. 1812 ON

ХРАПУНОВА
НОВАГО

KHRAPUNOV-NOVYI
C. 1860 ON

KIEL POTPOURRI JAR

KIEL
C. 1763 ON

KIEBL

KIEV
C. 1900 ON

ФАБРИКИ
ПЕТРА
ТЕРИХОВА.

KISELEV
C. 1835 ON

Kiel In ceramics; a faïence manufactory was started at Kiel, Holstein, Germany, in 1763 by J. S. F. Tännich of Strasbourg and was at first owned by the Duke of Holstein. After several changes it finally closed in 1788. It seems that all the finer wares were made in the period from 1763 to 1772. The characteristic faïence of that period painted in enamel colors in the style of porcelain ranks with the best of its type made in Europe. The tin glaze or the tin enamel glaze was of remarkable whiteness and the enamel colors were fresh and strong. The flower painting varied in quality but the finest was equal to Strasbourg. Attractive figure subjects and landscapes in the manner of Dutch painting were favorite motifs. Included among the characteristic wares were bishop bowls, wall fountains, flowerpots with four sides and plates and dishes with pierced basketwork rims or wavy edges. Of especial interest was a variety of potpourri having a pear-shaped body mounted on a spreading foot and having a pierced lid richly surmounted with applied fruits, flowers and leaves.

Kiev In Russian ceramics; a faïence factory was started at Kiev, actually at nearby Mejigorgje, in 1798, and was especially productive around 1820-1850. A small quantity of porcelain was also made. See *Russia; Miklashevskii.*

Kiku-no-go-mon In Japan, the Imperial or Honorific Crest of the Chrysanthemum: kiku (chrysanthemum) no (of) go (imperial or honorific) mon (crest). It is represented with sixteen petals.

Kikumon See *Japanese Porcelain Motifs.*

Kiln The furnace or oven in which pottery is fired. The pottery is placed in saggars to protect it from the flames and fumes during firing.

Kilta Service See *Arabia.*

Kinran-de In Japanese ceramics; the Japanese term applied to a gold brocade design, copied from the Chinese, used to decorate porcelain. See *Eiraku; Kutani.*

Kirchmayer, Joseph (1773-1845) Pupil of Johann Peter Melchior. Modeler at Nymphenburg, 1802-1819, or later. See *Melchior, J. P.*

Kirchner, Johann Gottlob (b. 1701) Modeler at the Meissen porcelain manufactory, 1727-1728 and again, 1730-1733. He was essentially a sculptor or stone carver and not a modeler. The series of colossal figures of animals started by him and subsequently finished by Kaendler for the Japanese Palace at Dresden are characteristically Baroque in subject and treatment. See *Baroque.* (307)

Kirschner, Friedrich (1748-1789) Miniaturist, engraver and faïence and porcelain painter at Ludwigsburg, from about 1770 to 1783, where he was a pupil of G. F. Riedel. See *Riedel, G. F.*

Kirimon See *Japanese Porcelain Motifs.*

Kiselev In Russian ceramics; the peasants Feodor and Peter Nikolaevich Terekhov founded a porcelain manufactory at Rechitsy in the Ghzel' area around 1830. About two years later, the competent ceramist Afanasii Leont'evich Kiselev joined the two brothers and raised the standard of this manufactory to that of one of the most important ones in Russia. At one time no less than five hundred workmen were employed. Kiselev's creative talent and his ability to organize benefited the entire community of the Ghzel' area. Early in the 1850's Kiselev started his own manufactory near Rechitsy which remained active until the end of the decade. Here he produced the finest porcelain, very thin and translucent. In addition he made ordinary china, the so-called tavern ware, faïence and porcelain figures. As a rule the porcelain tablewares were painted in traditional Russian color combinations, while the designs were in the style of folk art, as is to be expected from the Ghzel' area. Among the marks were A.K. and A. Kiselev. See *Russia; Ghzel'*.

Kitei, Waka Prominent studio-potter associated with the Kyoto circle of potters. He was the third generation of a family of Japanese potters who made excellent blue and white for seven generations and he is believed to have worked with Rokubei from around 1818-1829. He worked in the Dohachi style. See *Kyo; Rokubei; Dohachi, Ninami*.

Kiyomizu In Japanese ceramics; a term commonly given to wares in the tradition of Ninsei and his school produced by several local Kyoto kilns and associated more or less with the old pottery market which still exists on the slopes of the hill leading to Kyoto's ancient Kiyomizu Temple. The term *Old Kiyomizu* refers to wares made before the 19th century. See *Kyo; Ninsei*.

Kjellberg Friedl Holger Austrian-born ceramic artist working at the Arabia factory near Helsinki since 1924. Her specialties are hand-thrown bowls and vases with brilliant copper glazes, the so-called Sang de Boeuf and turquoise in the Chinese style. She developed the rice grain porcelain technique at Arabia in the early 1940's. See *Arabia*. (503)

Klaus, Karl Austrian artist whose designs were produced at the Alexandra Porcelain Works of Turin in the years preceding the First World War.

Klimt, Gustav (1862-1918) Austrian painter; studied mosaics, glass painting and ceramics in Vienna. He was one of the founders of the Vienna Secession, 1897, and he collaborated with the Wiener Werkstätte. He was the principal exponent of Art Nouveau painting in Vienna; his sphere of influence extended beyond Central Europe. See *Secession; Hoffmann, Josef*.

Klinger, Johann Gottfried (b. c. 1701-d. 1781) Painter and arcanist at Meissen, 1731-1746, and at Vienna, 1746-1781. One of the most important painters at Meissen.

Kloster-Veilsdorf In German ceramics; a porcelain manufactory was started at Kloster-Veilsdorf, Thuringia, in 1760 by Prince Friedrich Wilhelm von Hildburghausen. It was the outstanding Thuringian porcelain manufactory of the 18th century and is still in existence. The mark was CV either separated or in monogram in underglaze blue, and after 1797 it was a clover leaf. The best work was done prior to 1780 and was in the Rococo taste. The enamel colors were clear and fresh. Of especial interest was some admirable fruit and flower painting executed in an individual style. Attractive figure subjects and small garlands of flowers in the style of the French painter, Watteau, were also noteworthy. Some of the figure modeling was of excellent quality, in particular some figures from the Italian Comedy and some draped figures of gods and goddesses. After 1780 the Neo-Classic style was adopted and although the pieces were of finished workmanship, such as the vases, they were lacking in originality.

Knowles, Taylor and Knowles In American ceramics; a pottery was started at East Liverpool, Ohio, in 1854 by Isaac Knowles and Isaac Harvey, producing Rockingham and yellow wares. In 1870 when Mr. Knowles was the sole owner, he formed a partnership with Colonel N. Taylor and Homer S. Knowles, and the pottery was known as Knowles, Taylor and Knowles. In 1890 it became a company and "Co." was added to the name. In 1872 they began to manufacture white granite and around 1890 semi-porcelain or Hotel China was added to the production schedule. Notable is their fine porcelain of a Belleek type that they developed in the early 1890's and named Lotus ware. Probably the finest

KLOSTER-VEILSDORF
1760-1797

KNOWLES, TAYLOR AND
KNOWLES

C. 1872 ON

C. 1890

porcelain made in America, its manufacture was abandoned on account of costliness. Like many other American ceramic manufacturers, Knowles, Taylor and Knowles furnished blanks for the serious china painter. The firm advertised its Lotus ware as being adapted to the requirements of amateur and professional decorators, and made in artistic shapes designed for practical utility. The mark was Knowles, Taylor and Knowles enclosed in a circle surrounding a crescent and star, and Lotus ware below the circle. If it was decorated at the pottery, the date and initial of the decorator were included. White wares were marked with the distinguishing initials K T K or the name in a variety of designs. See *Pâte-sur-Pâte; Parian; Belleek; East Liverpool.* (458)

KO WARE INCENSE VASE

Knütgen A well-known family of German potters at Siegburg, first recorded in 1427. Anno Knütgen (who lived to be quite old, died after 1590) and his sons Bertram, Rütger and Hermann were leading makers of stoneware at Siegburg until 1590 when they moved to Höhr. Peter Knütgen who was active about 1570 and Christian Knütgen who was active about 1568 to 1605 were also prominent at Siegburg. Belonging to a later generation is Johann Knütgen recorded at Höhr from 1616 onward, and Wilhelm Knütgen at Grenshausen from 1620 onward. The stoneware ascribed to Anno Knütgen is unsigned and rarely dated; it appears to have been made from 1570 to 1590. In addition to the characteristic Siegburg types, he also introduced some interesting forms such as pilgrim bottles, occasionally with dragon handles. The work of Christian Knütgen is admirable for some finely executed biblical reliefs on tankards of the Schnelle type. His later work revealed a more pronounced feeling for Renaissance motifs which he executed with great refinement. (188, 189)

Ko In Japanese ceramics; the Japanese word for old; hence Ko-Kutani, Ko-Bizen, Ko-Seto.

Ko Yao In Chinese ceramics; Ko Yao or elder brother's ware is supposed to have been made by the elder brother Chang at Liu-t'ien in the Lung-ch'üan district of the province of Chekiang in the latter part of the Southern Sung dynasty, A.D. 1127–1280. Chinese records always associate Ko yao and Kuan yao together without making any particular effort to differentiate between the two wares. It was made of the same dark-colored clay and it is believed that the ware had a brown lip rim and an iron foot. It is assumed that the various Kuan glazes were also used on Ko ware. It had both large and small crackle. In fact, crackle was a special feature of Ko ware. The imitation of Kuan yao and the making of Ko yao were carried on at Lung-ch'üan at least until the end of the Yüan dynasty. Both wares were widely copied at Ching-tê-Chên from the 18th century. Eventually the term *Ko* was used simply to refer to the various kinds of buff and grey crackle wares without any reference to the original Sung pieces. The glazes are distinctive for their thickness and solidity, sometimes resulting in a soft surface texture like polished marble. The glazes are fat and undulating and often terminate in thick drops. The crackle varies in width and both the small and large crackle are occasionally combined on the same piece. Intentional crackle was obtained by several methods. One simple method was to add a special clay which was a kind of pegmatite to the glaze. Sometimes the crackle is accentuated by rubbing a coarse red or black ink into the fissures. See *Sung; Kuan Yao; Crackle.*

Kochi In Japanese ceramics; literally the Japanese word for Cochin China; given to a variety of wares with green and other colored lead glazes and with decoration in low relief (essentially commoner descendants of San Ts'ai or Three-Colored wares) ranging in appearance from a soft pottery through stoneware to a coarse porcelain. The provenance of this so-called Kochi ware still remains a mystery. It is almost a certainty that it did not come from Cochin China, but rather from some nameless Chinese southern provincial kiln. Kochi wares, which have in a general sense a late Ming look, have survived almost entirely in Japan in the form of small round boxes with covers molded in the forms of animals, birds, fruit and flowers in relief. These containers were favored by the Japanese tea masters who used them to hold incense for the tea ceremony. They were extensively copied by the Japanese studio potters in the early 19th century. Eiraku is well known for his use of this southern Chinese overglaze pottery technique. In the British Museum there are a number of Japanese pottery baskets and trays made of a fine pale buff ware with green, yellow and aubergine glazes in this style. On these pieces the designs are molded in low relief or outlined in raised threadlike lines serving as dikes, keeping the colored glazes apart, or again in colored glazes applied in broad areas without the containing lines. Some of these wares were made at Minato in the province of Izumi and others at Awaji in the province of Sanuki.

Koeks or **Kocks, Adriaenus**　and his son Pieter Adriaenus. See *Greek A.*

Koetsu, Hon'ami　See *Raku.*

Kofun or **Tomb Mound Period**　See *Yayoi; Haniwa; Japanese Periods.*

Koge　See *Iga.*

Kohiki　In Korean ceramics; a class of Punch'ŏng wares known in Japan as kohiki or powdered. The name is derived from the powdery white effect of the slip which was applied all over the ferruginous grey-brown body including even the foot. Nu-

merous examples of this type of ware are in the form of the Chinese ritual bronze called fu and have a distinctive primitive appearance. The decoration on these vessels is restricted to incised lines and squares, but some of the Kohiki bowls and bottles have floral designs painted in iron-brown under the glaze. There is another kind known as Muji-Hakeme in which the coating of white slip was limited to the upper half of the vessels. It is thought that Kohiki is among the earliest of the Punch'ŏng wares and is a direct forerunner of Hakeme. See *Punch'ŏng.*

Kok, J. Jurriaan　See *Rozenburg.*

Königsberg　In German ceramics; a small faïence manufactory was established at Königsberg, East Prussia, by John E. L. Ehrenreich in 1772. After changing hands several times it closed in 1811. The faïence mark was the monogram of Ehrenreich, HE, impressed with the date added. The forms and decoration were in the Rococo style and the influence of Marieberg wares was evident. The painted decoration was generally done only in blue, which in the best work was a rich vivid tone. Flowers realistically treated were a favorite motif. Later the manufactory produced a leadglazed earthenware marked with a K impressed. A second manufactory was in operation at Königsberg from around 1775 to 1785, making wares in the style of Wedgwood.

Korai or **Koryo**　The name of the Korean historical period, 912-1392. See *Korean Periods.*

Korea　In Korean ceramics; the pottery of the Silla period, 57 B.C.-A.D. 935, which is known through burial wares, is a type of grey stoneware vessel characteristic of which are those with a tall pierced openwork foot. Impressed and incised decoration of parallel lines, chain-pattern and the like recall a Chinese T'ang technique. It also includes some very original and natu-

KONIGSBERG
1778-1787

KOREAN BOWL WITH INLAID
SLIP DECORATION

ralistic figures. This Silla stoneware is usually unglazed, but other specimens have an olive-greenish or brownish feldspathic glaze. Under the Korai kings, 918-1392, the example of Sung China prevailed and its advanced techniques were adopted with remarkable success. Yüeh, Northern celadon and Ju exercised successive influence on the production of Korai celadon wares which, for all their general resemblance to these in style, nevertheless reveal a subtly different character. By the 12th century these wares attained a notable refinement. Korai celadons have a hard grey porcelaneous stoneware body, reddish at the exposed places and almost opaque, covered with a glaze that is usually bluish green, but is occasionally brownish or grey-green, or more rarely mouse-grey or putty color; the glaze generally shows a fine crazing. The traditional skill of Korean potters in modeling and pierced openwork resulted in a range of shapes of great and peculiar beauty. Decoration when used on this celadon was incised or carved, the latter when deeply carved having almost the appearance of low relief; or molded; or painted in slip; or painted in brownish black; or inlaid in black or white clay. The inlaid decoration, distinctively Korean, in which the designs are first incised and then inlaid in white and black slips to give a contrast of color under the celadon glaze, is the most famous Korean decoration. The invention of this technique probably sprang from the practice of incising and stamping. Most admirably drawn, the style of the inlaid designs ranges from the firm naturalism of willows and other trees, birds, feathery grasses and flowering plants and vines, to delicate formal flowers, daisy or starlike, and cloud scrolls. The later inlaid work, chiefly dating from the end of the Korai period, has a different and more coarse character. Characteristic motifs comprise groups of radiating or slanting strokes and starlike flowers which were bolder than in the earlier work. These later wares are known among the Japanese as *mishima*. In the 15th and 16th centuries of the Yi period, 1392-1910, two principal types of stoneware continued the Korai traditions; namely, the Mishima inlaid ware, and the ware with painted and incised decoration. From the latter was developed a characteristic type of ware with a ground of vigorously brushed-on white or grey slip resulting in a more or less striated effect, which, possessing a distinctive charm, was occasionally used as a decoration by itself. Other vessels were decorated with designs cut through the overall coating of brushed slip in sgraffiato style. The later Mishima ware was decorated in a coarsened version of the Korai style with dragons, cranes, willows and the like, in black and white inlay, but with fillings of the typical Mishima stars, strokes and dots impressed or made with a roulette. The more ordinary Mishima ware bore little else than the close-set starlike flowers, strokes, and occasionally larger rosettes and borders of petal patterns. With the decline of Korean prosperity their wares showed less and less refinement, but achieved nevertheless an artlessness, a satisfying rugged strength. Some of these 16th century bowls were among the spoils taken back to Japan by Hideyoshi where their primitive freedom and directness, a total disregard of mechanical perfection of finish, so profoundly influenced the wares made for the tea ceremony. Apart from the coarser wares both white and blue and white porcelains were made in native forms whose vitality and boldness more than offset their frequent lack of technical refinement. Painting in iron brown was transferred to porcelain; copper red was also used admirably. Though the history of these wares is still obscure, their free, swift brushwork, clear and rhythmical, wonderfully creative, that characterizes their best work is virtually unique. See *Celadon; Mishima; China,* in Far Eastern ceramics. (119-122)

Korean Karatsu   See *Karatsu.*

COLUMN KRATER

VOLUTE KRATER

Korean Periods The art of Korea is identified with the respective historical period in which it was produced. The following is a chronology of Korean art history.

Silla   c. 57 B.C.-A.D. 935
Korai (Koryo)   918-1392
Yi   1392-1910

Kornilov In Russian ceramics; among the 19th century Russian porcelain manufactories, one that made some of the finest wares was started by Mikhail Savinovich Kornilov at St. Petersburg in 1835. Until his death in 1885 it operated under his direction. From 1893 to 1917 it was under the name of the Brothers Kornilov. The manufactory was noted for the quality of the artists, while the technical equipment was far superior to that of most Russian manufactories. The kiln constructed in 1896 was the largest in Russia. A considerable amount of their export ware was shipped to the United States from around 1893 during and after the World's Fair at Chicago. The porcelain at the Fair was marked with a Russian bear and bore the inscription in English "Made by the Kornilov Brothers." Their export porcelain was of fine translucence and brilliant coloring. Among their marks were "Of the Brothers Kornilov in St. Petersburg" and B. K. See *Russia*.

Kothon See *Plemochoë*.

Kotyle See *Skyphos*.

Kousnetzoff See *Kuznetsov*.

Kovács, Margit (b. 1902) Outstanding artist-potter who through her work has raised Hungarian pottery to new technical and artistic heights. Her powerful and deeply individual work has received international appreciation and recognition, and though it is thoroughly European, it is deeply rooted in the national tradition of her country. See *Gádor, István*.

Koyomi-de See *Punch'ŏng*.

Krater In Greek antiquities; a large mixing bowl in which the wine and water were poured, as the Greeks generally diluted their wine with water. There are four varieties of krater, namely, column, volute, calyx, and bell, identified by their form and the position of their handles. The mouth in all four types was large enough to permit the ladling out of the wine mixture. The column krater is so-called from its columnar-shaped handles. The flat projecting lip rim is extended on each side by two lobes forming the top of the handles which rise from the shoulder of the body. The volute krater derives its name from the shape of the handles which extend and curve upward from the shoulder and terminate in large volutes above the lip rim. The calyx krater is so called because its body resembles in shape the calyx of a flower. The two horizontal handles are set low on the body near the base. The bell krater resembles an inverted bell. The two small horizontal handles are set high on the body, near the lip rim.

Krebs, Nathalie See *Saxbo*.

Kreussen In German ceramics; a flourishing manufacture for stove tiles or Hafner ware was in existence at Kreussen, near Bayreuth, Bavaria, during the 16th century. It seems that the manufacture of stoneware, which became an important production, dated from the late 16th century and was continued at least until 1732. All the artistic stoneware was of the 17th century. The stoneware was covered with a brown salt glaze of varying tone. One variety was decorated only with applied reliefs. In the other principal variety the reliefs were painted with bright opaque enamel colors of blue, red, green, yellow and white, sometimes with touches of gilding. This use of overglaze enamel colors at Kreussen was the first in Europe; the earliest date was recorded in 1622. The enameled decoration was executed in a similar style to that found on the German enam-

ВРАТЬЕВЪ
Корниловыхъ
KORNILOV
C. 1835 ON

CALYX KRATER

BELL KRATER

eled glass and was probably done by the same painters. Included among their productions were four- or six-sided flasks called Schraubflasch and made only at Kreussen, tankards of squat cylindrical forms with pewter lids, bell-shaped tankards and pear-shaped and globular-shaped jugs. The finest reliefs which were made from around 1700 to 1725 were well modeled, large and in rather high relief. The motifs for the reliefs included figure subjects, such as the Apostles, The Family or The Wedding and also coats-of-arms and inscriptions in typical Roman lettering. See *Vest, Georg.* (197, 247)

Kriegel and Company See *Prague.*

Krister Porzellan Manufactur See *Waldenburg.*

Krog, Arnold (1856-1931) Swedish architect and painter. Appointed art director at Royal Copenhagen in 1885. Later in the same year the first examples of Krog's celebrated underglaze painting were produced and by the time of the Paris Exhibition, 1889, the style was sufficiently matured to win a Grand Prix and the interest of all European ceramists. In the course of time a number of artists who admired Krog and his work and shared a similar outlook were attracted to Copenhagen; artists such as C. F. Lüsberg, Carl Mortensen, V. T. Fischer, Marianne Høst and Bertha Nathanielsen. Krog appears to have believed that the beauty of the porcelain surface could be enriched only by colors closely connected with it under the glaze and that areas of undecorated white porcelain should form an integral part of the overall aesthetic effect. His underglaze palette was developed around misty blues and greys which suited perfectly with his taste for depicting the mist-like quality in his northern landscapes. He left his dishes and plaques without borders and like the French Impressionist painters he permitted elements of his design to be cut through by the edge of the vessel. His de-

signs were always asymmetrically composed on surfaces intended to give the largest possible area for painting. Like the French decorators, the characteristics of Krog's style reveal that the precepts of Japanese art were well learned but not imitated. Krog was also deeply absorbed in figure modeling. It can be said that porcelain figures modeled by Krog and by others at Royal Copenhagen under his direction launched a modern style of figure-making. No longer were figures regarded as realistic toys or miniature versions of monumental sculpture. Figures were conceived directly in relation to the capabilities of their medium of slip-cast porcelain with a smooth glazed surface colored in pastel underglaze shades. This use of underglaze colors made the coloring seem really a part of the model. The style required smooth compact shapes with protrusions kept to a minimum. In the 1890's some of the modeling conveyed a remarkable feeling of abstraction for its period. In later years a more realistic style was to be pursued at Copenhagen. Examples of multicolored underglaze painting in the Copenhagen style were exhibited by Meissen at the Paris Exhibition of 1900. In the early years of the 20th century the art of making porcelain figures achieved a high degree of effectiveness in the work of German modelers who profited from the earlier discoveries of Copenhagen in the use of underglaze colors. However, unlike the earlier Copenhagen figures which favored animal subjects, the German figures showed a preference for human subjects. (485, 486)

Ku Yüeh Hsüan In Chinese ceramics; a distinctive ware made partly in the reign of Yung Chêng and partly in the reign of Ch'ien Lung during the Ch'ing dynasty. This ware tries to reproduce in porcelain the soft coloring on the enameled glass made by Hu, whose studio name was Ku Yüeh Hsüan, or ancient moon pavilion. According to the story the emperor expressed his admiration for this glassware and wished that the same effect could be simulated in porcelain. Therefore T'ang Ying set out to make a porcelain resembling glass and to copy the same style of decoration and the same soft coloring. He made a highly vitreous body with a milky texture and a glassy glaze on which the enameled decoration affected the soft coloring of the original glass. This type of porcelain is highly prized. It is known as Fang Ku Yüeh Hsüan or imitation Ku Yüeh Hsüan.

Kuan Chün Yao In Chinese ceramics; see *Chün Yao.*

Kuan Ti In Chinese art; a Chinese Confucian subject extensively used in Chinese painting, sculpture, textiles and ceramics. He is the god of war and is represented in full armor. He is generally seen seated with his right hand raised, or mounted on his horse or standing near his horse. He has a flowing beard. Until late in the 16th century he was known as Kuan Yü, a famous warrior. Confucius, K'uei Hsing and Kuan Ti are the three most commonly represented Confucian subjects. See *Chinese Gods.*

Kuan Yao In Chinese ceramics; the term literally means Imperial ware and it could be and was applied to all varieties of porcelains made at the Imperial potteries. The original Sung Kuan, which was called Ta Kuan by later writers, was first made at the Imperial pottery at K'ai-Fêng Fu in Honan during the early years of the 12th century. Apparently the Kuan yao potters followed the Imperial court when it fled south in 1127. The Northern Sung Kuan was made for only about fifteen or twenty years. According to Chinese records the color of the glaze is described as pale blue, green or grey; moon-white; deep green and bluish or greenish with a tinge of pale red. Much of the ware had both large and small crackle. The body of the original ware is not known. The Southern Sung Kuan was

made at Hangchow. Other potteries in the vicinity made wares of the Kuan type. The Hangchow Kuan followed closely the Northern Sung Kuan glazes. The body was dark brown or red which gave the ware a brown mouth and iron foot. That is, the stoneware body showed through the glaze where it was thin at the lip rim and the body was exposed at the raw edge of the foot rim. (93)

Kuan Yin In Chinese art; a Chinese Buddhist goddess. The figure of Kuan Yin was extensively produced in ivory, jade and blanc de chine. She is known as the goddess of mercy and is seen at times with an upturned vase, representing the source of water that produces growth. She is also represented as the mother goddess, holding a child or having a child near her. See *Chinese Gods.* (105, 108)

Kuan Yü See *Kuan Ti; Chinese Gods.*

Kuang Hsü The Kuang Hsü reign of the Ch'ing dynasty in China, 1874-1908. See *Chinese Dynasties.*

Kubachi See *Islamic Pottery, Later.*

Kuchi Beni A Japanese term meaning mouth rouge. See *Kakiemon.*

Kuchu See *Raku.*

Kudinov In Russian ceramics; a small porcelain manufactory was started in 1818 by N. S. Kudinov in the village of Lystsovo, near Moscow, and continued to operate until 1885. He took in his brother Semen in 1823; in time Semen started his own manufactory in the same village, which closed in 1861. The porcelain was of good quality and was decorated in the characteristic Russian taste with flower arrangements and designs in strong, vivid colors. The most common mark is NK in monogram. Semen's mark was relatively similar, no doubt to take advantage of the prestige achieved by his older brother. See *Russia.*

K'uei Hsing In Chinese art; a Chinese Confucian subject. He is the god of literature. He is depicted as a demon-faced creature and has one foot placed on the head of a monster which is a fish dragon. He is holding a brush and other implements of writing. See *Chinese Gods; Kuan Ti.*

Kuei Kung In Chinese ceramics; the term *kuei kung* or devil's work is often given to the delicate openwork that was characteristic of some of the later Ming porcelains. It was so called because the work was so delicate that it seemed beyond the realm of human skill. See *Ling Lung.*

Künersberg In German ceramics; a faïence manufactory was started at Künersberg, near Memmingen, Bavaria, in 1745 by Jacob Küner, a successful merchant, and was active until about 1767. The wares attributed to this manufactory were sometimes marked with the initials KB or Künersberg. Included among their productions which were widely diversified were lobed or gourd-shaped vases, cylindrical tankards, plates with wavy edges and jugs with very slender narrow necks. Figures were also made. Some of the finest German faïence is attributed to this manufactory. It was delicately and minutely painted either in soft high temperature colors or in overglaze enamel colors on a beautiful pure white ground. The most beautiful faïence ascribed to Künersberg was painted in the overglaze enamel colors in the style of porcelain. Gold was much used in this work in the form of delicate lacework and scrollwork borders frequently used round minutely painted landscape panels or chinoiseries. Other favorite motifs included sprays of flowers realistically treated, fruit, birds on branches and coats-of-arms. (390)

Kurlbaum and Schwartz In American ceramics; a porcelain factory started at Kensington, Philadelphia, by Charles Kurlbaum and John T. Schwartz, chemists. In 1853 at the Exhibition of the Franklin Institute, Philadelphia, some of their wares were represented and received favorable comment. The factory apparently ceased to operate in 1855. See *Tucker.* (451)

Kütahya See *Islamic Pottery, Later.*

Kutani In Japanese ceramics; porcelain known as Ko-Kutani (Old Kutani) was made probably from around 1650 until sometime around 1695 when the Kutani kilns seem to have declined. The Kutani kilns were started as "official" kilns for the house of Maeda, landed nobles in the feudal province of Kaga, which means that they were not intended for the common commercial market. The name *Kutani* is derived from the name of a remote village in the Ishakawa Prefecture, Kaga province, where the necessary clay deposit was discovered. The porcelain of Kaga province had several phases of activity and revival. The body of Ko-Kutani, which is the earliest, is a heavy porcelain, often coarse in texture and approaching stoneware. Both underglaze and overglaze decoration in a full palette of colors was used. The enamels were thickly applied to bold designs which include textile patterns, as well as birds and plants, and landscapes with figures. No doubt the most admired of Old Kutani is the superb Ao-Kutani (Green Kutani) in which the entire design is dominated by striking areas of a fairly bright green overglaze decoration. Perhaps it was the relatively rare success of Kutani potters to achieve a purely white porcelain that led them to devise the decorative technique known today as Ao-Kutani, in which the entire surface is covered mainly with green and yellow glazes leaving nothing of the porcelain itself showing. In another type of Ko-Kutani red predominates; while in a third variety the entire surface is covered with foliage painted in powerful green, blue, dull yellow and manganese purple. The drawing, design and color of

K.B.

KUNERSBERG
C. 1745 ON

K&S

KURLBAUM AND SCHWARTZ
1853

Ko-Kutani make it one of the most striking of all porcelains. A favorite and characteristic shape is the Japanese Hyotan (calabash), a large two-sectioned gourd commonly dried and used in earlier days as a container for rice wine. Ko-Kutani was seldom marked; or it bears various forms of the Chinese characters Fuki (Happiness). Early in the 19th century kilns in the Kaga province focused their production on reviving Old Kutani. Of these the most important was the Yoshidaya kiln reputedly built on the original site of the Ko-Kutani kilns. Especially well known was their ware decorated in an overall color scheme of green, yellow and "eggplant" purple. Around 1840 Iida Hachiroemon (d. 1849) introduced a brocade style known as Akaji Kinga or gold designs on red, an overdecorated ware lacking in refined taste. Later Eiraku's son, Wazen, worked at the kiln, making wares in the red and gold tradition. Eggshell porcelain was also made. Most of these kilns seem to have ceased operation shortly after 1868. Today the generic name *Kutani* has been given to a great variety of 19th century and later porcelains, stoneware and earthenware of which some was made in the same Ishakawa prefecture while others were made in quite different parts of Japan. See *Arita; Japanese Porcelain Motifs.* (139, 140)

Kuznetsov In Russian ceramics; the peasant Iakov Kuznetsov in 1810 founded a porcelain manufactory at Novo-Kharitonovo with the trade name Brothers Kuznetsov for his two sons, which they operated until the 1870's. In the meantime they started, rented, and bought other manufactories. In 1889 the M. S. Kuznetsov Company was organized. At the beginning of the 20th century the Kuznetsov porcelain combine was the largest porcelain company in Russia. They exported to Europe, India and China. Their wares always had good technical quality but the artistic value left much to be desired. The Kuznetsovs were also known for their faïence wares. The marks vary considerably, generally with the name M. S. Kuznetsov together with the name of the place of the actual manufactory that had made the ware. The most important manufactory which they bought was that of Francis Gardner. See *Russia; Gardner, Francis.*

Kwaart In Dutch ceramics; a clear lead glaze occasionally applied over and fired with the overglaze enamel colors of Delft and the wares of several other faïence factories to give more depth and sheen to the colors. See *Coperta.*

Kwangtung Yao In Chinese ceramics; there are many kilns located in the province of Kwangtung, which is the southernmost province in China, and it is reputed that some were operating as early as the T'ang dynasty and were making earthenware cooking vessels. The dating of the mottled Kwangtung wares, or Canton stonewares as they are generally called, is a difficult problem. It is certain that they were made at least as early as the late Ming dynasty. They are still made and are exported in large quantities. The kilns at Shekwan West which is close to Fatshan are probably the best known. It is a hard-fired ware and has a dark brown body of reddish tone. The glaze is thick and smooth and is characterized by mottling and dappling. The glaze may be olive-brown, bluish-black or green flecked and streaked with grey-green, white, buff and grey with often bright blue breaking through. At times the brown tone predominates but the most highly prized pieces are those in which the general tone is blue. Occasionally the mottled glazes bear a surface resemblance to the dappled Chün yao. This ware was also made into figures such as the god of war and other deities. The figures are generally covered with either a crimson-red flambé glaze or a celadon type of glaze, except for their faces and hands which are left unglazed. Other types of wares are also attributed to this province.

KUTANI VASE

ЗАВОДА
Б
КУЗНЕЦОБЫХЪ

KUZNETSOV
1815 ON

Kyathos In Greek antiquities; a kind of ladle or dipper in the form of a deep cup having a loop handle attached to the side of the cup and extending high above the rim. See *Oinochoë.*

KYATHOS

Kyhn, Knud See *Royal Copenhagen.*

Kylin A Chinese animal figure. See *Ch'i-Lin.*

Kylix In Greek antiquities; the most popular and most graceful of all drinking cups, in the form of a wide shallow bowl with two horizontal handles mounted on a stemmed foot. See *Kantharos; Skyphos; Rhyton.*

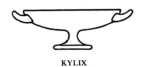

KYLIX

Kyo In Japanese ceramics; the name given to the wares made in and around Kyoto, roughly from the latter part of the 18th century onward. In a general sense Kyo ware may be divided into two phases: pottery and porcelain. The first period of its development, and with which the term is particularly linked, was marked by various elaborately enameled pottery wares in the Japanese taste, the so-called Ko-Kiyomizu (Old Kiyomizu). Their origin is traditionally traced to the famous late 17th century Japanese painter and potter, Ninsei. Down to the end of Japan's feudal period in 1868, certain provincial kilns, often of a very limited scale, were making a large number of wares more or less influenced by the school of Ninsei. Among these may be counted Akashi (Hyogo prefecture), Takamatsu (Kawaga prefecture), Mushiake (Okayama prefecture), Awaji (Hyogo prefecture), Akahada (Nara prefecture) and Soma (Fukushima prefecture). Banko ware with its characteristic style and Ando ware, both in Mie prefecture, are enameled pottery wares originally in the Kyo ware style.

The second period of the development of Kyo wares witnessed the growth of porcelains which came about after the Kyoto potters learned the technique of enameled Imari. Stimulated by the vogue for Chinese porcelains, these individual artist potters made imitations of Late Ming and Early Ch'ing wares, especially polychrome enameled porcelain, underglaze blue and white, celadon and Three-Color ware. Practically all of the great individual porcelain makers of this period, such as Okuda Eisen, Eiraku, Mokubei and Dohachi made pottery and faïence as well. In fact Dohachi is more associated with faïence than with porcelain. Also included among prominent studio-potters associated with the Kyoto porcelain circle are Choso Mikawa, Rokubei, Seifu, Okuda Kyuta, Waka Kitei, Mimpei and Chikusen. Many of these small kilns still flourish today. The development of a modern industrial society in Japan after 1868 put an end to the social and economic life which had cultivated the art of ceramics in Japan up to that time. In recent years in Japan such gifted studio-potters as Hamada, Kawaii and Tomimoto have attempted to continue Japan's heritage of ceramic art into the 20th century. See *Kiyomizu; Ninsei; Eisen, Okuda.*

Kyoto See *Kyo.*

Kyusu The Japanese name given to a teapot. See *Mokubei, Aoki.*

Kyuta, Okuda (d. 1852) Prominent Japanese studio-potter associated with the Kyoto circle of potters. He was well known for his unglazed kyusu teapots. See *Kyo; Mokubei.*

KYOTO CHARCOAL BOWL

L

La Belle Pottery Company See *Wheeling Pottery Company.*

La China See *Buen Retiro.*

La Courtille In French ceramics; a hard paste porcelain manufactory founded in Paris in 1771 by Jean-Baptiste Locré. This manufactory, which was also called Rue Fontaine-au-Roy, Basse Courtille or Manufacture de Porcelaine Allemande, produced a very translucent porcelain of excellent quality. It is generally believed to have been the most important and productive pre-Revolution factory in Paris. After several changes in ownership it closed in 1840. The mark was crossed torches with the flames pointing upwards in underglaze blue or incised. The forms and painted decoration were in the Neo-Classic style. The wares displayed fine workmanship and were admirable for their refinement and elegance. Especially noteworthy were some well-modeled biscuit figures. See *Pouyat.*

La Farge, John (1835-1910) American painter, craftsman, lecturer and writer. His immediate effect on his own generation was due to his help in reawakening the decorative arts.

La Fratta See *Alla Castellana Ware.*

La Moncloa Or Florida. In Spanish ceramics; a rather unimportant porcelain manufactory was established at La Moncloa, near Madrid, by Ferdinand VII in 1817 and continued until 1850. Some of the supplies at Buen Retiro were used here. The productions were chiefly imitations of contemporary French wares. Moncloa under a crown, impressed, was the usual mark. The mark M or Md under a crown was also used, as at Buen Retiro. See *Buen Retiro.*

La Rochelle In French ceramics; a faïence manufactory was established at La Rochelle, Charente-Inférieure, in 1749, aided by workmen and supplies taken from the faïence manufactory at Marans. It is believed that Pierre Roussencq of Marans was the first manager. It changed hands several times and closed in 1789. Although it is only reasonable that some of the work resembled Marans, the manufactory developed some more or less distinctive interpretations of the painted decoration found in the faïence at Rouen, Strasbourg, Moustiers and Nevers. Of particular interest was the painted decoration in the Nevers style with its strong drawings and clear high temperature colors. No regular factory mark is known; however, various initials and monograms are found. Two earlier faïence manufactories were active at La Rochelle during the early 18th century. They were relatively unimportant.

La Rue, Louis-Félix de French sculptor; modeler at Vincennes-Sèvres, 1754-1780. His works include some charming groups of little boys playing with a fish and conch-shell.

La Seynie In French ceramics; a hard paste porcelain was made at La Seynie, Saint-Yrieix, from 1774 at the Château de La Seynie by a company, one of whose members was the Comte de La Seynie. It changed ownership several times and closed in 1856. One of the marks was LS in monogram. See *Petite Rue Saint-Gilles.*

Lac-Burgauté In Chinese ceramics. See *Burgauté.*

Lace In ceramics; lace work or a lace effect in porcelain is achieved by a very simple process. A piece of real lace is dipped in porcelain slip; it becomes saturated and a coat or crust adheres to it which in the

LA COURTILLE
1773 ON

LA MONCLOA
1817-1850

$\mathcal{LS}$

LA SEYNIE
LATE 18TH CENTURY

firing becomes firm, the lace is burned away, leaving a porcelain model of itself. It was introduced at Meissen about 1770 although the credit for the invention is generally given to J. A. Hannong working at the Strasbourg manufactory where it was used around the same time.

Lachenal, Edmond (b. 1855) French sculptor and artist-potter; identified with the remarkable flowering of artist-pottery in France centered in Paris in the decades around 1900. He produced painted earthenware as well as elaborately glazed stoneware and porcelain. (515)

Lagrenée The Younger Porcelain painter; in 1785 appointed assistant art director with J. J. Bachelier at Sèvres. In 1793, when he was discharged for a brief period, he decorated porcelain independently in Paris; later returned to Sèvres. He introduced the antique (or Greco-Roman) style; delicate graceful Pompeian arabesques were much favored. See *Pompeian Taste.*

LANTERNIER, A. & CIE.
1891 ON

Lajoue, Jacques de (1686-1761) French painter and decorative artist. His name is sometimes linked with Meissonnier and Pineau as one of the three inventors of the more intensified or accelerated phase of the Rococo dating from around 1730. His work is not generally regarded to be as important in the movement of art as the work of either Meissonnier or Pineau. Some of his asymmetrical Rococo designs were especially fantastic and extravagant. His work as a whole belongs in the realm of fantasy. See *Engraved Designs.*

Lajvardina See *Islamic Pottery, Medieval.*

Lakin and Poole English potters operating a pottery at Hadderidge, Burslem, in the Staffordshire district, from around 1791 to 1795, where they made Wedgwood type wares, creamwares, and figures. Subsequently Lakin, Poole and Shrigley or Poole, Lakin and Shrigley.

Lamberton See *Sterling China Company.*

Lambeth In English ceramics; the term *Lambeth* is generally given to the faïence or delftware made in a group of London potteries at Aldgate and in the parishes south of the Thames and outside the City Walls, at Southwark, Vauxhall and especially at Lambeth during the 17th century. The faïence potteries at Lambeth were in existence at least until 1763, and other potteries in the vicinity were active until around the middle of the 19th century, although little faïence was made. No marks were used. Lambeth faïence was essentially influenced by the faïence made at Delft, Holland; however, some distinctively English styles were created around the middle of the 17th century. Some of the wares were also decorated in the tradition of Italian majolica. Included among their productions were globular jugs, ointment-pots, barrel-shaped mugs, plates and dishes, globular narrow-necked wine bottles, candlesticks, salt-cellars and stem-cups copied from silver, puzzle cups and posset-pots. Some of the wares were left entirely unpainted, others were painted in blue or in colors on the tin-glazed ground. It is often very difficult to distinguish the later 18th century faïence made at Lambeth from that made at Bristol and Liverpool. The principal inspiration for these wares was the Chinese porcelains exported to Europe. See *Faïence; Delft; Delftware; Bristol; Liverpool; Janson, Jacob.* (254-258)

Lambrequin A French term originally meaning pendent draperies applied to a variety of pendent lace-like ornament treated in a formal manner. The motif was found in the ornamental designs of such decorative artists as Bérain and Marot work in the Baroque style. See *Rouen; Style Rayonnant; Engraved Designs.* (269, 272)

Lancret, Nicolas (1660-1743) French painter; See *Watteau, A.* (278)

Lang Yao In Chinese ceramics; a Chinese term applied to Sang de Boeuf or ox-blood color porcelain. See *Sang de Boeuf.*

Lanternier, A. In French ceramics; started a porcelain factory at Limoges in 1855. The production was chiefly tableware and tea and coffee services for the export market. The marks include A. Lanternier and A.L.

Lanz, Johann Wilhelm Chief modeler at Strasbourg from around 1745 to 1754 and at Frankenthal, 1755 to around 1761 or later, where he became famous. He imbued his frequently stiff and doll-like figures with a singular artless simplicity. They were beautifully finished and showed a remarkable feeling for the plastic quality of porcelain. Though all the customary Meissen types were modeled by him, he also contributed many innovations, notably subjects from contemporary life such as beggars, peasants and gardeners, which were perhaps his best work. See *Frankenthal.* (281)

Laqabi See *Islamic Pottery, Medieval.*

Late Helladic Synonymous with Mycenaean. See *Helladic.*

Laub-und-Bandelwerk In ornament; a German term which literally means leaf and strapwork. This late Baroque style of ornament was very fashionable on glass, porcelain and faïence in the early 18th century. The Laub-und-Bandelwerk ornament was especially characteristic of German Baroque and was particularly important in ceramic art. See *Baroque; Engraved Designs.* (333)

Laüger, Max German artist-potter, teacher and experimenter; for a long period was influential at Karlsruhe, Baden, where the Karlsruhe Kunstgewerbeschule, a school for handiwork in the applied arts, flourished in the closing decades of the 19th century. He produced some notable earthenware at the nearby Kandern pottery,

decorated in Art Nouveau and in the subsequent Modern style.

Laughlin, Homer, China Company In American ceramics; this still-existing company was established in East Liverpool, Ohio, in 1874 by Homer and Shakespeare Laughlin. They produced chiefly white granite; in later years semivitreous china and higher grade wares were added to the production schedule. One of their marks represents the supremacy of the American Eagle over the British Lion.

Lavabo See *Wall Fountain.*

Le Foll, Alain See *Rosenthal.*

Le Nove See *Nove.*

Le Pautre, Jean (1618–1682) French architect, designer and engraver. His early work along with the work of Jean Marot (1619–1679), was characteristic of the reign of Louis XIII in which the Italian Baroque style was developed in a modified form. Their work was carried on by their respective sons, Pierre Le Pautre and Daniel Marot (c. 1662–c. 1752). The prolific designs of these two generations of artists represent a complete repertoire of the prevailing fashions during the reign of Louis XIV. Daniel Marot was the pupil of Jean Le Pautre. Pierre Le Pautre (c. 1648–1716) was made a dessinateur et graveur at the Bâtiments in 1699, and from that time until his death his decorative work had great influence. He combined in his style of ornament the nobility of the Louis XIV style with the gracefulness of the approaching Louis XV style. See *Marot, Daniel; Louis XIV; Baroque; Engraved Designs.*

Le Pautre, Pierre See *Le Pautre, Jean.*

Leach, Bernard (b. 1887) English artist-potter, born in Japan; studied drawing, painting and etching in London, 1903-1907. He returned to Japan in 1911 and studied pottery under Kenzan VI. He met Shoji Hamada, who accompanied him on his re-

LAUGHLIN, HOMER, CHINA CO.

C. 1899 ON

PRESENT

LEACH, BERNARD
C. 1921 ON

turn to England in 1920 and remained in England for three years. Hamada helped Leach to set up his pottery at St. Ives, which had a wood-burning fire kiln patterned after the Japanese chamber kiln. Here they began to experiment in producing Japanese-style stoneware with brushwork or wax resist decoration, and the earlier traditional English style of slipware pottery. Though Leach emphasized the potter's responsibility for the entire process of pottery-making, he also advocated the sharing of a pottery by a group of potters, particularly in the making of pottery for daily use. It was on these ideas that the pottery at St. Ives, Cornwall, was founded, where many would-be potters came as pupils. His influence has been effective not only through his pottery and the work of his students but also through his book, A POTTER'S BOOK, 1940, in which he strongly states his philosophy of pottery-making and gives a vivid description of the Oriental approach to technique. Essentially it became the potter's bible and focused the attention of potters on Chinese and Japanese values in pottery, and on stoneware as a perfect medium for the expression of something individual and yet universal in ceramics. The ideal potter became one who could claim that his pot was distinctively his own creation since he essentially carried out every process from the digging of his own clay to the firing in his own personally built kiln. Also and more significantly he was a seeker after an impersonal perfection of form and glaze, as he was more concerned in essence with the integrity of a tradition than striving to express the peculiarities of his own personal vision. This attitude strengthened the ideals of the Arts and Crafts Movement, and particularly the artist-potter's respect for his materials. As a result of this new and powerful impact the concept of artist-pottery underwent a notable development in the 1920's and 1930's, for until this time, although the artist-potter assumed responsibility for the pot as a work of art,

LEBES

LEBES GAMIKOS

the idea of subdivision of labor, inherent in the Industrial Revolution, was valid enough to warrant that the artist-potter would tend to use the skills of others wherever feasible for such tasks as turning and firing. Inevitably, potters who are concerned with a more personal approach to pottery have turned away to other less restraining styles, especially since the Second World War. Many of these potters are interested in painting and sculpture, and are concerned with a more personal expression in which the scope of color and range of form is less inhibited. See *Mashiko; Hamada, S.; Davis, H.; Cardew, M.; Braden, N.; Murray, W. S.; Coper, Hans; Arbeid, D.; Artigas, J. L.* (545)

Leach, David English artist-potter; apprenticed to the Leach pottery under his father, Bernard Leach, 1930-1933. He managed the Leach pottery for some years. After supervising a monastic pottery at Aylesford Priory, he established his own in Devonshire. See *Leach, Bernard.*

Lead Glaze See *Glaze; Galena.*

Lebes In Greek antiquities; or dinos, a large, round bowl used for mixing wine and water, made to be supported on a stand, as it was without a foot; it was also without handles.

Lebes Gamikos In Greek antiquities; a marriage bowl for ceremonial water placed in the home of the bride at the time of the wedding. This vase-shaped container was fitted with distinctive vertical, double-loop handles attached on the top of the shoulder and a conical lid provided with the pomegranate finial. The bowl rests on a conical or flaring high base or stand joined to the bowl. In another type the stand was omitted and the bowl rested on a simple ring base.

Lebrun, Charles (1619-1690) Celebrated French decorative artist. He was appointed First Painter to Louis XIV in 1662, and from that time until his death in 1690 he was virtually the arbiter of the arts of France.

Ledoux, Jean-Pierre Porcelain painter at Sèvres, 1758-1761, specializing in birds and landscapes.

Leeds In English ceramics; an English pottery manufactory at Leeds, Yorkshire, owned by Humble, Green and Company, which became Hartley, Greens and Company, made much cream-colored earthenware of the finest quality from 1774 to 1820. It was called The Old Pottery, and was reputed to have been started around 1760 by two brothers named Green. After 1820 it changed hands several times and continually declined. It finally closed in 1878. The pottery enjoyed a large domestic and export market. The most typical Leeds ware made until 1820 was characterized by a distinctive slightly greenish-yellow tone with a glass-like glaze. Useful wares were principally made. Especially characteristic were the pierced or punched decoration and the twisting handles terminating in flowers or leaves which were distinctive for their delicacy and refinement. Monochrome and polychrome painted decoration were used; however, much of the ware was not painted. The majority of the contemporary Staffordshire wares were made at Leeds. Modeled figures, especially on elaborate centerpieces, were also made. Luster ware, introduced at Staffordshire late in the 18th century was made at Leeds from about 1815. Silver luster from platinum and pink from gold were extensively used. Leeds was second in magnitude only to Wedgwood's factory at Etruria. The old Leeds wares were generally not marked; however, the impressed marks of Leeds Pottery or Hartley Greens & Co over Leeds Pottery were occasionally found. Before 1792 the Hunslet Hall Pottery was founded at Leeds by Petty and Rainforth. Their production was cream-colored ware in rivalry with the Old Pottery. The factory mark was Rainforth and Company. (404)

Leeuwarden See *Friesland.*

Léger, Fernand (1881-1955) French painter and designer; in the 1930's his architectural patterns for wall tapestries contributed much to stimulate a fashion for tapestries; he was also responsible for a number of impressive ceramic pictures.

Lei Hen See *Ting Yao.*

Leihamer, Johann (b. 1721) and his son, Abraham (1745-1774). Skilled faïence painters who played an important part in the Schleswig-Holstein faïence industry. Johann was a painter at Schleswig, around 1758, at Eckernförde, 1760-1767, and later with his son (who had married the daughter of Johann Buchwald and went along with him on his wanderings) at Criseby-Eckernförde, around 1764-1768, Kiel, 1768-1771, and Stockelsdorf, 1772-1774. See *Buchwald, Johann.* (296)

Lekanis In Greek antiquities; a shallow bowl or deep plate having a flat or almost flat cover provided with a distinctive disc-shaped finial. As a rule it was provided with two horizontal handles attached to the side of the bowl. It was regarded as a proper wedding gift and was used to hold cosmetics, trinkets and hot dishes.

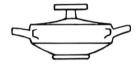

LEKANIS

Lekythos In Greek antiquities; the most common vessel for holding olive oil. There are three principal forms, all of which have a deep cup-shaped lip rim and a vertical loop handle extending from the narrow neck to the shoulder or to the top of the body. The forms are: one with a continuous curve from the neck to the base; one with the shoulder set off from the body and the third type with a broad body. The first two forms accent the vertical and look tall; the third accents the horizontal and looks squat. Many of the smaller lekythoi which contained per-

LEKYTHOS

fumed oil were placed on the graves. In time the larger lekythoi, often made as tomb offerings, were given a false bottom as the oil was costly and this was considered an unnecessary waste. (63)

Lenoble, Emile (1875-1939) French artist-potter; his work is identified with the great period of French artist-pottery when stoneware and glazes of notable beauty were produced. He used incised decoration freely and with great creativity, proving that it could be used with notable success on high-fired stoneware. In more recent times his son, Jacques Lenoble, has produced work in a rather similar manner. (529)

Lenoble, Jacques See *Lenoble, Emile.*

Lenox, Walter Scott See *Ceramic Art Company; Lenox Company.*

Lenox Company In American ceramics; in 1889 Walter Scott Lenox came to Trenton, New Jersey, to establish a pottery company which was named Lenox in 1906. It remains the undisputed master in the producing of fine porcelain dinnerware in America. See *Belleek; Ceramic Art Company.* (498)

Léonard, Agathon Modeler at Sèvres around 1900. He produced for the Paris Exhibition of 1900 a group of biscuit figures forming a table decoration or setting, Le jeu de l'écharpe, in which he conveyed the swirling movement of Art Nouveau with notable sensitivity. See *Art Nouveau.* (518)

Leonardi, Leoncillo A leading modern Italian ceramic sculptor, who, working very largely in the medium of brightly colored earthenware, has produced architectural details as well as figure-work of distinction. See *Majolica.*

Lepeltier, Odette (b. 1914) French sculptor concentrating on ceramic works. She belongs to that group of artists who have

tended to use earthenware especially with a tin glaze as a medium for figure making and for other purely decorative purposes, in the years after the Second World War.

Lerat, Jean and Jacqueline French artist-potters; prominent members of a group of potters working in the ancient pottery-producing area, near Bourges, since the Second World War. In figure-making this group shows a marked preference for strongly formed stoneware, and has in general been influenced by the work of Paul Beyer.

Les Islettes In French ceramics; a pottery at Les Islettes, or more correctly at Bois d'Epense, Meuse, began to make faïence under the direction of François Bernard and his son, Jacques-Henri, in 1785. The decoration was chiefly a coarsened version of Strasbourg. It continued to make the traditional popular faïence well into the 19th century, at the time when faïence fine enjoyed a period of great popularity. No factory mark occurs.

Lessore, Emile (1805-1876) French porcelain painter working for short periods at Sèvres and Mintons. He painted wares for Wedgwood at Etruria from around 1858 to 1863 when he returned to France, where he continued to work for Wedgwood until his death. Though he used the ceramic surface in the manner of a canvas, his bold sketchy style was not without influence. In recent years his granddaughters Louise Powell and Thérèse Lessore have decorated Wedgwood vases in modern styles.

Lesum In German ceramics; a faïence manufactory was established at Lesum, near Bremen, in 1755 by Johann Christoph Vielstich. By 1800 the production of faïence was completely supplanted by that of common earthenware. The factory is still in existence. The faïence was marked with VI with painters' initials. Included among their wares were tureens in the form of

LENOX COMPANY
PRESENT

LESUM
C. 1760 ON

birds and animals, cylindrical tankards and openwork baskets. The painted decoration was in high temperature colors that were generally rather dull; red was never used.

Lethaby, William Richard (1857-1931) English architect, designer, teacher, lecturer and writer on architecture and art; a leading designer before and after the turn of the century. He designed furniture, metalwork (chiefly fireplaces) and embroideries, painted pottery and tiles, woodwork and leadwork. Lethaby was a founder of the Art Workers' Guild, president of the Arts and Crafts Exhibition Society and a founder of the Design in Industry Association.

Levigation See *Clay, Preparation of.*

Liekki Ware See *Arabia.*

Lille In French ceramics; the earliest faïence manufactory was started here in 1696 by Jacques Féburier and Jean Bossu and was active until 1802. A third faïence manufactory was begun in 1740 by Jean-Baptiste Wamps and principally made tiles. No factory mark was used by any of these potteries. It is generally believed that their earlier wares resembled Delft and Rouen wares and that their later wares were influenced by the Strasbourg wares. The faïence manufactory founded by Doréz also made a soft paste porcelain. No mark is known to have been used. It is believed the porcelain was similar to that made at Saint-Cloud. A hard paste porcelain manufactory was started in 1784 under the patronage of the Dauphin by Leperre-Durot. It closed in 1817. The accepted mark was a dolphin stencilled in red. The wares had little quality and were of undistinguished Paris types.

Limbach In German ceramics; a porcelain manufactory was established at Limbach, Thuringia, in 1772 by Gotthelf Greiner. The early mark was LB in monogram or crossed L's, sometimes with a star added.

After 1787 the mark of a trefoil or clover leaf was adopted. Wares for daily use were chiefly painted in blue or in purple and were seldom of fine quality during the 18th century; better work was done during the 19th century. Figure modeling was also practiced. The characteristic figures were dressed in the contemporary fashion. Their faulty proportions and doll-like stiffness seemed to be a part of their singular charm.

Limburg In Dutch ceramics; an early center for peasant pottery. (211, 212)

Limerick See *Ireland.*

Limoges In French ceramics; a hard paste porcelain manufactory was established at Limoges, Haute-Vienne, in 1771 by the Grellet brothers, Massié and Fourneira under the protection of the Comte d'Artois. In 1784 it was purchased by the King to make a white porcelain which was later to be decorated at Sèvres. The usual mark was CD; Limoges with a fleur-de-lis was also recorded as a mark. The decoration was similar in style to that found on Paris and Sèvres porcelain. During the late 18th and 19th centuries the manufacture of porcelain flourished at Limoges, because of the local supplies of kaolin. Limoges was near Saint-Yrieix which was the chief source for kaolin and petuntse in France. Several porcelain manufactories were opened during the late 18th century and numerous ones came into existence during the 19th century. The important manufacturers of the first third of the 19th century, the Alluaud, Baignol and Tharaud families, were responsible for the many technical improvements that paved the way to the era of industrial prosperity and made Limoges the "porcelain town" that it still is at the present time. Among the marks were Limoges, the surname or initials of the manufacturer. See *Saint-Yrieix; Pouyat; Texeraud, L.; Lanternier, A; Vignaud, A.; Bernardaud, L.; Ahrenfeldt, C.; Haviland, D.; Fontanille and Marraud; Haviland, C. F.;*

LILLE
1784 ON

LIMBACH

1772-1788

1787 ON

LIMOGES
1771-1784

Haviland, T.; Raynaud and Company; Guérin-Pouyat-Elite. (494, 516)

Limoges Ware   In European ceramics; the name Limoges ware is given to a class of 19th century porcelain, such as vases, in which the technique of decoration was inspired by the 16th century Limoges painted enamels, mostly in white on a deep blue ground (or grisaille enamels). Many imitations of 16th century Limoges enamels were made in France at Sèvres around the mid-19th century. In England Worcester, who had noted the French examples, made a specialty of Limoges ware. See *Worcester.*

Limousin   In French ceramics; a source of kaolin. The town of Limoges was formerly the capitol of the old province of Limousin. See *Saint-Yrieix.*

Linck, Franz Konrad   (1732-1793) Court sculptor; master modeler at Frankenthal, 1762 to 1766, when he moved to Mannheim but he continued until 1775 or later to furnish models and designs. He not only added greatly to the range of Frankenthal figures but imparted a new quality to the already familiar types. No doubt his talent is best revealed in a series of single figures notable for a remarkable plastic feeling in the rhythmical and balanced composition of figures and draperies. Linck was an early follower of French Neo-Classicism. See *Frankenthal.*

Lindberg, Stig   See *Gustavsberg.*

Lindig, Otto   German artist-potter; played a formative role in the ceramic activities of the Bauhaus, whose influence on artist-pottery appears to have been chiefly in the direction of a thorough respect for the materials used and for simple natural wheel-thrown shapes. Like most modern German artist-potters, Lindig concentrated mainly on a restrained style of stoneware decorated solely by its glaze.

Lindner, Doris   See *Worcester.*

Ling Chih   In Chinese ornament; the ling chih fungus, *polyporus lucidus,* is a favorite motif in Chinese ornamental design. It was originally symbolic of good luck and later of longevity. The treatment of this motif was closely similar in appearance to the head of the ju-i scepter, which makes all wishes come true. See *Ju-i.*

Ling Lung   In Chinese ceramics; the term is applied to delicate openwork or pierced work. Cups and bowls of delicate openwork designs were made by potters working in the Wan Li reign of the Ming dynasty. See *Kuei Kung.*

Linthorpe Pottery   In English ceramics; set up by John Harrison at Middlesbrough, Yorkshire, with Henry Tooth as head; active 1879-1889. From the first the pottery was also connected with the name of Christopher Dresser. The pottery produced decorative earthenwares which combined the interest of glaze effects with the highly original forms of the professional designer Dresser. Henry Tooth probably left around 1882. Linthorpe is typical of a number of small art potteries set up particularly in Devon and the Midlands in the Late Victorian era, 1871-1901, whose general style was characterized by modeled decoration with thick colored glazes. See *Tooth, Henry; Ault, William; Brannam, C. H.; Aller Vale Art Potteries; Elton, Sir Edmund; Glaze,* in modern Western ceramics.

Lippert and Haas   See *Schlaggenwald.*

Lisbon   See *Portugal.*

Lithophane   In ceramics; the method of casting intaglio designs on thin transparent porcelain so as to produce a picture of light and shade when light shines through. This work is especially identified with the ceramic work at the Meissen and Berlin manufactories after the second quarter of the 19th century. (473)

Littler, William (b.c. 1724) Staffordshire potter making porcelain at Longton Hall around 1750-1760. About the same time, but for a longer period, he made Staffordshire salt-glazed stoneware. It is said Littler invented a deep blue glaze occasionally found on these wares. See *Longton Hall.* (415, 416)

Littleton, Harvey K. American artist-potter and glassblower; well established as a potter before he abandoned this craft in the late 1950's to work in glass.

Livermore, John (d.1658) One of the earliest slipware potters working at Wrotham, England, 1612 to 1649. Extant examples of his signed works date from this period.

Liverpool In English ceramics; faïence or delftware was made at Liverpool from around 1716 to about 1785. Cream-colored and white earthenware were subsequently made. Transfer printing on pottery was also a large part of their production. Most of the potters making faïence were principally engaged in the American export trade, and, as a result, little attention was given to any artistic productions. Liverpool faïence essentially resembled the faïence made at Bristol; however, the latter was generally superior. Huge punch bowls were a characteristic variety. Ship-bowls were among the best examples of Liverpool delftwares. Cream-colored earthenware, much of it being printed in blue or in black, and other Staffordshire types were produced at several potteries during the latter part of the 18th and 19th centuries. A printed ware manufactory was conducted by John Sadler and Guy Green in Liverpool during the latter part of the 18th century. They decorated by the transfer-printing process Liverpool earthenware and porcelain and also the wares from other parts of England, especially those from Staffordshire. Their earliest recorded work was in 1756. During the second half of the 18th century several of the potters producing faïence

wares also made porcelain. Richard Chaffers (d. 1765), a Liverpool potter, made a soapstone porcelain similar to that made at Worcester around 1756. See *Herculaneum; Faïence; Delftware; Bristol; Lambeth.*

Loc Maria In French ceramics; a faïence manufactory was founded at Loc Maria near Quimper in the department of Finistère by Jean-Baptiste Bousquet in 1690 and in 1743 it was taken over by Pierre-Paul Caussy of Rouen. The finest work was done from about 1743 to 1782 and closely imitated the wares made at Rouen. Around the last quarter of the 19th century, the manufactory began to make imitations of its 18th century productions. The modern mark since 1872 has been HB in monogram generally over Quimper.

Locker and Company See *Stevenson and Hancock; Derby.*

Loewy, Raymond See *Rosenthal.*

Löffelhardt, Heinrich German ceramic designer whose designs have been produced by porcelain factories at Arzberg and Schönwald. He has developed a Modern style in which the emphasis is mainly upon ceramic shape. This is clearly defined in a porcelain table service without decoration he designed for Arzberg in 1954.

Löffler, Berthold See *Wiener Keramik.*

Lohan or **Eighteen Lohan** In Chinese ornament; the Lohan or Arhat are the enlightened or personal disciples of Buddha. Sixteen are of Hindu origin and two more were added by the Chinese to increase the number to eighteen. Probably the group of 500 Lohan did not appear before the end of the 10th century. The Chinese popularly give the name of Lohan to a wider circle of Buddha's disciples who have been assigned to the retinue of the 500 Lohan. The images of the Lohan are derived chiefly from the art work of one or two painters of the T'ang dynasty and

LOC MARIA
1782 ON

from accounts found in Buddhist records. The Lohan and their attributes have been widely used in Chinese painting, sculpture and the decorative arts. In Japan the name *Rakan* is given to the Lohan and the name *Gohyaku-Rakan* is given to the 500 Lohan.

London Pottery See *Fulham; Lambeth; London Slipware; Janson, Jacob.*

London Slipware In English ceramics, a kind of pottery, known in England as Metropolitan, dating from around 1625-1675 and distinguished by pious inscriptions in poor lettering. See *Slipware.*

Long, W. A. An influential American potter producing original work toward the end of the 19th century. See *Lonhuda.*

Longton Hall In English ceramics; the earliest Staffordshire porcelain was made at Longton Hall, near Newcastle-under-Lyme, from 1751 or earlier. The manufactory was conducted by William Littler and apparently was active until 1760. It seems no factory mark is known to have been used. The identification of this porcelain depends upon its likeness to some salt-glazed stoneware also made by Littler. The stoneware which is marked with crossed L's has not been conclusively identified as the work of Littler; however, the evidence strongly indicates that it was his work. The porcelain wares ascribed to Longton Hall include dishes in the form of folded leaves, plates, sauce boats, butter dishes and tureens. Some figures attributed to the manufactory possess considerable merit. The painted decoration was in underglaze blue of a strong tone and in rather harsh enamel colors. (375)

Lonhuda Pottery In American ceramics; established at Steubenville, Ohio, in 1892, by Messrs. Long, Hunter and Day. The name was derived from the first syllables of their names. In 1895 Samuel Weller, who had operated a pottery at Zanesville, Ohio, since 1882, and wanted to enter the art pottery field, bought the Lonhuda Com-

LONHUDA POTTERY
1893 ON

pany, transferred the business to Zanesville and changed the name to Louwelsa. Their wares like those of Lonhuda closely resembled Rookwood standard wares. Long remained only a short time with the Weller firm and within a year he had become associated with the J. B. Owens Pottery Company, also at Zanesville. Fortified with Long's knowledge on underglaze decoration, the Owens factory entered the art pottery field. Here the earliest line, called Utopia, closely resembled Rookwood standard wares. It was also decorated with portrait heads of American Indians, horses, cats and dogs, as well as asymmetrical arrangements of floral sprays painted in colored slips under the glaze on shaded and blended grounds. After 1896 Long stayed only a short time with Owens. He then moved to Denver, Colorado, where he organized a new company, the Denver China and Pottery Company which produced Lonhuda ware. Here he introduced a new class of art ware known as Denura with various colored mat glazes, but chiefly green, and decorated with Colorado flowers modeled in relief in an Art Nouveau manner. Sometimes the surface was iridescent. Later, in 1905, Long founded the Clifton Art Pottery at Newark, New Jersey, where he made among other styles, an Indian ware which copied both the forms and decoration of American Indian pottery. See *Owens, J. B. Company; Weller, Samuel A. Company; Roseville Pottery Company; Fry, Laura A.*

Loos, Adolf (1870-1933) Austrian architect and designer; a leading personality in the Modern Movement. In a series of articles, 1897-1898, protesting against the extravagance of Art Nouveau, he recommended trying "to find beauty in form instead of making it rely on ornament." See *Secession.*

Loosdrecht In Dutch ceramics. See *Weesp.*

Losanti Ware In American ceramics; a kind of art pottery, a hard paste porcelain developed by Mary Louise McLaughlin in Cincinnati, Ohio, and exhibited at the Paris Exhibition of 1878. The following year Miss McLaughlin founded the Pottery Club of Cincinnati. A member of the club was Mrs. Marion Longworth Storer who founded her own pottery, Rookwood, in 1880. The name *Losanti* was derived from the former name of the city, Losantiville. See *Rookwood Pottery; McLaughlin, M. L.*

Lotus In ornament; the lotus flower was one of the principal forms of plant ornamentation employed by the ancient Egyptians. See *Denon, Baron.* The lotus flower was also one of the flowers of the Chinese Four Seasons, representing Summer. See *Chinese Four Season Flowers.*

Lotus Ware See *Knowles, Taylor and Knowles.*

Louis XIII King of France from 1610 to 1643. The style of Louis XIII, which is one of the principal styles of the French Renaissance, corresponds roughly to the first half of the 17th century.

Louis XIV or **Louis Quatorze Style** The name given to the French variety of the Baroque style of ornament developed in France during the reign of Louis XIV, 1643-1715, and unified under his personal rule after he became of age and assumed the reins of government in 1661. Under Louis XIV all the arts were strongly organized and developed. France became a center of great activity and dissemination in all branches of the arts. Her ascendancy in the arts under the Bourbon monarchs was evident to a greater or less extent in the style of ornament adopted in Europe through the remaining four decades of the 17th century and throughout the 18th century. Much later in the 19th century the Louis XIV style was revived with conspicuous success. Throughout the Second Empire, 1852-1870, Napoleon III, his Court and high society found all the qualities that appealed to them in the sumptuous and resplendent settings linked to the Grand

Monarque. See *Baroque; Louis XV; Historicism; Engraved Designs.*

Louis XV or **Louis Quinze Style** The name given to the French version of the Rococo or Rocaille style of ornament developed in France during the reign of Louis XV, 1715-1774. This style of ornament marked by asymmetry was evolved from the Baroque, usually called the Louis XIV style in France. It is generally accepted that the Louis XV style achieved its finest expression in the decorative arts from around 1740 to 1755-60. Owing to the discoveries at Pompeii and Herculaneum, which resulted in a universal enthusiasm for the antique, the Louis XV style was superseded by the early French Neo-Classic or Classic Revival, generally called the Louis XVI style in France. See *Rococo; Louis XVI; Revived Rococo; Historicism; Engraved Designs.*

Louis XVI or **Louis Seize Style** The name given to the early phase of the Neo-Classic or Classic Revival style of ornament developed in France. It was named after Louis XVI of France who reigned from 1774 to 1793, but it was evident some ten years or so before his accession. The Louis XVI style reasserted the taste for classic form and ornament and was dominated entirely by the principle of symmetry. Gradually, as the taste for the antique became more exacting, the Louis XVI style was eventually supplanted by the Empire style, the later phase of the Neo-Classic style of ornament. The influence of Classical art in the Louis XVI style is tempered by a distinctive lightness carried over from the Rococo, and the austerity and pedantry of the later phase are generally absent. The sentimental style, inspired by and embodied in the works of J. B. Greuze, J. J. Rousseau and Angelica Kauffmànn—to mention several characteristic figures—belongs to the period of the Louis XVI style. In ceramics; outstanding examples of the Louis XVI style in ceramic art in-

LOSANTI WARE
1880 ON

clude the porcelain of Sèvres, particularly the later figure-models of Falconet and those of his successors, and much of the faïence of Sceaux. Equally characteristic are the Meissen figures of M. V. Acier and the Höchst figures of J. P. Melchior and Derby and Tournay porcelains. See *Classic Revival; Louis XV; Empire; Revived Rococo; Engraved Design; Style Étrusque, Le; Pompeian Taste.*

Louis, Jean-Jacob (1703–1772) Working at Ludwigsburg 1762 to 1772, as chief repairer and modeler. The distinctive Venetain Fairs are ascribed to him. See *Venetian Fairs.* (329, 330)

Louis Philippe King of France, 1830-1848. The influence of the Napoleonic period was mitigated in the reign of Louis Philippe when the practice of copying every style from Gothic to Louis XVI with varying degrees of accuracy came into fashion. Until this time, under the Bourbon kings Louis XVIII, 1814-1824, and Charles X, 1824-1830, the style of the First Empire, 1804-1814-15, was still dominant. The Neo-Gothic and Revived Rococo made their debuts in the late 1820's. See *Historicism; Revived Rococo; Victorian.*

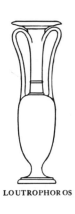

LOUTROPHOROS

Loutrophoros In Greek antiquities; a vase filled with water for the symbolic bridal bath, a wedding custom. It was a particular type of hydria, very much elongated, with a tall, narrow neck and a wide flat lip rim. The three handles were also elongated; two vertical loop handles extend upward from the top of the shoulder, while the third handle in the rear extends to reach the lip rim. Another special vase made for funeral rites was the loutrophoros amphora occasionally placed at the graves of those who died unmarried. This variety of amphora has an elongated body and a neck with a wide lip rim and two distinctive vertical engaged handles extending from the top of the neck to the top of the shoulder. As a rule the bottom of the vase was left open so that the water poured into the vase

at the grave would go directly into the earth.

Low Art Tile Works In American ceramics; a factory in Chelsea, Massachusetts, that was making tiles from 1877. In 1883, under the title of J. G. & J. F. Low, the factory produced tiles commercially for mantel facings, panels and stoves. In its employ was Arthur Osborne, whose excellent paintings in relief served to establish Low's reputation. In 1884 Low put out a catalogue of its art tiles.

Low Ford See *Ford Pottery; Dawson, John and Company.*

Louwelsa See *Weller, Samuel A. Company.*

Löwenfinck, Adam Friedrich von (1714-1754) German painter and pottery director; one of the most important figures in 18th century European ceramic art. By his introduction of enamel painted decoration on faïence, a technique borrowed from porcelain, he initiated a revolution which affected most of the German and French factories. Apprenticed at Meissen in 1726, he left for Bayreuth in 1736; at Ansbach 1737-1740; Fulda, 1741-1744-45; at Weissenau, 1745; founder and director of the Höchst faïence factory, 1746-1749; became a director at Haguenau, 1750-1754. Signed works by him reveal a wide variety in style. Apart from his personal achievement as a painter it is likely that several of the styles common to Höchst and Strasbourg, such as the naturalistically painted flowers or Deutsche Blumen, tablewares in the form of birds and fanciful Rococo forms were due to his influence. See *Strasbourg; Hannong, Charles-François; Löwenfinck, C. W. von; Löwenfinck, K. H. von; Löwenfinck, M. S. von; Overglaze.* (289)

Löwenfinck, Christian Wilhelm von (d. 1753) Younger brother of Adam Friedrich Löwenfinck, painter at Meissen 1726 and later, Höchst, 1747 and at Strasbourg 1748 and later.

LOW ART TILE WORKS
C. 1890

Löwenfinck, Karl Heinrich von (1718-1754) Younger brother of Adam Friedrich Löwenfinck; painter at Meissen, 1730 and later, at Fulda 1741-1743; at Strasbourg 1748 and later.

Löwenfinck, Maria Seraphia Suzanna Magdalena von (1728-1805) Painter and pottery-directress; daughter of J. P. Schick, painter and court official at Fulda; married Adam Friedrich von Löwenfinck in 1747. Became directress at Strasbourg-Haguenau from 1754 and later and again, 1760-1762. As the widow De Becke she was in charge of the faïence factory at Ludwigsburg from around 1763-1795.

Lowestoft In Chinese ceramics; see *Chinese Lowestoft*.

Lowestoft In English ceramics; a small porcelain manufactory operating at Lowestoft, Suffolk, from 1757 to 1802. The soft paste porcelain made at Lowestoft contained bone ash in its composition and in that respect resembles the soft paste made at Bow. Their productions, which had a rather naïve and unsophisticated charm, consisted chiefly of tablewares, various small objects such as pounce boxes, and also some small figures of cats, dogs and sheep. It seems that many commemorative gift pieces were made for country purchasers, such as mugs, tea caddies and birthday plaques. Dated and inscribed pieces bearing such inscriptions as "A Trifle from Lowestoft" were rather common. Among the finer wares were large well-painted punch bowls. Painted decoration in the Rococo and Chinese styles was especially favored. Much of the ware was painted in underglaze blue and the designs were frequently copied from Worcester patterns. The painted decoration in color was in imitation of the Chinese porcelain exported to Europe by the Dutch East India Company. There was no factory mark; however, the Worcester crescent and the crossed swords of Meissen were frequently copied. See *Chinese Lowestoft*.

Loza Fina Spanish term for faïence of fine quality.

Lu In Chinese art; a Chinese animal subject extensively used in Chinese sculpture, ceramics and painting. It is a deer and is symbolic of longevity. See *Chinese Animal Figures*.

Lu-hsing In Chinese art; a Taoist deity, who with Fu-hsing are two popular gods. They are the star gods of longevity, preferment and happiness, and with Shou Lao, who is believed to be a transformation of the founder of Taoism, make up the trinity of Taoism. Both are seen wearing official robes and one has a ju-i sceptre, which grants every wish, and the other is holding a baby who is reaching for a peach in his other hand. See *Chinese Gods; Shou Lao*.

Lucas, Daniel, Jr. See *Spode*.

Lück or **Lücke, Johann Christoph Ludwig** (d. 1780) Sculptor, mainly ivory carver; modeled at Meissen 1728–1729, and at Vienna about 1750; also porcelain arcanist.

Lück, Johann Friedrich (d. 1797) Relative, perhaps son of J. C. L. Lück. Repairer at Meissen, 1741-1757; believed to have been a modeler at Höchst around 1757 and subsequently at Frankenthal, 1758-1764. Returned to Meissen.

Lück, Karl Gottlieb (d. 1775) Most likely a son of J. C. L. Lück. Repairer and modeler at Frankenthal, 1756-1775, being made master modeler in 1766. Essentially his figures reveal the style of W. J. Lanz, but even more finely finished with elaborately worked costumes and coiffures. The rich openworked and Rococo-scrolled bases and arbors of latticework characteristic of many of the groups are also found at an earlier date and serve to give an aesthetic consistency to the detached figures. Perhaps the best of all his models are the single figures of Beggars, Dancers and Hawkers which reveal a singular characterization. See *Frankenthal*. (324)

LOWESTOFT MUG

Ludwigsburg In German ceramics; one of the seven most important porcelain manufactories in Germany during the 18th century was established at Ludwigsburg, Württemburg, in 1756, and in 1758 was taken over by Duke Charles Eugene of Württemburg, 1737-1793. It finally closed in 1824. The usual factory mark from 1758 to 1793 and occasionally later was two interlaced C's generally under a ducal coronet. Occasionally stags' horns from the Württemburg arms were used as a mark from around 1775; the initials F. R. generally under a crown were the mark of King Frederick of Württemburg, 1806 to 1816. The finest wares were made between 1764 and 1775. The most important productions of the manufactory were always the figures. Especially fine were some groups of dancers in the Rococo style. However, the chief contribution Ludwigsburg made to the ceramic art of figures were miniature groups made from about 1765 to 1770 in the Rococo style. Some miniature groups were representations of the Venetian Fairs and were replete with stalls and booths as well as buyers, peddlers and attendants. Vases and tablewares in the Rococo style reflected the influence of Frankenthal. The colors were splendid and the painted decoration was of a most finished workmanship. Figures and landscapes in panels, Rococo scrollwork, birds and bouquets of flowers were included among the favorite motifs. Especially noteworthy were some of the painted flowers. In the later years the forms and decorations were in the Neo-Classic and Empire styles. Faïence was also made at Ludwigsburg from 1757 and around 1776 cream-colored earthenware was added to the productions. The latter was of fine quality and frequently copied the porcelain wares. See *Beyer, J. C. W.; Ringler, J. J., Riedel, G. F.; Louis, J. J.* (329, 330)

Lunéville In French ceramics; a faïence manufactory was started here in 1731 by Jacques Chambrette who also established another branch factory at Saint-Clément. The potteries, after changing ownership several times, remained active throughout the 19th century. The early faïence was generally not marked and the wares were probably in imitation of those made at Strasbourg, Sceaux and Niderviller. Especially well-known are the big faïence dogs and lions which were used in pairs and were generally placed in the halls during the 18th century in France. Lunéville's chief claim to fame is due to the fine biscuit figures and groups. One variety made around 1750 and onwards was of a soft earthenware and the other variety from around 1766 was virtually a true porcelain. These figures were done by Paul Louis Cyfflé who at first was working for Chambrette and then started his own factory at Lunéville in 1766 which he sold in 1780. The best models for these figures were from everyday life and were imbued with a rare intrinsic charm. From 1766 the figures were marked Terre de Lorraine or T.D.L. impressed in relief with a stamp. Cream-colored earthenware in the English style and fine tablewares were also made at Lunéville. See *Faïence Fine.*

Lung In Chinese art; a mythical animal subject widely used in Chinese painting, textiles, ceramics and sculpture. He apparently belonged to nature worship and is believed to bring beneficial rains. There are various types of dragons such as of the sky, earth and sea and they assume different forms. Probably the best known, which is also the device of the Emperor and the emblem of Imperial power, has a bearded scowling head, straight horns, a scaly serpentine body, with four clawed feet, a line of bristling spines along his back and emitting flames from his hips and shoulders. For the last two hundred years the Imperial dragon has had five claws on each foot, while a dragon with four claws on each one of the four feet represents a prince of lower rank. The dragon is often depicted flying in clouds, rising from the

LUDWIGSBURG

1758-1793

1795-1806

1806-1816

LUNEVILLE
1766 ON

waves or playing with or pursuing a pearl. He is generally regarded as the foremost animal figure in Chinese art. See *Chinese Animal Figures; Claw and Ball Foot.*

Lung Ch'ing The Lung Ch'ing reign of the Ming dynasty in China, 1567-1572. See *Chinese Dynasties.*

Lung-Ch'üan In Chinese ceramics; see *Celadon.*

Luplau, Anton Carl (d. 1795) Modeler at Fürstenberg, 1765-1776; arcanist and master modeler at Royal Copenhagen where he greatly improved the standard of modeling and painting and imparted an unmistakable German flavor to its production.

Lüsberg, C. F. See *Krog, A.*

Luster Decoration In ceramics; a metallic film either completely covering or used as a design on the surface of pottery. This film of metal is reduced from an oxide or a sulphide. The luster pigment containing silver, copper, gold or platinum is applied with a brush over an already fired glaze. It is refired in the kiln in a reducing atmosphere caused by a smoke-producing material so that the carbon set free in this manner is united with the oxygen in the pigment and leaves a layer of pure reduced metal. There was always a great risk involved in the process. It is stated in 16th century documents that probably only six out of one hundred pieces were successful. When the metallic film was thin it often produced an iridescence of bluish, reddish or purple, or mother-of-pearl reflections. It was this color changing that gave the Near Eastern, Spanish and Italian luster painting of the 15th and 16th centuries their great beauty. The Hispano-Moresque lustered wares of the 14th, 15th and 16th centuries were of unrivalled beauty with their golden, tarnished-cop-

per and greenish luster. During the 17th century a hard bright-red copper luster was used and it is still being made at Manisses, a suburb of Valencia. Luster painting in Italy during the 16th century revealed a mastery of ruby red and golden yellow, bluish and mother-of-pearl iridescence of great beauty. Early in the 18th century Böttger at Meissen produced a purplish mother-of-pearl luster which was sparingly used on Meissen porcelain until around 1740. Late in the 18th century certain new processes were introduced in English industrial pottery to make pottery in imitation of copper and silver. This metallic film was rather thick and showed the natural color of the metal. Platinum salts were reduced to produce a silver surface and gold was used to produce a pink or purple luster. When this latter was applied over a red stoneware body it gave a coppery or ruddy gold effect. Much of the English luster ware of these types was made in Staffordshire during the late 18th and first half of the 19th centuries. The pearly luster used at Belleek and Worcester and other places around and after the middle of the 19th century was due to nitrate of bismuth. A similar method was invented in Paris by Gillet and Brianchon. See *Hispano-Moresque; Deruta; Italian Majolica; Gubbio; Belleek; Valencia; Islamic Pottery, Early.* (217-222, 231, 232)

LUNG DESIGN ON MING EWER

Luting In ceramics; the use of slip (liquid clay) to affix reliefs and the like to the surface of a vessel; also to join together two molded clay components.

Lycett, Edward See *Faïence Manufacturing Company.*

Lyman, Fenton and Company See *Bennington.*

Lyman, Fenton and Park See *Bennington.*

Lyons In French ceramics; it is generally accepted that some of the first French majolica was made at Lyons as early as 1510; however, the artistic productions ascribed to Lyons were from the latter part of the 16th century. Around 1733 production of painted faïence was revived when a manufactory was established by Joseph Combe and Jacques-Marie Ravier. It was active until 1770. Other faïence manufactories were also operating in Lyons during the 18th century but nothing is known of their history. The styles for Lyons faïence were similar to those of Moustiers. The painted decoration was almost always in high temperature colors. Especially fine were the pieces with pictures of saints and inscriptions, the so-called faïence patronymique. See *Istoriato*. (238)

M

Maastricht In Dutch ceramics; Petrus Regout (b. 1801) founded an important faïence manufactory, The Sphinx, in 1836, which still exists. They produced tin-glazed ware in imitation of English Spode and employed transfer-printed decorations. Sphinx ware is widely popular and it specializes in tableware and tea services. The accepted mark is a sphinx.

Ma-Chün In Chinese ceramics; see *Chün Yao.*

McKinley Tariff Act The McKinley Tariff Act of 1890 established the requirement that imported goods bear legible indication of the country of origin, and that requirement has continued to this day to be the law of the land. Section 6 of the Act of October 1, 1890 states: "That on or after the first day of March eighteen hundred and ninety-one, all articles of foreign manufacture, such as are usually or ordinarily marked, stamped, branded or labeled, and all packages containing such or other imported articles, shall, respectively, be plainly marked, stamped, branded or labeled in legible English words, so as to indicate the country of their origin; and unless so marked, stamped, branded, or labeled they shall not be admitted to entry." All acts after 1890 carry this provision.

Mackmurdo, Arthur Heygate (1851-1942) English architect and designer; one of the leading personalities of the Arts and Crafts Movement. See *Arts and Crafts Movement; Century Guild.*

McLaughlin, Mary Louise American artist-potter; a pioneer in the field of artist-pottery conducting her experiments in Cincinnati, Ohio. In the years immediately following the Philadelphia Centennial of 1876, Mary Louise McLaughlin, who was associated with a group of amateur china painters, developed a technique for underglaze painting in colored slips, similar to that represented at the Centennial by Charles Field Haviland's porcelain factory of Limoges. Later, decoration by colored slip was much used in American art pottery. See *Losanti Ware.* (460)

McNichol, D. E. Pottery Company In American ceramics; active at East Liverpool, Ohio, from around the 1860's, producing white granite and earthenwares.

Macquer, Pierre-Joseph See *Hellot, Jean.*

Maddock, John English potter; operated the Newcastle Street Pottery at Burslem in the Staffordshire district, 1842-1855, producing earthenwares, ironstone china and the like. Formerly it was Maddock and Seddon, 1839-1842, and subsequently John Maddock and Sons (Ltd.), 1855 to the present. They also opened the Dale Hall Pottery at Burslem in 1855. The name Maddock or John Maddock and Sons occurs in printed marks of various design. "Ltd." was added to the marks after 1896.

Maddock, John and Sons (Ltd.) See *Maddock, John.*

Maddock and Seddon See *Maddock, John.*

Mafra and Son In Portuguese ceramics; an earthenware manufactory at Caldas de Rainha founded by Manuel Mafra in 1853 and continued by his son Eduardo in 1887. Here Palissy ware was skillfully and realistically made for quite a few years. See *Saint-Porchaire.*

Magdeburg In German ceramics; a faïence manufactory was started at Magdeburg, Hanover, in 1754 by Johann Philipp Guischard. Open basketwork borders were a characteristic decoration for the early faïence wares which closely resembled those made at Münden. They were

MAASTRICHT
1891 +

MC NICHOL, D. E. POTTERY
COMPANY
1860'S ON

MADDOCK, JOHN
C. 1842-1855

MAFRA AND SON
1853 ON

also marked with an M like the Münden wares. In 1786 Guischard was granted a privilege to make cream-colored earthenware in the English style. In a few years his manufactory was one of the largest producers of cream-colored earthenware in Germany. They were marked with M or Guischard, impressed. The factory was active until 1839. In 1791 another manufactory was started by Johann Heinrich Wagener and chiefly made tile stoves. In 1799 Elias Karl Rousset and Georg Schuchard started a manufactory producing cream-colored earthenware in the English style. The wares were marked with the names impressed. It closed in 1865.

m

MAGDEBURG
FAIENCE 1754 ON

Magot or **Poussah**   A small grotesque figure, in a sitting position, of porcelain, ivory or wood, of Chinese or Japanese workmanship, inspired by the Chinese Pu-T'ai, the fat and jolly god of contentment. The porcelain magot was introduced in China during the late 17th century in the reign of K'ang Hsi, 1662-1722. A distinctive, but not invariable, feature is the movable head and hands, so perfectly weighted and balanced that the lightest touch makes them move in continuous animation. The French name is pagode. It was a favorite subject at all the earliest European porcelain factories. Notable were the magots of Chantilly which were close copies of the originals and retained their amusingly comic quality. (302, 346)

Maison de l'Art Nouveau   The name Art Nouveau, which was finally accepted in the majority of countries (the notable exception being German-speaking countries, where it was called Jugendstil or Jugend style) derives from S. Bing's first shop, Maison de l'Art Nouveau at 22 Rue de Provence, Paris. Bing, who was an early important collector of Japanese art, opened his shop in December, 1895; shortly afterward the name began to take root. Of the shop and its name Bing ob-

serves; "At its birth Art Nouveau made no claim to rising to the distinction of a generic term. It was simply the name of an establishment opened as a meeting ground for all keen young artists anxious to demonstrate the modernness of their tendencies." See *Art Nouveau.*

Maîtres Ornemanistes   Artists who engraved general repertories of designs from which ceramic modelers and painters very often took their inspiration. For example, the work of the ornemanist Jean Bérain was a formative influence in the so-called Laub-und-Bandelwerk style of interlacing scrollwork. See *Engraved Designs.*

Majolica or **Maiolica**   In ceramics; the term is applied to all varieties of Italian tin-glazed earthenware. This glaze, which is its distinguishing feature, is a lead glaze to which has been added tin ashes that results in a white and opaque glaze. By extension the term may be applied to all tin-glazed ware made in the Italian tradition characteristically painted in the polychrome majolica colors which are blue, green, yellow, orange and manganese purple. See *Faïence; Italian Majolica.* In the 19th century, Historicism, the tendency to imitate the past, an outstanding characteristic of the Victorian period, brought about a revived interest in Italian painted majolica of the 16th century. In England it was particularly the concern of Mintons in the 1850's and 1860's, and in Germany of the Royal Porcelain Manufactory in the 1860's; while in Italy, which was naturally the principal source for much of this work, there was for instance the Ginori factory at Doccia and the Cantagalli factory at Florence. Apart from the imitative painted work, the term *majolica* was also interpreted to include wares with a bright-colored glaze in which the interest is centered on the color itself and on bold relief decoration under the glaze. Undoubtedly some confusion was caused by the fact that the name *majolica* emerged from the 19th century into modern usage with a meaning which had little association with its historical prototype, the original majolica of the Italian Renaissance. Mintons, who showed their first pieces of colored-glaze majolica at the Great Exhibition, London, 1851, started the craze for it and were probably responsible for misnaming it. Regardless, it became perhaps the most characteristic earthenware of the Victorian period, as it filled a widespread need in the latter part of the 19th century. Its manufacture was started over a considerable part of Europe, without notable artistic pretensions, in the same kind of factories as had produced first the creamwares and then the printed wares in the early part of the century. In the United States, majolica in this colored-glaze sense appears to have been made as early as 1853 by Bennett of Baltimore and later from 1879 to 1890 by Griffen, Smith and Hill of Phoenixville who became the best known producer of majolica. See *Griffen, Smith and Hill; Cantagalli*. In the 20th century the modern Italian school of artist-pottery which appeared in the 1930's has mostly used the medium of brightly colored earthenware. This fact illustrates the dominant position of the faïence technique in Italian ceramics, for the experiments in stonewares and glaze effects which dominate the work of the artist-potter in other countries have played a comparatively minor role in Italy. See *Gambone, Guido*.

Makkum In Dutch ceramics; a faïence and tile manufactory was started at Makkum, Friesland, in 1675 by Freerk Jans Tichelaar and is still continued by his family. The principal productions were imitation Delft, crudely painted thick peasant-style dishes and tiles. The modern production has been limited chiefly to imitations of old Delft. A second manufactory conducted by the Kingma family produced only tiles and was active from around 1650 to 1835. See *Friesland*.

Malaga In Spanish ceramics. See *Hispano-Moresque*.

Maling See *North Hylton Pottery*.

Malinowski, Arno See *Royal Copenhagen*.

Mamluk See *Islamic Pottery, Medieval*.

Mamom See *Maya*.

Manara, Baldassare (d. before 1540) Member of a well-known Faenza family of potters. He excelled as a painter.

Mandarin In Chinese ceramics; the name given to a variety of porcelain jar made during the later part of the 18th century peculiar to the export trade. The ware is generally characterized by panels framed in underglaze blue, with figure subjects painted in red, pink and gold. This ware became popular and inspired the patterns used at several English porcelain manufactories.

Manganese In ceramics; the colors prepared from manganese are almost peculiar to pottery and are frequently of unusual beauty. Warm purplish and rich brownish colors are prepared from manganese and when it is mixed with an iron-bearing material is capable of giving an intense black. Manganese has from earliest times been known and used by potters of all classes of all countries. In general it produces purple tones in alkaline glazes and brownish tones with lead. It has the property to withstand the full heat of the high-temperature kiln. See *Colors; Manganese-Purple; Brown; Black*.

Manganese-Brown See *Manganese; Brown;*

Manganese-Purple In ceramics; many tones of purple are prepared alone from manganese or in association with other oxides. Manganese-purple is sometimes difficult to distinguish from the gold rose-pink

MAKKUM
TICHELAAR, F. J.
19TH CENTURY

(purple of Cassius). It is one of the four chief high-temperature colors as it will withstand the full heat of the faïence kiln. Occasionally manganese-purple is found as an underglaze color on soft paste porcelain but it cannot be used as an underglaze color on hard paste. As a monochrome and a conspicuous feature in the high-temperature palette it imparts great distinction to certain varieties of European faïence. On Dutch and northern French tiles it was greatly favored for monochrome painting. A manganese-purple enamel was employed with notable success at Marseilles and in monochrome painting on some late Chantilly porcelain. See *Purple of Cassius; Colors; Colored Grounds; Manganese.*

Manisses or **Manises** In Spanish ceramics; a suburb of Valencia where much if not the greater portion of luster-painted wares were produced in the 15th century and later. Around 1450 Manisses lustered ware became widely popular in Italy. It was at that time that the Italians first gave the term *majolica* to Valencian lustered wares. See *Valencia.*

Manka, Franz See *Altrohlau.*

Marans In French ceramics; a faïence manufactory was started at Marans, Charente-Inférieure, in 1740 by Pierre Roussencq. Around 1750 some workmen and materials were taken to La Rochelle where a new faïence manufactory was being organized. It is not known how long the factory remained active. Included among the marks are PR in monogram and MR. Included among the surviving examples is a wall fountain having painted decoration executed in a rather coarse version of the Rouen style.

Marbled Ware In English ceramics; the practice of blending together different colored clays to produce a ware resembling marble or agate dates to the ancient Romans during the first century. The English

MARIEBERG TERRACE VASE

potter, Dwight, working at Fulham during the late 17th century, decorated his stoneware with marbled bands made from white, brown and grey clay. This method was used for the solid agate ware produced in Staffordshire during the second quarter of the 18th century in which white, brown and blue-stained clays were blended to form a marble pattern. Wedgwood using the same method developed a ware which closely imitated natural agate and which was made into decorative vases. In another kind of marbling the surface of the ware was decorated with colored clay slips that were trailed, combed and mingled on the surface of the ware in the manner of the marbling on the papers employed in book binding. This method had been practiced on peasant pottery for many years. This marbling with colored clay slips, in which the parts essentially remain separate and distinct, was practiced in Staffordshire and many other places from the late 17th century onwards. Another method is the mottling of a fluid lead glaze by the use of metallic oxides producing indefinite splotches of color running into one another. This was the method used by Palissy in his so-called terres jaspées and by Whieldon and his followers in Staffordshire almost two centuries later. The same colors were used for both; namely blue from cobalt, copper-green and yellow from iron, and violet, purple and brown from manganese. Staffordshire earthenware with a lead glaze clouded and mottled with manganese brown and also with other colors is known as tortoiseshell ware. In a fourth type of marbling, which was practiced only at Marieberg near Stockholm, the opaque white tin glaze was marbled with coloring oxides. In Chinese ceramics; fine examples of marbled ware in which red and a light-colored clay have been mixed date from the T'ang dynasty. See *Agate Ware; Slipware; Tortoiseshell Ware.* (389, 391-396)

Maria, Giovanni One of the two artists (Nicola Pellipario being the other) whose names are particularly associated with the majolica made at Castel Durante. See *Castel Durante; Pellipario, Nicola.*

Marcks, Gerhard See *Bauhaus.*

Marieberg In Swedish ceramics; a faïence manufactory at Marieberg near Stockholm was started in 1758-1760 by Johann Eberhard Ludwig Ehrenreich and was active until 1788. The factory also made cream-colored earthenware and porcelain; however, it is best known for its faïence. The well-known crown marks were generally found on the faïence after 1763. The better wares were produced during the early years, and had one of three distinctive glazes, namely greyish, violet or marbled. The marbled glaze with its black-violet, grey, and less prominent red, blue, and brown streaks, was almost unique in faïence ceramics and was very effective and pleasing. High temperature colors except for a clear strong blue were rarely used. The enamel colors were particularly fine. Gilding was seldom used. The early wares, 1760-1766, were in the Scandinavian Rococo taste. Included among the productions were knobs in the form of fishes and birds, tureens with shell moldings and richly colored applied fruit, flowers and leaves and the so-called terrace-vases having a base formed of swirling waves or a winding flight of steps. The later faïence in the French Rococo and Neo-Classic styles retained an individual and fine quality. The cream-colored earthenware, which was usually marked with Sten over M B impressed, was decorated either with transfer prints or designs molded in relief. The soft paste porcelain was similar to that made at Mennecy. Especially characteristic were the reeded custard cups with painted floral motifs. The usual mark was an incised monogram MB. Hard paste porcelain was also made and the painted decoration was often monochrome. See *Berthevin, P.; Faïence Fine; Rörstrand.*

Mark In ceramics; a name, monogram, letter or other device impressed, raised, scratched, painted, printed or stenciled under or over the glaze on pottery, stoneware and porcelain indicating the factory where it was made, its date, maker or decorator. The custom of writing a mark of origin on pottery dates from early times, with signatures of painters occurring on ancient Greek pottery. The practice of inscribing a mark on the base undoubtedly had its provenance in Chinese porcelain. Although these Chinese marks were generally the name of reigning Emperors they were interpreted in Europe as potters' marks, with the earliest fully developed factory mark occurring on 16th century Medici porcelain in the form of the Cathedral dome of Florence. Meissen's adoption in 1724 of the crossed swords as a factory mark established the practice of using factory marks with some degree of regularity in Europe, with other porcelain as well as some faïence factories following the Meissen custom. Finally the custom of marking porcelain was sanctioned by law, and in 1766 French porcelain makers were required to put on their wares a mark already registered with the police authorities. A regular marking system was developed at such manufactories as Sèvres, Vienna and Frankenthal. However, since the system was never competently protected against imitation and was seldom compulsory, and in that respect different from the marks on silver, it is patent that the 18th century marks were far from reliable evidence as to the source of origin of a piece of pottery. Aside from the factory marks and full names of potters and painters, the latter generally occurring on Hausmalerei and special work fabricated outside the manufactory, it was a rather general practice in the 17th and 18th centuries for ceramic workers to add an identifying sign, such as an initial letter or a numeral, to their work. This was added purely for the information of those managing the factory. A mark in color or

MARIEBERG

FAIENCE C. 1760-1766

PORCELAIN 1769-1788

in gold was used by the painters and gilders, while the throwers and "repairers" used a scratched mark. Occasionally scratched marks were in reference to the composition and impressed or scratched numerals were sometimes used as mold numerals. Included among other marks were the ownership marks, dealers' marks and destination marks. See *McKinley Tariff Act; Backstamp; False or Fake Mark; Pattern Mark; Workman's Mark; Factory Mark; Body Mark; Date Mark; Decorator's Mark; Potter's Mark; Chinese Porcelain Marks; Japanese Porcelain Marks.*

Markup, Václav Czechoslovakian artist-potter; since the 1930's he has become known for his pottery figures.

Marot, Daniel (c. 1662-c. 1752) French designer, engraver and architect. His work, which was characteristic of the second phase of the Louis XIV style, 1661-1685-90, was distinctive for its splendor and elaboration. Marot possessed a profound knowledge of French classical design. He published a prolific number of designs remarkable for their lavish display of classical ornament which exerted enormous influence on contemporary taste. See *Le Pautre, Jean; Louis XIV; Baroque; Engraved Designs; Lambrequin.* (261, 299)

Marot, Jean See *Le Pautre, Jean.*

Marquet, Pierre Albert (1875-1947) French painter; became interested in the decoration of pottery at the incentive of José Llorens Artigas.

Marseilles In French ceramics; although some distinctive faïence in the manner of Nevers, Moustiers and Rouen was made at Marseilles during the late 17th and first half of the 18th centuries, the reputation of Marseilles faïence chiefly rests upon the fine enamel-painted faïence made during the third quarter of the 18th century. The earliest faïence of importance was made at Saint-Jean-du-Désert, a suburb of Mar-

seilles, in a factory conducted by Joseph Clérissy, in 1679. There were at least six other large and prosperous and also some minor faïence manufactories operating in Marseilles during the 18th century. However, with the exception of the early productions at Saint-Jean-du-Désert it is difficult to separate the Marseilles faïence into factory groups because many of the wares were not marked and the migration of the painters from one pottery to another tended to create a common style. The painted enamel decoration in the Rococo style was executed in a subtle free-flowing manner that imbued it with spontaneity and an effortless charm. It was gay and stimulating. The forms were also in the same easy and graceful French spirit. The enamel colors were of great beauty. Figures were also made in faïence, but they had little originality. The only porcelain of importance made at Marseilles was produced in the faïence manufactory of Joseph-Gaspard Robert from around 1773. His faïence and porcelain were decorated in a similar manner; especially typical were the extravagant Marseilles flowers. Marseilles potters treated the various subjects with typical southern French verve: fanciful chinoiseries; flowers in loose sprays painted with a fresh naturalness; charming trophies with fish, shells and all the fruits of the sea combined with fishing tackle and evocative of Marseilles, the seaport. Reflections of contemporary paintings were found on some wares: amorous scenes from Watteau, Boucher or Lancret; a seaport from Joseph Vernet or classical ruins inspired by the compositions of Hubert Robert. See *Clérissy, Pierre and Joseph; Viry; Perrin, Veuve.* (285-287)

Martin Brothers, Robert Wallace, Charles, Walter and Edwin All born in London between 1843-1860. Artist-potters producing individual studio-type salt-glazed stoneware from 1873 to 1914. The association of the four brothers in the making and selling of pottery was due mainly to

MARSEILLES
ROBERT, JOSEPH GASPARD
C. 1773-1793

MARTIN BROTHERS
1882-1914

Robert Wallace's initiative. In 1873 he set up a pottery studio and workshop for himself and his brothers at Fulham. In 1877 they moved to Southall and in 1879 they opened a shop and gallery in London. Charles took care of the shop and most of the business arrangements. Wallace was concerned above all with modeling; Walter was the principal thrower, and also the kiln-burner and chemist; Edwin was the principal decorator. They did not keep rigidly to precise roles. Most of their production comprised vases and similar decorative wares. Their work has enjoyed notable fame in recent years and they are often referred to as the first masters of modern English pottery. Their best work was done after they attended the Paris Exposition, 1900, where they saw the finer Japanese wares, which guided them to simple shapes and to more subtly wrought indefinite slips and glazes. Martin ware can almost always be identified and dated without difficulty. (482)

Marzacotto The Italian term given to the thin film of lead glaze on the surface of Italian majolica to increase the brilliancy of the colored decoration.

Mashiko In Japanese ceramics; an important center for handcrafted pottery. Mashiko is a small farming town about 50 miles north of Tokyo with a population of 25,000. About 40 families, mostly part-time workers of the farming community, are engaged in making pottery. Each family has its own kiln and bakes pottery only once every month or two. Clay deposits suitable for pottery-making were discovered near Mashiko in 1853. The people began trying in a very primitive way to supply low-grade kitchen utensils to the Tokyo market. However, in 1924, a young potter named Shoji Hamada, who is at the present time one of the leaders in Mingei-type (folk art) handcrafted pottery, settled down in Mashiko and started his life work. Through his influence Mashiko potters improved in making Mingei-type pottery, which is the specialty of Mashiko. The famous English potter Bernard Leach visited the town on several different occasions to study Mashiko pottery. See *Japanese Contemporary Pottery; Hamada, Shoji; Leach, Bernard; Yanagi, Soetsu.*

Mason, John (b. 1927) American ceramist; has executed numerous commissions of architectural ceramic wall reliefs and ceramic sculpture.

Mason, Charles James and Company Staffordshire potters active at the Patent Ironstone China Pottery, Lane Delph from 1829 to 1845. Formerly it was G. M. and C. J. Mason, 1813-1829, and subsequently Charles James Mason, 1845-1848. The name Fenton Stone Works first occurs in marks around 1825.

Mason Ironstone See *Ironstone China.*

Massier, Clément French artist-potter; son of a potter in Valluris. Around the turn of the 20th century he produced at his studio at Golfe-Juan, near Cannes, attractively decorated wares with luster-glaze effects. (489)

Massoul, Félix French artist-potter; he became concerned with pottery in the 1890's and is identified with the remarkable flowering of artist-pottery in France centered in Paris in the decades around 1900. He was known for his range of decorative styles, frequently influenced by his interest in archaeology.

Mathews, Heber (1905-1959) English artist-potter studied painting and design at the Royal College of Art; subsequently concentrated on the study of pottery under the tuition of William S. Murray, 1927-1931. Matthews was one of the early exponents of English contemporary ceramics and was adviser to the Council of Industrial Design. He exhibited widely all over the world. He used H.M. incised as his mark from 1931 to 1959. See *Murray, William S.*

MASON'S IRONSTONE
C. 1820 ON

MATHEWS, HEBER
1931-1958

Mathieu, Jean-Adam Enameler to Louis XV; charged with the supervision of modeling and decoration at Vincennes-Sèvres, about 1745-1753.

Mathildenhöhe In 1899 the Grand Duke Ernst Ludwig of Hesse-Darmstadt invited seven artists to live as a group in the artist colony of Mathildenhöhe in Darmstadt. The original group, "Die Sieben," comprised the architect and designer Peter Behrens of the Munich School; architect and designer Joseph Olbrich, one of the founders of the Secession in Vienna; designer Hans Christiansen; architect and designer Patriz Huber (1872-1902); sculptors Ludwig Habich (b. 1872) and Rudolf Bosselt (1871-1938); and painter Paul Bürck (b. 1878). The colony was officially opened in 1901 with an exhibition called A Document of German Art. The activity of the group was dominated by Behrens and Olbrich. See *Jugendstil; Behrens, Peter; Olbrich, Joseph.*

MAYER, THOMAS, JOHN
AND JOSEPH
1843-1855

Maund, Geoffrey English artist-potter. Has operated the Geoffrey Maund Pottery Ltd. at Croydon, Surrey, since 1952, where he makes handmade earthenware. Among his impressed marks since 1953 are G M in monogram.

Maximinenstrasse In German ceramics. See *Cologne.*

MAYER, J. AND E. POTTERY
COMPANY
1881 ON

Maya In pre-Columbian Central American ceramics; the earliest cities of the Maya were at Tikal and Uaxactum in the lowlands of Peten. Their Formative period was known as Mamom (earlier) and Chicanel (later). In the Classic period, 300-980, the real area of development independent of Teotihuacan was in the territory of the Maya who occupied the southeastern provinces of Mexico, Guatemala, Honduras and British Honduras. For ritual purposes the simple wares of the Formative period were supplanted by a polychrome ware known as Tzakol, usually with a cream or orange-colored base on which were painted designs in red and black. The polychrome decoration of the early Classic phase was geometrical or at least highly conventionalized. It varied from bands of black and red, rectangles and frets to stylized serpents. The insides of the plates and dishes were also painted with motifs usually in the form of animals and occasionally fish. The second phase of the Classic period known as Tepeu was one of great variety. The most striking were the polychrome vessels and a monochrome ware in which the ornament was carved in low relief. The designs on the carved vessels were generally limited to a narrow band of hieroglyphs that were used purely for ornament. Of the polychrome painted decoration the most beautiful of all were the scenes depicting Maya ceremonial life. See *Central American Pottery.* (8, 9)

Mayener Ware In German ceramics; a pottery fired to a stoneware hardness and of a red tone shading to violet, decorated with grooves and wavy lines, first made at Mayen in the Rhineland in the 8th century. See *Badorf.*

Mayer, Elijah Staffordshire potter. Operated the Cobden Works, Hanley, from around 1790-1804, where he made Wedgwood-type wares, creamwares and black basaltes of fine quality. The name was changed to Elijah Mayer and Son in 1805, when they added china to their production. Remained active until 1834.

Mayer, J. and E. Pottery Company In American ceramics; founded at Beaver Falls, Pennsylvania, in 1881. A fire in 1896 destroyed much valuable property at this factory.

Mayer, Thomas Staffordshire potter; operated Cliff Bank Works, Stoke, about 1826-1835, and Brook Street, Longport, about 1836-1838; produced earthenwares. His blue transfer-printed wares were extensively exported to America and American devices appear in the marks. (468)

Mayer, Thomas, John and Joseph Stafford-shire potters. Operated the Furlong works and Dale Hall Pottery at Burslem, 1843-1855, where they made earthenwares, china, parian and the like. Their products were varied and highly regarded. Interesting molded parian wares were a distinctive feature. They exhibited at the International Exhibitions of 1851, 1853 and 1855.

Mayodon, Jean French artist-potter working in the 20th century. His stonewares of the 1920's and 1930's were notable for their vigorous creativity combined with thorough technical knowledge.

Mazápan See *Toltec.*

Mazarine Blue In Chinese ceramics; it is generally accepted that the phrase *mazarine blue* refers to a brilliant deep blue monochrome glaze introduced during the reign of K'ang Hsi. See *Gros Bleu.* The term *mazarine blue* perhaps so-called from Cardinal Mazarin or the Duchesse de Mazarin was given in England to a deep rich blue and appeared in late 17th century records. The name was also given to the material or the costume of a mazarine blue color.

Mead, Dr. Henry (d. 1843) In American ceramics; apparently the first successful manufacture of porcelain in America was little more than an experiment, as there survives from it but one example. This was achieved by Dr. Henry Mead of New York City around 1816 and is a white, undecorated, soft paste porcelain vase with figural handles in the style of the French Empire. In his obituary it was stated that he was "a man of genius and enterprise being the first who ever manufactured porcelain or china ware in this country which he commenced at Jersey City. . . ." (447)

Meakin, Alfred (Ltd.) Staffordshire potters operating the Royal Albert, Victoria and Highgate potteries at Tunstall from 1875 onward. "Ltd." was added around 1913.

Meakin, J. and G. (Ltd.) In English ceramics; started the Eagle Pottery and Eastwood Works at Hanley in the Staffordshire district in 1851 where they produced earthenwares, ironstones and the like. In 1958 the Eastwood Pottery was sold and the Eagle Pottery was expanded and modernized. In 1947 they started a series of printed scenic patterns entitled Romantic England.

Medallion In ornament; a large medal or something resembling a large medal, such as a round or oval tablet, having a figure represented in relief, a portrait or a decorative motif. It was a favorite ornament during the Italian Renaissance. Portrait medallions were executed in Wedgwood's jasper ware and were remarkable for their beautiful coloring and classical composition. They were occasionally used for the enrichment of fine furniture such as commodes designed in the Adam style. See *Ceramic Plaques as Furniture Decoration.*

Medici Porcelain In Italian ceramics; the famous and very frequently beautiful soft paste porcelain which was the first to have been made in Europe. It was known to have been made under the protection of Francesco Maria de' Medici, Grand Duke of Tuscany, from about 1575 to 1587. Accounts relating to its invention are conflicting and some mention that it was made under Francesco's predecessor, Cosimo I. There are still extant about sixty specimens and two dated specimens, almost all of which bear a carefully painted mark of the dome of the cathedral of Florence with the initial F beneath. The forms are often similar to Urbino majolica and include pilgrim bottles, vases, dishes with broad flat rims and central convex bosses, ewers, twin flasks for oil and vinegar and small jugs with pinched lip spouts. As a rule the painting was in blue only with occasional touches of purple for outlining, and was

MEAKIN, ALFRED (LTD.)
C. 1875-1891

MEAKIN, J. AND G.
1912-C. 1950

MEDICI
1575 ON

inspired by the painted decoration on Chinese porcelains. Chinese motifs were mingled with characteristic majolica motifs such as grotesques and foliage. Painted figure subjects were relatively rare. The glaze was seldom pure white and was generally hazy with minute bubbles. (298)

Medieval Near East Pottery The extraordinary development of the art of the potter in the Near East dates from the 9th century. Near East potters were never able to make true porcelain because of a lack of suitable clays. At first they imitated its whiteness by covering a buff or pink earthenware with an opaque glaze containing tin oxide. From the 12th century onward they developed a translucent white material chiefly comprising glassy matter and white pipe clay. These materials restricted the Islamic potters to comparatively simple shapes. Their true genius was in painted and carved surface decoration and in devising the pigments and colored glazes in which it could be carried out. The Islamic potters made use of ornamental inscriptions and the calligraphic rhythms of writing pervaded all other themes of decoration. Plant forms, never naturalistic, evolved through phases of stylization to become purely geometrical figures. The arabesque was a compromise between plant and geometrical forms that could be adjusted to fill a space of any shape. Human and animal figures were banned only from buildings and objects of religious purpose; they frequently appeared on pottery, but are always more or less subordinate features in a decorative design. At first the designs were bold and imposing with little feeling of movement, but in the 12th century they became more delicate and intricate, and the figures frequently appear to be in lively motion. In Mesopotamia the potters of the 9th and 10th century discovered and perfected gold luster; this secret passed to Egypt under the Fatimid dynasty, 969–1171, and subsequently to Syria and Persia. In the mean-

while under the Samanid dynasty, 878–999, in East Persia and Turkestan, very original effects were produced by painting in clay slips of various colors under a clear lead glaze. For less ambitious lead-glazed wares the sgraffiato method was favored; the designs were cut through a layer of white slip to reveal the darker clay body. From the 12th century, particularly in Persia, the new white composite material effectively lent itself to finely carved and pierced decoration. Painting in various enamel colors as well as in gold luster were now done on the already fired glaze. Finally a satisfactory method was developed for painting in a few staple colors under the glaze without smearing the design; this economical technique eventually superseded all others. See *Islamic Pottery*. (154-169)

Megarian See *Roman Pottery*.

Mehlem, F. A. See *Poppelsdorf; Damm*.

Mehlhorn, Johann Georg (d. 1735) And his sons, arcanists and painters at Meissen. The father and his son Johann Gottfried were at Meissen from 1720 onward; another son, Johann Gottlieb, was mentioned as painter at Meissen from 1734, and about fifteen years later at Prague, Vienna, Holitsch and then in 1754 arcanist at Copenhagen. A third son, Johann Ernst, was also working at Meissen before 1735.

Mei p'ing In Chinese ceramics; the Chinese term given to a Prunus (plum) vase having a short narrow neck to hold a flowering branch of plum-blossom. (119)

Meigh, Charles English potter operating the Old Hall Works at Hanley in the Staffordshire district, 1835-1849, where he produced earthenwares and stonewares. Formerly it was Job Meigh and Son, around 1805-1834, and subsequently Charles Meigh, Son and Pankhurst, 1850-1851. The name of Charles Meigh is especially associated with the white stoneware

MEIGH, CHARLES AND SON
1851-1861

jugs with relief decoration that were popular toward the middle of the 19th century. It is interesting to note here that the decoration on these jugs was included in the mold from which they were cast, and thus scarcely any additional expense was involved beyond that of forming the original model. Relief decoration of this kind is to be distinguished from that of affixing clay motifs which have already been molded or modeled elsewhere, such as in jasper ware; it is also to be distinguished from relief decoration which has been carved on the surface. Notable among the jugs of the 1840's were those decorated with Gothic detail. The most famous of these and the one that set the style for most of the others was registered in 1842 by Charles Meigh. This jug, often known as the "Minister" jug, was vertical-sided and bore a relief figure in each of the eight Gothic niches and illustrates the Gothic taste of the 1840's. Inevitably in this Victorian era of stylistic eclecticism the Gothic jugs were balanced by Classical jugs, which were classical only in the spirit of their decoration. Bacchic scenes were highly favored and in 1844 Charles Meigh introduced a jug which was decorated with vines and with a Bacchic scene of dancing figures adapted from Nicholas Poussin's "Bacchanalian Dance" and which won for him a medal from the Society of Arts in 1847. A similar combination is found in the Silenus jug which was made by Mintons and also appeared in brown salt-glazed stoneware. Sporting scenes and drinking scenes were probably the two most frequent genre subjects to be used on the jugs of the 1840's and 1850's. The use of motifs associated with drinking was suitable as these jugs were probably chiefly used for serving beer at the table. Perhaps the most interesting from an art-historical point of view are the jugs which depict in their decoration or form the naturalism of the mid-19th century. These were often decorated with loose-running plant motifs growing from a gnarled or rusticated han-

dle, and were in marked contrast with the rather restrained formality which was to prevail in the 1860's. Relief-decorated wares of this kind were apparently not produced to any appreciable extent in Continental European factories. However, the United States witnessed an important development of relief-decorated wares in a variety of materials. See *Relief-Decorated Wares.* (469)

Meigh, Charles and Son   Operated the Old Hall Works at Hanley, 1851 to 1861. It was formerly Charles Meigh, Son and Pankhurst, 1850–1851.

Meigh, Job (and Son)   English potter operating the Old Hall Pottery, Hanley, about 1805–1834. "Son" was added about 1812. Subsequently became Charles Meigh.

Meiji   The Meiji period of Japan A.D. 1868-1912. See *Japanese Periods.*

Meillonas   In French ceramics; in 1759 Hugues de Marron, seigneur of Meillonas, started a pottery for making faïence at his chateau at Meillonas near Bourg-en-Bresse in Ain. De Marron was guillotined in 1794, but the pottery survived until 1830. It appears that around 1763 on-glaze enameled decoration was introduced by a Swiss painter, Protais Pidoux, formerly working at Aprey. The influence of Marseilles with that of Strasbourg is evident in their faïence.

Meissen   In German ceramics; a German porcelain manufactory was established in 1710 in the fortress of Albrechtsburg, at Meissen, where it remained until 1865, under the protection of Augustus the Strong, Elector of Saxony, with Johann Friedrich Böttger as manager. The Saxon State manufactory is still in existence, producing the porcelain always known in England as Dresden and in France as Saxe. From 1710 until the outbreak of the Seven Years War in 1756 the manufactory enjoyed an almost unrivaled supremacy. Much of the

MEISSEN

1725-1763

1934 ON

porcelain made during that period possessed the highest artistic merit and had the greatest influence on the history of European ceramic art. The leadership of Meissen passed to Sèvres when the Seven Years War started. Under the management of Count Marcolini, 1774 to 1814, the prosperity of the factory was revived, but it was no longer capable of creating new styles. Much of the success of Meissen was due to Johann Gregor Herold (1695-1775) who was the art director from 1720 to 1765. He improved the quality of Böttger's porcelain and brought it closer to the Chinese standard for porcelain. Shortly after 1720 he invented a new range of enamel colors and also fine colored enamel grounds. He also created and introduced several new kinds of painted decoration. Of particular interest were the chinoiseries; a new European miniature style with landscapes, especially harbor scenes, and small figures, bird motifs, and versions of Oriental flowers and realistically treated European flowers. The fame of Meissen to a large extent depends chiefly upon its porcelain figures. Johann Joachim Kaendler (1706-1775) the celebrated modeler, was working at Meissen from 1731 to 1775. He with the help of his assistants is virtually regarded as the creator of the European style of figure modeling. The best-known mark was the crossed swords from the Electoral arms of Saxony. It was first used around 1724, and the mark with slight variations such as dots or a star remained the factory mark until World War II. During the so-called Böttger period, 1710-1719, red stoneware and white porcelain were made. In the early Herold period, 1720-1731, chiefly painted wares were produced. Especially typical were the painted chinoiseries freely adopted from the Chinese Famille Verte. From about 1725 to 1730 the Japanese brocaded Imari pattern and the Kakiemon styles were more or less closely copied. The outstanding feature during the Herold and Kaendler or Late Baroque period, 1731 to

MEISSEN VASE

1740-1745, was the great development in figure modeling. Chinoiseries in painted decoration were supplanted by a miniature style of landscape painting with small figures. In the succeeding Rococo period, 1740-1745 to 1763, the fashion for Meissen figures reached its height. In the subsequent two periods, 1763 to 1774, and the Marcolini period, 1774 to 1815, the influence of Sèvres was evident and the decoration was in accordance with the contemporary Neo-Classic style. At the present time the workers at Meissen are kept busy making tablewares and reproducing Kaendler's models painted in a manner to appeal to contemporary taste. See *Zwiebelmuster; Indian Flowers; Deutsche Blumen; Porcelain; Böttger, Johann Friedrich; Ozier Pattern; Toy; Kirchner, Johann Gottlob; A. R.; Baroque; Herold, J. G.; Herold, C. F.; Heintze, J. G.; Löwenfinck, A. F. von; Löwenfinck, C. W. von; Klinger, J. G.; Hauer, B. G.; Kaendler, Johann Joachim; Eberlein, J. F.; Ehder, J. G.; Reinicke, P.; Meyer, F. E.; Punct, C. C.; Acier, M-V.; Schönheit, J. C.; Jüchtzer, C.G.; Hunger, C. C.; Colored Grounds; Flowers Modeled in Porcelain; Horn, J. C.; Mehlhorn, J. G.; Pfeiffer, M. A.; Scheurich, P.; Swan Service.* (301-320, 495)

Meissonnier, Juste Aurèle (1695-1750) French goldsmith, painter, sculptor, architect and designer. He was one of the principal designers whose ideas created the fashion for the Rocaille or Rococo style. Meissonnier, who is best known for his numerous collections of designs, is generally regarded as the most extreme of all the designers working in the Rocaille style. He was popular not only in France but in all the other countries of Europe which adopted the Rococo style of ornament. His best work was imbued with a quality of freedom and pliability that was remarkably striking. Unfortunately much of his work was marred by his fondness for complicated curves. Louis XV appointed him Designer to the Chamber and Cabinet of the King. Another principal designer and architect in the Rocaille style who was also best known for his collection of designs was Gilles-Marie Oppenord (1672-1742). He was appointed Chief Director of all Architectural and Decorative Work for the Regent. His designs at times retained some of the grandeur of the previous century. Both the work of Meissonnier and Oppenord was characterized by the principle of asymmetry, by complicated curves and by the predominance of shell work in their style of ornament. See *Louis XV; Rococo; Engraved Designs; Genre Pittoresque.* (314)

Melanesia See *Oceania.*

Melchert, James (b. 1930) American potter-sculptor of Oakland, California; his work owes much to "Pop" art, painting and graphics. Melchert may use clay merely as a convenient material to convey his purpose, without regard for the properties traditionally associated with clay, for traditional restrictions on the use of clay as a craft material are in some cases inhibiting restrictions. For example, he may shape a vase as though it were made of leather and he may decorate it with an imitation zip-fastener, clearly showing the influence of "Pop" art on ceramics. (559)

Melchior, Johann Peter (1742-1825) Sculptor; modeler for porcelain at Höchst, 1767-1779, Frankenthal, 1779-1793, Nymphenburg, 1798-1822. He was made master figure-modeler in 1770 at Höchst where his best work was done in a very individual style that gave to his subjects, dictated by the Neo-Classical fashion, certain elements of lightness and carefree gaiety retained from the preceding Rococo style. Especially typical early work is to be found in the many figures of children embodying in an original style the sentiment of the time. In Germany this style is especially identified with the SORROWS OF WERTHER written by Goethe in 1775. For a short time at Frankenthal he continued to exploit his elegiac, even sentimental, style in figures of children. However, this personal quality soon disappeared from his work as he became more deeply immersed in Neo-Classicism. At Nymphenburg his work shows no trace of his earlier and most familiar manner. It is always in biscuit and includes admirable portrait-reliefs of contemporaries, and figures and groups always in the Neo-Classical style, and always fine technical achievements. See *Louis XVI.* (325)

Mellor, Venables and Company In English ceramics; operated the Hole House pottery at Burslem in the Staffordshire district from 1834 to 1851. They produced a range of transfer-printed earthenwares for the American market. Of great interest were their two states series.

Melon Ware In English ceramics; modeled and colored in imitation of a melon, made by Whieldon, Wedgwood and other English potters in the latter part of the 18th century.

Memmingen See *Künersberg.*

Mennecy or **Mennecy-Villeroy** In French ceramics; a soft paste porcelain and faïence manufactory protected by the Duc de Villeroy was founded in 1734 and at first was operated in the Rue de Charonne in Paris. It was transferred to Mennecy in 1748 and to Bourg-la-Reine in 1773. These three manufactories essentially form a single manufactory. It was managed from the beginning by François Barbin. Little is known of his productions except for the porcelain. In 1766 the factory was bought by Joseph Jullien and Symphorien Jacques. It was in operation until 1806. For the last twenty years of its existence it chiefly made faïence. The factory mark for the Villeroy porcelain was DV. In 1773 Jullien and Jacques registered B R as a mark for their new factory. Early Mennecy porcelain to some degree imitated the wares from Saint-Cloud and Chantilly. The material, however, soon de-

.D.V.

MENNECY
1748 ON

veloped a distinctive character. The characteristic Mennecy glaze was brilliant and shiny, and the color of the finest was milky white. The inspiration for the mature Mennecy style was largely the work at Vincennes. The enamel painting of its finest work was distinctive for its individual treatment of borrowed motifs and for its fresh cool crisp colors. The figure modeling was not always very finished but it did have a charming simplicity. Biscuit figures of the Jullien and Jacques period were rather uninteresting. The porcelain productions at Bourg-la-Reine are difficult to distinguish from the work at Mennecy unless they are marked. (347-350)

MERCER POTTERY CO.
1875 ON

Mennicken In German ceramics; a family of stoneware potters working at Raeren and at Grenzhausen in the Westerwald. Their names and dates are known almost entirely from inscriptions and signatures on reliefs decorating the pottery itself. The most important, Jan Emens Mennicken of Raeren, active 1566 to 1594, frequently dropped the surname and his relatives apparently always did so. The work of Baldem Mennicken, active 1574 to 1584, was almost equally as important as that of his contemporary Jan Emens, who was presumably a relative. It is believed that Johann Mennicken (signing I M) went from Raeren to the Westerwald about 1595, where his mark is common on Grenzhausen stoneware jugs for the following two decades. See *Raeren*. (194)

THE METAL POT
1759-1764

Mercer Pottery Company In American ceramics; established in 1869 by James Moses at Trenton, New Jersey; claims to have been first in America to make semi-porcelain. White-ware dinner services were its principal production. See *Granite Ware; Ironstone*.

Mesopotamia See *Near East*, in prehistoric ceramics; *Islamic Pottery*.

Metal Mounts on Ceramics From about the 14th century onwards it was a widespread practice in Europe, particularly in Germany, to mount in silver such exotic materials as ostrich egg and coconut shells and semi-precious stones such as rock-crystal. Chinese porcelain had been so mounted from around the end of the 14th century. Islamic pottery, Roman red-ware and Rhenish stoneware offer examples of similar treatment. In the 16th and 17th century Rhenish stonewares were richly mounted in English silver. In the 17th and 18th century many German pottery tankards and jugs were mounted in pewter. Early Chantilly was mounted in gilt bronze (i.e., bronze doré or ormolu), a material then even more in favor than silver. Undoubtedly included among the masterpieces of the 18th century art are the gilt bronze mounts enriching Chinese as well as Vincennes, Sèvres and Meissen porcelains designed and made by such celebrated ciseleurs as Jean Claude Duplessis in the Louis XV period and Pierre Philippe Thomire in the later years of the 18th and early part of the 19th century. See *Duplessis, J. C., Thomire, P. P.* (104, 319, 352)

Metal Pot, The or **De Metale Pot** In Dutch ceramics; a pottery at Delft producing faïence, active from 1639 to 1764 or later under various proprietors. It was sold in 1691 to Lambertus van Eenhoorn, one of the great representatives of Delft polychrome, who continued to operate it until his death in 1721. See *Porcelain Bottle, The; Delft; Faïence.* (266)

Methey, André (1871-1920) Notable French artist-potter; exhibited at the Salon d'Automne and Salon des Independants; probably responsible for the return into fashion of tin-glazed decorative techniques. Though Methey was later to make on his own account a large quantity of decorative colorful pottery, much of his early fame was gained by means of pieces painted by many of the great artists of the Ecole de Paris. At the Salon d'Automne of 1907, plates, vases and dishes, produced at his workshop at Asnières near Paris, were decorated and signed by Maurice Denis, Bonnard, Odilon Redon, Georges Rouault, Vuillard, Friez, Maillol, Vlaminck and Derain.

Mettlach   See *Villeroy and Boch.*

Meyer, Friedrich Elias   (1723-1785) Modeler at Meissen, 1746-1761, and model master at Berlin, 1761-1785, where the style of figure-modeling was almost entirely his creation and that of his brother Wilhelm Christian Meyer, 1766-1783. The earlier work of the first-mentioned is essentially a continuation of his Meissen manner, and shows the same mannerisms—small heads turned to the side, smiling faces and very long limbs. Frequently he imparts to these figures a lively movement and expression that renders them completely charming. His brother Wilhelm Christian had been his pupil and in some instances their work cannot be distinguished. See *Kaendler, J. J.; Berlin.*

Meyer, Wilhelm Christian   See *Meyer, Friedrich Elias.*

Mexico   See *Central American Pottery.*

Mezza Majolica   In Italian ceramics; a term previously applied to the lead-glazed and other Italian pottery which preceded the true tin-glazed majolica. The distinction is erroneous since tin was already present to some extent in the white glaze of the majority of these earlier painted wares. The term was also given to lead-glazed wares with decoration incised through a white clay slip. It is more appropriate that these wares with incised decoration should be called sgraffiato wares.

Michelangelo Buonarroti   (1475-1564) Celebrated Florentine sculptor and painter. He inaugurated a new school of art that marked the beginning of the Baroque. See *Baroque.*

Michoacan   See *Tarascan.*

Micronesia   See *Oceania.*

Middelburg   In Dutch ceramics; the earliest recorded North Netherlands majolica manufactory was founded here in 1564 by Joris Andriessen of Antwerp, and was active until 1568 or later. Also mentioned here about the same time was the faïence-potter Adriaen Ingelsz. In the latter part of the 16th century it became an important center for the manufacture of tin-glazed tiles. See *Haarlem; Netherlandish Majolica; Dutch Tiles.*

Mikawa, Choso   (1796-1851) Prominent Japanese studio-potter associated with the Kyoto circle of potters. He learned pottery-making from Mokubei and specialized in imitating the wares of Ninsei. See *Kyo.*

Mikawachi   See *Hirado.*

Miklashevskii, Andrei   In Russian ceramics; started a porcelain manufactory in 1839 on his own estate in the Ukraine at Volodino in the Glukhov district of Chernigov province near the source of very fine kaolin. (It was so excellent it was generally known as Glukhov kaolin throughout Russia.) The wares were made by serfs and when Alexander II freed the serfs he closed the kiln in 1861. Serf artists, often trained by experienced artists, always instinctively added a Russian taste for strong colors and slightly exaggerated outlines to their work. Miklashevskii followed the usual custom in Russia and hired a foreigner to establish his porcelain manufactory. He selected Jacques Dart from the well-known Jacob Pettit manufactory in Paris, who remained in charge until his death in 1851. Essentially the porcelain wares were similar to those from Batenin and lacked the refinement that characterized the Imperial and Iusupov wares. It seems there was one

M

MIKLASHEVSKII, ANDREI
C. 1840-1861

MILAN

CLERICE, FELICE
1745 ON

RUBATI, PASQUALE
1756 ON

MILDE, ARIJ DE
C. 1680-1708

MING

HUNG WU
1368-1398

CHIEN WEN
1399-1402

section where the serfs were given a freer hand to decorate in native Russian manner, borrowing motifs from Ukrainian folk art. The customary mark was M. A. See *Russia.*

Milan In Italian ceramics; a faïence factory was active here in 1745 and still active in 1772 and was carried on by Felice Clerici. Notable among its productions were versions of the Japanese Imari brocaded pattern with decorations of flowers in red, blue and gold. Another faïence factory was started in 1756 by Pasquale Rubati, formerly a painter with Clerici, and carried on by his widow and son Carlo, who from 1796 was in partnership with E. Bonzanini. Their wares were painted in on-glaze enamels in imitation of enameled porcelain. A third faïence factory was carried on for a brief time, 1770-1775, by Cesare Confalonieri at Santa Cristina. FSC(Fabbrica di Santa Cristina) occurs as a mark.

Milde, Arij de (1634-1708) Dutch potter at Delft where he is recorded as a master potter in 1694. He is well known as the maker of the so-called red earthenware teapots which he made at his pottery De Gekroonde Theepot or The Crowned Teapot. These teapots were in imitation of the Chinese buccaro ware brought to Europe by the Dutch East India Company together with the tea for the brewing of which they were reputed to be especially suitable. The Delft teapots mentioned in an inventory as early as 1678 are of a ware of varying hardness, in De Milde's case approaching stoneware. As a rule they are small, with plain loop handles and short spouts, and like their Chinese prototypes are generally decorated with applied sprays of plum blossoms or with reliefs of dragons or other Chinese mythological creatures. The Dutch red teapots are significant as the European precursors of the very similar wares of Dwight and Elers in England and of the essentially very different stone-

ware of Böttger in Germany. See *Buccaro; Red Porcelain.*

Millot Kiln-master at Vincennes-Sèvres from 1746 to 1774; and from 1774 to 1786 in charge of pastes.

Mimbres Black-on-white. See *Mogollon.*

Mimpei, Kaja (d. 1870) Prominent Japanese studio-potter associated with the Kyoto circle of potters; studied under Ogata Shuhei who made Awata wares with Mimpei at Agano village around 1830. Around the same time Ogata Shuhei started a pottery at Awaji where Mimpei made excellent imitations of Ninsei. See *Kyo.*

Mina'i See *Islamic Pottery, Medieval;*

Ming The Ming dynasty of China was founded in 1368 with its capital at Nanking. The Ming period, which included the reigns of seventeen Emperors, extended until 1644. The art work of this period is referred to as Ming. In Chinese ceramics; the great Imperial porcelain manufactory was built at Ching-tê-Chên in 1369. The concentration of Chinese porcelain efforts at Ching-tê-Chên from the Ming period onward was probably due to the advantages of its situation. It was close to rich deposits of the necessary materials and was conveniently located for the transport of its productions to many parts of the Empire. The old ceramic centers of the Sung dynasty, 960-1279, such as Ting Chou, Ju Chou and Chün Chou, declined into secondary importance as the high-fired monochrome glazes of which celadon was the color most highly esteemed yielded pride of place to the polychrome and blue-painted porcelains. It is not to be supposed that celadon green glazes and other monochromes were not used in Ming times, but Ching-tê-Chên now took the lead in the porcelain world and here most of the wares were no doubt decorated with underglaze blue or with low-fired colored enamels or medium-fired colored glazes on a white body. Pure white porcelain with a specially selected glaze material used in the manufacture of the finer whites was highly esteemed in the earliest Ming periods. The only decoration permitted on the white wares was molded, carved, engraved or painted in white slip under the glaze. The last two decorative techniques were generally of a very slight and delicate kind to which the Chinese gave the name *an-hua* or secret decoration as it could only be seen clearly when the piece was held against the light or obliquely to it. There is little information on the wares of the first Ming period, Hung Wu, 1368-1398. But under Hung Wu's son, Yung Lo (1403-1424), certain types of white porcelain made at this time became almost legendary and were later widely copied. Porcelain bowls of white eggshell (known as T'o T'ai or bodiless) was one of the special triumphs. Fine white wares continued to be produced throughout the Ming dynasty. The decoration most widely used on Ming ware is that painted in blue under the glaze which was one of the noted specialties of the reign of Hsüan Tê, 1426-1435. This reign is considered as one of the classical periods in the history of porcelain. Next to the blue and white, Chinese writers have glorified the underglaze red of the earlier Ming periods. The Hsüan Tê underglaze red porcelain vies with Hsüan Tê blue and white for pride of position. This color, derived from copper, was given the general name of Chi Hung, usually rendered as sacrificial red. Of unusual refinement were the Hsüan Tê monochrome glazed wares, notably in blue, a brilliant copper-red or plain white frequently with secret (an-hua) decoration. It is generally agreed that the reign of Ch'êng Hua, 1465-1487, was the second great and classical period of Ching-tê-Chên porcelain. This opinion is substantiated by the potters of later times who used the reign marks of Hsüan Tê and Ch'êng Hua impartially on their wares. In the reign of Ch'êng Hua the tech-

nique of overglaze enameling appears to have attained its perfection. At this time the so-called Tou-Ts'ai or contrasted color style with its jewel-like enamel painting in several colors was added to designs first "penciled" in underglaze blue. Like the classical Hsüan Tê blue and white, Ch'êng Hua Tou Ts'ai also became classical and was copied repeatedly in later times. These three "classical" reigns are sometimes known collectively as early Ming. Ming polychromes are known under various names such as San Ts'ai (three colors), Wu Ts'ai (five colors) and Ts'a Ts'ai (mixed colors). The expressions three and five colors are not to be taken literally. The marks of Hung Chih (1485-1505) and Chêng Tê (1506-1521) were less famous. The Hung Chih wares continued without much novelty the styles of Ch'êng Hua, though a yellow enamel of the period was ingeniously used and became well known. Chêng Tê blue and white is notable for its often massive build and strong drawing in several styles virtually new. The tendency toward a broader, less "penciled" style of painting revealed itself early in the 16th century and was very marked in the colorful wares of the important reign of Chia Ching, 1522-1566, when bold, freely painted designs were favored either in a strong violet-toned underglaze blue or in enamels dominated by iron red. The 16th century also included a characteristic turquoise-blue enamel. Painting on the biscuit in enamel colors, mainly yellow, green and purple, was done at least as early as the 16th century and was used with striking boldness in the reign of Chia Ching. (This kind of decoration was to become widely popular in the following period, in the reign of K'ang Hsi, 1662-1722, when it was known as San Ts'ai or three-color decoration.) The Lung Ch'ing period, 1567-1572, and the reign of Wan Li, 1573-1619, in many respects continued the styles current under Chia Ching but with decreasing vitality. The imitation of earlier Ming styles initiated under Chia Ching became more

YUNG LO
1403-1424

HSUAN TE
1426-1435

CH'ENG HUA
1467-1487

HUNG CHI
1485-1505

CHENG TE
1506-1521

CHIA CHING
1522-1566

LUNG CH'ING
1567-1572

WAN LI
1573-1619

fashionable. Both the Chia Ching and Wan Li periods produced much painted porcelain steeped in Taoist symbolism. The color scheme popular in the late Ming period for polychrome enamels combined with underglaze blue is usually known by the name Wan Li Wu Ts'ai or Wan Li polychrome. During the reigns of the last three Ming emperors—T'ai Ch'ang, 1620, T'ien Ch'i, 1621-1627, and Ch'ung Chêng, 1628-1643—there is little to mention except that, although the Imperial factory declined due to the chaotic times which preceded the fall of the dynasty, private porcelain factories continued to operate and produced fine wares of excellent quality. Much of the porcelain made for export in late Ming times and in the so-called transitional period between Ming and Ch'ing is of distinct and fine character. The enameled ware of the red and green family introduced under the Sung dynasty, 960-1279, continued in favor to a great or less extent, though in very different styles in Ming. Noteworthy is a class of export ware, the so-called Swatow ware. Gilding was used from the earliest reigns of Ming. It was the final operation in the manufacture and always necessitated a separate firing at a low temperature. In some examples the gilding is applied in the form of gold leaf, but gilding painted on with a brush was much more customary. See *Stem Cup; Altar Cup; Tou Ts'ai; Five-Color Ware; Three-Color Ware; Ts'a Ts'ai; Underglaze Blue; Blue and White Ming; Underglaze Red; Swatow; Red and Green Family; Ling Lung; Sung; Ch'ing; Chinese Gods; Mohammedan Blue; Blanc de Chine; Celadon; Chinese Dynasties; China,* in Far Eastern ceramics. (98-105)

Mingei-Type Pottery   See *Mashiko.*

Minister Jug   See *Meigh, Charles.*

Mino   In Japanese ceramics; the name given to a period or era dating from the end of the Momoyama and early Edo period, which saw the production of several distinctive wares made in a number of new kilns in the Mino province, present-day Gifu Prefecture. These wares, intended for use in or noticeably influenced by the aesthetic of the tea ceremony, reveal a wide variety of different glazes and treatments. The same light yellow or golden mat glaze used at the Seto kilns, known as Yellow Seto, was successfully introduced into Mino kilns late in the 16th century. One of the marked features of this Mino area Yellow Seto ware is the decorative use of graceful incised sketches of leaf and plant motifs; another is the use of green splotches on the over-all yellow glaze. There was also the Temmoku type ware, especially a distinctive conical tea bowl for which lustrous black and dark brown glazes with various modest markings have always been most favored. It is recorded that late in the 16th century, owing to severe internal political disturbances in Japan, a group of very skilled potters from the Seto kilns took refuge in the comparatively settled Mino area. It is particularly from these movements that the development of the wares known as Shino, Seto Black and Oribe can be traced. To a great extent all these wares were the result of the influence upon ceramic design of the taste of one man, the tea master Furuta Oribe, active from about 1580 until his death in 1615. See *Temmoku; Chien Yao; Shino; Seto Black; Oribe.* At the present time Mino is one of the most important centers for handcrafted pottery. See *Japanese Contemporary Pottery.*

Minoan   In ancient Cretan art; the name given by Sir Arthur Evans (1851-1941) to the Cretan Bronze Age civilization, which he revealed at Knossos, after Minos, the great legendary King of Knossos. (Sir Arthur conducted excavations between 1899 and 1932.) Minoan art is divided into three periods:

Early Minoan	c.2800-c.2000 B.C.
Middle Minoan	c.2000-c.1500 B.C.
Late Minoan	c.1500-c.1100 B.C.

About 2000 B.C. there arose in Crete an

elaborate civilization based on royal palaces at Knossos, Phaistos, and Zakros in the east. These palaces housed the royal families and priests, served as administrative headquarters, stored foodstuffs and the like, and housed artists' workshops. About 1700 B.C. the Old Palaces came to an end; subsequently about 1600 B.C. or later New Palaces on a grander scale were built. Minoan Crete is now famous for the wondrous series of painted pottery, the best of which has been found on palace sites. It was also current elsewhere, and the tombs and houses of ordinary folk were furnished with pottery decorated in the same manner. The stylistic developments of Cretan pottery is as follows: the monochrome Neolithic wares survive into Early Minoan and are followed by vases decorated with dark paint on a light clay ground. In the last phase of Early Minoan the opposite technique occurs and remains typical of Middle Minoan. The imaginative abstract motifs probably derive ultimately from vegetable forms. In the Late Minoan period the painting is again dark-on-light. Many fine vases have been preserved from the period of the New Palaces. Two periods can be distinguished by style: the earlier, the naturalistic Floral and Marine styles; the later, Palace style. The latter was so named by Sir Arthur Evans and shows how Mycenaean and Minoan art combined in Crete. The Palace style, the last major phase in Minoan art, was especially but not exclusively confined to the palace at Knossos and was expressed particularly in the great amphorae and storage jars. It was most flourishing about 1450-1400 B.C. By this time a Mycenaean prince was installed on the throne at Knossos. Under the short-lived Mycenaean control of Knossos, the Minoan tradition was fused with a Greek way of looking at things. They adapted the peaceful Minoan culture to their more warlike spirit. In pottery the Floral and Marine styles remained popular but the motifs became increasingly stylized. The

vases have a peculiar bold, at times almost cold, monumental quality certainly not seen in the earlier Cretan painted vases. The sacred axe was used as a decorative motif. Helmets which have cheek pieces were also painted on jars and vases. See *Mycenaean; Kamares Style; Vasiliki Style.*

Minton In English ceramics; Thomas Minton (1765-1836), who served an apprenticeship at Caughley and also worked at Spode, founded a pottery at Stoke-on-Trent, Staffordshire, in 1796, which is still carried on by his successors. For the first two years only blue-printed and cream-colored earthenware were made. Porcelain was made from 1798 to 1811. It was started again around 1821 with the help of workers from Derby and became the chief production under Herbert Minton (1792-1858) who was the son of the founder. From 1836 to 1841 the firm was Minton and Boyle. After the death of Herbert Minton the works were continued by Colin Minton Campbell, first with Michael Hollins and later with the grandsons of Thomas Minton. In 1883 the present company was formed and became Mintons Limited. Numerous later productions from around 1820 onward were among the best of their time, rivaling those of Sèvres. This was largely due to the great number of well-known artists employed by the firm. In 1848 the French potter Léon Arnoux (1816-1902) became both art director and chemist; he was forever experimenting with new bodies, glazes and techniques, until his retirement around 1895. The Victorian majolica ware with its colored glazes was one of his early innovations and was to remain a staple product for most of the era. Marc Louis Solon, who was to become the most celebrated ceramic artist of the era, came to England in 1870 and practiced the pâte-sur-pâte technique at Mintons. Another significant event was the employment of the already established designer and water-color artist William Coleman (1829-

大明天
啟年天
製
T'IEN CH'I
1621-1627

年崇
製禎
CH'UNG CHENG
1628-1643

MINTON
C. 1873 ON

1904) who came to Mintons in 1869. He became director of Mintons' short-lived art-pottery studio initiated in 1871. During the second half of the 19th century Mintons was producing ambitious parian wares including elaborate centerpieces and compotes for richly painted dessert services, candelabra and a wide range of decorative figures. Mintons was among the few ceramic works in England to be noticeably influenced by Art Nouveau. The impetus in this direction was provided by Léon Victor Solon. At the opening of the 20th century Mintons was manufacturing earthenware table and ornamental ware, toilet ware, wall tiles, majolica, and bone china table and ornamental ware. The present-day production consists solely of bone china tableware, with a limited number of ornamental pieces. In 1968 the name of the company was changed to Minton Limited. See *Solon, L. V.; Solon, L. M.; Mintons Art-Pottery Studio; Boullemier, A.; Foster, H. W.; Toft, C.* (470, 475, 479)

Minton and Boyle See *Minton.*

Mintons Art-Pottery Studio In English ceramics; a short-lived venture set up in Kensington, London, by Mintons in 1871 under the charge of W. S. Coleman, an easel painter, who had worked for brief periods at both Copelands and Mintons. A great vogue for amateur ceramic painters was ignited in England by this project. More importantly it furnished a bridge between commercial production and the newer ideas of decoration which were taking shape at that time in the London schools of art.

Miró, Joan (b. 1893) Spanish Catalan painter, sculptor and ceramist; his production of ceramics has been abundant. In 1942 he proposed that the talented potter José Llorens Artigas collaborate with him, an offer Artigas accepted. The first experiments by Miró and Artigas, 1944-1946, possessed the primitive violence and dramatic resonance which was to characterize

their subsequent works. Since that time Miró, Artigas, and his son Joan Gardy Artigas have produced distinguished pottery, tilework and ceramic sculpture. Of these the latter are the most original. These were based on sculpture-objects Miró assembled himself, realized in fired clay. The few works whose conception and dimensions attain monumentality consist of separate modeled and fired elements assembled afterward. These include steles and figures with bodies made up of a rock fragment and the head of a sculptured stone; the most typical are the two Totems and the Portico. The pursuit of the monumental in ceramics acquired its full meaning a few years later with the Walls of the Sun and the Moon Miró created for the new UNESCO building in Paris, and the ceramic mural for Harvard University. See *Artigas, J. L.* (542)

Mirror Black In Chinese ceramics; the name given to the fine Chinese black glaze porcelain of the K'ang Hsi period. The black glaze which has bluish or brownish reflections was made by mixing iron of coffee-brown with the cobaltiferous ore of manganese. It is also called Wu Chin or black gold.

Mishima In Japanese ceramics; the small repetitive and radiating designs in the form of stars, circles, semi-circles, conventional flowers and bands. This type of decoration is distinctively Korean in its origin, and at first it was found only in those Japanese provinces where Korean potters had settled. Later it was used throughout Japan. The designs are generally impressed and are only rarely incised, and are filled with a white slip, sometimes in a grey glaze. The name is said to derive from the supposed resemblance of these rows of repetitive designs to the rows of radiating characters in the yearly Mishima calendar for which the town of Mishima in Japan was famous. See *Korea; Punch'ŏng.*

MINTON AND BOYLE
c. 1836-1841

Mitchell, Henry See *Doulton, Lambeth and Burslem.*

Mixteca Puebla Pottery In pre-Columbian Central American ceramics; in the late Aztec phase, 1400-1521, a beautiful, highly polished polychrome pottery decorated with a variety of motifs including human figures similar to those in the codices, religious and secular symbols, scrolls and feathers was made in the Mixtec country in the Oaxaca region. Very similar is the pottery from Tlascala and Cholula with the same highly polished surface and brilliantly colored decoration; the decoration, however, was generally of a geometrical character. See *Central American Pottery; Aztec.*

Mocha Creamware In English ceramics; mocha ware with its "creeping" liquid decoration on a thin slip was developed in the pre-Victorian part of the 19th century. It enjoyed a great vogue in the first four decades of the 19th century, and was produced by William Adams of Tunstall and many other Staffordshire potters. The moss-like decoration was obtained by touching the ground color of the ware, while wet, with a brush containing liquid black, brown, blue or green pigment, which spreads out in delicate traceries. It was so called because of its supposed resemblance to the mocha stone or moss agate. Mocha ware chiefly comprised bowls, jugs and mugs and was widely exported to America. It was made considerably later than 1837 and a small amount of it was made in America.

Mochica In pre-Columbian Andean ceramics; in the north coast, the ceremonial pottery of the Mochica culture reveals the peak of its development. The most striking feature is modeling in the round or in low relief combined with brush painting in red and white; later a little black was added when evidence of decline began to appear. Prominent among the many forms is a pot with a graceful stirrup spout and a jar frequently modeled to represent a human or animal body or the head only, with the opening formed by a simple neck expanding slightly upward. One of the most unusual manifestations is the portrait vase or jar from the Mochica culture. (This type of vase in the form of a man's head is designated as a portrait-vase because of the remarkable degree of realism.) There were also graceful funnel-shaped vessels and ladle-like vessels. Also frequent were whistle jars often in the form of birds. Whistle jars, which made their first appearance in Cupisnique pottery, are in the form of double vessels that when half full of liquid make a whistling sound if blown into at one end. Occasionally musical instruments were made of pottery, particularly end-blown trumpets. The decoration on Mochica pottery which is painted or modeled or a combination of both, gives a vivid picture of the life and customs of the people. See *Andean.* (16, 17)

Modern Movement The name universally recognized for the trend which was to become the basis for the philosophy and artistic ideals of the 20th century. The Modern Movement with its emphasis on form unhesitantly removed ornament and paid full attention to the capabilities of the material and honesty in the use of it, though without in any manner neglecting aesthetic consideration. See *Bauhaus; Art Nouveau; Behrens, P.; Riemerschmid, R.; Velde, Henry van de; Secession; Wagner, Otto; Hoffmann, Josef; Wright, F. L.*

Modern Style Essentially a period style, having a peculiar preference for certain kinds of form, a functionalist care for efficiency in use, a rational dislike of unnecessary ornament.

Mogollon In pre-Columbian Southwestern United States ceramics; the Mogollon, who lived in southwest New Mexico in the United States at least since A.D. 300, produced a distinctive ware around 1000 known as Mimbres black-on-white (though dark brown may supplant the black) in which outside influences, chiefly Anasazi, were combined with local traditions. The vessels were generally open bowls with the designs painted inside; by far the majority of them come from burials. The designs fall into two main types: a broad zone of finely painted geometrical decoration surrounding a blank circle; a few narrow black bands around the top with a lively but stylized representation of a human or animal figure at the bottom. These figures may make up a scene, for instance a man fighting a bear. It seems that the makers of this pottery left the area around the end of the 12th century, and it is surmised that at least some may have gone south to the Mexican province of Chihuahua, where Mimbres influence appeared around that time. Later features suggest the arrival of the Salado people. A distinctive pottery style was developed there and flourished until around the mid-15th century. It is characterized by crisply painted geometrical designs with occasional life forms, executed in red or black on a buff or white slip. Bowls are the most common form; other shapes include a highly stylized effigy vessel representing human or animal figures. See *Southwestern United States Pottery.* (4)

Mohammedan Blue In Chinese ceramics; the Chinese supplies of cobalt blue, which were used in the underglaze blue decoration, were supplemented by a superior blue imported from the Near East known as Mohammedan blue. During the Ming dynasty, 1368-1644, the finest blue and white ware was made from this blue. Supplies of Mohammedan blue were available during the Hsüan Tê reign, 1426-1435, Chêng Tê reign 1506-1521 and the Chia Ching reign, 1522-1566. Chinese records say that the tone of the blue varied. The blue and white wares were exceedingly fine during the Hsüan Tê period. The blue and white wares of the Ch'êng Hua reign, 1465-1487, are considered inferior to those of the Hsüan Tê period due to an insufficient supply of Mohammedan blue. During the Chêng Tê period the blue and white wares were highly regarded. The Mohammedan blue which was apparently plentiful was a dark color. The body of these wares was thick but of a fine texture. The glaze seemed to be bubbly which gave a kind of hazy effect to the blue. The blue had a soft tone and was applied in heavy outlines that were filled in with flat washes. During the Chia Ching reign the color of the Mohammedan blue was a rich violet blue that was distinctive for its intensity. The supplies of Mohammedan blue were practically exhausted during the Wan Li period, 1573-1619. Most of the Wan Li blue and white ware has a seemingly dull greyish blue. See *Ming; Blue and White Ming.*

Mokubei, Aoki (1767-1833) Kyoto scholar and antiquarian who became interested in pottery and from about 1784 began to operate a kiln. His wares were predominantly utensils for the sencha (Chinese infused) tea ceremony which made use of leaf tea instead of the customary powdered type and was much in fashion in Japanese scholarly circles at this time. Calligraphy and its enjoyment played an important role in Mokubei's work. Like his master Okuda Eisen he excelled in making copies of Chinese blue and white, celadon, Gosu-Akae and Kochi wares. But perhaps the most celebrated of his wares were his small unglazed pottery teapots (Kyusu) with long handles at the side. It is thought that the word *kyusu* derived from kubisho, meaning baked in a hurry. The prototype of the kyusu came from China where they were made by a Zen priest in the Wan Li period. Every Japanese kiln made kyusu because the popularity of the Chinese form of the tea ceremony during the Tokugawa and early Meiji period created a demand for them. Mokubei as a kyusu maker occupied a preeminent position. In his later years he painted pictures, often to the neglect of his pottery. He belonged to the Nango school and was the teacher of Tessai, the great 19th century painter of this school. See *Eisen, Okuda; Kochi; Gosu-Akae; Blue and White,* in Japanese ceramics; *Celadon,* in Japanese ceramics; *Kyo; Ninsei.*

Molding In ceramics; clay may be molded in several ways. Vessels may be formed by pressing clay into a single open mold with intaglio decoration and into two half molds, also with intaglio decoration, then being joined by luting together. Ornaments in relief may in a like manner be taken from a mold and affixed to the surface of a vessel by luting. Porcelain figures were formed by molding individual parts and joining them together. See *Slip-Casting.*

Mollica, Pasquale Pottery painter working at Naples in the second half of the 18th century. See *Naples.*

Momoyama 1573-1615 The following are the names of the eras for the Momoyama period.

Tensho	1573
Bunroku	1592
Keicho	1596

See *Japanese Periods.*

Monkey Band In German ceramics; the name given to the original set of more than twenty Meissen figures made by Kaendler around 1750 to ridicule the Royal orchestra at Dresden. Each figure represents a musician in the form of a monkey. These figures became widely popular and were copied at other manufactories including Vienna, Chelsea, Derby and Fürstenberg, and were extensively reproduced in the 19th century. See *Meissen.* (377)

Monochrome Painting In European ceramics; the principal example of the deliberate limitation of colors to two used in painting porcelain and pottery is blue and white after the Chinese prototype. Other colors

used in monochrome painting were: some red, black, rose-pink and rose-purple prepared from the purple of Cassius, manganese-purple, yellow and green. See *Colors.*

Montplaisir, Manufacture de See *Brussels.*

Monte Alban See *Central American Pottery; Zapotec.*

Monteith In English wares; the name given to a large bowl often made of silver, with a movable rim and scalloped edges from which wine glasses, punch ladle and the like could be hung so that they might be chilled in the cracked ice with which the bowl was filled. It is reputed that the name derived from a fantastical Scotchman, Monsieur Monteith, who wore a cloak with a scalloped border. The form without a movable rim appeared in 18th century English ceramics. (115)

Montereau In French ceramics; a manufactory was founded at Montereau, Seine-et-Marne, in 1775 by several Englishmen, Messrs. Clark, Shaw & Cie. It produced white earthenware of the English type. The manufactory prospered and in the early 19th century the manufactory at Creil was united with it. The productions at Montereau, which were numerous and as a rule of a rather ordinary character, were rarely marked. See *Faïence Fine.*

Montpellier In French ceramics; a faïence manufactory, started perhaps as early as 1684, was in existence here in 1718 under the direction of Jacques Ollivier. Became a Manufacture Royale in 1729. Montpellier was the seat of an influential faculty of medicine, and the equipment needed for the numerous hospital pharmacies of the region must have furnished the faïence potters with their outlet. From 1770 onward André Philipp who came from Marseilles conducted a faïence manufactory which was continued by his two sons, Antoine and Valentine, until 1828.

MANUFACTURE DE
MONTPLAISIR
1786-1790

MOORE BROTHERS
C. 1880 ON

MORGAN, WILLIAM DE
1882-1888

MOSBACH
1770 ON

MOSES, JOHN AND COMPANY
1884

JOHN MOSES

Moonstone Glaze   In English ceramics; a mat glaze introduced in 1933 by Wedgwood. Its "driven snow" effect has been used by Keith Murray, a Wedgwood artist, for contemporary design of both ornamental objects and tablewares.

Moore, Bernard (1853-1935) In English ceramics; in 1870 Bernard Moore and his brother Samuel took over their father's porcelain factory, St. Mary's Works, Longton, Staffordshire, and continued it as Moore Brothers. They produced a good variety of decorative porcelain and frequently used bronze and metallic colors. An advertisement in 1889 refers to them as manufacturers of Art Porcelain. They sold the business in 1905 and for the succeeding ten years or so Bernard Moore concentrated on wares with Chinese glaze effects which he produced at his studio pottery, Wolf Street, Stoke. He achieved remarkable control of high and low temperature glazes. Especially notable was his rouge flambé, the formula for which was used by Doultons of Burslem. The talented decorators of Bernard Moore's wares included John Adams, Hilda Beardmore, Dora Billington, Annie Ollier, Reginald R. Tomlinson and others. These artists signed their work with monograms of their initials.

Moore, Samuel and Company In English ceramics; operated the Wear Pottery at Southwick, Sunderland, Durham, from 1803 to 1874, producing earthenwares. Formerly it was owned by John Brunton, 1796-1803. Many marks were used from 1803 to 1874 incorporating the following names or initials: Moore and Company; S. M. and Company; S. Moore and Company, and Samuel Moore and Company.

Moore Brothers   See *Moore, Bernard.*

Morgan, William de (1839-1917) English potter and novelist; in the early 1860's made the acquaintance of William Morris, Dante Gabriel Rossetti and Sir Edward Burne-Jones. He was the chief exponent of Morris's craft movement in pottery. His pottery falls into two principal types: that painted in "Persian" colors (blues and greens) and that painted in luster colors. All the painted decoration on his pottery is said to have been designed by himself, but it was mostly carried out by others. His painters included Fred and Charles Passenger, Joe Juster, and J. Hersey. (483)

Morley   A family of Nottingham potters making stoneware from around 1690 until at least the mid-18th century.

Morris, William (1834–1896) English designer, craftsman, poet and socialist. The influence of Morris on the decorative arts in England and eventually abroad was so deep and far-reaching that there is scarcely a late 19th century designer who is not indebted to it. Morris's entire life was a crusade against the worthless standards of mid-Victorian mass production, which he traced to the influence of machine manufacture and the disappearance of honest and satisfying handcraftsmanship. His own special contribution to design was in the field of flat pattern-making, in which his output was profuse and his genius unrivaled. See *Morris, Marshall, Faulkner and Co.; Arts and Crafts Movement.*

Morris, Marshall, Faulkner and Co.,   Fine Art Workmen in Painting, Carving, Furniture and Metals. The establishment of this firm in 1861 by William Morris marks the beginning of a new era in the decorative arts, for it was through this firm that the influence of Morris and his associates, such as Burne-Jones, Rossetti, Ford Madox Brown, and Webb, was chiefly exercised. The firm started business at 8 Red Lion Square, London; in June 1865 it moved to 26 Queen Square. In 1875 it was reorganized as Morris and Co.; in April 1877 showrooms were opened at 264 (later 449) Oxford Street; in June 1881 the workshops were transferred to Merton Abbey. In the 1920's the showrooms were moved to 17 George Street, Hanover Square, London; in 1940 the firm went into voluntary liquidation. See *Morris, William.*

Morrison and Carr See *New York City Pottery.*

Mortensen, Carl See *Krog, A.*

Mortlake In English ceramics; a manufactory making brown stoneware was started at Mortlake, Surrey, by Joseph Kishere in 1800. The pottery was still in existence in 1843. They principally made jugs, mugs and flasks. The usual mark was Kishere Mortlake, impressed.

Mosaïk In German ceramics; a kind of scale-pattern or diapered color, in monochrome green, purple and other colors, employed for borders on German, especially Meissen, Ansbach and Berlin, porcelain, about 1760 onwards. The scale-pattern of Worcester was ultimately derived from the Meissen Mosaïk.

Mosbach In German ceramics; a faïence manufactory was started at Mosbach, Baden, in 1770 by Pierre Berthevin under the protection of the Elector Palatine. The marks generally attributed to the factory include MB under an Electoral Hat, MT in monogram and T; the mark CT may have been used also. After 1806 the initials of Carl Friedrich, Grand Duke of Baden, were found and from 1818 M or Mosbach, impressed, was the usual mark. In a general manner the various productions show a resemblance to the wares of Strasbourg. During the latter part of the 18th century gift jugs with inscriptions generally in black letters were made and were similar in style to the jugs made at Durlach.

Moser, Koloman (1868-1918) Austrian painter, designer and graphic artist; a founding member of the Vienna Secession, 1897. He began teaching in 1899 and became an influential figure in the Aus-trian decorative art movement; he established the Wiener Werkstätte, with Hoffmann and Wärndorfer, 1903. No doubt he was Austria's closest parallel to the French and Belgian exponents of curvilinear form. See *Secession.*

Moses, John and Company In American ceramics; started the Glasgow Pottery at Trenton, New Jersey, in 1863 producing earthenwares, principally yellow ware and Rockingham.

Moulins In French ceramics; the manufacture of faïence was carried on here at several factories from before 1730 until the 19th century. However, little is known of the history of these factories.

Mourning Jug In German ceramics. See *Freiberg.*

Moustiers In French ceramics; one of the most important centers in France for the manufacture of faïence. Several distinctive styles for the decoration of faïence were created at Moustiers that were extensively copied. The earliest faïence of artistic importance was made in a manufactory established in 1679 by Pierre Clérissy, remaining active until 1852. The blue and white Tempesta style from around 1680 to 1710 and the blue and white Bérain style from around 1710 to 1740 are principally associated with the Clérissy factory. Both styles were original and were of first-rate artistic importance. The subjects for the first style were often copied from the engraved designs by Antonio Tempesta, (1555-1630). The second style is named after Jean Bérain (1638-1711) whose decorative engravings inspired the designs. It is generally regarded as the most original work produced at Moustiers. The best in this style was remarkable for its smooth milky white tin-glaze ground and for its soft blue decoration. Another manufactory was founded in 1738 by Joseph Olerys in partnership with his brother-in-law Jean-Baptiste Laugier. The factory mark

MOUSTIERS

Cleriffy a Moustiers.

CLÉRISSY
C. 1680-1710

OLERYS AND LAUGIER
1738-C. 1790

FERRAT, JEAN-BAPTISTE
1770 ON

f d

FÉRAUD, JEAN-GASPARD
1779 ON

FOUQUÉ
C. 1770 ON

was OL and was active until 1790 or later. The work of this factory is chiefly identified with a "high temperature polychrome" style, named after Olerys and inspired by the faïence made at Alcora, Valencia, and used from 1740 onwards. The high temperature colors were a fine yellow, a soft blue, a green and a brown or violet; red was never used as a high temperature color at Moustiers. Another manufactory was operated from 1718 to 1791 by Jean Baptiste Ferrat and his descendants. This manufactory adopted the Strasbourg style of colored enamels from around 1770 onward. The designs were inspired to a large extent by the faïence made at Marseilles. Another manufactory was started in 1779 by Jean Gaspard Féraud and Joseph-Henri Berbegier and was active until 1874. They developed a new style of painting in high temperature colors from around 1779 onward. The work was well painted in soft colors and the tin glaze for the ground was extremely smooth and glossy. In addition to these manufactories there were many other minor manufactories. During the 19th century reproductions were made of the earlier styles. See *Clérissy, Pierre and Joseph; Viry, François; Fouqué, J.*. (276-278)

MUDÉJAR ORNAMENT

MÜNDEN
1737-C. 1793

Mt. Fuji A celebrated Japanese tea bowl. See *Fuji-san*.

Mudéjar The name given to the fusion of the art of Christian Spain with that of Moorish art. The most distinctive feature of Spanish art during the Middle Ages was the concurrent existence in Spain of two schools of art. This was due to the fact that in the 8th century the Spanish people were conquered by the Mohammedan Moors from across the Straits of Gibraltar. The Spaniards accepted from Mohammedan art that which was in harmony with Christian principles. These Oriental precepts in art were so deeply rooted that even after the Moors were finally expelled in 1607 during the reign of Philip III, this Moorish

influence was always to a greater or less degree present. This combination of Hispano-Moresque or Mudéjar art has always been a distinctive feature in all forms of Spanish art.

Muffle The fireclay box or interior of a kiln to which flames have no access.

Muffle Color In ceramics; an enamel color fired in a muffle kiln. See *Petit Feu*.

Muji-Hakeme See *Kohiki*.

Müller, Frantz Heinrich (1732-1820) Founder and manager of the Royal Copenhagen Porcelain Manufactory started in 1771-1772.

Müller, J.N. See *Schönwald*.

Müller, Karl See *Union Porcelain Works; Century Vase*.

Müller, Paul See *Selb*.

Münchener Vereinigte Werkstätten für Kunst in Handwerk See *Deutsche Werkstätten; Riemerschmid, Richard*.

Münden In German ceramics; a faïence manufactory was started at Münden, Hanover, around 1737 by Carl Friedrich von Hanstein who was granted a privilege in 1755. After 1793 it chiefly produced cream-colored earthenware in the English style. A mark of three crescents from the coat-of-arms of von Hanstein was an accepted mark. Especially typical of their wares were plates with open basketwork rims having forget-me-nots at the intersections of the plaited work and vases with double walls, the outer one being pierced in reticulated patterns painted in the four high-temperature colors. This kind of work was imitated at Magdeburg, Zerbst and Rheinsberg.

Munich School The name generally given to a group of seven artists living in Munich and working in the Jugend style: Otto Eck-

mann, Hermann Obrist, Richard Riemerschmid, Bernhard Pankok, August Endell, Bruno Paul and Peter Behrens. The
last-mentioned subsequently settled in
Darmstadt, 1899. In the opening years of
the 20th century this group began to turn
away from the curvilinear Jugend style to
the more simple and geometrical, working
more along the principles of the contemporary English arts and crafts designers.
See *Jugendstil*.

Muromachi 1333–1573 The following are
the names of the eras for the Muromachi
period.

Genko	1331	Choroku	1457
Kemmu	1334	Kansho	1460
Engen	1336	Bunsho	1466
Kokoku	1340	Onin	1467
Shohei	1346	Bummei	1469
Kentoku	1370	Chokyo	1487
Bunchu	1372	Entoku	1489
Tenju	1375	Meio	1492
Kowa	1381	Bunki	1501
Genchu	1384	Eisho	1504
Meitoku	1390	Daiei	1521
Oei	1394	Kyoroku	1528
Shocho	1428	Temmon	1532
Eikyo	1429	Koji	1555
Kakitsu	1441	Eiroku	1558
Bunan	1444	Genki	1570
Hotoku	1449	Tensho	1573
Koshu	1455		

See *Japanese Periods*.

Murray, Keith See *Wedgwood, Josiah*.

Murray, William Staite English artist-potter
and teacher; began working in high-fired
stoneware in the 1920's. He was interested
in Far Eastern techniques, especially glaze
effects. He possessed a remarkable genius
for pottery and produced many unique
pieces. His forms have an extraordinary
subtlety and suggestiveness, well indicated
by the titles he gave them, such as "The
Fawn" or "Autumn Wind and Rain." The
pots do not imitate the forms or effects
named, but the mood suggested by the title comes through in the form, color and

surface quality. Often the manner of his
masterly brushwork or incised decoration
projects the mood further still. Chief
among his pupils were Sam Haile, Heber
Mathews, Constance Dunn and Henry F.
Hammond. His influence through his
pupils has been great. In 1925 he became
head of the pottery school in the Royal
College of Art in London; his pottery career came to an end in 1940 when he went
to Southern Rhodesia. See *Leach, B.*

Mushiake See *Kyo*.

Mutz, Hermann German artist-potter of Al-
tona, in the Prussian province of Schleswig-Holstein, who, around 1900, was
producing attractive stoneware with
figured glazes. Around 1904 his son, Richard Mutz, started a studio pottery in Berlin
to make similar work with flowing glazes.
Notable are his figures which he produced
so successfully in stoneware at his Berlin
studio from models executed by the German sculptor Ernst Barlach, inspired by
his journey to Russia in 1906.

MURRAY, WILLIAM STAITE
1919-1940

Mutz, Richard See *Mutz, Hermann*.

Mycenaean In ancient Greek art; the name
given to Late Helladic art, about 1200-
1100 B.C., because it was at Mycenae, the
richest of Greek sites, where the first indi-
cations of it were found. The terms *Mycenaean* and *Late Helladic* are interchangeable.
From about 1400 to 1200 B.C. the Mycenaean Greeks ruled the Aegean world; they
were the heirs to the Cretan (now called
Minoan) empire which had for a long time
been the dominant power in the Aegean
world. The general aspect of Mycenaean
civilization is very Minoan; however, the
Minoans were not themselves Greeks or
even Greek-speaking. By and large,
Mycenaean art may be regarded as an extension of Minoan with only some original
features. The style of painting on the early
Mycenaean vases is almost exactly like Mi-

noan Floral and Marine styles. At about 1500 B.C. traces of the Palace style appear on the mainland more unmistakably and quickly than they do on Crete. From this time onward, though the general develop-

ment is in step with that of Minoan pottery differences between the Mycenaean and Minoan vases grow more marked and various local styles can be distinguished. See *Minoan; Near East,* in prehistoric ceramics.

N

Nabeshima In Japanese ceramics; the Nabeshima kilns for making porcelains were started by the prince of that name at Okawachi (also rendered Okochi) a few miles north of Arita, in 1722. Nothing but the very finest work was ever permitted to leave there, as the kilns were operated as an official manufactory by the House of Nabeshima. Their eventual decline came a little over a century later. Nabeshima porcelain was technically very perfect with a very smooth and flawless glaze; the colors used included a soft underglaze blue used for outlines, over which were added thin washes of bluish green, clear pale yellow and orange or vermilion red; blue enamel was occasionally used. The designs which were chiefly of flowers reveal a subtle rhythm and richness of invention. The technique of Nabeshima suggests that its best period was contemporary with the reign of Yung Chêng, 1723-1735, when it rivaled those contemporary wares in its perfection of material and designs. Most of the Nabeshima production was matched porcelains for formal table settings, the greatest part of which seems to have been in the form of a shallow dish or deep plate on a rather high foot rim used to serve main courses at formal meals. These are in their ultimate origin ceramic versions of utensils once commonly and still often seen in wood and particularly in lacquer ware. Almost always the Nabeshima potters decorated the rather high foot rim with an underglaze blue comb-tooth pattern which became its most distinguishing characteristic. Both the underglaze blue and the polychrome enameled Nabeshima are notable for the consummate skill with which the decorations have been applied, particularly the underglaze blue. Nabeshima celadon is one of the best of its kind in the Edo period. The wares have been widely copied. See *Arita; Imari; Japanese Porcelain Motifs; Blue and White*, in Japanese ceramics. (147-149)

Naestved See *Kähler ; Hizen.*

Nagoya See *Japanese Contemporary Pottery.*

Nan-Ting In Chinese ceramics; the Chinese name given to Southern Ting. See *Ting Yao.*

Nanking Ware or **Nankin Ware** In Chinese ceramics; the Ch'ing blue and white of the K'ang Hsi period, 1662–1722, exported to Europe and taken as the model by so many European potters. This was the Nankin ware, the blue china so enthusiastically collected by Rossetti, Burne-Jones, Whistler and other artists of the latter part of the 19th century, and which Wilde ruefully regretted he could "not live up to." This exported ware was usually in the pure Chinese tradition and was seldom made in forms especially for the export trade. Also called *Nankeen*. See *Blue and White Ch'ing; Chinese Lowestoft; Canton.*

NABESHIMA PLATE

Nanking Yellow In Chinese ceramics; a thin pale golden brown glaze that is invariably brownish. It was introduced during the K'ang Hsi reign and was chiefly found in narrow bands or in broad washes, separating or encircling blue designs. It was much used during the last half of the 17th century on wares sent to Europe, such as on small jars, bottles and similar articles.

NANKING VASE

Nantgarw In English ceramics; a porcelain manufactory was started at Nantgarw, Glamorgan, Wales, in 1813 by William Billingsley and Samuel Walker. From 1814 it was transferred to Swansea for a year or two and was reopened before 1817. It closed in 1822. The usual factory mark was Nantgarw, impressed, which was also used for a while at Swansea. The manufactory made a very translucent soft paste porcelain of a fine white color. Unfortunately it was apt to lose its shape in the kiln. Tablewares were the principal production. The painted decoration was in accordance with the contemporary decoration on Paris porcelain. Various dealers bought much of the porcelain and had it painted in London. See *Young, W. W.*

Naples In Italian ceramics; a factory making cream-colored earthenware in the English style was started here in 1760 by Nicola Giustiniani. It was successful and continued to flourish under his son Biagio, his grandsons Antonio and Salvatore, and particularly his great-grandson Michele. The earthenware was frequently decorated in excellent taste. The production also included figures in porcelain and other wares. The chief marks include Giustiniani and BG; N or FN, often part of the mark, probably stands for Napoli and Fabbrica. Another pottery making similar earthenware was operated here from the late 18th century onward by Cherinto del Vecchio and his son Gennaro. The marks included FDV and del Vecchio, both over N. A third pottery was started here about 1770 by Pasquale Mollica (who was named as painter both at the Giustiniani and del Vecchio potteries especially of the many Pompeian and Greek vase designs adapted for decoration). It was carried on by his descendants in the 19th century. See *Capo di Monte; Castelli.*

Nara The Nara or Tempyo period of Japan A.D. 645-794. See *Japanese Periods.*

Narghile Near East name for a hookah, a tobacco pipe having a long, flexible tube for stem passing through a water-filled bowl. Originally the bowl was made of coconut (Persian *nargil)*; later porcelain, glass and metal were also used.

Narumi China Company In Japanese ceramics; an important 20th century industrial manufactory located at Nagoya, for the most part producing tablewares for the export market.

Nassau Stoneware In German ceramics. See *Westerwald.*

Nast, J.N.H. See *Rue Popincourt.*

Nathanielsen, Bertha See *Krog, A.* (487)

Nathusius, Gottlob See *Althaldensleben.*

Natzler, Gertrud and Otto American, born in Austria, artist-potters. The Natzlers opened their first workshop in Vienna in 1933. They first won public recognition at the World Exposition in Paris, 1937, when they received a silver medal for a group of their ceramics. They came to the United States in 1939. The Natzlers reduced their art to its basic elements of throwing and glazing, refined these techniques to a high degree and united their separate efforts to a single end. Each piece is hand-thrown on the potter's wheel by Gertrud Natzler and bisque-fired in preparation for glazing. Glazes, developed by Otto Natzler, are applied by brush and fired. (555)

Nautilus Ware In English ceramics; ware made in imitation of a nautilus shell. A nautilus shell dessert service, comprising a center bowl, cream bowl and plates was illustrated in Wedgwood's first catalogue compiled in the latter part of the 19th century.

Nazca In pre-Columbian Andean ceramics; on the south coast, pottery achieved its highest development in the Nazca culture, most likely about the same time the Mochica culture flourished in the north, and surely later than Paracas Cavernas. It is thin, well-made and polished, but modeling in the round is scarce by comparison with Mochica pottery. The most typical form is a globular jar with two short tubular spouts joined by a flat-arched bridge. Nazca pottery is painted in as many as eight colors on a background slip; the customary colors are black, white, and differ-

PERSIAN NARGHILE

ent shades of red, yellow, brown, grey and violet, with the designs usually outlined in black. The majority of the early pots have a somber red background, while white grounds became popular later. Designs comprise stylized life forms, such as birds, fish or fruit, and themes inspired by religion or mythology. See *Andean.* (19)

Neale and Company See *Palmer, Humphrey.*

Neale and Wilson See *Palmer, Humphrey.*

Near East In prehistoric ceramics; undoubtedly the earliest groups for which there is evidence of a ceramic industry are those of the prehistoric Near East where pottery making dates back roughly seven to eight thousand years. Vertical kilns were used in Mesopotamia and Persia before 4000 B.C. and were evidently widely used in Egypt and Palestine by the 3rd millennium B.C. A simple method of making pottery less porous and one used before 5000 B.C. was to paint the outside of the pot with a clay slip. Soon after 2000 B.C. in Mesopotamia potters were able to give their pots a coating of glaze and so make them water-tight. One of the most widespread methods of glazing in the relatively primitive phases of the potter's art has always been the use of lead compounds, which fuse at relatively low temperatures, are usable with most types of potter's clay and are easily colored with metallic oxides, in particular with copper which produces a rich green color Though alkaline glazes had been used from pre-Dynastic times in Egypt and the use of glazed frit was common throughout the Near East by the Middle Bronze Age, it was not until the potters in Mesopotamia discovered a lead glaze that it became possible to get the known glazes to adhere to the clay surface. The practice of wheel-turning pottery was already in use from around 3000 B.C. Throughout the early history of Near East ceramics two principal traditions existed: namely a dark-surfaced polished or burnished ware, in most

instances without any decoration, and a painted ware commonly using a light ground with dark decoration. Painted pottery dating from about 6000 B.C. was made in Anatolia, and at an equally early stage in the eastern areas of Persia and Mesopotamia, the former remaining for a long period the principal center of painted wares in the prehistoric Near East. Probably the finest of all Near East painted wares were made in these two areas during the first two thousand years of settlement. Starting before 5000 B.C., potters in northern Mesopotamia developed a ware decorated with geometric patterns painted in a dark color varying from red to black on a mat cream-colored slip ground. It has been named Samarra after the site where it was first found. The pottery of the succeeding brilliant Tell Halaf culture of the 5th millennium B.C. surpassed the Samarra wares. Their potters achieved a technical standard not seen again in the Near East until three thousand years later when imported Mycenaean pottery appeared. The final stage of Mesopotamian ceramics of the succeeding 4th millennium B.C. was accompanied by marked artistic decline. Shortly after 4000 B.C. potters at Susa and Sialk in the Persian plateau region produced their finest painted wares, developing a variety of jar, bowl, chalice and goblet forms, some of which rivaled those of the earlier Halaf culture. To the west the earliest settlements of Egypt, Palestine and Cyprus also developed painted styles distinctively their own; but the majority were decidedly inferior to the wares from the east. Except for most of the 3rd millennium B.C., when large movements of groups of people from the north into the Near East brought with them a tradition of dark-surfaced burnished pottery, the tradition of painted pottery continued in favor until the end of the Iron Age. Although few wares compared with the earlier wares of Anatolia, Persia and Mesopotamia, finer wares were the more plentiful as ceramic techniques

NARUMI CHINA COMPANY
PRESENT

became more disseminated and used. The monochrome wares of the prehistoric Near East were the substance of the ceramic industry. As with the painted wares, they achieved their finest technical and artistic qualities in the work of the earlier potters. Many of the early shapes and decorations suggest the influence of containers made from a readily available material such as a stitched animal skin or a hollowed-out body of a gourd or similar vegetable. In Egypt in the last half of the 5th millennium B.C. the settlers of Badari and Deir Tasa in the central Nile valley made one of the finest varieties of pottery ever produced in the prehistoric Near East. The vessels of extreme thinness were well-fired and highly polished. A lustrous finish emphasized the surface color of black, brown, and red, the latter being often used with a black upper body. Essentially the forms are simple and give a feeling of reserve. The sole decoration was the occasional use of a light comb ripple. The Egyptians never surpassed the standard of this Badarian potting. According to present evidence the earliest of all pottery-making centers in the prehistoric world is located in west central and southern Anatolia where monochrome wares have been found in connection with cave-dwelling settlements of the late Mesolithic period and with the earliest communities of the central plateau. Both are no later than the middle of the 7th millennium B.C. The first production of both light- and dark-surfaced burnished wares was to begin a tradition which continued throughout the entire early history of the country. In Anatolia monochrome ware achieved its finest work in the technically excellent, but frequently rather overwhelming wares of the early Hittite Empire, 16th century B.C. The greater part by far of Hittite pottery used a highly burnished orange to red slip. Equally familiar with a burnished monochrome ware, the potters of Syria and Palestine very seldom achieved the excellent technical quality of their more advanced neighbors. In the 2nd millennium B.C. the Levant made its best monochrome ceramics with the invasion of the Hyksos tribes about 1800 B.C., whose skill in metalwork was reflected in their pottery. The finest period of production occurred between 1800-1600 B.C. At a later date, at the beginning of the Early Iron Age, 1050-700 B.C., Levantine potters once again demonstrated their ability to produce very artistic and technically sound work. It was only on the island of Cyprus that the comparative conservatism innate in plain pottery was broken. Throughout its history the Cypriot potter with admirable virtuosity embellished his wares with a wide variety of applied or incised ornament, imbuing them with a peculiar charm. Confident of his own skill, he ignored the technical advances of the mainland and even as late as the 15th century B.C. he was still making hand-shaped pottery without a potter's wheel. His skill is evident in the Base-Ring ware, a class of small vessels of the Late Bronze Age, 1600-1050 B.C., which were widely used throughout the Near East for the trade of drugs, ointments and scents. The ware is extremely fine, grey or brown, frequently little more than a millimeter thick, fired to an almost metallic hardness and coated with a thin polished black or brown slip. The forms are pleasing and usually reserved. It is with this ware that the island's renown in the ceramic world rests. See *Roman Pottery; Greece; Europe; Islamic Pottery; Minoan; Mycenaean; Ubaid; Sumerian; Cyprus.* (23-48)

Negative Painting In ceramics; see *Resist; Central American Pottery.*

Neo-Baroque or **Revived Baroque** See *Historicism; Louis XIV; Victorian.*

Neo-Classic In style of ornament. See *Classic Revival.*

Neo-Gothic or **Revived Gothic** See *Louis Philippe; Historicism; Victorian; Gothic; Meigh, Charles.*

Neo-Grec See *Greek Revival.*

Neo-Pompeian See *Pompeian Taste.*

Neo-Renaissance or **Revived Renaissance**
See *Historicism; Victorian.*

Neo-Rococo See *Revived Rococo.*

Netherlandish Refers to the earlier wares of Flanders and the Low Countries. See *Dutch; Belgium.*

Netherlandish Majolica See *Antwerp; Haarlem; Amsterdam; Middelburg; Majolica; Italian Majolica; Faïence; Dutch Tiles.*

Neu, Wenzel (c. 1708-1774) Repairer and modeler. He is believed to have worked at Fulda, 1765-1774, where he modeled the Four Seasons which may be considered the finest of German faïence figures.

Neustadt-Eberswalde In German ceramics; a small factory making cream-colored earthenware was operated at Neustadt-Eberswalde from around 1799 to about 1805 or later by Johann Heinrich Buchwald.

Nevers In French ceramics; during the 17th century much fine faïence distinctive for its bold drawings and rich colors was made at Nevers. The eminent position attained by Nevers during the 17th century was lost in the succeeding century. It remained a flourishing productive center but the quality of the decoration declined rapidly. Potteries are still in existence. No factory mark was ever used. Faïence figures were made from the earliest times. It seems that only high temperature colors were used at Nevers, and that the red always gave them trouble. Beautiful colors and strong drawings were characteristic of the Nevers style. A soft manganese purple was always a popular color at Nevers, especially for outline drawing. During the first half of the 17th century borders of continuous figures and later of flowers were much favored. Some of the polychrome painted decoration of this period ranks among the best of French faïence. Painted decoration in blue and manganese colors became fashionable during the second half of the 17th century and practically supplanted the earlier polychrome decoration of the first half of the 17th century. This was due to the vogue created by Chinese porcelains and the faïence made at Delft. The so-called Bleu Persan or Décor Persan was introduced during the second half of the 17th century and is probably the most important Nevers creation. The motifs chiefly consisted of foliage and birds of a French or Chinese character painted in opaque white and yellow on a deep blue, the celebrated Bleu de Nevers, ground. Sometimes, but very rarely, the blue ground was simply marbled in white. The forms were of Chinese shapes such as double gourd-shaped vases. See *Bleu Persan.* (239-244)

New Canton In English ceramics; see *Bow.*

New England Pottery Company In American ceramics; established in East Boston, Massachusetts, 1854, by Frederick Meagher for the manufacture of common white ware. In 1875 Thomas Gray and L. W. Clark took over the works and maintained the name. From about 1878 to about 1893 early ironstone china bore the mark of the Great Seal or Arms of the Commonwealth of Massachusetts. In 1886 the firm began to make a semi-porcelain ware in colored bodies which was artistically decorated and given the name Rieti ware. This was first marked with a mailed hand holding a dagger.

New Hall In English ceramics; a company of five Staffordshire potters started a porcelain manufactory at New Hall, Shelton, Staffordshire, in 1782, having in the preceding year bought the Bristol patent for hard paste porcelain and for the sale of china clay and china stone. Simply decorated wares in the manner of the cottage style formerly used at Bristol were typical.

NEW ENGLAND POTTERY
COMPANY

1883-1886

1886-1888

Later, from about 1810 to about 1825 when the factory is believed to have closed, a rather glassy bone porcelain was made and was marked with the name of the factory, New Hall, printed in red. This later ware was also decorated in a simple cottage style.

New Stone In English ceramics; the impressed mark Spode's New Stone occurred on Spode's stone-china body from around 1805 to 1820. Durable dinner services were made of this body. See *Stone-China; Spode*.

NEW YORK CITY POTTERY
1871 ON

New York City Pottery In American ceramics; started by Morrison and Carr around 1853–1855, producing Victorian majolica, stone china and white granite. Parian ware was also made here from the late 1870's. The impressed mark Morrison and Carr occurs in 1860. The partnership was dissolved in 1871. Carr continued to operate the pottery until he retired in 1888, when it closed. The pottery enjoyed considerable success. Among the marks of varying design the majority included the letters J.C. or N.Y.C.P. See *Carr, J.; Majolica; Parian*.

Newcastle-upon-Tyne In English ceramics; several potteries were active at Newcastle-upon-Tyne, Northumberland, in the late 18th and 19th century. Their production comprised inferior cream-colored and white earthenware, frequently transfer-printed, including figures. See *St. Anthony's Pottery*.

NEWCOMB
1896 ON

Newcomb Pottery In American ceramics; the Rookwood approach to pottery was already in effect at Newcomb College in New Orleans in 1895 at the newly formed ceramic department of the Newcomb Art School. In 1897 Newcomb pottery appeared on the market and in 1900 was awarded a bronze medal at the Paris International Exposition. Its popularity continued until 1915. Typical wares produced here in the years around 1900 were deco-

rated with Art Nouveau motifs colored and outlined with incising. See *Rookwood Pottery; Art Nouveau*. (512)

Newland, William (b. 1919) English, born in New Zealand, artist-potter and teacher; married Margaret Hine, an artist-potter. Trained at the Central School of Arts and Crafts in London. Newland belongs to that group of potters who are concerned with a more personal approach to pottery, in which the scope of color and range of form is less restricted than in the impersonal expression of form and glaze advocated by Bernard Leach. See *Leach, B*.

Nicaragua, Costa Rica and Panama In pre-Columbian Central American ceramics; the pottery of the southern part of Central America, embracing the states of Nicaragua, Costa Rica and Panama, is not as well known archaeologically as Mexico and the Maya region. Perhaps the first in point of time is the pottery found at Chiriqui and as a trade ware in Veraguas in Panama. Frequently called Biscuit ware, this pottery in appearance bears a close resemblance to modern European pottery after its first firing and before glazing, when it is technically called biscuit. The forms include bowls, vases and dishes in various shapes. Any of the forms may be modified by pedestal bases or wide hollow tripod supports containing pellets, the so-called cascabel feet. The decoration is either modeled in full relief or is applied in the form of conventionalized parts of an armadillo or less frequently of some other animal or fish. The most distinguishing feature of the Chiriqui ware is its excellent proportions and fine workmanship. These are revealed to great advantage by the light, even sandy color which is seldom marred by the "firing clouds." Closely related to Biscuit ware in respect to texture are the vessels from the highlands of Costa Rica and Nicaragua decorated with incising and applied figures. Many other monochrome wares, mainly red, brown or black, frequently decorated with simple incised designs or simple painting in one color on the natural surface, are found in the area. The remaining major wares include the polychrome pottery of Coclé in Panama and the so-called Nicoya polychrome pottery of Nicaragua. Both of these wares are characterized by many variations in shape and in decorative techniques. Nicoya polychrome ware, which probably belongs to the Post Classic period, 980-1521, is a blend of widely spread influences—Nahua, Maya, and South America. Features of this ware which distinguish this pottery as being apart from all other Central American wares are the size and heaviness of the base and the elaboration of the tripod supports often elaborately modeled in the form of animal heads, and an intangible quality in the contours of the vessels. See *Central American Pottery.*

Nicoya Polychrome Pottery   See *Nicaragua, Costa Rica and Panama.*

Niculoso, Francisco Pisano   (d. 1529) Italian majolica-type potter who was working at Seville 1503 to 1518, thus predating the emigration of Italian potters to Antwerp and Lyons.

Niderviller   In French ceramics; a faïence manufactory was started at Niderviller, Moselle, in Lorraine, in 1754 by Baron Jean-Louis de Beyerlé with the assistance of artists and workers from Strasbourg. Porcelain was also made after 1765. From late in the 18th century faïence fine wares were made. The manufactory is still in existence. Although the early wares were generally not marked, sometimes JLB in a monogram was found between 1754 and 1770. Crossed C's under a crown was one of the marks used from 1770 to 1793. Included among the late 18th century marks was Niderviller, impressed. The early wares in the Rococo style are generally regarded to be the most important and strongly reflect the influence of Strasbourg. The painted decoration was ex-

ecuted with admirable skill and taste. Figure painting in crimson monochrome was much favored. After 1770 the so-called Décor Bois decoration was frequently used and it is generally believed to have been an original Niderviller creation. A more individual style of work was attained in their faïence figures which were distinctive for their delicate modeling and coloring. The porcelain figures were frequently in biscuit, and often revealed the same finished and delicate workmanship found in the faïence figures. The later tablewares were rather undistinguished and were decorated in the contemporary Louis XVI style with sprigs of cornflowers and other similar patterns found on Paris porcelain. See *Décor Bois; Strasbourg; Faïence Fine.* (284, 361)

Niedermayer, Johann Josef   (d. 1784) Master-modeler at Vienna, 1747-1784. He is most likely the modeler of the majority of the typical Vienna figures of the Rococo era. His son Matthias became director at Vienna, 1805-1827. See *Vienna.*

Nielsen, Jais   (1885–1961) Danish painter, sculptor and ceramist. From 1921 to 1961 he worked at Royal Copenhagen where he created a great number of figures, bowls and vases. Biblical scenes were his main source of inspiration. His Good Samaritan created in 1923 is well known. (535)

Nielsen, Kai   (1884–1924) Danish painter, sculptor and ceramist. Worked at intervals for Bing and Grøndahl where his principal work was a series of sculptures executed in porcelain and named The Sea. This group represents the sea-mother with her sucking children surrounded by tritons riding on dolphins out of the water into the immortal world of fantasy. Amphitrite was the main piece of the group. (536, 537)

Nienhuis, Bert   (d. 1960) Dutch artist-potter; for many years an important figure in the artist-pottery of Holland. Around the beginning of the 20th century he was design-

NIDERVILLER

1754-1770

1770-1793

ing for De Distel, an art pottery at Amsterdam. His elaborately glazed wares exerted great influence.

Nieuwer Amstel   In Dutch ceramics. See *Weesp.*

NIHON KOSHITSU TOKI
COMPANY
20TH CENTURY

Nihon Koshitsu Toki Company   In Japanese ceramics; an important 20th century industrial manufacturer of ironstone tablewares located in the Ishikawa prefecture. They produce such well-known traditional patterns as Blue Willow, which bears a trademark including the inscription Double Phoenix N.K.T. Ironstone. See *Japanese Contemporary Pottery.*

Nilson, Johann Esaias (1721-1788)   See *Rococo; Engraved Designs.*

NINSEI

Nîmes   In French ceramics; a pottery was started here before 1548 by Antoine Sigalon or Syjalon, a Huguenot potter who made or caused to be made around 1554 wares in the manner of Italian majolica. It is believed that the kiln continued to be operated after his death in 1590 by members of his family until 1620. (236, 237)

Ninsei (d. 1695 ?) Japanese studio potter and painter, working at Awata and other districts of Kyoto; the foremost potter of Kyo wares. As Kakiemon is traditionally connected with the development of fine overglaze decorated porcelains (decorating in vitrifiable enamels) Ninsei is regarded as the originator of enameled pottery. In fact he may have anticipated Kakiemon. Ninsei, whose real name was Seiuemon, is himself an obscure figure. Regardless of his vague background, the specific contribution ordinarily ascribed to him is the creation of a school of flawlessly executed polychrome enameled pottery wares. Their most important feature is their exquisite imitation in ceramic terms of designs, themes and decorative techniques long popular in Japanese lacquer work. Ninsei and his school gave particular attention to the development of a

NISHIKI-DE PLATE, IMARI

jet black glaze that suggested the lustrous black of fine lacquer. They also made lavish use of gold and silver together with a rich variety of colors in their ceramic versions of the gilded inlay-lacquer for which Japan was celebrated. These elegant wares influenced the work of a great number of Kyoto potters down to the present day. Some of the best examples of the many-faceted inheritance of Ninsei's tradition are to be found among the wares of several studio potters of great distinction, whose work, while within the wide limits of Kyoto wares, reveals a notably large number of different styles. Among these individual potters were Ogata Kenzan, Mokubei, Dohachi and Eiraku. Ninsei principally made utensils for use in the tea ceremony. See *Kyo; Kenzan, Ogata; Mokubei, Aoki; Dohachi, Ninami; Eiraku; Eisen, Okuda.* (136)

Nishiki or **Nishiki-de**   The Japanese term for the polychrome enameled decoration on porcelain and pottery. See *Some Nishiki; Imari; Brocade Patterns.*

Nördstrom, Patrick   See *Royal Copenhagen.*

Noritake   In Japanese ceramics; probably the most important industrial ceramic manufactory in Japan at the present time. It was established at Nagoya in 1904 and for the most part produces porcelain tablewares for the export market. See *Japanese Contemporary Pottery.*

North Hylton Pottery or **Hylton Pottery**   In English ceramics; started at Sunderland, Durham, by William Maling in 1762 for his sons Christopher and John. Around 1797 John's son Robert joined the pottery. From 1780 to 1815 the pottery was operated by Phillips and Maling and subsequently John Phillips (and Company) until it closed about 1867. It should be noted that John Phillips also owned and operated the Sunderland or Garrison Pottery at Sunderland, and Phillips' marks without the Hylton address may refer to the Garrison Pottery. About 1817 the Malings

NORITAKE
PRESENT

started a new pottery at Ouseburn, New-castle. Among the early Maling wares were colorful patterns called in America Gaudy Dutch or Gaudy Welsh.

Northern Celadon In Chinese ceramics. See *Celadon*.

Norton, Captain John In American ceram-ics; a potter of Bennington, Vermont. See *Bennington*.

Norton and Fenton See *Bennington*.

Norton Pottery Company See *Bennington*.

Nottingham In English ceramics; salt-glazed stoneware was produced at Not-tingham from around 1690 to 1800. The most important stoneware was made from around 1700 to 1765. The grey body of the stoneware was concealed by a wash of fer-ruginous clay which gave it a warm brown tone and a slight metallic sheen. The wares, which were distinctive for their well-proportioned forms, included cylin-drical mugs, large and small jugs, two-handled posset-pots, teapots, tea caddies and other similar articles. The decoration, chiefly consisting of geometrical and floral motifs, was generally incised and im-pressed with small stamps. Sometimes conventional flowers were painted from the dark brown slip used as a wash over the ware. Occasionally a clay grit was sprin-kled on the surface to give it a roughened texture which was used in horizontal bands and on jugs in the form of a bear with a detachable head used as a cup. After the middle of the 18th century molded decora-tion in the Staffordshire manner was sometimes used, and at a still later date applied reliefs were often employed for decoration.

Nove In Italian ceramics; a faïence and por-celain manufactory was established in 1728 at Nove, Venezia, by Giovanni Bat-tista Antonibon. Except for a short interval between 1802 and 1824 the manufactory remained in the hands of the Antonibon family until late in the 19th century. No regular factory mark seems to have been used on the faïence. The mark of a six- or eight-pointed star in red and more rarely in gold or blue enamel, with or without the word Nove was used on porcelain but rarely on faïence until the 19th century when it was commonly used on all wares. Much faïence of good quality was made in the Rococo style and was painted in high temperature colors from around the mid-dle of the 18th century. The later faïence reflected the influence of Sèvres porcelain and was painted in enamel colors. Por-celain made at Nove was of a hybrid paste; no examples of hard paste porcelain are known. The best and most individual work belongs to a period from around 1760 to 1780. The material was rather opaque and grey and the colors were lively and clean. Especially prominent was a deep glossy red enamel. The forms and painted deco-ration for the best work were fanciful and typically Italian with masquerade figures, Italian landscapes, peasant scenes and similar subjects. The later work was chiefly copied from Sèvres and other manufacto-ries and had little distinction. Cream-colored earthenware of excellent qual-ity was also made at Nove. See *Faïence Fine*. (406)

Novyi In Russian ceramics; at the beginning of the 19th century, the three Novyi broth-ers, Ivan, Tikhon and Semen started a por-celain manufactory at Kuziaevo, near Moscow, which closed around 1860. Like many of the manufactories in the area they also made faïence. Figures were also pro-duced, but they were inferior to those made at the Gardner and Popov manufac-tories. Novyi tablewares and other por-celains possessed both technical and artistic excellence. They have a distinctive Russian provincial quality and for this rea-son are readily recognizable. Among their marks was the Russian N. See *Russia; Khrapunov-Novyi*.

POSSET-POT, POTTERY
ENGLISH 18TH CENTURY

NOVE
c. 1760-1780

БРАТЬЕВЬ
НОВЫХЬ
NOVYI
c. 1820-1860

Nowotny, August See *Altrohlau.*

Nuremberg In German ceramics; Nuremberg is generally regarded as the most important center for tile-work stoves from the 16th century onwards. Hafner ware jugs and mugs were also made. It seems also that many of the remaining examples of 16th century German majolica were made here. In 1712 two merchants established a faïence manufactory producing some of the most important faïence made in Germany. The best of this faïence was made from around 1715 to 1740 and was in a distinctive German Baroque style. Included among the productions were jugs with narrow necks, cylindrical tankards and plain and reeded dishes. Much of the painted decoration was in blue on a grey or pale blue ground. Other high temperature colors were also used; however, red was relatively rare. Especially fine was some work painted in blue in which web-like designs of Baroque scrollwork or foliage covered the entire surface. Panels with various subjects, such as coats-of-arms, landscapes and religious and mythological figure subjects, were finely painted and were enclosed within Baroque strapwork or scrollwork borders. No factory mark was used until about the middle of the 18th century when NB in monogram was used; however, painters' signatures were quite common. After 1770 the manufactory showed evidence of decline. The influence of Meissen porcelain was evident and some of the work was painted in enamel colors. See *Hafner.* (210, 245, 248, 249)

Nymphenburg In German ceramics; a German porcelain manufactory under the patronage of Prince Max III Joseph of Bavaria (d. 1777) was established in 1753 at Neudeck-ob-der-Au (when the well-known Viennese arcanist J. J. Ringler was there) and removed to Nymphenburg in 1761. It is one of the seven great 18th century German porcelain manufactories. From around 1755 to 1767 its productions in the Rococo style were unrivaled for their exquisite decoration and for the modeling of their figures made by Franz Anton Bustelli. The manufactory suffered a financial crisis in 1767 and never regained its earlier position. It operated as a Bavarian State possession until 1862 when it was leased privately. It still is in existence. The factory mark was the Bavarian coat of arms and it varied in size and shape. The figures in the Rococo style were remarkable for their simplification of form, for their flexible movement and for their flowing rhythmical lines. The models showed a humor and fantasy symbolic of the make-believe spirit of the Rococo. Many of the figures were not painted; however, when color was used it was treated in an original manner that did not disturb the lines. Of especial interest were some biscuit figures, busts and portrait reliefs in the Neo-Classic style modeled by Johann Peter Melchior. The painted decoration in the Rococo style on tablewares was outstanding for its beautiful color and execution. Naturalistic flowers, fruit, pastoral landscapes and figure subjects were much favored. Especially fine and characteristic were the beautiful gilt, blue and pink borders having a delicate lace-like quality. The tableware made in the Neo-Classic style was of fine quality; however, the painted decoration was in accordance with the prevailing fashion for porcelain and revealed little originality. The shield mark which was done in a variety of sizes and shapes, was used from 1754 to 1862. Modern marks include the shield, often with a star or crown above, sometimes with the word Nymphenburg; also the Frankenthal marks of a crowned CT and a checkered shield, as some of the Frankenthal molds found their way to Nymphenburg. See *Bustelli, F. A.; Melchior, J. P.; Auliczek, D.; Kirchmayer, J.; Schwanthaler, F.; Eberhard, F.; Scheurich, P.; Wackerle, J.; Rococo.* (321-323)

Nylund, Gunnar See *Rörstrand.*

NUREMBERG
1750 ON

NYMPHENBURG
C. 1754-1765

Meissen Rhinoceros, modelled by Johann Joachim Kaendler and Peter Reinicke, c. 1745. *The Antique Company of New York, Inc.; The Antique Porcelain Company.*

Chelsea Seals and Scent-Bottles, c. 1752–55. *The Antique Company of New York, Inc.; The Antique Porcelain Company.*

Meissen Garniture of Vases Symbolizing The Four Elements, modelled by Johann Joachim Kaendler, c. 1750. *The Antique Company of New York, Inc.; The Antique Porcelain Company.*

Chelsea Scent-Bottles and Bonbonnières, c. 1752–55. *The Antique Company of New York, Inc.; The Antique Porcelain Company.*

Meissen Five Senses, modelled by Johann Joachim Kaendler and Johann Friedrich Eberlein, c. 1745. *The Antique Company of New York, Inc.; The Antique Porcelain Company.*

Mennecy Figure of a Pierrot, c. 1740.
Collection: Mr. and Mrs. Charles W. Engelhard.

China Seller. Capo di Monte, 1743–59.
Collection: Mr. and Mrs. Edward M. Pflueger.

Meissen Harlequin Figures, modelled by Johann Joachim Kaendler, c. 1735–40.
The Antique Company of New York, Inc.; The Antique Porcelain Company.

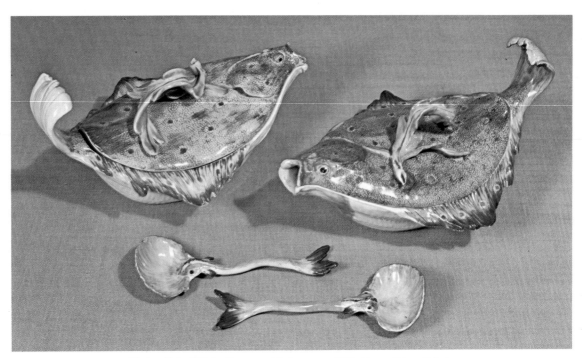

Chelsea Pair of Plaice Tureens with Spoons, c. 1755. *From a Private Collector.*

Meissen Rhinoceros, modelled by Johann Joachim Kaendler, c. 1743. *Collection: Edward Jackson Wiest, Esq.*

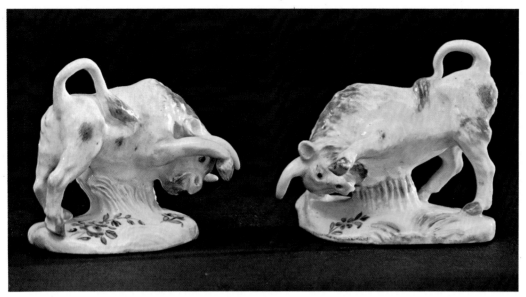

Derby Pair of Fighting Bulls, ascribed to Andrew Planché, c. 1750. *Collection: Edward Jackson Wiest, Esq.*

Astbury Pottery Pair of Equestrian Figures, c. 1730. *Collection: Mr. R. Thornton Wilson, Sr.*

Bow Singing Harlequin pretending to crank the tail of a Pug Dog
as if it were a Hurdy-Gurdy, c. 1755. *Collection: Mr. and Mrs.*
Frank H. Wyman.

Nymphenburg Figure of Capitano Spavento, modelled by Franz Anton
Bustelli, c. 1763. *The Antique Company of New York, Inc.; The Antique*
Porcelain Company.

Nyon In Swiss ceramics; the manufacture of porcelain was started at Nyon near Geneva around 1780 by Ferdinand Müller, believed to have come from Frankenthal, who a year later took as his partner, Jacob Dortu of Berlin, Marseilles and Marieberg. Dortu, who brought with him the secret for making a hard paste which was decorated in the fashionable Paris styles, became sole director, 1809-1813, when the company was liquidated. In 1814 the company became J. A. Bonnard et Cie and existed until well into the 19th century. Essentially from the past part of the Dortu period, the production centered on English earthenware and decorative wares in the Neo-Classical style, including Wedgwood's stonewares. The accepted mark was a fish in underglaze blue. See *Zurich*.

NYON
C. 1780 ON

NYMPHENBURG FIGURE

O

Oaxaca In pre-Columbian Central American ceramics; a region and at the present time a state in southern Mexico. Its capital Oaxaca lies 230 miles southeast of Mexico City. See *Central American Pottery; Zapotec.*

Öberg, Thure See *Arabia.*

Obrist, Hermann (1863-1927) Swiss sculptor and designer, a founding member of the Münchener Vereinigte Werkstätten; from 1888 devoted himself to decorative art, in 1892 founded an embroidery workshop in Florence which he moved to Munich in 1894. See *Munich School; Riemerschmid, Richard.*

Obsieger, Robert See *Wiener Keramik.*

Oceania In art; the name is used to designate the indigenous culture of the many clusters of islands which fan out from the coast of Asia into the Pacific Ocean. Those nearest the Indonesian archipelago are of great size: New Guinea, New Zealand and the continent-sized Australia. Eastward the islands decrease in size and the groups become more widely separated. Apart from Australia, geographers divide them into three areas: that just north and east of Australia is Melanesia, with Micronesia north of it; Polynesia extends farther east. In spite of the vast expanses of ocean between them these islands have been inhabited for a very long time. In a general sense Oceanic pottery is primarily a woman's craft; the use of the potter's wheel at least among women potters was unknown; slips were rarely used; coiling perhaps was the customary method of manufacture, together with the "paddle and anvil" method. Only archaeological pottery has been found in Polynesia and excavations in the Marquesas, Samoa and Tonga reveal that it was introduced there considerably more than two thousand years ago. In considering Oceanic pottery, attention must center on Fiji for there is in these islands the most southerly survival of living potters still employing traditional methods and Fiji pottery reveals the widest range in form and function to be found anywhere in the scattered pottery communities which lie outside the larger continental islands. Briefly, Fiji is representative, even if in part only, of all the pottery traditions which together make up the whole story of pottery diffusion throughout the Pacific. Fiji pottery was used for cooking and for water vessels. The latter, the most ornate vessel in Fiji, was frequently made for chiefs and used in various ceremonials, especially during the mixing and drinking of *kava.* Of interest are the water containers made in the Rewa district in the 19th century which were in the form of small canoes, each with a handle. In some examples they were joined together in pairs or even groups of three or four. In the same district the potters made what are now called fruit clusters. These were in the form of small pottery spheres joined at the body in groups of three or four and linked by a three- or four-part handle. Though each sphere had its own filling hole, the composite container as a rule was provided with only one pouring spout. A most distinctive water container was in the form of a turtle, complete in detail. In most water jars only the upper portion of the body was embellished. Characteristic of this decoration were applied stripes of clay forming a rope-like pattern, bordered by incised designs and relieved at intervals by applied knobs placed singly or in continuous or horizontal bands. In the Malolo group the water vessels were distinctive for their lack of relief decoration and in its place was an incised herringbone motif which is the marked feature of these containers. See *Pre-Columbian Pottery; Africa.* (22)

Oeil-de-Perdrix In French ceramics; a repetitive pattern or a diaper arrangement of dotted circles on various colored grounds. It was introduced on Sèvres porcelain around 1760.

Oesterreichischer Werkbund In Austrian arts and crafts; established in 1916. Craftsmen in Austria are well organized through the efforts of this organization. Its offices are in Vienna, and its outlet Wiener Handwerk is a showcase for Austrian handicrafts. See *Wiener Werkstätte; Deutscher Werkbund.*

Oettingen-Schrattenhofen In German ceramics; a faïence manufactory was started in 1735 at Oettingen, Bavaria, and moved in 1737 to Schrattenhofen. It was active well into the 19th century. Especially characteristic of their productions were cylindrical tankards with boldly painted Rococo motifs in high temperature colors. They were marked Schrattenhofen. The more common wares for daily use were not marked. It is generally believed that a brown ware similar to that made at Ansbach and at Bayreuth was also made. Later the manufactory made white and cream-colored earthenware.

Offenbach In German ceramics; a faïence manufactory was established at Offenbach, near Frankfurt-on-Main, in 1739, by Philipp Friedrich Lay. It seems that the factory was still active in the early 19th century. Included among the marks was an O with a double F written as one. Tablewares painted in high temperature colors in a peasant style with flowers, fruit, birds and figure subjects were the characteristic productions.

Ohnsorg, Kurt See *Wiener Keramik.*

Oil Spot Temmoku In Chinese ceramics. See *Honan Temmoku.*

Oinochoë In Greek antiquities; a jug resembling a pitcher, having a handle extending from the lip rim to the top of the shoulder, used for ladling and pouring wine. It is one of the most common of Greek vessels. The lip rim has either a rounded or trefoil-shaped pouring projection.

Oiron In French ceramics; near Thouars, Deux-Sèvres. The fine lead-glazed white earthenware with inlaid decoration generally known as Henri Deux ware, long attributed to Oiron, is now believed to have been made at Saint-Porchaire. See *Saint-Porchaire.*

Okochi See *Nabeshima.*

Olbrich, Joseph Maria (1867-1908) Austrian architect, craftsman and designer. Olbrich was a leader of the Vienna Secession, which he helped found in 1897. He was invited to the artist colony at Mathildenhöhe in 1899, where he designed practically all of the buildings. See *Secession; Hoffmann, Josef; Mathildenhöhe.*

Old Blue See *Historical Blue.*

Old Crown Derby China Works See *Derby.*

Old Moor's Head, The or **Oude Moriaenshooft** In Dutch ceramics; a faïence pottery started at Delft before 1690 by Rochus Jacobsz Hoppesteyn adjacent to his flourishing The Young Moor's Head. He sold it in 1690. After changing hands several times it was united with The Young Moor's Head in 1769 and ceased to operate in 1792. Some of the faïence made here imitated the style of the talented potter Rochus Hoppesteyn. See *Young Moor's Head, The; Delft; Faïence.* (294)

Old Nanking In Chinese ceramics; a name given to the blue and white porcelain made at Ching-tê-Chên. See *Ching-tê-Chên; Blue and White Ming; Blue and White Ch'ing; Nanking Ware.*

Old Prince, The or **De Oude Prins** In Dutch ceramics; the most important Amsterdam

OFFENBACH
C. 1740 ON

OINOCHOE

OINOCHE

tile factory. It was active from 1649 to 1802, and mainly produced flower tableaux and tiles, with landscapes, figures, flowers, especially tulips, children at play, ships and stories. It is believed that pottery for daily use was also made. The ware was especially well known and the tiles were exported abroad. See *Amsterdam*.

Olerys, Joseph　(1697–1749) French faïence painter born at Marseilles, working at Clérissy's faïence factory at Moustiers from before 1721. Around 1727 he was at the Alcora factory at Spain where he remained for ten years. Returned to Moustiers and in 1738 started a new factory with his brother-in-law Jean-Baptiste Laugier. His son Joseph Olerys (1754-1795) succeeded him in partnership with the Laugiers. (277)

Olerys, Joseph and Laugier, Jean Baptiste See *Moustiers*.

Ollivier　See *Rue de la Roquette*.

Olmec　In pre-Columbian Central American ceramics; the earliest important civilization was the Olmec of Mexico, its origins dating to the late second millennium B.C. At home on the coast of the Gulf of Mexico, the Olmecs influenced many distant areas, among them the high plateaus of central Mexico. The highland site of Las Bocas in the state of Puebla is well known for its Olmec style ceramics. Significant among these ceramics are the almost life size and quite realistic "baby" figures, which are closely related to the half-human, half-jaguar Olmec werejaguars. Both "baby" figures and werejaguars were thought to be early forms of the great gods of Mexico. The baby figures are white to pale yellow in color after firing, many of the figures were accented with red pigment. See *Central American Pottery*. (6)

On-Glaze　Same as overglaze. See *Overglaze*.

O'Neale, Jeffrey Hamet　English porcelain

ONONDAGA POTTERY CO.
c. 1890

painter at Chelsea and Worcester where his name appears in accounts of 1770 to 1773. Horses and other animals and figures in landscapes were his favorite subjects. See *Giles, J*.

Onion Pattern　In German ceramics. See *Zwiebelmuster*.

Onolzbach　In German ceramics. See *Ansbach*.

Onondaga Pottery Company　In American ceramics; this still-existing company was established in 1871 in Syracuse, New York, to manufacture white granite ware. Among their marks were the arms of New York State, 1874-1893, for white granite ware; the Imperial Geddo mark was used for the first china ware made by this company; semi-porcelain ware was marked Semi Vitreous, 1886-1898, and after 1897 the mark Syracuse China was used. Became the Syracuse China Corporation.

Opaque Porcelain　See *Granite Ware; Ironstone China*.

Orange　See *Yellow and Orange*.

Oribe　In Japanese ceramics; the name given to late 16th century examples made at the kilns in the Mino province, believed sufficiently representative of the taste of the tea master Furuta Oribe to be identified with his name. These wares, though numerous, share in common a remarkably large number of features. Oribe ware is usually divided into Green Oribe in which most or all of the surface has been covered with a thin green glaze, and Decorated Oribe painted with distinctive bold touches and commonly in several colors among which the same brilliant green is frequently conspicuous. Equally as characteristic as the bold design and color of this ware are the many elaborate and even unusual forms, notably including a variety of covered dishes and boxes and particularly trays with bail handles. Some extant examples are worked into fairly elaborate pieces, such as an incense burner in the form of a stylized lion. The lively charm of Decorated Oribe is regarded by many as a good antidote for the subdued sober style which so frequently resulted from the tea-cult influence. Therefore it is surprising to note that the Oribe techniques were even employed to produce a ware resembling Seto Black called Oribe Black, in which the surface decoration showed large areas of lustrous black glaze. See *Mino.* (132)

Oribe, Furuta (1543–1615) Celebrated Japanese tea master. See *Oribe; Rikyu, Sen-no; Mino; Cha-no-yu; Iga.*

Oribe Black See *Oribe.*

Oriental Lowestoft See *Chinese Lowestoft.*

Orientalizing See *Greece,* in ancient ceramics.

Orléans In French ceramics; in 1753 a privilege was granted to Jacques-Etienne Dessaux de Romilly to start a faïence and porcelain manufactory at Orléans, Loiret. It was active until 1812. According to contemporary records it seems that considerable faïence and porcelain, presumed to be a soft paste, were produced. However, it has always been difficult to identify early Orléans porcelain as well as faïence. It is believed that faïence decorated in the Strasbourg style with colored enamels was made during the early period. The mark registered for porcelain in 1766 was a crowned O. Later the manufactory also made faïence fine or lead-glazed earthenware in the English style and agate and marbled earthenware also in the English style. These wares were often marked with either the name of the proprietor or the place. Towards the end of the 18th century other porcelain manufactories were also active in Orléans.

Ormolu See *Metal Mounts on Ceramics.*

Ornamental Wares See *Useful Wares.*

Orvieto In Italian ceramics; pottery was made at Orvieto, Umbria, as early as the 13th century. It produced a primitive type of majolica during the 14th and early 15th centuries painted in copper green and manganese purple. This type of green and purple decorated majolica was also made at Siena and Florence in Tuscany and at Faenza; however, Orvieto was probably the earliest center. The forms, which were often clumsy and of poor proportions, included jugs with very wide mouths, small dishes with two handles and other similar articles. The decoration was in relief and distinctly reflected Gothic influence. Thick foliage, starry flowers, animals and masks were much favored for decorative motifs. Crowned figure subjects treated in a Gothic style drawn in outline on a cross-hatched ground were a popular Orvieto decorative manner. See *Italian Majolica.*

Østerbro In Danish ceramics; a third Copenhagen faïence manufactory was founded at Østerbro in 1763 by Peter Hofnagel. He employed workers from other Copenhagen potteries and after a lawsuit he withdrew in 1769. It seems that the wares were painted in blue or in manganese and occasionally with touches of gilding. The quality of the material in the pieces ascribed to him is rather imperfect.

Ott and Brewer Company In American ceramics; operated the Etruria Pottery at Trenton, New Jersey, from 1863 to 1893. It was under the direction of William Bromley, Sr., from the Belleek factory at Belleek, Ireland, from 1883. The pottery is especially remembered as a maker of American Belleek in the 1880's. Characteristic marks used by the company include Manufactured by Ott & Brewer Trenton N.J., U.S.A., and a crown pierced by a sword with Belleek above and O & B below. According to the opinion of certain experts, true Belleek was not made here until after 1883 and bore the crescent

ORLEANS
1766 ON

OTT AND BREWER

O.-B.
CHINA
C. 1866

BELLEEK

O & B
AFTER 1876

mark. See *Parian Ware; Belleek; Broome, I.; Bromley, W.* (446, 456, 459)

Ottoman-Turkish Pottery See *Islamic Pottery, Later.*

Ottweiler In German ceramics; a faïence and porcelain manufactory was started in 1763 at Ottweiler in the Rhineland by Etienne-Dominique Pellevé under the patronage of Prince Wilhelm Heinrich of Nassau. Lead-glazed earthenware in the English style was also made from 1784 onward. In 1794 the models and molds were transferred to Sarreguemines. The faïence was apparently not marked and is difficult to identify. The porcelain is generally marked with an NS (Nassau-Saarbrücken). The hard paste material varied in quality. Tablewares in the Rococo style are the most characteristic productions and are of good quality. Mythological subjects and scenes from the Italian Comedy framed in delicate gilt Rococo scrollwork were much favored and were painted in beautiful colors. The forms of some of the tablewares such as pear-shaped jugs were distinctly of French inspiration. Underglaze blue painting and purple monochrome were also used. The glazed earthenware or faïence fine was not marked. Faïence fine wares generally ascribed to this factory are plain white and are in the French Neo-Classic style.

Oude Amstel In Dutch ceramics. See *Weesp.*

Oude Loosdrecht In Dutch ceramics. See *Weesp.*

Oudry, Jean-Baptiste (1668-1755) French animal painter. Especially well known is his series "Les Contes de La Fontaine." Engravings of groups of game in the style of Oudry were adopted by the porcelain painters. See *Engraved Designs.*

Overglaze In ceramics; enameled decoration painted on a glaze previously fired, the colors then being fired onto the glaze

.NS.

OTTWEILER
C. 1763 ON

at a lower temperature (petit feu). The petit feu technique special to porcelain was later introduced on faïence, the decoration of which up to that time was painted directly on the raw glaze and then fired at a high temperature (grand feu). See *Petit Feu; Colors; Enamel; Löwenfinck, A. F. von.*

Owari Celadon In Japanese ceramics; the name given to a kind of wood-ash glazed ware made at Seto, which is in the ancient province of Owari, in the first part of the 11th century.

Owens, J. B. Company In American ceramics; J. B. Owens, who had started to make flowerpots in 1885 at Roseville, Ohio, was successful enough to build a new factory at Zanesville in 1891 where he installed his earlier modest equipment. Here he made majolica flowerpots, jardinieres, umbrella stands and popular fancy novelties. When W. A. Long, who was instrumental in establishing S. A. Weller in the art pottery field in 1895, took his knowledge of underglaze decoration to Owens, the firm started to make art pottery and employed a staff of artists to decorate the wares. The earliest ware, called Utopian, closely resembled Rookwood standard ware and Weller's Louwelsa. It also was decorated with portrait heads of American Indians, horses, dogs, as well as floral motifs in underglaze slip-painting, on dark or light grounds. In the following several years other lines were included; such as Henri Deux, Alpine, Corona, Venetian, Gun Metal and Mission. The last mentioned was decorated with scenes depicting old Spanish missions of the American Southwest. There was also a Rustic line made in rustic shapes to simulate branches of trees and the like; Aborigine with designs copied from early Indian pottery, and Art Vellum having underglaze decoration in warm rich tints of autumn leaves under a soft vellum finish. As a rule the name Owens and the name of the line were marked on the bottom of the ware. Owens art pottery, which did not survive the panic of 1907, was of fine quality and at its most flourishing period the firm employed a staff of decorators rivaling that of Rookwood in size. Owens remained in the ceramic business, providing architectural tiles until the start of the Depression. He retired to Florida, where he lived until his death in 1934. See *Roseville Pottery; Weller, S. A.; Lonhuda Pottery; Art Nouveau; Long, W. A.* (523)

Owl Jug In ceramics; a variety of armorial faïence jug made in the form of an owl and having a removable head forming a cup. It is generally accepted that the original faïence owl jug, of which there are about fifteen surviving examples, was made at Brixen in the Tyrol from around 1540 to 1570 and was used as an archery prize. The feathers were either applied in relief and painted in blue or simply painted on the body. On the breast of the owl was a coat-of-arms applied in high relief and painted in oil colors and in gold. Variations in detail occur. The faïence owl jug was copied in Rhenish stoneware and lead-glazed earthenware during the 16th century, and at a later time it was also made in other countries. (245)

Ox Blood In Chinese ceramics. See *Sang de Boeuf.*

Oxidation Firing See *Six Old Kilns.*

Oxidizing Fire or **Atmosphere** In ceramics; a clear bright flame in the kiln has a definite effect on the colors of the ceramic materials being fired. The majority of clays fire red in an oxidizing atmosphere and grey or black in a reducing or smoky atmosphere when the kiln is kept deficient in oxygen. In glazes iron tends to yellow or brown tones in an oxidizing atmosphere, and green under reducing conditions.

Ozier Pattern In German ceramics; relief border patterns presumably designed by Kaendler were introduced at Meissen for tablewares from around and after 1730. These relief border designs were extensively copied by other porcelain manufactories. One design is a zigzag basketwork pattern called the ordinair-ozier, and the other is a regular woven basketwork pattern with radial ribs, called the alt-ozier. Both patterns were introduced around or slightly after 1730. Around 1742 the neu-ozier design with curved S-shaped ribs was introduced.

OWL JUG, STONEWARE

BASKETWORK OZIER
PATTERN ON MEISSEN BOWL

P

Pa Chi Hsiang or **Eight Buddhist Emblems of Happy Augury.** See *Chinese Symbols and Emblems.*

Pa Hsien or **Eight Taoist Immortals** See *Eight Taoist Immortals.*

Pa Ku or **Hundred Antiques** See *Hundred Antiques.*

Pa Kua or **Eight Trigrams** In Chinese symbols. See *Eight Trigrams.*

Pa Pao or **Eight Precious Objects** See *Chinese Symbols and Emblems.*

Pa-pei In Chinese ceramics; the Chinese name for a stem-cup. See *Stem-Cup.*

Paccha See *Inca.*

Paddle and Anvil In primitive ceramics; a method in which early wares, apparently built up of broad bands of clay, were finished by a paddle and anvil. In this technique the walls of the vessels are thinned and shaped by beating them with a wooden paddle against a mushroom-shaped anvil of stone or some other material held against the inside which prevents the walls from collapsing and disguises the original structure. See *Oceania; Hohokam.*

Padua In Italian ceramics; potteries were active as early as the 15th century and majolica-making almost for a certainty dates from the 16th century and continued to be made until the 18th century.

Pagode See *Magot.*

Pai Ting In Chinese ceramics; the Chinese name given to Northern Ting or white Ting. See *Ting Yao.* (91)

Pai Tz'u In Chinese ceramics; a Chinese term for the white porcelain ware called Blanc de Chine. See *Blanc de Chine.*

Palace Style See *Minoan; Mycenean.*

Palermo See *Sicily.*

Palestine See *Near East,* in prehistoric ceramics.

Palissy, Bernard (c. 1510-c. 1590) French alchemist and potter. His reputation as a potter is chiefly predicated on literary sources, especially his own highly-colored writings. It is not possible with any degree of certainty to distinguish between his work and that of his assistants and followers, since the actual work of Palissy is not known to have ever been signed or marked. The outstanding merit of his work so far as it can be identified is in the use of finely colored glazes. After serving an apprenticeship as a glass painter he settled in Saintes around 1540 and began to conduct a series of experiments in ceramics. According to his own writings he succeeded in making a pottery which completely satisfied him. This was the so-called jaspée ware decorated in mingled colored glazes. Shortly after he produced the "rustiques figulines" upon which rested his later reputation as a potter. Around 1556 Catherine de Medici called him to Paris to make a grotto at the Tuileries which she was then having built. In 1574 he was recorded as "grottier et architecte des rustiques figulines du roy et de la royne." These "rustiques figulines" were the familiar pottery wares molded after nature with shells, lizards, snakes, fish, various kinds of leaves, rocks and moss and other natural subjects. The wares were principally decorative, unless they were large enough to be used in a garden or in a grotto, and included oval dishes, ewers, vases, plates and basins. They were remarkable for their skillful application of fine colored glazes of blue, yellow, purple brown and greyish white. Some of the best pottery was admirable for its free spirit and rhythmical designs in producing naturalistic subjects. The jaspée wares were notable for their skillful blending of glazes, either separate or mingled, producing an unrivaled harmony of colors. There is no evidence to prove that Palissy designed the molded forms decorated with fine French Renaissance motifs in which figure subjects were often introduced into the composition of the designs. Palissy's followers and imitators continued to produce wares in the Palissy style for many years. Palissy ware of the 19th century was by no means confined to a close imitation of the original style. In England the style was taken up by Mintons at Stoke-on-Trent, where close reproductions of original pieces were made, but where the term *Palissy* was also frequently used to describe the technical character of the ware rather than the style. See *Avisseau, J. C.; Mafra and Son.* (203-206, 257, 484)

Palmer, Humphrey English potter working from 1760 at the Church Works, Hanley, Staffordshire. He was living at the same time as Wedgwood, whose wares he imitated. In 1778 he secured financial aid from J. Neale, his London agent, and the firm was known as Palmer & Neale, and Neale & Co. Robert Wilson became a partner in 1786, and after 1802 the factory was carried on by his son, David Wilson. In the 19th century the firm was sold. They made tablewares of porcelain and cream-colored earthenware of good quality. They also made imitations of the fine black and jasper stonewares perfected by Wedgwood. Of particular interest were some delicately finished figures painted in clear and fresh enamel colors. Included among the marks were H.P., Palmer, Neale & Co., Neale & Wilson, and Wilson, all impressed. (403)

Palsjö In Swedish ceramics; a faïence manufactory was started at Palsjö, near Helsingborg, in 1765 by Michael Anders Coster.

Much of the production was simply painted in blue or in manganese and essentially resembled the wares made at Copenhagen. The mark was PF for Palsjö Fabrik.

Pan-t'o T'ai or **T'o T'ai** In Chinese ceramics; half-bodiless or porcelain of eggshell thinness. See *Eggshell; Ming.*

Panama See *Nicaragua, Costa Rica and Panama.*

Panathenaic Amphora See *Amphora.*

Pankok, Bernhard (1872-1943) German designer and graphic artist; a founding member of the Münchener Vereinigte Werkstätten. He furnished a room at the Paris Universal Exposition of 1900, and he contributed to JUGEND. From 1913 to 1937 he was director of the Staatliche Kunstgewerbeschule in Stuttgart. See *Munich School; Riemerschmid, Richard.*

Pao-Pie In Chinese ceramics; see *Celadon.*

Pao-Shih Hung See *Underglaze Red.*

Paquier, Claudius Innocentius du (d. 1751) Founder of the Vienna porcelain factory. From 1716 onward he started to experiment in porcelain-making; in the following year he was at Meissen and engaged the imposter arcanist C. C. Hunger from that factory. In 1719 with the assistance of S. Stöltzel he succeeded in making porcelain. In 1744 he sold his porcelain factory to the State. See *Vienna; Hunger, Christoph Conrad.*

Paracas Cavernas See *Andean.*

Paragon China Company Ltd. In English ceramics; operates the Atlas Works, Longton, since 1920, producing porcelain. Formerly the Star China Company operated the Atlas Works, 1900-1919. C. T. Weld and Sons Ltd. took over the Atlas Works in 1960, but continued it under the same title. The trade name Paragon has been used on marks from around 1900.

PARAGON CHINA COMPANY LTD.
C. 1957 ON

Parian In English ceramics; a variety of hard paste porcelain introduced by the Copeland manufactory at Stoke-on-Trent in 1846. It derived its name from the supposed resemblance of its marble-like paste to that of Parian marble. The usual proportions of kaolin and petuntse found in hard paste porcelain are considerably altered in the parian porcelain. It was principally used for biscuit figures.

Characteristic of the more ambitious work of the period following its introduction in England was the integration of parian sculptural elements in important table services; for example, a dessert service enriched with small-scale parian sculpture made by Mintons, displayed at the Great Exhibition, London, 1851, which Queen Victoria presented to the Emperor of Austria. An interesting development of the parian porcelain paste was the Irish porcelain of the Belleek factory which made use of a parian-like body. Another successful development was its use at Mintons by Solon who found the parian paste to be excellent in the use of pâte-sur-pâte decoration. The parian paste possessed the necessary degree of hardness, but as compared with the usual hard pastes it fired at a lower temperature which permitted a greater variety in the selection of colors. In American ceramics; in the 1850's and 1860's biscuit porcelain was being used in the style of parian at the United States Pottery at Bennington, Vermont, and elsewhere. The production of this version of parian at Bennington was mainly due to a certain John Harrison who had been brought from Copelands in England in 1846 by the earlier Bennington company of Norton and Fenton. This parian at Bennington was used for making figures and relief-decorated jugs either uncolored or with the white relief-pattern clearly defined against a colored pebbled or pitted ground. (It should be noted here that it is said that true parian was not made in the United States until after 1875, when it was produced by Ott and Brewer. However, this Bennington version is rightly to be regarded as parian in the sense that its use was patterned on English parian and it was intended for the same purpose.) In the last quarter of the 19th century parian ware was also made by Ott and Brewer of Trenton, Morrison and Carr of New York and Edwin Bennett of Baltimore. Somewhat earlier, around 1860, Farrar at the Southern Porcelain Company was imitating the parian jugs of Bennington in white and in blue and white.

Paris Porcelain In French ceramics; the term *Paris porcelain* is generally reserved for the hard paste porcelain made at numerous factories operating in Paris from around and after 1770. The painted decoration was essentially inspired by the contemporary styles in vogue at Sèvres. The delicate painting in the Louis XVI style was later supplanted by the more formal and severe style of the Empire. It is generally accepted that the manufactories Clignancourt, Rue Thiroux, Faubourg Saint-Denis and the Rue de Bondy, all four of which enjoyed some princely protection, and also La Courtille, which was operated privately, produced the finest Paris porcelains and that some of their best productions were equal to the hard paste porcelain produced at Sèvres. See *Rue de Bondy; La Courtille; Rue Amelot; Clignancourt; Petite Rue Saint-Gilles; Faubourg Saint-Denis; Rue de Crussol; Pont-aux-Choux; Rue Popincourt; Rue de la Roquette; Rue Thiroux.*

Partridge-Eye Pattern In French ceramics. See *Oeil-de-Perdrix.*

Party Eyes See *Andean.*

Passau In German ceramics; Passau, in Bavaria, was the source of the kaolin used at several 18th century German porcelain factories including Fürstenberg, Berlin, Nymphenburg, Ludwigsburg and Vienna. A porcelain factory was started here around 1779 by Karl Hagen and Friedel. The wares have not been identified, but it is believed that they were unimportant. They conducted a prosperous business in decorating coffee cups for the Turkish market, obtaining them white from other factories. Forgeries of porcelain made at the great 18th century German factories were also produced here in the 19th and 20th centuries.

Paste See *Body.*

Pastillage The French name given to decoration in slip trailed through a quill or a spouted vessel. See *Barbotine.*

Pastille Burner In English ceramics; an incense burner, usually of small size, made by Wedgwood, Spode, Coalport and other English potters. Especially charming are those in the shapes of fairytale cottages and castles, possessing all the beauty and grace of "once upon a time."

Pâte See *Body.*

Pâte Dure In ceramics; the French term applied to hard paste porcelain. See *Porcelain.*

Pâte-sur-Pâte In ceramics; the French term applied to the method of building decoration in low relief by successive layers of slip, usually white, applied with a brush on a colored, generally dark, ground. The process was developed at Sèvres around the middle of the 19th century. M. Solon who had worked at Sèvres came to work at Minton around 1870, where he remained for thirty-five years. He was very skilled in the pâte-sur-pâte method of decoration. As a result pâte-sur-pâte is perhaps best known in some of the Minton wares. Pâte-sur-pâte was adopted by all the important European potteries. In the late 19th century American potteries were also concerned with the development of this decorative technique. The most noteworthy was the pottery of Knowles, Taylor and Knowles of East Liverpool which showed such work with pâte-sur-pâte

decoration at the Chicago Exhibition of 1893. See *Solon, L. M.; Parian.* (479)

Pâte Tendre In ceramics; the French term for soft paste porcelain. See *Soft Paste.*

Pattern Mark A number or name painted or printed on the ware for the purpose of recording a decorative pattern. This practice was widely used in England, particularly on their transfer-printed wares. See *Marks, in ceramics; Backstamp.*

Paul and Virginia In ceramics; a widely popular Victorian theme inspired by a sentimental French novel, PAUL ET VIRGINIE by Bernardin de Saint-Pierre, 1788. The French painter, Pierre August Cot (1837-1883) portrayed the story of these unhappy lovers in his painting L'Orage or The Storm. In England the Staffordshire potters T. J. and J. Mayer of the Dale Hall potteries produced a parian porcelain pitcher with a Paul and Virginia pattern in white relief. In America the Fenton-directed Bennington pottery produced a Paul and Virginia parian pitcher, 1850-1858. (443)

Paul, Bruno (b. 1874) German architect, printmaker and decorative artist; a founding member of the Münchener Vereinigte Werkstätten and a contributor to JUGEND. Paul furnished industrial designs for the Deutsche Werkstätten. He was exhibited at the International Exposition of Art in Industry sponsored by R. H. Macy, New York, 1928. See *Munich School; Riemerschmid, Richard; Deutsche Werkstätten.*

Paul, Nikolaus Porcelain arcanist. See *Ringler, J. J.*

Pauline Pottery Company In American ceramics; a firm active in Edgerton, Wisconsin, from 1888 to about 1894, making underglaze decorated art wares. This pottery was originally established by Mrs. Pauline Jacobus in Chicago, 1883. The mark, impressed in the earlier pieces and

PAULINE POTTERY
C. 1883 ON

printed in black on the later ones, consisted of a crown with the letter C, for Chicago. Characteristic colors of Pauline pottery are vivid yellow, peacock blue and green, and soft creamy tints.

Peach-bloom In Chinese ceramics; a beautiful and refined porcelain ware first perfected during the K'ang Hsi period. The ware developed from the attempt to rival the Ming sacrificial red obtained from the use of copper to make the color. The Peach-bloom wares comprise seven small classic forms; such as a ring-necked bottle, a chrysanthemum vase with elongated neck, an amphora-shaped vase, a writer's water coupe, a writer's water jar which is shaped like a beehive, a dish and a flat rounded box for vermilion. The body is white and of a fine texture. The glaze is generally thin and even. On these wares that are perfectly formed the color varies from a pink to a liver color and is usually strewn with mottlings and splotches of greenish colors and brown. The Chinese call these wares chiang tou hung or bean red, p'in kuo hung or apple red, and p'in kuo ch'ing or apple green.

PELIKE

Pearl Ware In English ceramics; a white earthenware body containing a greater percentage of flint and white clay than cream-colored earthenware. A small amount of cobalt was added to the glaze for a still further whitening effect. Pearl ware was first made by Josiah Wedgwood in 1779 but never extensively used. It was important as a precursor of a granite ware later made by other potters. (Not to be confused with Wedgwood's granite ware in imitation of granite stone.) See *Cream-Colored Earthenware.*

Peasant Pottery As a rule pottery made for a local market; of simple technique decorated in traditional styles upon which the rapidly changing fashions created in the great cities have little or no effect. Such wares in general possess the virtues of simplicity and directness, imbuing them with singular charm. The art of the peasant potter usually clearly reveals an ancestry in its forms and decoration.

Pêche, Dagobert See *Wiener Keramik.*

Pécs See *Zsolnay.*

Peeling In ceramics; the name given to unintentional crackle caused by the body contracting more than the glaze. It is the opposite tendency of crazing in which the glaze contracts too much and as a result does not fit the body.

Peking Bowl In Chinese ceramics; a variety of porcelain bowl made during the Ch'ien Lung reign and the early 19th century. It is reputed that these bowls were especially produced for the Emperor, who used them as gifts. They are characterized by a dull opaque green, blue, yellow or crimson ground with an overall engraved scrollwork decoration.

Pelike In Greek antiquities; a variety of the amphora, provided with two vertical handles extending from the neck to the shoulder, used for the storage of wine. The ovoid-shaped body was wider at the lower portion than at the top and rested on a broad foot rim or base. See *Amphora.*

Pellipario, Nicola Also known as Nicola da Urbino. Perhaps the greatest of all majolica painters; still living in 1540. He was painter at Castel Durante about 1510 until 1525(?), at Fabriano in 1527 and from around 1528 onward at Urbino. His son Guido (d. 1576) known as Guido Durantino or Guido de Castello Durante settled at Urbino in 1520 and started a pottery for which his father sometimes painted. Guido took the surname of Fontana and had three sons, Orazio, Nicola, and Camillo. Orazio Fontana (d. 1571) who is known by signed works dating from 1542 onward, started a workshop of his own around 1565. Camillo Fontana (d. c. 1590) went with his brother Orazio to Florence to manage the Grand-Ducal pottery of Florence. He is reputed to have been an excellent painter, though his signed works are unknown. See *Castel Durante; Urbino; Istoriato.* (231)

Penig   In German ceramics; a town in the vicinity of Waldenburg in Saxony famous for its stoneware as early as 1490. See *Waldenburg.* (195)

Pennington, John   Painter of ceramics at Worcester and Etruria, late 18th and early 19th century.

Pennsylvania German   In American ceramics; a class of peasant or country pottery distinctive for its simple and direct modeling and vigorous decoration, clearly revealing the potter's indebtedness to his forebears overseas. Much of the best work dates from about the first half of the 19th century; the potters of Bucks and Montgomery counties furnished many interesting examples. (426-432)

Peony   In Chinese art; one of the flowers of the Chinese Four Seasons. It represents Spring. See *Chinese Four Season Flowers.*

Percier, Charles   (1764-1838) A French architect. See *Fontaine, Léonard; Empire.*

Pergolesi, Michele Angelo   (d. 1801) An Italian decorative artist, engraver and designer working in England prior to 1770. His treatment of antique and Renaissance motifs in the Neo-Classic manner is skillful and finished. Undoubtedly some of the painted decoration in the Neo-Classic manner used on porcelains was inspired by the designs of Pergolesi. See *Adam, Robert.*

Perlkrug or **Beaded Jug**   In German ceramics; the name given to a kind of stoneware jug on which scrolling foliage and flowers, birds and animals are formed out of little dots of clay.

Perrin, Veuve   In French ceramics; the most productive faïence factory at Marseilles was that operated by the Veuve (widow) Perrin (Pierrette Caudelot, d. 1793) for forty-five years after the death of her husband Claude Perrin (1696-1748) who had started it around 1740. About 1753 she took as a business associate Honoré Savy who, ten or more years later, started his own business, but achieved no notable commercial success. It is reported that the first experiments with overglaze enameled decoration on faïence at Marseilles were probably made shortly after 1750 at the Veuve Perrin. After 1793 the factory was carried on for at least two more years by the Perrins' son, Joseph. See *Marseilles.* (286, 287)

Persia   See *Near East,* in prehistoric ceramics; *Islamic Pottery.*

Perugia   See *Alla Castellana Ware.*

Pesaro   In Italian ceramics; potteries were in existence at Pesaro, near Urbino, from late in the 15th century. It was formerly believed that a luster ware similar to that made at Deruta was also made here during the Renaissance; unfortunately there is no evidence to substantiate this claim. This reputed luster ware was Pesaro's chief claim to fame; however, other varieties of majolica of some interest were made here during the 16th century. The manufacture of majolica declined during the 17th century; toward the latter part of the 18th century it was somewhat revived. See *Italian Majolica.*

Petit Feu   In ceramics; the French term for the low temperature required to fire or melt painted decoration executed in vitreous enamel colors into the glaze of porcelain or faïence which has already been fired. In order to have this low melting point a large amount of lead or other flux is added to the glassy colors themselves to increase their fusibility. These enamel colors are fired at a comparatively low tem-

VEUVE PERRIN
1753 ON

perature of 700° C to 900° C in a muffle kiln. They are often referred to as muffle colors. A much wider range of colors can be obtained in enamel colors than in the so-called high temperature colors or those colors which can stand the heat of the grand feu. See *Enamel*, in ceramics; *Grand Feu; Colors; Overglaze.*

Petite Rue Saint-Gilles In French ceramics; a hard paste porcelain manufactory was started in 1785 in Paris by François-Maurice Honoré. It was sometimes called the Boulevard Saint-Antoine manufactory. Around 1810 Honoré gave up the factory and acquired another at La Seynie. Early in the 19th century Honoré was associated with Dagoty who had started a manufactory in the Boulevard Poissonnière which remained active until 1867. The productions were principally tablewares decorated in accordance with the contemporary styles fashionable at Sèvres. The manufactories of Honoré and Dagoty chiefly flourished during the French Empire and in the subsequent years. The marked wares all date from the 19th century and generally included in the marks were the names of the proprietors. See *Paris Porcelain.*

Petri-Raben, Trude American potter born in Germany; in 1929 designed for Royal Berlin an entire service which is the prototype of modern white dinnerware. The service includes a "perfect" teacup; the delicacy of the bowl is complemented by the handle, the shape of which is easy to grasp and is primarily determined by the bowl. (500)

Petuntse In ceramics; the fusible feldspathic ingredient of hard paste porcelain. In China the stone was pulverized at the quarry and sent to the potter in the form of little bricks. In Chinese the term *petuntse* means little bricks.

Pew Group In English ceramics; the name applied to the charming stylized Staffordshire figures made of salt-glazed stoneware. They are represented as ladies and gentlemen, usually in country attire, seated on a high back settle and occasionally playing musical instruments. These pew groups date from about 1735-1745. (417)

Pewabic Pottery In American ceramics; an art pottery was started around 1900 at Detroit, Michigan, by Mary Chase Perry (1867-1961), who married William Stratton in 1918, in partnership with Horace J. Caulkins (who was making his fortune in the dental supply, china kiln and high heat furnace business) to whom it was an avocation. In 1903 Mary Chase Perry discovered her famous iridescent glaze which brought her international recognition. She named it Pewabic, which in Chippewa means clay in copper color, as a tribute to the Upper Peninsula copper mining region in Michigan where she was born in the copper-mining town of Hancock. The partnership of Mary Chase Perry and Horace Caulkins brought international fame to Pewabic. She was the artist who developed forms and rare glazes; he was the clay specialist who perfected an oil-burning kiln which soon received world recognition. She produced a ware of rather similar pattern to that of the Grueby Faïence Company. The relief leaf-shapes were strongly reminiscent of Grueby's, but the glazes were more flowing and less limited in variety. In 1923 Mary Chase Perry Stratton experienced her greatest triumph when she was selected to create the ceramic decoration for the Crypt at the Shrine of the Immaculate Conception in Washington, D.C. She was known as Detroit's most celebrated craftsman and her great work in tile and mosaics brought her many distinguished commissions for renowned buildings throughout the country. She was one of the founders of the Detroit Society of Arts and Crafts. Recently the University of Michigan has revived Pewabic Pottery on the site of its greatest flowering.

PEWABIC POTTERY
C. 1900

Pewter See *Metal Mounts on Ceramics.*

Pfalz-Zweibrücken In German ceramics; a porcelain manufactory was established here in 1767 under the protection of Duke Christian IV of Pfalz-Zweibrücken. In 1775 the Duke withdrew his patronage and the manufactory was leased privately. Nothing is known of the productions after 1775; however, it is believed that porcelain and also cream-colored earthenware in the English style were made. The factory mark was PZ in a monogram. Tablewares were the principal production. Especially typical was a decoration of small bouquets of flowers in colors. An inferior quality of hard paste porcelain was used for dishes for daily use which were chiefly blue and white.

Pfau See *Winterthur.*

Pfeiffer, Max Adolf The manager of the Schwarzburger Werkstätten for the manufacture of art porcelain, 1908-1913. At the end of the First World War, 1918, Pfeiffer became manager of the Meissen factory where from the following year the first significant Meissen figures of modern times were produced. A number of artists were involved, in particular Paul Scheurich and Max Esser.

Pharmacy Vase In ceramics; a variety of drug jar either without a spout for dry drugs or with a spout for liquid medicines. Some of the finest Hispano-Moresque wares and also Italian Renaissance majolica were made in the form of pharmacy jars. It was a custom in Italy during the Renaissance to display elaborate services of drug vases in the pharmacies which were at that time a favorite local rendezvous. See *Albarello.* (227, 229, 236)

Phiale In Greek antiquities; a shallow bowl without handles used to pour a libation. Frequently it was provided with a central boss that extended up into the center of the bowl. The boss was practical for holding the phiale from underneath while pouring.

Phillips, John (and Company) See *North Hylton Pottery; Sunderland Pottery.*

Phillips and Maling See *North Hylton Pottery.*

Picasso, Pablo (b. 1881) Painter, sculptor and ceramist, born at Malaga; his career as a ceramist began in 1947 when he worked in the Madoura pottery of Georges and Suzanne Ramié at Vallauris, a ceramic center near Golfe Juan on the French Riviera. His ceramic work is to be regarded as an integral part of his general artistic production. On his plates are found almost all the motifs Picasso treated in his paintings and drawings, primarily bullfight scenes and mythological figures, executed in a broad brush stroke technique which is particularly suitable for ceramic ware. For all their crudeness, these paintings completed in a few moments without corrections are extremely expressive. Picasso turned and molded his clay ware before matching the paintings to the molded forms, and it is his ability to create such combinations that primarily accounts for his unique success in the field of ceramics. Picasso realized the unity of painting and pottery; this higher conceptional art is destroyed when there is a division between the potter and the painter. Especially characteristic of Picasso is his tendency to give the shape of the vessel a representational meaning through the painting. Thus a vase may be transformed into a female figure, an owl or the like. Except when Picasso deliberately intends to make a figure, his objects always retain the character of vessels, even though their functional character is occasionally strongly overshadowed by other elements. (550)

Pie Crust In English ceramics; unglazed cane ware made in imitation of pie crust in the early 19th century to substitute for pie crust in times of a flour shortage. An example is the well known "Game Pie Dish."

PFALZ-ZWEIBRUCKEN
1767-1775

Pien Hu In Chinese ceramics, the term given to a pilgrim flask.

Pietersz, Harman (d. 1616) Dutch faïence-potter who moved from Haarlem to Delft in 1584. The earliest local record of a faïence at Delft refers to him.

Pigalle, Jean Baptiste (1714–1785) French sculptor; one of the most popular sculptors of his time. His earlier work includes Child with Cage (model at Sèvres) and his famous Mercury Fastening his Sandals. See *Sèvres*.

Piggin In English ceramics; a small shallow pottery vessel with a long handle at one side used for ladling out the liquor brewed in the tyg. It was principally made during the 17th and 18th centuries. See *Tyg*.

Pijnacker, Jacobus and Adriaen See *Two Little Ships*.

Pilgrim Flask The name given to a flattened vessel which was generally almost circular in shape designed with two loops or rings on the shoulders to hold a cord. As a rule it had a short neck. The body generally rested on a short spreading foot or base. Variations in form occurred. Pottery pilgrim flasks were made in China at least as early as the T'ang dynasty, 618-906. In Europe especially noteworthy are the Italian majolica pilgrim flasks painted in the polychrome istoriato style, dating from the early 16th century. (237, 242, 303)

Pilkington's Tile and Pottery Company In English ceramics; a pottery established at Clifton Junction, near Manchester, in 1892. Pilkington pottery was made under the close supervision of William and Joseph Burton. Some of the glazes were formulated by them, others by Abraham Lomax. The throwing was done by Edward Radford. The Burtons were inspired by some of their successful tile glazes to produce in 1904 a range of pottery which showed a remarkable variety of glaze effects. Owing to a revived interest in luster painting, Pilkington's in 1906 began producing luster-painted earthenware by a number of artists such as Gordon M. Forsyth and Richard Joyce. The firm closed in 1938, but reopened their pottery department (as opposed to their main concern, the making of tiles) in 1948 and continued it until 1957. The trade mark included the initial P. Roman numerals occur under this mark to denote the year of potting. Some wares bear only the words Royal Lancastrian. The initials or monogram of the designer or artist occur on most items, such as LFD for Lewis F. Day and C enclosing a crane for Walter Crane. See *Glaze*, in modern Western ceramics.

Pillement, Jean (1728-1808) A noted French painter, decorative artist and engraver. He created a delightful type of chinoiserie which was very popular in England. See *Rococo; Engraved Designs*.

Pillivuyt A French family of 19th and 20th century potters and manufacturers. Pillivuyt & Cie was started at Foëcy around 1800; later, around 1880 at Paris and Mehun-sur-Yèvre. Still active.

Pillow In Chinese ceramics; the pottery pillow or chên of oblong rectangular form, generally being slightly concave on the top, is of early origin and is among the articles found in ancient tombs. It appears from extant examples dating from the T'ang dynasty that tomb pillows as well as those used in daily Chinese life are rarely more than one foot in length. A passage in the T'ao Shou reveals that the Chinese regarded the use of porcelain pillows as "most efficacious in keeping the eyes clear and preserving the sight, so that even in old age fine writing can be read." It seems reasonable to assume that the existence of this curious belief among the Chinese accounted for much of the usage of porcelain pillows. Pillows were also made of other materials, and were occasionally in-

PILKINGTON'S

1904 ON

RICHARD JOYCE
1906 ON

PILLIVUYT

C. H. PILLIVUYT
& Cie Paris.
PARIS. FOËCY. MEHUN.

1880 ON

MEHUN
C.P.
& Cie
FRANCE

1891 ON

TZ'U CHOU PILLOW, SUNG

serted with porcelain plaques, but the majority by far were made of porcelain.

P'in Kuo Ch'ing Apple green. See *Peach-bloom.*

P'in Kuo Hung Apple red. See *Peach-bloom.*

Pinder, Bourne and Company A pottery in Nile Street, Burslem, in the Staffordshire district, active 1862-1882, producing earthenwares. Formerly Pinder, Bourne and Hope, around 1851-1862. The company was purchased by Doultons in 1878, but the title was retained until 1882 when it became Doulton and Company, Ltd.

Pineapple Ware See *Whieldon, T.*

Pineau, Nicolas (1684-1754) A prominent French decorative artist of the 18th century, who is generally regarded as one of the chief pioneers in the Rococo style of ornament. The work of interior decoration that he executed for many of the palaces and châteaux of France rewarded him with a great reputation. In 1716 he was commissioned by Peter the Great to work at St. Petersburg where he stayed until 1727. Among his notable achievements in Russia were his chinoiseries at the Peterhof Palace. See *Engraved Designs.*

P'ing In Chinese ceramics; the Chinese term for a vase.

Pingsdorf In German ceramics; the name given to a fine unglazed pottery made of pale clay and enriched with red strokes, circles, wavy lines and dots, made in the same workshops as the Badorf pottery from the 9th century. It was copied over a wide area and continued in use until the 13th century. See *Badorf.*

Pinte In German ceramics; a variety of small tankard or cylindrical-shaped mug generally having roll moldings at the mouth and at the foot. The form, which was taken from a wooden prototype, was a characteristic form for Rhenish stoneware during

the 16th and early 17th centuries. See *Schnelle.*

Pinxton In English ceramics; a small porcelain manufactory was started at Pinxton, Derbyshire, in 1796 by William Billingsley with the help of John Coke. Between 1796 and 1801 the manufactory made a translucent glassy soft paste porcelain having bone ash as one of its ingredients. The porcelain was often of fine quality; unfortunately it was sometimes misshapen. The forms were essentially simple and the wares were decorated in the current Derby styles. There was no recognized factory mark. In 1801 Billingsley left and in 1804 the business was taken over by John Cutts. An inferior and coarse porcelain that was almost opaque was then made until the manufactory closed in 1813.

Piranesi, Giovanni (1704-1784) A celebrated Venetian architect, draughtsman and etcher. He studied art at Rome and was greatly inspired by the classic works of art. He wrote many books; however, his outstanding contribution to the decorative arts was a book of engravings, entitled DIVERSE MANIERE, published in 1769. This book, which proved to be an endless source of supply and inspiration, was filled with fine classical ornament for mural decorations. It is now generally believed that Piranesi strongly influenced French and English designs in the Neo-Classic style as well as Italian. See *Classic Revival; Engraved Designs.*

Pirkenhammer (also **Birkenhammer**) In Bohemian ceramics; a porcelain manufactory, still in existence, was started here in 1802 by Friedrich Hölke and J. G. List. Included among the marks were H K in monogram (Hölke and Karlsbad); F & R (Fischer and Reichenbach) c. 1810-1845; C. F. (Christian Fischer) 1846-1857; F & M (Fischer and Mieg) 1857 and later; while the mark of the crossed hammer with or without the name of the place is a modern one dating from around 1876. Brezovà is

PIRKENHAMMER

H·K
1802-1810

F&R
1810-1845

C.F
1846-1857

F&M
1857 ON

Prag
PIRKEN HAMMER
Made in
CzechoSlovakia
1918 ON

PINDER, BOURNE AND
COMPANY
1862-1882

SEVRES PLAQUE, LOUIS XVI

PLEYDELL-BOUVERIE, K.
1925 ON

2↓

PLYMOUTH
1768-1770

the more recent Czechoslovakian name for this German porcelain-manufacturing town. See *Austria, Czechoslovakia and Hungary.*

Pithos In Greek antiquities; a big storage jar, for the storage of large quantities of wine, water or grain. Frequently it was so large that it was sunk into the ground except for the upper part and mouth. This feature made access to the contents much easier and also protected and strengthened the jar. The larger pithoi were built up by the coil method, rather than thrown on the potter's wheel. Some extremely large pithoi, large enough to hold a man, were constructed over a wooden core and were fired at the place where they were made.

Place, Francis (d. 1728) English portrait painter, engraver and architect. Reputed to have made experiments toward the manufacture of porcelain at the Manor House, York. A coffee cup of grey, black and brown marbled stoneware in the Victoria and Albert collection is attributed to him.

Plaque A decorative plate or tablet of metal, porcelain or some other material of rectangular, round or oval form, either plain or decorated, chiefly intended to be hung as a wall ornament or to be inserted in a fine article of cabinetwork. Sèvres plaques were occasionally inserted in some Louis XV and Louis XVI cabinetwork, such as tables and cabinets, and Wedgwood plaques were occasionally used in English cabinetwork designed in the Neo-Classic style. See *Jasper Ware; Ceramic Plaques as Furniture Decoration.*

Plaue-on-Havel In German ceramics; a manufactory was started at Plaue-on-Havel, Brandenburg, in 1713 by Samuel Kempe, a runaway workman from Meissen. They were especially well known for their good imitations of Böttger's red stoneware. In a few examples the forms

were exact replicas of Böttger's; most of them, however, were marked with a curious heaviness, lacking gracefulness.

Plemochoë or **Kothon** In Greek antiquities; a container for perfume, larger than the alabastron, in the form of a covered bowl mounted on a high or low spreading foot. The flat lid which fitted the small opening or mouth at the top of the flattened, shallow, circular-shaped body was provided with a finial.

Pleydell-Bouverie, Katherine English artist-potter; specializes in stoneware with wood ash glazes. Her pottery is more or less similar in character to the work of Bernard Leach and William S. Murray. Simplicity and purity of form predominate and, as if in the interest of form, the glazes are generally sober in color—grey, olive, russet, buff and brown. See *Braden, N.; Leach, B.*

Pløen, Erik Modern Norwegian artist-potter; the forms of his vessels in stoneware are characteristically strong and severe, frequently revealing interesting glaze effects over incising.

Plumbago See *Graphite.*

Plumbate See *Toltec.*

Plum Blossom See *Prunus.*

Plymouth In English ceramics; a manufactory producing the first hard paste porcelain in England was active in Plymouth, Devonshire, between 1768 and 1770, when it was transferred to Bristol. The manufacture of hard paste porcelain was due to William Cookworthy, a chemist of Plymouth who discovered the secret for making Chinese porcelain and then after many years of searching found the necessary materials in Cornwall. In 1768 he received a patent and established a manufactory at Coxside, Plymouth. Occasionally the porcelain was of good quality; however, it was often technically imperfect and inclined to be misshapen. The alchemist's sign for tin in underglaze blue, blue enamel, red or gold was the usual mark. The decoration revealed little originality. The painting in underglaze blue had a rather blackish tone. The enamel colors with the exception of a deep red and leaf green were usually impure in tone. See *Cookworthy, W.*

Polynesia See *Oceania.*

Pompeian Taste Decorative motifs generally derived from those classical objects found at Pompeii and Herculaneum, a vast repertory of which the Comte de Caylus had provided in his RECUEIL. In ceramics, for example, arabesques reflecting Pompeian taste appeared on French porcelain in the 1780's. Almost one hundred years later, during the Second French Empire in the 1860's, Pompeian, known as the Neo-Pompeian style, had its hour of glory. See *St. Petersburg; Caylus, Comte de.*

Pont-aux-Choux In French ceramics; a manufactory producing white earthenware was started in Paris around 1740. Its reputation is due to the cream-colored earthenware of fine quality and color which they began to produce around 1765. In 1772 it was advertised as a Manufacture Royale. The decoration, which was molded in relief, chiefly consisted of flowers, foliage and other similar motifs and was in imitation of silversmith's work. The fleur-de-lis in gold occurred as a mark; however, the wares were not regularly marked. In 1777 the fleur-de-lis was registered as a porcelain mark by the proprietor of Pont-aux-Choux. However, porcelain bearing this mark is rarely found. See *Paris Porcelain; Faïence Fine.* (405)

Ponti, Gio See *Doccia.*

Poor, Henry Varnum (b. 1888) American painter and muralist; later tried his hand at pottery. He was one of the exponents of figure decoration on pottery.

Popov In Russian ceramics; the A. G. Popov porcelain manufactory was started by the German Karl Melli, in 1806 at the village of Gorbunovo, about thirty miles from the Francis Gardner manufactory. The undertaking was unsuccessful, and in 1811 he sold it to the merchant Aleksei Gavrilovich Popov (d. 1850's). After changing ownership several times it closed in 1875. Its finest period was from 1811 to the 1850's, when it ranked among the best of the porcelain manufactories in Russia at that time. Its wares were not quite equal to those of the Imperial Porcelain manufactory; they were equal to the Francis Gardner wares, which at times they surpassed, especially the porcelain figures. Apart from their costly wares they also made less expensive porcelain as was customary in other Russian manufactories, usually known as tavern china. The porcelain figures were the most celebrated part of the Popov production. Figures of a jocose character were especially charming. The mark A was most commonly used. See *Russia; Gardner, Francis.*

Popp In German ceramics; several members of the Popp family are linked in the history of an important faïence factory started at Ansbach around 1708–1710. Johann Georg Christoph Popp (d. 1791) was a painter at the factory from around 1715 and became proprietor in 1769. The mark A P for Ansbach-Popp occurs as a factory mark after 1769. See *Ansbach,* in German faïence.

Poppelsdorf In German ceramics; a still existing faïence factory was started at Poppelsdorf, near Bonn in the Rhineland, in 1755 at the instance of Clement Augustus of Cologne who wished to establish a porcelain factory. At first it was in the charge of merchants and officials; in 1798 it was taken over by Engelbert Cremer and in 1825 Ludwig Wessel became the proprietor. His firm are the present owners. Essentially the wares possess little artistic importance; later cream-colored earthenware was chiefly made. No factory mark

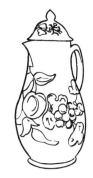

PLYMOUTH CHOCOLATE POT

PONT-AUX-CHOUX
1777 ON

POPOV
1811-C. 1850

POPPELSDORF
MEHLEM, F. A.
C. 1836 ON

was used. A factory was also conducted here from 1836 by F. A. Mehlem of Bonn, later using the mark FAM Bonn 1755. In 1886-1887 they acquired the Höchst molds and materials from the Damm factory. Much of their wares were exported to the United States. See *Damm.*

Porcelain (Fr. porcelaine; Ger. porzellan; It. porcellana; Du. porselein or porcelein; Sp. porcelana; Sw. porslin; Da. porcellaen; Pg. porcelana) The name given originally to the Chinese ware brought to Europe by the Portuguese traders. It is usually agreed to be derived from the Italian porcellana, itself a derivative of porcella, for cowrie-shell (lit. a little pig) which in its whiteness and smooth compact texture porcelain appeared to resemble. True porcelain was made in China as early as the T'ang dynasty, 618-906. The Chinese used the term *porcelain* in a broad sense. In addition to the fine hard white, more or less translucent, vitrified material which is required in the European definition, the Chinese included fine hard dusky and grey materials which had been fired to such a vitrifiable state that they emitted a musical note when struck. The musical note was the principal test of early porcelain in China. In European ceramics; European porcelain falls into two main classes, the true porcelain also called hard paste porcelain or pâte dure and the artificial porcelain known as soft paste porcelain or pâte tendre. True porcelain is made of kaolin or china clay and of petuntse or china stone. Kaolin is a nonfusible silicate of aluminum, and petuntse is a fusible silicate of aluminum, and when these two related materials are fired at a temperature of 1300° C-1400° C they produce a white more or less translucent vitrified material. This material may be glazed with a compound of petuntse with lime or some similar fluxing material. True porcelain or feldspathic porcelain is so hard that ordinary steel will not cut it. The secret for making true porcelain in Europe was discovered by Johann Fried-

rich Böttger of Meissen in 1708, and in the following year he made a suitable glaze for it. The ware was first placed on the market at Leipzig in 1713. Although the secret became known elsewhere due to a few runaway workmen from Meissen, it was not until after the middle of the 18th century that any considerable number of hard paste porcelain manufactories were established. Unglazed porcelain is called biscuit or bisque. The terms *porcelain* and *china* are synonymous. The artificial or soft paste porcelain was made with glassy substances before Böttger discovered true porcelain. See *Soft Paste Porcelain; Parian Ware; Bone China; Enamel,* in ceramics; *Glaze.*

Porcelain Bottle, The or **De Porceleyne Fles** In Dutch ceramics; a pottery producing faïence at Delft, owned in partnership in 1655 by Wouter van Eenhoorn, the father of two famous potters Lambertus and Samuel, and Quirinus Aldersz van Cleynoven. The latter became sole proprietor in 1663 until his death in 1697. From that time onward there was a succession of proprietors until 1904 when a company was formed which has carried on the business to the present time. It is the only early Delft pottery to enjoy a continuous existence. The wares made here try to maintain the high artistic tradition common to the Delft faïence of the 17th and 18th century. During the ownership of Captain Henricus Arnoldus Piccardt who purchased The Porcelain Bottle in 1804, the manufactory made the so-called faïence patriotique. This ware is generally marked Piccardt Delft. Piccardt engaged English potters and with their help produced ware in imitation of English faïence which was at that time widely popular on the Continent. After his death the pottery was operated by his daughters until 1876 when it was purchased by Joost Thooft who revived the early Delft style. The first to introduce a bottle as his factory mark was Jacobus Har-

THE PORCELAIN BOTTLE
19TH CENTURY

THE PORCELAIN CLAW
17TH-18TH CENTURIES

lees who bought the pottery in 1771. In the later 1950's an experimental pottery group carried out some exciting work here as an integral part of the factory. See *Faïence Parlante; Delft; Faïence.*

Porcelain Claw, The or **De Porceleyne Klaeuw** In Dutch ceramics; started at Delft in 1662 for the production of faïence. The familiar claw mark was eventually registered in 1764. Changed ownership several times. In 1840 the proprietors J. van Putten and Company united it with the Three Bells Pottery. See *Delft.*

Porcelain Plaques as Furniture Decoration See *Ceramic Plaques as Furniture Decoration.*

Porcelaine de la Reine See *Rue Thiroux.*

Porcelaneous Of the nature or resembling true or feldspathic porcelain. See *Porcelain.*

Porsgrund In Norwegian ceramics; a still-existing porcelain factory was started here in 1887 producing industrial wares, principally table services of fine quality. Noteworthy are the modern designs for table wares of Tias Eckhoff, senior designer at Porsgrund from 1952 to 1957, in which a sculptured elegance is effectively combined with the principle of functionalism.

Portanier, Gilbert French artist-potter; working at Vallauris, near Golfe Juan, French Riviera. The influence, even though superficial, of Picasso is seen in his pottery vases dating from around the mid-1950's.

Portland Vase The most famous of Josiah Wedgwood's reproductions is his jasper ware copy of the Portland vase with white figures in relief. The original, an example of Greco-Roman work in glass, is the sepulchral urn which contained the ashes of the Roman Emperor Alexander Severus and his mother Mammaea which was buried about 234 A.D. and was dug up by order of the Barberini Pope, Urban VIII,

between 1623-1644. It was bought by Sir William Hamilton in 1782, sold to the Duchess of Portland in 1785 and after her death in 1786 was lent to Josiah Wedgwood so that he might reproduce it. After four years of experiment to get the correct color, surface and texture, the copy was completed. The vase is also known as the Barberini vase. It is believed that about fifty reproductions were made before Wedgwood's death and that not over sixteen pieces exist at the present time. (425)

Portobello In English ceramics; a variety of Staffordshire earthenware made around 1739 decorated with applied reliefs of ships and the figure of Admiral Edward Vernon, with inscriptions commemorating the capture of Portobello, Panama, by him in 1739. This so-called Portobello ware is very characteristic of the wares made by Thomas Astbury. See *Astbury, Thomas.*

Portobello In Scottish ceramics; a pottery was operated by the Scott Brothers at Portobello, near Edinburgh, from 1786 to 1796, producing cream-colored earthenware and other popular Staffordshire types. The mark Scott Brothers was also used at the Southwick Pottery at Sunderland. The Portobello Works were subsequently carried on by several potters including Thomas Rathbone and Company, about 1810-1845. See *Southwick Pottery.*

Portrait Vase In ceramics; the name given to a kind of vase in the form of a man's head. See *Mochica.*

Portugal The majolica made in Portugal during the Renaissance cannot be readily distinguished from that of Italy, Spain and the Netherlands. In all periods tile work, in particular, has been plentiful and of remarkable quality. In the 17th century the Portuguese trade with China was reflected in a distinctive class of Portuguese majolica in which designs were adapted

PORSGRUND
1891 ON

PORTOBELLO
SCOTT BROTHERS
C. 1786-1796

from late Ming wares. It was composed of dishes, vases with two handles, drug pots, helmet-shaped ewers and bowls, as well as many tiles painted in strong blue generally with manganese-purple outlines. In the 17th century both polychrome and blue and white tiles were produced in great quantity, frequently simulating and being used in place of wall tapestries. In the 18th century faïence, tablewares and figures were produced at a number of centers as well as at Lisbon, where many noteworthy faïence tiles were also produced. Porcelain was also made at Lisbon in the 18th century. At Caldos de Rainha, Palissy wares were skillfully and realistically made for quite a few years at an earthenware factory founded by Manuel Mafra in 1853 and continued by his son Eduardo in 1887. (252)

Posset-Pot In English ceramics; a small cylindrical pottery drinking vessel made during the 17th and 18th centuries. The posset-pot was fitted with a cover and two handles and with a small spout projecting from the side of the cup through which the posset was sucked. Posset was an old English drink and is especially associated with Christmas Eve. It is usually a mixture of warm ale or wine with hot curdled milk, sugar, spices and bits of bread or oatcake. During the 17th and 18th centuries there was a penchant for curious drinking vessels in pottery. See *Tyg.*

Post-Classic Period See *Pre-Columbian Pottery.*

Pot Lids In English ceramics; small pottery boxes, generally round, with transfer-printed covers, were made in great quantities in the second half of the 19th century and were used for packaging cosmetics and foods such as fish pastes and honey. The art of transfer printing on pottery with colored pictures was perfected by Jesse Austin in 1846, working at the Messrs. Pratt's Pottery, Fenton, Staffordshire. Pictures were printed on various types of ta-

bleware but chiefly on pot lids. They included portraits of famous people, historical scenes and buildings, rural scenes and the like, in great variety. See *Historical Blue; Transfer-Printed Wares.*

Potiche In ceramics; the name given to a vase generally having a polygonal or rounded body of almost cylindrical form with slightly pronounced shoulders. The neck is slightly smaller in width than the body. It is fitted with a cover of conforming design with a finial. This form of vase was widely used in Chinese ceramics. (99, 121)

Potpourri The French term *potpourri,* which literally means rotten pot, is applied to a mixture of dried petals of different flowers mixed with spices and kept in a jar or container for its perfume qualities. It was mentioned in England as early as 1749. In ceramics; the name is given to a container designed with a delicate perforated cover used to hold a mixture of potpourri. It was made in a variety of forms, such as bowls, jars and vases. Many were made by European potters in porcelain, faïence and pottery. (326)

Potschappel In German ceramics; a porcelain factory was started at Potschappel, which is about twenty-five miles from Meissen, by Carl von Thieme in 1872. They made quality wares, often in the Meissen manner. The marks of varying designs often included T; CT; Dresden, and Potschappel.

Potsdam In German ceramics; a faïence manufactory was started at Potsdam, near Berlin, around 1739 by Christian Friedrich Rewend and remained in the Rewend family until 1775. There were several changes in ownership and it was still active in 1800. It has been established that the mark P over R was occasionally used until 1775. The manufactory did not develop any distinctive style. The wares essentially resembled the wares made at Delft. The

POTICHE, K'ANG HSI

POTSCHAPPEL
1872 ON

Dresden

painted decoration in underglaze blue and in polychrome in the Delft style was carefully executed.

Potsdam Rococo   See *Rococo.*

Potsherd   In ceramics; a fragment of pottery or earthenware; a broken piece of pottery.

Potter, Christopher   See *Rue de Crussol.*

Potter   See *Pottery.*

Potter's Mark   A character or other device representing the name of the potter as found on some Chinese porcelains and much of the pottery of Japan, as that of the celebrated Japanese potter, Ninsei. See *Mark,* in ceramics.

Potter's Wheel   The invention of the potter's wheel occurred late in the fourth millennium B.C. and its use spread slowly from the Near East to Europe and America. One of the earliest areas was in Sumer, a region in Mesopotamia, about 3250 B.C. In Egypt it was used as early as around 2750 B.C. and at Troy around 2500 B.C. Wheel-made pottery dates from Crete around 2000 B.C.; mainland Greece 1800 B.C.; south Italy 750 B.C.; upper Rhine basins 400 B.C.; south England 50 B.C.; Scotland 400 A.D.; the Americas 1550 A.D. The Greek wheel, which was around two feet in diameter, was made of wood, terra-cotta or stone. The underside of the disc was provided with a socket which fitted over a low fixed pivot. The entire wheel ran without vibration, as it was perfectly balanced. The usual practice was to have a boy turn the wheel by hand, regulating the speed at the command of the potter. Some wheels were notched around the edge, which allowed a firmer grip. Once it was started in motion the large size and weight afforded ample momentum. Having a boy to turn the wheel permitted the potter to use both hands in forming the vase and to concentrate his efforts on it. Apparently the kick-wheel or foot-operated wheel was

introduced later and was not in use in the classical period. Prior to the introduction of the potter's wheel it is presumed that each family made its own pots, and since most household tasks were done by the women, it seems reasonable that they also made the pots. With the introduction of the potter's wheel and the improved kiln this work undoubtedly was taken over by the men. The tools of the potter are primarily his skillful fingers and a few simple implements.

POTPOURRI, NIDERVILLER

Pottery   In ceramics; the term was formerly used to describe all kinds of ceramic wares, that is porcelain, stoneware and earthenware. At the present time the term *pottery* is regrettably applied only to earthenware and is not applied to translucent porcelain or to vitrified stoneware. The body of pottery is not vitrified. Slipware, majolica, faïence and delftware are all varieties of earthenware. Essentially the word pottery (Fr. poterie) in its broadest sense includes all objects fashioned from clay and then hardened by fire. The very existence of pottery depends upon two important natural properties of that great and widespread group of substances known as clay, that is the property of plasticity and the property of being converted when fired into one of the most indestructible of ordinary things. Pottery denotes the place where all kinds of ceramic wares are made; the man who makes them being a potter.

Pouchol, Paul   French painter and ceramist; working in the 20th century. Exhibited at the Salon des Indépendents, 1935. Produced tin-glazed earthenware figures and other items for purely decorative purposes in the years following the Second World War.

Poulsen, Christian   Modern Danish artist-potter; using stoneware as a medium. His simply modeled vessels are covered with very thick glaze in carefully calculated colors.

POTSDAM
1740 ON

Poussah See *Magot.*

Pouyat French family of pottery-proprietors. Pierre Pouyat started a faïence factory at Saint-Yrieix, near Limoges, around 1760, and after the discovery of kaolin became the owner of large quarries around 1780. His son François (1752-1830) was the associate and later successor of Laurentius Russinger (formerly of Höchst and other German factories) at La Courtille or Rue Fontaine-au-Roy in Paris. Pouyat and his family owned La Courtille from around 1800 until they closed it around 1840. François' son, Jean Pouyat, in association with Russinger, started a prosperous porcelain factory mainly for export ware at Limoges, in 1842, which is still active today. The mark was J.P. over L.

Powder Blue Ware In Chinese ceramics; porcelain of the Ch'ing period, especially of the K'ang Hsi reign, which is characterized by a beautiful and rather even ground of bright soft blue with a slightly clouded appearance. As a rule the ground is covered with very close and minute blurry particles; occasionally the ground is not so closely speckled. Since it is not possible to lay an even ground of underglaze blue by means of a brush, it was necessary to devise some other method. It is generally believed that the ground on powder blue ware was applied by blowing on the blue and then carefully applying the glaze after the blue was entirely dried. Sometimes gold or silver decoration was applied over the glaze. When decorative designs were to be painted on the ware a piece of paper was cut in the proper shape and was temporarily laid on the portion to be reserved in white, while the blue was blown or sprayed on. Later the designs in the white portions were painted in underglaze blue, and, after the article was glazed and fired, with overglaze enamels.

Powolny, Michael See *Wiener Keramik.*

Pozzi, Ambrosio See *Rosenthal.*

J.P.
L.
FRANCE.

POUYAT, J.
1891 ON

K&C
PRAG

PRAGUE
1836-1862

Prague In Bohemian ceramics; a factory making lead-glazed earthenware in the English style and porcelain was started here by Carl Kunerle and Joseph Emanuel Hübel with a privilege dating from 1795. Among the marks were P, Prag, Prager and K & C (for Kriegel & Co.); the latter was used from 1836 to 1862. See *Austria, Czechoslovakia and Hungary.* Workshops under the name of Artel were organized here in 1908. Ceramics was one of their products. See *Secession; Artel.*

Pratt, Felix In English ceramics; it is reputed that Felix Pratt and his successors, who were Staffordshire potters of Fenton, made a variety of pottery from around 1780 to 1820 with relief decoration of figures, fruits, leaves and other motifs painted over with orange, green and blue underglaze or high temperature colors. There is no doubt that this variety, which was rarely marked, was made by other contemporary English Staffordshire potters. Around the middle of the 19th century the manufactory was making wares with a stipple-printed decoration in several different colors. They were marked F. & R. Pratt. The familiar pot lids are in this style. See *Pot Lids; Transfer-Printed Wares.*

Pratt Ware In English ceramics; a modern term frequently used to describe late 18th and early 19th century creamwares and pearlwares painted with designs in high temperature (underglaze) colors including blue, brown, ochre and dull green; those colors often applied with a sponge. The name was chosen after Felix Pratt; however, the so-called Pratt coloring is found on wares of a great many potteries, especially those of Leeds and Bristol. See *Pratt, Felix; Sponged Ware.* (461)

Pre-Columbian Pottery In American ceramics; the commonest technique for making medieval pottery vessels in the New World was the primitive one of building up from coils or rings of clay smoothed with the hand or a small implement such as a bit of gourd. Hand modeling was frequently employed and casting from molds was widespread and was in use by the early part of the first millennium B.C. Porcelain is unknown, glaze is rarely used as an ornament and never as a waterproofing agent. Of fundamental importance is the complete absence of the potter's wheel, because unhampered by a mechanical device, the vessels fashioned by hand working were of much wider range and variety. The use of the oxidizing flame for firing red, brown and orange wares and of the reducing flame for firing black and grey ones was mastered at an early time. Slips and paints of many colors were used in finishing the pots, and freehand designs were painted on them. In many instances the surfaces were highly burnished with a pebble or some similar object. Tempering materials varied from place to place. The first known appearances of pottery in America are in the second millennium. The highest of the New World civilizations are found in Mexico and the countries on its southern border and in Peru. Notable examples of pottery come from other regions, especially the Southwest of the United States, Panama, Nicaragua and Costa Rica. In certain regions of the Southwest, household vessels were first made of baskets, most of which were made by the coiling method. Sometimes they were daubed with clay to make them water tight. In time clay alone was used for bowls and pots. Features of the basket persisted for centuries; not only were the shapes retained but even the texture was copied in the design. The pottery made in medieval America, up to the coming of the Europeans in the early 16th century, ranges from the basket imitations to the inimitable fresco vase. It has been useful to set up a simplified framework of periods, namely, Formative, Classic and Post-Classic, for the principal centers of cultural development. Though the terms differ in significance as applied to certain areas, in a general sense the Formative Period marks the introduction of pottery starting at different points in the second millennium B.C. The subsequent Classic Period covers the greater part of the first millennium A.D. and is widely considered as the climax in the development of the arts. The Post-Classic Period extends to the Spanish conquest in 1521. At this period, with a few exceptions, the aesthetic development diminished, and the production increased. See *Southwestern United States Pottery; Central American Pottery; South American Pottery; Oceania; Africa.* (1-21)

Prehistoric Periods
Old Stone Age (Paleolithic) 30,000-10,000 B.C.
Middle Stone Age (Mesolithic) 10,000-3,000 B.C.
New Stone Age (Neolithic) 6,000-50 B.C.
Bronze Age, Early c.3000-c.2,000 B.C.
    Middle c.2,000-c.1500 B.C.
    Late c.1500-c.1100 B.C.
Iron Age, began c.1100 B.C.
These dates mark a period of civilization through which it is believed most races have passed at one time or another. It must have been earlier in some countries, and is certainly known to have been later in others. For this reason the dates have no absolute chronological value.

Prehistoric Pottery See *Near East; Europe; Shang; Jomon; Pre-Columbian Pottery; Oceania; Beaker Folk; Mycenaean; Minoan; Cyprus.*

Preissler, Daniel (1636-1733) and his son Ignaz (b. 1676). Silesian and Bohemian Hausmalerei active from around 1720 to 1739. They decorated Chinese, Meissen and Vienna porcelain in Schwarzlot (black enamel) red and purple monochromes and gold. Dated examples are extremely rare and no signed examples are known. See *Schäper, Johann; Schwarzlot.* (333, 334)

Preuning, Paul See *Hafner.*

Pricking See *Sponse.*

Priestman, James American sculptor; in the early 1880's modeled a series of plaques

PRIESTMAN, JAMES

with relief designs of heads of cattle and other specialties which were highly esteemed. They were executed in parian by Bennett of Baltimore and also at the Chesapeake Pottery. The parian plaques of the former bore copyright and patent marks in 1884 and 1885.

Primaticcio, Francesco (1504-1570) Bolognese school; painter, sculptor and engraver. See *Engraved Designs*.

Primitive Pottery A class of vessels made by the primitive races of mankind, whether before the beginning of civilization or at the present time. Certain modern races still produce pottery by the same crude method as the Neolithic races of Europe and Asia, and with remarkable similarity of result. The materials and methods of primitive pottery are always of the simplest. (Clay had been used to model figures for religious or magical purposes long before it was used to make vessels.) See *Pre-Columbian Pottery; Oceania; Africa*.

Printed Wares See *Transfer-Printed Wares*.

Procopé, Ulla See *Arabia*.

Proskau In German ceramics; a faïence manufactory of considerable importance was established at Proskau, Silesia, in 1763 by Count Leopold von Proskau (d. 1769). It changed hands several times and was active until 1850. The manufacture of lead-glazed earthenware was started in 1788 and in 1793 the manufacture of faïence was abandoned. The best period was from 1763 to 1769. The mark was generally a P. The productions were essentially a liberal imitation of the faïence made at Strasbourg and were painted in enamel colors. The wares were marked by a pronounced penchant for freely modeled and applied leaves, fruit, flowers and bouquets of flowers. Vases filled with flowers and the lids of tureens heaped with fruit were typical. From 1770 to 1783 the mark was DP; the

PROSKAU

1763-1769

1770-1783

PRUNUS MOTIF

D standing for Count Dietrichstein. Essentially the productions of this period were a continuation of the earlier work. Tureens in the form of fruit or vegetables and modeled figures generally in the classical style were made. Chiefly useful wares were made from 1783 and were marked with Proskau, impressed. The lead-glazed earthenware or steingut principally followed English models. The faïence made between 1783 and 1793 was again marked with a P and was in the Neo-Classic style.

Prunus or **Plum Blossom** One of the flowers of the Chinese Four Seasons, representing Winter. No doubt the most popular tree in Chinese and Japanese flower painting on ceramics was the early flowering plum (prunus mume) opening its blossoms about the time of the Chinese New Year, which dates from the earliest spring. Of great beauty is the K'ang Hsi ginger jar whose entire surface is covered with delicate plum blossoms reserved in white on a pure sapphire blue ground broken by a network of lines resembling cracked ice, symbolizing the approach of spring. The swift and sensitive brushwork of the Japanese has eloquently captured the peculiar linear rhythm of the flowering plum in countless beautiful designs, as in the enameled porcelain of Kakiemon. The plum blossom became a favorite decoration at Meissen, Chantilly, Saint-Cloud, Chelsea, Worcester, Bow and other European factories. See *Ginger Jar; Shochikubai; Chinese Four Seasons Flowers*. (110, 347)

Psykter In Greek antiquities; a wine cooler in the form of a bulbous vase with a deep hollow stem. It was almost entirely filled with wine and often floated in a large krater of cold water, as the Athenians preferred to drink their wine slightly chilled. Occasionally psykters were provided with small loop handles set high on the shoulder through which a cord was passed and served as a handle. It seems that only the psykters with handles were given covers.

Pu-Tai Ho-Shang In Chinese art; a Chinese Buddhist subject. He is the god of children and earthly happiness. He is generally represented with a smiling cheerful face and a fat and unclothed belly, and he is usually in a reclining position resting against bags of money. The subject was widely used in Chinese ceramics. In Japan he is called Hotei. See *Chinese Gods; Hotei.* (362)

Pucci, Emilio See *Rosenthal.*

Puebla In pre-Columbian Central American ceramics; a region and at the present time a state in central Mexico. Its capital, Puebla, lies 65 miles southeast of Mexico City. See *Central American Pottery; Olmec.*

Pueblo Periods

Developmental Pueblo	700-1050 A.D.
Great Pueblo	1050-1300 A.D.
Regressive Pueblo	1300-1700 A.D.
Historical Pueblo	1700 on

See *Anasazi.*

Puente del Arzobispo See *Talavera de la Reina.*

Pug Mill A cylinder, either vertical or horizontal, equipped with knives, similar to a food chopper on a large scale which cuts up the clay and forces it out in a cylindrical shape ready for potting.

Punch Bowl In English ceramics; porcelain and earthenware punch bowls largely inspired by Chinese export porcelain were much favored. Of particular interest were the punch bowls made at Bristol from around 1750 painted with ships, which appear to have been made in some examples for foreign sea-going captains. See *Ship Bowl.*

Punch'ŏng In Korean ceramics; in recent years this term has been applied to a large class of wares made in the early part of the Yi period. This name is the Korean rendering of the Chinese fên ch'ing, signifying pale blue or green, and is correct in so far as the glaze is of celadon type and has a tendency to assume a greenish or bluish tone when vessels are fired in a reducing atmosphere. However, the essential characteristics of punch'ŏng are that it is a stoneware, made of the same greyish clay as Koryo celadon though somewhat more coarse in texture, and that the surface is covered entirely or partly with a coating of brushed white slip before the glaze is applied. For centuries in Japan punch'ŏng ware has been widely admired and carefully studied. It is known as *mishima,* a term that is believed was derived from the almanacs issued by the Mishima Shrine in Izu Province, during the latter part of the 16th century, which were noted for their columns of finely printed characters. A common type of the ware is decorated with a stamped ground of white mesh or hatching known in Korea as "rope curtain pattern" which is thought to bear a resemblance to the almanacs; the name *koyomi-de* or *almanac ware* is also in popular use in Japan for this kind of punch'ŏng. The other common type of mishima is decorated with over-all patterns of white flower-heads resembling daisies and is known as hana mishima or flower mishima. The minute designs for these two standard types of mishima were generally stamped into the body, after which white slip was brushed over the entire surface. The excess slip was then wiped off, leaving the pattern filled with the residue. In brief, it was a quick and mechanical technique of producing inlaid decoration, and the result was not comparable with the earlier inlay. Frequently the effect was impaired by traces of the excess slip which could not be completely removed and gave a greyish white tinge to the entire surface. For this reason punch'ŏng ware, which was a utilitarian ware used for the serving and storage of food, has frequently been called a debased form of inlaid celadon. A different class of punch'ŏng ware is decorated with bold floral designs that were carved out and filled with white slip. It is known in

PSYKTER

Japan as hori mishima or carved mishima. See *Hakeme; Kohiki.*

Punct, Carl Christoph (d. 1765) Court sculptor, 1763; modeler at Meissen, 1761-1765. His figures are skillfully modeled in a transitional style displaying a compromise between Rococo and Neo-Classicism. As a rule his figures have a Rococo-scrolled base.

Purple See *Manganese-Purple; Purple of Cassius.*

Purple of Cassius In European ceramics; a pigment precipitated from chloride of gold producing a gold rose-pink color, frequently called rose or rouge d'or, varying from a pale rose to a deep strong purple according to the method of its preparation. It is so called because the process was discovered by Andreas Cassius of Leyden, at some time prior to 1685. It was used on faïence before the close of the 17th century and was one of the first enamels (muffle-kiln colors) made by Böttger for his Meissen porcelain around 1715. It preceded the introduction of the rose-pink enamel in China, the Famille Rose, 1720-1725. Notable examples of this enamel color are the rich plum and warm rose-pink in some Meissen flower painting, 1725-1730; the soft mulberry-purple monochrome painting on early Vincennes, about 1755; the smooth rose-pink ground-color (or Rose Pompadour) of Sèvres, 1757-1764 or later; the rare lilac or pale purple-blue ground-color of Sèvres

which also contains gold-pink. There were also the rich crimson-clarets of Chelsea, Derby and Worcester. In the middle of the 19th century a pink prepared from chromium and tin was introduced to the enameler's palette, and from that time onward chrome-pink frequently supplanted the rose-pink prepared from purple of Cassius. See *Colors; Colored Grounds; Manganese-Purple.*

Puzzle Jug In ceramics; a variety of drinking jug generally having pierced openwork around the neck which made it impossible to use in the normal manner. The only way liquid could be drunk was by sucking it through an inconspicuous opening in the spout at the end of a tube which went around the neck and through the handle to the bottom of the jug. Variations in detail occurred. The puzzle jug was of early origin and was known during medieval times. During the 17th and 18th centuries unusual pottery drinking vessels were quite popular and the puzzle jug made in faïence and in earthenware was much favored. (255)

Pyxis In Greek antiquities; a rather small container in several forms fitted with a cover to contain rouge and other toilet articles used by women. The cover was provided with a finial or bronze ring. Occasionally notches were cut into the foot ring to make individual bracket-like feet.

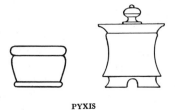

PYXIS

Q

Queen's Ware In English ceramics; cream-colored earthenware came to be known as Queen's Ware when Josiah Wedgwood made a tea set for Queen Charlotte, wife of George III of England, in 1765. This and subsequent orders pleased her sufficiently for her to permit it in the future to bear the name of Queen's Ware. It was with this tableware that Wedgwood laid the foundation for his fame and fortune and with which he launched the British pottery business. This same Queen's Ware was used for making the famous Green Frog service. See *Cream-Colored Earthenware; Frog Service.*

Quimbaya See *Ecuador and Colombia.*

Quimper In French ceramics; see *Loc Maria.*

Quodlibetz In ceramics; the name, meaning *what you please,* is given to a painted decoration in which letters, scissors, playing cards and other miscellaneous articles are casually grouped together without any particular plan and are painted in a manner to cast shadows. This decoration was much favored in late 18th century Royal Copenhagen porcelain.

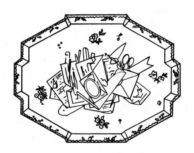

QUODLIBETZ DECCORATION,
ROYAL COPENHAGEN TRAY

R

R and S The distinguishing initials appearing in a popular 19th century European porcelain mark of varying design. See *Tillowitz; Suhl.*

Raeren In German ceramics; it is generally accepted that the most outstanding of all Rhenish salt-glazed stoneware was made at Raeren, near Aix-la-Chapelle in the Rhineland, from around 1560 to 1600. The material for the earlier wares was always brown. During the first half of the 16th century the influence of Cologne was evident. The wares of the best period were admirable for the perfectly balanced proportions of their forms and for the well-placed friezes or medallions in relief. Of outstanding interest were the huge jugs almost 20 inches high with either double or arcaded friezes of reliefs depicting biblical and mythological stories, circular pilgrim bottles with finely modeled armorial bearings and foliage in rather high relief, cylindrical pharmacy vases, jugs with long beak-like spouts, large globular Bartmann jugs and tall conical tankards often simply decorated with small medallion reliefs. From about 1580 a grey body ware was introduced; however, it did not entirely supplant the brown body ware until early in the 17th century. The grey body stoneware, which permitted finer relief work, was slightly colored with blue. Probably the greatest figure in the history of Rhenish stoneware was Jan Emens working at Raeren from around 1566 to 1594. Baldem Mennicken, the second great Raeren potter, signed his work from 1575 to 1584. From early in the 17th century there was a growing tendency for over-elaboration in which the elegant and refined simplicity of the earlier work was lost. See *Rhenish Stoneware; Mennicken.* (194)

Raffaelle-Ware In French ceramics; pre-

RAEREN STONEWARE JUG

RAKU

sumably made in imitation of Italian majolica, shown by Sèvres in 1849 at an exhibition of French Industry in London.

Ragnolis, Nicolaus de A majolica plaque formerly built into the wall above the door of the church of S. Michele at Faenza bears the name of Nicolaus de Ragnolis and the date 1475. See *Faenza.*

Rainforth and Company See *Leeds.*

Rakka See *Raqqa.*

Raku In Japanese ceramics; essentially Raku ware as it is known today is less a special variety of pottery than it is an artistic tradition embracing several different wares joined by common ideals of taste. With its emergence the ceramic art of Japan began to evolve from the almost complete anonymity of its earlier periods. The hereditary line of Raku ware masters begins with a certain Sasaki Chojiro (1516-1592) whose bowls attracted the attention of the tea master Sen-no Rikyu (1521-1591). Rikyu was the arbiter of the wabi tea cult which emphasized the identity of utility and beauty, and aspired to an artistic code stressing what was subdued, sober and unassuming in the arts of decoration. Chojiro's work conformed exactly to the principles of this school and the patronage of Rikyu provided the impetus to found what has become in fact a hereditary "dynasty" of potters. The identification both of the ware and of the line of potters producing it comes from a seal for marking these wares presented to Jokei II in the Raku line by Hideyoshi (1536-1598) de facto ruler of Japan at the time. The seal bore the single Chinese character, raku (enjoyment). It appears that Chojiro, whose original occupation was the making of decorative roof tiles, first began to produce tea ceremony utensils around 1572.

As a rule Raku ware itself is a fairly soft, low-fired pottery with a variety of sober glazes. Sometimes it was wheel-thrown; however, more frequently it was hand-modeled and worked over with a bamboo spatula. Raku potters trace fourteen generations down to the present day in direct succession from Chojiro. However, this does not include many other potters working in the Raku tradition. Many of this latter group are "dilettante potters" working at ceramics as an artistic pastime and who produced celebrated pieces in the Raku manner. One such was Hon'ami Koetsu (1556-1637) who was intimate with Jokei and particularly with Donyu (1574-1656), the third generaton head of the Raku line and by all accounts the most exceptional potter among the fourteen generations. Koetsu made the celebrated tea bowl Fujisan, which he so named because the hazy greyish-white glaze on the upper half suggests the snow-capped Mt. Fuji, and the lower half, the misty scenery at the foot of Mt. Fuji at daybreak. This early 17th century Raku piece together with a later 16th century Painted Shino piece with the typical opaque white Shino glaze and a design painted in iron-rust brown showing a bamboo trellis are Japan's two most celebrated tea bowls. Especially notable among the descendants of Koetsu is his grandson Kuchu who made famous tea bowls and other tea utensils from the same earths that had once been used for Shigaraki wares. Among the work of Donyu is a famous tea bowl, Jukushi (Ripe Persimmon) which refers to the color of the glaze. (130, 133)

Ramié, Georges and Suzanne See *Picasso.*

Raphael Sanzio (1483–1520) The great Italian painter. See *Engraved Designs; Raphaelesque.*

Raphaelesque In decoration; the term is often applied to a style of painted decoration executed by Raphael in the Loggia of the Vatican. He received his inspiration for this work in the beautiful decorations in painting and in stucco found in the Golden House of Nero. See *Bérain, Jean, the Elder; Grotesque; Urbino; Arabesque; Engraved Designs.* (233, 234, 239)

Raqqa See *Islamic Pottery, Medieval.*

Ratskrug or **Ratskanne** In German ceramics; the name given to a type of Siegburg stoneware jug, with a high conical foot. The form is derived from a metalwork shape. See *Rhenish Stoneware.*

Ratti, Agostino (1699-1775) Painter in oils; worked on Savona majolica around 1720-1721.

Rauenstein In German ceramics; a porcelain manufactory was started at Rauenstein, Thuringia, in 1783 by Christian Daniel, Johann Georg and Johann Friedrich Greiner. Their productions were principally coarse imitations of the contemporary wares made at Meissen. Included among the marks were R either with or without a star and R-n with or without crossed hoes.

Ravilious, Eric See *Wedgwood, Josiah.*

Raynaud and Company In French ceramics; a still-existing porcelain factory started in 1919 at Limoges. Included among their marks are the distinguishing initials R and T & V. The latter was a French pottery active from the late 19th century until the Second World War. Some of their patterns were taken over by Raynaud and Company.

Rayy See *Islamic Pottery, Medieval.*

Rebekah at the Well Teapot In American ceramics; made in brown or Rockingham glaze, this teapot was designed and modeled by Charles Coxon at the E. & W. Bennett Company of Baltimore in 1852. He adapted it from an earlier model produced by S. Alcock and Company of Burslem, England, the original being a parian jug with a blue ground and a raised figure of Rebekah in white. Subsequently Rebekah at the Well teapots were made at a number of potteries. See *Bennett, Edwin.*

RAPHAEL, PAINTED DESIGN
IN THE VATICAN

RAUENSTEIN
1783 ON

RAYNAUD & CIE.
1919 ON

Rechitsy See *Kiselev.*

Recuay See *Andean.*

Red In ceramics; red colors practically always result from an oxide of iron. The red on the Turkish earthenware, the so-called Rhodian ware, was prepared from a highly iron-bearing ochre known as Armenian bole or simply bole. At a high temperature the color develops to perfection under an alkaline glaze but if lead is present it tends to turn brown. For this reason it is uncertain and is frequently not included in the high temperature palette of faïence. A calcined sulphate of iron was employed on Delft ware and other faïence from the late 17th century onward. Reds obtained from reduced copper used in the Sang de Boeuf glaze and other decoration on Chinese porcelains were unknown to European potters before the second half of the 19th century. The rouge-d'or (purple of Cassius) so-called to distinguish it from rouge-de-fer or iron-red, is more appropriately called rose-pink or rose-purple. Apart from the copper-red a translucent red glaze is unknown, while the smooth opaque iron-red enamel ground-color of Chinese porcelain is rarely found on European porcelains before the 19th century. It is difficult to say whether the excellent full-toned red found on Delft faïence of the late 17th and early 18th century was not applied as a muffle color at a second firing. On porcelain the painters of Schwarzlot used a distinctive red enamel, which they also occasionally used as a monochrome. On Meissen porcelain red monochrome was a marked feature of the Baroque period, in the same manner as rose-pink was of the Rococo porcelain at Sèvres and elsewhere. Iron-red ground colors are seldom found; however, they do occur on early Meissen around 1730, and Du Paquier's Vienna porcelain. See *Colors; Colored Grounds; Purple of Cassius; Islamic Pottery, Later.*

Red and Green family In Chinese ceramics; a particular group of colored enamels extensively used on porcelains during the Ming dynasty. The enamels used in the Red and Green family are chiefly red, green and yellow, occasionally supplemented with turquoise green. Underglaze blue was omitted. Since this kind of decoration was used on pottery during the Sung dynasty it is therefore possible that it had been used on wares dating from the Hung Wu reign of the Ming dynasty. However, most of the Red and Green family wares in present day collections date from the Chêng Tê reign with the greatest number of examples being found on porcelain of the Chia Ching reign. See *Ming.*

Red Dragon Pattern See *Meissen; Kakiemon.* (306)

Red Earthenware Teapots In Dutch ceramics; see *Milde, Arij de.*

Red-Figure Ware In ancient Grecian ceramics; in contrast to the black-figure technique wherein the figures are painted in black silhouettes on a red ground, in the red-figure technique it was the background which was black, drawn by a brush or a more precise tool around the figures which were therefore reserved and stood out against the black in the color of the clay (red-brown in Attic pottery). Within these reserved shapes inner details of anatomy and drapery, which had been shown on black-figure vases by incising, were painted in black, permitting the artist much greater fluency. Sometimes the black pigment was thinned to produce a golden brown, which was often used for the muscles and hair on the body. Inscriptions were often painted on the black background in red (or reddish purple) and touches of the same color were used sparingly on the accessories of the figures themselves; white painting was extremely rare. The red-figure technique was invented in Athens between 530-520 B.C., most likely by one of the painters who worked for the potter Andokides, who had studied under Exekias and done much black-figure work, sometimes combining the two techniques on the opposite sides of the same vase. By extension the term *red-figure* is also given to the same technique used on wares whose clay body is not red-brown but varies from cream to muddy brown. As in the earlier black-figure the subjects for red-figure vases are at first chiefly taken from mythology. As time progressed the artist drew his inspiration increasingly from everyday life, but the mythological legends possessed an enduring popularity. Ornamental bands and designs were used on Attic vases to frame the figured scenes and to decorate the areas of the vase not occupied by these scenes, namely, the mouth, neck, shoulder, spaces around the handles and base of the body. Though secondary, they always play an important role in the composition, helping to link the figured scenes to the shape of the vase. Included among the repertoire of favorite motifs were meanders, palmettes, tongues, eggs, ivy, laurel, lotus, scrolls, rays, spirals, crosses, dots and simple lines. In contrast to the somber black-figure scenes, a more spirited, humanistic tone was injected into the red-figure painting. The various moods of painting correspond to the temperament of the individual artist. It was the generation of artists working from 480 to 450 B.C. that created the "classical" type of humanity in which a uniform conception of ideal beauty supplanted the livelier characterization of individual differences. A diminishing power and feeling marked the red-figure painting of the late classical period, 420-400 B.C. See *Greece*. (62)

Red-Gloss Ware   See *Roman Pottery*.

Red Porcelain or Red China   In European ceramics; popular 17th and 18th century names for imported unglazed stoneware (the so-called Buccaro ware) made in China, and imitations by Arij de Milde,

Böttger at Meissen and others. In Germany at Ansbach and Bayreuth they made a soft red earthenware with a brown glaze which they called brown china or brown porcelain, a ware especially in vogue in the 1740's. There are also the wares by Dwight at Fulham, by the Elers and by other Staffordshire potters, including Wedgwood who called his red ware Rosso Antico. See *Plaue-on-Havel; Bodenbach*.

Red Stoneware   In European ceramics; a term applied particularly to unglazed redware of the Chinese Yi-hsing type. See *Red Porcelain*. (199, 407)

Reducing Fire or **Atmosphere**   See *Oxidizing Fire* or *Atmosphere*.

Reduction Firing   See *Six Old Kilns*.

Redware or **Red-Clay Pottery**   In ceramics; clays used for redware pottery are also used for common red brick, floor tiles and the like. This clay burns at a low temperature to a rather soft and porous body ranging in color, depending on the temperature, from pinkish-buff to reds and reddish browns. As a rule it is covered with a soft lead glaze. A similar red body has been used for the pottery of ancient Greece and the Arretine wares of ancient Rome. See *Red Porcelain or Red China; Earthenware; Colors*.

Reeves, Ann Wynn   (b. 1929) English ceramist and oil painter; shares a studio with her husband, silversmith and ceramist Kenneth Clark. She specializes in colored glazes with a majolica technique and has completed several large architectural ceramic murals. See *Clark, Kenneth*.

Refractory   In ceramics; a term used of pottery, particularly porcelain bodies and glazes, and of materials used in making them, referring to the property of resisting heat or capable of enduring high temperature and not readily melting or fusing out of shape. This property is obtained generally by employing silica in the form of sand, quartz or calcined flint.

Régence The period in French history, 1715-1723, when Philippe, the Duke of Orleans, was appointed Regent for Louis XV, King of France 1723-1774.

Regency In history the name *Regency* covers that period from 1811 to 1820 when George, Prince of Wales, acted as regent for his father, King George III. In the decorative arts the name *Regency* is given to an English development of several styles from about 1795 to 1820. This development included a Greek revival, an Egyptian revival and a Chinese revival.

Regensburg In German ceramics; a porcelain-decorating workshop was active at Regensberg, Bavaria, from around 1782-1793 under the management of Johann Welland and his son Franz Matthias. Their principal productions were small, handleless Turkish coffee cups for the export market. It is believed a porcelain factory was active here around 1830 and owned by Dominicus Auliczek II. See *Auliczek, Dominicus.*

Registry Marks From 1842 to 1883 when the British Patent Office employed the lozenge-shaped Registry mark on English manufactured goods, manufacturers used the mark in addition to the trademark which indicated that the design was registered in the British Patent Office. When this mark appears it is possible to tell the exact year, month and date of an object by using the following table. (It should be noted that in this period ceramic objects were always listed as Class IV.)

It will be noted that there are several departures from the general pattern in the above codes.

After 1883 a more simple system of con-

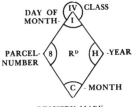

REGISTRY MARK
PATTERN ONE
YEAR LETTER AT TOP
1842-1867

REGISTRY MARK
PATTERN TWO
YEAR LETTER AT RIGHT
1868-1883

secutive numbering was introduced. Beginning at 1 in 1884 the Registration Numbers had reached some 368,000 by the end of the century. Below are listed the first registrations issued in each year of objects in all classes. It should be noted that before the beginning of 1892 a slight numerical overlap occurs between the registrations of each December and January.

Rd. No.		Rd. No.	
1884	1	1895	246975
1885	19754	1896	268392
1886	40480	1897	291241
1887	64520	1898	311658
1888	90483	1899	331707
1889	116648	1900	351202
1890	141273	1901	368154
1891	163767	1902	385500
1892	185713	1903	402500
1893	205240	1904	420000
1894	224720	1905	447000

Regout, Petrus See *Maastricht.*

Rehau In German ceramics; the porcelain factory Zeh, Scherzer & Co. was started at Rehau, Bavaria, in 1880. They made table, coffee, and tea services and wares for daily use. The distinguishing initials Z.S.& Co. appeared in marks of varying design.

Reinhart, Oscar See *Hafner.*

Reinicke, Peter (d. 1768) Modeler at Meissen, 1743-1768. See *Kaendler, J. J.*

Rekston See *Stockton Art Pottery.*

Relief-Decorated Wares During the lengthy early and middle Victorian times in England, one particular kind of ceramic vessel, the jug, was regarded pre-eminently as the subject for relief decoration. It was patent that these jugs were in universal use for table purposes. Essentially these jugs can be considered as a manifestation of popular art, since they were produced in quantity for the widest market and their decoration was included in the mold from which they were cast. Hence scarcely any extra expense was involved. Relief-decorated wares of this kind apparently were not made to any notable extent in Continental Europe. See *Meigh, Charles.* In the mid-19th century period the United States saw an important development of relief-decorated wares in a variety of materials. The outstanding production of English-style jugs and related wares was made at the Fenton factory in Bennington, Vermont. Many of the designs were of English derivation but they were chiefly produced in a type of parian porcelain, while in England the material was usually stoneware. Other firms such as E. and W. Bennett of Baltimore, the American Pottery Company of Jersey City, and Taylor and Spieler of Trenton were also producing jugs in the English manner. (441-444, 469, 470)

REHAU
1891 ON

Relief Decoration In ceramics; various methods are employed to obtain decoration in relief. One method is by free incising or piercing and by freehand modeling. The latter is relatively rare since each piece can never be duplicated. Two common processes are used, either by pressing or casting in molds made from a hand-modeled specimen or from a specimen in some other material such as metal. In pressing, the soft clay is pressed into either plaster or slightly baked clay molds. In casting, a liquid mixture of clay and water is poured into a porous mold which absorbs the water. In another method the relief ornament is stamped or impressed with stamps cut in intaglio and generally made of metal. The soft clay surface is impressed or pads of clay applied to the surface are impressed. In still another method the molded reliefs are separately made and applied to the surface with slip.

Remmy, John (d. 1762) German potter; started a stoneware factory in New York around 1735. The business was carried on through three generations of Remmys, all of the name of John, until it failed in 1819-1820. One great-grandson continued at South Amboy, New Jersey, until 1833. About 1810, Henry Remmy, a grandson of the first John Remmy, went to Philadelphia, where the firm is still established. By 1900 the Philadelphia works had grown to extensive proportions. Here they manufactured chemical bricks and stone and porcelain ware of every variety for chemical purposes. In addition to these specialties the factory produced an extensive line of salt-glazed ware for daily use, such as jugs, mugs, pitchers, crocks and coin banks, mainly decorated in underglaze blue.(434)

Remojadas In pre-Columbian Central American ceramics; a site in central Vera Cruz where the "smiling figures" were first found in some quantity in the early 1950's. For this reason these ceramic sculptures which are among the few seemingly light-hearted human representations from ancient Mexico have been stylistically named after the site. They date from the Classic period, 300-980. See *Vera Cruz.*

Renaissance The name *Renaissance,* which literally means rebirth, is given to a widespread movement of complex character that had its inception in Italy in the 14th century. Its effect on art is identified with the discovery of man as an individual and his inherent human right to enjoy the beauty of this world, and with the revival of classic culture. The earliest manifestation of the Renaissance was in the study of classic literature and in the humanists of the 14th century. After literature, the arts all contributed to this new age of classic culture. In architecture the Gothic style was supplanted by the Renaissance style. Once again were employed the Roman Classic Orders which had been in abeyance for almost one thousand years. This revival in classic art began in the first quarter of the 15th century in Florence and spread from Italy into France and ultimately into all the countries of Europe. Italian Renaissance art was aided by the patronage of the Medici family of Florence and in the 16th century by the papal court of Rome, which became the leading art center during the 16th century and was where the art of the High Renaissance culminated, 1500-1540. The entire alphabet of classic ornament was employed by the Italians during the Renaissance. Repetitive running motifs, which were a legacy of ancient architecture, were much used, such as the guilloche and egg and dart. Included among the favorite decorative motifs were the acanthus leaf, the anthemion, flowers, fruit and foliage, arabesques, rosettes, roundels, scrolls, vase forms, medallions, swags, paterae, lozenges, cartouches, cornucopiae, banderoles, candelabra and grotesques. Cherubs, cupids, atlantes, terms, caryatids, masks, dolphins, chimeras, satyrs, human and animal figures were all included among the innumerable classic motifs. Religious subjects, historical, mythological and allegorical stories, as well as garden scenes and marriage processions, were all favorite decorative themes. In ceramics; the humanistic culture was very much in evidence in the istoriato style of pictorial painting on Italian, Lyons and other majolica. See *Engraved Designs; Michelangelo Buonarroti; Sansovino, Jacopo; Baroque; Gothic; Saint-Porchaire; Palissy, B.; Tuscany; Rhenish Stoneware.*

Rendsburg In ceramics; a faïence manufactory was established at Rendsburg, Holstein, Germany, in 1764 by Caspar Lorenzen and Christian Friedrich Clar. It changed hands several times and finally closed in 1818. The faïence was chiefly painted in underglaze blue or manganese and only rarely in other high temperature colors. Chinese plants and flowers were much favored for decorative subjects. The wares included such articles as bishop bowls, potpourris, cane handles and snuff

CR
N

RENDSBURG
1764-1800

boxes. After 1772 the manufactory only produced white and cream-colored lead-glazed earthenware. Much of this ware was unpainted; occasionally the design was picked out in blue. Late in the 18th century the manufactory made some imitation black basalt ware and a red stoneware with a slight glaze. Included among the marks were CR joined together and Ren.I and R F; the last two being for the lead-glazed earthenware. See *Faïence Fine.*

Rennes In French ceramics; potteries were in existence in Rennes, Ille-et-Vilaine, Brittany, from the 16th century. Two faïence manufactories were active during the 18th century; however, no regular factory mark was used. One factory was started in 1748 by Forasassi, a Florentine, in the Pavé Saint-Laurent, Rue des Capucines. The other factory was started in 1749 by François-Alexandre Tutrel in the Rue Huë. The two manufactories made all types of wares; however, they seldom achieved a high standard in their workmanship. The high temperature colors found on the wares of one factory were characterized by a dull dark green and a bubbled manganese; red was not used.

Repairer In ceramics; the name given to the workman who did the molding, assembling and finishing of a decorative vessel or figure. The incised and impressed marks found on figures and other objects in porcelain are frequently those of the repairer and not of the artist who made the original model. However, exceptions occur.

Reserve In decorative processes; the term *reserve* means to retain unaltered; to remain or keep in a particular condition or state, or to leave intact or untouched. For example, the term *in reserve* is frequently used in ceramics to describe a decorative feature or process, such as a piece of blue and white porcelain having the design in reserve. In other words the ground of the design is in blue while the design is in white, which is actually the color of the white body of the porcelain that remained intact or untouched. See *Blue and White Ch'ing; Shonzui.* (110)

Resist In ceramics; a method of decorating pottery by which a resist substance such as wax is used to produce a design. The resist, which is applied on the surface of an object before it is dipped in the colored glaze, is burnt away in the kiln leaving a pattern, generally in white or the color of the body, in reserve on a colored ground.

Restauration See *Restoration.*

Restoration The reigns of Louis XVIII, 1814-1824; Charles X, 1824-1830; Louis Philippe, 1830-1848. See *Louis Philippe; Revived Rococo.*

Reval In ceramics; a faïence manufactory was started at Reval, Estonia, around 1775 by Karl Christian Fick of Stralsund and closed in 1792. The wares were chiefly in the Rococo style and reflected the influence of Stralsund faïence. Included among their productions were figures, vases pierced in openwork, tureens applied with flowers and fruit and all other kinds of tablewares. The colored enamels used in the painted decoration had a distinctive and pleasing tone. Of particular interest were some very fine animal figures of dogs, bulls, elephants and tigers. Included among the marks were Reval Fick and RF.

REVAL
1775-1792

Revelry See *Coalport.*

Revived Baroque or **Louis Quatorze** See *Revived Louis XIV*

Revived Gothic or **Neo-Gothic** See *Louis Philippe; Historicism; Victorian; Viollet-le-Duc, E. E.*

Revived Louis XIV See *Historicism; Louis XIV Style; Revived Rococo; Victorian.*

Revived Louis XV See *Revived Rococo; Historicism; Victorian.*

Revived Louis XVI   See *Historicism; Victorian.*

Revived Renaissance or Neo-Renaissance
See *Historicism; Victorian; Revived Rococo; Saint-Porchaire; Palissy, B.*

Revived Rococo   As its name implies, a renewed interest in the mid-18th century Rococo style. It is important to distinguish Revived Rococo from the more deliberately pastiche styles which were to follow before the end of the 19th century. In effect, the Revived Rococo represented from the beginning the borrowing merely of motifs which could be utilized to fit a new wave of romanticism and affectation. In porcelain it meant the use of swirling, sinuous, asymmetrical motifs frequently in relief and gilded, together with a marked interest in applied decoration of flowers. It was not adopted everywhere and its time of adoption varied widely from factory to factory. In France, it apparently made little impact at Sèvres; however, it was typical of the work at other factories. In Bohemia certain factories, such as Schlaggenwald, embraced wholeheartedly the Rococo motifs, while others were still producing wares of an Empire character in the middle of the 19th century. The Revived Rococo forms with their sinuous outlines and relief decoration afforded very little scope for the porcelain painter. This fact, as well as the spirit of the Rococo style, which is one of lightness and fantasy, brought forth a period in which porcelain figure modeling was intensely developed, particularly in the Bohemian factories. Not only were actual 18th century models revived, such as Meissen, but more importantly an immense number of new models were created around the mid-19th century. There were figures in contemporary costumes, many folk types and even theatrical figures, and figures of gallants and lovely ladies in romantic versions of mid-18th century costumes which have long continued to have popular appeal. These figures were often provided with Rococo

scrollwork bases. Noteworthy was the mid-19th century practice of painting directly on the unglazed porcelain, that is, biscuit. In the latter part of the 19th century this technique was to become increasingly popular for inexpensive figure-work. In England where the Empire style was comparatively of short duration, the Revived Rococo developed early. By 1830 it was completely developed at such factories as Derby, Davenport, Rockingham and Coalbrookdale. From the late 1840's soft-paste porcelain made at Sèvres in the 1750's and 1760's was imitated in English bone china, at Minton, Copeland and Coalport. Shortly after the middle of the 19th century the Revived Rococo yielded to styles which embodied Classical, especially Louis Quatorze, and Renaissance motifs. However, the Rococo was not without appeal to some Second Empire artists in the 1850's, and at a number of porcelain factories a further revival of the Rococo, known as the Third- or Neo-Rococo developed in the last decade or so of the 19th century. See *Victorian; Historicism; Louis Philippe; Coalport; Engraved Designs.*

Rewend, Christian Friedrich   See *Potsdam.*

Rheinsberg   In German ceramics; a faïence manufactory was founded at Rheinsberg, Brandenburg, in 1762 by Baron von Reisewitz(d. 1763). The factory was bought by Karl Friedrich Lüdicke in 1770, which date marked the beginning of a flourishing manufacture. Around 1786 cream-colored earthenware and black basalt ware in the English style became the principal productions and after 1800 the only productions. The factory remained active until 1866. The mark for faïence after 1770 was R L in monogram. The painted decoration on the faïence was generally in polychrome. Much of the productions resembled the wares made at the manufactories in Thuringia. Other types such as tureens in the form of birds and fruit and vases with pierced double walls show the influence of

RHEINSBERG
C. 1770 ON

Münden. The lead-glazed earthenware and the black basalt ware were marked with the name Rheinsberg, LRBG or R impressed.

Rhenish Stoneware In German ceramics; salt-glazed stoneware was made in the Rhineland from late in the Middle Ages; however, it was without artistic importance. From around the middle of the 16th century and for about the ensuing seven decades a salt-glazed stoneware was made at four great centers, namely Cologne, Raeren, Siegburg and Westerwald, that ranks at its best with the finest of German Renaissance art. It has not been determined whether stoneware was first made at Cologne or Siegburg; however, the former was undoubtedly the first of the different leading centers to produce wares having real artistic merit. See *Cologne; Raeren; Siegburg; Westerwald; Stoneware; Salt Glaze.*

Rhodes, Daniel (b. 1911) American designer-craftsman, teacher and writer; has achieved eminence as a potter. As a writer of pottery and design his influence has been significant. He is the author of STONEWARE AND PORCELAIN: THE ART OF HIGH-FIRED POTTERY, 1959. Some of his recent work is representative of a movement toward abstract pottery that has been evident in the United States since the later 1950's and which appears to be partly analogous to the sculptural style of some of the Italian pottery. The prominent leader in this group has been Peter Voulkos of California. See *Voulkos, P.* (562)

Rhodes, David (d. 1777) David Rhodes and Jasper Robinson operated an enameling workshop not far from the Leeds pottery in 1760-1761 and perhaps later. Their work appears on Leeds, Wedgwood, Derbyshire, and Liverpool wares. By 1768 Rhodes was working in London; then he became head of the Wedgwood enameling workshops at Little Cheyne Row, Chelsea.

Rhodian Ware See *Islamic Pottery, Later.*

Rhyton In Greek antiquities; a Greek word derived from *rysis,* a flow or stream. A cup or vessel with a handle in the form of an animal's horn, an animal's head or an entire animal, which has a hole or small opening at the bottom which permits a stream of wine to flow from the vessel.

Riccoboni, Louis See *Engraved Designs.*

Rice Grain Pattern In Chinese ceramics; a porcelain having perforated designs. It derived its name from the shape of the perforations which were similar to grains of rice. The perforations were filled with glaze. It was sometimes supplemented with decoration in underglaze blue. The rice grain pattern is characteristic of the Ch'ien Lung period, 1736-1795. Perforated decorative designs filled in with glaze were used in the Near East by Persian potters as early as the 12th century on a composite paste of powdered quartz and alkaline frit; the glaze was also made of a similar alkaline frit thus making certain that it would adhere. Rice grain pattern still retains its appeal to potters. (505)

Richard-Ginori See *Doccia.*

Ridgway In English ceramics; from the end of the 18th century the Ridgway family had extensive connections in the potteries district at Hanley, North Staffordshire. Job Ridgway (1759-1813) in partnership with his brother George Ridgway (c. 1758-1823) started the Bell Works, Shelton, Hanley, in 1792. The partnership continued until 1802 when Job Ridgway started a separate pottery at Cauldon Place, Shelton, titled Job Ridgway and Sons. They made earthenware. Subsequently Job's sons John (1785-1860) and William (1788-1864) operated Cauldon Place and Bell Works from 1814-c.1830 under the title of John and William Ridgway, producing earthenwares and porcelain. Blue transfer-printed wares of

RIDGWAY
1880 ON

American views for the American market were an important part of their production. John Ridgway, who was appointed potter to the Queen, owned the Cauldon Works under the title John Ridgway (and Company) c. 1830-1855. In time it was taken over by Brown, Westhead, Moore and Company, subsequently Cauldon Ltd. William Ridgway and his son Edward John (1814-1896) operated Bell Works together with several other potteries at Hanley under the title of William Ridgway and Son, c. 1830-1854. Shortly afterward it was purchased by Joseph Clementson. The present firm of Ridgway Potteries, Ltd. includes in its list of potteries the Bedford Works, Shelton, at one time operated by E. J. Ridgway and Son. See *Cauldon Ltd.*

Rie, Lucie (b. 1902) English artist-potter born in Austria, trained in the Vienna Arts and Crafts School; settled in England in 1938 at Albion Mews, London. She became one of the most accomplished potters working in England. Clarity of outline and precision of detail characterize her stoneware. See *Coper, Hans.* (504)

Riedel, Gottlieb Friedrich (1724-1784) An influential figure in German porcelain. Painter at Meissen, 1743-1756; also working at Höchst. Director of painting at Frankenthal, 1757-1759, and director of painting and design at Ludwigsburg, 1759-1779. Then worked for a time as an independent engraver at Augsburg. See *Kirschner, F.*

Riemerschmid, Richard (1868-1957) German architect and designer; a founding member of the Münchener Vereinigte Werkstätten Für Kunst in Handwerk, with Obrist, Pankok and Paul. He became one of the leaders of modern German decorative art. He was an active designer in many media, including porcelain and stoneware, and around 1906 he designed a porcelain dinner service for Meissen. Apart from his work for Meissen he was also interested in stoneware. He was particularly concerned with bringing a modern feeling into the traditional German stoneware of Westerwald, a district in the Rhineland. He designed for the Reinhold Merkelbach pottery in Grenzhausen, Westerwald. From 1912 to 1924 he was director of the School of Applied Arts in Munich. See *Munich School.* (496)

Riese, Johann Carl Friedrich Model master at Berlin, 1789-1834. His figures and groups were almost entirely in the Classical style, using biscuit as material. His son, Wilhelm, also modeled at Berlin and succeeded him as model master. See *Berlin.*

Rikyu, Sen-no (1521-1591) Celebrated Japanese cha-jin or tea master; regarded as one of the most important figures of the Momoyama period. Chosen by Hideyoshi to remodel the rules of the tea ceremony, the strict rules and etiquette prescribed by Rikyu still constitute the basic principles as taught by the various schools that came after him. The principles established by Rikyu called for utter simplicity in all matters and for the tea room to be decorated in the severest style. His favorite pupil was Furuta Oribe (1543-1615) who became one of the most distinguished tea masters of all time. In contrast to Oribe, Kobori Enshu (1579-1647) a noted tea master, introduced a profusion of rich and beautiful objects into the tea ceremony, thereby departing from the severe style of Rikyu. See *Cha-no-yu; Iga; Raku.*

Ring Jug In German ceramics; an early type of tall stoneware jug made at Dreihausen, Siegburg and other centers, provided with several small handles attached vertically on the shoulder which held loose stoneware rings, no doubt to create a festive noise as the jug was passed around. (193)

Ringler, Joseph Jakob (1730-1804) Painter and the most influential of all the porcelain arcanists. He was first at Vienna, c. 1744 onward, where through his friendship with the director's daughter he learned the se-

RIE, LUCIE
C. 1938 ON

cret of porcelain making, especially the knowledge of kiln construction. Subsequently he was arcanist at Höchst, Strasbourg, Nymphenburg and other places, and finally at Ludwigsburg where he settled down and held the post of director from 1759 until his death. Other manufactories owed their porcelain production to two of Ringler's assistants at Höchst, Johann Benckgraff and at Fürstenberg, Berlin, Fulda and Cassel, Nikolaus Paul. See *German Porcelain*.

Robert, Joseph Gaspard See *Marseilles*.

Robertson, Hugh C. An influential American potter; he was particularly interested in the reproduction of Oriental and high-fired glazes, and their use for original designs. See *Chelsea and Dedham*.

Robertson, James and his sons Alexander and Hugh. See *Chelsea and Dedham*.

Robineau, Adelaide Alsop Born in Middletown, Connecticut, in 1865; lived most of her life in Syracuse, New York, where she died in 1929. One of the earliest artist-potters in America, she began her career in ceramics as a china painter. In 1899 she married Samuel E. Robineau and in the following year they began to publish the magazine KERAMIC STUDIO, which became the official mouthpiece of an organization of china painters. In 1903 she began to make and decorate pottery. She was continually experimenting with new glazes, forms and techniques. Her individual porcelains won international honors. In 1911 her Scarab Vase, which is her most celebrated work, won the Grand Prize for Ceramics at the Turin International Exhibition. Though it is known as the Scarab Vase, it was entitled "The Apotheosis of the Toiler," and was so named for its overall carved design portraying a beetle rolling up his ball of food, to symbolize the toiler and his work. (524)

Robinson, Jasper See *Rhodes, David*.

Rocaille A style of ornament. See *Rococo*.

Rock and Wave Pattern A border pattern used on Isnik plates. (179)

Rockingham In English ceramics; a general pottery from around 1745 to 1842 was located on the estate of the Marquis of Rockingham, Swinton, Yorkshire, and became known by his name because it was located on his estate. From 1826 when the manufactory was financially helped by the heir to the Rockingham estates, the name Rockingham was formally adopted, and the griffin, which was the family crest, was used as the mark. After 1830 the word Royal was added to the mark. It is not possible to identify the very early wares. A stoneware was made from around 1765. It was not until after 1778 when the Brameld family became associated with it, that the factory became important. From 1787 to 1806 the factory was in partnership with Leeds pottery. The earthenwares made during this period, which were not marked, cannot be distinguished from the wares of Leeds. After 1806 the Brameld family became the owners and the wares were marked with either Brameld or Rockingham, impressed. Included among the wares made under Brameld were cream-colored and blue-printed earthenware, marbled and tortoiseshell earthenware, black basalt and other stoneware. Especially characteristic was a manganese-brown lead glaze known all over England as the Rockingham glaze. Porcelain was included in the productions after 1820. Due to the royal patronage the wares became quite fashionable. They were in a rather ornate Revived Rococo style and were often excessively gilded. In American ceramics; Rockingham generally denotes a coarse pottery with a brown tortoiseshell mottled glaze, from which many household items were made. The solid brown Rockingham was not produced in as large quantities as the mottled type. From around 1840 to 1900 almost every

ROCKINGHAM
C. 1830 ON

sizable pottery in America produced Rockingham. However, the principal center came to be East Liverpool, Ohio. The brown color in American Rockingham is inherent in the glaze itself. It is seldom marked, and it is incorrect to give the generic name Bennington to this ware, as most of it was made elsewhere. See *Bennington; Yellow Ware.*

Rockingham Glaze In English ceramics; see *Rockingham.*

Rococo At the present time the word is used interchangeably with the French word *Rocaille* meaning rock work or grotto work. Originally the term *Rocaille* was used to describe the artificial grottoes found in French gardens which were decorated with natural stones of irregular outline and stalactites and other ornamentation made of shells. The term *Rocaille* or *Rococo* is the name now given to a singular form of asymmetrical ornament evolved from the Baroque in France where it was in vogue from around 1720-1760. Certain natural forms were used as the foundation of the style which was richly fantastic. It was marked by a profusion of rocks or rocaille and shells or coquillage, with flowers, foliage and fruits. Various forms of ornamental curves, especially C-scrolls, figured prominently. The style was more suitable for interiors and the arts of decoration than for architecture. Included among its chief pioneers were Pineau and Audran. From around 1730 the movement was accelerated and intensified in the designs of such men as Oppenord and Meissonnier. This movement, which carried the style in France to its culmination, was marked by an extravagant and a more thorough use of asymmetry. Sometimes the word *Rococo* is restricted in its use to this later and more advanced phase. In France this style of ornament, which reached its finest expression in the decorative arts from around 1740 to 1755-1760, is called the Louis XV style, and in other countries it is

ROCOCO DESIGN BY BOUCHER

called the Rococo style. Due to the revived interest in classic art a reaction took place in France which resulted in the style of Louis XVI. In England the Adam brothers were the guiding spirit of the Classic Revival. In ceramics; included among the chief Rococo exponents in France were François Boucher and Jean Pillement, both of whom also created in widely differing manners some of the fantastic chinoiseries which are closely related to the style. In Germany the engraver F. X. Habermann, J. E. Nilson and J. C. and J. M. Hoppenhaupt were notable exponents, the last-named sharing in the invention of the early and late varieties of what is known as Potsdam Rococo, exemplified in the decoration of the palace of Sans Souci (1745-1769). The amazing outburst of Rococo art at Würzburg and Nymphenburg and elsewhere in Bavaria in the 1730's and 1740's and later was largely inspired by François de Cuvilliés. The appearance of Rococo coincided with the European vogue of porcelain, which, as it happened, furnished a plastic material admirably suited to embody it. A general relaxation and emancipation from Classical principles in favor of sheer amusement and surprise brought a taste for fanciful vessels in the form of vegetables, birds and fishes, curious scent bottles and "toys" of all kinds to satisfy a craving for novelty. The naturalism of flowers painted on Meissen and other porcelains essentially may be regarded as a reaction against Baroque formality and symmetry. Practically all the European porcelains of the period from around 1745 to 1775 include noteworthy examples of Rococo art, but that of Nymphenburg is especially admirable. In French porcelain the best Chantilly brings together the Japanese with the Rococo asymmetry, and early Vincennes includes some delightful examples, but in general, as Sèvres itself, ranks rather as early Louis XVI. Some late Chelsea is as extravagant as any examples made in Germany. Notable is the Potsdam Rococo of Berlin porcelain. There is also the Scandinavian and Baltic variety such as Herrebøe, Stockelsdorf and Eckernförde. Charming examples of the style can be seen in the faïence of Rouen, Höchst, Strasbourg, Lunéville and Niderviller, and of Alcora, while also essentially Rococo are the delightful compositions of flowers and fishes and the Pillement chinoiseries of Marseilles. See *Revived Rococo; Engraved Designs; Louis XV.*

Rodin, Auguste (1840–1917) Celebrated French sculptor. He executed a great many etchings and sgraffiato on porcelain for the Sèvres manufactory. See *Sèvres.*

Rogers, John (1829–1904) See *Rogers Groups.*

Rogers Groups In American ceramics; story-telling figure groups created and patented by John Rogers (1829–1904) in New York, between the years 1859–1892. Cast in reddish plaster and given three coats of oil wash to keep the surface from chipping, each Rogers Group bears the date of patent and John Rogers, New York. The average height of each figure group was from twenty to twenty-four inches; some of the later groups were as tall as forty-seven inches. John Rogers executed no less than eighty clay models and sold more than one hundred thousand plaster reproductions. The name of the group was impressed in the front of the statue base. These groups, redolent with sentimentality, expressed the spirit of the Victorian era. John Rogers is remembered today not because he was a great sculptor but because he pictured in detail the America of his day, its costumes, furniture, current events and social activities. The subject matter of his groups, even those inspired by the Civil War, were near to the heart of the people, such as his Parting Promise and Taking the Oath. Included among some of the well-known Rogers groups are The Fugitive's Story, 1868, The Tap on the Window, 1874, Weighing the Baby, 1877, Faust and Marguerite, 1886, and Fighting Bob of Sheridan's "The Rivals," 1889.

Rokubei (d. 1799) Prominent Japanese studio-potter associated with the Kyoto circle of potters. He excelled in the preparation and application of enamels and in the refined quality of his designs found on his faïence wares. The Rokubei kiln is still active and enjoys a fine reputation. See *Kyo.*

Roman Pottery In ancient ceramics; the type of pottery most widespread in the Roman world is that characterized by a red-gloss surface obtained by dipping the pot in a liquid consisting of the finest clay particles in suspension in water and then firing it in a clear oxidizing flame. A fine film of tiny clay particles is deposited all over its surface which reflects light in a manner not unlike the fibers of silk. The red color is the result of using an iron-bearing clay which in an oxidizing kiln leaves unaffected the red ferric oxide in the clay. (The technique is closely related to that used in Greek pottery.) The pots were made by pressing clay into a mold which had itself been decorated by means of separate stamps and occasionally of rouletted designs. When shaped, the bowls were fired either in a reducing atmosphere to produce a black surface or in an oxidizing atmosphere to produce red, a color which ultimately triumphed over black in the course of the 2nd or 1st century B.C. The ornament of these bowls, which are now commonly but erroneously called Megarian bowls after the town of Megara, is clearly derived from metalwork. It has been said that both the red-gloss method and the use of impressed molds were the technical roots from which emerged almost overnight red Arretine pottery, complete in the perfection both of its physical and artistic qualities. Apparently its existence was short, scarcely exceeding the period c. 30 B.C.-A.D. c. 30. A certain Marcus Perennius Tigranus now emerges as an outstanding manufacturer of red-gloss pottery with figural relief decoration in the pottery center of Arretium (now Arezzo).

Early Arretine made at his workshop has never been surpassed in this class of red-gloss relief-decorated ware in which the influence of repoussé metal work is easily recognizable. Noteworthy were the carefully composed figural designs in classical arrangement impressed with stamps on the wheel-turned clay mold. In making a pot the mold was mounted on the potter's wheel and clay pressed into it and smoothed on the inside by the thrower, who most likely at this point worked the rim of the bowl above the edge of the mold. The clay was then allowed to dry, and in drying it contracted sufficiently to enable the shell to be removed from the mold. The bowl-shaped shell might then be given greater height by the addition of a foot which was luted on. Roman potters also decorated red-gloss pottery with incising which imitated the facets of cut glass, and applied ornament either in the form of small pads of clay or trailed on in the slip technique. It was also made without decoration, its quality depending on the fine surface finish and shape. This great family of Roman red-gloss pottery (also called Sigillata or Terra Sigillata or "figured clay") was made at other Italian centers than Arretine. There can be little question that Arretine pottery, of which an abundance was made, claimed the greatest fame in early Imperial times. It found its way to the most distant ports—to Britain and to India. That it enjoyed an enviable position is shown by the fact that the stamp Genuine Arretine appears on pottery which is not Arretine. Apparently the Roman red-gloss industry tended to move nearer both to its best established customers, the Roman legions, and to newly Romanized provinces. In the early course of the 1st century A.D. it made its appearance in south Gaul and in the reign of Claudius (41–54) the industry began to move to central Gaul, where Lezoux, near Vichy, was the chief center. Eventually Gaulish red-gloss pottery copied from the Roman superseded it, as it was superior to it, and

was in its turn copied in other provinces of the Empire. Apart from the Roman red-gloss ware, Roman potters also made a coarser earthenware without a surface treatment to give a degree of impermeability to liquids. In the Near East, at least since the 2nd millennium B.C., potters knew how to give their pots a coating of glass or glaze to make them watertight. One of the easiest and therefore most common methods of glazing in the relatively primitive phases of the potter's art has invariably been the use of lead compounds, because they fuse at relatively low temperatures, are usable with most types of potter's clay, and readily receive coloring by means of metallic oxides, in particular copper, which produces a rich green color. A fairly large class of colored lead-glazed pottery with relief decoration made in a mold after the manner of Arretine ware is found in Asia Minor dating from the 1st century B.C. The glaze is usually green; the form and decoration is in imitation of metalwork, such as a distinctive low cup with two ring handles which is by far the most common shape. Occasionally the designs were drawn in clay slip, sometimes with additional chromatic effects made by the use of white or colored slips under the glaze. Lead glazing appears to have spread early in Italy. By the middle of the 1st century A.D. green and yellow glazed wares were made in certain centers in Gaul and from about 200 A.D. onward in the Rhineland. A method of making a brilliant turquoise-blue glaze was known in Egypt at a very early date. It was obtained by utilizing the fluxing properties of natron (a soda compound found in a natural form in Egypt) in combination with copper compounds acting as coloring media on a quartz body. The technique, in various adaptations and using a number of different coloring media, survived the phases of Egyptian culture to emerge in Roman times with an even more glass-like and brilliant glaze and a richer, fuller tone of copper turquoise blue. This ware, formerly known as faïence but now more properly called glazed quartz frit ware, is a composite paste of powdered quartz and alkaline frit. The glaze is also made of a similar alkaline frit, thus ensuring that it would adhere. The chief disadvantage of the glazed quartz frit ware is its lack of plasticity, which kept it from surviving as a potter's material. The gorgeous colors of its alkaline glaze can scarcely be surpassed. In the Islamic period a ware emerged which joined this surface splendor of color with a material capable of embodying the virtues of wheel-throwing. This was obtained by using a clay which contained a high proportion of silica (sand, powdered quartz or the like) for lacking this an alkaline glaze cannot adhere to its body. A considerable quantity of alkaline-glazed pottery was made in the western provinces of the kingdom of Parthia. See *Greece; Shawabty Figures; Near East; Europe; Islamic Pottery; Castor Ware.* (69-78)

Romanesque   The name is given to a style of ornament developed in Europe in the 11th century and attaining its highest development in the 12th century. The principal elements of this style were borrowed from Roman and Byzantine art. The Romanesque style spread very quickly into the countries which were formerly a part of the Western Roman Empire, the characteristics of the style changing in each respective country in accordance with the character of the inhabitants. The Romanesque style was gradually supplanted in the different European countries by the Gothic style which was the glory of the medieval age. The style lingered in some countries longer than in others. In art; the term *Romanesque,* which simply means of Roman origin, is applied to all branches of European art based on Roman art from the fall of the Western Roman Empire in A.D. 475 until the Gothic period. See *Gothic; Byzantine.*

Rome   In Italian ceramics; by the end of the 14th century pottery was produced here painted in copper-green and dark manganese-purple on a more or less imperfect white ground, the so-called mezza majolica. It is known that majolica-making was carried on here in the 16th century. Some extant majolica wares in the Urbino style dating from 1600 and later may be attributed to Rome. Two minor porcelain manufactories were started in Rome in the second half of the 18th century. See *Volpato; Cuccumos, Filippo.*

Rookwood Pottery   In American ceramics; in 1880 Mrs. Marion Longworth Nichols Storer established her own pottery at Cincinnati, Ohio, and named it Rookwood, which was to achieve an international reputation in the later years of the 19th century. Ten years later Mrs. Storer withdrew, but by then the pottery was a successful company. In 1892 the manufactory was moved to a group of buildings near the Cincinnati Art Museum where it still operates in a limited way. From 1883 until 1913 this significant pottery was managed by William Watts Taylor. The individual pieces produced there were all signed by the decorators and until 1900 all were hand-thrown. Like the majority of the European potteries of the era, the Rookwood style was strongly influenced by Japan, and in the case of Rookwood, much of the Japanese influence came directly from the Far East, as Mrs. Storer, who had been profoundly inspired by the Japanese exhibit at the Philadelphia Centennial of 1876, hired a Japanese, Kataro Shirayamadani, as one of the pottery's decorators. A large part of the Rookwood decoration comprised asymmetrical compositions of flowers painted in colored slips under the glaze on a dark shaded ground. Great concern was given to the figured grounds and glazes which included such singular effects as tiger-eye, a crystalline glaze initiated in 1884, as well as pleasing mat surfaces. The pottery's

ROOKWOOD
1900

greatest moment of acclaim occurred at the Paris Exhibition of 1889, when it was the recipient of a gold medal. It was also prominent at the Paris Exhibition of 1900, and from that time Rookwood became generously represented in the collections of European museums. Vases were the principal product. Among the most outstanding decorators working at Rookwood before 1900 were Albert R. Valentien, A. van Briggle, Matthew E. Daly, Kataro Shirayamadani and E. P. Cranch. Characteristic marks are: from 1880 to 1882 an overglaze painted Rookwood Pottery, Ohio; from 1882 to 1886 an impressed mark, Rookwood and the year; in 1886 the monogram mark consisting of a reversed R and P was adopted. In 1887 a flame point was placed above the monogram and one point was added for each year thereafter. Therefore the mark for 1900 had fourteen flames. In 1901 the same mark was used with the addition of a Roman numeral below to indicate the first year of the new century. Since that time the mark comprises the monogram, the fourteen flames and the Roman numeral of the particular year of the 20th century in which the object was made. See *Newcomb Pottery; Grueby, W.H.; McLaughlin, Mary Louise; Glaze,* in modern Western ceramics. (520)

Rörstrand In Swedish ceramics; a faïence manufactory was started at Rörstrand, near Stockholm, in 1725 by the Swedish Chamber of Commerce at the request of Johann Wolff. There were several changes in management. Its most flourishing period dates from 1753. Lead-glazed earthenware in the English style, known as flintporslin in Sweden, was included in the productions from around 1773 and by 1800 it had entirely supplanted faïence. From that time the wares had little artistic merit until a modern revival. Marks were rarely found from 1745. They included Stockholm or Rörstrand, occasionally both together either written in full or abbreviated, with the date, approximate

price and a painter's mark. The most characteristic work was in the Rococo style from around 1740 onward. Of particular distinction were the often fanciful Rococo forms and several original designs composed of chinoiseries and Rococo motifs. The practice of painting in opaque white on a greyish blue ground or bianco sopra bianco was much favored. The finest polychrome painted decoration was in high temperature colors. Some of the wares after 1760 reflected the influence of Marieberg and were painted in enamel colors and were decorated with applied fruit, flowers and foliage. The wares were widely diversified and in addition to the tablewares included tea trays, stoves and other very large pieces of faïence. Though other faïence factories of less importance were started at one time or another in Sweden none rivaled Rörstrand or Marieberg whose styles they copied and from where the majority of potters and painters working for them came. In the 19th century, in 1856-1857, bone china was added to their production while some hard paste porcelain was made here from the 1870's. At the end of the century Art Nouveau appeared in much of their work, initiated by the art director Alf Wallander. In the 20th century the designers Louise Adelberg and Gunnar Nylund pioneered in modern industrial tablewares which use to some degree the principal of functionalism, a development of the 1930's and 1940's. Such services are often in plain white with emphasis on the ceramic shape. Here, as elsewhere in Scandinavia, these industrial wares follow the general tendencies of the modern style, but a strong craft tradition indigenous to the Scandinavian countries is clearly evident in some of the modern table services which appear to express more clearly than others the nature and limitations of their material. From the middle of the 1950's the most significant design has concerned tablewares of strictly functional design and composition generally heat proof, and frequently in

S.ockholm

·HB

RORSTRAND
C. 1745

plain colors or else decorated with large simple motifs. Such services or sets of vessels are characteristic of the industrial wares produced not only at the three great Swedish factories—Rörstrand, Gustavsberg and the Upsala-Ekeby combine—but also at the ceramic factories of Finland. At Rörstrand such tableware has been designed by Hertha Bengtson and Marianne Westman. See *Bone China; Wolff, J.; Ingman, E. M.; Arabia.* (513)

Rosanjin, Kitaoji (1883-1959) Japanese artist-potter; belongs to that group of potters who devoted their life work to the revival and continuation of some of the traditional Japanese pottery styles. His wares show a deference to such traditional styles as Bizen, Oribe and Shino. (544)

Rose, John and Company See *Coalport.*

Rose, The or **De Roos** In Dutch ceramics; a pottery at Delft producing faïence from 1662 to 1858 under various proprietors including Jan Jansz Culick, a skillful potter who owned a third of this pottery in 1662. Celebrated among their early wares is a series of blue and white plates depicting scenes from the New Testament enclosed by borders and clouds in the manner of Italian grotesques, though the painting within is unmistakably Dutch. Chinese sets of five vases, three of baluster shape and two of beaker, were made there and became a common production at Delft. Known as Kast-stel or cupboard set they were intended for the five ledges on the molded cornice of the important Baroque style cupboard, an essential piece of furniture in every well-to-do house. See *Delft; Faïence.* (268)

Rose-Engine Turning See *Engine-Turned Decoration.*

Rose Medallion In Chinese ceramics; the name given to a green enameled dinner ware with medallions of people, pink flowers, birds and butterflies that became a popular export ware from late in the 18th century. Its popularity continued throughout the 19th century. Much of the ware was decorated at Canton and shipped from that port.

Rose-Pink See *Purple of Cassius; Colors; Colored Grounds; Monochrome Painting.*

Rose Pompadour In French ceramics; a pink ground color appearing on Sèvres in 1757 and attributed to Jean Hellot. The attribution is questionable. See *Sèvres.* (356, 357)

Rosenthal In German ceramics; this still-existing porcelain factory was started at Selb, Bavaria, in 1879 by Philip Rosenthal. One of the great German factories producing industrial wares. Important early designs include the Darmstadt and Donatello table services, dating from 1905 and 1907 respectively, and the Isolde service, 1910, which broke away from the attempt to integrate the handle in the general form. The original versions of these porcelain services were left white and without decoration; this feature to emphasize form was to become a characteristic of the Modern style. After the Second World War Philip Rosenthal, Jr., introduced a drastic reformation of style, directed against the slavish imitations of period style and the cult of purely functional form. His aim was to strike a proper balance and produce porcelain ware which combines functional perfection with aesthetic merit and individual appeal. To achieve this he enlisted the aid of the best contemporary artists and initiated the firm's Studio line. Included among the artists: Tapio Wirkkala, Finland; Bjorn Wiinblad, Denmark; Hans Theo Baumann, Germany; Raymond Loewy, United States; Ambrosio Pozzi, Italy; Walter Gropius and Louis A. McMillen (The Architects Collaborative); Emilio

THE ROSE
EARLY 18TH CENTURY

ROSENTHAL
C. 1880 ON

Pucci, Italy; Alain Le Foll, France, and many others. The elder Philip Rosenthal used to sign his porcelain with the family name. Their wares have always enjoyed a fine reputation. (497)

Roseville Pottery Company Established at Roseville, Ohio, in 1892; opened a second factory at Zanesville in 1898. Two years later, in 1900, the firm's aggressive manager, George Young, attracted by the success of Weller and Owens in the art pottery field, introduced Rozane, the name being a combination of the names Roseville and Zanesville. Rozane art ware, an underglaze decorated pottery made from local clays, won popular favor. It was cast in molds and ground-tinted by spraying and blending the colors by means of comprehensive air brushes. Then the decoration was painted with slip-colors on the damp clay and when thoroughly dry the ware was subjected to its first firing. Finally the glaze was applied and the ware was fired a second time. To match the Zanesville competition Roseville introduced new lines. The original Rozane became Rozane Royal to distinguish it from other new lines which included Rozane Woodland, Rozane Egypto, Rozane Mara (to compete with Weller's Sicardo) and Rozane Mongol. The last mentioned had a rich red color glaze resembling Chinese Sang de Boeuf, and was an important contribution to American art pottery. The names of the individual lines were not marked on the ware. Among the marks was a circle enclosing a rose and the name Rozane ware, the incised name Rozane, believed to have been used until 1906, and R. P. Co., used to around 1912. During this period Roseville was operating four factories. From around 1910 the production of art pottery, all of which was made at Zanesville, was increased and the mark was changed to an R enclosing a small v in the upper part of the letter R. New lines were introduced with increasing frequency. Even during the business depression of the 1930's,

R

ROSEVILLE POTTERY
COMPANY
1910 ON

Roseville continued to bring out new lines, which included Morning Glory, Laurel, Blackberry and Sunflower. However, after the Second World War art-pottery of this class began to lose its popularity. Finally, in 1954 this large commercial art-pottery, the last of the big three—all notably at Zanesville—ceased to operate. See *Weller, S. A.; Owens, J. B.; Art Nouveau.*

Rossetti, Dante Gabriel (1828-1882) English poet and painter; an impassioned medievalist. In all matters of taste Rossetti's influence has been enormous. He may be said to have rejuvenated the decorative arts both directly and indirectly in England.

Rössler, Wolf (1650–1717) One of the principal Hausmalerei of Nuremberg, 1680-1690. Signed pieces bear the initials WR in monogram. The most important pieces of the monogrammist WR are notable for their rich enamel colors. Biblical, pastoral and mythological subjects were favored themes for his painted decoration. (249)

Rosso Antico In English ceramics; the name given by Wedgwood to his unglazed red stoneware, dating at the latest from 1763, which was a refinement of the earlier red stonewares introduced by the Elers. The rose-engine-turned tablewares in this material bearing imitation Chinese seal-characters and occasionally ascribed to Elers, were in many instances manufactured by Wedgwood. After the introduction of his black basalt ware, the same styles and designs were applied to the red ware, which was then named rosso antico. Wedgwood always favored his black more than his red stoneware, as the latter, he is reputed to have said, reminded him too much of "red teapots." See *Engine-Turned Decoration; Wedgwood; Red Porcelain or Red China.* (422)

Rothman, Jerry (b. 1933) American potter-sculptor; working at Paramount, California. His work is representative of a new movement toward abstract pottery that has been evident in the United States since the later 1950's. The prominent leader in this movement has been Peter Voulkos of California. See *Voulkos, P.*

Rottenberg, Ena A 20th century designer furnishing designs for the Viennese Augarten porcelain factory. See *Vienna*. (501)

Rotterdam In Dutch ceramics, the principal tile-making center in Holland in the 17th century. Faïence-making dates here from 1612. The important Flower Pot or Bloempot faïence factory began before 1665 and continued in business until 1873. Members of the Aelmis family who operated the Flower Pot from 1691 to 1787 chiefly made tiles and tile pictures, but some blue and white trays are known. Cornelis Boumeester (1652-1733) was also a noted maker of tile pictures. He was well known for his many pieces with views of Rotterdam, seascapes with shipping, whaling scenes, and, much more seldom, landscapes with figures. The Aelmis pottery made free use of engravings while the compositions of Boumeester were usually original creations. See *Dutch Tiles; Tiles*.

Rouen In French ceramics; painted faïence of great distinction was made at the numerous factories located at Rouen, Seine-Inférieure, Normandy, from around and after 1670 which had a great formative influence on the faïence styles adopted in France, Germany and Holland. Evidence of decline was perceptible from around 1770-1780. A Rouen innovation introduced late in the 17th century was a decoration of lambrequins and formal scrolls; the term *lambrequin* being used to include all types of formal pendent lace-like ornament. The term *style rayonnant* was given to a characteristic type of Baroque design because of the radial treatment of its motifs, made from around 1690 to 1740. At its best the painted decoration which in-

cluded lambrequins, festoons, formal scrolls, flowers, cornucopias, armorial bearings and rarely figure subjects, had a splendid vitality and formality which was typically Baroque in spirit. Blue was the principal color used for this lambrequin style and its variants with their symmetrical radiating formal designs; however, other high temperature colors, especially a dull red, were also found. Rouen developed a distinctive and beautiful polychrome style reflecting Chinese and Baroque influence, 1720-1750. Probably the most beautiful and original Rouen polychrome decoration was in the Rococo style, 1745-1770. The style was remarkable for its ingenious and fanciful treatment of Rococo motifs. Pastoral landscapes, mythological subjects and Chinese motifs were given a new expression that was completely captivating. The simpler types of designs included the familiar à la corne. From around 1770 to 1780 faïence painted in colored enamels and inspired by Strasbourg, Meissen and Marseilles was made. The first French soft paste was made at Rouen. A patent was granted in 1673 to Louis Poterat which included the manufacture of porcelain. It seems that very little was actually made. See *Abaquesne, Masséot*. (269-275, 299)

Rouge Box In Chinese ceramics; the name given to a small container for holding vermilion which was used for signature seals. The box, which is usually made of porcelain, is circular and is rather flat. The cover is the same size and shape as the body part which holds the vermilion. The Japanese rouge box is generally made of lacquer.

Rouge de Cuivre In Chinese ceramics; the French name given to the underglaze red, which is a copper color, used during the Hsüan Tê period, 1426-1435. It was used either alone or with underglaze blue.

Rouletting In ceramics; an incised method of decorating, comprising simple repetitive patterns produced by the use of a roulette (a small wheel or disk having the desired pattern on its outer edge). Of very early origin, it was used, for instance, in ancient Roman times either alone or as an auxiliary for decorating pottery. (408)

Rouse and Turner See *American Pottery Company.*

Roussencq, Pierre See *Marans.*

ROYAL COPENHAGEN
C. 1775 ON

Royal Aller Vale and Watcombe Pottery Company In English ceramics; active at Torquay, Devon, from around 1901 to 1962, producing earthenwares. Formerly Aller Vale Art Pottery and Watcombe Pottery Company. See *Watcombe Pottery Company; Aller Vale Art Potteries.*

Royal Bayreuth See *Tettau.*

Royal Copenhagen In Danish ceramics; a porcelain manufactory was started around 1771-1772 in Copenhagen by F. H. Müller and is still in existence. A royal privilege was granted in 1775, and around 1779 the manufactory was taken over by the King. Its best period was from around 1780 to 1800; however, a modern revival dates from 1885. The factory mark was three wavy lines, one under the other, generally in underglaze blue symbolizing the three waterways through Denmark, The Little Belt, The Great Belt and The Sound. The hard paste porcelain made from around 1772 to 1779 was generally painted in underglaze blue, purple or iron red. Stylized floral patterns were much favored for this painting. The wares reflected the influence of Meissen and Fürstenberg. From around 1780 the Rococo style was supplanted by the Neo-Classic style. The painted decoration was in accordance with the contemporary German fashions. Medallion portrait heads in a grey monochrome or in black silhouette were very fashionable. Charming wreaths of small flowers painted in polychrome were also characteristic. A pale gilding was used on the severely clas-

ROZENBURG VASE

sic molded borders. The many figures were essentially copied from the models of other manufactories. Blue and white wares for daily use were also made and were generally decorated with slight formal floral patterns of German origin. In the early part of the 19th century the manufactory kept up with developments in the main European factories but rarely created usual styles of its own. Some time later in the century the production of figures, however, was given new life by the introduction of models by the celebrated Danish sculptor Thorwaldsen. In 1867 the factory ceased to be Royal except in name, as it was sold to a merchant named A. Flack, who was given permission to retain the name and mark. The revival at Copenhagen dates from 1882 when its effects were sold to the Aluminia ceramic factory. Under Philip Schou, who was appointed director in 1884, a period of reorganization and experimentation was initiated at Royal Copenhagen. Arnold Krog, who was appointed art director in 1885, introduced a style of underglaze painting which revealed a newly awakened understanding of nature and materials based on Japanese precepts. A technical development of the late 1880's was the introduction of painting in colored porcelain paste to achieve a relief effect, a method used by C. F. Lüsberg and later by Krog. Late in the century the great concern with the color possibilities and textural effects of glazing as a means of artistic expression, another facet of influence from the Far East, affected Copenhagen. No doubt the Danish tradition for glazes on stoneware can be traced to the spadework done in the early 20th century by Patrick Nördstrom at Copenhagen. In time Copenhagen as well as Bing and Grøndahl developed a perfect glazing technique and their experimental work was to benefit the Danish stoneware production as a whole. The tradition of figure-making was carried on. During the inter-war period porcelain was still used, as in the figures in a narrative style mod-

eled by Gerhard Henning and Arno Malinowski. But from the 1930's onward stoneware was chiefly used as a material for
figure-making, such as those of Knud
Kyhn, Jais Nielsen and Helge Christoffersen. The fashion for dinner services of
strictly functional design and composition, usually heat resisting, is seen in a service designed in 1957 by Magnus
Stephensen. See *Luplau, A. C.; Thorwaldsen,
B.; Bayer, J. C.; Hald, A.; Müller, F. H.; Aluminia; Quodlibetz; Glaze,* in modern Western
ceramics; *Salto, Axel; Krog, Arnold; Japanism;
Flora Danica.* (379-381, 477, 485-487, 506,
509, 533, 535, 551, 552)

Royal Crown Derby Porcelain Company, Ltd.
Established in 1876. See *Derby.*

Royal Danish Porcelain Manufactory See
Royal Copenhagen.

Royal Doulton   See *Doulton.*

Royal Dux   See *Dux.*

Royal Lancastrian   See *Pilkington's Tile and
Pottery Company.*

Royal Porcelain Manufactory   See *Berlin.*

Royal Sphinx   See *Maastricht.*

Royal Worcester See *Worcester; Worcester
Royal Porcelain Company, Ltd.*

Royal Worcester Ltd. See *Worcester Royal Porcelain Company, Ltd.*

Rozane Ware See *Roseville Pottery.*

Rozenburg In Dutch ceramics; established
in the last quarter of the 19th century at the
Hague. From 1885 to 1889 the well-known
painter T. A. C. Colenbrander was its artistic leader. Here he introduced his original and striking patterns inspired by
Javanese batik-printed textiles. Under the
leadership of J. Jurriaan Kok a striking Art
Nouveau style was achieved in porcelain at
Rozenburg which was expressed not only
in the decoration but also in the form. Per-

haps the most perfected expression of the
Art Nouveau style in ceramics was to be
found in the wares of Rozenburg made
around 1900 and the years immediately
following. Especially notable were the porcelain vases designed by Kok and painted
by J. Schellink at Rozenburg. See *Colenbrander, T. A. C.* (517)

Rubati, Pasquale See *Milan.*

Rubens, Peter Paul (1577-1640) Celebrated
Flemish painter. The paintings of Rubens
influenced the art work of Europe, especially Catholic Europe, for the first half of
the 17th century. After studying in Italy
and Spain for eight years he returned to
Antwerp in 1608 and in the following year
he was appointed court painter. During his
years of study he had acquired such facility
in arranging large scale compositions and
of using light and color to increase the
general effect of more movement and contrast that he had no rival north of the Alps.
He accepted commissions from the rulers
of Spain, France and Flanders. In so doing
he was instrumental in spreading Roman
Baroque art through Europe. Rubens devoted much time to the study of antique
carvings in which field he became a leading
authority. This same vitality, richness, fullness and movement were also evident in
his ornament. It is easy to understand why
Rubens is regarded as the originator of
the Baroque movement in the Netherlands
and one of its principal transmitters in
Europe. See *Baroque.*

Ruby Back Porcelain In Chinese ceramics;
see *Canton.*

Rudolstadt In German ceramics; a faïence
factory was started at Rudolstadt in the
Thuringia region in 1720 by Johann Philipp Frantz and D. C. Fleischhauer of
Dorotheenthal. It remained active until at
least 1791. It is believed that most of the
wares are of the usual Thuringian types. In
1882 L. Straus & Sons started a porcelain
factory at Rudolstadt, producing luxury

ROZENBURG
C. 1885-1900

RUDOLSTADT
STRAUS AND SONS
C. 1882 ON

RUE AMELOT
1786-1793

RUE DE RONDY
C. 1780-1793

RUE DE CRUSSOL
C. 1789

RUE DE LA ROQUETTE

OLLIVIER
C. 1770 ON

SOUROUX
1773 ON

DUBOIS, VINCENT
1774 ON

and fanciful articles. It is no longer in business. Included among the many marks were the Schwarzburg coat-of-arms and the initials R W enclosed in a diamond with a crown above. See *Volkstedt.*

Rue Amelot In French ceramics; a hard paste porcelain manufactory was located on the Rue Amelot in 1786 under the protection of the Duc d'Orléans. The mark L P was registered in 1786. It is believed that the manufactory at an earlier time was located in the Rue des Boulets and the Pont-aux-Choux, respectively. Essentially the wares were of little artistic importance. Especially typical of its painted decoration was a design of strewn flowers, generally of roses. See *Paris Porcelain.*

Rue de Bondy In French ceramics; a hard paste porcelain manufactory was started in 1780 on the Rue de Bondy, Paris, by Dihl with the patronage of the Duc d'Angoulême. In 1795 it was moved to the Rue du Temple and in 1825 to the Boulevard Saint-Martin. It closed in 1829. Tablewares were the principal productions and they varied in decoration from simply painted floral designs to richly painted and gilded elaborate designs. Especially characteristic and charming were the simply decorated wares with sprig patterns of cornflowers. Biscuit figures were also made. Included among the marks were A G in monogram either with or without a crown. See *Paris Porcelain.*

Rue de Crussol In French ceramics; a hard paste porcelain manufactory was started in Paris in 1789 by Christopher Potter, an Englishman. He named it the "Manufacture du Prince de Galles," and operated it until around 1792. Subsequently it changed hands several times. Included among the marks were Potter, E B and P B in underglaze blue. The productions were decorated in the contemporary Paris styles. See *Paris Porcelain.*

Rue de la Roquette In French ceramics; a leading center in Paris for the manufacture of faïence and porcelain. A faïence manufactory was conducted by Digne around 1750. Spouted pharmacy vases painted in the Rouen style are ascribed to this manufactory. Another manufactory at a somewhat later date was operated by Ollivier and made principally tile stoves. It is believed that a soft paste porcelain manufactory was conducted here by François Hébert and that the mark of crossed arrows was used. A hard paste porcelain manufactory was conducted here by Souroux who registered S as a mark in 1773. From 1774 a hard paste porcelain manufactory was operated by Vincent Dubois. Hard paste porcelain with the mark of two crossed arrows with the points pointing upward is believed to have been made at Dubois' manufactory. These pieces bearing this mark are similar to the usual Paris types. See *Paris Porcelain; Chicaneau, Pierre.*

Rue de la Ville L'Evêque Also Faubourg Saint-Honoré. See *Chicaneau, Pierre; Saint-Cloud.*

Rue du Temple See *Rue de Bondy.*

Rue Fontaine-au-Roy See *La Courtille.*

Rue Popincourt In French ceramics; a hard paste porcelain manufactory was established in 1782 in Paris by J. N. H. Nast. After 1784 it was known as Rue Amandiers Popincourt. The manufactory, which was active until 1835, enjoyed a flourishing business; however, the productions were of little artistic importance. All types of wares were made, including tablewares, clock cases, ink stands and biscuit figures. The mark was Nast stencilled in red. See *Paris Porcelain.*

Rue Thiroux In French ceramics; a hard paste porcelain manufactory was started around 1775 by Leboeuf under the protection of Marie Antoinette. The mark registered in 1776 was an A and the wares were known as "porcelaine de la Reine." After changing hands several times it was still active in 1869. The 18th century porcelain was admirable for its fine quality and for its delicately and slightly painted floral designs of cornflowers and roses executed in excellent taste. See *Paris Porcelain*.

Rusafa   See *Islamic Pottery, Medieval*.

Russia   Porcelain and faïence were not made in Russia until the 18th century. The manufacture of tin-glazed earthenware was introduced in the 18th century but little of artistic value was produced. The manufacture of porcelain has had a continuous existence in Russia from 1758 when the Imperial manufactory at St. Petersburg was established. The Imperial

Ruskin Pottery   In English ceramics; started by W. Howson Taylor (1876-1935) at Smethwick near Birmingham, in 1898. It closed in 1935, several months before the death of Mr. Taylor. This art pottery produced earthenwares principally decorated solely with elaborate glaze effects. See *Glaze*, in modern Western ceramics.

manufactory was followed by the establishment of a few relatively important private manufactories near Moscow. Of these only the Francis Gardner continued into the 19th century. From the reign of Alexander I, 1801-1825, smaller porcelain manufactories came into existence. In the 18th century Russian manufactories began to make figures in glazed or unglazed (biscuit) porcelain in the manner of Meissen. In the ensuing century these figures became characteristically Russian, representing all classes, many in brilliantly colored native costumes and characteristic attitudes. The vitality and striking charm of these call forth the atmosphere of old Russia. See *Gardner, Francis; Iusupov; Batenin, Sergei; Novyi; Popov; Kudinov; Fomin; Safronov; Kiselev; Kornilov; Khrapunov-Novyi; Sabanin; Miklashevskii; Kuznetsov; Ghzel'; Sipiagin; Dunashov*.

Russian Imperial Manufactory   See *Russia; Iusupov; St. Petersburg*.

Rustiques Figulines   See *Palissy, B.*

Ruyckevelt, Van   See *Worcester*.

RUE THIROUX
1776-1790

RUSKIN POTTERY
C. 1898 ON

RUE DE BONDY EWER AND
BASIN

S

S and S See *Southwick Pottery*.

Saar Basin In German ceramics; the fine quality clays of the Saar Basin were employed not only at Sarreguemines (German Saargemünd) but also at Ottweiler, Saarbrücken and especially at the 19th century pottery of Mettlach where the Brothers Boch of Septfontaines joined with the family of Villeroy to start a great ceramic industry in 1841. See *Sarreguemines; Ottweiler; Villeroy and Boch*.

Saargemünd See *Sarreguemines*.

Sabanin, Vavila Dmitrievich (d. c.1874) In Russian ceramics; worked for his relative A. G. Popov, whose porcelain manufactory was the third most important in Russia, before starting his own kiln in the village of Klimovka in Vladimir province around 1850. The early porcelains were equal to those of Popov. Especially charming were the figures. The later wares were less successful. Ceased operations around 1875. Among the marks were Of the Factory of V. Sabanin. See *Russia*.

Sabrina In English ceramics; the name given to earthenware with a crystalline glaze made at the Worcester Royal Porcelain Company for around the first thirty years of the 20th century. It was the outcome of research and experiment which proved that porcelain hardened by firing to a degree which leaves it still porous, treated by saturation with certain metallic salts, and subjected to suitable atmospheric conditions before final firing, acquires a distinction of color and beauty of appearance not obtainable by superficial methods. During the process in which the porcelain is impregnated with its colors, and also during the process of firing, the various mineral salts which are absorbed by the paste crystallize and produce starry points and luminous clouding seen in many specimens. Beyond determining the general scheme of color and design, the final effects were not under the control of the operator. The name *Sabrina* was derived from the Roman goddess of the River Severn, on whose bank the Worcester factory stands. See *Worcester; Crystalline Glaze*.

Sacrificios See *Teotihuacan; Huaxtec*.

Sadler, John (1720-1789) Engraver for transfer-printing at Liverpool, 1756-1770. He was a partner of Guy Green. See *Liverpool; Green, G*.

Safavid See *Islamic Pottery, Later*.

Safronov In Russian ceramics; a manufactory was started in the village of Korotkaia near Moscow in 1830 by Anton Trofimovich Safronov which made porcelain of fine as well as mediocre quality. It was active for around fifteen or twenty years. See *Russia*.

Saggar or **Sagger** In ceramics; a refractory fireclay box in which ware is packed in a kiln to protect it from the direct action of the flames and fumes. The term is supposed to be a corruption of *safeguard*.

Saint-Amand-les-Eaux In French ceramics; a faïence manufactory was started at Saint-Amand-les-Eaux, Nord, by P. J. Fauquez. The factory was active until the French Revolution. Around 1800 the factory was acquired by the Bettignies family, who operated it until 1882. Much of the faïence was in imitation of Rouen and Strasbourg. The early painted decoration was in high temperature colors, while during the second half of the 18th century the polychrome painted decoration was in enamel colors. A factory mark of F's and P's in

monogram was sometimes found. Cream-colored and white earthenware in the English style was also made in the late 18th and 19th centuries. Soft paste porcelain was also made from around 1771 to 1778 and was resumed after 1800, principally producing copies of Sèvres and other soft paste porcelain.

St. Anthony's Pottery In English ceramics; active at Newcastle-on-Tyne, Northumberland, from about 1780–1878, producing creamwares, earthwares, and the like. It was operated by Sewell from around 1804 to 1828, when some fine lustered pottery was made. From 1828 to 1852 it was Sewell and Donkin and subsequently Sewell and Company.

Saint-Clément In French ceramics; a faïence manufactory was started at Saint-Clément, Meurthe-et-Moselle, in 1758 by Jacques Chambrette as a branch of the Lunéville factory. It changed hands several times and was active until late in the 19th century. The factory produced a fine enameled and gilt faïence closely resembling the faïence made at Sceaux. Figures were made in faïence painted in enamel colors, and also in biscuit in the manner of Lunéville. Much cream-colored earthenware of a good quality was also produced. It seems no factory mark was in use until the 19th century when St. Clément and St Ct were employed. See *Faïence Fine.*

Saint-Cloud In French ceramics; a soft paste porcelain manufactory, also making faïence, was active at Saint-Cloud, Seine-et-Oise, from before 1678 to 1766. It is regarded as the first important French porcelain manufactory. It was started by Pierre Chicaneau (d. 1678) and letters patent were granted to his family in 1702. Saint-Cloud had a branch manufactory in the Rue de la Ville L'Evêque, Paris. A sun face and a fleur-de-lis were registered as marks in 1696; however, the latter is very rare. The well-known factory mark St C over T, usually in blue and often accompanied by other letters, dots, and crosses, was apparently not used until after 1722. It seems that Saint-Cloud figures never bore the factory mark. Much of the charm of Saint-Cloud porcelain is in the material itself which at its best is a rather warm ivory tone with a distinctive firm and smooth texture. The porcelain often closely resembled the Chinese Blanc de Chine. Of particular interest were the forms with their beautiful and refined lines. Baroque lacework scrolls painted in blue were a favorite decoration and were executed with delicacy and grace. Figures, which were often left unpainted, were admirably modeled. The porcelain from around 1730 to 1750 strongly reflected the influence of Meissen. Chinese Famille Verte porcelain and the Japanese Kakiemon styles were frequently the inspiration for the painted decoration. (300, 343, 344)

Saint-Jean-du-Désert In French ceramics; an early center for French faïence. Italian potters were working at Saint-Jean-du-Désert, which is a suburb of Marseilles, as early as the 16th century. See *Marseilles; Clérissy, Pierre and Joseph.*

St. Petersburg In Russian ceramics; the Russian Imperial Porcelain Manufactory was established in 1744 under the protection of the Empress Elizabeth. However, it was not until almost twenty years later that the manufacture of hard paste porcelain was successfully conducted. Evidence of artistic decline became perceptible around 1825; however, since 1917 the manufactory has enjoyed a modern revival. The marks were principally monograms and imperial emblems according to the different reigns. Under Catherine II, 1762-1796, good porcelains were made in the fashionable French, German and Viennese styles. The Rococo yielded to the Neo-Classic. A famous dinner service, known as Arabesque, and comprising almost one thousand pieces, was made, 1784-1785. Decorated with Pompeian scrolls and

SAINT-CLOUD TEAPOT

SAINT-CLOUD

PORCELAIN 1696 ON

PORCELAIN 1722 ON

1762-1796

1894-1917

SALAMANDER WORKS
1848

small cameo-medallions, its inspiration was from one produced at Sèvres. Later Sèvres porcelain in the Empire style was closely imitated. Classical vases decorated with minutely worked copies of oil paintings and broad areas of plain gilding were typical of this taste. In the last quarter of the 18th century figures modeled in the round were produced in painted enamels and in biscuit. Russian folk-types were popular subjects. In the succeeding Empire style idealized peasant figures prevailed. See *Russia*. (383, 384)

Saint-Porchaire In French ceramics; a white earthenware with inlaid decoration was made at Saint-Porchaire from around 1525 to 1560. There are about sixty surviving examples. The ware is quite unlike any other ceramic ware both in respect to its extreme fragility and in the unusual technique of its inlaid decoration. The intricate inlaid decoration, comprising French Renaissance motifs, was produced by impressing the soft white clay body with metal stamps and filling the impressions with different colored clays, chiefly brown, black and reddish or ochre yellow. It was covered with a transparent ivory-colored lead glaze. Some of the elaborate specimens such as ewers, candlesticks and salt-cellars were of architectural forms and were lavishly ornamented with applied Renaissance motifs such as statuettes, cupids, masks, grotesques and cherubs. Occasionally the reliefs were lightly touched with colored glazes of green, purple and blue. The ware is also called Henri Deux or Henri II. This Renaissance style was revived in the mid-19th century. In France the style appeared at Choisy-le-Roi and other factories, while in England some elaborate work in this manner was done at Minton and Wedgwood. See *Gien*. (201, 202)

Saint-Verain In French ceramics; a fine earthenware which can be distinguished by its color which is always a rather dark

shade of blue, made at Saint-Verain, Nièvre, in the 17th century.

Saint-Yrieix In French ceramics; the chief source of kaolin and petuntse in France was at Saint-Yrieix, near Limoges, Haute-Vienne, and thus Limoges came to be the great ceramic center that it is still today. Marc-Hilaire Vilaris, an apothecary of Bordeaux, assisted the Sèvres chemists in the discovery of the kaolin of Saint-Yrieix in 1768. A porcelain medallion in the Musée Adrien-Dubouché in Limoges bears on the revere side in inscription, "First porcelain of Limousin clay 1771." The town of Limoges was formerly the capital of the old province of Limousin.

Salamander Works In American ceramics; active at 54 Cannon Street, New York City, in 1848. Included among their wares were brown glazed earthenware pitchers with relief decoration. See *Relief-Decorated Wares*.

Salopian In English ceramics; see *Caughley*.

Salt, Ralph (1782–1846) English potter working at Hanley in the Staffordshire district from around 1820–1846. Chiefly known for his earthenware figures and chimney ornaments painted in colors in the manner of the Staffordshire figure-maker John Walton, with similar bocages. His figures are marked with his surname. He was succeeded by his son, Charles (d. c. 1864). See *Walton, John*.

Salt Cellar A container or vessel used on the table for holding salt. Salt cellars played an important part on the table in the medieval and Renaissance periods, and for this reason a wealth of ornament was lavished on them. Especially typical of this taste is the 16th century French Saint-Porchaire standing salt. This type of salt container varied in height from about seven to sixteen inches. It was placed in the center of the table and had a special social significance as it divided the host and his more important guests from the less important guests who sat "beneath the salt." "White" salt-glazed stoneware was made from the very end of the 17th century; however, the Staffordshire potters continued to improve it, making it both whiter and lighter in weight. Large quantities of this improved ware were made between the years 1740 and 1760 when practically every pottery throughout the country was making it. The growing popularity of cream-colored earthenware brought about its downfall.

Salt Glaze In ceramics; a thin hard film of glaze made on the surface of stoneware by throwing salt into the kiln at the point of highest temperature during the only firing. The brown color which is so characteristic of salt-glaze ware is made by applying a wash of clay rich in iron oxide to the surface of the stoneware before it is fired in the kiln. Black was also obtained by a wash of ferruginous clay. The colors blue and purple are produced from cobalt and manganese oxides, respectively. In English ceramics; the name is familiarly used for Staffordshire salt-glazed stoneware. The majority of salt cellars made no distinction between the highest and the lowest. The low salt dish or open salt was a fashionable 18th century form. (202, 350, 363) See *Glaze; Rhenish Stoneware; Staffordshire.* (408-420)

Salto, Axel (d. 1961) Danish artist-potter working at Royal Copenhagen where he concentrated on glaze effects. In the 1930's he introduced vases with sculptured relief decoration in which his "grooved," "budding" and "germinating" sculptured relief style is used primarily as a vehicle for emphasizing the play of color in the glaze. His style expressed strongly the relationship of material and glaze. See *Glaze*, in modern Western ceramics; *Royal Copenhagen.* (506, 551, 552)

Samarra See *Near East,* in prehistoric ceramics.

Samian In Roman ceramics; clay wares of Samos. Pliny uses the word in this sense when he writes in 77 A.D., "the Samian to this day is appreciated as a tableware." However, as early as the second century B.C. in the plays of Plautus the word Samian is clearly used in the generic sense of "made of clay." Pliny's wording suggests that the manufacture had been long established in Samos while the earlier reference implies that the wares were so well known to the Romans that the word became synonymous with clay. The identity of this very early ware has never been satisfactorily established.

Samson and Company In French ceramics; a still-existing manufacturer, located in Paris since the early 19th century, specializing in the reproductions of collectible wares of various countries and periods, such as Chelsea, Meissen and Famille Verte. It is claimed that all Samson's imitations bear one of several trade marks. For example, many Samson copies of English porcelains bear a painted mark resembling two crossed S's; while a rectangular pseudo-Chinese hallmark in red with a running S beside it appears on copies of Oriental Lowestoft. The consoling feature of a Samson mark is the establishment of the manufacturer, as up to this time no one has copied Samson.

SAMSON AND COMPANY

San Ts'ai In Chinese ceramics; see *Three-Color Ware.*

Sanda See *Celadon,* in Japanese ceramics.

Sanders, Herbert (b. 1909) American artist-potter and teacher; his work includes decorative and utilitarian pottery and porcelain forms. Many of these are glazed with the crystalline glazes for which he is especially well known. He is the author of POTTERY AND CERAMIC SCULPTURE, 1964.

Sang de Boeuf In Chinese ceramics; a beautiful red-glazed porcelain of the Ch'ing dynasty, especially of the K'ang Hsi reign. The body of the ware is white or greyish white and is of a fine texture. The red glaze, which is made from copper, is glassy with minute pores and bubbles. There is always a minute delicate crackle that is hardly distinguishable. The red glaze has a tendency to run or fall, and, especially in the K'ang Hsi pieces, forms a welt at the base but does not run over. In many of the later pieces the glaze was allowed to run over the bottom and had to be ground off. The red glaze often slips down from the lip rim and sometimes off the shoulder exposing portions of buff or greenish white. The color appears to be a blend of tiny blotches of blood-colored particles, or at times larger splotches, when it is called strawberry red. Many pieces are streaked with grey. Sometimes the ware is the color of ashes of roses or a harmonious blend of red, rose, grey and green. The foot is usually well formed and does not have any red glaze underneath. The glaze under the base is occasionally olive green, clear or mottled. Sometimes it has red or pink splotches, or at times it is a buff or pale green crackle. Usually the inside has a greenish or buff crackled glaze. Sang de Boeuf is also called Ox Blood and Lang Yao. See *Chi Hung.*

Sang de Pigeon In Chinese ceramics; a crimson or liver red porcelain ware commonly called Sang de Pigeon. It is stated that this ware was first made late in the K'ang Hsi reign. However, the only examples known at the present time are of the Yung Chêng reign as well as those produced during the late 19th century. The red glaze is produced from copper oxide and is at times a deep rich color. The texture of the glaze is perfectly even and is usually dull, pitted with minute pores, or at times it is glossy.

Sango Toki In Japanese ceramics; an important industrial manufactory producing

SATSUMA VASE

porcelain dinner services started in 1932 at Sango, a section of Seto. See *Japanese Contemporary Pottery.*

Sansovino, Jacopo (1486-1570) Italian architect and sculptor who arrived in Venice from Rome in 1527. His architectural forms and style of ornament provided the initiative for a new style that was the harbinger of the Venetian Baroque. See *Renaissance; Baroque.*

Santa Maria Urn See *Argentina and Chile.*

Sarreguemines (Fr.) or **Saargemünd (Germ.)** In European ceramics; a considerable faïence manufactory was started at Sarreguemines, in Lorraine, around 1770 by Paul Utzschneider and managed throughout the 19th century by his descendants. The wares were generally marked with the name of the town, Sarreguemines or U.S. in a triangle or U & Cie in an octagon. The production was of a wide variety including cream-colored wares and stonewares in the Wedgwood style, and fine red, brown, lustered and marbled lead-glazed earthenwares. See *Saar Basin.*

Satsuma In Japanese ceramics; shortly after the beginning of the 17th century kilns were established at Chosa Village in the Shimazu fief of Satsuma, present Kagoshima Prefecture, by two Korean potters, father and son, Kim Hae and Kim Hwa. The Chosa kilns, which were active for only a short period, produced pottery of the Karatsu type chiefly intended for the tea ceremony. Today the term *Old Satsuma* is reserved only for the earliest wares of the Chosa kilns, though the same variety of Karatsu continued to be made long after. Included among the other kilns in the Kagoshima Prefecture producing Satsuma pottery were those at Tateno, Ryumonji and Nayeshirogawa. Later, toward the end of the 18th century, polychrome enameled Satsuma pottery on a cream-colored ground and crackled glaze in the Kyo ware tradition was first made. The nishiki or

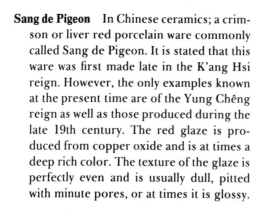

brocaded pattern in colored enamels and gold was much favored. From around 1850 onward brocaded satsuma export wares with crowded designs and extravagant enameling and gilding were developed to appeal to 19th century European taste. In time Satsuma export wares were also produced in quite different parts of Japan. See *Karatsu.*

Sattler, Wilhelm and his son. See *Aschach.*

Sava See *Islamic Pottery, Medieval.*

Savin, Maurice Louis (b. 1894) French painter, sculptor and ceramist. Exhibited regularly at the Salon d'Automne. Also shown in Switzerland, England and Japan. His work is more that of a ceramic sculptor than of a potter of vessels. In the years after the Second World War he tended to use earthenware, especially with a tin glaze, as a medium for figure making and for other purely decorative purposes.

Savona In Italian ceramics; a considerable faïence manufacture was carried on during the 17th and 18th centuries at the Ligurian coast towns of Savona, Albissola and Genoa. However, little exact information is available about their productions which are generally grouped under Savona, probably the leading center. The faïence made at Delft was the principal influence. Chinese, Spanish and French influences were also evident in some of the designs. Included among the characteristic wares were pharmacy vases, vases with two handles, plates and dishes with flat rims and tea table wares. The early work was only in blue and white. Later other high temperature colors were used and much effective work was achieved in different polychrome styles. The painted decoration was often admirable for its fine drawings. Of particular interest was a variety with cupids, horsemen and other figure subjects depicted against a mountain landscape and painted either in blue or in polychrome on a greenish toned ground. Other equally

interesting styles were also developed. See *Faïence.*

Savy, Honoré See *Perrin, Veuve.*

Sawankhalok See *Indo-China.*

Saxbo In Danish ceramics; a pottery established in 1929; its production was chiefly a collaboration between Nathalie Krebs, the proprietor, and Eva Staehr-Nielsen. In its classic form, the Saxbo stoneware was precisely shaped and decorated solely by its figured glaze effects. Since the mid-1950's the range of Saxbo ware has considerably expanded to include new decorative techniques and materials. (553)

Saxe In French ceramics; the term *Saxe porcelain* was the name given in France to Meissen porcelain. See *Meissen.*

Scale Pattern In European ceramics; a diaper arrangement or a repetitive pattern resembling overlapping fish scales. Especially characteristic was the English Worcester scale-blue used from around 1765 to 1785, and the more unusual scale-pink. Similar monochrome patterns in purple, green, yellow and other colors were used particularly for borders on Meissen, Berlin and Vienna porcelain from around and after 1760 and were known as Mosaïk.

Scarab Vase See *Robineau, A. A.*

Sceaux In French ceramics; a porcelain and faïence manufactory was started at Sceaux, Seine, probably as early as 1735 with Jacques Chapelle as manager and later owner, under the patronage of the Duchesse de Maine. The manufactory changed hands several times. The wares revealed little artistic merit after 1810. From late in the 18th century cream-colored earthenware was also added to the productions. It is doubtful that much porcelain was made before 1763. The mark S X was submitted for porcelain in 1773. The influence of Mennecy and Sèvres was evident in the

SCALE BORDER ON WORCESTER PLATE

SCEAUX
1773 ON

SCHNABELKRUG, SIEGBURG
STONEWARE

SCHLAGGENWALD
1832-1846

$\dfrac{S}{CB}$

SCHLESWIG
1756 ON

porcelain. Flower painting in blue similar to that found on Mennecy porcelain was much favored. Some of the painted decoration was obviously done by the same artist who painted the faïence. The faïence, which was of fine quality, was painted in enamel colors and gilt in the style of porcelain, and ranks among the best of its kind. The early faïence wares reflected the styles of Mennecy and Vincennes. The faïence in the Louis XVI style was distinctive for its refinement and elegant simplicity. The painted decoration included birds, flowers, foliage, cupids and exquisite pastoral scenes executed in the style of contemporary Sèvres painting. Tablewares were the principal production. Finely modeled faïence figures frequently closely copied from Sèvres were also made. Included among the faïence marks were O P and S P, the latter being of a later date. (283)

Schäper, Johann (1621-1670) Celebrated German artist-enameler; one of the most influential of the German Hausmalerei working at Nuremberg, painting mainly in black enamel (schwarzlot) on glass and faïence. Schäper's technique was derived from the later Dutch painters of window-glass roundels, and reveals a similar use of lines scratched through the pigment with a needle point to appear white on a black ground. Extant examples of his signed paintings on faïence appear on about twelve jugs. The subjects were principally landscapes, generally with ruins, painted in bands around the vessel or in circular or oval panels. His style of painting was highly regarded by his contemporaries, and, as a result, his name is often given to a school of painting carried on by a number of followers using a similar black-enamel technique, notably J. L. Faber, Hermann Benckerett and the Bohemians Daniel and Ignaz Preissler. See *Schwarzlot; Faber, J. L.; Benckertt, Hermann; Preissler, Daniel.* (248, 333, 334)

Scharvogel, Julius German artist-potter who, around 1900, started an art studio in Munich where he produced stoneware with thick, flowing glazes. Formerly he had worked for the German potters Villeroy and Boch at their Mettlach pottery. In 1906 he was appointed director of the Grand Ducal Ceramic Factory in Darmstadt where he was responsible for stoneware with studied glaze effects.

Scheid, Karl German artist-potter, whose reputation dates from after the Second World War; worked for a time in the early 1950's with Harry Davis in England. His work is excellently decorated and glazed.

Scheier, Edwin and May American 20th century artist-potters; most of their pieces are made on the wheel and are notable for their simplicity. As a rule the principal decoration is the simple and effective striping which follows the motion of the wheel, a characteristic of Scheier pottery.

Schepers, Livio Ottavio And his son Gaetano. Of South Netherlands (now Belgium) origin; potters at Capo di Monte from 1743 onward. Gaetano was in charge of the manufactory at Buen Retiro for a brief period from 1759. His son Carlos (d. 1783) was director at Buen Retiro, 1770-1783; another son Sebastiano was active there as potter and chemist until 1802.

Scheurich, Paul German figure modeler working at the Schwarzburger Werkstätten, 1908-1913, and in the post-war period at Meissen, Nymphenburg and Berlin. His modeled figures for Berlin possessed the finest effect. See *Schwarzburger Werkstätten; Pfeiffer, M. A.* (526)

Schihan, Gunda See *Wiener Keramik.*

Schilkin, Michael See *Arabia.*

Schlaggenwald In Bohemian ceramics; a porcelain manufactory was active here from around 1793 to 1866. In addition to the name of the place the marks include S and L & H in a shield, the latter the mark of Lippert and Haas, 1832 to 1846. See *Austria, Czechoslovakia and Hungary.*

Schleswig In German ceramics; a faïence factory was started here in 1755 (which at this time belonged to Denmark) by the arcanist Johann Christian Ludwig von Lücke who left in the following year. Its best productions were those made from 1756 to 1773. It closed in 1814. Schleswig faïence is characterized by a good quality glaze and a preference for Rococo in both modeled and painted decoration. Although painting in muffle-colors was sometimes used, the characteristic Schleswig decoration is a high-temperature manganese-purple (especially adopted since the importation of blue and white was forbidden in Copenhagen, the factory's principal market). Combined with it are typical greyish and yellowish greens. Some of the finest pieces are bowls for bishop, a kind of punch favored here, in the form of a bishop's mitre. Some outstanding pieces in blue and white with figure subjects within rich Rococo scrollwork of characteristic Scandinavian type are notable. The factory employed many good artists, preeminently Johann Leihamer, an accomplished figure painter who was to play an important role in the Schleswig-Holstein faïence industry.

Schleswig-Holstein See *Leihamer, Johann; Buchwald, Johann; Schleswig; Eckernförde; Kiel; Stockelsdorf; Rendsburg; Kellinghusen.*

Schmuz-Baudiss, Theo Art director at the Royal Porcelain Factory in Berlin, 1908-1926, where his arrival in 1902 initiated an important period of activity. He was particularly concerned with the use of rich floral patterning and he was responsible for some elegant and sumptuous services.

Schnabelkrug or **Schnabelkanne** In German ceramics; a Rhenish stoneware jug with a long beak-like spout. It was a very popular form for the Siegburg wares made during the late 16th and first half of the 17th centuries. See *Rhenish Stoneware.* (189)

Schnelle In German ceramics; a tall tankard having straight sides tapering upwards

and generally having roll moldings at the mouth and at the foot. The form, which was taken from a wooden prototype, was a characteristic form for Rhenish stoneware during the 16th and early 17th centuries. See *Pinte; Rhenish Stoneware.* (190)

Schönheit, Johann Carl (1730-1805) Modeler at Meissen, 1745-1805.

Schönwald In German ceramics; a porcelain factory (a sister company to the Kahla porcelain factory in Thuringia) was started here in 1879 by J. N. Müller. In 1898 it was incorporated and the firm became Porzellanfabrik Schönwald A.G. In 1927 the firm was united with the still existing Kahla. The modern style of table service has been notably established here since the Second World War.

Schrattenhofen In German ceramics; see *Oettingen-Schrattenhofen.*

Schraub-Flasch In German ceramics; a four- or six-sided flask made with a metal screw stopper. It is identified with the brown salt-glazed stoneware made at Kreussen, near Bayreuth, during the 17th century. Each corner was marked by a fantastic caryatid or a column and the panels were framed in rope or chain designs executed in relief. See *Kreussen.* (247)

Schrezheim In German ceramics; a faïence manufactory of considerable importance was started at Schrezheim, near Ellwagen in Württemberg, in 1752 by Johann Baptist Bux with a privilege from the Prince-Archbishop of Trèves. Evidence of decline was perceptible before 1800. The factory was active until 1862. The mark was a sprig of box conventionalized to resemble an arrow-head. Especially characteristic were tureens in the form of vegetables, fruits and different animals' heads. Helmet-shaped ewers, cylindrical tankards, jugs, coffee pots and pitchers were included in their productions. The painted decoration was generally in polychrome; blue and

SCHNELLE, SIEBURG
STONEWARE

SCHONWALD
1898 ON

SCHREZHEIM
1752 ON

white was seldom found. During the 19th century the manufactory principally reproduced the 18th century wares in a lead-glazed earthenware.

Schuchard, Georg In German ceramics; started a partnership with E. K. Rousset in 1799 at Magdeburg for producing cream-colored earthenware in the English style. Schuchard succeeded Rousset in 1806 and his family continued the work until 1865. The wares were marked with the name or distinguishing initials, impressed.

SCHWARZBURGER
WERKSTATTEN FUR
PORZELLANKUNST
1908 ON

Schumann, Carl Porzellanfabrik A. G. See *Arzberg.*

Schwanthaler, Franz (1760-1820) And his more famous son, Ludwig. Modelers at Nymphenburg during the first half of the 19th century.

Schwarzburger Werkstätten Für Porzellankunst In German ceramics; the manufacture of art porcelain was started at Unterweissbach in Schwarzburg-Rudolstadt in 1908 by Max Adolf Pfeiffer who served as manager until 1913 when the Schwarzburg workshops were associated with another factory. The sculptor, Ernst Barlach, was represented by a number of unusual powerful figures in white porcelain without any coloring. Some of his figures of Russian subjects were inspired by his Russian tour in 1906. Paul Scheurich and Max Esser also modeled for Pfeiffer. See *Pfeiffer, M. A.; Scheurich, P.*

SCHWERIN
1753 ON

Schwarzlot In ceramics; a German term meaning black lead generally given to a style of painted decoration in black enamel, occasionally with a touch of red, such as for flesh tones, and gilding. This technique was used in window glass painting by the Dutch glass painters and later was first used on faïence by Johann Schäper around 1660. It was later used on Meissen porcelain especially for harbor scenes. Vienna porcelain also used this kind of decoration. Some of the Viennese examples were of incomparable beauty. See *Schäper, J.* (248, 333, 334)

Schwerin In German ceramics; a faïence manufactory was started at Schwerin, Mecklenburg, in 1753, by Johann Adam Apfelstädt and is still in existence. The wares were sometimes marked with A Sverin or A S for Apfelstädt-Schwerin. The 18th century productions were essentially without any particular distinction.

Scott, Anthony See *Southwick Pottery.*

Scott Brothers See *Southwick Pottery.*

Scratch Blue Ware In English ceramics; a salt-glazed stoneware having a nearly white body with incised decoration filled with blue color, made at Staffordshire from around 1748 to 1776. This almost white body was obtained by introducing ground flint as an ingredient into the clay mixture. The incised designs were chiefly patterns of conventionalized flowers. It is thought that this scratch blue ware may also have been made at Liverpool and in other parts of England.

Screen, Table Screen or **Ink-Screen** In Chinese art; a small screen in the form of an oblong, square or circular plaque set in an ornamental stand, generally of wood and occasionally of bronze, having a total height of around 12 to 14 inches. The plaques for table screens are made chiefly of jade, ivory, and porcelain, and are praiseworthy for the artistic merit of their decoration. They are elaborately decorated with Chinese motifs consisting of Buddhist and Taoist figures and legends, pavilions, mountain landscapes, lakes, bamboo trees, flowers and animal subjects. The richly carved ivory screens were made principally in the 18th century. Fine examples of porcelain ink-screens are found in private collections dating from the 16th century. K'ang Hsi Famille Verte oblong plaques mounted in crisply carved wood stands are especially typical of the Ch'ing dynasty. It is stated in literature on the Chinese decorative arts that the ink-stick used for making ink in calligraphy was rubbed on the ink-stone behind the ink-screen or yen p'ing. It is also observed that the screen protected the writer's work from the splash of the brush. According to the definition of the term *screen*, which means to protect or conceal, either one or both uses seem a reasonable assumption. See *Writing Equipage.*

Scroddled Ware   In American ceramics; occasionally called lava ware or solid agate ware; often confused with the more easily made marbled ware, which was never produced at Bennington and has surface decoration only. Scroddled ware comprises different-colored clays (generally brown to reddish-brown and grey) mixed with cream-colored clay. The different-colored clays were mixed together in such a way that the striations went through the entire piece and were visible outside and inside. The article was given a clear glaze and then fired. The variegated clay fused together, not unlike a marble cake, with a solid body of different mixed striations. Scroddled ware was not produced in quantity at Bennington because the demand was small and the process costly. See *Bennington.* (440)

Scrolls, C and S   In ornament; a decorative curve in the form of the Roman capital letters C and S from which each receives its name. C and S scrolls were a favorite Baroque style of ornament. During the Rococo style C and S scrolls lost their sculpturesque Baroque quality. Decorative curves were a pronounced feature of the Rococo style, with slender and graceful C and S scrolls figuring prominently.

Sebring Pottery Company   In American ceramics; established at East Liverpool, Ohio, in 1887, for the manufacture of white granite and other decorated wares in dinner and tea services. Later semi-porcelain was added to their production.

Secession   The Austrian version of Art Nouveau; a term deriving from the union of advanced Viennese painters and sculptors founded in 1896 under the name Wiener Sezession. It is irrevocably connected with the architects Josef Hoffmann and Joseph Olbrich. Before 1900 the Secessionists began to create a style that bypassed Art Nouveau and led directly to the Modern Movement with its completely new stylistic ideals. The Secession was almost entirely concentrated in Vienna, which rapidly became an international center for new directions in art and design that were spread across Austria and Europe through the Wiener Werkstätte, founded in 1903, under the influence particularly of Josef Hoffmann. Two years later in 1905 the Wiener Keramik workshop was organized by Michael Powolny and Berthold Löffler. Also notable were the art products of Ernst Wahliss' Alexandra Porcelain Works of Turn. In the strictly industrial field of porcelain production the spirit of Austrian design in these years was apparent in the products commissioned by the firm of Joseph Boch of Vienna. In Prague, in 1908, a group of architects, artists and designers formed an organization under the name Artel to further the decorative arts along similar lines of thought. In later years the influence of Austria in industrial ceramics has stemmed chiefly from the Augarten porcelain factory started at Vienna in 1922. See *Wiener Keramik; Artel; Turn; Vienna.*

Second Empire   1852-1870. All the ingredients of the style, both form and decoration, were taken from the previous styles extending over a period of 500 years. However, a distinctive richness, sumptuousness, brilliance and vivid colors gave to the work of this era an undeniable unity that offset its mode of imitation. See *Victorian; Historicism.*

PORCELAIN INK-SCREEN,
K'ANG HSI

SEBRING POTTERY CO.
C. 1887 ON

Seefried, Peter Antonius   (d. 1831) A pupil of Bustelli. Modeler at Kelsterbach, 1767-1769, and Nymphenburg, 1756-1767 and 1769-1810.

Seifu, Yokei   (1806-1863) Prominent Japanese studio-potter associated with the Kyoto circle of potters. He made porcelain and some faïence decorated in underglaze blue and brocade enamels in imitation of Chinese wares. Seifu III established a reputation as one of the best known makers of Japanese porcelains; especially notable were his celadon and underglaze red monochrome wares. The kiln is still active. See *Kyo.*

Seiji   The Japanese name for celadon. See *Celadon.*

SELB

MULLER, PAUL
c. 1890

H&Cͦ
SELB
BAVARIA
GERMANY

HEINRICH AND COMPANY
1896 ON

Seixas, David G.   American potter working at Trenton from around 1812 to 1816. A documented survival of his work at Trenton is a molded dark green glazed earthenware pitcher with a repetitive raised-diamond quilted pattern not unlike the pineapple decorated Staffordshire examples of the early 1800's. From 1817 to 1822 Seixas was working at Philadelphia where he used clays from the area of Wilmington, Delaware, and managed to imitate, with notable success, English Staffordshire models, though production appears to have been limited to useful rather than ornamental wares.

Selb   In German ceramics; a porcelain factory was started at Selb, Bavaria, in 1890 by Paul Müller which was purchased by Lorenz Hutschenreuther of Selb in 1917. The still-existing Heinrich & Co. was established in 1896 at Selb, Bavaria, for the manufacture of porcelain. The production included tablewares for daily use, tea and coffee services, luxury porcelain and hotel wares. Marks of varying design included H & Co. Their wares were popular and much of it was exported to the United States in the years prior to the First World War. See *Hutschenreuther, L.; Rosenthal.*

Seljuq   See *Islamic Pottery, Medieval.*

Seltmann, Christian   See *Weiden.*

Semi-Porcelain   In American ceramics; a porcelain-like body lacking translucency developed in the early 1880's; seemingly lighter and more pleasing than White Granite or Ironstone China. Also called Hotel China or Hotel Ware. See *Ironstone China; Stone-China.*

Semi-Vitreous or **Semi-Vitrified**   In American ceramics; a term describing a white ware occasionally found in American ceramic marks dating from the later part of the 19th century. Apparently the terms *semi-porcelain* and *semi-vitreous* were used interchangeably. See *Semi-Porcelain; Stone-China.*

Serapis-Fayence   In Austrian ceramics; made at the Alexandra Porcelain Works started at Turn by Ernst Wahliss around 1880. See *Turn.*

Seto   In Japanese ceramics; Seto, in the ancient province of Owari, was a leading center for the production of Sue wares and is one of the traditional sites of the Six Old Kilns period. Seto wares are of the greatest importance in a consideration of medieval Japanese ceramics. The direct stimulus for most of the early Seto wares was the imported celadon ware of the Southern Sung and Yüan Chinese dynasties, 1127-1368. Owing to the relatively low stage of technical progress and the nature of the materials available to Japanese potters, the Japanese equivalents of Sung celadons tended toward a greenish or yellowish brown. It is these thick greenish and yellowish brown glazes, all made from compounds of iron fired in an oxidizing kiln, which became the hallmark of the Old Seto stonewares of the Six Old Kilns era. As the easier oxidation firing methods became increasingly popular among Japanese potters, their stonewares were more and more dominated by the thick yellows and browns toward which this method of firing tends. The surface decoration, perhaps peonies or stylized grass or reeds, on the unfired body of these wares, was done by incising and sometimes by stamping with a die. Among their wares were wide-mouthed jars and bottle-shaped vases, the latter probably most often used for religious ceremonies, especially as containers for rice wine offerings. During the Mino period the Seto kilns were especially active in producing a light yellow or golden mat glaze known today as Yellow Seto. After the first part of the 17th century and through the 18th century fine continuations of Old Seto wares were produced, though with many innovations and changes. In the Edo period the Seto kilns supplied a large part of the domestic pottery made for daily use. From the beginning of the 19th century the Seto kilns began to produce porcelain wares. The best imitations of Shonsui blue and white porcelains were made by the Seto potters, Kato Tamikichi (d. 1824) and his successors at Seto. Among Tamikichi's most famous pupils were Sosendo Jihei (d. 1865) and his nephew Shentoen Hansuke, who copied most skillfully Shonsui and Ch'eng Hua blue and white. Eggshell porcelain was also made. Seto made much over-elaborated porcelain ware, in the most unrefined taste, for the European export market. Ceramic wares of various kinds have continued to be produced there until the present day. See *Six Old Kilns; Mino; Bizen; E-Seto; Seto Black; Shonsui; Owari Celadon; Ame-Gusuri.* (131)

Seto Black In Japanese ceramics; the name now generally given to a ware with a distinctive lustrous black ferruginous glaze produced at the kilns in the Mino province for about four decades, starting roughly around 1573. Most of the extant pieces are tea bowls, short and circular in shape. The rare beauty of this ware is the wonderful lustrous lacquer-like glaze. Occasionally the ware is called hikidashi-guro (pulled-out black) as it is thought that during the

firing of these wares the effect was in part caused by suddenly pulling them out from the kilns while still hot, the sudden contact with the cooler air causing certain changes in the structure of the glaze and its ingredients. See *Mino.*

Seuter, Bartholomäus (1678–1754) German Hausmaler; his family were well-known Augsburg craftsmen. (250)

Seven Gods of Good Fortune or **Seven Fortune Gods** In Japanese art; Fukurokuju, Ebisu, Benzai-ten (or Benten), Daikoku-ten, Jurojin, Hotei and Bishamon-ten. These seven gods (the number seven based on a holy number) were used as symbols of Kotobuki; that is good fortune, abundance (of food) and longevity. It is not known when these gods, which were of ancient Chinese and Indian origin, were established in Japan, but they were already popular in 1420. Benzai-ten, the only woman in the group, Goddess of Music, originated in India. She was known in Japan as early as Heian and is represented with a biwa. Ebisu is represented with a fishing rod and tai (sea-bream). Daikoku-ten, God of Darkness in ancient India, was the God of Anger who subjugated the Devil God. Those who worshipped him would always win wars. He carries a sack of gold. Hotei, a Zen priest of China, carries a sack in which he kept presents given to him by people. Bishamon-ten, defender of Buddhism, gave people money, good fortune, virtue and children, or he is the God of Victory in war. Clad in armor, he wears a crown in the shape of a bird. In his left hand he holds a pagoda and in his right hand a holy staff, symbols of his dual role. Essentially Jurojin and Fukurokuju are one and the same. Either one may be regarded as a Chinese god of Good Fortune and Longevity. For this reason one or the other, usually Fukurokuju, is sometimes replaced by Kichijo-ten.

Seville In Spanish ceramics; the manufacture of pottery was centered at Trina, a suburb of Seville. Ordinary glazed pottery with impressed relief decoration was made as early as the 11th century, comprising water and oil jars and two-handled vases. Of particular interest are the tiles which were made by various processes. It is claimed that tiles impressed with designs in relief and covered with colored glazes were made at Seville as early as 1260. Mosaic tile work or alicatados was made at Seville during the 14th century. In this method the already fired pieces in the different colored glazes were cut into the desired shapes to form the design. Green, white, brown and blue were the principal colors. Another method known as Cuerda Seca or dry cord was introduced around the middle of the 15th century. In this process a dry cord of grease and manganese was painted into the impressed outlines of the design, which kept the different colored glazes separate. After the tile was fired the so-called dry cord left a dull brown line between the colored glazes. Pharmacy vases, dishes and ewers were also decorated in this manner. In another process introduced late in the 15th century, known as Cuenca or cell type, a stamped design having limiting lines in relief served to separate the colored glazes. Early in the 16th century tiles were made in the tradition of Italian majolica. See *Tiles.* (216)

SEVRES
1778

SEVRES VASE

Sèvres In French ceramics; The national porcelain manufacture of France; originally established as a soft paste porcelain manufactory in 1738 at Vincennes under the patronage of Louis XV. In 1753 it was proposed to move the manufactory to Sèvres between Paris and Versailles. In 1769 a hard paste porcelain was made and was marked with a crowned version of the crossed L's which were in use from 1745-1753 to 1793. Date letters were first added in 1753. The factory mark from 1793 to 1804 was R F or R F in monogram for République Française, over Sèvres. Numerous marks were used during the 19th century, many of which included the word Sèvres. The factory is still in existence. The so-called Vincennes period dates from 1738 to 1753. During the second period, 1753 to 1772, the finest and most finished soft paste porcelain was made. Much of the reputation of Sèvres is associated with this work. From 1772 to 1804 both hard paste and soft paste porcelain were made. From 1804 to 1830 the style of the Empire prevailed. In 1804 the manufacture of soft paste was abandoned and was revived around 1850. Many technical improvements and innovations including the pâte-sur-pâte process were introduced around and after the middle of the 19th century. Faïence was also added to the productions. The influence of Meissen was evident in the productions made at Vincennes. However, the light and graceful Vincennes style of painted flowers, landscapes, and figure subjects, as well as the simple and graceful forms, had an intrinsic French charm. Perhaps the most important productions were the modeled flowers in vogue around 1750. The figures were all original models. In 1751 a porcelain biscuit was introduced and colored enamel figures were extremely rare after that date. Although some of the Sèvres figures and groups were superb they were seldom as interesting as those made at Meissen and Vincennes. Perhaps the most characteristic of all Sèvres decoration is painting in panels reserved on a colored ground. Turquoise or bleu celeste was introduced in 1752, yellow or jaune jonquille in 1753; apple green in 1756 and the now famous pink or Rose Pompadour in 1757. The early underglaze dark blue or gros bleu introduced around 1749 was supplanted before 1760 by the strong blue enamel or bleu de roi. These grounds were distinctive for their technical excellence and for their incomparable smoothness. A very finely wrought gilding is closely connected with the grounds. Occasionally to soften the brilliance of these grounds repetitive patterns were introduced and were an interesting Sèvres invention. Gilt or colored diaper arrangements of dots, stars, pebbles and other devices were employed. A late diaper arrangement was the so-called jeweled decoration. High temperature ground colors, including black, dark blue, brown and tortoiseshell were invented after 1770 and were used either in or on the hard paste porcelain glaze which did not take the earlier ground colors too well. From about 1765-1770 it became the practice to hire "outside" sculptors of repute to make reduced versions of their famous monumental works. Among these were the sculptors Pigalle, Clodion and Houdon. In the beginning of the 19th century the painters at Sèvres depicted the Napoleonic era on porcelain with remarkable skill. Noteworthy is the famous Table of the Marshals. In the last quarter of the 19th century flambé and other glazes and the decoration of Oriental porcelain were emulated. A new kaolinic porcelain very similar to the Chinese was introduced. The last two decades of the 19th century witnessed an extension of the range of high-temperature or underglaze colors. A number of artists used the pâte-sur-pâte decorative technique with notable distinction. Outstanding among these were Taxile Doat and for a brief time the sculptor Auguste Rodin. Stoneware for architectural use was perfected in the 1890's. The great variety and accomplishment of the productions of the Sèvres National Manufacture exhibited at the Paris Exhibition of 1900 was indeed a notable event. See *Flowers Modeled in Porcelain; Fond Ecaille; Oeil-de-Perdrix; Caillouté; Jeweled Decoration; Louis XVI; Classic Revival; Colored Grounds; Ceramic Plaques as Furniture Decoration; Swebach, J. F.; Béranger, A.; Deck, T.; Doat, T.; Ledoux, J. P.; Evans, E.; Aloncle, F.; Bachelier, J. J.; Fournier, L.; Pâte-sur-Pâte; Falconet, E. M.; Boizot, L. S.; Millot; Hellot, J.; Macquer, P. J.; Mathieu, J. A.; Duplessis, J. C.; Lagrenée, The Younger; Cornaille, A. T.; Chanou; Bulidon, H.; Blondeau; La Rue, L. F. de; Brongniart, A.; Léonard, A.;* *Dammouse, A.; Bracquemond, F.; Isabey, J. B.* (351-360, 518)

Sewell; Sewell and Donkin; Sewell and Company See *St. Anthony's Pottery.*

Sezession See *Secession.*

Sgraffiato or **Graffiato** In ceramics; an Italian term literally meaning a scratched decoration. There has been a growing tendency in modern times to restrict the use of this word to decoration scratched with a pointed instrument through a coating of slip or engobe to the body beneath, resulting in a design of two contrasting colors. Although according to the etymology of the word this arbitrary usage is incorrect, it does provide a term for a distinctive type of decoration. The term *incised decoration* is used for designs simply scratched in the soft clay without any color contrast. Incised decoration was frequently used on some of the finest Chinese porcelains; however, in Europe its use was almost limited to the simply decorated peasant wares. Sgraffiato decoration is of early origin. Perhaps the most notable early examples of the sgraffiato process are found on Islamic pottery. The process was widespread both in time and in place. It is also spelled Sgraffato, Sgraffito, and Graffato. See *Tz'u Chou.* (390)

Shang or **Yin** In Chinese archaic ceramics; the earliest pottery of aesthetic interest found in China believed to date from late Neolithic times, about 2000 B.C., shows two distinct traditions. First, painted pottery in the form of funerary jars and utilitarian vessels; a kind of smooth burnished buff earthenware, hand-modeled and painted with swirling motifs in red and black. Second, a rarer and plain type, the so-called black pottery frequently in almost metal-like shapes and often wheel-turned to a notable fineness. The Shang dynasty, (?) 1523- (?) 1028 B.C., the first historical period, is notable for its achievements in bronze casting. Characteristic of this era and the succeeding Chou dynasty, (?) 1122- c. 256, is a grey-bodied earthenware made in relatively simple shapes and decorated with such simple Neolithic techniques as cord impressions, incising and applied pads of clay. Shang wares are distinctive for two rare types. First, a fine-grained white pottery fired to considerable hardness with carved designs in the manner of Shang bronzes. Second, a coarse but thinly made stoneware on which the first primitive feldspathic glaze, probably accidental at first and later deliberate, made its first appearance. See *China,* in Far Eastern ceramics.

Shawabty Figures In ancient Egyptian ceramics; about 2100 B.C. small figures representing the deceased in his mummy wrapping began to be placed in the tombs. These were known as shawabty figures. The original meaning of shawabty is uncertain but it most likely derived from the word for persea tree, suggesting that the earliest figures were of persea wood. In the New Kingdom and later dynastic periods, however, when they were made in great quantity, most were of glazed faïence, which is the ware now preferably called glazed quartz frit. See *Roman Pottery.*

SHELL MOTIF

Shell In ornament; a decorative motif of shell form widely used in the arts of decoration. In the Baroque period the shell motif was always symmetrically treated, while in the Rococo style it was given many fanciful new forms of irregular outline. See *Rococo; Coquillage.*

Sherratt, Obadiah (c. 1775-c. 1845) English potter, toy- and figure-maker working at Burslem in the Staffordshire district from around 1822 onward. His name is mainly associated with earthenware bull-baiting pieces and related subjects noted for their earthiness and healthy vulgarity. The figures were mounted on table-like stands or bases provided with feet.

Shibuemon Japanese potter. See *Kakiemon.*

Shigaraki In Japanese ceramics; pottery appears to have been made in or near Shigaraki near Omi on the shores of Lake Biwa since very early times. Always listed as one of the traditional sites of the Six Old Kilns, it was an important center for the production of Sue ware. Later the production of the Shigaraki kilns came under the influence of the famous tea ceremony masters of the day, who recognized in the heavy unrefined wares being made for use in local agricultural communities the sober, subdued aesthetic qualities which they sought in their tea ceremony. As a result the Shigaraki potters were led to making wares which capitalized on these same characteristics. In Shagaraki ware the clay body is dominantly reddish-brown and the material tends to show considerable amounts of small impurities imbedded in it. It has a light, transparent, and at times almost glasslike glaze of a distinctive watery bluish-green tint where it has been permitted to accumulate into a layer thick enough to show color. This glaze was trickled over the Shigaraki ware in a carefully calculated carelessness which characterizes the products of this kiln, and during firing it frequently cracked and split, but only in such areas where it was sufficiently thick. The contrast between this glasslike decoration and the rough and stonelike surfaces on which it is found is completely rewarding aesthetically. Early wares of this type, with comparatively little assistance from Continental models, in which the Japanese potter developed a skill whose greatest expression is found in concealing its consummate skill, embody the ideals of the tea cult and as such they are milestones in Japanese aesthetic history. At the present time it is an important center for handcrafted pottery. See *Iga; Six Old Kilns; Tamba; Japanese Contemporary Ceramics.*

Shino In Japanese ceramics; a term of obscure origin given to a considerable variety of ceramics made at the kilns in the

Mino province from around the end of the 16th and first part of the 17th century. It includes Painted Shino which is decorated with usually strong brushwork painting in iron oxides under a fairly opaque greyish-white feldspar glaze, and Grey Shino in which the body of the ware was covered with a red clay slip and lightly carved before it was decorated with the distinctive greyish-white glaze. One of the numerous remarkable features of Painted Shino is the manner in which it combines the distinctive aspects of traditional Japanese painting with the skill of the Shino potter and his beautiful opaque whites. See *Mino; Raku.* (129)

Ship Bowl In English ceramics; faïence ship-bowls commissioned by the sea captains of trading ships generally inscribed with the captain's name as well as that of the ship and generally with good luck wishes. Many of these bowls were made by Liverpool potters from around 1750-1775 and also at Bristol, both for English sea captains and for the captains of ships from other countries stopping at Bristol.

Shirayamadani, Kataro See *Rookwood Pottery.*

Shochikubai In Japanese ornament; the Japanese term for the pine, bamboo and plum, a set of three lucky symbols widely employed in Japanese art. This motif had its origin in China. The pine, plum tree and bamboo were known as the Three Friends and were believed to be emblematic of the founders of the Three Religions of China—Confucius, Lao Tzŭ and Buddha. Shochikubai was a favorite decoration on Japanese porcelain, and versions of it reveal a subtle rhythm and spontaneity that are far above the level of mere decoration. See *Japanese Porcelain Motifs.*

Shonsui or **Shonzui** In Japanese ceramics; the identity of Gorodaiyu Shonsui is still unsolved. Three theories prevail in Japan today, namely, that he was a Japanese who went to China to make or buy porcelain; a

Chinese merchant who exported Chinese porcelain to Japan; a combination of the two, that is, the name Gorodaiyu and Shonsui refer to two different people. The last perhaps is the most popular theory in Japan today. Numerous scholars date genuine Shonsui porcelain wares from around 1632-1652 and regard them as the logical descendant of the blue and white porcelain made at Ching-tê-Chên for the Japanese market. The most typical designs of Shonsui wares which set them apart from other late Ming blue and white are the geometric patterns which usually form part or whole of the background. Geometric patterns were also used on the so-called colored Shonsui. Everyone agrees that the best imitations of Shonsui blue and white porcelains were made by the Seto potters, Tamikichi and his successors at Seto. Shonsui was copied at Arita kilns and by a host of famous Kyo studio potters, including Mokubei, Dohachi, Eiraku Hozen, Wazen, Shuhei and Chikuzen. See *Blue and White,* in Japanese ceramics; *Arita.* (153)

Shorthose, J. English potter working at Hanley, Staffordshire, from about 1785 to around 1823. Included among his principal productions were cream-colored and blue-printed earthenware, black basalt stoneware and porcelain. The marks found on his wares were Shorthose; Shorthose & Heath; and Shorthose & Co., impressed or printed in blue, sometimes with two crescents and an impressed S.

Shosoin In the early days in Japan every important temple had within its compound several storehouses called godowns for storing the objects used in religious ceremonies. The name *Sho-so,* meaning Chief Repository, was given to the principal one or pair of these storehouses, and its premises, generally surrounded by a wall and including the repository itself, were called Shosoin. At the present time the name refers only to the renowned Imperial Repository near the Hall of the Great Bud-

SHOCHIKUBAI: PINE, BAMBOO AND PLUM

dha of the Todaiji Temple at Nara. This Chief Repository was originally the Shosoin of the Todaiji Temple and housed the personal effects of the Emperor Shomu, who reigned 724-747, as dedicated by his widow, the Empress Dowager Komyo in 756. As a collection, its almost countless thousands of relics comprising jewels, glass, silver, ceramics, musical instruments, textiles, masks, arms and armor, wearing apparel, and the like, is priceless for the study of Chinese as well as Japanese art. Ceramics do not form the most important portion of the collection. Notable, however, is the so-called Shosoin Three-Color ware. See *Sue Ware.*

Shosoin Three-Color Ware   See *Sue Ware.*

Shou Lao   In Chinese art; a Chinese Taoist subject. He is the god of long life and is generally believed to be a transformation of Lao Tzü who was the founder of the religion. He is represented as an old man with a long beard and he has a large protuberance on his bald head. He is clothed in flowing robes on which is shown the character shou or longevity. He is seen seated and sometimes he is seen riding on the back of an animal or a bird. See *Chinese Gods; Lu-hsing.*

Shrine Set   In Chinese ceramics; a garniture of Chinese porcelain comprising five pieces: a central censer or incense burner, two pricket candlesticks and two trumpet-shaped beakers.

Shrinkage   Clay shrinks when drying and in the firing to become pottery. For this reason the body and glaze must be matched so that the shrinkage is about the same. Also all figures must be hollow. See *Crazing; Peeling.*

Shu Fu Ware   In Chinese ceramics; during the Yüan dynasty, 1280-1368, a porcelain ware was produced at Ching-tê-Chên known as Shu Fu or Privy Council ware. It is the earliest porcelain known to have

SIEBURG STONEWARE
RING FLASK

been ordered by the Imperial officials. The ware has an opaque glaze of pale bluish-green with relief decoration of lotus flowers and similar flowering plants with the Chinese characters, shu fu, found in the design. Bowls and flat-bottomed plates having square-shaped foot rims are the most common.

Shuhei, Ogata   (1783-1839) Kyoto studio-potter; brother of Ninami Dohachi. He specialized in kyusu (unglazed earthenware teapots in the Mokubei manner); stoneware tea bowls covered with a fine creamy crackle glaze and decorated in underglaze blue, and red enameled porcelains. His wares, which were mostly porcelain, were in excellent taste and he executed his designs with skill and precision. He started a pottery at Awaji around 1830. See *Kyo; Dohachi, Ninami; Mokubei, Aoki; Ninsei; Eisen, Okuda.*

Shun Chih   The Shun Chih reign of the Ch'ing dynasty in China, 1644-1661. See *Chinese Dynasties.*

Sialk   See *Near East,* in prehistoric ceramics.

Siam   See *Indo-China.*

Sicily   In Italian ceramics; majolica, in more or less coarse copies of Castel Durante wares was made here chiefly at Palermo, but also at Trapani, Caltagirone, and other sites in the late 16th and early 17th century. Painting of trophies in grey in the manner of Castel Durante on a dull-colored ground was a popular decoration.

Siegburg   In German ceramics; potteries were in existence at Siegburg in the Rhineland from the 14th century. During the second half of the 16th century it was one of the four most important centers for Rhenish salt-glazed stoneware. Its best productions were from about 1550 to 1590. The town was sacked by the Swedes in 1632 and the potteries never recovered. Siegburg made a grey or nearly white stoneware. On the finer specimens the stoneware was almost white and the salt glaze was thin and colorless. Included among the many interesting forms identified with Siegburg stoneware are the Trichterbecher or a cup with a funnel-shaped mouth, a jar with a handle designed as a candle socket, a small jug in the form of an owl, ring flasks, goblets, and the Schnabelkrug or a jug with a beak-like spout. The more richly decorated wares with beautiful applied reliefs of animals, birds, leaf scrolls and biblical figure subjects date from around 1560. Especially praiseworthy were the tall tapering tankards or Schnellen with reliefs of biblical subjects arranged in three long strips on the front. (186-191)

Siena   In Italian ceramics; potteries were in existence at Siena, Tuscany, as early as 1265 and by 1500 Siena was a flourishing center for the manufacture of majolica. Unfortunately only very little majolica can be ascribed to Siena for the 15th and 16th centuries. The painted decoration on some pharmacy vases and dishes attributed to Siena reveals a similarity to that found on a type of Faenza majolica. Ample contemporary records show that majolica was produced throughout the 16th century. A minor revival of majolica occurred during the 18th century. See *Italian Majolica; Benedetto.*

Sigillata   See *Roman Pottery.*

Sikyatki Polychrome   See *Anasazi.*

Silenus Jug (Mintons)   See *Meigh, Charles.*

Silesia Hafner Ware   In German ceramics; during the 16th century a small but significant variety of Hafner ware dishes were made in Silesia. This variety is characterized by the use of lines in the designs incised with a sharp tool which served to keep the different colored tin glazes or tin-enameled glazes of yellow, green, blue, purple, white and brownish black sepa-

rated. Occasionally relief decorations were also added. See *Hafner.*

Siliceous or **Silicious**   A glass glaze composed of silex (sand) and an alkali, as soda or potash. The same as glass glaze.

Silicon   In English ceramics; the name given to an unglazed brown stoneware, somewhat like terra-cotta in appearance, but smoother and much harder, introduced at Doultons of Lambeth in the early 1880's. It was cut and carved, and vases were even made with perforated decoration; it was frequently decorated with inlays or pâte-sur-pâte work in clays of a contrasting color, and gilding was employed sparingly. The attraction of the ware, however, was clearly the texture of the natural fired surface, and the decoration appears never to have been permitted to conceal more than a small part of it.

Silla   The name of the Korean historical period, c. 57 B.C. to A.D. 935. See *Korean Periods.*

Silver   See *Metal Mounts on Ceramics.*

Silver-Forms   In ceramics; silver-forms have been commonly copied by potters, particularly in porcelain. Early Meissen, Vienna, French faïence and porcelain, Worcester and Wedgwood forms furnish many examples. See *Helmet Ewer.* (115, 269)

Sinceny   In French ceramics; a faïence manufactory was started at Sinceny, Aisne, France, in 1733 and managed by Denis-Pierre Pellevé of Rouen who brought artists and potters from that city. The factory was active until 1864. From 1733 to 1775 Rouen styles in high temperature colors were made. Essentially this early faïence, which was of fine quality, differed from Rouen faïence only in a decidedly whiter tin glaze, in a stronger blue, a paler red and a more frequent use of yellow. Figure modeling was also done. During the sec-

SINCENY
1733 ON

ond period from 1775 to 1795 painters from Strasbourg were working at Sinceny and the painted decoration was in enamel colors in addition to the earlier high temperature colors. This faïence in enamel colors and gilding in the Strasbourg style was seldom as interesting as the earlier work. The letter S with a dot on each side is generally recognized as the actual factory mark; Sinceny written in full has also been found; S C Y was found in the second period.

Singerie In ornament; a French term applied to a decorative grotesque composition in which monkeys and apes were playfully treated. Singeries were introduced by Bérain in his fanciful compositions. These amusing monkey pieces were further elaborated by Watteau and were fashionable in the Rococo style of ornament. See *Watteau, Antoine.*

Fabrique de Vsevolojskoy

SIPIAGIN
1815 ON

Sipiagin In Russian ceramics; the short-lived early 19th century Vsevolozhskii porcelain manufactory, near Moscow, passed to Nikolai Sipiagin in the late 1820's for another short period. In 1850 Nikolai's son reopened the manufactory and in 1865 it was leased to I. A. Ikonnikov who in 1875 bought A. G. Popov's molds for figures and plates which he reproduced. See *Russia; Popov.*

Six Dynasties A period in Chinese art history, c. 222-589. See *Chinese Dynasties.*

Six Old Kilns In Japanese ceramics; during the Kamakura and early Muromachi periods, roughly from around the 12th to the early 14th century, pottery made in Japan centered about six sites, which were all in earlier times leading centers for the production of Sue wares and which are still known today as the Six Old Kilns. The traditional list of these sites is Seto, Tokoname, Shigaraki, Tamba, Bizen and Echizen, the last being of minor significance. It is customary to trace most modern Japanese ceramic techniques to this

period and particularly to relate them with Kato Shirozaemon Kagemasa, called also Toshiro, a Japanese potter who is reputed to have gone to China and returned to Japan around 1227. He is believed to have settled in the area known as Seto in the modern Aichi Prefecture and to have begun making pottery in which the ceramic techniques of long duration in Japan were developed and modified with the introduction of new skills from the Continent. Technically the most outstanding development during this period was a change from reduction firing (in which the supply of air is limited during firing) to the more readily handled oxidation firing (in which the air is admitted freely). For example, glazes using oxides of iron as coloring agents in a reducing kiln atmosphere yield green and grey celadon, while the identical iron oxides in an oxidation kiln atmosphere produce yellow and russet browns and blacks which are a distinctive feature of most wares of this era. Of these, the wares made at the Seto kilns possess the greatest importance as they are typical of the many kinds of stonewares made in what may be called the first or early period of Japanese ceramic art. Although the Six Old Kilns are grouped together principally because they represent very early centers of ceramic production, in almost all cases wares continued to be produced in these areas, and in some instances are very active today. In much of the 16th century and later ware the aesthetic ideals of the tea cult became increasingly important in the output of the Six Old Kilns as they did in practically all areas of Japanese ceramics. See *Sue Ware; Japanese Periods; Bizen; Seto; Shigaraki; Tamba.*

Skawonius, S. E. See *Upsala-Ekeby.*

Skinning In ceramics; the name given to the process whereby the biscuit is uncovered by grinding away the glaze. This procedure is sometimes used on forgeries which have a perfectly good and genuine body and mark, originally of a comparatively inexpensive sort, which may be left to impart the appearance of authenticity to the more expensive kind of decoration. For example, a vase of Chinese blue and white may in this fashion be transformed into Famille Noire.

Skyphos or **Kotyle**   In Greek antiquities; a deep wine cup with two horizontal handles attached near the lip rim. Unlike the Kylix, which was mounted on a stemmed foot, the bowl of the skyphos rested directly on a slight foot or ring base. It was both copious and serviceable. See *Kylix.*

Slater, Walter   See *Doulton, Lambeth and Burslem.*

Slip   In ceramics; clay thinned with water to a liquid or semi-liquid condition. It is used for the decoration of pottery, and used to join or to lute the several pieces of an unfinished vessel or figure after it is removed in sections from the mold. Slip is used to fix handles, finials and other similar parts to the body of a vessel. The equivalent French term is *barbotine.* See *Engobe; Slipware.*

Slip-Casting   In ceramics; molding by means of multipartite plaster-of-Paris molds with internal intaglio decoration. After the mold is assembled, slip (liquid clay) is poured into it. The plaster quickly absorbs the water and leaves a thin film of clay clinging to the mold. This was repeated until the lining was sufficiently thick when, after it had dried, it was removed from one mold. This process allows sharp decorative detail on vessels with thin walls. See *Molding.* (409, 410)

Slipware   In ceramics; the practice of decorating pottery by applying a semi-liquid clay-mixture called in England slip (French, barbotine) is of great antiquity. As a rule the commoner clays used by the

potter bake red, and a covering (French, engobe) of white pipe-clay or some lighter colored earth was frequently used to provide a cleaner-looking surface more appropriate for painted decoration. Perhaps an accidental scratching of this surface-covering showing the darker body beneath may have suggested the decorative technique now called sgraffiato, though designs obtained by simple incising in the body are practically as old as the art of pottery itself. White decoration reserved on a dark ground, easily made by sgraffiato, may have suggested designs in white clay directly applied. Sometimes the designs are in a dark clay on a lighter ground and in one English variety both light and dark clays are combined in feathered or marbled effects produced by working the semi-liquid slip with a comb or brush. The so-called Gabri wares of Persia are notable early examples of the sgraffiato technique, but the technique has been widespread in time and place. Perhaps the richest and most varied use of the slip method appears in the Egyptian wares of the Mamluk period decorated with a great variety of designs incised through the slip-covering and also trailed with a liquid white clay mixture from a pipe or spouted vessel. Under the lead glaze these designs become yellow on the deep red or brown ground. Similar processes were employed in the 17th and 18th century in various places in Europe. These examples of slipware were probably the work of peasant potters, who for a daily living made very ordinary crockery. The main centers in England were Wrotham and particularly North Staffordshire. Combed wares were also produced in many places. The meaning of the term *slipware* in this connection is usually extended to include related wares with simple incised decoration as well as pottery decorated with white or colored clays applied to body of a contrasting color. See *Sgraffiato; Slip; Sussex; Toft, Thomas; Colored Grounds; Castor Ware; Roman Pottery; Barbotine; Combed Ware.*

SKYPHOS

SQUAT LAKYTHOS

Slop-Basin The term *slop-basin* is applied to a bowl usually of silver or porcelain used with the tea service for holding slops, or the rinsings of tea. The name *slop-basin* was mentioned in English records as early as the latter part of the 18th century. It is derived from the word *slop* meaning refuse liquid of any kind such as rinsings of tea, coffee or other beverages, or the dirty water of a household.

Smaltino In Italian ceramics; a contemporary 16th century term given to a greyish or pale bluish tin glaze used on majolica. A tin glaze of this tone is especially identified with the majolica made at Venice.

Smear Glaze A semi-glaze or thin deposit on the surface of pottery produced by smearing the inside of the saggar with the glazing preparation. This vaporizes in the heat of the kiln and settles on the surface of the enclosed item. Smear glaze was a development following salt glaze and is frequently mistaken for it.

EST 1846
OLD ROYAL
BONE CHINA
ENGLAND
SMITH, SAMPSON
C. 1945-1963

Smith, Sampson (Ltd.) In English ceramics; operated Staffordshire potteries at various addresses at Longton, from about 1846–1963. Included in their production were earthenwares, figures and, in the 20th century, china. "Ltd." was added to the name around 1918. From 1954 the firm was one of the Alfred Clough group. See *Flat-Black Figures*.

Smith, Fife and Company In American ceramics; a porcelain factory active in Philadelphia in 1830, the year it exhibited two porcelain pitchers at the annual exhibition of the Franklin Institute of Philadelphia. Apparently the manufacture did not continue for any length of time. Essentially the form and decoration was similar to that of the Tucker porcelain factory. See *Tucker*.

Snuff Bottle In Chinese art; a very small vessel or container used to hold snuff, generally fitted with a tiny stopper attached to a tiny spoon. Although snuff bottles are known to have been made as early as the K'ang Hsi reign, 1662-1722, they usually date from the Tao Kuang reign and the middle of the 19th century. Snuff bottles were made in a great variety of shapes, sometimes with rounded bottoms having the appearance of smooth stones or little eggs. They were made of jade, glass, porcelain, semi-precious stones, crystal, onyx, agate, amethyst, coral, red lacquer and amber. Those made of porcelain were decorated in the same manner as the other Chinese wares, such as Famille Verte, Famille Rose, Underglaze Red, Underglaze Blue and Tea Dust. See *Famille Verte; Famille Rose*.

Society of Arts Established in England in 1754. At the present time its full title is the Royal Society for the Encouragement of Arts, Manufactures and Commerce, which explains its purpose.

Society of Arts and Crafts An American national society founded in Boston in 1897 stemming from the English Arts and Crafts Movement. Like the English Arts and Crafts Exhibition Society, established in 1888, this society held exhibitions to stimulate public appreciation for the work of American artists working in the arts and crafts.

Soft Chün In Chinese ceramics; see *Chün Yao*.

Soft Paste or **Soft Paste Porcelain** In European ceramics; European porcelain falls into two principal classes; true porcelain or hard paste porcelain made of kaolin and petuntse, and artificial porcelain, known as soft paste or pâte tendre, made with glassy substances. Many successful and artistic imitations of true porcelain were made in Europe during the 17th and 18th centuries by using glass or the materials of glass fused and ground up and mixed with clay or some other ingredient. The ingredients used in soft paste have varied widely over a period of years. Generally the required temperature to fire soft paste is about 1100° C. The glaze was added in a second firing at a lower temperature and lead was freely used as an ingredient in the glaze in order that it would fuse more readily. A clear lead glaze was never used in the usual feldspathic hard paste porcelain of Europe. In reality soft paste is soft in appearance and artistically its decoration is more pleasing in color than true porcelain. Its glaze was easily scratched and was soft. Because of its great production hazards and also because the finished product was not very durable, the making of soft paste was gradually abandoned as the process and materials for true porcelain became better understood. Its production was practically given up in France and England early in the 19th century, the French having been the principal producers of this artificial porcelain. See *Porcelain; Bone China; Sèvres.* (298-300, 343-359)

Soldner, Paul (b. 1921) American artist-potter; constantly experimenting. His most recent work has been with Japanese Raku ware. Soldner's work has had a considerable influence on American artist-potters.

Solis, Virgil (1514-1562) German painter, designer and engraver. See *Engraved Designs.*

Soliva, Miguel Painter at the Alcora manufactory in Spain, 1727-1750. Scenes painted and signed by him reveal his brilliant skill in reproducing engraved pictures in colored glazes. His decorative panels and figure subjects rank as the best painting done at Alcora.

Solon, Léon Victor (1872-1957) English ceramic designer; became art director and designer at Mintons where in collaboration with J. W. Wadsworth he designed an earthenware series, which may be regarded as a prominent manifestation of Art Nouveau in English industrial wares. He also made a reputation in other media, including bookbinding. In 1909 he emi-grated to the United States. He was responsible for the coloring of architectural details and sculpture on the Museum of Fine Arts in Philadelphia and Rockefeller Center in New York.

Solon, Louis Marc (1835-1913) French ceramist, outstanding among 19th century artists. He worked first at Sèvres, perfecting the process of pâte-sur-pâte introduced there in 1847. In 1870 Solon moved to England and was employed by Minton until 1904. He is known not only for his magnificent work in the pâte-sur-pâte or cameo style but also for pieces with sgraffiato or incised decoration. See *Pâte-sur-Pâte.* (479)

Sölvesborg In Swedish ceramics; a faïence factory started by Baron Gabriel Sparre was active here from 1773 to 1793. Its manager and chief painter was Peter Akermark who had come from Marieberg, the styles of which and also of Rörstrand were borrowed. The mark was S B for Sölvesborg.

Soma See *Kyo.*

Some Nishiki The Japanese term for a porcelain technique in which the body is decorated in underglaze blue and overglaze colors or polychrome enamels. See *Nishiki; Imari.*

Sometsuke The Japanese name for underglaze blue and white porcelain.

Sorgenthal, Konrad von (d. 1805) Director of the Vienna porcelain manufactory, 1784-1805, its most prosperous period. Especially typical were designs on red, green, yellow or blue grounds framed by gilt ornament, a style created at Sèvres some time before.

Souroux See *Rue de la Roquette.*

South American Pottery In pre-Columbian ceramics; the main archaeological remains in South America are found in the mountainous regions in the west and on the west

S: B
G: S.Q

SOLVESBORG
1773 ON

coast, and within this part of the continent the central Andean area, consisting of highland Peru and Bolivia and the coast of Peru, was the home of the highest ancient civilizations. More is known of them than of the less significant ones of Colombia, Ecuador, north Chile or northwest Argentina. In each of these countries the great diversity in topography hindered free communication, which resulted in the growth of many tribes and many varieties of material products. It was not until the 15th century owing to the rise of the Inca Empire that the peoples of Peru and the adjacent countries were welded into a coherent whole. Even then Colombia and much of the coast of Ecuador remained the same. See *Pre-Columbian Pottery; Andean; Ecuador and Colombia; Argentina and Chile; Inca.* (15-21)

South Hylton   See *Dawson, John and Company.*

Southern Porcelain Company   In American ceramics; a pottery and porcelain factory started at Kaolin, South Carolina, between Aiken and Augusta, in 1856 by H. W. Farrar, formerly at Bennington and Jersey City, who was attracted to the white clays of the area. He made brown-glazed pottery of the Rockingham type, white granite and unglazed porcelain or biscuit. In this he imitated the parian porcelain of Bennington, making relief-decorated jugs either uncolored or with the white relief-pattern clearly defined against a blue pebbled or pitted ground. These date from around 1860. He also made some glazed porcelain without color; however, a few examples were enriched with gilded decoration. The outbreak of the Civil War interrupted the factory's progress which closed in 1878. See *Parian Ware.* (444)

Southwestern United States Pottery   In pre-Columbian ceramics; the best early pottery in the United States came from the Southwest, which comprises the states of Arizona and New Mexico, southern Utah

and Colorado and part of northern Mexico. From early times this region was inhabited by three main groups of people, each with its typical pottery types. The plateau which occupies the north and middle of the region was the home of the Anasazi whose descendants were the Pueblo Indians. The desert valleys of the Gila and Salt rivers, which lie south and west of the plateau, were the seat of the Hohokam. In southwest New Mexico in a hilly region where the Mimbres valley runs down toward the Mexican border was a third group, to whose culture the name of Mogollon has been given; but their pottery is not as well known as that of the other two groups. See *Pre-Columbian Pottery; Anasazi; Hohokam; Mogollon; Mimbres.* (1-5)

Southwick Pottery   In English ceramics; a pottery operated at Sunderland, Durham, by Atkinson and Company from 1788 to 1799, producing earthenwares. The successors were Anthony Scott and Company, 1800-1897. The following includes some of the changing styles of marks that were incorporated in the printed designs: A Scott and Company, Scott, Southwick, c. 1800-1824; Scott and Sons, c. 1829–1838; Scott Brothers, c. 1838–1854; Scott, c. 1838-1872 and c. 1882-1897; S and S c. 1872-1882. See *Portobello.*

Spatterware   See *Sponged Ware.*

Speckner, Lorenz (1598-1670 or later) and his son, **Johannes Lorenz** (1638 or earlier-1673-74) German potters working at Kreussen. (245-247)

Sphinx or **Royal Sphinx Ware**   See *Maastricht.*

Spietz, Johann   See *Bornholm Island.*

Spode   In English ceramics; a pottery was started at Stoke-on-Trent, Staffordshire, around 1770 by Josiah Spode (1733-1797) who had previously worked for Thomas Whieldon. His son, Josiah Spode II (1754-

SOUTHERN PORCELAIN COMPANY
1856-1864

SPODE
c. 1805-1830

1827), carried on the business. He introduced porcelain around 1800 and stone-china around 1805. The porcelain was a hybrid bone-ash paste. He is generally given credit for establishing the standard composition for English bone china or bone porcelain. The porcelain made under Josiah Spode II was technically of fine quality; however, the painted decoration and the forms were often ostentatious. Especially typical were ornately gilded vases with colored grounds. Some wares with simplified Japanese designs were generally more pleasing. William Taylor Copeland, who had become a partner in 1813, succeeded to the business in 1833, Josiah Spode III having died in 1829. The firm was Copeland and Garrett from 1833 to 1847, and then Copeland, late Spode or W. T. Copeland until 1867, when it became W. T. Copeland and Sons. See *Copeland, W. T.; Bone China; Stone-China; Copeland and Garrett.*

Sponged Ware In American ceramics; decorating the surface of pottery by dabbing with a sponge or something of the sort. It resembles the rather coarse and mostly late examples of what in England is commonly called Pratt ware, after one of the Staffordshire manufacturers of this class of ware. Pratt ware is a modern term used of late 18th and early 19th century creamwares or pearl wares decorated in high temperature colors including blue, yellow, ochre and dull green, those colors being quite often applied with a sponge. It seems that the term *spatterware* which is commonly used in America to describe this class of ware should be avoided, partly as having no historical basis, but still more because it gives a totally misleading idea of the technique of production. Though it is perfectly possible to blow pigment onto ware, in powder or liquid form, this ware is clearly decorated by dabbing with a sponge or something similar. For this reason *sponged ware* is at least a more accurate term. The term *spatterware* is rather un-

familiar in England and it is perhaps a modern dealer's term of United States origin. Of great interest are the sponged wares made by a number of Staffordshire potters for the American trade between the years 1820–1850. They include a delightful range of patterns (nearly forty) and are seen mostly on tablewares. Among the popular patterns are the Red Schoolhouse, Star, Tulip, and Peafowl and its numerous variants. (464-466)

Sponse In ceramics; a Dutch term applied to a paper on which the design has been marked out with a point. The paper was then laid on the surface of an item and pounced with black powder, which thus after the paper was removed provided the outlines of the design for subsequent painting over.

Spotted Celadon In Chinese ceramics; see *Celadon.*

Sprigged Ware In English ceramics; a contemporary English name given to 18th century wares decorated in applied reliefs principally of flowers, foliage, and stems. These applied reliefs were pressed in intaglio molds and were secured to the body of the vessel by a mixture of clay and water or slip. The stems were done in free hand modeling and were also applied with slip. Early examples of this technique were found in Rhenish stoneware and in Astbury and Whieldon earthenwares and salt-glazed stonewares of Staffordshire. The technique was known as sprigging.

Sprigging See *Sprigged Ware.*

Sprimont, Nicholas (1716-1771) Of Flemish origin; manager of Chelsea porcelain factory, 1749-1758, and proprietor, 1758-1769.

Staehr-Nielsen, Eva See *Saxbo.*

Stafford Knot In English ceramics; in the form of a loose knot, or pretzel-shaped; used as a mark by a number of Stafford-

SPODE PLATE WITH "JAPAN" PATTERN

STAFFORD KNOT

STAFFORDSHIRE PEW GROUP

STAMNOS

shire potters in combination with their distinguishing initials. Legend has it that a local sheriff in medieval times wanted to hang three men at the same time with one rope and that he accomplished his purpose by forming a triple noose, which because of the county of origin (Staffordshire) became known as the Stafford knot. Such a proceeding would be very difficult and highly improbable. In heraldry this knot was the badge of the Stafford family in the 15th century.

Staffordshire   In English ceramics; practically all of the information regarding early Staffordshire pottery and the potters working in North Staffordshire is traditional. It has been the custom to associate types of Staffordshire wares with the names of individual potters; however, these types were undoubtedly made by more than one potter. Marks did not come into anything resembling general use until the latter part of the 18th century, and it has always been difficult to identify the wares of a particular pottery. The tremendous growth of the ceramic industry in North Staffordshire during the 18th and 19th centuries was essentially due to the abundance of clays in the district. The earliest Staffordshire wares of any artistic merit were the slipwares first made during the latter part of the 16th century. Toward the end of the 17th century the Elers brothers produced a red stoneware in imitation of the Chinese buccaro wares. From around 1725 earthenware covered with colored lead glazes in the types associated with Astbury and Whieldon were made concurrently with the solid agate ware and the almost white salt-glazed stoneware in imitation of porcelain. Apparently faïence was never made. Later in the 18th century Wedgwood perfected the cream-colored earthenware with an almost colorless lead glaze. The figures made at Staffordshire in salt-glazed stoneware or in earthenware covered with colored lead glazes have an intrinsic charm. Of particular interest

were the so-called pew groups with charming stylized seated figures. From around 1785 the earthenware figures were generally painted in enamel colors. The 19th century Staffordshire figures with their simple modeling and bold colors are an attractive form of peasant art. Toby jugs were a characteristic Staffordshire production. The fine black basalt and jasper stonewares made by Wedgwood were extensively imitated by other contemporary potters. Porcelain was also manufactured at Staffordshire. Outside Staffordshire the principal potteries in the second half of the 18th century were centered at Bristol, Durham, Liverpool, Newcastle, Swansea and Yorkshire. Leeds in Yorkshire was second in magnitude only to Wedgwood's Etruria factory. See *Spode; New Hall; Minton; Davenport; Ironstone China; Stoke-on-Trent; Marbled Ware; Agate Ware; Tortoiseshell Ware; Scratch Blue Ware; Crouch Ware; Stoneware; Wood, Ralph; Wood, Enoch; Elers; Astbury, John; Whieldon, Thomas; Toft, Thomas; Pratt, Felix; Cream-Colored Earthenware; Wedgwood, Josiah; Mayer, Elijah; Turner, John; Palmer, Humphrey; Hollins, Samuel; Shorthose, J.; Basalt; Jasper Ware; Adams, William; Walton, J.; Engine-Turned Decoration; Pratt Ware; Doulton and Company; Ridgway; Meigh, Charles; Clews, James and Ralph; Furnival, Jacob and Thomas; Maddock, John; Aynsley, John and Sons; Meakin, Alfred; Flat-Back Figures.* (385-425, 461-470, 472, 475, 479, map, page 333).

Stamnos   In Greek antiquities; a jar or vase to hold wine or water, provided with two small horizontal handles attached to the shoulder of the body. The mouth was large enough to allow for ladling out the wine.

Stangl Pottery   See *Fulper Pottery.*

Stanniferous Ware   Holding or containing tin. See *Tin Glaze.*

State Porcelain Manufactory   See *Berlin.*

Statuary Porcelain   See *Spode; Parian.*

Steingut In German ceramics; the German term for cream-colored or white earthenware with a lead glaze. See *Cream-Colored Earthenware.*

Steinzeug In German ceramics; the German term for stoneware. See *German Stoneware; Stoneware.*

Steitzische Vasenfabrik in Cassel See *Cassel.*

Stem-Cup In Chinese ceramics; a small porcelain vessel introduced during the Hsüan Tê reign, 1426-1435. It has a wide, rather shallow bowl, and a tall foot or stem which flares gently toward the bottom. The glaze is a pure white of fatty texture and on the bowl are painted three fishes, or three fruits, in underglaze red. The stem-cup was so much appreciated that it was copied at the Imperial factory during the Yung Chêng reign. This form was later imitated in European ceramic wares. (98)

Stephan, Pierre Modeler at Derby, Coalport and Etruria, 1770-1795. He is reputed to have modeled a series of English Admirals and Generals for Derby.

Stephens, Tams and Company See *Greenwood Art Pottery Company.*

Stephensen, Magnus See *Royal Copenhagen.*

Sterling China Company In American ceramics; started in 1917 at East Liverpool, Ohio, in a modest way, producing such basic wares as cups, mugs and bowls. In the ensuing years the firm grew and prospered. After the Second World War Sterling introduced the first new Hotel China shape in many years in the form of the Russell Wright line. In 1954 Sterling took over the Scammell lines of china. At the present time Sterling produces the well-known Lamberton china together with the large line of Sterling china.

Steubenville Pottery In American ceramics; a pottery started at Steubenville, Ohio, in 1879 for the manufacture of earthenware.

Stevenson and Hancock In English ceramics; when the Derby Porcelain Works closed in 1848 some of the former artists and workmen opened a small factory in King Street, Derby, which they called the Old Crown Derby China Works. Stevenson and Hancock and subsequent owners operated this factory from about 1859 to 1935. The distinguishing initials SH appeared in the distinctive Crown Derby mark (crowned D with crossed batons and six dots) from around 1861 to 1935. Stevenson and Hancock succeeded Stevenson, Sharp and Company who operated the factory around 1859; they in turn had succeeded Locker and Company who had operated the factory from around 1849–1859. See *Derby.*

Stevenson, Andrew Staffordshire potter active at Cobridge, about 1816-1830, producing earthenwares. (466)

Stevenson, Sharp and Company See *Derby.*

Stile Bello or **Beautiful Style** In Italian ceramics; a name often given to the istoriato style and the elaborate decoration inspired by humanist taste that flourished during the first half of the 16th century at Faenza, Urbino and other centers producing majolica. See *Istoriato.*

Stirrup Vessel In Andean ceramics; a kind of Cupisnique vessel or pot characterized by the stirrup-shaped handle serving as a spout. The body of the pot may take many forms. This distinctive type of stirrup vessel had been a ceramic tradition for more than two thousand years, persisting right up to the time of the Spanish conquest in the 16th century. In ancient Cretan and Mycenaean ceramics; the stirrup jar, the most characteristic of all later Mycenaean vases, appeared in Crete about 1580 B.C. It was not introduced to Greece before 1400 B.C. and was probably connected with the growing trade in oil. Also called a false neck vase, because what looks like the spout is simply a solid rod of clay and the

STEM CUP, HSUAN TE

STEUBENVILLE POTTERY
1879 ON

STOCKELSDORF STOVE

STOCKELSDORF
1771 ON

STOCKTON ART POTTERY
C. 1891 ON

true spout rises vertically beside the stirrup-shaped handle. The well-known Octopus jar from Gournia also has a false neck. (15, 17, 52)

Stockelsdorf   In German ceramics; a faïence manufactory was started at Stockelsdorf near Lübeck in 1771; it apparently was a branch continuation of an earlier stove factory. The finer wares upon which the reputation of the factory depends were probably made prior to 1788 and displayed a high standard of artistic excellence. Stoves were perhaps the most important production and rank among the best of their kind. They are generally of pyramidal form and were molded in a fanciful Rococo style with scrollwork and applied flowers and leaves. Others were in the Neo-Classic style. The painting in enamel colors was exceedingly fine; flowers in the Strasbourg manner, figure subjects and landscapes were much favored. The most typical forms in useful and ornamental wares were helmet-shaped ewers of Rococo form with shell molding, trays, wall fountains, four-sided jardinières and large pear-shaped vases. Very large trays or tea table tops are a characteristic production of the faïence factories in the Baltic region and nowhere were they more charmingly painted than at Stockelsdorf. Included among the marks was Stff for Stockelsdorf faïence. (296)

Stockton Art Pottery   In American ceramics; a firm active in Stockton, California, 1891-1902, and originally called the Stockton Terra Cotta Company. They were noted for a special art ware which they called Rekston. This was characterized by heavy colored glazes on enamels and included such pieces as jardinières, umbrella stands and vases.

Stoke-on-Trent   In English ceramics; the name of a federated town in North Staffordshire. A number of small towns in which the pottery industry of North Staffordshire was originally centered were

united to form Stoke-on-Trent. They included Burslem, Stoke, Tunstall, Longton, Longport, Fenton, Shelton, Lane Delph (now Middle Fenton), Lane End, Cobridge and Hanley. See *Staffordshire.*

Stölzel, Samuel   (d. 1737) Kiln master for Böttger at Meissen, 1713-1719; arcanist at Vienna 1719-1720; returned to Meissen as a potter and color master, 1720-1737. See *Paquier, C. I. du.*

Stone-China   In English ceramics; a dense hard earthenware having china stone as an ingredient in its composition. Stone-china, which was generally of a greyish or bluish tone, was introduced by Josiah Spode II at his manufactory at Stoke-on-Trent in 1805. He hoped that this ware would supplant the coarse Chinese export porcelain. The painted decoration was generally composed of Oriental motifs which were transfer-printed in blue with touches of red. The ironstone china patented in 1813 by Charles James Mason is supposed to contain pulverized slag of iron; however, it is essentially very similar to Spode's stone-china. Trade names for the stone-china ware made by the various potters included ironstone china, new stone, semi-porcelain, opaque porcelain, granite ware, and kaolin ware. Between such names there is often very little technical distinction. For the most part they are simply individual names for the hard earthenware body which had appeared in Staffordshire in the early part of the 19th century and was usually used thereafter for transfer printing. See *Ironstone China.*

Stoneware   In ceramics; a name given to all types of clay pottery except porcelain having a body fired to a state of vitrification that is non-porous. Stoneware is always hard and is always fired in a high temperature kiln, generally ranging from 1200° C to 1400° C. Vitrified feldspathic stoneware was made in China before the 7th century and is commonly regarded as the forerunner of porcelain. Kaolinic and feldspathic stonewares are kindred to porcelain, generally lacking only the whiteness and translucency of porcelain, and are sometimes referred to as porcelaneous stonewares. Stoneware was made in certain northern parts of Germany as early as the 15th century. Grey and red stoneware bodies were the most common until around the middle of the 17th century in Europe. The glaze for stoneware has to be a special quality to stand the heat of the kiln. A salt glaze was the most common. Due to the non-porous nature of the material stoneware does not require a glaze. A distinctive variety of an almost white salt-glaze stoneware in imitation of porcelain was made at Staffordshire around the second quarter of the 18th century. In America stoneware did not come into general use until after the Revolution. Probably the first stoneware kiln or furnace in America was erected in 1730 by William Crolius near the Collect Pond in New York. The German term for stoneware is *Steinzeug*, and the French is *Grès*. See *Buccaro Ware; Elers; Fulham; Nottingham; German Stoneware; Salt Glaze; Bouffioulx; Beauvais; Crolius, W.*

Store Kongensgade   Or Delfs Porselins Eller Hollandsch Steentoys Fabrique. In Danish ceramics; a faïence factory was founded in 1722 at Copenhagen and conducted by Johann Wolff. Its best work was from 1727 to 1749 when Johan Pfau was the director. It closed shortly after 1770. The principal mark was IP in monogram. The early work was obviously inspired by the blue and white of Delft and Nuremberg. The later work was in the Scandinavian Rococo style. Some later designs were also versions of Chinese plant designs. Painting in blue was the usual style; however, some polychrome painting was also done. The characteristic bishop bowls identified with Baltic ceramics were included in their wares. See *Wolff, Johann.* (297)

Storer, Maria Longworth   See *Rookwood.*

Stove   In ceramics. See *Hafner.*

Stralsund   In Swedish ceramics; a faïence manufactory was established at Stralsund, Pomerania, Germany, in 1756 by Johann Ulrich Giese, of Sweden, to which Stralsund belonged between 1720 and 1814. It was active until 1792. Its best work was made in a four-year period between 1766 to 1770 when the factory was leased to Johann Ehrenreich who had founded the faïence manufactory at Marieberg. The wares made during this period closely resembled Marieberg faïence. The marks included the three nails of the Crucifixion with the initials of the proprietor and painter and the date. Especially characteristic were tureens and vases in the Rococo style decorated with applied reliefs of flowers, birds, small figures and foliage and potpourri vases with richly pierced covers and wavy bases. The painting was in enamel colors and was characterized by a prominent use of green. A powerful violet blue and also manganese were employed for shading, especially on openwork dishes and similar pieces.

Strapwork   In ornament; a narrow band that has been folded, crossed or interlaced in many different designs. It was often worked into very elaborate and intricate designs. A characteristic feature of the Flemish Baroque style was its prominent use of elaborate strapwork. See *Laub-und-Bandelwerk.*

Strasbourg   In French ceramics; a faïence manufactory was conducted by the Hannong family from 1720 to 1781 at Strasbourg, Alsace, producing some of the finest of French faïence. Shortly before 1750 the practice of painting in enamel colors and gilding, which previously had been almost exclusively limited to porcelains, was introduced at Strasbourg and established a fashion which was followed at the majority of French and German faïence manufactories. The manufacture of porcelain was started around 1752 but was

STORE KONGENSGADE
1727-1749

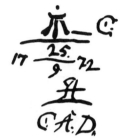

STRALSUND
1772

STRASBOURG
FAIENCE 1740-1760

STRASBOURG TUREEN

transferred to Frankenthal in 1755. Around 1766 porcelain was again made at Strasbourg. The wares generally fall into three periods corresponding to the chief proprietors; C. F. Hannong, 1721-1739; Paul Hannong, around 1740-1760, and Joseph Hannong, 1762-1781. The early wares did not have a factory mark; however, the initials of painters were rather common. P H in monogram appeared as a faïence mark around and after 1740; the initials P H were on the porcelain. From 1762 the monogram J H was used, plus initials and numerals. Strasbourg faïence was distinctive for its pure and brilliant white glaze and for its magnificent and rich enamel colors. The early faïence was chiefly painted in blue in a style derived from Rouen. The stylized so-called Indian flowers, adapted from Meissen, were introduced around 1740 and were supplanted around 1750 by the naturalistic treatment of flowers or Deutsche Blumen, also from Meissen. However, regardless of the inspiration, the Strasbourg flowers were superb and were copied in practically every faïence factory in France and Germany. The figures included all the characteristic Meissen types. The so-called Trompe l'Oeil wares such as tureens in the form of vegetables and dishes molded with fruits painted in natural colors were made at Strasbourg and were perhaps the finest of their type. From 1762 to 1781 the faïence production was to a great extent a repetition of the middle period; however, the porcelain reflected the influence of the Louis XVI style. Under Strasbourg's influence other manufactories were started in Alsace and in Lorraine. In Niderviller, near Sarrebourg, the faïence works were the diversion of two cultured aristocrats, the Baron de Beyerlé and his wife, herself a painter and poet, who had gained possession of the estate in 1748. They lured workers away from the Strasbourg Hannongs, among them François-Antoine Anstett who was a director of their manufactory from 1754-1779. Beyerlé's faïence,

STURZBECHER, SIEGBURG
STONEWARE

which bears the mark N.B., is well known for the refinement of its forms, inspired by silversmiths' work, and for its painted decoration of landscapes or flowers executed in delicate shades. See *Faïence; Trompe l'Oeil; Haguenau; Hannong, Charles-François; Löwenfinck, A. F. von; Anstett, François-Antoine; Niderviller; Hannong, Paul-Antoine; Ringler, J. J.* (279-282)

Strasbourg Flowers   See *Strasbourg.*

Stratton, Mary Chase Perry   See *Pewabic Pottery.*

Strebelle, Oliver   Belgian designer, ceramist and teacher, who first became prominent after the Second World War. He is especially well known for his ceramic sculptures.

Stuart Period   In English history, 1603-1714; the reigns of James I, 1603-1625; Charles I, 1625-1649; the Commonwealth, 1649-1660; Charles II, 1660-1685; James II, 1685-1688; William and Mary, 1688-1702; Anne, 1702-1714.

Stubbs, George   (1724-1806) English portrait and animal painter; a friend of Josiah Wedgwood for whom he modeled some reliefs of horses.

Studio-Potter   Essentially the conception of a studio-potter relates to a potter producing pottery under studio conditions, that is, the working room of one. See *Artist-Potter.*

Studio Pottery   Hand-made pottery (as opposed to machine-made factory wares) made by one potter or a small team. For the most part true studio pottery is of an individual nature.

Sturzbecher   In German ceramics; a Rhenish stoneware cup having a stem but no foot. The stem was in the form of the figure of a man. When the bowl of the cup was inverted the figure of the man was upright.

It is especially identified with the salt-glazed stoneware made at Siegburg during the second half of the 16th century. (188)

Style Étrusque, Le The name given by contemporaries to a more simple, more austerely classical phase of the Louis XVI style, which emerged about 1785 and developed after the French Revolution into the Directoire and Empire styles. Its immediate source of inspiration was the painting on Greek vases, collections of which were reaching France and England in increasing numbers. Sir William Hamilton's first collection of vases was acquired by the British Museum in 1772; in France, Comte de Caylus' vases were given to the Cabinet des Médailles during his lifetime or bequeathed at his death in 1765, and in 1786 the Sèvres factory purchased a large collection assembled by Vivant de Denon. The archaeologists of that time erroneously believed them all to be of Etruscan origin. See *Victorian; Louis XVI.*

Style Rayonnant In French ceramics; the name given to the most characteristic type of lambrequins comprising festoons, lacework, closely diapered borders and formal scrolls in a radial arrangement in which a severe symmetry was preserved. The Baroque Style Rayonnant and related decorations was in fashion from around the late 17th century to about 1730-1740, and the motifs were usually executed in blue on a white ground. The style was copied at Lille, Saint-Cloud, and Paris, where black outlines usually supplanted the blue of Rouen, at Nevers, Strasbourg, Moustiers and Marseilles. The vogue and influence of this class of Rouen ware achieved its climax around 1709-1710. See *Rouen.* (270-272)

Sue Ware In Japanese ceramics; the contemporary name (which is still used today) given to the earliest examples of true pottery in Japan. This important new variety which was first found in burial mounds of the late 5th and early 6th centuries, marks a fairly distinct departure from the indigenous potting methods of Jomon and Yayoi wares. The introduction of this hard-baked non-porous grey pottery is believed to have been to a great extent due to the importation of Korean potters around this period. Sue potters used a more refined variety of clay than the makers of Yayoi ware and baked or fired it at much higher temperatures resulting in a harder, much more durable product. They were devotees of the potter's wheel whose demands determined the nature of much of the surface decoration. Their work developed more uniformity and precision which to a great extent can only be acquired at the sacrifice of freedom. Their most important contribution was progress in the use of surface glazes. It is to these advanced techniques and their early development in Sue wares that later Japanese ceramic art is deeply indebted. Much early pottery, especially from about the 6th century onward, showed thin smears of a glaze-like substance thought to be the result of wood ash coming into contact with the surface of the vessel during firing. In fortunate combinations various impurities, particularly ashes, when once introduced, then combined in different kinds of chemical reactions to fuse at high temperatures with silica in the surface of the ware, produce, when cooled, thin streaks of a hard and semi-transparent glaze. Briefly, Sue potters had accidentally discovered the principle of fused silica glaze as potters had done long before in China and were to do many times again in different parts of the world. In Japan, Sue wares were the first to be fired at sufficiently high temperatures for such fusion to occur. This fused silica type of glaze is the most common and most easily produced variety of glaze, in which wood ash acts as a flux to assist in the fusing of silica in the form of sand or quartz, either naturally on the surface or added deliberately for the sole purpose of producing a glaze. The flux

STYLE RAYONNANT ON
ROUEN PLATE

may be either alkaline (for instance, lime or ash) or an oxide of lead, in this latter instance resulting in the familiar lead glaze. Most important among the Shosoin wares are the so-called Shosoin Three-Color wares, the earliest of which are of 8th century origin and are the earliest extant examples of Japanese ceramic art in which complicated glazings were deliberately used for decorative effects. Their source of inspiration was the lead-glazed Three-Color ware of the T'ang dynasty, 618-907, and like their prototypes some of the Shosoin wares are decorated with streaked and dappled green, brown and white glazes alternating over their surfaces in a variety of arresting designs. However, the majority by far are in only two colors, green and white. Fired at lower temperatures than the earlier Sue ware, most likely at less than 1000 degrees, all of these polychrome lead-glazed wares are unmistakably Japanese and are quite different, chiefly in style, glaze and color of body, from the Chinese originals. Apart from the Shosoin ware there are many other good examples of the same general type of ware including a distinctive monochrome lead-glazed ware, particularly green, which has been excavated around Nara. These are generally called Nara Three-Color and Nara Green. Wares with wood-ash glazes, either accidental or planned, were also produced at this time. Certain sites producing Sue ware began to develop local characteristics which mark the beginning of the Six Old Kilns era. See *Shosoin; Yayoi; Japanese Periods; Six Old Kilns; Glaze.*

SUHL
1891 ON

Suhl In German ceramics; a porcelain factory making table services and ornamental pieces was started at Suhl, Prussia, in 1861, by Erdmann Schlegelmilch. The distinguishing initials E S are found in marks of different design. An accepted mark bears the initials R S (Reinhold Schlegelmilch) and Prussia. It was a very popular export ware. See *Tillowitz.*

Sui A period in Chinese art history, c. 581-618. See *Chinese Dynasties.*

Sukhothai See *Indo-China.*

Sullivan, Louis (1856-1926) American architect; an important pioneer of modern design. In his ORNAMENT IN ARCHITECTURE, 1892, he said, "Ornament is mentally a luxury, not a necessity." See *Modern Movement.*

Sumerian In ancient Near East culture; the Sumerians were the first great cast of actors in the drama of civilization in southern Mesopotamia. The exact time of their arrival remains uncertain; however, they were already a heterogeneous people when their acquaintance is first made in Ubaid times, about 4500-3500 B.C. Ubaid pottery ranges from monochrome chocolate-colored painted fabrics of high quality to coarse green overfired pottery, both painted and unpainted. The succeeding Uruk period, c.3500-3100 B.C., is named after the famous site that is today called Warka. This was followed by the Jamdat Nasr period, c.3100-2900 B.C., named after the site where the culture was first recognized, and Early Dynastic period, c.2900-2370 B.C., when the Sumerian city states were subdued. In the Neo-Sumerian period, c.2230-2000 B.C., fine works of art in the Sumerian tradition were produced. The vital contribution made by the Sumerians to the development of civilized life will remain as one of man's greatest achievements, for they were the peoples who invented writing and made man civilized. See *Ubaid.* (25)

Summer, George Heywood Maunoir (1853-1940) English designer, archaeologist, painter and etcher; joined the Art Workers' Guild and was associated with Arthur Mackmurdo and the Century Guild.

Summerly, Felix See *Summerley's Art Manufactures.*

Summerly's Art Manufactures In English decorative arts; started in 1847 by Felix Summerly, a pseudonym for Sir Henry Cole, who believed that it would promote public taste if well-known painters and sculptors could be persuaded to produce designs for manufactured articles of daily use. This interesting enterprise, directed entirely toward improving contemporary industrial products, lasted for about three years. Examples were sold under the name of Summerly's Art Manufactures. In ceramics the distinguishing initials F.S. in monogram were found in marks of differing design. See *Cole, Sir Henry.*

Sunderland In English ceramics; several potteries were active in Sunderland, County Durham, during the late 18th and early 19th centuries, making a rather inferior quality of cream-colored and white earthenware. The decoration was principally transfer-printed. See *North Hylton Pottery; Sunderland Pottery; Dawson, John and Company; Southwick Pottery; Moore, Samuel and Company; Union Pottery.*

Sunderland Pottery or **Garrison Pottery** In English ceramics; a pottery at Sunderland, Durham, c. 1807-1865, producing earthenwares. The marks were as follows: J. Phillips, Sunderland Pottery, c. 1807-1812; Phillips and Company, Dixon and Company, c. 1813-1819; Dixon, Austin and Company, c. 1820-1840; Dixon, Austin, Phillips and Company, c. 1824-1840; Dixon, Phillips and Company, c. 1840-1865. A later Sunderland Pottery Company (Ltd.) was active from around 1913 to 1927. Its trade name was Sundrex. See *North Hylton Pottery; Sunderland.*

Sundrex See Sunderland Pottery.

Sung In Chinese ceramics; the Sung dynasty ruled over China from A.D. 960 to 1127 and over the southern half from A.D. 1127 to 1279. The Tartar tribes invaded north China in 1127, and the reigning Sung emperor left his capital at K'ai-Fêng Fu and established his court at Hangchow which became the Southern Sung capital. The Sung emperors were patrons of the arts, and all the arts flourished during their reigns. Ceramic art enjoyed one of its most brilliant phases. T'ang earthenware with its low-fired lead glazes was supplanted by high-fired porcelaneous ware with feldspathic glazes. Porcelain and high-temperature glazes came into vogue late in the T'ang dynasty and by the Sung dynasty the fashion for porcelain was established. The term *porcelain* is used in the broad Chinese sense which includes, in addition to the white translucent body, grey and dusky bodies which have been fired to such a state of vitrification that they emit a musical note when struck. This musical note was the principal test of early porcelains in China. Painting in underglaze blue and overglaze enamels which was so typical of the later wares produced at Ching-tê-Chên was not in vogue during the Sung period. Monochromes were in vogue and color effects were achieved by mixing coloring oxides in the glaze. In this manner a wide range of delicate and elusive tints were achieved; some were undoubtedly accidental and were chiefly due to the opalescent nature of the bubbly glazes. An important feature was crackle, which in the beginning was accidental but later purposely obtained. The refinement of form and color was a distinctive feature of the Sung monochromes. Potters in the ensuing centuries returned to them again and again for inspiration. The ornament on the Sung wares was obtained by carving, etching, applying stamped reliefs or by pressing in molds. The designs were notable for their free-flowing quality and delightful freshness. The Yüan dynasty, 1280-1368, is generally regarded in

SUMMERLY, FELIX
c. 1846-1850

ceramics as an extension of the Sung dynasty. See *Chien Yao; Chün Yao; Ju Ware; Kuan Yao; Ko Yao; Ting Yao; Celadon; Tz'u Chou; China,* in Far Eastern ceramics; *Ming; Ch'ing Pai.* (89-97)

SUPPER SET, K'ANG HSI

Supper Set In Chinese ceramics; a number of small ornamental trays which when grouped together form a large tray of varying shape. The trays can be used individually or joined together. Especially praiseworthy are the K'ang Hsi Famille Verte supper sets consisting of 13 petal-shaped trays which form a lotus flower. In another characteristic grouping four triangular trays form a circle which is surrounded by eight trays forming a rosette.

Susa See *Near East,* in prehistoric ceramics; *Islamic Pottery, Early.*

Sussex In English ceramics; during the late 18th and early 19th centuries slipware was made in a number of towns in Sussex. Essentially most of it was rather crude. However, at Brede and Chailey in Sussex and at Bethersden in Kent, a more interesting variety of slipware was made. The designs, comprising stars, circles, foliage and formal patterns, were incised or impressed and were inlaid with white clay. Included among the wares were pocket flasks and drinking mugs in the form of pigs.

Swan Service In German ceramics; a Meissen table service made for Count Brühl and his wife originally comprising two thousand two hundred individual items modeled by Kaendler and assisted by Johann Friedrich Eberlein, working on it from 1737–1741. The service was so named in the 19th century no doubt because of the aquatic theme of its elaborately modeled decoration—swans, river gods, mermaids, shells, rushes and other similar motifs. It is said to be the most beautiful, the most magnificent table service ever made by a porcelain factory. (314)

Swansea In English ceramics; the Cambrian Pottery in Swansea, Glamorganshire, Wales, was operating at least as early as 1765 and was active until 1870. The reputation of Swansea rests upon a soft paste porcelain made from 1814 to 1822, having some of the qualities of whiteness and translucency associated with Nantgarw porcelain. Included among the marks were the names of the town, the pottery and the different proprietors (Dillwyn, 1802-1817; Bevington, 1817-1824; Dillwyn, 1824-1850; Evans and Glasson, 1850-c. 1861; D. J. Evans and Company, c. 1861-1870). The forms for Swansea porcelain which was only made here from 1814-1822, were distinctive for their refined simplicity and were in the contemporary Neo-Classic taste. Much of the ware was decorated in London to the order of dealers. The painted decoration executed at Swansea included flowers, fruit, birds, figure subjects and landscapes. As a rule the earthenware had little or no artistic merit. Practically all the different kinds of current Staffordshire wares were imitated, such as cream-colored and white earthenware, blue-printed ware, marbled and black basalt ware. Painting in colors was done and figures were also made. Many fine Etruscan patterned wares, such as vases, were made here around 1847-1850. Another pottery called the Glamorgan Pottery was active from around 1813 to 1839, making earthenware similar to that made at Swansea. See *Young, W. W.* (471)

Swatow In Chinese ceramics; the red and green enameled painting on porcelain introduced under the Sung Dynasty continued in favor more or less, though in very different styles, throughout the Ming period and was chiefly used on a notable variety of wares, largely plates and dishes, exported to Japan and the islands of the southwest Pacific from (it is believed) the port of Swatow in southern China. Hence their name. The red and green enameled variety of Swatow with underglaze blue sparingly applied was eagerly collected in Japan under the name of Gosu-Akae (akae means red). A subdivision of the class with little or no red is called Ao-Gosu (blue-green). Gosu is apparently a dialect word meaning blue. In Japan the wares are most usually found in the form of large bowls made during the Ming period decorated in red and green enamels or in underglaze blue. Swatow wares are characterized by a rather unrefined finish and a gritty foot rim caused by placing it on sand in the kiln. Made for the common market, these wares have a free, uninhibited quality in their style of painted decoration that makes them in some ways more attractive than the well-behaved Imperial porcelains. Swatow wares were highly prized in Japan and as a result were widely imitated. Okuda Eisen is especially remembered for his Gosu-Akae style of decorated porcelains. Pieces of this type have red and green enamels sometimes combined with underglaze blue. See *Gosu-Akae.*

Swebach, Jacques-François-José (1769-1823) Called Desfontaines or Fontaines. Painter,

working at Sèvres, 1802-1814, and at St. Petersburg, 1815-1820. He specialized in military subjects and was engaged at Sèvres to celebrate Napoleon's victories on porcelain.

Swinton In English ceramics. See *Rockingham.*

Swiss Lady In American ceramics; the name given to a pottery article made at Bennington, Vermont, 1849-1858, in the form of a lady with a bell-shaped hoop skirt, used in public bars as a cover over coins on a bar counter. As a rule the figure was covered with a flint enamel glaze. See *Bennington.*

Syjalon, Antoine (1524–1590) A Huguenot potter working from the middle of the 16th century at Nîmes, France, where he produced some faïence of fine quality. (236, 237)

Syracuse China Corporation See *Onondaga Pottery Company.*

Syria See *Near East,* in prehistoric ceramics; *Islamic Pottery.*

SWANSEA
PORCELAIN 1814-1822

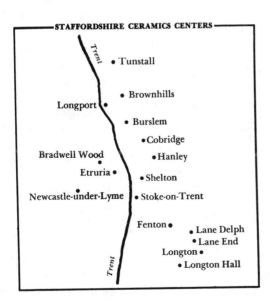

STAFFORDSHIRE CERAMICS CENTERS

- Tunstall
- Brownhills
- Longport
- Burslem
- Cobridge
- Bradwell Wood
- Hanley
- Etruria
- Shelton
- Newcastle-under-Lyme
- Stoke-on-Trent
- Fenton
- Lane Delph
- Lane End
- Longton
- Longton Hall

T

Ta Kuan In Chinese ceramics; see *Kuan Yao.*

Table des Maréchaux or **Table of the Marshals** See *Ceramic Plaques as Furniture Decoration; Sèvres.*

Taft, J. S. and Company See *Hampshire Pottery.*

T'ai Ch'ang The T'ai Ch'ang reign of the Ming dynasty of China, 1620. See *Chinese Dynasties.*

Takamatsu See *Kyo.*

Takatori In Japanese ceramics, shortly after the beginning of the 17th century kilns were started at several locations in present Fukuoka Prefecture, Kyushu, which made the ware known as Old Takatori, a designation reserved for products made prior to around 1640. The founder of these kilns is recorded to have been a Korean potter named Pal San. Most Takatori wares, which are Karatsu-type wares, were intended for the tea ceremony and it is believed that Takatori potters were instructed in their design and taste by the tea master Kobori Enshu. See *Karatsu.*

Talavera de la Reina In Spanish ceramics; majolica and faïence were made at Talavera de la Reina and at neighboring Puente del Arzobispo in Castile from early in the 16th century, continuing into the 18th century. No factory marks were ever used. They developed an original style of painting remarkable for its vigor but having little refinement. The colors were dominated by a powerful green, a canary yellow and a thick orange, and to some extent by a heavy blue. Horsemen, hunting scenes, buildings, trees, animals, birds, figures and coats-of-arms were much favored as motifs. The distinctive and interesting forms were to a large extent of traditional Spanish shape and included broad flat-bottomed jugs, helmet-shaped ewers, very large basins and dishes and globular jars and two-handled vases. During the 18th century the wares reflected the influence of the faïence made at Alcora. It has also been suggested that the scented red pottery or buccaro made in Central and South America and imported to Spain was also made here. See *Caussada, Jacinto; Tempesta, A.* (292)

Talbot A 19th century French family of potters working at La Borne, near Bourges, who were very prominent in the field of figure-making in this very early pottery-producing district. Their pottery figures may be regarded as popular art and were notable for the liveliness and strength the Talbots imparted to them.

Tamba In Japanese ceramics; wares produced in the Tamba kilns in modern Hyogo and Kyoto Prefectures represent a ceramic tradition sufficiently ancient to be included among the Six Old Kilns. Included among their products is a distinctive heavy stoneware very greatly resembling that of the Iga and Shigaraki kilns. Extant examples having a reddish-brown body together with a greyish-green glaze are reminiscent of the characteristics of much Iga ware. Like many of the very early centers, Tamba has continued to produce various wares down to modern times. See *Six Old Kilns; Shigaraki.*

Tamikichi, Kato See *Seto.*

Tanagra Statuette A small terra-cotta figure or statuette found in large numbers at Tanagra, Greece. Tanagra figures were used as household gods or ornaments and were placed in temples or buried in tombs. Genre figures and statuettes or graceful girls in standing or seated positions made during the 4th and 3rd centuries B.C. are particularly noted for their charm and artistic quality. Many of these figures have painted decoration. See *Terra-Cotta*. (64)

T'ang   The T'ang dynasty of China, A.D. 618 to 906, has been called the great age of Chinese art and literature. Sculpture, painting and the lesser arts flourished during T'ang times. In Chinese ceramic art; T'ang pottery reached a high plane of development. T'ang pottery in collections is mostly from the tombs as was the pottery of the Han period. Included among the specimens of T'ang articles are bowls, dishes, ewers, jars, figures in costume and armor, horses and camels. Numerous models buried with the dead are of objects that surrounded them in life. The body of T'ang ware varies from a soft pottery to a porcelaneous ware. It is usually a soft white material similar to plaster of Paris and varies in color from white to pinkish white to buff. Although some figures are unglazed, they usually have a neutral glaze that has a tendency to yellow, and both types are decorated with unfired colors The same glaze, which is colored with blue, green and brownish-yellow, is used on the finer figures. The decoration was more or less of simple technique. It consisted of pressing in molds, incising with a pointed tool and stamped reliefs applied on the surface. Frequently the ground was cut away with a knife, leaving the design in relief. The stamped reliefs were usually medallions or palmettes, frequently having intricate designs. Stamped reliefs also included small figures of animals, rosettes and occasionally human figures. Another incised ornament has the design outlined with a pointed instrument with the enclosed spaces covered with variously colored glazes which comprises the so-called T'ang Three-Color ware. High-fired glazes such as celadon green, chocolate brown, cream white, flambé and grey were introduced during the T'ang period. The lead glaze on T'ang pottery colored with oxides that produce green, blue and brownish yellow differs from the Han glaze in that it has a paler hue, since it is applied on a light colored body or on a white slip. See *China*, in Far Eastern ceramics. (87, 88)

Tao Kuang   The Tao Kuang reign of the Ch'ing dynasty, 1821-1850. See *Chinese Dynasties*.

Tarascan   In pre-Columbian Central American ceramics; a people from the Tarascan country, a region northwest of Tenochtitlan (Mexico City) in what is today the state of Michoacan, who even at the time of the most powerful Aztec expansion in the 15th century were successful in maintaining their artistic independence. Unusually striking are the Tarascan figures in clay in which the potter succeeded in catching a remarkable variety of expressions and attitudes. Always in Tarascan modeling the entire figure is transfused with a communicative spirit. It is not known how long they inhabited the region. See *Central American Pottery*.

Tatler, Elijah   See *Cartlidge, Charles*.

Tavern China   See *Popov; Kiselev*.

Taylor, Howson   (1876-1935) English artist-potter, experimented in glaze technique from 1898 onward in his Ruskin pottery at Smethwick, near Birmingham. See *Ruskin Pottery*.

Taylor and Company   In American ceramics; active at Trenton, New Jersey, 1865-1870; succeeded by Taylor and Goodwin, 1870-1872. Same as the Trenton Pottery Company. (445)

Taylor and Speeler   In American ceramics; first of the Trenton potteries; started to manufacture Rockingham and yellow wares at Trenton, New Jersey, in 1853. They continued with this for about two decades. By 1855 the firm, now Taylor, Speeler and Bloor, the latter being a successful East Liverpool potter who provided financial aid, was making white ware or white granite. Their success attracted other potters and initiated the great pottery industry at Trenton. See *White Ware; Trenton.*

Taylor, Smith and Taylor Company In American ceramics; this still-existing factory was started in 1896 at East Liverpool, Ohio, for the manufacture of ironstone, earthenware and china for daily use.

Taylor, Speeler and Bloor See *Taylor and Speeler.*

Tê-Hua In Chinese ceramics; a location in the Ch'üan-Chou district of the province of Fukien noted during the later part of the Ming period for the beautiful pure white porcelain known as Blanc de Chine. See *Blanc de Chine; Ming.*

Tea Caddy A small container for tea, derived from the Malay word *kati* or the Chinese *catty,* which means a measure of weight equal to about one and one-third pounds avoirdupois and signified the small box in which tea was sent to Europe. In the 18th century tea caddies were made in a wide variety of materials such as wood, silver and porcelain. See *Tea Table Wares.* (305, 362, 374)

Tea Dust In Chinese ceramics; a glaze on porcelain ware developed during the Ch'ien Lung period which was a yellowish green or yellowish brown color sprinkled with a tea-green color.

Tea Table Wares In European ceramics; the use of tea in Europe dates from around the middle of the 17th century. Generally exported along with the tea from China were the unglazed red stoneware teapots, the so-called Buccaro ware, reputed to be best for brewing it. The forms of these teapots served as prototypes for the earliest European examples which were made at least as early as 1672 in a red ware like the Chi-

nese, as Delft faïence proved unsuitable. Subsequent variations in shape were made according to 18th century styles. The typical 18th century European tea service comprised a teapot and teapot stand, cups (at first without handles like the Chinese), bowls for tea leaves and sometimes for sugar basins, and jugs for milk, cream and hot water. When the tea service was provided with an oval tray it was occasionally called a cabaret set (the term is not contemporary). Also should be mentioned the flat sugar box and cover and the tea caddy. The very large rectangular tea trays made at the Scandinavian factories are especially notable. (111)

Teco Pottery In American ceramics; an art pottery started in the early years of the 20th century at Terra Cotta, Illinois, using mainly mat green glazes reminiscent of Grueby's but with forms tending to be more organic. One of the chief designers was German-born Fritz Albert who had been trained in Berlin. See *Grueby, W. H.*

Tegelen In Dutch ceramics; pottery was made here as early as the days of Roman occupation in Holland. From the 17th century Tegelen potteries have been chiefly making peasant pottery ornamented in relief and decorated with colored slips. Many of the motifs are derived from Tegelen folklore.

Telechany In Polish ceramics; a faïence factory specializing in stoves was carried on here from the close of the 18th century by Count Michael Oginski, whose wares were occasionally marked with the initials C.O. The wares show a preference for chinoiserie decoration.

Tell Halaf See *Near East,* in prehistoric ceramics.

Temmoku In ceramics; a comprehensive term given to a large variety of Chinese pottery, stoneware and semi-porcelain

TAYLOR, SMITH & TAYLOR

VITREOES

1901 ON

PRESENT

with a rich thick glaze in which predominate bluish, purplish-black or reddish-brown colors. In particular the term applies to one variety called Chien yao. See *Chien Yao; Honan Temmoku; Kian Temmoku.* The term *temmoku* is also a Japanese term, and it is the name given to those tea bowls of the Chien yao type having mottlings or fine streaks like the breast of a partridge or the fur of a hare. During the Ming period these bowls were much favored by the Japanese due to the importance of the tea ceremony. By extension the term is now given to tea bowls with a dark brown glaze.

Tempesta, Antonio (1555-1630) Engraver; copies of his designs were frequently used on Nevers, Marseilles (Saint Jean-du-Désert), Talavera, and Moustiers faïence. His name is attached to the earliest styles adopted at Moustiers. See *Engraved Designs; Viry, F.G.*

Tempesta Style See *Tempesta, A.*

Tempyo The Tempyo or Nara period of Japan; A.D. 645-794. See *Japanese Periods.*

Teotihuacan In pre-Columbian Central American ceramics; the Classic period; 300-980, is best exemplified in central Mexico by the site of Teotihuacan, where the earliest vessels were similar to those of the Formative period, 1500 B.C.-A.D. 300. The early phase of the Classic period was one of development and experiment, which resulted in the rich and colorful wares using new shapes and techniques of the succeeding phase. Perhaps the most striking is that known as fresco or cloisonné pottery. In this technique the entire surface of a vessel was covered with a thin film of colored plaster. The greater part of this was cut away, leaving thin walls to form partitions or divisions between the plaster of other colors which was then applied to the intervening spaces. After smoothing, the surface revealed a clean design. Unfortunately, the process was technically unsound and the wares were

very fragile. Pastel shades were usually employed, pink, blue, green and white. Related to this technique is that known as Champlevé, in which black or dark brown slip is scraped or cut away, leaving the design in low relief; then the scraped background is filled in or painted with cinnabar. The molded figures were well made; some were of striking beauty; and all are characterized by over-elaboration and great attention to iconographic detail. In the last phase, beginning after 700, a decline set in, and the figures revealed a coarsening of workmanship. The destruction of Teotihuacan marks the beginning of the Post Classic period, 980-1521. Outside the valley of Mexico but still sufficiently close to be influenced from it was the city of Cholula, whose pottery appeared to follow the styles of the valley. At first it resembled the Formative and Teotihuacan, and later the polychrome trade wares of Sacrificios and Tlascala. See *Central American Pottery.*

Tepeu See *Maya.*

Teramo See *Castelli.*

Terekhov and Kiselev See *Kiselev.*

Terrace Vase In Swedish ceramics; a distinctive Rococo vase identified only with the wares made at Marieberg. The body of the vase was mounted on a base formed either of swirling waves or a winding flight of steps. Sometimes a rabbit or some other kind of animal was at the foot of the steps. See *Marieberg.*

Terra-Cotta Clay baked without a glaze; the Italian words *terra-cotta* simply mean burnt earth. Among the many purposes for which terra-cotta was used by the ancient Greeks may be mentioned parts of buildings such as bricks and roof tiles and architectural ornament; tombs and coffins; statues and statuettes for sepulchral or votive purposes or for the decoration of houses; such objects for daily use as

CO

TELECHANY C. 1790 ON

domestic jars and pots, lamps, braziers and spindle whorls; molds for the potter and models of works of art, particularly in bronze for the sculptor. The small terra-cotta figures used as ornaments or household gods, buried in tombs or dedicated in temples, have been discovered in large numbers at almost all the well-known sites of antiquity such as Tanagra, Rhodes, Athens, Sicily and some of the towns of southern Italy. The coloring of the baked figures was fairly universal. The front of the figure was covered with a creamy white slip on which colors were painted in tempera colors. The people of Etruria also used terra-cotta both for ornamental and utilitarian purposes. The uses of terra-cotta among the Romans were much the same as among the Greeks and Etruscans. After the downfall of the Roman Empire in the west, the artistic use of terra-cotta came to a halt, until it was revived during the 14th and 15th century as an adjunct to medieval architecture. Sculptors of the Italian Renaissance used terra-cotta as a medium for making reliefs, busts and even groups of numerous life-sized figures. In the 16th century a more realistic style made its debut, and this was accentuated by the custom of painting the figures in oil colors. The introduction of enameled reliefs in terra-cotta is closely associated with the Florentine sculptor Luca della Robbia. From the Italian school the development of architectural terra-cotta slowly spread through Europe. In the 17th and 18th century the architectural use of terra-cotta again fell away, due no doubt to the increasing use of marble. Around the middle of the 19th century the interest in terra-cotta as a ceramic material was revived and centered on its use for large objects such as garden vases, even fountains, and architectural features. In America the use of terra-cotta in architecture is linked with the search for a fireproof building material. Chicago, New York, Boston and Perth Amboy had the most important plants producing terra-cotta. Ornaments

designed by architects such as James Renwick, Thomas Hastings, Louis Sullivan and Bernard Maybeck were made from molds and were supplied to builders in cities throughout the United States. From the office of Adler and Sullivan in Chicago came the most effective designs. Glazed terra-cotta and fire bricks for interior use were a specialty of the Boston Terra-Cotta Company. In conclusion it should be mentioned that the distinction between pottery figures and models in baked clay known as terra-cotta is one not readily drawn. It may be said that the name *terra-cotta* is more appropriately applied to a figure baked more lightly than most kinds of earthenware, which is the work of a sculptor and not of a potter. The smaller Greek terra-cottas, like the related Chinese grave-figures of the Han and T'ang dynasties and the Japanese Haniwa of the Jomon period, are essentially the potter's art, while the figures and reliefs, for example those by della Robbia who was originally a carver of marble, rank as sculpture though they use the typical tin-glaze of the potter.

Terra de Pipa   The Spanish term for a kind of pottery which imitated the English cream-colored earthenware.

Terra Sigillata   Pottery made of clay (terra) suitable for being impressed with seals (sigilla). See *Roman Pottery*.

Terraglia   In ceramics; the Italian term for cream-colored earthenware or creamware.

Terre de Lorraine or **Clay of Lorraine**   A hard pipe-clay composition which in eastern France is used like biscuit. See *Faïence Fine*.

Terre de Pipe   In French ceramics; a French term for a lead-glazed soft earthenware having a white body. See *Cream-Colored Earthenware*.

Teruel   In Spanish ceramics; certain notable classes of blue- or green-and-purple painted tin-glazed ware with strong designs seemingly inspired by Manisses are attributed to this town. Apparently the best wares date from the 15th century and early 16th century.

Tettau In German ceramics; a still-existing porcelain factory, Die Porzellanfabrik Tettau, was started here in 1794 by Georg C. F. Greiner with a royal privilege, producing chiefly table services. In 1897 it was destroyed by fire; on the same site a larger, modern factory was built. Their wares have always enjoyed a good reputation. Among the marks are Royal Tettau; Königl. pr. Tettau; T.; PRIV 1794. A familiar mark dating from around 1891 to 1905 bore the inscription Royal Bayreuth above a decorative design centering the initial T with Germany written below.

Texeraud, Léon In French ceramics; started a porcelain factory at Limoges in 1923. The production chiefly consists of tea and coffee services, tablewares for daily use and fanciful articles. The marks include L.T. and the trade mark Elite.

Thailand See *Indo-China.*

Tharaud See *Limoges.*

Thieme, Carl See *Potschappel.*

Thiirslund, Jens See *Kähler.*

Thomire, Pierre Philippe (1751-1843) French bronze founder working in the Louis XVI and French Empire style. His bronze mounts are remarkable for their jewel-like quality. See *Metal Mounts on Ceramics.*

Thompson, C. C. Pottery Company In American ceramics; active at East Liverpool, Ohio, from around 1870 onward. They were large producers of yellow ware and Rockingham; also included in their production was white granite and cream-colored earthenware.

Thorsson, Nils See *Aluminia.*

Thorwaldsen, Bertel or **Thorvaldsen** (1770-1844) Danish sculptor. Noteworthy are his statues of pagan deities modeled with much of the antique feeling for breadth and purity of design. The most widely popular among Thorwaldsen's works have been some of his bas-reliefs such as Night and Morning. At the Royal Copenhagen porcelain factory the production of figure modeling was given fresh life with the introduction of models by Thorwaldsen. See *Bing and Grøndahl.*

Three Bells, The or **De Drie Klokken** In Dutch ceramics; active at Delft from 1671 onward producing faïence. Changed ownership several times. In 1840 the proprietors, J. van Putten and Company, united it with the Porcelain Claw Pottery. See *Delft.*

Three-Color Ware or **San Ts'ai** In Chinese ceramics; porcelain and sometimes stoneware decorated on the biscuit with medium-fired colored glazes used in washes over engraved, carved, or relief-edged designs set in a single colored ground. They are the most characteristic Ming polychromes. The glazes include dark violet blue sometimes verging on black, turquoise inclining to blue, brownish purple or aubergine, green and yellow. To these can be added a colorless glaze which over the more or less white biscuit resulted in a more or less clean white. The term *three-color* has no exact numerical significance; the addition of another color was perfectly permissible. To keep these glazes from touching each other, three technical devices were used. The most usual and most characteristically Ming, as it was a Ming innovation, is the so-called cloisonné technique. In this method the designs were drawn in raised lines of clay which served as walls, like the cloisons of enameling on metal work, keeping the glazes apart. In the second method the designs were outlined with strongly incised or engraved lines which served as dikes. This device (sgraffiato) goes back to T'ang times. The

TEXERAUD, L.
1923 ON

THOMPSON, C. C., POTTERY
1884 ON

THE THREE BELLS
17TH-18TH CENTURIES

third, also pre-Ming, was by carved reliefs and perforation. Sometimes all three were combined on the same piece. The cloisonné group (the "carved" may be taken in conjunction with it) which includes superb large wine jars, flower vases, incense burners and barrel seats, is remarkable for the splendor of color and the breadth and freedom of treatment. The designs are picked out with colored glazes but the mass of color is the background which is often a dark purple blue, a beautiful turquoise and more rarely leaf green or aubergine brown. Wares of this class have been attributed to the Hsüan Te period, 1426-1435, but they probably did not make their debut until the Hung Chih period, 1488-1505. Regardless, the ware was not made to any extent after the Ming period except for recent bad imitations. The engraved or sgraffiato type of decoration is found on wares before and after Ming. Probably the finest work of the kind under Ming was that belonging to the Chêng Tê period, 1506-1521. In the succeeding Ch'ing dynasty, 1644-1912, the potters of the K'ang Hsi period, 1666-1722, developed their enameled decoration from two Ming styles: the three-color painting usually applied on the biscuit and the overglaze five-color painting which on K'ang Hsi wares is known in Europe as Famille Verte. Enameled painting on biscuit was used to a great extent in the K'ang Hsi period. The wares with the medium-fired glazes include the brinjal bowls (the word *brinjal* is of the same derivation as the word *aubergine*) having a ground color of dark manganese purple with incised decoration in leaf-green, yellow and greenish white. There are also dapple glazes, possibly made in imitation of the Three-Color ware of the T'ang dynasty, 618-906, with patches of green, yellow and purple. These are variously called tiger-skin and egg-and-spinach. The usual Three-Color enamels were essentially the same as the glazes; the yellow and green frequently used as ground colors were of a soft tone

and texture, while the aubergine was of distinctive quality. Designs were drawn in a brownish black outline, and this same color covered with a wash of the green enamel provided the much-favored black ground of the big vases. See *Ming; Five-Color Ware; Ch'ing.* (100, 101)

Three Friends See *Shochikubai.*

Throwing In ceramics; the way to make any circular clay article on a rotating potter's wheel. The shape into which the plastic clay is squeezed is controlled by centrifugal force and the pressure of the potter's hand. After the article or pot is dry, it may further be turned on a lathe of the wheel to modify the profile or to impart a smoother surface texture.

Thuringia In German ceramics; a number of faïence and porcelain manufactories were situated in the forest region of Thuringia during the 18th century. Although some of the faïence produced here was of a very high standard, especially that produced in certain potteries having princely protection, the majority of faïence had little artistic importance. Essentially the manufacture catered to the middle class. The painted decoration was distinctive for its vigor, but it had very little refinement. Especially characteristic was the use of strong, powerful high-temperature colors, which included a bright blue, a dry red, a greyish green, all tones of yellow and manganese. Cylindrical tankards were characteristic productions. Among the motifs which were conventionally treated were birds, trees, figure subjects and coarse chinoiseries. A number of porcelain manufactories were started here around 1770, essentially due to a plentiful supply of local clay. The porcelain industry is still flourishing. The rather coarse and greyish tone hard paste porcelain was produced by a cheaper process. Most of it had little artistic merit. Gotha and Kloster-Veilsdorf are the exceptions which included in their productions some excellent figures. Some of the factories such as Limbach, Wallendorf and Volkstedt were principally engaged in producing porcelain for the middle class market. These wares often closely imitated Meissen, even to the Meissen mark. Minor factories of much the same kind were at Ilmenau, Rauenstein and Groszbreitenbach. See *Dorotheenthal; Erfurt; Abtsbessingen; German Porcelain; Gotha; Kloster-Veilsdorf; Limbach; Rauenstein; Groszbreitenbach; Volkstedt; Ilmenau; Wallendorf; Rudolstadt.*

Tiahuanaco In pre-Columbian Andean ceramics; at about the same time as Mochica and Nazca styles of pottery were flourishing, there was a third highly developed style of pottery found in the southern highlands in the neighborhood of Tiahuanaco near Lake Titicaca in Bolivia. In the best period the ground is always a red slip, and the overlaying colors—brown or grey, yellow—are outlined by black or white. In the same vicinity, probably slightly earlier, a related though distinct style is found at Pucára, some distance north of Lake Titicaca. See *Andean.*

Tichelaar, Freerk Jans See *Makkum.*

Tickenhall In English ceramics; some very early English slipware, perhaps of the 16th century, is generally attributed to Tickenhall, Derbyshire. The pottery is very hard and has a red body covered with a dark brown glaze. The rather primitive designs are made from small flat pads of white clay in the form of flowers, animal heads and similar motifs. A characteristic and popular form was a tall cylindrical mug having two loop handles near the base.

Tielsch, C. and Company See *Altwasser.*

T'ien Ch'i The T'ien Ch'i reign of the Ming dynasty in China; 1621-1627. See *Chinese Dynasties.*

T'ien Shun The T'ien Shun reign of the Ming dynasty of China; 1457-1464. See *Chinese Dynasties.*

Tiffany, Louis Comfort (1848-1933) America made her chief contribution to Art Nouveau in the work of the American designer, Louis Comfort Tiffany, who after turning to the decorative arts experimented first with glass. After he fashioned his Favrile (meaning hand-made) glass, heretofore used only in stained glass windows and mosaics, into unique small objects, he explored the field of metal crafts, ceramics, enameling and the making of fine jewelry from original designs. Favrile pottery executed under the supervision of Louis Comfort Tiffany at the Tiffany Furnaces, Corona, Long Island, made its appearance in 1906. Prior to this, shades of Favrile glass had been made for lamp bases of Grueby pottery with beautiful effect, but Tiffany having now entered into the field of ceramics, wanted only his vases used as bases for lamps. Each example of Tiffany pottery was individually designed and hand-made. Some were molded, others were thrown. Shapes and decorations were fused to suggest plant and flower forms, in a free expression of organic growth. Decorations and colors were made in the clay itself or evolved in the firing without the use of applied paints or enamels. Some lamps had porcelain bases with plastic clays used as ornamentation. The earliest of these vases produced for lamp bases were deep ivory in color, occasionally shaded with brown. Later they were produced in shades of green and the surfaces ranged from soft to rough. Some were white, without glaze, others were covered with a thin coating of bronze. He perfected a distinctive mat glaze in colors ranging from delicate to deep green, to which was added a crystalline effect. Each piece had the initials L C T carved into the base. The Tiffany Studios, which he first organized under the name of Louis C. Tiffany Company, Associated Artists to promote the decorative arts in the United States, were discontinued in 1933.

Tiffany Studios See *Tiffany, L. C.*

Tiger-Eye Glaze An aventurine glaze resembling the luminous appearance of a tiger's eye. Also called Gold-Stone. See *Rookwood.*

Tiger Skin Ware In Chinese ceramics; see *Hu P'i.*

Tiger Ware In ceramics; a contemporary English term given to Rhenish stoneware having a mottled brown glaze, because of the supposed resemblance of the glaze to the skin of a tiger. It was made during the 16th and 17th centuries and is particularly identified with the stoneware made at Cologne and Frechen. Especially characteristic were tiger ware jugs, frequently richly mounted in silver. See *Rhenish Stoneware.*

Tigranus, Marcus Perennius See *Roman Pottery.*

Tikal See *Maya.*

Tile Picture In ceramics; a set of tiles painted to form a picture. At Rotterdam, Holland, an early tin-glazed example dates from 1594; another with the subject of the Prodigal Son dates from 1601. See *Tiles.*

Tiles In ceramics; the use of pottery tiles for wall decoration had its origin in the Near East; the earliest specimens dating from the ninth century. Seville was an important center for the production of tiles made by various processes. Mosaic tile work or Alicatodos, which was a Moorish style, was very fashionable in Seville at the beginning of the 15th century. Valencia produced numerous blue-painted and occasionally luster-painted tiles during the latter part of the 15th century. Late in the 15th century painted tiles were made in Italy employing the Italian majolica technique and were of great beauty. Practically all the tiles made in Italy were used in pavements and only rarely for ceilings and never for wall decorations. The Italian majolica technique spread to Spain and to the Netherlands at the beginning of the 16th century where it was used as wall

TIGER WARE JUG,
ELIZABETHAN

decoration. They developed in the majolica technique a style of pictorial painting over a large number of tiles which had never been done in Italy. The pictures made in Spain and Portugal were in imitation of the tapestries. France, Germany and Switzerland also adopted the technique of majolica tiles. The great development of Dutch tiles in the form of small tiles and in large pictures dates from the 17th century and was principally active in Rotterdam and Friesland. A special feature in Dutch tiles during the 17th century was the gradual abandonment of polychrome painting in favor of monochrome painting in either blue or manganese purple. Chinese motifs were relatively rare. A charming variety of small figure subjects such as horsemen, soldiers, cavaliers, ladies, peasants and children were much favored. Especially fine and important were the sets of tiles painted to form pictures. The making of so-called Dutch tiles spread to England, France and Germany. During the 18th century throughout Europe the style of painted decoration was in accordance with the prevailing fashion; the Rococo style being later supplanted by the Neo-Classic style. See *Seville; Dutch Tiles.* In American ceramics; the decorative painting of tiles had been done in Trenton, New Jersey, before the Centennial Exhibition; after 1876 in Chelsea, Massachusetts, a new ceramic art industry arose. The first in the field was Hugh Robertson, but much more successful was John G. Low. To a large degree, the superior quality of Low tiles is the result of the work of Arthur Osborne, whose ceramic paintings or "plastic sketches" in relief created effects of depth that still receive the highest admiration. See *Low Art Tile Works; Union Porcelain Works.*

Tillowitz In German ceramics; a porcelain factory making table services and ornamental pieces was started at Tillowitz, near Flakenberg, Silesia, in 1869 by Reinhold Schlegelmilch. The distinguishing initials

T'ang Dynasty Pottery Figure of a Prancing Horse, 618–906 A.D. *Collection: John T. Dorrance, Esq.*

Hoechst Figure of a Rearing Horse, modelled by Johann Godfried Becker, c. 1775. *Collection: Mr. and Mrs. Charles W. Engelhard.*

Worcester Billing Doves Tureen, c. 1760. *The Antique Company of New York, Inc.; The Antique Porcelain Company.*

Fuerstenberg Pair of Vases for Pot-Pourri, by Johann Christof Kind, 1765. *The Antique Company of New York, Inc.; The Antique Porcelain Company.*

Famille Rose Pair of Hawks, K'ang Hsi period, c. 1720. *Collection: The Honorable Nelson A. Rockefeller, Governor of the State of New York.*

Meissen Pair of Hoopoes, modelled by Johann Joachim Kaendler, 1736. *Collection: Mr. and Mrs, Russell B. Aitken.*

Vincennes Vase Filled with Vincennes Flowers, 1745–50. *From a Private Collector.*

Meissen Elephant with Persian and Blackamoor, modelled by Johann Joachim Kaendler and Peter Reinicke, 1743. *Collection: Mr. and Mrs. Russell B. Aitken.*

Meissen Pair of Bustards, modelled by Johann Joachim Kaendler, c. 1735. *From a Private Collector.*

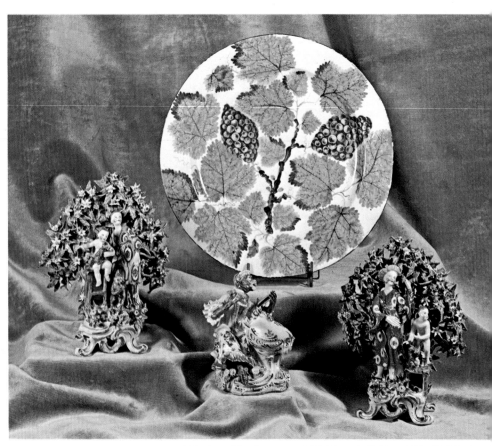

Bow Dish, Pair of Chinoiserie Groups and Monkey with a Sweetmeat Dish (One of a Pair), c. 1750–60. *The Antique Company of New York, Inc.; The Antique Porcelain Company.*

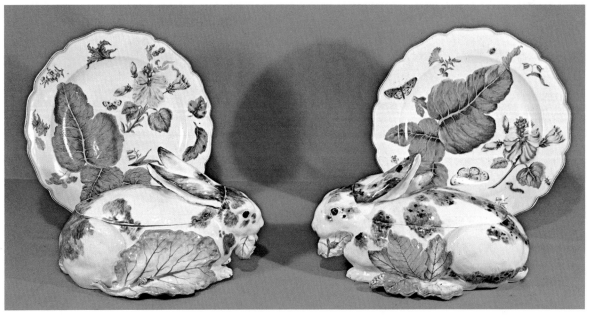

Chelsea Pair of Rabbit Tureens, c. 1754. *Collection: The Campbell Museum.*

Meissen Pair of Parakeets, c. 1733. *Collection: Mrs. Walter B. Ford II.*

Meissen Group of Two Parrots and Three Figures of Parrots, modelled by Johann Joachim Kaendler, c. 1740–45. *The Antique Company of New York, Inc.; The Antique Porcelain Company.*

Sèvres Breast Bowl of the Queen Marie Antoinette, designed by Lagrenée, 1787.
The Antique Company of New York, Inc.; The Antique Porcelain Company.

Sèvres Garniture signed Lecot, c. 1771. *The Antique Company of New York, Inc.; The Antique Porcelain Company.*

R S are found in marks of different design. It was a very popular export ware, and is referred to as R & S. See *Suhl.*

Tin-Enamel Glaze   See *Tin Glaze.*

Tin Glaze   In ceramics; a lead glaze made white and opaque by the addition of oxide (ashes) of tin. It provides a perfect background for painted decoration as the dense white glaze effectively conceals any color in the clay surface. The glaze may also be colored by the addition of metallic oxides. Tin-glazed pottery which is essentially the same everywhere is known by different names in different countries: maiolica in Italy, faïence in France, fayence in Germany and delftware in England. The use of tin glaze, sometimes also called tin-enamel glaze, was known in the ancient Near East and was used in Mesopotamia by the 9th century. From there, due to the Islamic conquests in North Africa, it spread eventually to the Omayyad kingdom of Spain and then to the rest of Europe. See *Faïence; Majolica; Glaze.*

Tinaja   In Hispano-Moresque ceramics, a kind of unglazed earthenware jar or vessel with a tall flaring collar, an egg-shaped body and two solid half-crescent-shaped handles attached vertically on the shoulder, employed for the storage of foodstuffs. Tinajas were produced in all parts of Moslem Spain with so little variety in design that to determine in which province they were manufactured would be difficult, if not impossible. Relief or incised patterns were made on the damp clay surface of the jar by stamping with molds, punches and sharp implements. Some of the jars are glazed wholly or partially. A green vase with Christian motifs is a later development of the tinaja. (215)

Ting Yao   In Chinese ceramics; a white ware first made at Ting Chou. Although it was probably made as early as the T'ang dynasty it was perfected during the Northern Sung period. After the Sung court fled

south in 1127, Ting ware was also made in the neighborhood of Ching-tê-Chên. However, the production of Ting ware continued in the original locality. The fine plain white Ting ware had tear stains, lei hên, or straw-colored patches, generally on the outside of the bowls, caused by a thickening of the glaze. Chinese writers refer to the Ting ware with engraved decoration as hua hua, impressed decoration, yin hua, and painted decoration, hsiu hua; however, no specimen of the latter has been found. The three favorite motifs were the lily, the peony and the phoenix. The finer white Ting wares are distinguished by the names fên ting, or flour ting, and pai ting or white ting. The fine Ting wares had a close-grained greyish-white porcelaneous body with a smooth ivory white glaze that was beautifully mellowed. The name *t'u ting* or *earthy ting* was given to a coarser ware with a thicker and more yellow glaze that was finely crackled. As a rule the Ting bowls had a raw edge, as though placed in the furnace in an inverted position. This edge was commonly concealed with a metal band. The different Ting wares were widely copied in other localities during the Sung period as well as in the succeeding periods. (90, 91)

Tinworth, George   English modeler. He was the first of the artists from the Lambeth School of Art to be associated with Doultons in the late 1860's. It was on his modeling that his reputation was chiefly based. He achieved most of his contemporary fame through his terra-cotta panels illustrating biblical scenes in high relief. In 1883 an exhibition devoted entirely to Tinworth's work was held in London. See *Doulton, Lambeth and Burslem.* (481)

Tippe, Aurora   Russian artist-potter; her sophisticated, asymmetrically formed, stoneware bowls with a mat glaze shown at the exhibition of contemporary ceramics held at Prague in 1962 made a significant contribution.

TILES, DUTCH FAIENCE

TILLOWITZ
C. 1870 ON

Tirschenreuth In German ceramics; a porcelain factory was started at Tirschenreuth, Bavaria, in 1838, which was purchased by Lorenz Hutschenreuther of Selb in 1927. The letters PT occurring in the marks are for Porzellanfabrik Tirschenreuth. See *Hutschenreuther, L.*

Tittensor, Charles (b. 1764) English potter working at Shelton in the Staffordshire district around 1815-1823, where he produced earthenware figures of the Walton type and transfer-printed wares. Some rare examples of figures bearing the mark Tittensor appear to be earlier than the working period of Charles Tittensor, and other potters with this surname may have also used it. See *Walton, John.*

Tlascala See *Mixteca Puebla Pottery.*

T'o T'ai In Chinese ceramics; see *Eggshell.*

Tobe In Japanese ceramics; an important center in the Ehime Prefecture for handcrafted pottery. Tobe ware was first produced in 1775 by order of the feudal lord of Tobe. The potters were invited from Arita, where pottery had already been made from early days by using Amakusa china clay. A china clay similar to Amakusa could be obtained nearby and Tobe learned from Arita the use of such material. At the present time very interesting tea utensils and vases are being made in Tobe. See *Japanese Contemporary Pottery.*

Tobi Seiji In ceramics; see *Celadon.*

Toby Jug In English ceramics; a characteristic pottery beer jug first made around 1769 by the Ralph Woods, father and son, working in Staffordshire. It was in the form of a seated man usually holding a pipe, with the handle attached to his back. The three-cornered hat which he wore was very often detachable and formed a lid. The front corner of the hat also served as a pouring spout. It is very probable that the name

TIRSCHENREUTH
C. 1840 ON

as well as the form was taken from undated engravings of Toby Philpot who was the subject of a song called The Brown Jug, published in 1761. Many jugs of similar form with different subjects were made such as The Thin Man and The Planter. The toby jug is a very characteristic Staffordshire production and has been endlessly imitated since it was first made. In American ceramics; several popular pottery articles usually with a flint enamel glaze deriving from the toby jug or pitcher were made at Bennington, Vermont, 1849-1858. They include a toby bank, toby snuff jar and toby bottle, also called "coachman" bottle. See *Bennington; Staffordshire; Wood, Ralph.* (399, 438)

Toft, Charles (1831–1909) English modeler working at Mintons around 1870. Signed portrait busts in parian ware testify to his skill as a modeler, but he is best known for his intricate and painstaking copies of Henri Deux wares, bearing his signature Toft or C. Toft, made at Mintons from around 1870 to 1877. Later he was chief modeler at Wedgwood and in 1889 he started a small pottery at Stoke. His son, Albert Toft (1862–1949) who was working for Wedgwood, became a sculptor.

Toft, Thomas English Staffordshire potter. He and his brothers, James, Charles and Ralph, were working in North Staffordshire during the late 17th and early 18th centuries. Due to the fact that some very fine surviving examples bear the name of one of the Toft family, it became the practice at one time to apply the name of Toft loosely to all the different kinds of slipware made in Staffordshire. The type of slipware bearing the name of Toft was distinctive for its skillfully executed designs. Slips of reddish brown, dark brown and olive green were cleverly counterchanged under a yellow lead glaze. Inscriptions, trailed lines and diamond-shaped and other repetitive patterns were skillfully manipulated. Sometimes the slip was impressed with stamps. Large signed platters have designs of Adam and Eve, grotesque borders, lions, foliage and other similar motifs. The signed Toft wares seldom have a date. Examples by Thomas Toft are most frequently found; more than thirty signed examples are recorded. See *Staffordshire*. (214)

Tokoname   In Japanese ceramics; one of the most important towns for handcrafted pottery, which was one of the leading centers of the production of Sue wares. From one section around this small town a special fine dark salmon-colored clay named Shudei can be obtained. This clay was in demand for making much-admired Japanese tea utensils from early times. See *Japanese Contemporary Pottery; Six Old Kilns.*

Tokugawa   In Japanese periods; the Tokugawa or Edo period in Japan, 1615-1868. See *Japanese Periods.*

Toledo   In Spanish ceramics; it seems that several potteries imitating Talavera wares were active here in the 16th, 17th and 18th centuries. However, their productions have not been identified with any certainty. The typical big Spanish oil jars (tinajas) with impressed relief decoration were made here as well as at Seville and other locations, and signed examples bearing the place name are recorded.

Toltec   In pre-Columbian Central American ceramics; the beginning of the Post Classic period, 980-1521, dates from the founding of Tula in 980, the principal city of the Toltecs whose influence spread far and wide. At the beginning of the Toltec era three broad types of pottery appear to have prevailed. The earliest ware found at Tula was a polished brown or buff ware with painted decoration in red. The most characteristic form was a heavily built tripod with legs of almost conical form. The legs seem to be an integral part of the bowl and not attached to it, as is the case with most American tripod supports. This type

appears to have preceded the Mazápan style of pottery which is also a ware with red decoration on a buff body. The identifiable feature of this ware is the use of parallel wavy lines as the only decorative motif. Included among the forms are plates with tripod supports, biconical cups, bowls and cylindrical vases. The third main type is the pottery known as Coyotlatelco. The chief form is a bowl with tripod supports, while the decoration comprising bands, frets and scrolls is painted in red on a cream ground. Two outstanding types of pottery made in large quantities and traded wherever Toltec influence was evident are Fine Orange ware, so called because it was made from a remarkably fine-grained paste of an orange color, and Plumbate. The distinguishing feature of Fine Orange is the complete absence of some kind of a tempering medium such as sand, calcite, or the like, which was used in practically every other Central American ware. There are two varieties which for convenience have been labeled X and Z. In both the paste is of an even color and fine texture. The surface of X is rather hard and lustrous, and harsh to touch; the surface of Z is smooth, chalk-like and mat, frequently with a red or white slip. Bowls and jars are the prevailing forms; the decorative techniques varied greatly. Perhaps the most notable ware in Central America is the so-called Plumbate pottery. It is hard and well fired in an area where all other wares are comparatively soft; it differs from almost all other wares of its time by depending on a lustrous appearance and incised decoration for its aesthetic qualities when other wares tended to rely on a fine finish and the skillful use of polychrome painting. Essentially it was a monochrome ware, varying from greyish black to dark olive; the decoration was incised before the slip was applied. The forms were numerous; there was a great variety of vases and jars. Frequently the figures of gods or animals were luted onto the sides of vases; or an entire vase

TOBY JUG, STAFFORDSHIRE

might be made in the form of an animal or bird. The quality of the finish and workmanship is very poor. The two most important factors contributing to the lustrous finish were the high temperature of firing in a reducing kiln and the use of a very specialized form of clay. Plumbate ware dates from around 1000. Though examples are found, at various sites, the greatest quantity occurs on the Pacific slopes of Guatemala and in Salvador. See *Central American Pottery*. (13)

Tomb Mound Period or **Kofun** See *Yayoi; Haniwa; Japanese Periods.*

Tomb Pottery See *Han; T'ang.*

Tomimoto, Kenkichi (b. 1896) Japanese stoneware potter; one of the leaders of the folk art movement. A close associate of Bernard Leach during the latter's first stay in Japan, he is best known for his beautifully brushed patterns on stoneware. Tomimoto is venerated in Japan as one of the great contemporary potters. See *Leach, Bernard; Hamada, S.*

Tonking See *Indo-China.*

Tooth, Henry English potter who began his career as a potter, as head of the newly organized Linthorpe pottery, Middlesbrough, Yorkshire, started in 1879. He must have left Linthorpe in 1882, for the same year he went into partnership with William Ault and in 1883 the Bretby Art Pottery was established at Woodville, in south Derbyshire, as Tooth and Ault. In 1887 when Ault withdrew and set up his own pottery at Swadlincote, near Woodville, the pottery continued as Tooth and Company. The third man in this group is the professional designer Christopher Dresser who produced a highly unusual series of designs for both Linthorpe and Ault Faïence, as the pottery was called. These three men were responsible for a group of late Victorian art pottery of great

TOOTH & CO.
BRETBY ART POTTERY
1884 ON

distinction and originality. See *Linthorpe Pottery; Tooth and Company.*

Tooth and Company (Ltd.) In English ceramics; in 1883 the Bretby Art Pottery was established at Woodville in south Derbyshire as Tooth and Ault, producing earthenwares. Continued as Tooth and Company from 1887 onward when Ault withdrew. Among the marks were H T in monogram, Bretby and name marks such as Clanta introduced around 1912.

Toro, Bernard (1672-1731) French ornamental sculptor. At the present time he is best known for his drawings and engravings which display remarkable verve and fantasy often touched with the grotesque. Many features in his work are dependent on the decorative work of Bérain. He together with Claude Audran helped to "lighten" the Louis XIV style. See *Bérain, Jean; Engraved Designs.*

Tortoiseshell Ware In English ceramics; earthenware made at Staffordshire around the middle of the 18th century having a lead glaze mottled with manganese brown and occasionally with other colors to produce a tortoiseshell effect. See *Staffordshire; Whieldon, Thomas; Marbled Ware; Fond Ecaille.* (393-395)

Toshiro See *Six Old Kilns.*

Totonac See *Huaxtec.*

Toulouse-Lautrec, Henri de (1864-1901) French painter and printmaker. One of the most outstanding figures in the development of French Art Nouveau.

Tournay or **Tournai** In Flemish ceramics; a soft paste porcelain manufactory was started by 1751 at Tournay, in Flemish Doornik, Belgium, by F. J. Peterinck, with a privilege from the Empress Maria Theresa. Evidence of decline became perceptible around 1800. From around 1817 to 1850 the factory was principally engaged in making forgeries of Sèvres, Chelsea and Worcester. In the beginning the wares were marked with a tower taken from the Tournay coat-of-arms; however, after 1760 it was found only on the finer grades of porcelain. The more general mark from 1756 to 1781 was the crossed swords with crosses in the angles; it was used on all types of wares. Many of the very fine pieces from around 1780 to 1800 were unmarked. This manufactory is generally regarded as one of the most important 18th century manufactories for soft paste porcelain. From around 1755 the porcelain was technically of a fine quality, having a not unpleasant slightly yellowish tone. Much of the decoration was in imitation of Meissen and Sèvres. The most common of all Tournay porcelain is in blue and white; the so-called Meissen onion pattern was much favored. The shapes and forms for the tablewares were in the Rococo style but showed a certain restraint and simplicity that was pleasing and original. German flowers, exotic birds in the Sèvres style, figure painting and landscapes in Sèvres or Meissen style were of fine quality and were carefully painted. The figures were generally unmarked; in style they showed a strong resemblance to those of Chelsea, Worcester and Mennecy. The majority were in glazed white porcelain. During the last two decades of the 18th century the Louis XVI style was adopted.

Tou-Ts'ai In Chinese ceramics; a Chinese term meaning contrasted colors, used to describe the characteristic style of enamel painting developed in the Ch'êng Hua period, 1465-1487, in which shining red, yellow, apple-green and other enamels were applied in thin, even, almost translucent washes over pale underglaze blue outlines. This classical Ch'êng Hua style of tou-ts'ai enameling with washes of thin, softly brilliant color combined with underglaze blue became classical, and was revived under Chia Ching, Wan Li, Yung Chêng and Tao Kung. The wu ts'ai or five-color style associates enamel painting supplemented

with underglaze blue in a broader style. See *Ming*.

Toy In ceramics; the name given in England to porcelain scent bottles, étuis, snuff boxes, patch boxes and other similar small objects made in the Rococo style in the fanciful and delightful forms of miniature figures, fruits, animals and other similar forms. This variety of so-called toys was originally introduced at Meissen. Especially delightful and charming were the toys made at Chelsea and at Mennecy. (331)

Trac, F. An important German relief-cutter and modeler working at Siegburg from about 1560 onward, generally signing his work F.T. He is believed to have worked for Anno Knütgen and was the most influential of the earlier workmen responsible for the artistic relief decoration on Rhenish stonewares. Toward 1560 he began to produce original reliefs mainly of biblical subjects adapted from Heinrich Aldegrever applied to the tall tapering tankards of the Schnelle type. Each piece generally bears on the front three reliefs in long panels or strips. Since his reliefs were freely used by other workmen after 1568, it is assumed that he died about that time.

Trailing In ceramics; slip or liquid clay trailed on pottery with a spouted can. See *Slipware*.

Transfer-Printed Wares In ceramics; a method first used in England by which an impression from an engraved metal plate inked with enamel colors is made on a thin piece of paper and transferred to the surface of pottery or porcelain and subsequently melted into the glaze. The method was used as early as 1753 on Battersea painted enamels on copper. It has never been conclusively ascertained who invented the process. Several different persons claim the credit for the invention of printing, among whom were John Sadler and Guy Green of Liverpool who operated

TOURNAY PORCELAIN
GROUP, GLAZED WHITE

TOURNAY

C. 1751 ON

C. 1756-1781

a successful printed ware manufactory from 1756. At first the printing was done over the glaze in red, purple and black. From around 1760 the method was used for underglaze printing in blue. The underglaze blue-printed method was much used at Staffordshire and other centers producing English white earthenware and stone china during the early 19th century. A process known as bat printing was introduced late in the 18th century. In the third decade of the 19th century the practice of printing the outlines of a design in black or grey or pale purple and subsequently to be painted over in colors came into general use, notably at the Coalport and Rockingham (Swinton) porcelain works. However, this technique had been occasionally used some five decades earlier at Battersea, where the entire design was frequently faintly printed in brown and colored over by hand, and at Bow. Printed wares were mostly cheap wares and for this reason the printing remained in most instances monochrome. Blue was the favorite color, but by the second quarter of the century many other underglaze colors were available, especially black and shades of green, red, purple, brown and yellow. Many experiments, however, were made in polychrome printing. Later in the 19th century methods for transferring stipple-prints in several colors were introduced. F. and R. Pratt of Fenton exhibited examples of these at the London Great Exhibition, 1851. It was used to some extent for tableware but it was also used for the decoration of pot lids. Still later, lithographic transfers came into use of birds, flowers and pictorial subjects completely printed in natural colors in facsimile imitation of painting. The fashion for decorating pottery with printed scenes faded away in the third quarter of the 19th century, but it left behind the long-lasting practice of decorating simple pottery tablewares with floral designs either to be left monochrome or to be tinted by hand. Other European countries were slow in taking up

TRICHTERBECHER,
SIEBURG STONEWARE

the technique of transfer printing. It was used with distinction and charming effect on Marieberg faïence. It became the characteristic mode of decoration in the early 19th century at Montereau and Creil. It was also in use at Sèvres, at Choisy-le-Roi and in the 19th century at many places in Germany. The development of printed pottery in America was cut short owing to the vast quantity and the almost endless range of attractive, often exotic, patterns and colors produced and exported by the Staffordshire and Liverpool potteries. It is generally believed that American printed wares were first made around 1840. See *Historical Blue; Flow Blue; Backstamp; Bat Printing; American Pottery Company; Pot Lids; Stone-China.* (374, 406, 436, 437, 467, 468)

Trapani   See *Sicily.*

Trek   In Dutch ceramics; the name given to the outline in blue, manganese-purple or black generally as used in blue-painting on Delft faïence.

Trembleuse   In ceramics; a French term meaning a trembler applied to a saucer either with a raised ring around the well or with a deeply sunk well to keep the cup secure. It was used by persons who were unable to use the usual saucer.

Trenton   In American ceramics; contemporary comments on the ceramic exhibition of the Centennial Exhibition held in Philadelphia in 1876, report that the chief centers of production are Trenton in New Jersey and East Liverpool in Ohio. See *Taylor and Speeler; Willets Manufactory Company; Ott and Brewer; Mercer Pottery Company; Ceramic Art Company; Lenox Company; Columbian Art Pottery; Knowles, Taylor and Knowles; Moses, John and Company.*

Trenton Pottery Company   See *Taylor and Company.*

Triana   In Spanish ceramics; a suburb of Seville where the manufacture of pottery was centered. See *Seville.*

Trichterbecher In German ceramics; a Rhenish salt-glazed stoneware cup having a funnel-shaped mouth. Although it was made in different centers producing stoneware in the Rhineland during the 16th and 17th centuries, it is a particularly characteristic form for the salt-glazed stoneware made at Siegburg. (187)

Triller, Erich and Ingrid Swedish artist-potters; since the mid-1930's they have been producing finely glazed stoneware.

Trofei In Italian ceramics; a contemporary Italian term for a decoration used on Italian Renaissance majolica. It consisted of attributes or symbols such as armor, weapons and musical instruments that were appropriate to war and music respectively. It was much favored at Castel Durante and Faenza. See *Trophies; Italian Majolica.*

Trompe l'Oeil The term, which means deceive the eye or fool the eye, is applied to a school of painting that goes back to the legendary Greek Zeuxis who was reputed to have painted grapes so realistically that birds swooped down to pick at them. Roman and Pompeian decorators employed this style of painting for murals to give the illusion of spaciousness to small rooms. During the 17th and 18th centuries this technique was given to cards, scissors and other similar articles by realistic painters. Although the articles were painted on the canvas they were executed in such vivid perspective that they appeared to be pasted on. In ceramics; the term is given to 18th century faïence wares such as tureens in the form of vegetables, fruits, birds, boars' heads and other similar natural objects and dishes molded in a similar manner with vegetables and fruits painted in natural colors. The tureens were a Meissen innovation while the latter were a Strasbourg innovation. It is generally accepted that this style had its origin in the Italian della Robbia school. These so-called trompe l'oeil wares were very popu-

lar and were produced at many faïence manufactories. Perhaps nowhere was the style more aptly interpreted than at Strasbourg. See *Décor Bois; Quodlibetz.* (281, 293, 301, 309-313, 365)

Trophies In ornament; attributes or symbols appropriate to pastoral life, love, music, war, hunting, fishing, science, agriculture and astronomy were employed as decorative motifs. Trophies of love included bows, arrows, torches and quivers; pastoral emblems such as crooks and the large straw hats of shepherdesses, and attributes of war such as body armor. All these symbols were especially favorite themes for ornament during the Louis XV and Louis XVI styles. Trofei were also a characteristic form of decoration for large Italian majolica plates made during the 16th century.

Trotter, Alexander American potter; started a factory for the manufacture of Queen's ware under the name of Columbia pottery around 1808 in Philadelphia. The ware enjoyed a fine reputation. Trotter retired from the business around 1813.

Ts'a Ts'ai In Chinese ceramics; a Chinese term meaning mixed colors used to describe any combination of colors; it has no special application. It occurred in the Imperial lists of the Ming dynasty during the Chia Ching period, 1522-1566 and later periods. See *Ming.*

Ts'ung In Chinese ceramics; a ritual vessel used in the worship of the earth. It was supposed to contain the divining rods. It was in the form of a rather tall rectangular vase with a circular foot rim and neck rim. A set of the Pa Kua symbols was molded in relief on each side of the body. Sometimes vertical ribs extended the length of the vessel. See *Eight Trigrams.*

T'u In Chinese art; a Chinese animal subject widely used in Chinese ceramics and art. It is represented as the hare that is seen in the moon where it is mixing an imaginary

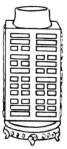

TS'UNG, MING

liquid of an elixir to prolong life. See *Chinese Animal Figures.*

T'u Ting See *Ting Yao.*

Tucker & Hulme
China Manufacturers
Philadelphia
1828
—

TUCKER AND HULME

Manufactured
by Jos Hemphill
Philad—

JOSEPH HEMPHILL
1832

Tucker In American ceramics; though several partially successful attempts were made toward the manufacture of porcelain by progressive potters in the United States prior to the year 1825, the honor of being the first to supply the home market with a purely American product of this character belongs to William Ellis Tucker, who established the first important American hard paste porcelain factory at Philadelphia in 1826. In the course of time several partners were involved. Thomas Hulme became a partner in 1828 and though he was active for less than one year, wares survive bearing the mark Tucker and Hulme. In 1831 Alexander Hemphill joined Tucker. As a result of this partnership the production was expanded. After the death of William Tucker in 1832, the firm was continued by Alexander's father, Judge Joseph Hemphill, with William's brother, Thomas, as manager. The factory which was carried on in the name of Hemphill closed in 1838. The range of their production included dinner services, tea and coffee services and ornamental wares. See *Mead, Dr. Henry; Columbian Pottery; Bonnin and Morris; Smith, Fife and Company; Kurlbaum and Schwartz.* (448-450)

Tucker and Hemphill See *Tucker.*

Tucker and Hulme See *Tucker.*

Tudor Period In English history, 1485-1603; the reigns of Henry VII, 1485-1509; Henry VIII, 1509-1547; Edward VI, 1547-1553; Mary, 1553-1558; Elizabeth I, 1558-1603.

Tulip Ware In American ceramics; the name given to a variety of folk pottery made by the Pennsylvania German potters, charac-

TULIP WARE PLATE

terized by a stylized design of tulips and leaves symmetrically arranged. Tulips were always a favorite motif in all kinds of Pennsylvania German decoration. See *Pennsylvania German.* (427)

Tuncahuán See *Ecuador and Colombia.*

T'ung Chih In Chinese periods; the T'ung Chih reign of the Ch'ing dynasty, 1862-1873. See *Chinese Dynasties.*

Tung Yao In Chinese ceramics; see *Celadon.*

Turkish Pottery Apparently fine pottery vessels were not made in Turkey until about the end of the 15th century. The wares made at Isnik (ancient Nicaea) in northern Anatolia henceforward surpassed in brilliance of technique all their contemporaries in the Near East where the once flourishing art of the potter had fallen into decline. Their low-fired body is a composition of white clay and glassy matter, with a carefully prepared porcelain-like surface on which the designs were painted under a transparent alkaline glaze. The earliest class, about 1480-1525, reveals the influence of imported Chinese porcelain both in the blue and white color scheme and in the Chinese floral designs mingled with arabesques of Near East origin. In the second class, which was made from about 1525-1550, the blue is augmented at first by a clear turquoise and later by a range of soft grey and olive greens, purple and black. The Turkish love of garden flowers is revealed in the painted decoration, at first in simple stylized designs and later in fantastic compositions, whose bold linear rhythm suggests the luxuriance of natural growth. The patterns for other wares are literally copied from 15th century Chinese blue and white porcelain. After 1550 a new and simplified color scheme was developed and included black for outlines, blue, copper-green and an intense scarlet composed of a clay named Armenian bole, which appears in perceptible relief under the glaze. Floral and arabesque patterns continued in favor; ships, birds, and animals were rare, and human figures are seldom found until about mid-17th century. Sometimes the decoration was painted on a ground of pale blue or red slip. After 1600 the colors and drawings greatly deteriorated; however, the wares continued to be made into the 17th century. See *Islamic Pottery, Later.* (174-180)

Turn In modern Bohemian ceramics; the Alexandra Porcelain Works was started at Turn, near Teplitz, Bohemia, by Ernst Wahliss around 1880. The factory made an effort to produce a strictly artistic line of products in porcelain and faïence. The work was broadly similar in spirit to that made at Powolny's Wiener Keramik workshop started in 1903. Especially notable was the serapis-fayence made here in the years preceding the First World War, enriched with heavy-lined, intricate and almost abstract patterning from the designs of such artists as Karl Klaus. See *Wiener Keramik; Secession.* The Amphora factory was started at Turn in 1892 by Riessner and Kessel for the manufacture of porcelain figures, which were widely exported.

Turner, John (d. 1786) An English potter working at Stoke from around 1755 and at Lane End from around 1762, Staffordshire. He made cream-colored earthenware and stonewares which were equal in quality to those made by Wedgwood. Of particular interest were his fine white and buff-colored stonewares and his blue jasper wares. His factory was quite active and enjoyed a good reputation. He exported wares to Holland. The business was carried on until 1803 by his sons, John and William. The marks were Turner or Turner & Co, impressed. (402)

Turning See *Throwing; Rose-Engine Turning.*

Turquoise In ceramics; a clear turquoise color of remarkable beauty may be prepared from copper in an alkaline glaze, tending to green or blue depending on

whether lead is present or absent. Though this is widespread in the Near East, apparently it is never found on European pottery before the 18th century. A muffle-kiln enamel of this color used on 18th century porcelain is prepared perhaps from a mixture of copper and cobalt oxides rather than only copper. The beautiful sea-green or turquoise ground-color prepared by Herold at Meissen shortly after 1725 is of this kind and forecast the more powerful clear turquoise (or bleu celeste) invented by Hellot at Sèvres around 1752. A striking turquoise tin-enamel perhaps derived from copper only was used as a ground-color on Delft faïence in the late 17th and first half of the 18th century. It found many imitators. In enamel painting a beautiful turquoise-blue is found on Meissen porcelain from around 1725 onward. See *Colors; Colored Grounds.*

Tuscany In Italian ceramics; the rapid growth of Italian majolica during the 15th century was due principally to the potters working in Faenza and Tuscany, the chief centers at the latter being Siena and Florence. Of particular interest was a Tuscan variety of majolica, probably of Florentine derivation and dating from around 1410, painted principally in rich translucent green within outlines of manganese purple or brownish black. Heraldic lions, foliage, figures and busts were among the favorite motifs. Especially outstanding and dating from around 1430 were the well-known Florentine jars or vases painted in blue and sometimes known as oak leaf jars from the conventionally treated leaf motifs. The original inspiration for the leaves as well as much of the painted decoration on Tuscan wares until about 1475 was derived from Valencian earthenware dishes and tiles which were exported in large quantities to Italy and particularly to Pisa during the 15th century. This imitative phase was brought to a close around 1475 by the rich and magnificent Gothic foliage of typically coiled

TURN

ALEXANDRA PORCELAIN
WORKS

C. 1880 ON

1891 ON

AMPHORA PORCELAIN
WORKS
AFTER 1892

leaves. This original treatment of Gothic leaves is especially identified with the majolica made at Tuscany and Faenza during the last quarter of the 15th century. See *Italian Majolica; Siena.* (228)

Two Little Ships, The or **De Twee Scheepjes**
In Dutch ceramics; a faïence manufactory started around 1621 at Delft and bequeathed in 1635 to Albrecht Cornelisz de Keiser or Keyser, which marked the beginning of the career of this famous faïence-potter who died in 1667. His ware was of superior quality, very thin and light, and covered with pure white glaze. He especially imitated the Japanese style. His son, Cornelis Albrechtsz de Keiser, succeeded him as owner, and he worked in partnership with his mother and brothers-in-law Jacobus and Adriaen Pijnacker. The latter sold the flourishing manufactory in 1694. After a succession of various owners this famous pottery closed in 1798. See *Delft; Faïence.*

TWO LITTLE SHIPS
1759-1770

Tyg In English ceramics; a pottery drinking vessel made in great numbers at the various English pottery centers from the beginning of the 17th century. It was a very large cup or mug, generally designed with three or four handles on the side in order that it could easily be passed from one person to the other. These tygs were often decorated with names, quaint inscriptions, mottoes and emblems. See *Posset-Pot; Piggin.* (213)

Tzakol See *Maya.*

Tzu Chin In Chinese ceramics; crackled ware of the K'ang Hsi period varying in colors from a pale grey to brown tones and sometimes nearly black. The most noted ware is known as Tzu Chin, or lustrous brown, which includes various colors such as golden brown, golden black, café-au-lait and chocolate brown. It is also called Batavian ware. The glaze is sometimes in varying effects, such as brown mottled with black or a mottling and shading of

brown with a harmonizing color. During the later part of the K'ang Hsi period and in the Yung Cheng and Ch'ien Lung times a decoration of Famille Rose color in panels was used on a ground of the café-au-lait color. See *Batavian Ware.*

Tz'u Chou In Chinese ceramics; a wide variety of wares were made at Tz'u Chou, which was a pottery center as early as the Sui dynasty, A.D. 589-618. Especially characteristic were the shapely vases with their strong, free-flowing designs that were painted in black slip, incised, or carved. Tz'u Chou pottery had a buff-grey, buff or grey stoneware body which often had porcelaneous quality. Occasionally it had a light reddish or reddish-buff stoneware body. The body was covered with a dressing or wash of white slip. Numerous potteries made wares of the Tz'u Chou type. Different methods were employed in decorating the Tz'u Chou wares. The following are the characteristic kinds of decoration. In one variety of Tz'u Chou wares the designs were painted in black or black brown slip under a creamy or transparent glaze that was sometimes minutely crazed. Occasionally the black slip decoration had sgraffiato details. In another variety the designs were painted in black under a colored glaze of pale blue or turquoise or deep green that was sometimes finely crazed. Sgraffiato was another type of Tz'u Chou ornament. In this type the stoneware body was covered with a thick black, brown or creamy glaze and the ornament was formed by cutting away the ground around the design and exposing the color of the body. Sometimes the design was engraved in outline and filled in with a black glaze through which the details were scratched. Another kind of Tz'u Chou ware was painted in red and brown or black slips under a usually transparent glaze that was sometimes crazed. The painted slip decoration frequently had sgraffiato decorations. A kind of Tz'u Chou ware had enameled decoration. The decoration was painted in black or brown slip and in three colored enamels, that is, iron red, green and yellow. In another late technique actual leaves were applied to the body. After it had been washed in slip, the leaves were removed and then the piece was glazed and fired. (94)

TZ'U CHOU GALLIPOT

U

U-no-hanagaki   See *Fuji-san.*

Uaxactun   See *Maya.*

Ubaid   In ancient Near East culture; about 4500 B.C., there arose in southern Mesopotamia a culture called by archaeologists Ubaid, after the site where the culture was first recognized. Although the question is still debated, it is generally accepted that the bearers of Ubaid culture were a people now known as Sumerians. This is not the name they themselves used; they are now called Sumerians because another people, several hundred years later, called the land Sumer. See Sumerian. (25)

Underglaze Colors   Pigment colors painted on the clay body of a ware under the glaze before firing. See *Colors.*

Underglaze Blue   In ceramics; blue pigment color painted on the clay body of the ware under the glaze before firing. In Chinese ceramics; the blue and white wares of the Ming and Ch'ing dynasties are considered to be the finest ever produced. See *Underglaze Red; Blue and White Ming; Blue and White Ch'ing; Blue and White,* in Japanese ceramics.

Underglaze Red   In Chinese ceramics; red pigment colors painted on the clay body of the ware under the glaze before it was fired. It is said to have originated in China. Painting in the difficult underglaze copper red reached its highest development during the Hsüan Tê period, 1426-1435, and the reign was famous for this ware. Of particular importance are the white porcelain stem-cups decorated with three fishes in underglaze red of this period. The Chinese books give the color various names indicating the esteem with which it was regarded in its most perfected forms: hsien hung (fresh red or blood red); chi hung

(sacrificial red); pao-shih hung (refers to its supposed use in its preparation of rubies or other stones). The art of making this copper-red is alleged to have been lost after the time of Ch'êng Hua, though marked specimens of the Chêng Tê and Chia Ching reigns are known. During the K'ang Hsi reign and later in the Ch'ing period an underglaze red was called Rouge de Cuivre. It was then used either singly or with underglaze blue. See *Rouge de Cuivre; Underglaze Blue; Ming; Chi Hung.* (98, 103)

Unfired Colors   The so-called cold colors; rare and uncharacteristic in ceramics. See *Colors.*

Union Porcelain Works   In American ceramics; a factory for the production of soft paste porcelain was begun in 1848 by Charles Cartlidge at Greenpoint, Brooklyn, New York, an important center for porcelain. The mark Greenpoint sometimes was used by this firm, which closed in 1856. Between the years 1857 and 1861, the factory was reopened and operated by William Boch and Brothers. In 1861, Thomas C. Smith took over the company and renamed it the Union Porcelain Works and by 1864-1865 had changed over to hard paste porcelain. During the 1870's Karl Müller, a sculptor, joined the company and was responsible for designing some of the most noted pieces of American porcelain. Of these the Century Vase which he designed for the Philadelphia Centennial of 1876 is the most celebrated. The wares of this company are noteworthy for their design and the high quality of workmanship. The company remained active until the turn of the century. Its pieces frequently bore the mark Union Porcelain Works Greenpoint N.Y. By around 1891 hard paste porcelain tiles had become an

UNION PORCELAIN WORKS

1878

1880

important item in its manufacture. See *Century Vase; Cartlidge, C.; Boch, William and Brother.* (452, 453, 455)

Union Pottery In English ceramics; a pottery active at Southwick, Sunderland, Durham, around 1802, producing earthenwares. Very little is known about this pottery.

United States Pottery In American ceramics; see *Bennington.*

United States Pottery Company See *Bennington.*

Unterweissbach See *Schwarzburger Werkstätten Für Porzellankunst.*

Upsala-Ekeby In Swedish ceramics; a combine which includes additional factories in Gävle and Kurlskrona, organized in 1886 at Upsala fifty miles north of Stockholm. One of the three great Swedish factories, Rörstrand and Gustavsberg being the other two, producing industrial wares, principally table services. From the middle of the 1950's the most significant design has concerned tablewares of strictly functional design and composition, generally heat-proof, and frequently in plain colors or else decorated with large simple motifs. Such services or sets of vessels have been designed by Sven Eric Skawonius for Upsala-Ekeby.

Urbino In Italian ceramics; Urbino is generally regarded as the most important center for the manufacture of Italian majolica around and after the middle of the 16th century. It was under the patronage of the Duke of Urbino. Castel Durante and Gubbio are also included in the Duchy of Urbino. Although potteries were in existence at Urbino from 1477, the manufacture of majolica did not achieve any artistic

importance until around 1520 when Guido Pellipario, the son of Nicola Pellipario working at Castel Durante, settled at Urbino. He adopted the name of Fontana, and his pottery in addition to one conducted by his son, Orazio Fontana, were the two most important during the best period for Urbino majolica. Especially associated with Urbino majolica is the istoriato or pictorial style of painting developed by Nicola Pellipario while working at Castel Durante and the decoration of grotesques on a white ground with a pronounced use of modeled decoration. Nicola Pellipario was also working at Urbino from around and after 1528. The istoriato style of painting was in vogue in Urbino from around 1530 to 1580. Around 1570 the decoration of grotesques inspired by Raphael's painting in the Loggia of the Vatican began to appear and finally supplanted the istoriato style. These Urbino grotesques were accompanied by an increasing use of modeled decoration such as handles in the form of dolphins, figures modeled in the round, applied reliefs of masks and other similar kinds of plastic decoration. This type of work was continued into the 17th century. Practically nothing is known about Urbino majolica during the second half of the 17th century. See *Italian Majolica; Castel Durante; Raphaelesque; Istoriato; Pellipario, Nicola.* (232-234)

Urbino Style See *Castel Durante.*

Urfirnis See *Vasiliki Style.*

Useful Wares In ceramics; essentially wares may be divided into two principal categories, useful and ornamental. The latter are of a purely decorative character, while useful wares are those to be used in the service of food.

UPSALA-EKEBY
1918 ON

URBINO PLATE

V

Vaisseau à mat In French ceramics; an ambitious piece of soft paste porcelain introduced at Sèvres about 1760. It is shaped like a masted ship with a pierced or perforated cover, used as a potpourri vase. (356)

Valencia In Spanish ceramics; Valencia has been a principal center for Spanish pottery including blue and white, lustered and other earthenwares from the 13th century until the present day. The fame of its lustered productions was apparently well established around the beginning of the 15th century. The greater part of these beautiful Hispano-Moresque lustered wares were made during the 15th century and early 16th centuries. During this time they received princely and aristocratic patronage not only in Spain but also and especially from the Pope and Papal Princes in Italy. Especially praiseworthy were the armorial dishes of that period. The luster varied from a soft golden or greenish tone to a reddish purple similar to tarnished copper, sometimes having bluish or mother-of-pearl reflections. Later in the 16th century the luster was inclined to be a brownish yellow golden tone which was not as desirable and in the succeeding two centuries it was a rather hard bright reddish color like polished copper, which was even less desirable. The lustered earthenware comprised such pieces as vases, dishes, pharmacy jars and bowls. Coats-of-arms, arabesques, interlacements, starry flowers, trefoil leaves, vine leaves arranged in bands or in concentric circles, repetitive patterns of small circles, rosettes and small flowers, Arabic script and many other motifs were included in the decorative designs. Blue and white wares were made concurrently with the lustered wares; however, they were seldom as fine. Beautiful blue and white Valencia tiles were also made from the 15th century. See *Luster Decoration; Tuscany; Hispano-Moresque; Manisses.* (217-222)

Valentien, Albert R. See *Rookwood Pottery.*

Vance Faïence Company In American ceramics; established at Tiltonville, Ohio, in 1900; produced a variety of art faïence in colored glazes and underglaze and overglaze decoration. The pottery reproduced the hound-handle pitcher, having acquired the mold from the pottery at Bennington. See *Hound-Handle Pitcher.*

Variegated Wares Earthenwares made by mingling different colored clays throughout the body as in agate ware; also by the mixture of colors in the slip glazes as in marbled or mottled wares.

Varsovie See *Warsaw.*

Vasiliki Style In ancient ceramics; vases coated with black paint and mottled in the firing; the Vasiliki style, from Vasiliki, east Crete; dating from the Early Minoan period of Cretan art. The dark painted surface corresponds to the Urfirnis of mainland wares, with the dark brown, yellowish or reddish appearance produced by uneven firing in the kiln. By covering parts of the surface of the vase, patterns of various shapes could be produced at will, forerunners of abstract art. Sometimes there is also painted decoration. See *Minoan.*

Veilleuse In ceramics; the name derives from the French veiller, to keep a night vigil. It originally referred to any night lamp, but soon came to be given to a warmer for food or drink. The pottery or porcelain veilleuse is a hollow pedestal on which sits a covered bowl or teapot. The bowl or teapot has a projecting bottom that fits into the pedestal to bring its con-

357   VENICE

tents nearer to the warming flame of the small lamp. Beginning in the middle of the 18th century as food warmers, simple in form and decorated with varying degrees of elaboration, they were popularized in porcelain by the great German factories at Nymphenburg and Höchst. Soon potteries throughout Europe adapted the form into a tea warmer. Figures were also ingeniously disguised as tea warmers. (450)

Velde, Henry van de (1863–1957) Belgian painter, architect, writer and designer; has been considered the creator and theoretical founder of Art Nouveau, apart from his important role as a pioneer in the Modern Movement. Van de Velde made his debut as a decorative designer in 1893. In 1901 he accepted an invitation from the Grand Duke of Saxe-Weimar to head the Weimar School for Arts and Crafts, where he introduced his own methods of art instruction. He remained there until the outbreak of World War I. He also took part in the founding of the Deutscher Werkbund in 1907. He was active in many media, including porcelain, and around 1905 he designed a porcelain service for Meissen. Apart from his work for Meissen he was also interested in stoneware. He designed stoneware vases for production with figured glazes by Reinhold Hanke of Höhr, Westerwald, a district in the Rhineland known for its stonewares at least as early as the 16th century. (495)

Venetian Fair In German ceramics; a distinctive miniature porcelain group ascribed to the modeler Jean-Jacob Louis (1703–1772) and made at Ludwigsburg about 1767–1770. This class is one of the chief Ludwigsburg contributions to the art of the porcelain figure. Venetian Fairs with stalls and booths, showmen, players and musicians, peddlers and buyers of all classes are believed to have been inspired by the fairs instituted at Ludwigsburg by Duke Charles Eugene after his return from a visit to Venice in 1767. (329)

Venice In Italian ceramics; it is generally accepted that majolica was not made in Venice before 1525. As a rule the tin glaze did not have as much tin oxide as was generally used in the glazes for majolica, and as a result it was partially transparent. Perhaps the most characteristic tin glaze for Venetian majolica had a bluish or greyish tone, given the contemporary name of smaltino. The earliest Venetian majolica reflected Oriental inspiration, due to the trade relations existing with Oriental countries. Lotus flowers and scrolled foliage in the Chinese style were typical. The close trade relations between Venice and Nuremberg in the 16th century resulted in a distinctive class of great beauty having armorial bearings of important Nuremberg families. Another 16th century variety was in the istoriato Urbino style with pictorial subjects. Another type had coiled foliage and flowers painted in colors reserved on a blue ground with panels containing figure subjects or busts. Of particular interest was a late 17th century thinly potted resonant variety of majolica with a smaltino glaze. It had molded decoration of flowers, foliage, cupids, and masks, apparently taken from silver models, with landscapes painted in colors often enclosed in painted Baroque scrolls. Other distinctive varieties of majolica ware were also made during the 16th and 17th centuries, such as one variety with a rich decoration of luscious fruits. During the 18th century one of the porcelain manufactures produced faïence with painted flowers. See *Italian Majolica; Faïence.*

Venice In ceramics; there were three porcelain manufactories operating in Venice during the 18th century. They were conducted by Francesco and Giuseppe Vezzi, c. 1720 to c. 1740; by Nathaniel Friedrich Hewelcke, 1757 to 1763, and by Geminiano Cozzi, c. 1764 to 1812. The porcelain attributed to the Vezzi manufactory was a true porcelain of varying qual-

VENICE

$V_{en:}{}^a$

VEZZI
C. 1720 ON

V

HEWELCKE
C. 1757 ON

V.F

COZZI
C. 1764 ON

ity. It is presumed that the marks were Venezia, Ven a or V a. The painted decoration included figures from the Italian Comedy, charming naturalistic flowers and motifs of Chinese and Japanese inspiration. Underglaze blue painting of a clean quality was also found. The wares comprised globular shaped teapots, small bowls, saucers and cups without handles. The porcelain attributed to Hewelcke, who was a dealer from Dresden, was marked with a V and was not free from imperfections. Much of the porcelain ascribed to this factory had an unusual primitive charm. The porcelain made at the Cozzi manufactory was a hybrid soft paste porcelain with a thin glaze, generally marked with an anchor. The productions chiefly consisted of tablewares, vases and figures and were frequently in imitation of Meissen. Especially admirable were the fine colors including a rich red, a beautiful bluish purple and a clear emerald green. The gilding was of fine quality and soft in tone. The painted decoration in the Rococo style was often distinctive for its fanciful Italian interpretation. Their versions of Meissen Rococo border patterns had an abandon that was entirely delightful. Of outstanding interest were some delicately modeled white glazed and biscuit figures and groups showing an unusual and frequently very charming miniature style. (337)

VICAR AND MOSES BY THE RALPH WOODS

Vera Cruz See *Huaxtec; Remajodas; Central American Pottery.*

Verdone, Giuseppe Modeler at Capo di Monte, Naples, Italy, about the middle of the 18th century.

Vergette, Nicholas (b. 1923) English ceramist and teacher who studied painting initially, then turned to pottery and mosaics; well known for his ceramic enamel and ceramic mosaic architectural wall panels. He was invited to teach on a year's grant at the School for American Craftsmen, Rochester Institute of Technology, New York, in 1958. He settled in Illinois in 1959.

Verrière In French ceramics; the wine glass cooler was a fashionable piece of French 18th century tableware. Especially charming were the faïence models decorated in overglaze polychrome enamels.

Vest, Georg, the Younger (b. 1586) The most important member of a celebrated family of Kreussen potters, whose name is closely associated with Kreussen stoneware. An important manufacture of stoneware at Kreussen was apparently a development of a flourishing local Hafner industry in which the most famous figures were a family of modelers named Vest, who had come from Austria. Members of the Vest family are recorded at Kreussen, near Bayreuth, Bavaria, Germany, as early as 1512. See *Kreussen; Hafner.*

Veuve Perrin See *Perrin, Veuve; Marseilles.*

Vezzi, Francesco and Giuseppe See *Venice.*

Vicar and Moses In English ceramics; the name given to a popular and well-known pottery figure group first made around 1770 by the Ralph Woods, father and son, of Burslem, Staffordshire. The group portrays a parson asleep in the pulpit with his good friend and parish clerk Moses delivering the sermon. Bears impressed mark Ra. Wood Burslem. See *Wood, Ralph.*

Victoria, A. G. See *Altrohlau.*

Victorian The age of Victoria, 1837-1901, bears the indelible stamp of revivalism. From the 1840's most of the great ceramic factories moved inexorably toward more and more historicism. The potters were dazzled by their increasing technical efficiency and by their ability to copy almost every historical style. After the comparatively easy conquest of classical wares, especially the unglazed red-figure pottery of classical antiquity, normally identified with Greece, but in the 1840's still described as Etruscan or Etrurian because it was mainly known through finds in Italy, the potters turned with excitement toward more modern themes. It was only natural that the potters of France should first feel the challenge of French Renaissance wares. The work associated with the 16th century potter, Bernard Palissy, appears to have held a particular attraction for the mid-18th century public. The first potter to revive this style was Charles Avisseau of Tours. In England, the Palissy style was adopted by Minton at Stoke-on-Trent. Another French Renaissance ware which attracted considerable attention was the inlaid ware known as Saint-Porchaire. In England Saint-Porchaire or Henri Deux provided the incentive for some elaborate work by the Minton and Wedgwood factories. The imitation of painted majolica was adopted in several countries. In addition to the imitative work the term *majolica* was also interpreted in England and later in other countries to include wares with relief decoration under colored glazes. Among the colored-glaze productions of the mid-19th century the French introduced about 1844 a technique known as émaux ombrants (shading enamels) which was of some interest. In England, and especially in France, the fashion for ceramic painting, and particularly pottery painting, spread to amateurs in the sense that it was done for the pleasure of the painter rather than the factory which furnished the ware and later fired the painted product. A great vogue for amateur ceramic painting was initiated in England by Minton's Art-Pottery Studio. In marked contrast to the more sophisticated ceramic wares, the mid-19th century period witnessed the debut in England of the notably naïve Staffordshire flat-back figures. In porcelain from 1830 the French factory of Sèvres continued to exercise great influence. The Empire style of porcelain persisted for the many prestige wares at Sèvres through the reigns of Louis XVIII, Charles X and Louis Philippe. In a certain sense the Revived Rococo was the first of the imitative styles brought on by the Industrial Revolution. It is important to distinguish this renewed interest in mid-18th century Rococo work from the more deliberately potpourri styles which were subsequently essayed in the 19th century. Of prime importance was the development of parian porcelain in the later 1840's, which it appears was first formulated by Copeland. In England it resulted in a revival of figure-making, where on the analogy of marble the parian statuettes were, for the most part, uncolored until considerably later in the century. An interesting development of the parian porcelain body was the Irish Belleek having a parian-like body with a characteristic iridescent glaze. Another interesting development of the parian body was its use for pâte-sur-pâte decoration, dating after the arrival of Marc Solon at Minton in 1870. Noteworthy in the United States was the Bennington version of parian. In the 19th century the young porcelain industry in the United States mirrored the influence of different European sources. Shortly after the middle of the 19th century the Revived Rococo yielded to styles which embodied chiefly classical and Renaissance elements. Many potters and manufacturers explored such exotic styles as Persian and Turkish. In the 1880's the influence of Javanese batik-printed textiles were reflected in patterns produced in Holland at the Rozenburg pottery. But by far the foremost influence was that of Japan, not only in the development of Art Nouveau and the Modern styles, but also in the development of modern artist-pottery. See *Historicism; Arts and Crafts Movement; Morris, William; Aesthetic Movement; Art Nouveau; Japanism; Modern Movement; Cole, Sir Henry; Pâte-sur-Pâte; Biedermeier; Parian; Revived Rococo; Chenavard, Aimé; Tucker, W. E.; Transfer-Printed Wares; Meigh, Charles; Relief-Decorated Wares; Jasper Ware; Engraved Designs.*

Victorian Majolica   See *Majolica.*

VIENNA

VIENNA PORCELAIN FACTORY
C. 1750-1820

BOCK, J.
EARLY 20TH CENTURY

AUGARTEN
20TH CENTURY

VIGNAUD
1911-1937

Vienna In Austrian ceramics; a hard paste porcelain manufactory was established at Vienna in 1719. It was the second European hard paste porcelain manufactory, the first being at Meissen. The productions generally fall into three groups: 1719 to 1744 under the management of Claudius Innocentius du Paquier; 1744 to 1784 under the Austrian State; 1784 to 1864 under the management of Konrad von Sorgenthal (d. 1805). Evidence of decline became perceptible after 1805 and the factory closed in 1864. No factory mark was used during the early period. A shield mark with the arms of Austria was adopted after 1744, the form varying considerably. After 1749 the shield mark was in underglaze blue. After 1783 in addition to the shield mark the last two numerals of the year were generally impressed, and after 1800 the last three numerals. The early wares were notable for beautiful specimens in the Baroque style. The Baroque decoration included interlacing scrolls and foliations, pendent swags of drapery, and palmettes which often covered the entire surface with a delicate web of decoration. The beautiful Vienna iron-red was also prominent in these early wares. During the second period the tablewares were in the Rococo style and to a large extent were in imitation of Meissen and Sèvres. Of particular interest were the figures and groups which showed an individual quality although the types were of Meissen inspiration. The best figures were executed in a lively and vivacious style that was completely captivating. The third period is notable for its superb tablewares in the Neo-Classic style painted in miniature style and richly gilded. They were remarkable for their great refinement and perfection of workmanship. The forms were distinctive for their elegant simplicity; urn-shaped vases were especially typical. Perhaps the principal innovation was a style of highly wrought gilding in relief. Interesting new ground colors of technical perfection also contributed to the refine-

ment of the wares. Practically all the figures were of biscuit and were chiefly copied from Sèvres. The material had a warm white tone that was pleasing. See *Schwarzlot; Paquier, C.I. du.* In modern Austrian ceramics; Joseph Böck was owner of a porcelain firm here that reflected the early 20th century Art Nouveau spirit of Austrian design. The marks of varying design included B, J B and Jos. Böck. In later years the influence of Austria in modern industrial ceramics has stemmed chiefly from the Augarten porcelain manufactory started in Vienna in 1922. Its aim seems to be to produce its own version of elegance in the modern taste, reflecting in part the simple, but significant, work of the Wiener Werkstätte and in part an earlier tradition of elegance and richness. Included among the designers have been Josef Hoffmann and Ena Rottenberg. See *Secession; Hunger, C. C.; Stölzel, S.; Niedermayer, J. J.; Beyer, J. C. W.; Grassi, Anton; Dannhauser, L.; Sorgenthal, K. von.* (332-336)

Vienna Secession See *Secession.*

Vieux Paris In French ceramics; porcelain wares made by the various manufactories in Paris particularly during the 18th century. The term *Vieux Paris,* or *Old Paris,* is given to those wares that are without an accepted identifying mark but which are known to have been produced in the Paris kilns because of their colors and decoration which are characteristic of Paris wares.

Vignaud, A. In French ceramics; started a porcelain factory at Limoges in 1911 for making tablewares. In 1937 the name was changed to Vignaud Brothers.

Vilaris, Marc-Hilaire See *Saint-Yrieix.*

Villeroy and Boch In German ceramics; this still-existing firm of great German potters was established in 1841, by the families of Villeroy and Boch, to merge into a single body the resources of their potteries at

Frauenberg 1760, Wallerfangen 1789, Septfontaines 1766, Mettlach 1809 and Schramberg 1820. Their combined potteries in 1899 employed six thousand workers, a great number for those days. They covered almost every field of ornamental and useful pottery. Steins, of which countless thousands were exported to the United States from Germany from around 1860-1900, were a big production item at their pottery in Mettlach. Well known is the Mettlach castle mark bearing the monogram VB. Originally it was the Abbey of Mettlach, which Jean-François Boch bought in 1809 and converted into a pottery. From 1853 a factory for general earthenware was operated at Dresden by Villeroy and Boch, making tablewares in cream-colored earthenware in the English style and tiles.

Vincennes In French ceramics; a hard paste porcelain manufactory was established at Vincennes, near Paris, in 1765 by Pierre-Antoine Hannong. In 1777 a heraldic label showing the patronage of Louis-Philippe, Duc de Chartres, was registered. The factory changed hands, and after 1788 there is no further record of its productions. The wares were similar in form and in painted decoration to the current fashions for Paris porcelains. The important soft paste porcelain manufactory was moved to Sèvres. See *Sèvres*.

Vinovo In Italian ceramics; a porcelain manufactory was started at Vinovo, near Turin, by Giovanni Vittorio Brodel and Pierre-Antoine Hannong in 1776 under Royal patronage. In 1780 it was taken over by Dr. V. Gioanetti, (d. 1815) a chemist, under whose guidance it flourished. It was active until 1820. Included among the marks were a cross over a V, sometimes accompanied by the initials D G; occasionally the cross was used alone. The material for the porcelain resembled a soft paste, actually it was of a hybrid composition. Generally it had a rather warm and pleas-

ing creamy tone. The decoration was in the late 18th century French style, comprising such typical motifs as small bouquets, sprigs of cornflowers and classical scrolls. The enamel colors were of a good quality; especially fine were the soft warm tones of yellow and brown. The figures were admirable for the texture of the material. Essentially they were nicely finished but revealed little originality. They were in white glazed and unglazed porcelain as well as in painted enamel colors.

Viollet-le-Duc, Eugène-Emmanuel (1814–1879) French architect and writer on archaeology; his chief interest was in the art of the Gothic period. As a writer on medieval architecture and related arts he is preeminent. The influence of his writings can scarcely be over-estimated.

Virgiliotto, Calamelli, Maestro (d. before 1570) Noteworthy potter and painter working at Faenza.

Viry, François-Gaspard and other members of a well-known family of faïence-painters active at Moustiers and Marseilles. François I, 1614-1689, worked at Moustiers from about 1682 onward; his son François II, 1659-1697, was a faïence-painter at Saint-Jean-du-Désert, Marseilles, where he succeeded Joseph Clérissy. Another son, Gaspard, 1668-1720, was a painter at Moustiers where he probably originated the Tempesta style, that is in the manner of the Florentine, Antonio Tempesta. See *Clérissy, Pierre and Joseph; Moustiers; Marseilles*.

Vista Alegre In Portuguese ceramics; a still-existing porcelain factory was started here in 1824 by José Ferreira Pinto Basso. Included among the marks are the letters V A.

Vitreous or **Vitrified** In ceramics; like glass; hard, glassy and impermeable.

VILLEROY AND BOCH
19TH CENTURY

VINCENNES
1777 ON

VINOVO
C. 1780 ON

Vitreous Body or **Vitrified Body** In ceramics; a body converted to a glass-like substance by fusion at high temperature.

Vogelesdekor In German ceramics; the name given to a pattern comprising scattered flowers interspersed with small exotic birds and groups of dots, particularly identified with the 17th century Hanau faïence-style of painted decoration.

Vogelmann, Carl Modeler, arcanist and potter working at Kelsterbach from 1764 to 1766; subsequently working at several porcelain factories. He was responsible for some interesting porcelain figures at Kelsterbach.

VOLKMAR, CHARLES
1879-1888

Volkmar, Charles American painter and artist-craftsman, studied in Paris under Harpignies and others; known for his paintings of landscape and cattle. While in Paris he became interested in the Limoges process of underglaze painting. In 1879 he returned to the United States and built a kiln at Greenpoint, Long Island, where he made vases and tiles. In 1895 he established the Volkmar Keramic Company. His wares were decorated with underglaze blue designs of historical buildings and portraits of persons prominent in America. Later, with Kate Cory, Volkmar opened a pottery at Corona, New York, and in 1903 he founded a pottery at Metuchen, New Jersey, where his production included tiles and lamps. See *Volkmar, Leon.*

VOLKSTEDT
C. 1760 ON

Volkmar, Leon (b. 1879) American artist-potter and teacher, born in France; son of Charles Volkmar, the well-known painter. Regarded as one of the most fundamental of modern potters, he always tried for simple forms with fine color and texture. Near East influence was strong in his work.

Volkmar Keramic Company See *Volkmar, Charles.*

Volkstedt In German ceramics; a soft paste porcelain manufactory was started in 1760

VOLKSTEDT-RUDOLSTADT
BEYER AND BOCK
C. 1890 ON

by Georg Heinrich Macheleid at Volkstedt, Thuringia. The mark was a hay-fork from the Schwarzburg arms. Shortly after, Macheleid obtained a privilege from the Prince of Schwarzburg-Rudolstadt to make hard paste porcelain. The factory changed hands many times and is still in existence. During the 19th century it obtained a bad reputation for making forgeries. The early mark was one or two crossed hay-forks; the latter mark was drawn to resemble the crossed swords of Meissen, who protested. In 1787 it was changed to either a single fork or crossed forks with incurvate prongs and having a line at the point where they crossed; however, the former mark apparently continued to be used. Around 1799 the letter R was used as a mark. The early porcelain was not free from imperfections and relief decorations were often used to conceal these defects. Meissen wares were freely copied, and the majority of their productions were essentially a coarse version of Meissen. Among their finer productions were tablewares and vases with excellent painted decoration in the Rococo style of figure subjects enclosed in Rococo scrollwork and of naturalistic flowers. The figures were executed in the manner of peasant art and were sometimes imbued with a singular charm. See *Thuringia.*

Volkstedt-Rudolstadt In German ceramics; a porcelain factory was started at Volkstedt-Rudolstadt by Beyer and Bock in 1890 producing tablewares for daily use. The marks of varying design included the distinguishing initials B or BB.

Volpato In Italian ceramics; a manufactory for porcelain and cream-colored earthenware in the English style was started at Rome in 1785 by Giovanni Trevisan, called Volpato (d. 1803). Members of the family operated the manufactory until 1831. Finely finished biscuit figures were perhaps its most important production.

Volute Krater See *Krater.*

Voulkos, Peter (b. 1924) American ceramist; first established a reputation in the United States and Europe for his vigorous and masterfully thrown pots and jars, generally finished in iron-reds or resist patterns in dark slips under mat glazes. In 1957 he turned in a radically new direction characterized by sculptural forms put together from thrown or slab units and coated with rough glazes or slips. The impact of his work has been strongly felt by the younger generation of potters. See *Abstract Pottery; Rhodes, Daniel.* (560, 561)

Voyez, Jean (John) (c. 1740-died after 1791) Modeler for Wedgwood, 1768-1769; however, because of a quarrel between them he left and took Wedgwood's processes to Humphrey Palmer for whom he then modeled. He also worked for Ralph Wood of Burslem and perhaps also worked on his own account. His signed works include reliefs on the Judgment of Paris. In 1773 he issued a catalogue of intaglios and cameos made by J. Voyez, sculptor, but these were not necessarily in the medium of ceramics. See *Wood, Ralph.* (398)

Voysey, Charles Francis Annesley (1857–1941) English architect and designer; generally regarded as the most important designer before and at the turn of the century.

Vsevolozhskii See *Sipiagin.*

Vsevolozhskii Porcelain Works See *Sipiagin.*

Vulci In ancient ceramics; a site in Etruria where from the tombs, the great majority, at least the finer specimens, of ancient Greek vases have been extracted.

Vyse, Charles English artist-potter, having a studio on Cheyne Row, Chelsea, London, 1919-1963. After his marriage, aided by his wife's chemical knowledge, he made earthenware figures and groups from around 1919-1930, with notable success. He and Nell Vyse experimented widely in wood-ash glazes and in reproducing some of the early Chinese glazes for their stonewares with studied glaze effects. Among his marks were his signature or initials with the year of production added.

19 V 27
CHELSEA.
VYSE, CHARLES
1937

W

Wa Wa In Chinese ceramics; the Chinese name given to a decorative design of playing children.

Wackerle, Josef Perhaps the most characteristic German modeler around the beginning of the 20th century. He was art director at Nymphenburg, 1906-1909. He modeled a series of human figures of remarkable charm and personality for Nymphenburg and later for the Berlin manufactory.

Wagenfeld, Wilhelm (b. 1900) German designer working in the Modern style in several media, especially ceramics and glass, in which he furnished designs for useful wares. After the Second World War he made designs for tablewares produced by the Rosenthal porcelain factory at Selb, Bavaria.

Wagner, Otto (1841–1918) Vienna's most progressive architect at the turn of the century; Hoffmann and Olbrich were his students. In his influential publication MO-DERNE ARCHITEKTUR in 1896 he expounded the relationship between modern life and modern forms, for example: "Nothing that is not practical can be beautiful." See *Secession*.

Wahliss, Ernst Of Turn and Vienna. See *Turn*.

Waldenburg In German ceramics; potteries were in existence at Waldenburg, Saxony, as early as the Middle Ages. A salt-glazed stoneware having a grey or light brown body with a brown surface was made here from around the middle of the 16th century. This early stoneware had little artistic merit, and it was not until later in the 16th century that more richly decorated wares were found. Their principal productions were all kinds of drinking vessels of distinctive form decorated with reliefs, such as circular wreaths, medallions, and allegorical figure subjects. Peculiar to Waldenburg are the decorative bands of dotted or zigzag roulette lines just below the mouth and around the foot. In 1831 the Krister Porzellan Manufaktur, A-G, was started here producing table and coffee services and gift articles. Later the firm was relocated to Landstuhl/Pfalz (Palatinate) and the works were merged with Rosenthal Porzellan, A-G, established at Selb, Bavaria, 1879. Among the accepted marks of varying designs are the distinguishing initials K P M. See *Penig; Hedgehog*.

Wall, Dr. In English ceramics; the name frequently attached to the early period of Worcester porcelain, 1751-1783, since Dr. Wall was one of the founders. Although Dr. Wall died in 1776 the period is generally extended to 1783, which date marks the death of William Davis, who was the first manager and who is commonly credited with the early productions. See *Worcester*.

Wallander, Alf See *Rörstrand*.

Wallendorf In German ceramics; a porcelain manufactory was started at Wallendorf, Thuringia, in 1764 by Johann Wolfgang Hammann. It was conducted by the same family for many years and in 1898 was formed into a company. Originally the mark was a W made to resemble the crossed swords of Meissen; after 1778 it was simply a small w. The productions were principally useful wares for a middle class market. The painted decoration was largely in imitation of Meissen; the so-called Meissen onion pattern was a very popular design. The figures, which were generally not marked, included all kinds of

K P M
WALDENBURG
C. 1831 ON

WALLENDORF
C. 1764-1778

subjects; many were copied from Meissen models. Of particular interest were some charming figures in contemporary dress executed in the manner of peasant art. They had the same naïve charm associated with the somewhat primitive figures made at Limbach.

Wall Fountain The decorative wall fountain, which was usually affixed to the wall, was a container for holding water with a spigot at the bottom. It was generally made of pewter, copper or pottery and the lavabo or wash basin, which was placed beneath it was made to match it. In the Spanish home the wall fountain and lavabo were made of colorful pottery and were invariably placed in a niche lined with colored tiles. They were often in the dining room and provided a striking and colorful note to the décor of the room. Large wall fountains and basins were a distinctive accessory of French provincial furniture. They were chiefly found in the dining room. Especially colorful were the ones made of faïence. Later they were sometimes made of tôle. Frequently the wall fountain and lavabo were attached to a kind of tall and narrow panelled cupboard stand. The stand had a tall narrow back panel to which the wall fountain was attached, while the basin rested on the cupboard portion which was fitted with a single cupboard door. (279)

Wall Period See *Worcester.*

Wall Pocket In ceramics; a decorative object made of faïence, porcelain or pottery, having the shape of a vase, with one side being flat so that it can be hung on a wall. It is also called a wall vase. (413)

Wall Vase See *Wall Pocket.*

Walton, John English potter working at Burslem in the Staffordshire district, late 18th and early 19th century. He was known mainly for his small figures and chimney ornaments in earthenware, painted in col-

ors often with spreading bocages. His Flight into Egypt group is typical of the 1815-1825 period. It may be said that he developed a style which was emulated by others, such as the figure-makers, Ralph Salt, Ralph Hall, Charles Tittensor and Edge and Grocott. His figures are generally clearly marked Walton.

Walzenkrug In German ceramics; a cylindrical mug that became the drinking vessel of the people in the 18th century. Beer mugs have been of this shape ever since.

Wan In Chinese ceramics; the Chinese name given to a bowl.

Wan Li The Wan Li reign of the Ming dynasty in China, 1573-1619. See *Chinese Dynasties; Ming.*

Wan Li Wu Ts'ai See *Five-Color Ware.*

Warburton, John In English ceramics; a family of potters making wares at Hot Lane, Cobridge, Staffordshire, during the second half of the 18th century. He and his successors were among the first potters to make cream-colored earthenware. A Jacob Warburton (1740-1826) was a partner in the New Hall Porcelain Company. The mark Warburton, impressed, was used, but it was extremely rare. See *New Hall.*

Warring States Early period in Chinese art history, c. 403-221 B.C. See *Chinese Dynasties.*

Warsaw In Polish ceramics; the Belvedere faïence factory at Warsaw was founded by King Stanislas Poniatowski with the help of Baron Franz Schütter in 1774. The wares were marked Varsovie. The best known pieces formed part of a service painted in muffle-colors and gold in the Japanese brocaded Imari style with Turkish inscriptions, reported to have been made in 1776 as a gift from the King to the Sultan of Turkey. Forgeries of the Turkish service are occasionally found. The more customary style appears to have been inspired by

WALTON, JOHN
C. 1818-35

WARSAW
BELVEDERE
1774 ON

the Chinese as interpreted in German porcelain. (295)

Wärtsilä   See *Arabia.*

Warwick China Company   In American ceramics; organized in 1887 in Wheeling, West Virginia, for the manufacture of semi-porcelain table and toilet goods. The first stamp was a helmet and crossed swords. From 1893 to 1898 the mark Warwick Semi-Porcelain was used and from 1898 Warwick China.

WARWICK CHINA CO.
C. 1887 ON

Washington, Martha   In American ceramics; a porcelain dinner service made in China and decorated with the monogram of Martha Washington surrounded by a gold sunburst and a chain of fifteen links, each containing the name of one of the States. Presented to Martha Washington by Captain Jacob van Braam, and extensively copied during the last quarter of the 19th century. (116)

Waster   In ceramics; a pot or fragment of a pot which has been spoiled and thrown away.

Watcombe Pottery Company   In English ceramics; active at South Devon from 1867 to 1901, producing earthenwares, portrait busts, figures and terra-cotta ornamental wares. It was subsequently combined with the Royal Aller Vale Pottery.

WATCOMBE POTTERY
1875 ON

Water-Dropper   In countries where writing is done with a brush, the water-dropper is a usual part of the scholar's writing equipage. See *Writing Equipage.* (126)

Water Leaf   In ornament; a decorative motif resembling an ivy leaf. The profile of the folded water leaf with its wavy edge and strongly marked ribbings was a favorite decorative motif during the Louis XV style.

Water Pipe   See *Narghile.*

Watteau, Antoine   (1684–1721) A celebrated French painter. Watteau was the founder of a new school of painting which marked a revolt against the stately and heroic classicism of the Louis XIV style and which initiated the Louis XV style. Watteau was to influence French art until the return of classical antiquity when French art was completely dominated by the painter, Jacques Louis David (1748-1825). Among the followers of Watteau were Lancret, Pater, Boucher, and Fragonard. Watteau lived most of his life during the reign of Louis XIV. He gained much of his knowledge of decorative art and ornamental design in the atelier of the brilliant painter and decorative artist, Claude Gillot, (1673–1722). Gillot introduced the decorative fêtes champêtres, in which he was later excelled by Watteau. The ornamental designs of Watteau and Gillot were undoubtedly inspired to some extent by the work of Bérain; however, they imparted far more vivacity to their work. The use of numerous curves in the work of Gillot and Watteau anticipated the Rocaille or Rococo style. Especially fashionable were their chinoiseries and singeries and their decorative designs of ingenious compositions in which Turks and other quaint doll-like figures from the Italian Comedy figured prominently. See *Louis XV; Rococo; Bérain, Jean, the Elder; Engraved Designs.*

Wazen   See *Eiraku; Kutani.*

Wear Pottery   See *Moore, Samuel and Company.*

Weaver, James   See *Spode.*

Webb, Aileen Osborn (Mrs. Vanderbilt Webb) (b. 1893) The person most responsible for the burgeoning crafts movement in the United States at the present time. See *American Craftsmen's Council.*

Wedging   See *Clay, preparation of.*

Wedgwood, Josiah   (1730–1795) Celebrated

English potter and founder of the manufactory at Etruria, Staffordshire; the firm is still in existence. Numerous potters having the name of Wedgwood were working in Staffordshire from the 17th century. After the death of his father in 1739, who operated the Churchyard Pottery at Burslem, Josiah Wedgwood began to work in the family pottery where he served an apprenticeship from 1744 to 1749. He joined Thomas Alders, a potter at Stoke, and in 1754 he joined Thomas Whieldon at Fenton. In 1759 he started a new pottery of his own in the Ivy House, Burslem, making all the current Staffordshire types including salt-glazed stoneware. In 1764 he moved to larger premises in the Brick House Works, later called the Bell House. In 1768 he had as his partner Thomas Bentley, a Liverpool merchant, who inspired in Wedgwood an appreciation for the antique. They completed a new factory in 1769 which Wedgwood named Etruria. In 1780 Bentley died, and in 1790 Wedgwood formed a partnership which included his three sons and a nephew. Undoubtedly Wedgwood's early productions were of the Whieldon type. While working with Whieldon he perfected a green glaze used especially on teapots and other vessels known as cauliflower and pineapple wares. Wedgwood always paid great attention to detail. He perfected cream-colored earthenware and an almost colorless glaze for it. Around 1765 he named it Queen's Ware. Ranking among his important and characteristic work were his marbled, onyx, agate and pebbled vases which he made by mingling different colored clays. In addition to the basalt or black basaltes stoneware, which he introduced around 1769, he also made cane ware and red stoneware; the latter being named Rosso Antico. His jasper wares were remarkable for the exquisite quality of the workmanship. Sometime around 1779 Wedgwood introduced a white earthenware which he named pearl ware. From around 1792 to 1810 platinum or silver, gold or pink and copper luster

painting were employed at Etruria. Included among the productions was a bone china made from 1812 to 1816. The pre-Etruria wares were seldom marked. From 1769 to 1780 the marks included Wedgwood and Bentley and W & B. From 1771 the name Wedgwood was found on useful wares and after 1780 on all varieties of wares. The early successes of Wedgwood's cane ware encouraged further research and the development of other colored clays. In 1805 Wedgwood introduced celadon; in 1850, lavender blue and in 1930, champagne. These self-colored bodies were, apart from bone china, the most significant technical and artistic development by Wedgwood in the 19th century. The manufacture of bone china, discontinued in 1812 owing to the enormous popularity of Queen's Ware, was resumed in 1878. In the following century, in the 1930's, Wedgwood produced the most distinguished English industrial wares, both tablewares and ornamental pieces. In the 1930's the architect Keith Murray was commissioned by Wedgwood to produce a series of contemporary designs suitable for their moonstone glaze introduced in 1933. Later in the same decade, Wedgwood tried to revive the English tradition of printed pottery with designs made by the painter and graphic artist, Eric Ravilious. The result of this collaboration was the Persephone earthenware table service. Also in the same decade, in 1936, the firm introduced Alpine Pink, a self-colored pink translucent bone china. The Barlaston period dates from 1938 when the foundation stone was laid to found a new plant in the hamlet of Barlaston, the home for several generations of members of the Wedgwood family, and the decision ultimately to abandon Etruria. See *Staffordshire; Basalt Ware; Jasper Ware; Cream-Colored Earthenware; Pearl Ware; Luster Decoration; Whieldon, Thomas; Leeds; Bamboo Ware; Alpine Pink; Cauliflower Ware; Marbled Ware; Cane Ware; Colored Bodies; Moonstone Glaze; Nautilus Ware; Hackwood, W.; Stubbs, G.; Rosso Antico;*

WEDGWOOD, JOSIAH

WEDGWOOD

C. 1759 ON

WEDGWOOD

C. 1878 ON (PORCELAIN)

C. 1940 ON (CREAMWARE)

Wedgwood, Josiah, Works or Factories. (396, 397, 401, 421-425, 507)

Wedgwood and Bentley Period   c. 1768-1780. See *Wedgwood, J.*

Wedgwood and Whieldon Period   1754-1759. See *Whieldon, T.; Wedgwood, J.*

Wedgwood and Company (Ltd.)   Staffordshire potters operating the Unicorn and Pinnox Works at Tunstall since 1860. Although the mark of this firm is Wedgwood & Co. it is often mistaken for that of the well-known firm of Josiah Wedgwood and Sons (Ltd.). The latter, however, does not include "& Co." in its marks. Wedgwood and Company, who include in their production earthenwares and stone china, was formerly Podmore, Walker and Company, active at Tunstall about 1834-59. The corporate name has been changed to Enoch Wedgwood (Tunstall) Ltd.

Wedgwood, Enoch Ltd.   See *Wedgwood and Company (Ltd.).*

Wedgwood, Josiah, Works or **Factories**   They are in chronological sequence: Churchyard Works, 1648-1749, at Burslem; Cliff Bank Works (Josiah's partnership with John Harrison), 1753-1754, at Stoke; Fenton Lòw (partnership with Thomas Whieldon), 1754-1759, at Fenton; Ivy House, 1759-1763, at Burslem; Brick House or Bell Works, 1763-1769, at Burslem; Etruria, 1769-1940, at Etruria; Barlaston, 1940- , at Barlaston.

Weesp   In Dutch ceramics; the first successful porcelain manufactory in Holland was established at Weesp in 1759 by Count Gronsfeldt-Diepenbroek. Weesp hard paste was very white and of fine quality. It was similar in form and in decoration to the contemporary German wares. Figures were also made and they were of fairly good quality. The accepted mark was a version of the Meissen crossed swords with three dots around them in underglaze

blue. In 1771 the manufactory was bought by Johannes de Mol (d. 1782) and transferred to Oude Loosdrecht. A new mark was adopted: MOL. The production was essentially similar to the earlier wares. The quality of the porcelain was fine. It flourished until 1782 and in 1784 it was moved to Oude Amstel near Amsterdam. After another change in ownership it was removed to Nieuwer Amstel in 1809. It ceased to operate around 1820. The wares produced at Oude Amstel and Nieuwer Amstel are rather undistinguished. The style of decoration was influenced by the contemporary wares of France as well as of Germany.

Weiden   In German ceramics; a porcelain factory was started at Weiden, Oberpfalz, by the Bauscher Brothers in 1881. They specialized in Hotel China. In 1927 the firm was purchased by Lorenz Hutschenreuther. See *Hutschenreuther, L.* A still-existing porcelain factory chiefly producing table services was started at Weiden, Oberpfalz, in 1911 by Christian Seltmann. The marks of varying design include Seltmann and C.S.

Weimar School for Arts and Crafts   In 1901 the Grand Duke of Saxe-Weimar invited Henry van de Velde to become head of the school. With the outbreak of World War I in 1914 his post was taken over by Walter Gropius, who began to prepare plans for reorganizing the school. The new school, combining an academy of art and a school of arts and crafts, opened in 1919; it was named the Staatliches Bauhaus. See *Bauhaus.*

Weissenau   In German ceramics; Adam Friedrich von Löwenfinck conducted an experimental faïence manufactory at Weissenau near Mayence in 1745. See *Löwenfinck, A. F. von.*

Weller, Samuel A. Company   Samuel A. Weller, who operated a pottery at Zanesville, Ohio, since 1882, started negotia-

WEDGWOOD AND COMPANY
1862-1890

WEESP
C. 1759 ON

M.O.L
✳

OUDE LOOSDRECHT
C. 1771-1782

Amstel
M.O.L
AMSTEL
C. 1800-1820

tions with W. A. Long to acquire the Lonhuda Pottery in Steubenville, Ohio, and with it the necessary knowledge of the methods and glazes involved. About 1895 he entered the art pottery field by continuing Lonhuda under the new name of Louwelsa. This line closely resembled Rookwood standard wares with underglaze decorations of flowers, fruits, portraits of American Indians and animals painted on spray-blended grounds of darker colors. As a rule the name *Louwelsa* was impressed on the bottom of the ware and the mark or monogram of the artist was occasionally added. Before 1903 there were no less than twenty-three decorators on the Weller staff, which continued to expand until as many as fifty decorators may have been working there at one time during the peak of production in the 1920's. The Louwelsa line was popular, and was made for around twenty years; regrettably it was not dated. In 1901 J. Sicard, formerly connected with the studio of Clément Massier of Golfe-Juan, France, came to the United States to continue experiments in metallic luster glaze effects at the Weller pottery. He developed an art ware called Sicardo-Weller decorated with floral and other motifs in metallic lusters on an iridescent ground of contrasting tints. It is said that the effect was novel and artistic. Other new lines were added and by 1904 the list included such styles as Aurelian which was similar to Louwelsa but the ground color was applied with a brush rather than spray-painted, and L'Art Nouveau with a semi-mat finish generally decorated in relief designs. By 1918 Weller was introducing two new lines each year, but as the names of these later styles did not appear on the ware, the names have little or no interest. In 1922 the business was incorporated; Weller died in 1925 and was succeeded as president by his nephew, Henry Weller (d. 1932). By this time three factories were in operation producing not only art pottery, but also garden ware and utility kitchen wares. The firm never recov-

ered from the business depression of the 1930's; it was officially dissolved in 1949. See *Roseville Pottery; Owens, J. B.; Massier, Clément; Lonhuda Pottery; Art Nouveau.*

Wells, Reginald   (1877–1951) English artist-potter; mainly concerned with the simple effect of glazes on his so-called Coldrum pottery; first working at or near Wrotham, Kent, around 1909. Next he was at Chelsea, London, around 1910-1924, then at Storrington, Sussex, around 1925-1951. He produced studio-type pottery, stonewares and figures.

Welsh Ware   In English ceramics; see *Combed Ware.*

Wessel, Ludwig   See *Poppelsdorf.*

Westerwald   In German ceramics; an important district for the production of Rhenish salt-glazed stoneware during the 17th and 18th centuries. The stonewares produced in the three principal towns, namely Höhr, Grenzau and Grenzhausen, did not achieve any artistic importance before 1590. As a rule it is difficult to separate their productions. Westerwald stoneware is often erroneously referred to as Nassau ware, since the towns were not incorporated in the Duchy of Nassau until the 19th century. The white stoneware made at Höhr around 1590 was difficult to distinguish from the later Siegburg wares. Several potters from Raeren settled at Grenzhausen, and the style was essentially a continuation of the Raeren wares. Large grey stoneware jugs with reliefs and impressed patterns painted in blue were typical of all the Westerwald wares. There was a general tendency for over-elaboration in the use of excessive applied and impressed ornament. In the second half of the 17th century some new types of decoration were introduced. Small applied reliefs in the form of rosettes, lozenges, angels' heads and the like began to be freely used in repeated patterns, diapers and borders. About 1680 there was intro-

WEIDEN

BAUSCHER BROTHERS
1881 ON

SELTMANN, CHRISTIAN
1911 ON

WELLS, REGINALD F.
C. 1910 ON

duced the well-known motif of dots in relief clustered to form flowers, foliage, and the like, which were effectively combined with incised lines. The cobalt-blue glaze was now supplemented with a manganese-purple glaze. About 1700 white ware was reintroduced and an attempt was made to meet the fashionable demand for white tea and coffee pots with the traditional Rhenish carved decoration. Figures, sometimes in contemporary costume, and lion saltcellars were among the forms found in the 18th century wares which may be well compared with the Staffordshire salt-glazed stoneware of the same time. An important new type of decoration was cut with a knife or impressed with sharp-edged stamps, the cut lines of the designs effectively separating the cobalt blue and manganese purple glazes. In this technique were rendered bold and fantastic birds and beasts, and scrolling foliage in a highly effective style of peasant art. Another peasant type, probably also of Westerwald origin, is decorated with patterns of flowers, foliage and animals executed completely in incised lines. See *Rhenish Stoneware; Stoneware; Mennicken.*

Westman, Marianne See *Rörstrand.*

Wheeling Pottery Company In American ceramics; organized in 1879 in Wheeling, West Virginia; in 1887 a second company was formed, under the same management, called La Belle Pottery Company. The two companies joined in 1889. They made white granite ware, plain and decorated, and La Belle factory made Adamantine china. They also introduced Cameo china, a thin china decorated with designs in various colors and in blue and gold.

Whieldon, Thomas (1719–1795) English Staffordshire potter. He started a pottery at Fenton Low or Little Fenton in 1740. He was one of the outstanding potters of his time and he made practically every type of current Staffordshire ware. His name is especially associated with a variety of pot-

WHEELING POTTERY

C. 1879 ON

C. 1893 ON

tery having mingled colored lead glazes. In order to produce this effect he dusted the cream-colored body of the pottery with various coloring oxides which were more or less irregularly absorbed into the thick lead glaze, producing indefinite patches of color running into one another. The colors were distinctive for their beauty and included green, yellow, purple, grey and dark brown. These same colored glazes were used over relief decorations. Sometimes Whieldon mottled only with manganese brown, producing a ware which is sometimes called tortoiseshell ware. Unfortunately, Whieldon never marked any of his wares. Included among his earlier productions were teapots and other vessels in the natural form of vegetables and fruit and known as pineapple and cauliflower wares. Josiah Wedgwood was in partnership with Whieldon from 1754 to 1759. See *Staffordshire.* (393-395)

Whistling Jar In pre-Columbian Andean ceramics; a variety of jar in the form of a more or less globular vessel, occasionally carinated (ridged), with two vents connected by an arched bridge. One of these is in the form of a human figure combined with a small globular whistle through which air must pass when water is poured in or out through the other which is the spout. The whistling jar made its first appearance in Cupisnique pottery. See *Andean.* (16, 21)

White In European ceramics; it seems that a white ware has always had a particular attraction for the potter. White-burning clays, however, are rare and are usually lacking in plasticity. For this reason potters were for centuries content to cover a red- or buff-bodied ware with a white-clay slip. An alternative to the slip-covering was a tin-glaze, a technique used in Europe at least as early as the 14th century, which made possible the beautiful white-surfaced majolica and faïence. Following the soft-paste porcelain phase, the discovery of the use of kaolin or white china-clay in hard paste or true porcelain by Böttger in 1709 brought the final phase in the production of satisfactory white-bodied ware in Europe. Apart from the white-burning clays, certain novel ingredients used to make white pottery should be noted. For example, at Bow and elsewhere in England the pure white ash of calcined bones was used in porcelain. First introduced in Staffordshire salt-glazed stoneware and later adopted in cream-colored earthenware was a white powder obtained by calcining and grinding flints.

White, George See *Doulton, Lambeth and Burslem.*

White Granite In ceramics; a hard white pottery. It is also called Ironstone China. See *Ironstone China, Granite Ware.*

White Star, The or **De Witte Starre** In Dutch ceramics; a Delft faïence pottery active 1660-1803. The initials of the various proprietors occur in the marks, such as A K (Albertus Kiehl) 1761 to 1772. See *Delft.*

White Ware See *Granite Ware.*

Wien See *Vienna.*

Wiener Keramik In modern Austrian ceramics; a workshop organized by Michael Powolny and Berthold Löffer in 1905 at Vienna. Later in 1912 it was merged with the workshop of one of Powolny's pupils, Franz Schleiss, under the name Wiener und Gmundener Keramik Werkstätte. Included among the products of the Wiener Keramik workshop was black and white majolica generally decorated with geometric patterns in a manner connected with Cubism, from designs by such artists as Josef Hoffmann, Dagobert Pèche and Michael Powolny. The work of the latter is especially known for the lively style of his earthenware figures of children. Products broadly similar to these were being made at the factory of Ernst Wahliss at Turn. Following the work of Powolny, Robert Obsieger was for many years a significant teacher. Included among his more notable students were Kurt Ohnsorg and Gunda Schihan. See *Turn; Secession; Wiener Werkstätte.*

Wiener Sezession See *Secession.*

Wiener und Gmundener Keramik Werkstätte See *Wiener Keramik.*

Wiener Werkstätte Founded in Vienna in 1903 by Josef Hoffmann in conjunction with Koloman Moser and others; under the leadership of Hoffmann these workshops continued the line of the English Arts and Crafts Movement and were more interested in form and material than in ornament. As in the case of the Bauhaus in Germany, the Wiener Werkstätte was a strong influence on both industrial and art-pottery. See *Secession; Deutsche Werkstätten; Deutscher Werkbund; Oesterreichischer Werkbund.*

Wiinblad, Bjorn See *Rosenthal.*

Wildenhain, Frans (b. 1905) American designer-craftsman born in Germany; studied at the Bauhaus in Weimar; a potter whose work is characterized by great variety. He came to the United States in 1947. Whimsical shapes, functional forms and ceramic sculpture are all within the scope of his work.

Wildenhain, Marguerite (b. 1898) American artist-potter born in France, teacher and writer; received her art training at the Bauhaus in Weimar. She came to the United States in 1940 and settled in California as a potter, ultimately opening her own school at Pond Farm, Guerneville. She is the author of POTTERY: FORM AND EXPRESSION, 1959. (556)

Wilkomm See *Dreihausen.*

THE WHITE STAR
1761-1772

Willems, Joseph Modeler at Chelsea porcelain factory working from around 1750-1766.

Willets Manufacturing Company In American ceramics; established at Trenton, New Jersey. The factory is noted for Belleek pieces made during the late 1880's and 1890's. Many of Willets' forms were reproductions of the shell and coral forms of Irish Belleek. The characteristic mark was a snake coiled to form a W with Belleek above and Willets below.

WILLETS
C. 1888 ON

William IV King of England, 1830-1837. As a rule the years of his reign are included in the Victorian period, the years of the reign of Queen Victoria, 1837-1901.

Willow Pattern In English ceramics; a decorative design executed in a pseudo-Chinese manner introduced at the Caughley manufactory around 1780. It is reputed that this design, which was employed for underglaze blue transfer-printing on English porcelain and pottery, was engraved by Thomas Minton. The design was copied and adapted by many other potters in both France and Germany as well as in England. It is probably the best-known of all transfer-printed designs, depicting a river with a bridge across it and trees along the bank. The two birds associated with the scene in its later characteristic form are, according to legend, supposed to represent the souls of two lovers flying away from an irate father.

Wilson, Robert See *Palmer, Humphrey.*

Wincanton In English ceramics; see *Bristol.*

WILLOW PATTERN PLATE,
SPODE

Winckelmann, Johann (1717–1768) A famous German archaeologist. He went to Rome in 1755 and studied Roman antiquities and gradually acquired an unrivaled knowledge of ancient art. He was a prolific writer and his books covered all phases of ancient Roman and Grecian art. Scholars gained their first real information about the treasures excavated from Pompeii and Herculaneum from his books. French and English classic designs were greatly indebted to Winckelmann's archaeological researches. See *Classic Revival; Engraved Designs.*

Winchcombe Pottery See *Cardew, Michael.*

Winterthur In Swiss ceramics; Hafner-ware of the 16th century ascribed to Winterthur includes tall tankards either glazed in plain colors or splashed with manganese-purple on a yellow ground and ornamented with applied reliefs. The manufacture of faïence tile stoves at Winterthur was mainly associated with a family named Pfau. The earliest recorded member, Ludwig Pfau the Elder (d. 1623), is known by works bearing the date 1591. The family continued to work as stove-makers until the middle of the 18th century. (253)

Wirkkala, Tapio (b. 1915) Finnish designer-craftsman, sculptor and graphic artist. Like many other great artists Wirkkala has found his inspiration in nature. See *Rosenthal.*

Wolff, Johann Born in Holstein and worked as a painter in the faïence factory at Nuremberg. The making of faïence in northern Europe began with Wolff's arrival in Copenhagen in 1721 and the establishment of Store Kongensgade in 1722 under the patronage of Christian VI of Denmark and conducted by Wolff, 1722-1723. His stay was abruptly terminated as his work proved unsatisfactory. Wolff was also a problem at Rörstrand, where he worked from 1725 to 1728 when he was dismissed. See *Store Kongensgade; Rörstrand.*

Wood, Aaron (1717–1775) Brother of Ralph Wood. Mold-cutter and modeler at Burslem, Staffordshire. The most celebrated mold-cutter of his time, Aaron Wood worked for the majority of important

Staffordshire potters, including Whieldon. The Pew groups have been attributed to him.

Wood and Sons (Ltd.) Staffordshire potters operating the Trent and New Wharf Potteries at Burslem since 1865. Son was changed to Sons around 1907; Ltd. was added in 1910.

Wood, Beatrice American artist-potter; one of the foremost ceramists in the United States; has been making pottery from about 1939. The aesthetic value and charm of her work springs from her independence from currently accepted traditions. She is, however, capable of producing a Bauhaus piece or achieving a subtle Chinese or Japanese glaze effect. Because of her open receptivity, her work is always filled with fresh excitement. In her pottery decoration and modeled clay figures appear a fantasy sometimes reminiscent of Klee, sometimes of Chagall, but always characteristically Beatrice Wood.

Wood, Enoch (1759–1840) English modeler and potter working at Burslem, Staffordshire. In 1783 he was working in partnership with his cousin, Ralph Wood, at Burslem. The firm was known as Enoch Wood & Co., in 1790, and in the same year was changed to Wood and Caldwell. This partnership with James Caldwell continued until 1818. The pottery was known as Enoch Wood & Sons until 1846 when it ceased to operate. They made practically every kind of Staffordshire pottery including cream-colored and blue-printed earthenware, black basalt and jasper stoneware and perhaps porcelain. Their blue-printed earthenware made chiefly for the American market was of excellent quality. More than sixty American views were produced, as a rule with an elaborate "shell" border. Enoch Wood modeled numerous busts; especially familiar are the busts of John Wesley and George Whitefield, the preachers. His numerous pottery figures were generally painted in enamel colors. Included among the marks are E Wood, Wood and Caldwell and Enoch Wood & Sons.

Wood, John Wedge Staffordshire potter working at Burslem and Tunstall, 1841-1860. He produced earthenwares. As several printed marks occurring on his wares bear the name of J. Wedgwood, this mark has often been mistaken for the mark of the familiar Josiah Wedgwood firm. However, this latter firm never used marks with the initial J. The marks of John Wedge Wood frequently have a slight gap or dot between "Wedg" and "Wood."

WOOD, JOHN WEDGE
C. 1841-1860

Wood, Ralph (1715–1772) English Staffordshire potter; he and his son Ralph, (1748–1795) also a potter, were working at the Hill factory, Burslem. The marked Ralph Wood wares are mainly toby jugs, reliefs and figures; however, there is no good reason for supposing that these rare impressed marks (R.Wood, Ra. Wood-/Burslem) indicate the Woods as modelers, or are other than factory marks. It is generally accepted that most of their marked work was modeled by John Voyez. Ralph Wood used the technique of mingled colored lead glazes associated with the wares of Thomas Whieldon. However, his glazes differed from the latter in that the patches were kept more distinct, which produced more of a painted effect. Of course the blurred edges and streaked colors obviously showed that the colors were not actually painted. About 1780 these pleasing color-glazes were supplanted by enameling. See *Whieldon, Thomas; Staffordshire; Toby Jug.* (398-400)

Worcester In English ceramics; a porcelain manufactory was established at Worcester in 1751, and in the following year it absorbed Lowdin's porcelain manufactory at Bristol. During the first forty years of its existence it was the most productive English porcelain manufactory. It ranks second only to Chelsea in artistic importance. There were many changes in the manage-

WOOD AND SONS
C. 1907 ON

WORCESTER

WORCESTER
C. 1755-1790

FLIGHT
C. 1788-1792

FLIGHT AND BARR
C. 1792-1807

BARR, FLIGHT AND BARR
C. 1807-1813

FLIGHT, BARR AND BARR
C. 1813-1840

ment. The name of Dr. John Wall is frequently attached to the early period of Worcester porcelain, 1751-1783, since Dr. Wall was one of the founders. Although Dr. Wall died in 1776 the period is generally extended to 1783, which date marks the death of William Davis, who was the first manager and who is commonly credited with the early productions. In 1783 the manufactory was bought by Thomas Flight, who was the London agent for the firm, for his sons John and Joseph. In 1792 a year after the death of John Flight, Martin Barr was taken into the company. From 1792 to 1807 the partnership was called Flight and Barr and in 1807 it became Barr, Flight and Barr and in 1813 Flight, Barr and Barr. In 1840 it was amalgamated with the Chamberlain pottery of Worcester and in 1852 it became Kerr and Binns. In 1862 it became the Worcester Royal Porcelain Company. For a long time the factory did not have any regular mark, although a script W was sometimes used. The crescent was used enough to be regarded as a factory mark. From around and after 1790 there were numerous marks. The early Worcester porcelain was a kind of soft paste porcelain containing soapstone or steatite. The early productions were principally tablewares of practical and plain forms, technically well finished. Underglaze blue painting was much used for almost fifty years. The process of transfer printing was largely adopted around 1756 and the underglaze blue around 1760. The so-called Worcester-Japan patterns which were free adaptations of the Japanese Imari and Kakiemon styles were made almost from the beginning and remained in vogue for a long time. More ambitious pieces began to appear from around 1770. Colored grounds imitated from Sèvres were made, including turquoise, apple-green and lavender. The plain dark blue was occasionally marked with the scale pattern, which can be regarded as virtually a Worcester innovation. The scale blue as well as the less

common scale pink were fashionable from around 1765 to 1785. The gilding was of excellent quality and was frequently finely chased. Probably the painting of exotic birds in panels on a colored ground is the best known of all Worcester decoration. Chinoiseries in the Chelsea style and landscapes in panels on colored grounds were also favored. In the middle period, which extends from around 1783 to 1840, the decoration was in accordance with the successive styles, the early Neo-Classic being supplanted by the Empire. The Kerr and Binns Company, 1852-1862, was remarkable for the interest it aroused among contemporaries. Of the many young artists Thomas Bott, engaged in 1853, worked on the so-called Limoges enamels made of porcelain. Painted with a semi-opaque white enamel on a deep rich blue ground giving a striking cameo-like effect, they were called Limoges because their style was suggested by the Renaissance painted enamel work on copper which was executed at Limoges. Besides their prestige work Worcester expended the same exacting care on their wares for daily use. For Kerr and Binns' (also referred to as W. H. Kerr & Co.) finest production a printed shield-shaped mark was used. This mark incorporates the last two figures of the year and provides a space at the lower lefthand corner for the artist's signature or initials. The customary factory mark comprises a circle incorporating four cursive W's with a crescent centering the figure 51. This mark with the addition of a crown was retained by the new Worcester Royal Porcelain Company formed in 1862 and is used to this day. In the early 1870's and particularly for the Viennese Exhibition of 1873, Worcester produced a Japanese style which was mainly associated with the modeler James Hadley and which was to have a considerable influence on the porcelain of the period. The work was not imitative, as they looked to Japan for lessons, not models. Other styles which later influenced

Worcester—Persian, Italian and Indian—were used in the same perceptive spirit. The interest in glaze techniques resulted in Worcester's earthenware Sabrina ware, patented by 1894 with its fine crystalline glaze, which was made in the first thirty years of the 20th century. Great hand painting on fine bone china continued to be a dominant feature in the 20th century. The acquisition of James Hadley and Sons factory in 1905 brought in more fine decorators to join such artists as the Stintons (John, James and Harry) and Harry Davis. A movement into limited editions began in 1935 with the series of American birds modeled by Dorothy Doughty, followed by the horses and bulls of Doris Lindner, the fish, flowers and game birds of Van Ruyckevelt, the Victorian figurines of Baroness Van Ruyckevelt, all in fine bone china, and the porcelain figures of Machin. See *Scale Pattern; Transfer-Printed Ware; Hadley, J.; Bott, T.; Sabrina; Grainger Company; Baxter, T.; Chamberlain, R.; Giles, J.; Donaldson, J.; O'Neale, J.H.* (370–374, 546)

Worcester Royal Porcelain Company, Ltd.
Worcester obtained its Royal Warrant in 1788, but the actual title of the Worcester Royal Porcelain Company dates from 1862, which title the firm that actually makes bone china and porcelain has had ever since, although the wares have for nearly one hundred years been marketed under the name of "Royal Worcester." In 1958 a new company called Royal Worcester Limited was formed, which is now a holding company of which the Worcester Royal Porcelain Company Ltd. is a manufacturing subsidiary. See *Worcester.*

Workman's Mark An initial, numeral or simple character used by a workman in a factory. See *Mark,* in ceramics.

Wright, Frank Lloyd (1869–1959) American architect; one of the first architects to believe in the machine and to understand its basic character and its effects on the relation of architecture and design to or-namentation. These ideals were expressed in his manifesto, THE ARTS AND CRAFTS OF THE MACHINE, 1901.

Wright, Russell (b. 1904) American industrial designer; the range of his art in industry includes tableware, glassware, furniture, wallpapers, rugs, fabrics and flatware. He pioneered the change to a more modern style of tableware design. In 1938 he designed and produced at Steubenville a set of earthenware which was simple, functional, undecorated and employed solid colors rather than decals. This modern dinnerware was an immediate success.

Wrisbergholzen In German ceramics; a faïence factory started by Baron von Wrisberg was active here, in the region of Hanover, from around 1735 to 1834, under a succession of managers. The wares, bearing the mark W R in monogram, revealed no great creativity and in the use of high-temperature colors frequently resembled those of the nearby Brunswick faïence factory.

Writing Equipage In Chinese ceramics; since calligraphy and painting are considered by the Chinese among the highest accomplishments, the potter expended great skill in creating and decorating the various writing accessories. The following comprise the principal writing equipage. The pencil brush or pi was provided with a fine porcelain handle or pi kuan. The brush rest or pi ko was given many delightful forms. Especially characteristic was a miniature range of mountains in the form of three or five hills. A brush pot or jar or pi t'ung, generally cylindrical in form, was designed for the brush to stand in and a bed or pi ch'uang for the brush to recline on. The brush bath or the vessel for washing the brush or pi hsi was generally in the form of a shallow bowl and occasionally it was shaped like a lotus flower, chrysanthemum or blossom. There was also a hand-rest or chên shou and a paperweight or

WORCESTER

KERR AND BINNS
C. 1852-1862

WORCESTER
C. 1862 ON, WITH
VARIATIONS

WRISBERGHOLZEN
1735 ON

chên chih in the form of a coiled lizard and other fanciful forms. In order to make the ink or mo there was an ink-pallet or mo yen and an ink-cake, which was also given a bed or mo ch'uang. Ink-stones made of pottery or porcelain with a depression to form a well and an unglazed space for rubbing the ink-stick were not as efficient as real stones with a fine and smooth texture. The ink-stick was rubbed on the ink-stone behind the ink-screen or yen p'ing. The water-dropper or shui ti was given various ingenious shapes, such as a peach. Especially typical was the water-dropper modeled in the form of a frog. The small water pot or shui ch'êng with its miniature ladle was also given many unusual shapes. Finally, the seal vermilion was kept in a seal box or rouge box or yin sê ch'ih which was generally circular or square and occasionally octagonal or multifoil. The decorative handles for the seals were of an endless variety and included handles modeled in the form of dragons, lions and turtles. Many of these writing accessories were also made in other materials such as jade, ivory and metal. See *Table Screen or Ink-Screen; Handrest.*

Wrotham In English ceramics; a variety of English slipware was made at Wrotham, Kent, during the 17th and 18th centuries. Tygs with many handles, mugs with two handles, posset-pots and candlesticks were especially characteristic productions. The slipwares were decorated with applied and stamped reliefs in white clay, comprising rosettes, fleur-de-lis, stars, masks and similar motifs. Applied and stamped inscriptions were also found.

Wu Chin Ware In Chinese ceramics; see *Mirror Black.*

Wu Ts'ai In Chinese ceramics; see *Five-Color Ware.*

Würzburg In German ceramics; a short-lived porcelain factory was started at Würzburg in Lower Franconia around 1775 by Johann Caspar Geyger (d. 1780). They produced a class of tablewares of considerable interest. The history of the factory has not yet been fully established. One of the factory's accepted marks are the initials CGW.

C . G
W

WURZBURG
1775 ON

Y

Yaki In Japanese ceramics; the Japanese word for ware or kiln. See *Yao.*

Yanagi, Soetsu Japanese art critic and lecturer, tea master, specialist in the fields of fine arts. Appreciation of Japanese folk art begins with Yanagi; he discovered it. In 1935, after Yanagi had been collecting early examples of folk art for a number of years, a well-known philanthropist and art lover, Magosaburo Ohara, offered to build a folk art museum in Tokyo to house Yanagi's collection of "people's art." As soon as the public had the opportunity to appraise the charm of folk art, a great demand developed, which led to its revival. Yanagi set down precisely what Japanese folk art was and what its qualities were. First of all, artists and geniuses were not a part of folk art; it was done by anonymous craftsmen for the use of the common people. It was unpretentious, everyday craftsmanship. According to Yanagi, the greatest thing was living beauty in daily life; in bringing beauty into life, crafts must play a vital part. The quality of extravagance that is always associated with deluxe art objects was absent, and any excess of decoration was considered objectionable. Folk art had to be simple in shape, in color and design. Finally, he believed people's art was normal art, that nothing was healthier than normal things. See *Mashiko.*

Yao In Chinese ceramics; the Chinese word for ware. See *Yaki.*

Yasabei See *Bunzo, Hozan.*

Yatsushiro See *Agano.*

Yayoi In Japanese prehistoric ceramics; following the prehistoric Jomon earthenware, the art of Japanese pottery is next observed in Yayoi ware, generally so named because it was first excavated at a Neolithic site in Tokyo known by that name. Yayoi ware is believed to have been made in a subsequent period when in relatively rapid succession bronze and iron-working techniques, introduced by a new influx from the Continent, came into use alongside of Neolithic stone implements. The new wares, like those of the Jomon style, were made throughout Japan but the many varieties possess certain distinctive common characteristics which allow them to be grouped into a single category. Both Jomon and Yayoi wares were fired or baked at quite a low temperature, with the result that neither could be very durable. As a rule Yayoi ware was made with a more carefully washed variety of clay than is found in the Jomon style, though bits of stone and pebble are to be found in relatively refined Yayoi ware. More important by far, the Yayoi potters seem to have used either a throwing wheel or some similar device, for their work shows evidence of mechanical production both in its symmetry and in certain features of its decoration. Yayoi ware was made for a period of at least several hundred years. It is technically superior to Jomon, the ware that yielded to it, but both in form and decoration it is less imaginative. In addition to ceramic vessels, both the Jomon and Yayoi potters produced a large variety of other earthenware objects including semi-sculptural figures and small-scale reproductions of buildings. The purpose of many of these was probably connected with early religious practices. Pottery in the Yayoi tradition, which is smoother in finish than Jomon and is decorated with simple geometrical designs, continued to be made into the Kofun or Tomb Mound period. Dating from around the beginning of the 4th century A.D., this period derives its name from the practice of erecting elaborate burial mounds, a practice that continued until the introduction of Buddhism in Japan when cremation became the burial practice customary among the upper classes. It is chiefly from excavations of such burial mounds that the history of the ceramic art of the time must come. Though the pottery gave evidence of increasingly important contacts with continental culture, pottery in the earlier relatively indigenous tradition continued to be made. Contemporary literature of this period mentions hereditary guilds of potters working with indigenous techniques, to whom they gave the name of Haji-be or Earthenware Workers' Guild. Hence in modern times the name *Haji* has come to be given to the plain, unglazed, porous red earthenware frequently found in burial mounds. The ware, which tends to be brittle and fragile, represents a later development of the same indigenous techniques which were used in the Jomon and Yayoi wares. See *Jomon; Japanese Periods; Haniwa; Sue Ware.*

Yellow and Orange In ceramics; yellow and orange pigments used in decorating pottery are generally obtained from antimoniate of lead and from iron. They are classified as high-temperature colors as they can endure the full heat of the majolica and faïence kiln and are painted on the unfired tin glaze. They cannot be used under the glaze on porcelain. Many shades of petit-feu or muffle-kiln colors can be made from them. See *Colors; Colored Grounds; Monochrome Painting; Jasper Ware.*

Yellow Seto See *Seto; Mino.*

Yellow Ware In American ceramics; a term which particularly tends to be associated with a class of simple kitchen and tableware having a body similar to that covered with a brown (a Rockingham) glaze. In yellow ware, however, the body is covered with a transparent or colorless glaze which intensifies the buff to yellow or cane color body. For this reason it has been dubbed yellow ware, in the same manner

that the ware with a brown glaze is referred to as brown ware. Both belong to pottery in an industrial age, after 1830. In time the principal center in America for the manufacture of Rockingham and of yellow ware came to be East Liverpool, Ohio. A great quantity was made from 1830 to 1900.

Yen-yen In Chinese ceramics; the Chinese name given to a vase of baluster form with a long trumpet-shaped neck.

Yi The name of the Korean historical period, 1392–1910. See *Korean Periods.*

Yi Hsing Yao In Chinese ceramics; an unglazed stoneware produced at Yi-hsing-hsien in Kiang-su province. It is a reddish or brownish stoneware. Its greatest productive period was during the latter part of the Ming dynasty and during the Ch'ing period. The articles most commonly produced were usually small and dainty and included teapots, wine cups, tea cups, bottles and dishes. This ware was taken to Europe by the Portuguese traders in large quantities where it was given the name of buccaro. See *Buccaro.* (111)

Yin The Shang or Yin period in Chinese art history, ?1523–?1028 B.C. See *Chinese Dynasties.*

Yin Hua See *Ting Yao.*

Yin Yang In Chinese symbols; a circle divided by a wavy line. It is a symbol of the dual powers of nature or symbol of Creation, yin representing the female and yang the male element. See *Eight Trigrams.*

Ying Ch'ing In Chinese ceramics; an arbitrary name given to a ware made during the Sung dynasty. One theory advanced by some modern collectors is that the Ying Ch'ing wares should be regarded as of the Ju type. This ware has a hard white body that is highly translucent and burns brown where exposed. The glaze is thick and generally full of bubbles which gives it a soft effect. The glaze is white with a faint bluish tinge which is darker where the glaze runs thicker. The glaze is sometimes crazed. The lip rim of the bowl was generally glazed and the bottom was often not glazed and sometimes revealed the marks of the ring on which it was fired. Unglazed lip rims were relatively rare. Some of the specimens were very skillfully potted and were sometimes worked as thin as eggshell porcelain. The quality of this ware varies widely; this is due to the variety of locations where it was made. It is believed that much of this ware was made in Honan since the decorative designs have a strong similarity with designs on northern Sung celadon. Some of the ware was without decoration. When decoration was added it was incised, carved or molded in relief by pressing the object in an intaglio mold. The decoration was covered with a transparent glaze. Included among the favorite motifs were boys among flowers, lotus flowers, ducks and fishes. Beautiful vase forms and ewers were especially distinctive. See *Sung; Ju Ware.*

Ying-Hsuing In Chinese ceramics; a term meaning bear and eagle. The name was given to a form of vase made during the Ming period that consisted of two cylindrical vases of conforming shape joined together with the figures of a bear and an eagle linking the vases on one side. These vases were reputed to have been presented to soldiers for heroic deeds.

Ying Ts'ai In Chinese ceramics; the Chinese name given to hard enamels, the Famille Verte or Green Family. See *Famille Verte.*

Ymagynatyf Pottery Active at Chelsea, London, from around 1922 to 1939 producing studio-type pottery. Ymagynatyf, incised or impressed, with initials of the potter is the mark.

Yokkaichi In Japanese ceramics; in the 18th century a rich merchant in the town of Kuwana, which is across the bay from Nagoya, started making tea utensils, learning the techniques from Kyoto. He named the product Banko ware. In the 20th century the town of Yokkaichi, adjacent to Kuwana, developed as an industrial town and potters gradually moved there. At present Yokkaichi has become the center of Western style export ware; only a few potters make traditional type Banko ware. See *Japanese Contemporary Pottery.*

Yoshidaya See *Kutani.*

Young Moor's Head, The or **Het Jonge Moriaenshooft** In Dutch ceramics; a faïence manufactory at Delft operated from around 1661 by Jacob Wemmersz Hoppesteyn, a very talented faïence-potter. Upon his death in 1671 his widow and his son Rochus Jacobsz Hoppesteyn operated the pottery together until 1679 when Rochus became sole proprietor until his death in 1692. From that time onward the pottery changed hands a number of times until 1792 when it ceased to operate. The faïence jugs and plates made by Rochus Hoppesteyn are superbly beautiful and rank among the great rarities of Delft. See *Old Moor's Head, The; Delft; Faïence.* (265)

Young, William Weston (1776–1847) Painter at Swansea and Nantgarw, specializing in the painting of flowers, birds and butterflies, early 19th century. He was manager of Nantgarw from 1819 to 1822, where he mainly decorated the existing stock.

Yu-ch'ui P'ing In Chinese ceramics; the Chinese name given to a club-shaped vase.

Yüan The Yüan period of China, 1280-1368. See *Chinese Dynasties.*

Yucatan See *Central American Pottery.*

Yüeh Yao Or Yüeh Chou yao. In Chinese ceramics; celadon wares made at the kilns in the old district of Yüeh, which is now called Shao-Hsing, in the province of Chekiang. Yüeh ware was first produced during the period of the Six Dynasties and was fully perfected during the T'ang period.

THE YOUNG MOOR'S HEAD
1680-1692

The body is a hard light grey porcelaneous stoneware that burns deep orange or reddish-brown where exposed. It is covered with a beautiful transparent glaze of various tones of green although greyish-greens and olive greens predominate. Yüeh ware was beautifully proportioned in classic forms. The decoration which was also executed in a refined and classic manner included incising, delicately molded appliqués and modeling in low relief. A variety of articles was made, such as vases, bowls, small plates, wine pots, teapots and small boxes. (89)

Yung Chêng The Yung Chêng reign of the Ch'ing dynasty in China, 1723-1735. See *Chinese Dynasties.*

Yung Lo The Yung Lo reign of the Ming dynasty in China, 1403-1424. See *Chinese Dynasties.*

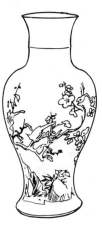

YUNG CHENG VASE

Z

Zapotec In pre-Columbian Central American ceramics; the home of the Zapotecs whose culture had its roots in the Formative period was Monte Alban, which is in the province of Oaxaca and lies south from the valley of Mexico and west from the Maya area. The influence of the Teotihuacanos and the Maya was apparent in their pottery. See *Central American Pottery; Teotihuacan; Maya.*

Zdekauer, Moritz See *Altrohlau.*

Zeh, Scherzer and Company See *Rehau.*

Zeisel, Eva American designer, born in Hungary. In collaboration with the Museum of Modern Art, New York City, she developed a "modern" porcelain table service, 1941-1945, produced by the Castleton China Company of New Castle, Pennsylvania. Such modern services use in some degree the principle of functionalism together with a sculptural sense of elegance. Since the Second World War practically every major ceramic factory in Europe, America and Japan has produced at least one modern service, which is very frequently in plain white, like the Zeisel service, or else with sparse decoration. The tendency to emphasize form at the expense of decoration is a characteristic of the Modern style and was evident in table services dating from the beginning of the 1900's, such as Rosenthal's Darmstadt, 1905, and Donatello, 1907, table services which were in the original versions left white. (502)

Zell In German ceramics; a pottery making faïence fine or cream-colored earthenware in the English style was started at Zell, Baden, by Lenz, whose family still operates it. From 1818 onward the mark Zell, impressed, was used.

Zenith Pottery See *Gouda.*

Zerbst In German ceramics; a faïence factory was started at Zerbst, Anhalt, by the arcanist Johann Caspar Ripp of Hanau, who in 1720 with a potter friend named Daniel van Keyck of Delft, applied to the Prince of Anhalt-Zerbst for assistance in founding it. Ripp remained only for four years, but Keyck remained as the manager for twenty years. From 1758 to 1768, the factory enjoyed a flourishing period. It changed ownership several times and closed in 1861. Occasionally the mark Z was used. No distinctive style was created though the wares following the current vogue in blue and white and high-temperature polychrome were occasionally of good quality.

Zoar In American ceramics; pottery made by the Society of Separatists called Zoarites who came from Württemberg, Germany, and settled at Zoar, in Tuscarawas County, Ohio, where they prospered from about 1819 to 1898. Buff- or black-glazed redware and common brown ware are typical of their production.

Zopf In German decorative art; the term, literally meaning pigtail, is given to a German phase of the Classic Revival, characterized by silhouette portraits and the serious and solemn painting of figures in contemporary costumes.

Zsolnay In Hungarian ceramics; a ceramic factory started at Pécs in 1862 producing chiefly wares for everyday use. The Art Nouveau style was strongly expressed by this firm in a series of boldly shaped lustered vases. Around 1900 the Zsolnay firm also made some pieces with distinctive painted decoration designed by the Hungarian painter Joseph Rippl-Rónai. The factory was continuously seeking to dis-

ZERBST
C. 1720 ON

ZSOLNAY
C. 1862 ON

381

cover new materials and glazes, experimenting with novel technological processes.

Zuid Hollandsche See *Gouda.*

Zurich In Swiss ceramics; a porcelain and faïence manufactory was founded at Zurich in 1763 by a company. From around and after 1790 faïence and lead-glazed earthenware were the principal productions. The manufactory changed hands several times and remained active until the end of the 19th century. The mark was a Z with or without dots. A soft paste porcelain was made for the first two years. Hard paste porcelain was made from around 1765, and in the ensuing decade the manufactory produced porcelain of great beauty, admirable for its extremely delicate enamel painting. The principal productions were tablewares in the Rococo style and they were of the most finished workmanship. Minutely painted Swiss landscapes and scenes with figures were much favored and are the best known. The coloring was distinctive for its subdued richness and for the manner in which it fused into the brilliant glaze almost as in soft paste porcelain. This beautiful coloring was found in their treatment of Meissen flowers and fruits. The more common wares were largely in imitation of the so-called onion-pattern identified with Meissen. The porcelain figures were principally inspired by Ludwigsburg models. The glaze had the same smoky tone found in the tablewares. The figures included musicians, peasants, soldiers and other subjects in contemporary costume. The best of the figures were notable for their charming simplicity. The faïence was decorated in a manner similar to the porcelain. The lead-glazed earthenware or faïence fine was decorated with transfer printing. See *Nyon.* (382)

Zwiebelmuster In German ceramics; a German term literally meaning onion pattern. The design was of Chinese inspiration and was composed of formal flowers and foliage and conventionalized peaches mistaken for onions which they did resemble. The decoration was generally in underglaze blue and occasionally in purple. It was introduced at Meissen around 1739 as a decoration for common blue and white wares for daily use, and was much copied by other manufactories.

ZURICH
C. 1763 ON

The Photographs

For notes on the photographs see pages 485-524

1. Cooking pot. American, New Mexico, probably Zuñi Creek. Developmental or Great Pueblo period. *Cambridge University Museum of Archaeology and Ethnology*

2. Bird jar. American, New Mexico, probably Zuñi Creek. Developmental to Great Pueblo period. *Cambridge University Museum of Archaeology and Ethnology*

3. Effigy vessel, in form of a bird. American, New Mexico, Socorro. Late Developmental or Great Pueblo period. *Museum of the American Indian, Heye Foundation*

5. Bowl, Sikyatki Polychrome. American, N.E. Arizona, Hano near Polacca, after 1895. *University Museum, University of Pennsylvania*

4. Bowl, Mimbres ware. American, New Mexico, Mimbres valley. Great Pueblo period, 11th-12th century. *Cambridge University Museum of Archaeology and Ethnology*

6. Seated "baby" figure. Mexico, Puebla, Las Bocas. Formative period. *Museum of Primitive Art, New York*

7. Standing "laughing" figure. Mexico, Vera Cruz, Remojadas. Classic period. *Museum of Primitive Art, New York*

8. Pot. Mexico, probably Ulua valley. Maya culture, early Classic period. *British Museum*

9. Cylindrical jar. Mexico. Maya culture, Classic period, probably 600-900. *Museum of Primitive Art, New York*

10. Effigy vessel in the form of a Mexican hairless dog. Western Mexico, Colima. Classic period. *British Museum*

11. Effigy vessel in the form of a warrior. Western Mexico, Colima. Classic period. *Museum of Primitive Art, New York*

12. Figure with applied ornament. Western Mexico, Guanajuato, Chupícuaro. Classic period. *Museum of Primitive Art, New York*

13. Vase with cascabel feet, Plumbateware. Central America, Isla de los Sacrificios. Post-Classic period, probably 11th-13th century. *British Museum*

14. Bowl, black-on-orange ware. Central America, Aztec II period, 1325-1400. *Cambridge University Museum of Archaeology and Ethnology*

16. Double whistle-spout vessel in form of a bird. North coast Peru. Mochica culture, end of Formative period. *Metropolitan Museum of Art, Gift of Nathan Cummings, 1964*

15. Stirrup-spouted vessel, Formative period. North coast Peru. Cupisnique in the Chavín style. *British Museum*

17. Stirrup-spouted vessel, so-called Portrait vase. North coast Peru. Mochica culture, Classic period, c. 17th century. *British Museum*

18. Double-spouted vessel. South coast Peru, Paracas Cavernas. Formative period. *Metropolitan Museum of Art, Gift of Nathan Cummings, 1964*

19. Vessel in the form of a seated figure. South coast Peru. Nazca culture, end of Formative period, c. 1st B.C.-A.D. 2nd century. *Museum of Primitive Art, New York*

20. Effigy jar in the form of a man, Chancay black-on-white. Central coast Peru, Chancay valley. Later Post-Classic period. *Horniman Museum, London*

21. Double whistle-spout vessel in the form of an animal. Colombia, Cauca valley, Quimbaya style. Later Post-Classic period. *Horniman Museum, London*

22. Drua (drinking vessel), varnished earthenware. Fiji, Viti Levu, Rewa district, probably early 20th century. *Museum of Primitive Art, New York*

23. Bowl, painted pottery. Anatolian (Turkey) Hacilar, Early Chalcolithic, 5th millennium B.C. *Museum of Archaeology, Ankara*

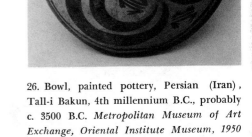

24. Dish, painted pottery. Northern Mesopotamia (Syria), Tell Halaf, c. 4500-5000 B.C. *University Museum, University of Pennsylvania*

25. Bowl, painted pottery. Southern Mesopotamia (Iraq), Ubaid, c. 4000 B.C. *University Museum, University of Pennsylvania*

26. Bowl, painted pottery, Persian (Iran), Tall-i Bakun, 4th millennium B.C., probably c. 3500 B.C. *Metropolitan Museum of Art Exchange, Oriental Institute Museum, 1950*

27. Vessel, painted pottery. Persian, Tall-i Bakun, 4th millennium B.C. *Metropolitan Museum of Art Exchange, Oriental Institute Museum, 1950*

28. Large storage jar, painted pottery. Persian, Sialk, c. 3100 B.C. *Metropolitan Museum of Art, Joseph Pulitzer Bequest, 1959*

29. Spouted jug, monochrome pottery. Anatolian, Yortan, early 3rd millennium B.C. *Metropolitan Museum of Art, Gift of Burton Y. Berry, 1961*

30. Vessel, dark grey pottery. Persian, Susa, end of 3rd millennium B.C. *Metropolitan Museum of Art, Acquired by exchange, Teheran Museum, 1948*

31. Cup, painted terra-cotta. Central Anatolia, early 2nd millennium B.C. *Metropolitan Museum of Art, Rogers Fund 1967*

32. Vessel, tripod, painted pottery. Persian, Tell Choka, Persepolis, 2nd millennium B.C. *Metropolitan Museum of Art, Acquired by exchange, Teheran Museum, 1948*

33. Spouted jar, painted pottery. Persian, Sialk, c. 1100-1000 B.C. *Metropolitan Museum of Art, Gift of the Teheran Museum, 1939*

35. Votive figure. Northern Mesopotamia (Syria), c. 1400 B.C. *Metropolitan Museum of Art, Gift of George D. Pratt, 1933*

34. Female "bird-headed" figures. Southern Mesopotamia, Ubaid II period of Ur, c. 3rd millennium B.C. *University Museum, University of Pennsylvania*

36. Oil lamp, unglazed pottery. Palestinian, reputed to be from Kfar Malik, c. 1900 B.C. *Metropolitan Museum of Art, Gift of Miriam S. Schloessinger, 1961*

37. Vessel, black-topped pottery. Egyptian Pre-Dynastic, early 4th millennium B.C. *Metropolitan Museum of Art, Rogers Fund, 1907*

38. Vase, painted pottery. Egyptian, Pre-Dynastic, first half of the 4th millennium B.C. *Metropolitan Museum of Art, Gift of Miss Helen Miller Gould, 1910*

40. Hippopotamus, bright blue-glazed quartz frit ware. Egyptian, Meir, XII Dynasty, c. 1900 B.C. *Metropolitan Museum of Art, Gift of Edward S. Harkness, 1917*

41. Kohl tubes, bright blue-glazed quartz frit ware. Egyptian, XVIII Dynasty, c. 1400 B.C. *Metropolitan Museum of Art, Carnarvon Collection, Gift of Edward S. Harkness, 1926*

39. Jar, painted pottery. Egyptian, second half 4th millennium B.C. *Metropolitan Museum of Art, Rogers Fund, 1920*

42. FAR LEFT. Amphora, white-glazed quartz frit ware. Egyptian, XVIII Dynasty, c. 1360 B.C. *Metropolitan Museum of Art, Carnarvon Collection, Gift of Edward S. Harkness, 1926*

43. LEFT. The Carnarvon goblet, bright blue-glazed quartz frit ware. Egyptian, XXII Dynasty, rein of Sheshonq I, 935-914 B.C. *Metropolitan Museum of Art, Gift of Edward S. Harkness, 1926*

44. LEFT. Vessel in the form of a leather bag, monochrome polished red ware. Cypriot, Early Bronze Age, 3000-2000 B.C. *Metropolitan Museum of Art, The Cesnola Collection, Purchased by Subscription, 1874-1876.*

45. RIGHT. Beaked jug, monochrome, polished red ware. Cypriot, Early Bronze Age, I-II, c. 3000-2300 B.C. *Metropolitan Museum of Art, The Cesnola Collection, Purchased by Subscription, 1874-1876*

46. UPPER RIGHT. Jug of White Slip type. Cypriot, Late Bronze Age I-II, c. 1550-1230 B.C. *Metropolitan Museum of Art, The Cesnola Collection, Purchased by Subscription, 1874-1876*

47. RIGHT. Vase, Base-Ring ware, monochrome, black surface. Cypriot, Late Bronze Age I, c. 1550-1400 B.C. *Metropolitan Museum of Art, The Cesnola Collection, Purchased by Subscription, 1874-1876*

48. Oinochoë, painted pottery. Cypriot, Cypro-Archaic I, c. 7th century B.C. *Metropolitan Museum of Art, The Cesnola Collection, Purchased by Subscription, 1874-1876*

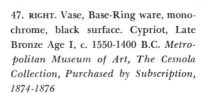

49. Jug, flame-mottled decoration. East Crete, Vasiliki, Early Minoan II, c. 2500-2400 B.C. *Metropolitan Museum of Art, Gift of the American Exploration Society, 1907*

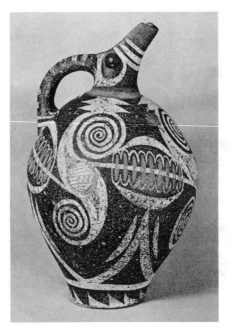

50. RIGHT. Jug, painted pottery. Cretan, Phaistos Middle Minoan II, c. 1900-1700 B.C. *Heraklion Museum, Crete*

51. FAR RIGHT. Jug, painted pottery. Cretan, Phaistos, Late Minoan I, c. 1550 B.C. *Heraklion Museum, Crete*

52. Octopus stirrup-vase, painted pottery. Eastern Crete, Gournia, Late Minoan I, c. 1500 B.C. *Candia Museum, University of Pennsylvania Museum Excavations*

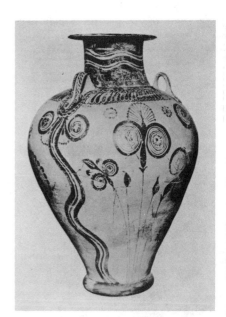

53. Jar, painted pottery. Cretan, Knossos, Late Minoan II, c. 1425 B.C. *Heraklion Museum, Crete*

54. Kylix with painted decoration. Mycenaean Greece, Zygouries near Corinth, c. 1300-1230 B.C. *Metropolitan Museum of Art, Gift of the Greek Government through the American School of Classical Studies, 1927*

55. FAR LEFT. Stirrup-jar with painted decoration. Mycenaean Greece, 1200-1125 B.C. *Metropolitan Museum of Art, Louisa Eldridge McBurney Gift Fund, 1953*

56. LEFT. Krater with painted decoration, Mycenaean from Cyprus, probably Enkomi, c. 1400-1375 B.C. *Metropolitan Museum of Art, The Cesnola Collection, Purchased by Subscription, 1874-1876*

57. Colossal Dipylon krater. Greek, Attic-Geometric, 8th century B.C., probably c. 750 B.C. *Metropolitan Museum of Art, Rogers Fund, 1914*

58. Amphora. Greek, Proto-Attic, c. 675-650 B.C. *Metropolitan Museum of Art, Rogers Fund, 1911*

59. Oinochoë, black-figure animal style. Greek, Proto-Corinthian, c. 640-625 B.C. *Metropolitan Museum of Art, Rogers Fund, 1922*

60. Amphora, black-figure. Greek, Attic. c. 550-525 B.C. *Metropolitan Museum of Art, Rogers Fund, 1917*

61. Panathenaic amphora, black-figure. Greek, Attic, late 6th century, c. 530 B.C. *Metropolitan Museum of Art, Rogers Fund, 1914*

62. Amphora, red-figure. Greek, Attic. c. 530-520 B.C. *Metropolitan Museum of Art, Purchase 1963, Joseph Pulitzer Bequest*

63. Lekythos, white-ground ware. Greek, Attic, 5th century B.C. *Metropolitan Museum of Art, Rogers Fund, 1909*

64. Tanagra figure, terra-cotta. Greek, 4th century B.C. *Metropolitan Museum of Art, Rogers Fund, 1906*

65. Amphora, Buccaro ware. Etruscan, c. 610-560 B.C. *Metropolitan Museum of Art, Purchase by Subscription, 1896*

66. Amphora, black-figure. Etruscan, c. 575-550 B.C. *Metropolitan Museum of Art, Gift of Nicolas Koutoulakis, 1955*

67. Askos in the form of a duck. Etruscan, 4th century B.C., probably c. 375-350 B.C. *Metropolitan Museum of Art, Rogers Fund, 1919*

68. Mug in the form of a Negro's head, terra-cotta. Etruscan, 4th century B.C. *Metropolitan Museum of Art, Gift of El Conde de Lagerillas, 1956*

ANCIENT WORLD

69. Clay mold for an Arretine bowl. Roman, Arretium, c. 25-10 B.C. *Metropolitan Museum of Art, Rogers Fund, 1919*

70. Arretine cup, red-gloss pottery. Roman, Arretium, c. 10-15 A.D. *Metropolitan Museum of Art, Gift of J. Pierpont Morgan, 1917*

71. FAR LEFT. Jar, red-gloss pottery. Roman, probably Lezoux, central Gaul, late 2nd century A.D. *British Museum*

72. LEFT. Beaker, red-gloss pottery. Roman, probably Rheinzabern, Rhineland, 3rd century A.D. *British Museum*

73. Scyphus (cup) green lead-glazed earthenware. Roman, Asia Minor, probably Syria, end of 1st century B.C. or 1st century A.D. *Metropolitan Museum of Art, Fletcher Fund, 1942*

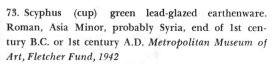

74. Askos (jug) green lead-glazed earthenware. Roman, probably Italy, 1st century A.D. *Metropolitan Museum of Art, Gift of J. Pierpont Morgan, 1917*

75. Jar, turquoise-glazed quartz frit ware. Roman Egyptian, perhaps Memphis, probably 1st or 2nd century A.D. *Metropolitan Museum of Art, Rogers Fund, 1944*

76. Covered vase, turquoise-glazed quartz frit ware. Roman Egyptian, perhaps Memphis, probably 1st century A.D. *Metropolitan Museum of Art, Rogers Fund, 1944*

77. Vase, glazed quartz frit ware. Roman Egyptian, perhaps Memphis, 1st or 2nd century A.D. *Metropolitan Museum of Art, Gift of Edward S. Harkness, 1927*

78. Vase, blue-green alkaline-glazed earthenware. Roman, probably Western Mesopotamia, 1st century B.C. or A.D. *Metropolitan Museum of Art*

80. Beaker, buff clay. Britain, Berkshire, Lambourn, c. 1600 B.C. *British Museum*

79. Food vessel, buff clay. Britain, Northumberland, Early Bronze Age, 1700-1300 B.C. *British Museum*

81. TOP LEFT. Tomb model of a house, terra-cotta. Chinese, Han Dynasty, 206 B.C.-A.D. 220. *Metropolitan Museum of Art, Rogers Fund, 1951*

82. LEFT. Tomb vessel, "hill" jar, glazed earthenware. Chinese, Han Dynasty, 206 B.C.-A.D. 220. *Metropolitan Museum of Art, Kennedy Fund, 1913*

83. Tomb vessel, granary urn, glazed earthenware. Chinese, Han Dynasty, 206 B.C.-A.D. 220. *Metropolitan Museum of Art, Kennedy Fund, 1913*

84. Tomb figure of a spearman, earthenware. Chinese, c. 3rd century A.D. *Metropolitan Museum of Art, Gift of Ralph M. Freydberg, 1964*

85. RIGHT. Tomb figure of a musician, earthenware. Chinese, Six Dynasties, 222-589. *Metropolitan Museum of Art, Rogers Fund, 1925*

86. FAR RIGHT. Tomb figure of a dancer, earthenware. Chinese, Six Dynasties, 222-589, probably 6th century. *Metropolitan Museum of Art, Fletcher Fund, 1928*

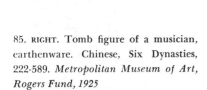

87. Tomb figure of a Mohammedan cloth merchant, earthenware. Chinese, T'ang Dynasty, 618-906. *Philadelphia Museum of Art: George Crofts Collection, gift of Charles H. Ludington*

89. Funerary jar, Yüeh ware, porcelaneous grey stoneware. Chinese, Sung Dynasty or earlier. *Metropolitan Museum of Art, Fletcher Fund, 1937*

90. Bowl, Ting ware, white porcelaneous body. Chinese, Sung Dynasty, 960-1279, probably c. 11th-12th century. *Metropolitan Museum of Art, Rogers Fund, 1923*

88. Tomb figure of a guardian (Locopala), glazed earthenware. Chinese, T'ang Dynasty, 618-906. *Metropolitan Museum of Art, Rogers Fund, 1911*

91. Cup stand, Ting ware, white porcelaneous body. Chinese, Sung Dynasty, 960-1279. *Metropolitan Museum of Art, Gift of Mrs. Samuel Peters, 1926*

92. Dish, Ju ware, glazed stoneware. Chinese, Sung Dynasty, 960-1279, early 12th century. *Philadelphia Museum of Art: Gift of Major General & Mrs. William Crozier*

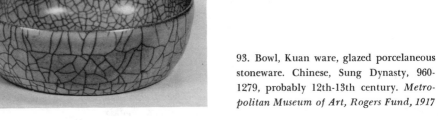

93. Bowl, Kuan ware, glazed porcelaneous stoneware. Chinese, Sung Dynasty, 960-1279, probably 12th-13th century. *Metropolitan Museum of Art, Rogers Fund, 1917*

94. Gallipot,Tz'u Chou ware, glazed stone-ware. Chinese, Sung Dynasty, c. 1108. *Metropolitan Museum of Art, Rogers Fund, 1925*

95. Flower pot, Chüen ware, glazed porcelaneous stoneware. Chinese, Sung Dynasty, 960-1279. *Metropolitan Museum of Art, Gift of John D. Rockefeller, Jr., 1945*

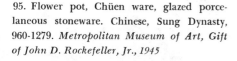

96. Wine jar, Lung-Ch'üan celadon, porcelaneous stoneware. Chinese, Sung Dynasty, 960-1279. *Metropolitan Museum of Art, Fletcher Fund, 1934*

97. Bowl, Chien ware, glazed stoneware. Chinese, Sung Dynasty, 960-1279. *Metropolitan Museum of Art, Bequest of Mrs. H. O. Havemeyer, 1929, Havemeyer Collection*

98. Stem cup, porcelain. Chinese, Ming Dynasty, Hsüan Tê period, 1426-1435. *Metropolitan Museum of Art, Rogers Fund, 1919*

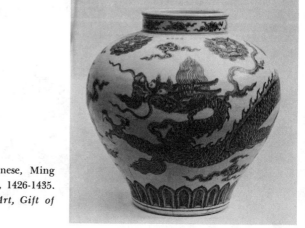

99. Potiche, porcelain. Chinese, Ming Dynasty, Hsüan Tê period, 1426-1435. *Metropolitan Museum of Art, Gift of Robert E. Tod, 1937*

100. LEFT. Gallipot of mei-p'ing form, Three-Color ware, porcelain. Chinese, Ming Dynasty, Chia Ching period, 1522-1566. *Metropolitan Museum of Art, Bequest of John D. Rockefeller, Jr., 1960*

101. RIGHT. Double gourd-shaped vase, Three-Color ware, porcelain. Chinese, Ming Dynasty, Chia Ching period, 1522-1566. *Metropolitan Museum of Art, Bequest of John D. Rockefeller, Jr., 1960*

102. Double gourd-shaped vase, porcelain. Chinese, Ming Dynasty, Chia Ching period, 1522-1566. *Metropolitan Museum of Art, Harris Brisbane Dick Fund and Anonymous Gift, 1965*

103. Bowl, porcelain. Chinese, Ming Dynasty, Chia Ching period, 1522-1566. *Metropolitan Museum of Art, Rogers Fund, 1917*

104. Bowl, porcelain. Chinese, Wan Li period, 1573-1619, with English silver-gilt mounts, c. 1585. *Metropolitan Museum of Art, Rogers Fund, 1944*

105. Figure of Kuan Yin, enameled porcelain. Chinese, Late Ming. *Ex. Coll. Winston Guest, Photo Taylor and Dull*

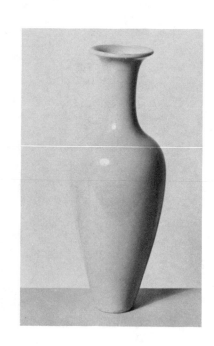

106. RIGHT. Baluster-form beaker with flaring trumpet neck, Famille Noire style, porcelain. Chinese, Ch'ing Dynasty, K'ang Hsi period, 1662-1722. *Metropolitan Museum of Art, Bequest of John D. Rockefeller, Jr., 1960*

107. FAR RIGHT. Vase, porcelain with Clair-de-Lune glaze. Chinese, Ch'ing Dynasty, K'ang Hsi period, 1662-1722. *Metropolitan Museum of Art, Bequest of Mary Stillman Harkness, 1950*

108. Figure of Kuan Yin, Blanc-de-Chine porcelain. Chinese, Fukien province, Tê-hua, Ch'ing Dynasty, K'ang Hsi period, 1662-1722. *Metropolitan Museum of Art, Bequest of Mary Clark Thompson, 1924*

109. Dog of Fo, pair, porcelain. Chinese, Ch'ing Dynasty, K'ang Hsi period, 1662-1722. *Metropolitan Museum of Art, Michael Friedsam Collection, 1931*

110. Jar, ginger jar type, porcelain. Chinese, Ch'ing Dynasty, K'ang Hsi period, 662-1722. *Metropolitan Museum of Art, Bequest of Bernard M. Baruch, 1965*

111. Teapot, unglazed red stoneware. Chinese, Yi-hsing, probably early 18th century. *Victoria and Albert Museum*

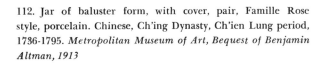

112. Jar of baluster form, with cover, pair, Famille Rose style, porcelain. Chinese, Ch'ing Dynasty, Ch'ien Lung period, 1736-1795. *Metropolitan Museum of Art, Bequest of Benjamin Altman, 1913*

113. Vase, porcelain with flambé glaze. Chinese, Ch'ing Dynasty, Ch'ien Lung period, 1736-1795. *Metropolitan Museum of Art, Bequest of Mrs. H. O. Havemeyer, 1929, Havemeyer Collection*

115. Monteith (punch bowl), China Trade Porcelain for the English market. Chinese, early 18th century. *Metropolitan Museum of Art, Purchase 1960, Winfield Foundation Gift*

114. Vases, five, China Trade Porcelain for the English market. Chinese, 18th century. *Metropolitan Museum of Art, Gift of the Winfield Foundation, 1951, the Helena Woolworth McCann Collection*

116. Plate, porcelain. Chinese, late 18th century,
c. 1795. *Metropolitan Museum of Art, Gift of R.
Thornton Wilson, 1942*

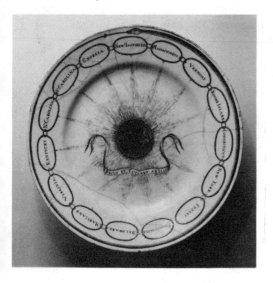

117. TOP. Plate, China Trade Porcelain for the
American market. Chinese, late 18th century, c.
1785. *Metropolitan Museum of Art, Rogers Fund,
1917*

118. BOTTOM. Platter, China Trade Porcelain for
the American market. Chinese, late 18th-early 19th
century. *Metropolitan Museum of Art, Gift of the
Winfield Foundation, 1951*

119. LEFT. Gallipot of mei-p'ing form, porcelaneous stoneware. Korean, Korai
Dynasty, 918-1392, probably late 12th century. *Metropolitan Museum of Art,
Fletcher Fund, 1927*

120. RIGHT. Gallipot, porcelaneous stoneware. Korean, Korai Dynasty, 918-
1392, 13th-14th century. *Metropolitan Museum of Art, Purchase, 1927, Fletcher
Fund*

121. Potiche, porcelain. Korean, Yi Dynasty, 1392-1910, c. 17th-18th century.
Victoria and Albert Museum

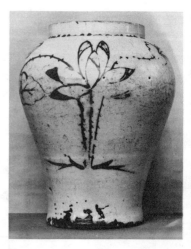

122. Covered jar, porcelain with Clair de Lune glaze. Korean, Yi Dynasty, 1392-1910, c. 17th-18th century. *Metropolitan Museum of Art, Seymour Fund, 1965*

123. Covered jar, greyish stoneware with celadon glaze. Thailand, Sawankhalok, 14th-early 15th century. *British Museum*

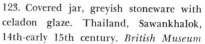

124. Incense burner in the form of two monsters, stoneware with celadon glaze. Thailand, Sawankhalok, 14th-early 15th century. *Metropolitan Museum of Art, Rogers Fund, 1963*

125. Kendi (drinking vessel), stoneware. Thailand, Sawankhalok, 14th-early 15th century. *Metropolitan Museum of Art, Seymour Fund, 1964*

126. RIGHT. Water-dropper in form of a seated figure, stoneware. Thailand, Sawankhalok, 14th-early 15th century. *Metropolitan Museum of Art, Gift of Mr. and Mrs. J. W. Klejman, 1964*

127. FAR RIGHT. Jar, earthenware. Japanese, Middle Jomon period, perhaps 2nd millennium B.C. *Tokyo National Museum*

FAR EAST WORLD

129. Uno-Hanagaki tea bowl, Shino type ware. Japanese, late 15th century. *Tokyo National Museum*

128. Haniwa figure of a warrior, earthenware. Japanese, Ancient Burial Mound Age, c. 3rd-7th century. *Tokyo National Museum*

130. Tea bowl, Raku type ware. Japanese, 16th century. *Mitsui Collection, Tokyo*

131. Tea bowl, Yellow Seto ware. Japanese, Momoyama period, 1573-1615. *Hatakeyama Collection, Tokyo*

132. Dish or tray, Oribe ware. Japanese, Momoyama period, 1573-1615. *Tokyo National Museum*

133. Fuji-san tea bowl, Raku type ware. Japanese, made by Hon'ami Koetsu (1556-1637). *Sakai Collection, Tokyo*

134. Jar, Karatsu ware. Japanese, Edo period, 17th century. *Idemitsu Collection, Tokyo*

135. Tea bowl, Hagi ware. Japanese, c. 1640. *Victoria and Albert Museum*

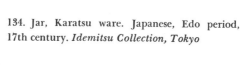

136. Tea bowl, earthenware. Japanese, made by Ninsei, mid-17th century. *Tokusawa Collection, Tokyo*

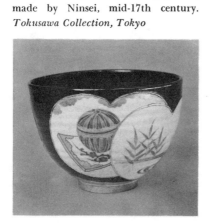

138. Figure of Hotei, Bizen stoneware. Japanese, Edo period, c. 1800. *British Museum*

137. Tray or dish, earthenware. Japanese, made by Kenzan, painted by Korin, late 17th-early 18th century. *Tokyo National Museum*

139. Dish, Kutani porcelain. Japanese, Edo period, 17th century. *Idemitsu Collection, Tokyo*

140. Wine ewer, Kutani porcelain. Japanese, Edo period, 17th century. *Hosokawa Collection, Tokyo*

141. Dish, Imari porcelain. Japanese, Edo period, 18th century. *Takasu Collection, Tokyo*

142. Dish, Imari porcelain. Japanese, Edo period, 18th century. *Tokyo National Museum*

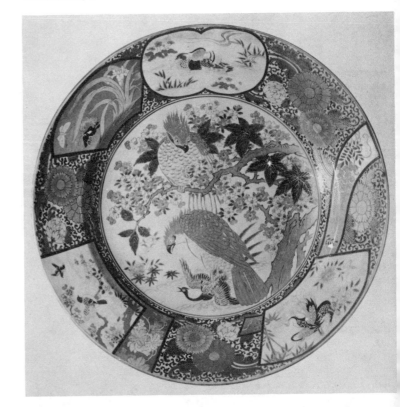

143. Dish, Imari porcelain. Japanese, Edo period, about 1700. *Metropolitan Museum of Art, Gift of J. J. Klejman, 1960*

144. Dish, Kakiemon porcelain. Japanese, Edo period, 18th century. *Tokyo National Museum*

145. Wine ewer, Kakiemon porcelain. Japanese, Edo period, 18th century. *Takasu Collection, Tokyo*

146. Wine ewer, Kakiemon porcelain. Japanese, Edo period, 18th century. *Kenoshita Collection, Tokyo*

147. Dish, Nabeshima porcelain. Japanese Edo period, 18th century. *Yamanaka and Company, Osaka*

148. Dish, Nabeshima porcelain. Japanese, Edo period, c. 1760. *Philadelphia Museum of Art: Gift of Mrs. Herbert C. Morris*

149. Dish, Nabeshima porcelain. Japanese, Edo period, 18th century. *Tokyo National Museum*

151. Bowl, porcelain. Japanese, by Nanimi Dohachi (1783-1855). *Tokyo National Museum*

150. Dish, Hirado porcelain. Japanese, Edo period, c. 1750. *Author's Collection, Photo Taylor and Dull*

153. Bowl, Shonsui style, porcelain. Japanese, by Kawamoto Hansuke, Edo period, 19th century. *Tokyo National Museum*

152. Tea bowl, Kairaku-en porcelain. Japanese, Edo period, c. 1830. *Tokyo National Museum*

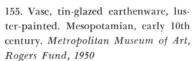

154. Bowl, tin-glazed earthenware. Mesopotamian, 9th-10th century. *Metropolitan Museum of Art, Harris Brisbane Dick Fund, 1953*

155. Vase, tin-glazed earthenware, luster-painted. Mesopotamian, early 10th century. *Metropolitan Museum of Art, Rogers Fund, 1950*

156. Bowl, slip-painted glazed earthenware. Persian, Nishapur, 10th century. *Metropolitan Museum of Art, Harris Brisbane Dick Fund, 1963*

157. Bowl, Sari type, slip-painted glazed earthenware. Persian, late 10th-early 11th century. *Metropolitan Museum of Art, Rogers Fund, 1958*

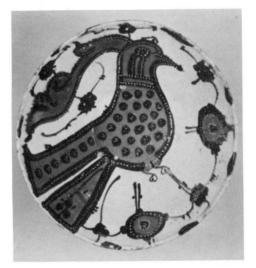

159. Bowl, alkaline-glazed, composite body. Persian, 12th century. *Metropolitan Museum of Art, Harris Brisbane Dick Fund, 1963*

158. Bowl, tin-glazed earthenware, luster-painted. Egyptian, Cairo, early 11th century. *Metropolitan Museum of Art, Gift of Mr. and Mrs. Charles K. Wilkinson, 1963*

ISLAMIC POTTERY

161. Figure, camel, alkaline-glazed, composite body. Persian, probably Rayy, 12th century. *Metropolitan Museum of Art, Purchase 1964, Fletcher Fund*

160. Bowl, in bird shape, alkaline-glazed, composite body. Persian, probably Rayy, 12th century. *Metropolitan Museum of Art, Harris Brisbane Dick Fund, 1963*

163. Bowl, Laqabi ware. Persian, Rayy or Kashan, 12th century. *Metropolitan Museum of Art, Gift of Horace Havemeyer, 1929, The H. D. Havemeyer Collection*

162. Jug, underglaze painted ware, composite body. Persian, Kashan, dated 612 AH (A.D. 1215-1216). *Metropolitan Museum of Art, Fletcher Fund, 1932*

164. Tankard, black silhouette-painted slipware. Persian, Rayy, second half of 12th century. *University Museum, University of Pennsylvania*

165. Bowl, tin-glazed earthenware, luster-painted. Persian, Rayy, late 12th-early 13th century. *Metropolitan Museum of Art, Purchase, 1963, Joseph Pulitzer Bequest*

166. Bowl, Mina'i ware, composite body. Persian, Kashan, dated 1186. *Metropolitan Museum of Art, Purchase, 1964, Fletcher Fund*

167. Bowl, Mina'i ware, enameled composite body. Persian, late 12th-early 13th century. *Metropolitan Museum of Art, Rogers Fund, 1957*

168. Vase, composite body, turquoise-blue glaze. Mesopotamian Raqqa, late 12th-early 13th century. *Metropolitan Museum of Art, Bequest of Horace Havemeyer, 1956, Havemeyer Collection*

169. Albarello (drug pot), luster ware. Mesopotamian, Raqqa, late 12th-early 13th century. *Metropolitan Museum of Art, Gift of Horace Havemeyer, 1948, Havemeyer Collection*

ISLAMIC POTTERY

170. Dish, Kubachi ware, glazed composite body. North Persian, early 17th century. *Metropolitan Museum of Art, Fletcher Fund 1917*

171. Bowl, Gombroon ware, glazed composite body. Persian, 16th-early 17th century. *Victoria and Albert Museum*

172. Bottle, glazed composite body. Persian, Kirman (?), 16th-early 17th century. *Metropolitan Museum of Art, Rogers Fund, 1914*

173. Large bowl, glazed composite body. Persian, Meshhed, 16th-17th century. *Metropolitan Museum of Art, Gift of Nasli Neeramaneck, 1964*

175. Pitcher, glazed composite body. Turkish (Isnik), c. 1525-1550. *Metropolitan Museum of Art, Harris Brisbane Dick Fund, 1966*

174. Large shallow bowl, glazed composite body. Turkish (Isnik), late 15th-early 16th century. *Metropolitan Museum of Art, Harris Brisbane Dick Fund, 1966*

176. Mosque lamp, glazed composite body. Turkish (Isnik), c. 1525-1550. *Metropolitan Museum of Art, Harris Brisbane Dick Fund, 1955*

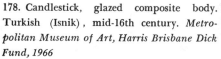

177. Plate, glazed composite body. Turkish (Isnik), c. 1525-1550. *Metropolitan Museum of Art, Bequest of Benjamin Altman, 1913*

178. Candlestick, glazed composite body. Turkish (Isnik), mid-16th century. *Metropolitan Museum of Art, Harris Brisbane Dick Fund, 1966*

180. Jug, glazed composite body. Turkish (Isnik), c. 1600. *Metropolitan Museum of Art, Rogers Fund, 1918*

179. Plate, glazed composite body. Turkish (Isnik), 2nd half of 16th century. *Metropolitan Museum of Art, Purchase 1966, Harris Brisbane Dick Fund*

182. Deep bowl, slipware, glazed and incised. Byzantine, 13th-14th century. *Dumbarton Oaks Collection*

183. Jar, slipware, glazed and incised. Byzantine, perhaps Greece, 13th century. *Dumbarton Oaks Collection*

181. TOP AND BOTTOM. Shallow bowl, slipware, glazed and incised, interior and exterior. Byzantine, probably from the Chersonese, 13th century. *Dumbarton Oaks Collection*

184. Shallow bowl, slipware, glazed and incised. Byzantine, perhaps Thessalonica, late 13th century. *Dumbarton Oaks Collection*

185. Deep bowl, slipware, glazed and incised. Byzantine, 13th-14th century. *Dumbarton Oaks Collection*

186. Jakobakanne (a kind of jug), salt-glazed brownish-yellow stoneware. German, Siegburg, 15th century. *Victoria and Albert Museum*

187. LEFT. Trichterbecher (a kind of cup), salt-glazed brownish-yellow stoneware. German, Siegburg, 1st half of 16th century. *Metropolitan Museum of Art, Gift of John Stenne, 1910*

188. RIGHT. Sturzbecher (a kind of cup), salt-glazed grey stoneware. German, Siegburg, c. 1570-1590. *Metropolitan Museum of Art, Gift of R. Thornton Wilson, 1954, in memory of Florence Ellsworth Wilson*

189. Schnabelkanne (a kind of jug), salt-glazed white stoneware. German, Siegburg, c. 1590. *Metropolitan Museum of Art, Gift of J. Pierpont Morgan, 1917*

190. ABOVE. Schnelle (a kind of tankard), salt-glazed white stoneware. German, Siegburg, dated 1573. *Metropolitan Museum of Art, Gift of R. Thornton Wilson, 1954, in memory of Florence Ellsworth Wilson*

191. FAR LEFT. Cup, salt-glazed white stoneware. German, Siegburg, c. 1569-1595. *Metropolitan Museum of Art, Gift of R. Thornton Wilson, 1954, in memory of Florence Ellsworth Wilson*

192. LEFT. Bellarmine jug, light-brown salt-glazed stoneware. German, Cologne, c. 1530. *Kunstmuseum, Düsseldorf*

194. LEFT. Large jug, brown salt-glazed stoneware. German, Raeren, dated 1576. *Kunstmuseum, Düsseldorf*

195. RIGHT. Tankard, salt-glazed grey stoneware. German, Saxony, probably Penig or Zeitz, c. 1560 or later. *Metropolitan Museum of Art, Gift of R. Thornton Wilson, 1954, in memory of Florence Ellsworth Wilson*

193. Loose-ring-handled jug, brown salt-glazed stoneware. German, Dreihausen, 16th century. *Victoria and Albert Museum*

196. RIGHT. Jug, salt-glazed grey stoneware. German, Saxony, Freiberg, c. 1675. *Victoria and Albert Museum*

197. ABOVE. Humpen (a kind of tankard), brown salt-glazed stoneware. German, Kreussen, dated 1675. *Metropolitan Museum of Art, Gift of R. Thornton Wilson, 1954, in memory of Florence Ellsworth Wilson*

198. FAR LEFT. Pilgrim bottle, blue-glazed stoneware. French, Beauvais, late-16th-early 17th century. *Metropolitan Museum of Art, Gift of J. Pierpont Morgan, 1917*

199. LEFT. Mug, unglazed red stoneware. English, probably Staffordshire, late 17th century. *Victoria and Albert Museum*

200. Jug, lead-glazed earthenware. French, Avignon, late 16th century. *Metropolitan Museum of Art, Gift of J. Pierpont Morgan, 1917*

201. RIGHT. Tazza (standing cup), Henri Deux ware, lead-glazed earthenware. French, Saint-Porchaire, 1525-1560, probably c. 1535. *Metropolitan Museum of Art, Gift of J. Pierpont Morgan, 1917*

202. LOWER LEFT. Salt cellar, Henri Deux ware, lead-glazed earthenware. French, Saint-Porchaire, 1525-1560, probably c. 1540-1550. *Metropolitan Museum of Art, Gift of J. Pierpont Morgan, 1917*

203. Oval dish, lead-glazed earthenware. French, in the manner of Palissy, 2nd half of 16th century. *Metropolitan Museum of Art, Gift of Julia A. Berwind, 1953*

205. Cup on low foot, lead-glazed earthenware. French, in the manner of Palissy, 2nd half of 16th century. *Metropolitan Museum of Art, Gift of Julia A. Berwind, 1953*

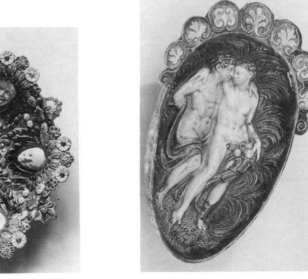

204. Dish, lead-glazed earthenware. French, in the manner of Palissy, late 16th century. *Metropolitan Museum of Art, Gift of J. Pierpont Morgan, 1917*

EUROPE: RENAISSANCE
LEAD-GLAZED EARTHENWARE

206. Ewer, lead-glazed earthenware. French, made by a follower of Palissy, late 16th-early 17th century. *Metropolitan Museum of Art, Gift of Julia A. Berwind, 1953*

207. LEFT. Group, Nurse and Child, lead-glazed earthenware. French, Avon, near Fontainebleau, beginning of 17th century. *Metropolitan Museum of Art, Gift of J. Pierpont Morgan, 1917*

208. RIGHT. Figure, The Bagpipe Player, lead-glazed earthenware. French, Avon, beginning of 17th century. *Metropolitan Museum of Art, Gift of Mrs. Russell S. Carter, 1944*

210. Jug, Hafner ware, lead-glazed earthenware. German, Nuremberg, c. 1550. *Metropolitan Museum of Art, Gift of R. Thornton Wilson, 1950, in memory of Florence Ellsworth Wilson*

209. Figure, Neptune astride hippocamp, lead-glazed earthenware. French, Avon, early 17th century. *Metropolitan Museum of Art, Gift of Mrs. Francis P. Garvan, 1966*

213. Tyg (cup), lead-glazed slipware. English, Wrotham, dated 1649. *Victoria and Albert Museum*

211. LEFT. Beggar beaker in the form of a nun, lead-glazed earthenware. Dutch, Limburg, dated 1605. *Metropolitan Museum of Art, Gift of R. Thornton Wilson, 1962, in memory of Florence Ellsworth Wilson*

212. RIGHT. Beggar beaker in the form of a monk, lead-glazed earthenware. Dutch, Limburg, dated 1605. *Metropolitan Museum of Art, Gift of R. Thornton Wilson, in memory of Florence Ellsworth Wilson*

214. Dish, lead-glazed slipware. English, Staffordshire, c. 1675. *Victoria and Albert Museum*

215. Tinaja (jar), unglazed earthenware. Spanish, probably Toledo, 15th-16th century. *Hispanic Society of America*

216. Plate, earthenware with "dry cord" glazing. Spanish, Seville, 15th century. *Hispanic Society of America*

217. RIGHT. Armorial brasero (deep dish), tin-glazed earthenware, reverse and obverse, luster-painted. Spanish, Manisses (Valencia), c. 1430. *Hispanic Society of America*

218. Albarello (drug jar), tin-glazed earthenware, luster-painted. Spanish, Manisses (Valencia), c. 1435. *Hispanic Society of America*

219. Armorial brasero (deep dish), tin-glazed earthenware, luster painted, Spanish, Manisses (Valencia), mid-15th century. *Hispanic Society of America*

220. UPPER LEFT. Armorial plate, tin-glazed earthenware, luster-painted. Spanish, probably Manisses (Valencia), c. 1480. *Hispanic Society of America*

221. UPPER RIGHT. Armorial bowl of escudella ab orelles type, luster-painted. Spanish, Manisses (Valencia), late 15th century. *Hispanic Society of America*

222. LEFT. Plate, tin-glazed earthenware, luster-painted. Spanish, Manisses (Valencia), early 16th century. *Hispanic Society of America*

223. BELOW. Tondo (circular relief), tin-glazed terra-cotta. Italian, Florentine, c. 1450-1460. *Metropolitan Museum of Art, Purchase, 1921, Joseph Pulitzer Bequest*

224. LEFT. Armorial dish, majolica. Italian, Faenza, c. 1480. *Metropolitan Museum of Art, Fletcher Fund, 1946*

225. Wine cooler, majolica. Italian, probably
Faenza, late 15th century. *Metropolitan Museum
of Art, Fletcher Fund, 1946*

226. LEFT. Tazza (standing cup), majolica. Italian, probably Faenza, c. 1500.
Metropolitan Museum of Art, Gift of George Blumenthal, 1941

227. RIGHT. Spouted drug vase, majolica. Italian, Faenza or Florence, c. 1460-
1480. *Metropolitan Museum of Art, Fletcher Fund, 1946*

228. FAR LEFT. Albarello (drug jar), majolica. Italian,
Florence, c. 1470. *Metropolitan Museum of Art, Fletcher
Fund, 1946*

229. LEFT. Drug vase, majolica. Italian, Faenza, late 15th
century. *Metropolitan Museum of Art, Gift of J. Pierpont Morgan, 1965*

231. BELOW. Scudella (dish on a low foot), majolica.
Italian, Castel Durante, 1538; lustered at Gubbio.
*Metropolitan Museum of Art, Gift of Everit V. Macy,
1927, in memory of his wife, Edith Carpenter Macy*

230. Albarello (drug jar), majolica.
Italian, Faenza, c. 1470-1480. *Metropolitan Museum of Art, Gift of J. Pierpont Morgan, 1965*

232. Dish, majolica. Italian, Urbino, 1533; lustered at Gubbio. *Metropolitan Museum of Art, Gift of V. Everit Macy, 1927, in memory of his wife, Edith Carpenter Macy*

233. Oval dish, one of a pair, majolica. Italian, Urbino, c. 1560-1570. *Metropolitan Museum of Art, Bequest of George Blumenthal, 1941*

234. Wine cooler, majolica. Italian, Urbino, c. 1560-1570. *Metropolitan Museum of Art, Michael Friedsam Collection, 1931*

235. Albarello (drug jar), tin-glazed earthenware. French, Rouen, 16th century. *Metropolitan Museum of Art, Gift of J. Pierpont Morgan, 1917*

236. RIGHT. Spouted drug-pot, tin-glazed earthenware. French, Nîmes, 2nd half of 16th century, probably c. 1580. *Metropolitan Museum of Art, Gift of J. Pierpont Morgan, 1917*

237. FAR RIGHT. Pilgrim bottle, tin-glazed earthenware. French, Nîmes, dated 1581. *Metropolitan Museum of Art, Samuel D. Lee Fund, 1941*

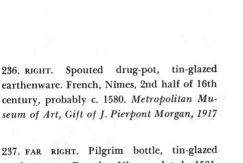
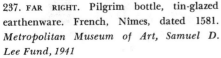

EUROPE: TIN-GLAZED EARTHENWARE

238. Dish, tin-glazed earthenware. French, Lyons, 16th century, probably c. 1580-1585. *Metropolitan Museum of Art, Gift of J. Pierpont Morgan, 1917*

239. Dish, tin-glazed earthenware. French, Nevers, dated May 1644. *Metropolitan Museum of Art, Gift of J. Pierpont Morgan, 1917*

241. Ewer, tin-glazed earthenware, décor Persan. French, Nevers, c. 1650-1675. *Metropolitan Museum of Art, Gift of J. Pierpont Morgan, 1917*

240. Plate or stand for ewer, tin-glazed earthenware, décor Persan. French, Nevers, c. 1650-1675. *Metropolitan Museum of Art, Gift of J. Pierpont Morgan, 1917*

243. Plate, tin-glazed earthenware, décor Persan. French, Nevers, c. 1675. *Metropolitan Museum of Art, Gift of J. Pierpont Morgan, 1917*

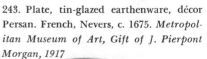

242. Pilgrim bottle, tin-glazed earthenware, décor Persan. French, Nevers, c. 1650-1675. *Metropolitan Museum of Art, Gift of J. Pierpont Morgan, 1917*

244. Plate, tin-glazed earthenware. French, Nevers, c. 1660-1680. *Metropolitan Museum of Art, Gift of J. Pierpont Morgan, 1917*

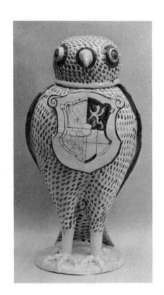

245. LEFT. Drinking vessel in the form of an owl, faïence. South German, perhaps Nuremberg, 1598-1608. *Metropolitan Museum of Art, Gift of R. Thornton Wilson, 1950, in memory of Florence Ellsworth Wilson*

246. RIGHT. Jug, faïence. German, Hamburg, 1st half of 17th century. *Metropolitan Museum of Art, Gift of R. Thornton Wilson, 1950, in memory of Florence Ellsworth Wilson*

247. LEFT. Schraub-flasch (flask), with pewter screw-stopper, faïence. German, Kreussen, c. 1660-1670. *Metropolitan Museum of Art, Gift of R. Thornton Wilson, 1954, in memory of Florence Ellsworth Wilson*

248. LOWER LEFT. Jug, faïence, with gilt bronze mounts. German, Nuremberg, c. 1665. *Metropolitan Museum of Art, Gift of R. Thornton Wilson, 1950, in memory of Florence Ellsworth Wilson*

249. LEFT. Jug, faïence, with metal mounts. German, Nuremberg, c. 1690. *Metropolitan Museum of Art, Gift of R. Thornton Wilson, 1950, in memory of Florence Ellsworth Wilson*

250. RIGHT. Enghalskrug (form of jug), faïence, with silver gilt mounts. German, Augsburg, c. 1730. *Metropolitan Museum of Art, Gift of R. Thornton Wilson, 1950, in memory of Florence Ellsworth Wilson*

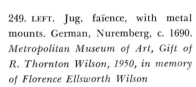

EUROPE: TIN-GLAZED EARTHENWARE

251. LEFT. Jug, Habaner ware, faïence with pewter mounts. Upper Hungary or Moravia, dated 1619. *Metropolitan Museum of Art, Gift of R. Thornton Wilson, 1951, in memory of Florence Ellsworth Wilson*

252. RIGHT. Saucer, one of a pair, tin-glazed earthenware. Portuguese, probably Lisbon, late 17th century. *Metropolitan Museum of Art, Gift of R. Thornton Wilson, 1967, in memory of Joan Bergire Drayton, 1967*

253. LOWER RIGHT. Barber's basin, tin-glazed earthenware. Swiss, Winterthur, dated 1701. *Metropolitan Museum of Art, Gift of R. Thornton Wilson, 1954, in memory of Florence Ellsworth Wilson*

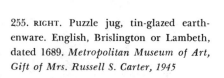

254. Fuddling cup, tin-glazed earthenware. English, London, Lambeth, c. 1650. *Metropolitan Museum of Art, Gift of Mrs. Russell S. Carter, 1938*

255. RIGHT. Puzzle jug, tin-glazed earthenware. English, Brislington or Lambeth, dated 1689. *Metropolitan Museum of Art, Gift of Mrs. Russell S. Carter, 1945*

256. FAR RIGHT. Punch bowl, tin-glazed earthenware. English, London, Lambeth, 1705. *Metropolitan Museum of Art, Gift of Mr. and Mrs. Leslie R. Samuels*

257. Oval dish, tin-glazed earthenware, Palissy style. English, London, Lambeth, dated 1664. *Metropolitan Museum of Art, Gift of Mrs. Francis P. Garvan, 1941*

258. Dish, Blue Dash Charger, tin-glazed earthenware. English, Lambeth or Bristol, c. 1700. *Metropolitan Museum of Art, Gift of Mrs. Russell S. Carter, 1945*

259. LEFT. Dish, Blue Dash Charger, tin-glazed earthenware. English, Lambeth or Bristol, c. 1700. *Metropolitan Museum of Art, Gift of Mrs. Frederic V. S. Crosby, 1930*

260. BELOW. Wig stand, tin-glazed earthenware. Dutch, Delft, c. 1675. *Victoria and Albert Museum*

261. LEFT. Tulip vase, tin-glazed earthenware. Dutch, Delft, c. 1694. *Victoria and Albert Museum*

262. ABOVE. Large dish, tin-glazed earthenware. Dutch, Delft, c. 1712. *Metropolitan Museum of Art, Gift of R. Thornton Wilson, 1954, in memory of Florence Ellsworth Wilson*

263. Plate, tin-glazed earthenware. Dutch, Delft, c. 1700-1725. *Metropolitan Museum of Art, Gift of Mrs. Catherine van Vliet de Witt Sterry, 1908*

264. UPPER RIGHT. Cistern, tin-glazed earthenware. Dutch, Delft, c. 1700 or later. *Metropolitan Museum of Art, Charles E. Sampson Memorial Fund, 1969*

267. Plate tin-glazed earthenware. Dutch, Delft, c. 1710-1715. *Metropolitan Museum of Art, Gift of J. Thornton Wilson, 1950, in memory of Florence Ellsworth Wilson*

265. Teapot, tin-glazed earthenware. Dutch, Delft, c. 1690. *Metropolitan Museum of Art, Gift of R. Thornton Wilson, 1950, in memory of Florence Ellsworth Wilson*

266. RIGHT. Vase, one of a pair, tin-glazed earthenware. Dutch, Delft, c. 1700-1710. *Metropolitan Museum of Art, Gift of J. Thornton Wilson, 1950, in memory of Florence Ellsworth Wilson*

268. FAR RIGHT. Jug, tin-glazed earthenware. Dutch, Delft, c. 1700-1725. *Metropolitan Museum of Art, Gift of Henry C. Marquand, 1894*

269. Helmet-form ewer, faïence. French, Rouen, c. 1700-1720. *Metropolitan Museum of Art, Gift of J. Pierpont Morgan, 1917*

270. Plate, faïence. French, Rouen, c. 1700-1720. *Metropolitan Museum of Art, Gift of J. Pierpont Morgan, 1917*

271. Plate, faïence. French, Rouen, c. 1700-1720. *Metropolitan Museum of Art, Gift of J. Pierpont Morgan, 1917*

272. Plateau, faïence. French, Rouen, c. 1710-1720. *Metropolitan Museum of Art, Gift of J. Pierpont Morgan, 1917*

273. Dish, faïence. French, Rouen, c. 1728. *Metropolitan Museum of Art, Gift of J. Pierpont Morgan, 1917*

275. Dish, faïence. French, Rouen, c. 1750. *Metropolitan Museum of Art, Gift of J. Pierpont Morgan, 1917*

274. Large table-tray, faïence. French, Rouen, c. 1730-1740. *Metropolitan Museum of Art, Gift of J. Pierpont Morgan, 1917*

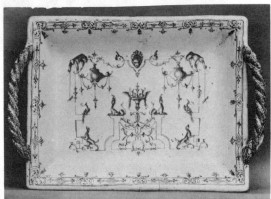

276. Tray, faïence. French, Moustiers, c. 1720-1740. *Metropolitan Museum of Art, Gift of J. Pierpont Morgan, 1917*

278. Plate, Camargo pattern, faïence. French, Moustiers (?), c. 1750. *Metropolitan Museum of Art, Gift of J. Pierpont Morgan, 1917*

277. Écuelle (soup bowl), faïence. French, Moustiers, c. 1745. *Metropolitan Museum of Art, Gift of J. Pierpont Morgan, 1917*

279. Wall fountain, tin-glazed earthenware. French, Strasbourg, c. 1730. *Collection of Mr. & Mrs. H. Graves Terwilliger*

280. Tureen, enameled faïence. French, Strasbourg, c. 1750-1760. *Metropolitan Museum of Art, Gift of R. Thornton Wilson, 1950, in memory of Florence Ellsworth Wilson*

281. UPPER RIGHT. Tureen in the form of a duck, enameled faence. French, Strasbourg, c. 1750. *Ex-Collection James Donahue, Photo Taylor and Dull*

282. BELOW. Dish with matching stand, enameled faïence. French, Strasbourg, c. 1762-1781. *Metropolitan Museum of Art, Gift of J. Pierpont Morgan, 1917*

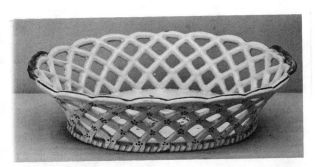

283. Cruet frame and two cruets, enameled faïence. French, Sceaux, c. 1760. *Metropolitan Museum of Art, Gift of R. Thornton Wilson, 1950, in memory of Florence Ellsworth Wilson*

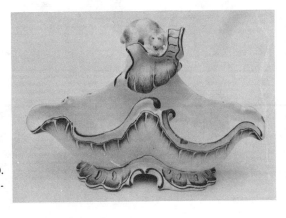

284. RIGHT. Sauceboat, enameled faïence. French, Niderviller, c. 1760-1770. *Metropolitan Museum of Art, Gift of R. Thornton Wilson, 1950, in memory of Florence Ellsworth Wilson*

286. Covered bowl and stand, enameled faïence. French, Marseilles, c. 1760. *Metropolitan Museum of Art, Gift of R. Thornton Wilson, 1950, in memory of Florence Ellsworth Wilson*

285. Plate, enameled faïence. French, Marseilles, c. 1750-1770. *Metropolitan Museum of Art, Gift of R. Thornton Wilson, 1950, in memory of Florence Ellsworth Wilson*

287. RIGHT. Plate, enameled faïence. French, Marseilles, c. 1750-1770. *Metropolitan Museum of Art, Gift of R. Thornton Wilson, 1950, in memory of Florence Ellsworth Wilson*

289. UPPER RIGHT. Small vase, enameled faïence. German, Fulda, 1741-1744. *Metropolitan Museum of Art, Gift of J. Thornton Wilson, 1950, in memory of Florence Ellsworth Wilson*

291. RIGHT. Vase, faïence. Spanish, Alcora, c. 1730-1740. *Metropolitan Museum of Art, Gift of R. Thornton Wilson, 1954, in memory of Florence Ellsworth Wilson*

288. Plate, Carp pattern, faïence. German, Ansbach, c. 1730. *Metropolitan Museum of Art, Gift of R. Thornton Wilson, 1950, in memory of Florence Ellsworth Wilson*

290. RIGHT. Plateau, faïence. German, Künersberg, c. 1760. *Metropolitan Museum of Art, Gift of R. Thornton Wilson, 1950, in memory of Florence Ellsworth Wilson*

293. Cabbage tureen on leaf stand, faïence. South Netherlands, Brussels, c. 1753. *The Campbell Museum, Camden, New Jersey,*

292. Incense burner in the form of a lion, faïence. Spanish, Talavera de la Reina, late 18th century. *Hispanic Society of America*

294. BELOW. Teapot and brazier, enameled faïence. Dutch, Delft, c. 1761-1769. *Metropolitan Museum of Art, Gift of Henry G. Marquand, 1894*

295. Dish, enameled faïence. Polish, Warsaw, 1776. *Metropolitan Museum of Art, Gift of R. Thornton Wilson, 1950, in memory of Florence Ellsworth Wilson*

296. RIGHT. Potpourri vase, enameled faïence. Schleswig-Holstein, Stockelsdorf, c. 1772-1774. *Metropolitan Museum of Art, Gift of R. Thornton Wilson, 1954, in memory of Florence Ellsworth Wilson*

297. FAR RIGHT. Bishop-bowl in form of a mitre, faïence. Denmark, Copenhagen, c. 1740. *National Museum, Copenhagen*

EUROPE: PORCELAIN

298. LEFT. Ewer, Medici porcelain. Italian, Florence, c. 1575-1587. *Metropolitan Museum of Art, Gift of J. Pierpont Morgan, 1917*

299. RIGHT. Ewer, soft-paste porcelain. French, Rouen, c. 1680-1695. *Metropolitan Museum of Art, Gift of J. Pierpont Morgan, 1917*

301. Teapot, Böttger stoneware. German, Meissen, 1715. *Metropolitan Museum of Art, Gift of R. Thornton Wilson, 1943, in memory of Florence Ellsworth Wilson*

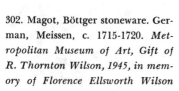

300. Vase, one of a pair, soft-paste porcelain. French, Saint-Cloud, 1700-1725. *Metropolitan Museum of Art, Gift of J. Pierpont Morgan, 1917*

302. Magot, Böttger stoneware. German, Meissen, c. 1715-1720. *Metropolitan Museum of Art, Gift of R. Thornton Wilson, 1945, in memory of Florence Ellsworth Wilson*

303. Pilgrim bottle, Böttger stoneware. German, Meissen, c. 1715-1720. *Metropolitan Museum of Art, Gift of R. Thornton Wilson, 1943, in memory of Florence Ellsworth Wilson*

304. "Callot" figure, Böttger porcelain. German, Meissen, c. 1718. *Metropolitan Museum of Art, Gift of Judge Irwin Untermeyer, 1948*

305. RIGHT. Tea caddy, porcelain. German, Meissen, c. 1725-1730. *Metropolitan Museum of Art, Gift of R. Thornton Wilson, 1954, in memory of Florence Ellsworth Wilson*

306. Sugar boxes, Red Dragon pattern, porcelain. German, Meissen, c. 1740. *Ex-Collection Winston Guest, Photo Taylor and Dull*

307. FAR LEFT. Untierkanne, porcelain. German, Meissen, 1730. *Collection of Mr. & Mrs. Edward M. Pflueger*

308. LEFT. Magpies, enameled porcelain. German, Meissen, 1733. *Metropolitan Museum of Art, Collection of Irwin Untermeyer, 1964*

EUROPE: PORCELAIN

309. LEFT. Tea jug in the shape of a seated squirrel, enameled porcelain. German, Meissen, 1735. *Metropolitan Museum of Art, Gift of Irwin Unter-meyer, 1964*

310. RIGHT. Teapot in the form of a seated monkey, enameled porcelain. German, Meissen, 1735. *Metropolitan Museum of Art, Gift of Irwin Unter-meyer, 1964*

313. Teapot, enameled porcelain. German, Meissen, 1737. *Metropolitan Museum of Art, Gift of Irwin Untermeyer, 1964*

312. Pair of boxes in the form of a cluster of grapes, porcelain. German, Meissen, c. 1750. *Ex-Collection James Donahue, Photo Taylor and Dull*

314. Candlestick and fruit dish, one of a pair, from the Swan Service, porcelain. German, Meissen, 1737-1741. *Metropolitan Museum of Art, Gift of R. Thornton Wilson, 1950, in memory of Florence Ellsworth Wilson*

314A. Plate from the Swan Service. *Ex-Collection Winston Guest, Photo Taylor and Dull*

315. Figure, Harlequin, enameled porcelain. German, Meissen, c. 1738. *Victoria and Albert Museum*

316. Figures, Tailor and Tailor's Wife Riding Goats, enameled porcelain. German, Meissen, 1740. *Metropolitan Museum of Art, Collection of Irwin Untermeyer, 1964*

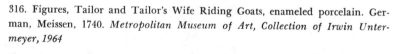

317. Group, Harlequin and Columbine, dancing, enameled porcelain. German, Meissen, 1744. *Metropolitan Museum of Art, Collection of Irwin Untermeyer, 1964*

318. Figure, Mme. de Pompadour, enameled porcelain (two views). German, Meissen, 1750-1752. *Metropolitan Museum of Art, Gift of Irwin Untermeyer, 1964*

319. Candelabrum, one of a pair, porcelain; mounted in gilt bronze. German, Meissen, 18th century. *Metropolitan Museum of Art, Gift of Ann Payne*

320. Guelder-rose vase, one of a pair, porcelain. German, Meissen, Marcolini period, c. 1780. *Philadelphia Museum of Art, Gift of Mrs. Henry Breyer, Sr.*

321. LEFT. Figure, Pantalone, white-glazed porcelain. German, Nymphenburg, c. 1755-1760. *Metropolitan Museum of Art, Gift of R. Thornton Wilson, 1950, in memory of Florence Ellsworth Wilson*

322. LOWER LEFT. Figure, Columbine, porcelain. German, Nymphenburg, c. 1755-1760. *Victoria and Albert Museum*

323. Crinoline Figure of a Lady, enameled porcelain (two views). German, Nymphenburg, 1754-1755. *Metropolitan Museum of Art, Gift of Irwin Untermeyer, 1964*

324. Group, The Naughty Children, porcelain. German, Frankenthal, c. 1770. *Metropolitan Museum of Art, Gift of R. Thornton Wilson, 1950, in memory of Florence Ellsworth Wilson*

325. Group, Disturbed Slumber, porcelain. German, Höchst, c. 1770. *Metropolitan Museum of Art, Gift of R. Thornton Wilson, 1950, in memory of Florence Ellsworth Wilson*

326. Potpourri vase, enameled porcelain. German Höchst, c. 1750-1765. *Collection of Mr. & Mrs. H. Graves Terwilliger*

327. Milk jug, porcelain. German, Fürstenberg, c. 1755-1765. *Metropolitan Museum of Art, Rogers Fund, 1906*

328. Group, Two Miners, enameled porcelain. German, Fürstenberg, c. 1760. *Metropolitan Museum of Art, Gift of R. Thornton Wilson, 1950, in memory of Florence Ellsworth Wilson*

330. Group, The Coiffure, porcelain. German, Ludwigsburg, c. 1770. *Metropolitan Museum of Art, Collection of Irwin Untermeyer, 1964*

329. Group, Venetian Fair, enameled porcelain. German, Ludwigsburg, c. 1767-1770. *Metropolitan Museum of Art, Gift of R. Thornton Wilson, 1950, in memory of Florence Ellsworth Wilson*

331. Scent bottle in the form of Harlequin, enameled porcelain. German, c. 1775. *Metropolitan Museum of Art, Gift of R. Thornton Wilson, 1950, in memory of Florence Ellsworth Wilson*

332. Teapot, porcelain. Austrian, Vienna, c. 1725. *Metropolitan Museum of Art, Gift of R. Thornton Wilson, 1954, in memory of Florence Ellsworth Wilson*

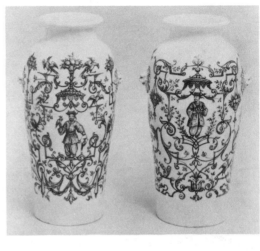

333. Vases, pair, porcelain. Austrian, Vienna, c. 1720-1730, decorated in Bohemia, c. 1730. *Metropolitan Museum of Art, Gift of R. Thornton Wilson, in memory of Florence Ellsworth Wilson*

334. FAR LEFT. Ollio pot, porcelain. Austrian, Vienna, c. 1730, decorated in Bohemia, c. 1730-1735. *Metropolitan Museum of Art, Gift of R. Thornton Wilson, 1945, in memory of Florence Ellsworth Wilson*

335. LEFT. Tankard, porcelain; metal mounts. Austrian, Vienna, c. 1731. *Metropolitan Museum of Art, Gift of R. Thornton Wilson, 1945, in memory of Florence Ellsworth Wilson*

336. Covered vessel, porcelain. Austrian, Vienna, c. 1735-1740. *Metropolitan Museum of Art, Collection of Irwin Untermeyer, 1964*

337. LOWER LEFT. Vase, porcelain. Italian, Venice, c. 1725-1730. *Metropolitan Museum of Art, Gift of R. Thornton Wilson, 1950, in memory of Florence Ellsworth Wilson*

338. LOWER RIGHT. Coffee pot, porcelain. Italian, Doccia, c. 1760. *Metropolitan Museum of Art, Gift of George F. Baker, 1931*

EUROPE: PORCELAIN

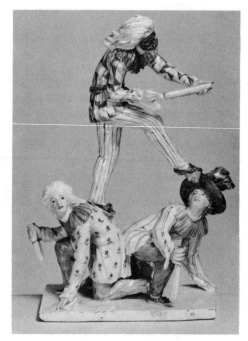

339. FAR LEFT. Figure, Pantalone, enameled soft-paste porcelain. Italian, Capo di Monte, c. 1750-1752. *Metropolitan Museum of Art, Gift of R. Thornton Wilson, 1950, in memory of Florence Ellsworth Wilson*

340. LEFT. Group, Acrobats, enameled soft-paste porcelain. Spanish, Buen Retiro, 1760-1770. *Metropolitan Museum of Art, Collection of Irwin Untermeyer, 1964*

341. BELOW. Group, Children with Goat, enameled soft-paste porcelain. Spanish, Buen Retiro, 1760-1770. *Hispanic Society of America*

342. LEFT. Benitier (Holy Water Basin), enameled soft-paste porcelain. Spanish, Buen Retiro, c. 1770. *Metropolitan Museum of Art, Gift of Irwin Untermeyer, 1964*

343. RIGHT. Cachepot, soft-paste porcelain. French, Saint-Cloud, c. 1730. *Metropolitan Museum of Art, Gift of R. Thornton Wilson, 1950, in memory of Florence Ellsworth Wilson*

344. FAR RIGHT. Small rouge jar, soft-paste porcelain. French, Saint-Cloud, c. 1725-1735. *Metropolitan Museum of Art, Gift of R. Thornton Wilson, 1942*

345. Small tulip vase, soft-paste porcelain. French, Chantilly, c. 1730-1740. *Metropolitan Museum of Art, Gift of R. Thornton Wilson, 1950, in memory of Florence Ellsworth Wilson*

346. Chinese Magot, enameled soft-paste porcelain. French, Chantilly, c. 1730-1740. *Musée National de Céramique, Sèvres*

347. Jars, pair, soft-paste porcelain; molded silver rims. French, Mennecy, c. 1740. *Metropolitan Museum of Art, Bequest of Edward C. Post, 1930*

348. Gruel bowl in the form of a fish, soft-paste porcelain. French, Mennecy, c. 1740-1750. *Metropolitan Museum of Art, Gift of R. Thornton Wilson, 1954, in memory of Florence Ellsworth Wilson*

349. Small box in the form of a slipper, soft-paste porcelain. French, Mennecy, c. 1750. *Metropolitan Museum of Art, Gift of R. Thornton Wilson, 1943, in memory of Florence Ellsworth Wilson*

350. Salt dish, soft-paste porcelain. French, Bourg-la-Reine, c. 1773-1785. *Metropolitan Museum of Art, Gift of R. Thornton Wilson, 1950, in memory of Florence Ellsworth Wilson*

351. UPPER LEFT. Bowl (detail), soft-paste porcelain. French, Vincennes, c. 1745. *Musée National de Céramique, Sèvres*

352. UPPER RIGHT. Bouquet of at least 480 flowers of various kinds, soft-paste porcelain, mounted in gilt bronze. French, Vincennes, 1749. *Dresden Museum, Dresden*

353. LEFT. Powder flask, soft-paste porcelain; gilt-bronze mounts. French, Vincennes or Sèvres, c. 1750-1755. *Metropolitan Museum of Art, Gift of R. Thornton Wilson, 1950, in memory of Florence Ellsworth Wilson*

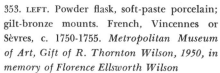

354. Group, Les Mangeurs de Raisins, soft-paste biscuit porcelain. French, Vincennes or Sèvres, after 1752. *Musée National de Céramique, Sèvres*

355. Group, La Lanterne Magique, soft-paste biscuit porcelain. French, Sèvres, c. 1760. *Metropolitan Museum of Art, Bequest of Ella Morris de Peyster, 1958*

357. Candelabrum vase, one of a pair, with rose Pompadour, enamel ground, soft-paste porcelain. French, Sèvres, c. 1758. *Metropolitan Museum of Art, Gift of the Samuel H. Kress Foundation, 1958*

356. Potpourri vase with rose Pompadour, enamel ground, soft-paste porcelain. French, Sèvres, 1757. *Metropolitan Museum of Art, Gift of the Samuel H. Kress Foundation, 1958*

358. Wall sconce, one of a pair, enameled soft-paste porcelain. French, Sèvres, c. 1761. *Metropolitan Museum of Art, Gift of the Samuel H. Kress Foundation, 1958*

359. RIGHT. Ice-pail, enameled soft-paste porcelain. French, Sèvres, probably c. 1780-1790. *Metropolitan Museum of Art, Bequest of Emma Townsend Gary, 1937*

360. Circular top of Table des Maréchaux, porcelain; mounted in gilt bronze. French, Sèvres, 1810. *Musée National de Malmaison.*

361. Group, Louis XVI and Benjamin Franklin signing a Treaty of Alliance, biscuit porcelain. France, Niderviller, c. 1780-1785. *Metropolitan Museum of Art, Gift of William Henry Huntington, 1883*

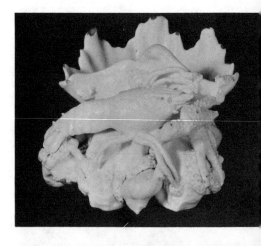

362. LEFT. Tea caddy, soft-paste porcelain. English, Chelsea, Incised Triangle period, 1745-1750. *Metropolitan Museum of Art, Collection of Irwin Untermeyer*

363. RIGHT. Shell salt dish, one of a pair, soft-paste porcelain. English, Chelsea, Incised Triangle period, 1745-1750. *Metropolitan Museum of Art, Collection of Irwin Untermeyer*

364. BELOW. Plate, Hob-in-the-Well pattern, enameled soft-paste porcelain. English, Chelsea, Red Anchor period, c. 1752. *Metropolitan Museum of Art, Collection of Irwin Untermeyer*

365. Tureen in the form of a cauliflower, soft-paste porcelain. English, Chelsea, Red Anchor period, c. 1752-1756. *Ex-Collection James Donahue, Photo Taylor and Dull*

366. LEFT. Group, The Music Lesson, enameled soft-paste porcelain. English, Chelsea, Gold Anchor period, c. 1765. *Metropolitan Museum of Art, Gift of Irwin Untermeyer, 1964*

367. RIGHT. Vase in the form of an eel-basket, soft-paste porcelain. English, Chelsea, Gold Anchor period, c. 1760. *Metropolitan Museum of Art, Gift of Mr. and Mrs. Howard Eric, 1940*

368. Vase, soft-paste porcelain. English, Chelsea, c. 1755-1765. *Metropolitan Museum of Art, Bequest of John L. Cadwalader, 1914*

369. Sugar bowl, soft-paste porcelain. England, Chelsea, Gold Anchor period, c. 1761. *Metropolitan Museum of Art, Gift of Mrs. Francis P. Garvan, 1954, in memory of Francis P. Garvan*

371. BELOW. Plate, one of a pair, soft-paste porcelain, Imari style. English, Worcester. Dr. Wall period, c. 1770-1780. *Metropolitan Museum of Art, Gift of Mr. and Mrs. Luke Vincent Lockwood, 1939*

370. Dessert basket and cover, soft-paste porcelain. England, Worcester, Dr. Wall period, c. 1770-1780. *Metropolitan Museum of Art, Gift of Henry G. Marquand, 1894*

372. RIGHT. Plate, Blind Earl's Pattern, soft-paste porcelain. English, Worcester. Dr. Wall period, c. 1770. *Metropolitan Museum of Art, Gift of Mr. and Mrs. Luke Vincent Lockwood, 1939*

373. FAR RIGHT. Plate, Hop Trellis pattern, soft-paste porcelain. English, Worcester. Dr. Wall period, c. 1770-1780. *Metropolitan Museum of Art, Gift of Mr. and Mrs. Luke Vincent Lockwood, 1939*

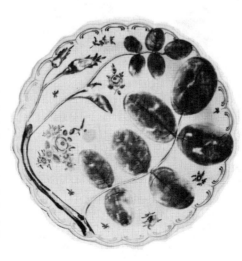

374. LEFT. Tea caddy, soft-paste porcelain. English, Worcester, Dr. Wall period, c. 1765. *Metropolitan Museum of Art, Gift of Mr. and Mrs. Luke Vincent Lockwood, 1939*

375. RIGHT. Vase with cover, enameled porcelain. English, Longton Hall, c. 1755. *Metropolitan Museum of Art, Collection of Irwin Untermeyer*

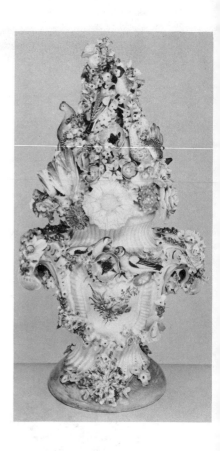

376. LOWER LEFT. Vase, one from a garniture of five pieces, soft-paste porcelain. English, Bow, c. 1760-1780. *Metropolitan Museum of Art, Gift of Irwin Untermeyer, 1951*

377. Figures, Monkey Musicians, enameled soft-paste porcelain. English Derby, c. 1760. *Metropolitan Museum of Art, Purchase 1966, Charles E. Sampson Memorial Fund*

378. Spouted cup, soft-paste porcelain. English, Lowestoft, c. 1760-1770. *Metropolitan Museum of Art, Gift of R. Thornton Wilson, 1937*

379. Tray and six ice cream cups, porcelain. Danish, Copenhagen, probably before 1779. *Kunstindustrimuseet, Copenhagen*

380. LEFT. Tureen, porcelain. Danish, Copenhagen, 1789-1790. *Kunstindustrimuseet, Copenhagen*

381. ABOVE. Serving dish from the Flora Danica service, porcelain. Danish, Copenhagen, 1789-1802. *Kunstindustrimuseet, Copenhagen*

384. BELOW. Plate, porcelain. Russian, St. Petersburg, c. 1760. *Metropolitan Museum of Art*

382. LEFT. Figure, Bird Vendor, enameled porcelain. Swiss, Zurich, c. 1775-1779. *Metropolitan Museum of Art, Gift of R. Thornton Wilson, 1943, in memory of Florence Ellsworth Wilson*

383. RIGHT. Figure, Samoyed woman, porcelain. Russian, St. Petersburg, early 19th century, *Victoria and Albert Museum*

STAFFORDSHIRE:
EIGHTEENTH CENTURY

385. Coffee pot, lead-glazed red earthenware. English, Staffordshire, c. 1740. *Metropolitan Museum of Art, Gift of Mrs. Russell S. Carter, 1944*

386. TOP. Teapot, lead-glazed black earthenware. English, Staffordshire, c. 1740-1750. *Metropolitan Museum of Art, Gift of Mrs. Russell S. Carter, 1945*

387. BOTTOM. Bowl, lead-glazed black earthenware. English, Staffordshire (?), c. 1750-1760. *Metropolitan Museum of Art, Gift of Mrs. George D. Pratt, 1922*

388. LEFT. Figure, Cavalryman on Horseback, lead-glazed creamware. English, Staffordshire, c. 1750. *Metropolitan Museum of Art, Bequest of Marion E. Cohn, 1966, Cohn Collection*

389. Dish, marbled or combed lead-glazed slipware. English, Staffordshire, early 18th century. *Victoria and Albert Museum*

390. Jug, lead-glazed slipware, marbled and incised. English, Staffordshire, dated 1766. *Victoria and Albert Museum*

392. Figure of a duck, lead-glazed agate ware. English, Staffordshire, c. 1750. *Metropolitan Museum of Art, Gift of Mrs. Russell S. Carter, 1944*

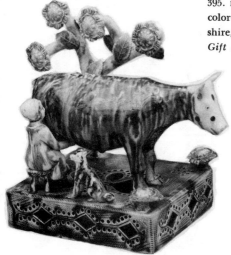

391. TOP. Bowl, lead-glazed agate ware. English, Staffordshire, c. 1745. *Metropolitan Museum of Art, Gift of Mrs. Russell S. Carter, 1944*

393. BOTTOM. Tureen stand, tortoiseshell ware. English, Staffordshire, c. 1750-1755. *Metropolitan Museum of Art, Purchase, 1967, Charles E. Sampson Memorial Fund*

394. RIGHT. Teapot, mottled color-glazed creamware. English, Staffordshire, c. 1750-1755. *Metropolitan Museum of Art, Gift of Mrs. Russell S. Carter, 1944*

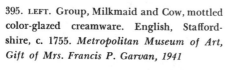

395. LEFT. Group, Milkmaid and Cow, mottled color-glazed creamware. English, Staffordshire, c. 1755. *Metropolitan Museum of Art, Gift of Mrs. Francis P. Garvan, 1941*

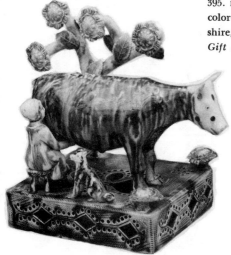

396. RIGHT. Ewer, creamware with color-glazed mottling. English, Staffordshire, Etruria, 1769-1780. *Metropolitan Museum of Art, Rogers Fund, 1940*

397. Teapot, in the form of a cauliflower, color-glazed earthenware. English, Staffordshire, Burslem, c. 1763. *Victoria and Albert Museum*

398. LEFT. Jug, Fair Hebe, color-glazed earthenware. English, Staffordshire, Burslem, dated 1788. *Metropolitan Museum of Art, Gift of R. Thornton Wilson, 1943, in memory of Florence Ellsworth Wilson*

399. RIGHT. Toby jug, The Planter, color-glazed earthenware. English, Staffordshire, Burslem, c. 1780. *Metropolitan Museum of Art, Gift of R. Thornton Wilson, 1943, in memory of Florence Ellsworth Wilson*

400. Squirrel, color-glazed earthenware. English, Staffordshire, Burslem, c. 1780. *Metropolitan Museum of Art, Gift of Mrs. Russell S. Carter, 1945*

401. Trial plate from the Green Frog service, creamware. English, Staffordshire, Etruria, 1774. *Josiah Wedgwood & Sons, Ltd.*

402. Plate, enameled creamware. English, Staffordshire, Lane End, c. 1790. *Metropolitan Museum of Art, Gift of Mrs. Bernice Chrysler Garbisch, 1852*

403. Figures of children, Winter and Summer, creamware. English, Staffordshire, Hanley, c. 1780. *Metropolitan Museum of Art, Gift of R. Thornton Wilson, 1950, in memory of Florence Ellsworth Wilson*

404. ABOVE. Vase, one of a pair, creamware. English, Yorkshire, Leeds, late 18th century. *Metropolitan Museum of Art, Gift of Mrs. Heywood Cutting, 1942*

405. LEFT. Tureen and stand, creamware. French, Paris, c. 1750. *Metropolitan Museum of Art, Gift of R. Thornton Wilson, 1950, in memory of Florence Ellsworth Wilson*

407. Punch-pot, unglazed red stoneware. England, Staffordshire, c. 1750-1760. *Metropolitan Museum of Art, Rogers Fund, 1913*

406. Coffee pot, enameled creamware. Italian, Nove, c. 1815. *Victoria and Albert Museum*

408. Bowl, salt-glazed stoneware. English, Staffordshire, c. 1740-1745. *Metropolitan Museum of Art, Gift of Carlton Macy, 1934*

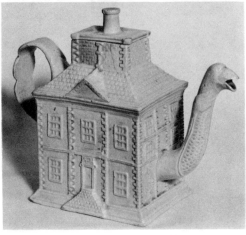

411. Teapot, white salt-glazed stoneware. English, Staffordshire, c. 1755. *Metropolitan Museum of Art, Gift of Carlton Macy, 1934*

409. TOP. Teapot in the form of a crouching camel, white salt-glazed stoneware. English, Staffordshire, c. 1745. *Metropolitan Museum of Art, Gift of Carlton Macy, 1934*

410. BOTTOM. Teapot in the form of a house, white salt-glazed stoneware. English, Staffordshire, c. 1745. *Metropolitan Museum of Art, Gift of Carlton Macy, 1934*

412. LEFT. Goat and Bee milk jug, salt-glazed stoneware. English, c. 1750. *Metropolitan Museum of Art, Gift of Mrs. Screven Lorillard, 1953*

413. RIGHT. Wall vase, white salt-glazed stoneware. English, Staffordshire, c. 1750-1755. *Metropolitan Museum of Art, Gift of Carlton Macy, 1934*

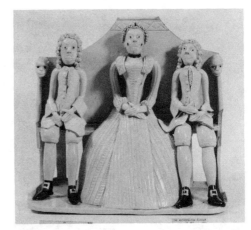

417. Pew Group, white salt-glazed stoneware. English, Staffordshire, c. 1745. *Metropolitan Museum of Art, Gift of Carlton Macy, 1934*

418. Rattle, white salt-glazed stoneware. English, Staffordshire, c. 1740. *Metropolitan Museum of Art, Gift of Mrs. Russell S. Carter, 1945*

414. TOP. Punch-pot, white salt-glazed stoneware. English, Staffordshire, c. 1755. *Metropolitan Museum of Art, Gift of Carlton Macy, 1934*

415. MIDDLE. Teapot, salt-glazed stoneware. English, Staffordshire, c. 1755. *Metropolitan Museum of Art, Gift of Carlton Macy, 1934*

416. BOTTOM. Teapot in the form of a cabbage, white salt-glazed stoneware. English, Staffordshire, c. 1760. *Metropolitan Museum of Art, Gift of Carlton Macy, 1934*

419. RIGHT. Figures, adapted from Chinese Dog of Fo, salt-glazed stoneware. English, Staffordshire, c. 1750. *Metropolitan Museum of Art, Gift of Carlton Macy, 1934*

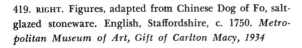

STAFFORDSHIRE: EIGHTEENTH CENTURY

420. Figures, Turkish, white salt-glazed stoneware. English, Staffordshire, c. 1755-1760. *Metropolitan Museum of Art, Gift of R. Thornton Wilson, 1943, in memory of Florence Ellsworth Wilson*

421. Vase, "Etruscan" ware, black basalt. English, Staffordshire, Etruria, c. 1780. *Metropolitan Museum of Art, Purchase 1966, The Charles E. Sampson Memorial Fund*

422. LEFT. Vase and bough pot, unglazed red stoneware. English, Staffordshire, Etruria, early 19th century. *Josiah Wedgwood and Sons, Ltd.*

425. Portland Vase, jasper ware. English, Staffordshire, Etruria, 1793. *Josiah Wedgwood & Sons, Ltd.*

423. ABOVE. Plaque, Dancing Hours figures, jasper ware. English, Staffordshire, Etruria, 1775. *Josiah Wedgwood & Sons, Ltd.*

424. RIGHT. Plaque, Apotheosis of Homer, jasper ware. English, Staffordshire, Etruria, 1784. *Josiah Wedgwood & Sons, Ltd.*

426. Barber's basin, painted slip-ware. American, Pennsylvania German, dated 1769. *Metropolitan Museum of Art, Rogers Fund, 1953*

428. Bowl, reddish-brown glazed earthenware. American, Pennsylvania, Bucks County, made by David Haring (1801-1871), c. 1835. *Metropolitan Museum of Art, Gift of Mrs. Robert W. de Forest, 1933*

429. Beanpot, reddish-brown glazed earthenware, slip decoration. American, Pennsylvania, c. 1800. *Philadelphia Museum of Art: The Titus C. Geesey Collection*

427. TOP. Plate, lead-glazed red earthenware, slip decoration. American, Pennsylvania, dated 1821. *Metropolitan Museum of Art, Gift of Mrs. Robert W. de Forest, 1933*

430. BOTTOM. Plate, slipware. American, Pennsylvania, Montgomery County, made by Samuel Troxel, dated 1846. *Metropolitan Museum of Art, Gift of Mrs. Robert W. de Forest, 1933*

431. FAR LEFT. Bowl, lead-glazed earthenware, slip decoration. American, Pennsylvania, c. 1800. *Metropolitan Museum of Art, Gift of Mrs. Robert W. de Forest, 1933*

432. LEFT. Jar, slipware. American, Pennsylvania, Montgomery County, c. 1800-1850. *Metropolitan Museum of Art, Gift of Mrs. Robert W. de Forest, 1933*

433. LEFT. Crock, salt-glazed grey stoneware. American, Massachusetts, Charlestown, 1850-1868. *Henry Ford Museum, Dearborn*

434. RIGHT. Coin bank, salt-glazed grey stoneware. American, Pennsylvania, Philadelphia, late 19th century. *Philadelphia Museum of Art*

435. RIGHT. Pitcher, earthenware, Rockingham glaze. American, New Jersey, Jersey City, 1838-1845. *Newark Museum, Newark, New Jersey*

436. FAR RIGHT. Pitcher, lead-glazed creamware. American, New Jersey, Jersey City, 1840. *Newark Museum, Newark, New Jersey*

437. Platter, lead-glazed white earthenware. American, Maryland, Baltimore, c. 1890-1900. *Philadelphia Museum of Art: Bequest of R. Wistar Harvey*

438. Toby or Coachman bottle, earthenware, flint enamel glaze. American, Vermont, Bennington, 1849-1858. *Metropolitan Museum of Art, Rogers Fund, 1914*

439. Figure, lion, earthenware, flint enamel glaze. American, Vermont, Bennington, 1852-1858. *Metropolitan Museum of Art, Rogers Fund, 1941*

440. Scroddled ware wash-hand set, glazed earthenware. American, Vermont, Bennington, 1853-1858. *Henry Ford Museum, Dearborn*

441. LEFT. Hound-handle pitcher, earthenware, Rockingham glaze. American, Vermont, Bennington, 1852-1858. *Metropolitan Museum of Art, Gift of Mrs. Russell Sage, 1913*

443. LEFT. Pitcher, Paul and Virginia pattern, parian porcelain. American, Vermont, Bennington, 1852-1858. *Metropolitan Museum of Art, Gift of Dr. Charles W. Green, 1947*

444. RIGHT. Pitcher, parian porcelain. American, South Carolina, Kaolin, c. 1862. *Metropolitan Museum of Art, Gift of Robert M. Jackson, 1920*

442. Niagara Falls pitcher, smear-glazed parian porcelain. American, Vermont, Bennington, c. 1853. *Metropolitan Museum of Art, Gift of Dr. Charles W. Green, 1947*

AMERICAN: NINETEENTH CENTURY

445. Figure, Greek Slave, parian porcelain. American, New Jersey, Trenton, c. 1869. *Newark Museum, Newark, New Jersey*

446. Baseball Vase, parian porcelain. American, New Jersey, Trenton, 1876. *New Jersey State Museum, Trenton, Brewer Collection*

447. Vase, soft-paste porcelain. American, New York, 1816. *Philadelphia Museum of Art: Exchanged with Franklin Institute*

449. LEFT. Vase, one of a pair, porcelain. American, Pennsylvania, Philadelphia, c. 1835. *Philadelphia Museum of Art: Purchased, Temple Fund*

448. LEFT. Pitcher, one of a pair, porcelain. American, Pennsylvania, Philadelphia, 1827-1828. *Newark Museum, Newark, New Jersey, Gift of Miss Margaret Ely Webb, 1926*

450. RIGHT. Veilleuse (tea warmer), porcelain. American, Pennsylvania, Philadelphia, c. 1836. *Philadelphia Museum of Art: Bequest of Bertha L. Landis*

451. LEFT. Pitcher, porcelain. American, Pennsylvania, Philadelphia, 1851-1855, *Philadelphia Museum of Art: Gift of Titus C. Geesey*

452. RIGHT. Pitcher, porcelain. American, New York, Greenpoint, c. 1855. *Metropolitan Museum of Art, Edgar J. Kaufmann Charitable Foundation Fund, 1968*

453. Century Vase, porcelain. American, New York, Brooklyn, 1876. *Brooklyn Museum, Gift of Carll and Franklin Chace*

454. Plaque, biscuit porcelain. American, Massachusetts, Chelsea, c. 1878-1880. *Brooklyn Museum, Gift of Arthur W. Clement*

455. Oyster plate, porcelain, Palissy style. American, New York, Greenpoint, 1881. *Metropolitan Museum of Art, Edgar J. Kaufmann Charitable Foundation Fund, 1968*

456. Pitcher in the form of a nautilus shell, Bel-. leek ware. American, New Jersey, Trenton, 1887. *Newark Museum, Newark, New Jersey*

457. Dish in the form of a swan, Belleek ware. American, New Jersey, Trenton, c. 1889-1894. *Brooklyn Museum, Gift of Arthur W. Clement*

458. Sweetmeat dish, Belleek ware. Ohio, East Liverpool, c. 1890-1898. *Brooklyn Museum, Gift of Arthur W. Clement*

459. Vase, Belleek ware. American, New Jersey, Trenton, end of 19th century. *Metropolitan Museum of Art, Edgar J. Kaufmann Charitable Foundation Fund, 1968*

460. RIGHT. Ali Baba vase, pottery, colored-slip decoration. American, Ohio, Cincinnati, 1880. *Cincinnati Art Museum; Rookwood loan*

461. Sugar bowl, creamware. English, Ferrybridge, c. 1805. *Victoria and Albert Museum*

462. Saucer, Gaudy Dutch, lead-glazed earthenware. English, Staffordshire, c. 1825. *Metropolitan Museum of Art, Gift of Mrs. Robert W. de Forest, 1933*

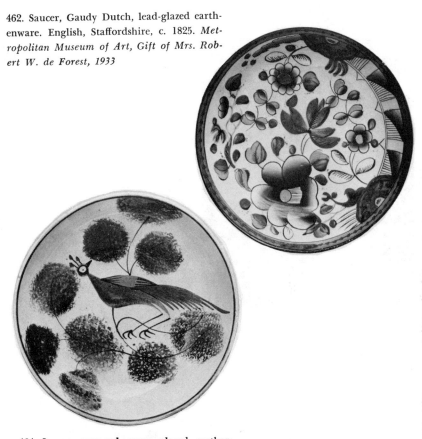

463. Teapot, Gaudy Dutch, lead-glazed earthenware. English, Staffordshire, c. 1825. *Metropolitan Museum of Art, Gift of Mrs. Robert W. de Forest, 1933*

464. Saucer, **sponged ware**, glazed earthenware. English, probably Staffordshire, early 19th century. *Metropolitan Museum of Art, Gift of Mrs. Robert W. de Forest, 1933*

466. Pitcher, sponged ware, glazed earthenware. English, probably Staffordshire, early 19th century. *Metropolitan Museum of Art, Gift of Mrs. Robert W. de Forest, 1933*

465. Plate, sponged ware, **glazed earthenware**. English, probably Staffordshire, early 19th century. *Metropolitan Museum of Art, Gift of Mrs. Robert W. de Forest, 1933*

469. Minister jug, smear-glazed white stoneware. English, Staffordshire, Hanley, 1842. *Victoria and Albert Museum*

467. TOP. Platter, transfer-printed earthenware in medium blue. English, Staffordshire, Cobridge, 1823-1829. *Louis Lyons, New York, Photo Taylor and Dull*

468. BOTTOM. Platter, transfer-printed earthenware in dark blue. English, Staffordshire, Stoke, 1829. *Louis Lyons, New York, Photo Taylor and Dull*

470. Silenus jug, smear-glazed white stoneware. English, Staffordshire, Stoke, c. 1840-1845. *Victoria and Albert Museum*

471. Vase, "Etruscan," earthenware. English, Wales, Swansea, c. 1850. *Victoria and Albert Museum*

472 B. LEFT. Candlestick in the form of a dolphin, glazed earthenware. English, Staffordshire, Etruria, c. 1870. *Josiah Wedgwood Sons, Ltd.*

472. A. Chestnut dish with matching spoon, glazed earthenware. England, Staffordshire, Stoke, 1855. *Victoria and Albert Museum*

474. BELOW. Vase, porcelain. English, Shropshire, Coalport, c. 1830. *Victoria and Albert Museum*

473. Lithophane, porcelain. German, Berlin, 1825-1850. *Metropolitan Museum of Art, Gift of W. L. Hildburgh, 1936*

475. LEFT. Vase, The Seasons, porcelain. English, Staffordshire, Stoke, 1848. *Minton Ltd., Photo Pottery Gazette*

476. BELOW. Teapot, reticulated porcelain. English, Worcester, 1862-1878. *Philadelphia Museum of Art: Gift of George M. Gilbert in memory of Gwendolyn Taylor Gilbert*

477. Figure of Mercury, biscuit porcelain. Denmark, Copenhagen, c. 1870. *Victoria and Albert Museum*

478. Sweetmeat dish, Belleek ware. Ireland, Fermanagh, Belleek, c. 1868. *Victoria and Albert Museum*

480. Dish, painted pottery. English, London, Lambeth, 1876. *Victoria and Albert Museum*

479. BELOW LEFT. Vase, The Toy Seller, pâte-sur-pâte on parian porcelain. English, Staffordshire, Stoke, dated 1899. *Minton, Ltd., Photo Pottery Gazette*

481. Tankard, stoneware. English, London, Lambeth, 1874. *Victoria and Albert Museum*

482. FAR LEFT. Vase, stoneware. English, Middlesex, Southall; made by the Martin Brothers, dated 9-1886. *Victoria and Albert Museum*

483. LEFT. Vase, earthenware, lustered. English, London, Fulham; made by William de Morgan, 1888-1898. *Metropolitan Museum of Art, Purchase 1923, Edward C. Moore, Jr. Gift*

484. BELOW. Dish, lead-glazed earthenware, Palissy manner. English, Essex, Castle Hedingham; made by Edward Bingham, c. 1870-1885. *Metropolitan Museum of Art, Gift of H. Burlingham, 1927*

485. Jar, porcelain. Denmark, Copenhagen, 1888. *Kunstindustrimuseet, Copenhagen*

487. Wall plaque, porcelain. Denmark, Copenhagen, 1901. *Royal Copenhagen Porcelain Manufactory*

486. Figure group, pair of owls, slipcast porcelain. Denmark, Copenhagen, 1901. *Royal Copenhagen Porcelain Manufactory*

488. LEFT. Vase, glazed earthenware. Denmark, Copenhagen, Valby; made by Thorwald Bindesboll, 1893. *Kunstindustrimuseet, Copenhagen*

489. RIGHT. Vase, earthenware, lustered. French, Golfe-Juan; made by Clément Massier, dated 1889. *Metropolitan Museum of Art, Gift of John C. Moore, 1940*

490. Vase, porcelain with flambé glaze. French, Limoges; made by Ernest Chaplet, 1870-1886. *Metropolitan Museum of Art, Gift of George Haviland, 1923*

491. Vase, glazed stoneware. French, Beauvais, made by Auguste Delaherche, late 19th-early 20th century. *Metropolitan Museum of Art, Gift of Edward C. Moore Jr., 1922*

492. Vase, glazed stoneware. French, Bourg-la-Reine, made by Adrien Dalpayrat, 1897. *Metropolitan Museum of Art, Edward L. Moore Gift Fund, 1926*

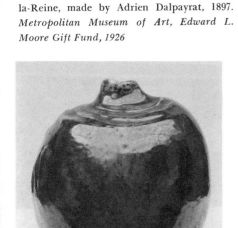

493. Bowl, glazed stoneware. French, made by Alexandre Bigot, c. 1895. *Metropolitan Museum of Art, Edward C. Moore, Jr., Gift Fund, 1926*

494. Cup and saucer, porcelain. French, Limoges, 1899. *Metropolitan Museum of Art, Gift of R. Hanse, 1926*

495. Plate, porcelain. German, Meissen, c. 1905. *Hessisches Landesmuseum, Darmstadt*

496. Mustard pots, glazed stoneware. German, Grenzhausen, c. 1897. *Museum of Modern Art, New York*

497. Coffee pot, Donatello service, porcelain. German, Bavarian, Selb, 1907. *Hessisches Landesmuseum, Darmstadt*

498. Plate, with bouillon cup and saucer, Woodrow Wilson service, porcelain. American, New Jersey, Trenton, 1918. *Lenox China Company*

THE TWENTIETH CENTURY
WORLD: USEFUL WARES

499. Part of a service, porcelain. Austrian, Vienna, c. 1928. *Osterreichisches Museum für Angewandte Kunst, Wien*

500. ABOVE. Part of a dinner service, white porcelain. German, Berlin, 1923-1933. *Museum of Modern Art, New York*

501. BELOW. Part of a service, porcelain. Austrian, Vienna, c. 1939. *Osterreichisches Museum für Angewandte Kunst, Wien*

502. RIGHT. Part of a service, porcelain. American, Pennsylvania, New Castle, 1941. *Photo Museum of Contemporary Crafts, New York*

503. ABOVE. Cup and saucer, Grain of Rice pattern, porcelain. Finnish, Arabia, 1942. *Oy Wärtsilä AB, Helsinki*

504. RIGHT. Teapot, pitcher and cream pitcher, stoneware. English, London, made by Lucie Rie, 1952-1954. *Museum of Modern Art, New York*

505. Pieces from the "Donatella" service, porcelain. Italian, Milan, c. 1954. *Museo di Doccia*

506. Pieces from a service, porcelain. Danish, Copenhagen, 1957-1958. *Royal Copenhagen Porcelain Manufactory*

507. Pieces from a service, black basalt. English, Staffordshire, Barlaston, 1964. *Josiah Wedgwood and Sons, Ltd.*

508. Pieces from a service, Kilta ware, ovenproof earthenware. Finnish, Arabia, 1953. *Oy Wärtsilä AB, Helsinki*

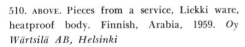

509. Pieces from a service, Patella ware, ovenproof porcelain. Danish, Copenhagen, 1967. *Royal Copenhagen Porcelain Manufactory*

510. ABOVE. Pieces from a service, Liekki ware, heatproof body. Finnish, Arabia, 1959. *Oy Wärtsilä AB, Helsinki*

511. RIGHT. Pieces from a service, Novum 65, porcelain. German, Bavaria, Selb, 1965. *Lorenz Hutschenreuther AG*

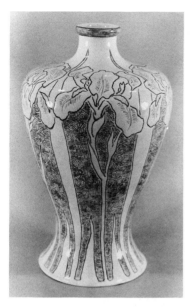

514. Jug, glazed stoneware; silver mounts. French, made by Bigot and Colonna, c. 1900. *Metropolitan Museum of Art, Edward C. Moore, Jr. Fund, 1926*

512. LEFT. Vase, glazed earthenware. American, Louisiana, New Orleans, c. 1897. *Cincinnati Art Museum, Gift of Mary Schearer*

513. RIGHT. Vase, porcelain, Swedish, Rörstrand, c. 1900. *Victoria and Albert Museum*

515. Vase, glazed stoneware. French, made by Edmond Lachenal,. c. 1900. *Hessisches Landesmuseum, Darmstadt*

516. ABOVE. Vase, porcelain. French,. Limoges, made by de Feure and Gérard, c. 1898-1904. *Metropolitan Museum of Art, Edward C. Moore, Jr. Gift Fund, 1926*

517. RIGHT. Vase, porcelain. Dutch, The Hague, c. 1900. *Osterreichisches Museum für Angewandte Kunst, Wien*

THE TWENTIETH CENTURY
WORLD: ORNAMENTAL WARES

518. Figure of a dancer, biscuit porcelain. French, Sèvres, 1900. *Hessisches Landesmuseum, Darmstadt*

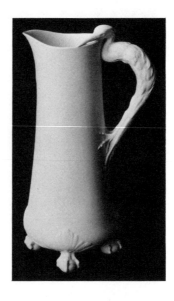

519. Pitcher, glazed white porcelain with heron-shaped handle. Italian, Milan, c. 1900-1910. *Museo di Doccia*

520. Vase, glazed earthenware. American, Ohio, Cincinnati, by Artus van Briggle, c. 1900. *Collection of Dr. & Mrs. Robert Koch, Photo Museum of Contemporary Crafts, New York*

521. Bowl, glazed earthenware. American, Colorado, Colorado Springs, by Artus van Briggle, c. 1902. *Collection of Dr. & Mrs. Robert Koch, Photo Museum of Contemporary Crafts, New York*

522. LEFT. Vase, faïence. American, Massachusetts, Boston, c. 1900. *Metropolitan Museum of Art, Edgar J. Kaufmann Charitable Foundation Fund, 1969*

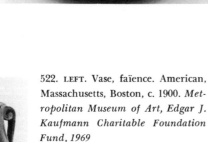

523. LEFT. Umbrella stand, glazed earthenware. American, Ohio, Zanesville, c. 1905. *Metropolitan Museum of Art, Gift of Ronald S. Kane*

524. RIGHT. Scarab vase, porcelain. American, New York, Syracuse, made by Adelaide Alsop Robineau, 1910. *Everson Museum of Art, Syracuse, New York*

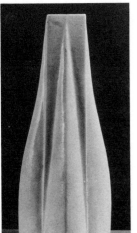

525. Vase, glazed earthenware. Bohemian, Prague, c. 1911. *Osterreichisches Museum für Angewandte Kunst, Wien*

527. RIGHT. Vase, porcelain. Italian, Milan, 1929. *Museo di Doccia*

526. Figures, Daphne and Apollo, glazed white porcelain. German, Berlin, c. 1925. *Victoria and Albert Museum*

529. Vase, glazed stoneware. French, Choisy-le-Roi, made by Emile Lenoble, c. 1920's. *Metropolitan Museum of Art, Gift of Charles J. Liebman, Jr., 1965*

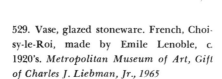

528. Vase, glazed stoneware. French, Fontenay-aux-Roses (Seine), made by Emile Decoeur, c. 1920's. *Metropolitan Museum of Art, Gift of Charles J. Liebman, Jr., 1965*

530. Vase, glazed stoneware. French, Sainte-Radegonde, made by René Buthaud, c. 1925-1930. *Metropolitan Museum of Art, Gift of Charles B. Liebman, Jr., 1965*

531. LEFT. Vase, Argenta ware, glazed stoneware. Swedish, Gustavsberg, c. 1920-1930. *Metropolitan Museum of Art, Purchase, 1934, Edward C. Moore, Jr. Gift Fund*

532. RIGHT. Cup, glazed stoneware. Danish, Naestved, early 20th century. *Metropolitan Museum of Art, Gift of Edward C. Moore, Jr., 1922*

533. Figure, Javanese Girl, glazed porcelain. Danish, early 20th century. *Metropolitan Museum of Art, Gift of Edward C. Moore, Jr., 1929*

534. Figure of an ape, glazed stoneware. Danish, Copenhagen, early 20th century. *Metropolitan Museum of Art, Purchase, 1922, Edward C. Moore, Jr., Gift*

536. LEFT. Group, Silenus, glazed white porcelain. Danish, Copenhagen, early 20th century. *Metropolitan Museum of Art, Purchase 1923, Edward C. Moore, Jr., Gift Fund*

537. Figure, Amphitrite, glazed white porcelain. Danish, Copenhagen, early 20th century. *Metropolitan Museum of Art, Gift of Bing & Grondahl, 1946*

535. LEFT. Group, The Good Samaritan, glazed stoneware. Danish, Copenhagen, c. 1923. *Royal Copenhagen Porcelain Manufactory*

538. Figure, In Surf, glazed stoneware. Danish, Copenhagen, 20th century. *Metropolitan Museum of Art, Gift of Bing & Grondahl, 1946*

539. LEFT. Jug, slipware. English, Winchcombe, made by Michael Cardew, c. 1938. *Victoria and Albert Museum*

540. ABOVE. Vase, stoneware. American, New York, Alfred, made by Thomas Samuel Haile, 1942. *Detroit Institute of Arts*

541. LEFT. Vase, glazed stoneware. Signed Artigas, Paris 1931. *Metropolitan Museum of Art, Purchased 1932, Edward C. Moore, Jr., Gift Fund*

542. UPPER LEFT. Vase, stoneware. Spanish, made by Artigas and Miro, 1941. *Musée National d' Art Moderne, Paris*

543. LEFT. Square dish, stoneware. Japanese, made by Shoji Hamada, after 1930. *Philadelphia Museum of Art: Gift of Mrs. Albert M. Greenfield*

544. Vase, Bizen ware type. Japanese, made by Kitaoji Rosanjin, 1953. *Museum of Modern Art, New York, Gift of the Japan Society*

THE TWENTIETH CENTURY
WORLD: ORNAMENTAL WARES

546. RIGHT. Figure of a female bluebird, porcelain. English, Worcester, 1937. *Metropolitan Museum of Art, Gift of Mr. and Mrs. Thomas F. Staley, 1960*

545. Vase, stoneware. English, Cornwall, St. Ives, made by Bernard Leach, c. 1958. *Metropolitan Museum of Art, Rogers Fund, 1960*

547. RIGHT. Hen coop, stoneware. Danish, Copenhagen, 1958. *Bing and Grondahl*

548. LOWER LEFT. Dolphins, biscuit porcelain. German, Bavaria, Selb, 1967. *Lorenz Hutschenreuther, A.G.*

549. LOWER RIGHT. Jug in the form of a rooster, glazed earthenware. Spanish, Valencia, Segorbe, 20th century, before 1938. *Hispanic Society of America*

550. Wine pitcher, tin-glazed earthenware. French, Vallauris, made by Pablo Picasso, c. 1951. *Victoria and Albert Museum*

551. Vase, glazed stoneware. Danish, Copenhagen, made by Axel Salto, 1937. *Kunstindustrimuseet, Copenhagen*

552. RIGHT. Vase, glazed stoneware. Danish, Copenhagen, made by Axel Salto, 1956. *Royal Copenhagen Porcelain Manufactory*

553. RIGHT. Saxbo ware bowl, glazed stoneware. Danish, 1960. *Kunstindustrimuseet, Copenhagen*

554. Vase, glazed stoneware. American, Michigan, Bloomfield Hills, made by Maija Grotell, 1958. *Photo Museum of Contemporary Crafts, New York*

556. Vase, glazed stoneware. American, California, Guerneville, made by Marguerite Wildenhain, 1964. *Photo Museum of Contemporary Crafts, New York*

555. RIGHT. Vase, glazed stoneware. American, California, Santa Susana, made by Gertrud and Otto Natzler, 1958. *Photo Museum of Contemporary Crafts, New York*

557. RIGHT. Vase, stoneware, English, London, made by Dan Arbeid, 1956. *Victoria and Albert Museum*

558. BELOW. Vase, earthenware. Hungarian, made by István Gádor, c. 1963. *Victoria and Albert Museum*

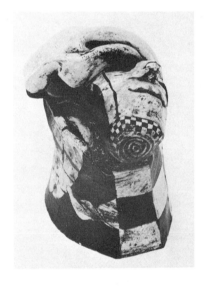

559. RIGHT. Checkered ghost, fired clay. American, California, Oakland, made by James Melchert, 1965. *Photo Museum of Contemporary Crafts, New York*

560. LEFT. Vase, glazed stoneware. American, California, Berkeley, made by Peter Voulkos, 1956. *Photo Museum of Contemporary Crafts, New York*

561. LOWER LEFT. Vase, stoneware. American, California, Berkeley, made by Peter Voulkos, 1962. *Smithsonian Institution, Washington, D.C.*

562. LOWER RIGHT. Vase, unglazed stoneware. American, New York, Alfred Station, made by Daniel Rhodes, 1967. *Johnson Wax Collection*

1. Grey cooking pottery with an entirely corrugated exterior surface, comprising thin constructional coils which were pinched into wavy form with notable effect. Ht. 6″

2. Pottery decorated in black over a white slip was introduced in Developmental Pueblo times. Many kinds of this so-called black-on-white are found during Developmental and Great Pueblo times. The forms are relatively few and simple; this asymmetrical variety perhaps derived from a bird form. The black ornament is produced either with a mineral paint or with pigment obtained by burning vegetable matter. The designs are essentially geometrical, and are in all sorts of combinations. Ht. 6½″

3. Effigy jar in black-and-white pottery. Ht. 7½″ (See 2)

4. This Mimbres black-on-white bowl is actually dark brown-on-white. The vessels were usually open bowls with the designs painted inside; most of them come from burials. Dia. 10″ (See 2)

5. About 1425 a kind of pottery called Sikyatki Polychrome was made by the Hopi, which is considered a high point of Southwestern Indian ceramics. Its outstanding feature is the painted asymmetrical design of highly stylized birds or parts of birds. This remarkably beautiful bowl was made by Nampeyo, the wife of a Tewa-speaking Hopi, one of the workmen of Dr. Walter Fewkes who in 1895 excavated the ruin of the Pueblo Sikyatki and discovered the beautiful old pottery.

6. This white-slipped hollow baby figure with red pigment on its helmet has the typical drooping mouth of the Olmec culture. Ht. 13⅜″

7. These clay figures were first found in some quantity in the early 1950's and are stylistically named for the site, Remojadas, with which they were first definitely associated. The very few complete figures found show them to be boy or girl dancers with a liveliness usually not found in Pre-Columbian pottery. Ht. 18¾″

8. In the early phase of the Classic Period a polychrome ware known as Tzakol was developed for ritual purposes. The designs in black and red were painted on an unslipped surface, usually cream or orange color. The polychrome decoration was geometrical or at least highly conventionalized; this example displays a rich variety of rectangles, steps and frets. Ht. 5¼″

9. The tall cylindrical vase or jar was the most characteristic shape of the second part of the Classic Period of Maya culture (known as the Tepeu phase) when polychrome painting achieved a brilliant level. This example with a continuous design of narrative painting in polychrome is especially striking. Ht. 5½″

10. Especially typical of Colima culture are these delightful effigies, the little fat hairless dogs of the region. Ht. 12⅕″

11. The singular, lighthearted manner in which the potters of the area portrayed, almost caricatured, the warriors is remarkably evident in this effigy vessel. Ht. 14¾″

12. A class of pleasing clay figures was made here, rather flatter than most, having features indicated by fillets of clay neatly applied to form slanting eyes. They are unpainted and unslipped, and are frequently referred to as the "pretty lady" type. Ht. 13¼″

13. Plumbate ware is perhaps the most remarkable ware in Central America. The ornament was incised before the application of the slip, which varied in color from greyish black to dark olive. Ht. 8½″

14. This bowl on a tripod base, like many bowls of this class, had the floor roughened by sharp criss-cross incising to make a grater for some kind of soft grain. Dia. 9¼″

15. The art style of the Chavín people, who appeared in the Central Andes about 800 B.C., was the first to overcome Peru's geographical barriers. They were devoted to a feline cult and signs of their cat worship are widely distributed through Peru. The North coast expression of the Chavín style is known as Cupisnique. The stirrup spout is the most striking feature of the majority of Cupisnique pots, a feature that remained in use

for over 2000 years. The Cupisnique pots, as in this dark monochrome example, are generally heavy and massive in comparison with later models. Ht. 7⅜″

16. The beginnings of the Mochica culture, which supplanted the Chavín culture, became evident toward the end of the Formative Period, which is about when the whistling jar came into use. Cream and orange slip on orange ware. Ht. 5¾″

17. The Mochica culture was developed in the Moche and nearby valleys by a remarkable people who produced some of the finest Pre-Columbian pottery. This stirrup vessel painted in red, cream and white attests to their skill in modeling. Ht. 12⅝″

18. In the South coastal region Peruvian pottery relied on polychrome painting which is in striking contrast to the North coast with its bichrome styles and marked emphasis on modeling. The globular jar with two spouts connected by a bridge was the traditional South coast form, just as the stirrup vessel was characteristic of the North. In this example the incised designs serve as an outline for the bright, resin-based pigments (yellow, red, and a very deep green) applied after firing. Ht. 3¾″

19. Pottery reached its highest development on the South coast in the Nazca culture. It was later than Paracas Cavernas, and probably contemporary with the Mochica culture in the North. Human figure jars generally have a single spout joined to the back of the figure by a bridge. Polychrome painted on a background slip. Ht. 8⅞″

20. Pottery of the central coast of Peru was overshadowed by the more vivid and original pottery of North and South Peru. Chancay dating from the late Post Classic Period is the most distinctive. Ht. 15⅖″

21. Modeled in the form of an animal playing a set of panpipes which obscure the whistle; negative-painted in black on red. Negative painting is highly characteristic of the Quimbaya zone which lies in and around the central part of the Cauca valley. It is either in two colors (black on red) or in three (black on white and red). This vessel is an interesting combination of the Peruvian style double whistling jar with the mammiform feet characteristic of Central America. Ht. 5⅛″

22. Decorated with stick-incised and applied nubbins. Quadruple handle, four spheres joined, with spout and filling hole. This type is very characteristic of Rewa 19th century forms, and varied from one to four spheres. Ht. 6¼″

ANCIENT WORLD

23. Many of the earliest signs of settled life so far discovered have appeared in plateau sites such as Catal Hüyük, c. 6500-5700 B.C., and Hacilar, c. 5700-5000 B.C. in Turkey, Sarab and Hajjifiruz in Iran and Jarmo, c. 6200-6000 B.C., and Hassuna, c. 5500-5000 B.C., in Iraq. When man learned the practice of irrigation around the end of the 5th millennium B.C., his center of activity shifted from the Turkish, Iranian, and Iraqi plateaus to the portion of Mesopotamia which lies between the Tigris and Euphrates rivers south of modern Baghdad. Throughout the early history of pottery-making there were two principal traditions; one a dark-surfaced burnished or polished ware, more often than not entirely undecorated, the other a painted ware. Evidence indicates that painted wares followed an initial

stage when only plain wares were made, but that the time intervening was not great. This example of painted pottery from Hacilar on the plateau of southwestern Turkey is painted in a red-brown pigment on a cream-slip ground, both being highly burnished. The technical quality of the fabric and the well-executed geometric patterns mark a high point in the early ceramics of Anatolia.

24. Painted pottery was made at an equally early stage in the eastern part of Persia and Mesopotamia, the former long remaining the principal center of painted ceramics. In these two regions the first two thousand years of settlement witnessed the making of what are probably the finest of all Near Eastern painted wares. Before

5000 B.C. the agricultural communities in northern Mesopotamia were producing a luxury fabric named Samarra after the site where it was first discovered, and before 4500 B.C. a highly sophisticated polychrome pottery named Halafian after Tell Halaf in northern Syria where it was first isolated. Decorated with geometric and natural designs painted in bistre and black paint combined with shades of red, Halafian ware when fired exhibits a fine finish unequaled by Near Eastern potters for centuries afterward.

25. At about the same time, the first known settlers in southern Mesopotamia produced painted pottery showing some northern Halafian influences. Called Ubaid ware after the site where much of it was excavated, this pottery consists of fine and coarse wares made by hand or on a slow wheel. A variety of vessels painted with geometric patterns in brown or black paint were fired to a reddish or yellowish-green color. Although there is much merit in the wares of the Ubaid culture (c. 4500-3500 B.C.), they can come only as an anticlimax to those of Tell Halaf.

26. Beginning at a time roughly contemporary with the first painted pottery of Mesopotamia, the earliest communities on the Persian plateau had developed their own particular styles of painted pottery. The finest of the early wares were those made shortly after the beginning of the 4th millennium B.C. Though the painted pottery at Tall-i Bakun in the Persepolis region did not achieve quite the degree of sophistication of the superbly elegant painted pottery of Susa, known as Susa A, predominantly a funerary ware, Tall-i Bakun was not without highly skilled potters. On this bowl the design has probably been abstracted from ibex horns. The broad, confident sweep of the painter's brush displays remarkable dexterity and the sensitive adaptation of design to space is equally notable. Dia. 7⅜"

27. Decorated with vertically-directed geometric motifs; the shape may have ultimately derived from an animal horn and would probably have been used as a drinking vessel. Ht. 8⅛"

28. The introduction of the potter's wheel and kiln now permitted new forms and a new control, as for example this large storage jar from Tepe Sialk in Iran. The carefully painted paneled decoration comprising three panels of ibexes alternating with three geometrical panels in dark brown on a buff ground represents another exciting high point in Near Eastern pottery making. Ht. 20⅞"

29. More restrained and relying more on form, the monochrome wares were the mainstay of pottery production. As with painted wares, they attained their greatest heights in the early settlements of the Ancient World. The initial production of both light and dark surfaced, well-polished or burnished wares was started in West Central and Southern Anatolia from earliest times, a tradition which was to continue in the ensuing centuries. The form of this example of black-burnished ware with a cutaway spout is pleasingly effective. Ht. 5⅛"

30. Intended for suspension. Unglazed dark-surfaced grey pottery with incised decoration filled with white; the birds and some horizontal and vertical bands have been painted a dull reddish color. Directly under each lug, close to the base, is a hole. Perhaps the most interesting deduction to be drawn from the example is the persistence of the Persian tradition for painted pottery.

31. Painted pottery was relatively rare in the Near East during the greater part of the 3rd millennium when mass movements of people into the Near East from the north brought with them a tradition of dark-surfaced burnished pottery. It was only with the renascence of Eastern influence toward the end of the 3rd millennium that painted pottery was again favored. In Anatolia a new painted pottery appeared about 2300 B.C. when groups from the East settled in the region of Cappadocia. The wares, made entirely by hand, were decorated with geometric motifs and paneled ornament reminiscent of early Persian wares and indicating the origin of the cultural influences. This example with a high handle (restored) and pointed base has an orange body with black-painted decoration. Ht. 2⅜"

32. Though few productions at this time compare with the early painted wares of Anatolia, Mesopotamia and Persia, the finer wares were more plentiful. The form and decoration of this example with an unglazed reddish body and blackish-brown geometric ornament is remarkably pleasing to the eye. The tripod support

which lends itself to an almost infinite range of variation has been handled with remarkable sophistication. Ht. 6¼"

33. The decorative inventiveness of the early potters of Iran, their sense of form and balance, the assurance with which they executed their designs, transformed these vessels of simple clay into pleasing works of art. This example, probably intended for ritual purposes, is painted in red pigment on a polished buff clay slip. Ht. 14½"

34. Long before clay was used for the manufacture of utilitarian vessels ancient man had learned to fashion and bake human and animal figures of clay for magical or religious purposes. For this reason he was aware of its plastic and durable qualities which, in time, he was to develop into a full-scale industry to meet the ciety. This unique clay figure with hair indicated by applied bitumen was found in the loose soil. It is believed that this class of figures with bird-shaped heads, square, broad shoulders and the prominence of breasts represents a goddess or demon.

35. This figure molded of reddish-buff clay, with applied pads of clay, possesses the formative charm of a gingerbread figure.

36. About the beginning of the 2nd millennium lamps became customary; they were a clay version of a simple bowl form first used in stone from about the 9th to the 7th millennium B.C. The Bronze Age forms usually have only one spout. Ht. 2⅛"

37. In early Pre-Dynastic times the Egyptian potters had learned how to make well-shaped vessels with a red-polished surface, purposely carbonized around the top to a shiny black for decoration. The red color was produced by a wash of fine red clay. The black is an oxide of iron obtained by limiting the access of air in the process of baking, which it has been suggested was done by placing the pot's mouth down in the ashes, which was the part to be burnt black. An interesting feature of this black-topped vessel is the relief decoration on either side in the form of an ape. Ht. 10"

38. This class of painted ware using white decoration on a polished red ground was introduced in Egypt early in the 4th millennium B.C.

Geometric patterns occasionally mingled with animal and human figures are characteristic.

39. In the latter half of the 4th millennium B.C. the Egyptian potters turned to a light-surfaced ware. Using mat red to dark brown pigment, they covered this finer buff-colored surface with human and divine figures, reed ships with branches as sails and bearing emblems on the standards resembling those which later belonged to the different Nomes or provinces of Egypt; rows of wild animals and birds and other haphazard space-fillers. The wavy lines represent water and the triangles desert. This haphazard decorative manner also appears in the earliest Egyptian wall-paintings found in a tomb of the later Gerzean period at Hierakonpolis. This example is one of the finest known.

40. Evidence suggests that wares of powdered quartz were made by 3100 B.C. As early as the 20th century B.C. painting was being effectively done in black pigment on turquoise blue glazed quartz frit ware. This example from the tomb of the Steward Sonbi at Meir belongs to the well-known turquoise blue glazed hippopotami of this period with the reeds and water plants in purplish black upon their bodies to indicate their habitat. L. 8"

41. Kohl tube in the shape of a reed, the common container for kohl. Reign of Amenhotep III. Inscribed in black with the names of Amenhotep III and the Royal Daughter and Royal Wife Sitamun (a rare mention of this second Queen). Kohl tube container in the form of a palm column with pierced and low relief decoration. Reign of Amenhotep III. The scene depicts cats flanking figures of goddesses Hathor and Taweret and a band of papyrus umbels and buds.

42. Evidence suggests that toward the end of the XVIII Dynasty the Egyptian potter extended his color range for glazes to embrace black, red, apple-green, purple, yellow and white. This example of an amphora with two handles is of rare white, decorated with petals, blossoms and buds of the blue lotus, *lotus caerulea*, in blue and black. Ht. 6"

43. During the XXII Dynasty a series of these fragile lotiform goblets with relief decoration were made in the workshops of Hermopolis. In the present example the scene represents life in the marshes and recalls the early life of the

God Horus who was born and hidden by his mother Isis in the swamps of the Delta. Birds and animals are pictured being caught among the papyrus plants and taken away in light skiffs. A band of swimming fishes above another band representing water helps to place the scene. This superb and miraculously preserved goblet is the best known of the series. Ht. 5¾″

44. The firing temperature for the great majority of the earliest pottery was relatively low, resulting in a surface partly porous and fritted where impurities had burnt out of the clay. A simple method to lessen the porosity was to smooth the surface of the vessel while it was still wet so that any imperfections would be covered over before firing. In this example of polished red ware a more ambitious and also very early method was used; that is, to paint the outside of the vessel with a slip of a very highly refined clay. On drying this "coating" could be burnished with a pebble or bone, and perhaps polished after firing. The resultant luster not only made the surface more attractive but also increased its practical value. Both of these methods were practiced before 5000 B.C. in some parts of the Near East. The pronounced skeuomorphic character of this vessel (copying the features appropriate to one substance in another) is a forerunner of the influence of Pop Art in ceramics of today. Ht. 8″

45. This form of jug with a tall cutaway spout may possibly reflect the influence from nearby Anatolia. The entire surface is coated with a well-polished red slip enriched with an incised geometrical pattern. Ht. 10⅜″ (See preceding)

46. With horned handle; belongs to a class of early White Slip wares of the Late Bronze Age which were exported to the mainland in considerable quantities. The decoration, frequently in an attractive reddish brown, was mainly inspired by the stitchery of leather vessels. Ht. 10⁷⁄₁₆″

47. One of the most successful products of the potters of Cyprus. This class of pottery was widely used in trade in the Late Bronze Age throughout the Near East to provide containers for such luxury items as scents, cosmetics and drugs. The ware is made of highly refined clays, fired at a high temperature and finished with polished brown or black slips. This example is unusually tall. Ht. 17¹³⁄₁₆″ (See 44)

48. This style of painted decoration on a white ground with a minimum of secondary decorative detail was one of the most effective of all Cypriot products. Ht. 11″

49. Vasiliki style; the mottled decoration on this so-called teapot jug has been done with fire; belongs to Pre-Palace period.

50. Kamares style; so-called beaked jug painted in white and light brownish-red on a black ground. This class of light-on-dark appears in the last phase of Early Minoan and remains characteristic of Middle Minoan. The stylized motifs probably derive from nature; overall decoration was favored. Ht. 10¼″

51. Floral style, painted in dark colors on a light ground. In the Late Minoan period naturalistic motifs of plants and marine life were used for the overall decoration. The Cretans appreciated the decorative value of flowers. The wall paintings at Amnisos, Knossos and elsewhere offered a wealth of flower and plant representations which certainly served as models for the vase painters. The Cretans, who had a lively use of color and decorative sense, painted lilies, crocuses, grasses, reeds and the like on their Floral style vases. Papyrus in its natural or stylized form occurs often; the plant itself must have been introduced from the mainland. Besides the overall decoration a more frequent use of floral friezes lending a horizontal emphasis began to occur.

52. Marine style, the aristocrat of Late Minoan art. Eastern Crete may have been the home of the Marine style, at least the finest examples have been found there, especially the well-known Octopus stirrup-vase from Gournia, the most ambitious example of the Marine style. This Octopus stirrup-vase, also excavated at Gournia, is amazingly similar.

53. Palace style; three-handled jar with papyrus decoration. Shows how Mycenaean and Minoan combined in Crete. Ht. 27⁵⁄₁₆″

54. The form of this high-stemmed goblet has been evolved from the popular so-called Ephyrean goblet, the name being derived from an old name for Corinth, Ephyre, in which vicinity this class was first found. On this example Mycenaean restraint has reduced the Cretan marine motif to a lifeless linear style.

55. The Marine style decoration based on Cretan prototypes clearly reveals the Mycenaean tendency to formality and stylization. Ht. 10¼"

56. Most surviving examples of the Mycenaean pictorial style have been found in Cyprus. Chariots and the hunt were favorite subjects for pictorial scenes, most of which are found on kraters. Probably the Mycenaean vase painters used contemporary wall paintings for inspiration, but they lacked the talent to adapt the work successfully.

57. Decorated with funeral scenes; Prothesis (lying in state). The upper frieze shows the dead man on a bier surrounded by mourners. The lower shows the three-horse chariots and warriors, some of them carrying shields, which escorted the funeral procession to the grave. Vases of this kind were erected as monuments on graves. There is a hole in the bottom of the vase through which libations were poured. Ht. 40½"

58. Depicts combat between Herakles and the Centaur Nessos who had attacked his bride Deianeira. On shoulder horses grazing; on neck lion attacking deer. The painting is identified with the Orientalizing phase which occurred between the Geometric and the mature Attic black-figure style. Ht. 42¾"

59. Animal friezes relate to the Orientalizing phase.

60. Painted by Exekias, one of the leading painters of Attic black-figure ware. Depicts a marriage procession; perhaps representing the marriage of Herakles and Hebe.

61. Attributed to the Euphéletos Painter, found at Vulci. The event for which the prize was given was a foot race. Reverse side depicts Athena between columns surmounted by cocks. Bears inscription, *I am* [a prize] *from the games at Athens.* Ht. 24½"

62. Attributed to the Andokides Painter. The rim of the vase coated with white slip bears two subsidiary scenes painted in black-figure technique. In each Herakles wrestles with the Nemean lion. The principal scenes enclosed in two large panels are in the red-figure technique. On the front Herakles is shown struggling with Apollo for the possession of the Delphic tripod. Each protagonist is accompanied by an interested spectator. To the left of Herakles stands his protector Athena, holding her owl in her hand; behind Apollo is his sister Artemis, holding a bow and arrow and smelling a flower. The reverse scene is more tranquil, depicting Dionysos with two of his followers, a satyr and a maenad. Ht. 22⅝"

63. Made as a grave offering; reputed to be from Thebes, white ground with outline drawing and color. Depicts child leading his mother to Charon's boat which ferries the souls of the dead across the water to another world. Probably by the Painter of Munich 2335, which simply means that a key piece to a particular style of painting is in the Munich Museum (2335 being the accession number) and that this vase is painted in a similar manner. This system was devised as in most instances Greek vase painters did not sign their work.

64. It has been said of the Tanagra figures that they are all sisters but few of them are twins. Though the same mold was used many times variety was achieved by such means as attaching the arms in different ways, changing the pose of the head, adding different attributes and the like. These slight differences introduced a refreshing element of originality and saved the statuettes from being monotonous. This example wears a himation and a sun hat (tholia) and carries a fan. Ht. 7½"

65. Figure of the goddess of animals is molded in relief on each handle of this graceful vase. Such remarkably pleasing proportions are relatively rare in Bucchero ware.

66. Etruscan vase painting, admittedly derivative, took much of its technique but not always its inspiration from Greek styles. However, the Etruscan genius for blending and assimilating these influences produced in the end an unmistakably Etruscan work, quite distinct from its Greek models. The painting on this example is attributed to the Paris Painter. As is usual on neck amphorae of this shape there are several pictures which depict banqueters, heralds and centaur, neatherds and bull. Ht. 13¹³⁄₁₆"

67. Unguent flask used for the pouring of libations; on either side a floating female figure showing the influence of the Greek outline style of drawing. Notably lively in form and decoration.

68. An appealing example of genre executed in a mannered style. Ht. 6"

69. Kalathiskos Dancers; Classical style. Signed by Pilemo, workman in the Marcus Perennius Tigranus factory. Molds of this kind were made by impressing with pattern stamps and rouletting the horizontal borders. Details were occasionally incised by hand. Dia. 7¼"

70. Molded relief decoration in the Classical style; perhaps from the workshop of M. Perennius Bargathes. Ht. 7³⁄₁₆"

71. Found at Felixstowe. In this example the trailed slip technique has been combined with the use of decorative motifs pressed in a mold and then luted to the body with a remarkably lively effect. Ht. 7¾"

72. With trailed slip decoration, the form bears a striking similarity to Celtic metal work. Ht. 6¼"

73. Molded relief decoration; depicting on one side a satyr riding a sea goat; other side a Maenad riding a sea panther. This class of color-glazed wares constituted one of the most luxurious kinds of pottery in the worldly Eastern Mediterranean centers of Hellenized Roman culture. The style of decoration and the form of the ring handle on this cup, which is one of the most common shapes for vessels of this class, has been derived from contemporary repoussé metal work. Ht. 2¾"

74. Belongs to same class of color-glazed wares as the scyphus. Ht. 5⅓" (See preceding)

75. In the Roman period the glaze of the Egyptian quartz frit ware tends to be stronger in tone and more glasslike in appearance. In this example the decoration in high relief was apparently done by carving. It is possible that this decorative method may trace unbroken ancestry to dynastic times when objects of glazed quartz frit ware were enriched with carving and occasionally even by piercing to produce an openwork design. The usual decoration is mixed Egyptian and classical, the latter generally predominating. Ht. 7½"

76. With incised decoration of ivy band and rope pattern. The decorative technique of incising exploits with consummate success the brilliant glaze coloring as the incised designs appear as darker lines where the glaze flows into them. Most of the glazed quartz frit ware seems to date from the first three centuries A.D., but it appears likely that the method of making a brilliant turquoise blue in an alkaline glaze survived into Islamic times. Ht. 6¾"

77. With applied relief decoration. Roman-Egyptian potters of glazed quartz frit ware obtained this kind of relief decoration by applying shreds of the body material, generally to suggest laurel wreaths colored green on a dark blue or deep purple ground. Ht. 6¾"

78. Reputedly found at Salemiyeh, Syria. A comparable technique to the Egyptian glazed quartz frit ware was used in Syria and in the western provinces of the Parthian kingdom. Here, however, the body of this alkaline-glazed pottery was far more plastic. Parthian pottery was made in considerable quantities; it was not as brilliant in its blue and green tones as the Egyptian ware. Usually it was simply decorated with incised lines; occasionally, as in this example, pads with impressed designs were applied to the surface for decoration. Despite its elementary character it was significant as a forerunner of the alkaline-glazed pottery of the Islamic Near East. Ht. 14⅛"

79. Essentially, prehistoric pottery in Europe was without important significance for the subsequent development of ceramic art. This food vessel was probably made by semi-Nomadic people. Of coiled construction; with small molded lugs and profuse incised and impressed herringbone and zigzag decoration. Ht. 5½"

80. With circular impressions arranged vertically. Made by the Beaker Folk who probably used it as a drinking vessel. Ht. 7⅜"

FAR EASTERN WORLD

81. Painted red, yellow and black. For a long time the Chinese followed the custom well known in other countries of placing in the tomb of a deceased person models in clay of his household goods and of his retainers and servants. The furnishings of the Han graves were occasionally

very elaborate, including such things as models of houses, farm buildings with grain towers, sheep, pigs, dogs and their kennels, ox-carts, cooking stoves, domestic vessels of all sorts, servants to wait upon the deceased, dancers and musicians to entertain and guardian spirits to protect him. Ht. 52⅜"

82. Lead-glazed earthenware, with designs molded in relief. So-called "hill" jar because the cover in the form of a conventionalized group of hills represents the Islands or Mountains of the Blest, important in the mythology of Taoism which gained many followers in the Han period. Ht. 8⅝"

83. Lead-glazed earthenware. Lead glaze was introduced in the Han period, perhaps from Western Asia. Ht. 12⅛"

84. Warrior figures such as this model were to protect the deceased, perhaps from demons. Ht. 14¼"

85. One of a set of six figures, covered with unfired pigments. Ht. c. 5½"

86. One of a set of nine figures, unglazed pottery with traces of a brilliant polychromy. Notable for a fluency of line and a delicate sense of balance in composition. Ht. 5¾"

87. Westerners, Central Asiatics and peoples from the southeast are found in tomb pottery. They served the Chinese in different ways, such as grooms for camels and horses, and as in this example a merchant. .

88. Green and yellow lead-glazed earthenware. During the T'ang dynasty the fashion for furnishing tombs with all manner of figures must have ultimately reached the dimensions of a mania; it is recorded that in 741 an Imperial order was necessary to restrict the number of objects that might be placed in a single tomb. Many of the better class of figures were now lead glazed, frequently with a rich green and yellowish-brown, probably obtained by dusting onto the unglazed surface the metallic oxides which were in firing taken up by the lead glaze. In general, the T'ang modeler's art was marked by a new naturalism and lively movement. Ht. 33⅞"

89. Carved with overlapping lotus petals under a transparent olive-green glaze. Inscriptions on two extant examples of this class of funerary

vessel show that they were intended to contain wine; possibly the spouts having holes that do not enter the main body were to hold flowers. The ancient Yüeh kilns achieved their acme of excellence in the Five Dynasties period, 907-959, and exercised a strong formative influence on Sung wares. The green was highly esteemed and it is recorded that in the 10th century it became a private color (pi sê) reserved for the Princes of Yüeh and Wu who governed Hangchow, 907-976. Ht. 16"

90. Engraved lily design under a thick ivory-white glaze. Ting ware chiefly comprising bowls and dishes is one of the classical Sung wares made for the Court. The distinction between the two principal varieties, white Ting and flour Ting is not very marked. The bowls seem to have been fired in an inverted position, and the rims, being unglazed, are frequently mounted with bands of metal.

91. Covered with a thick creamy-white glaze. The cup or bowl stand was a characteristic form for Sung wares.

92. Probably the rarest of all Sung wares produced for only a few years to the order of the Northern Court at Ju Chou (modern Lin-ju Hsien) in Honan province in the early 12th century. Characteristics of the ware are a carefully prepared buff stoneware body and a highly refined light greenish-blue glaze, deliberately marked with a delicate crackle of "broken-ice" fissures. Probably fewer than thirty examples are extant outside of China.

93. Glazed grey porcelaneous stoneware broadly crackled; one of the classical Sung wares made for the Court. Its great beauty depends almost entirely on the quality of the glaze which is thick but very smooth and fine-grained, dense and only slightly translucent.

94. Of great interest and beauty is the painted (in black or brown) and incised class of Tz'u Chou wares with remarkably bold, free-flowing designs. In this example the body was primed with a dressing or wash of slip. The design was painted in black; later with a blunt instrument the lines were scratched or incised through to the slip; finally covered with a lead glaze.

95. Covered with a rich and variegated glaze, the effect of furnace transmutation. The forms of Chün ware are chiefly from bronze prototypes.

96. Decorated with a peony design under a lustrous and smooth olive-green celadon glaze. Ht. 8¾″

97. Covered with a lustrous black glaze, freely and thickly applied, marked "like hare's fur." Chien ware owes its great and distinctive charm to these intense black glazes with brown and silvery markings.

98. Decorated with three fishes in underglaze copper-red. Painting in underglaze red was fully mastered in the Hsüan Tê period, in fact it was famous for it.

99. Broad jar of potiche form; design of clouds and dragons painted in underglaze Moham-medan blue. The dragon, traditional symbol of supernatural powers and the authority of the Emperor, was a widely popular motif on Chinese porcelains, particularly in his natural habitat of water and clouds. Though underglaze blue painting was done throughout the Ming dynasty, there were two periods of greatest activity and artistic achievement, namely the reigns of Hsüan Tê and Chia Ching.

100. In this example of Three-Color ware me-dium-temperature glazes were applied directly to a pre-fired but unglazed (biscuit) porcelain. To keep the glazes apart the designs were outlined in applied "cloisons" of clay serving as dikes. (In other examples the designs might be either incised or executed in carved openwork, in the case of the latter the vessel was double-walled.) This beau-tifully modeled gallipot with a dark blue ground, decorated with lotus plants in turquoise, yellow and white, has all the colorful richness peculiar to this technique. Ht. 14⅜″

101. Reticulated vase decorated with Taoist figures in a garden; using pale aubergine, yellow and beige medium-temperature glazes on a blue ground. Ht. 14″ (See preceding)

102. Painted in underglaze blue. The animal, bird, plant and tree motifs are taken from Taoist mythology and are symbolic of abundance, that is, a full and long life. Ht. 18″

103. Painted in underglaze copper red. Bowls were one of the shapes most often found among wares of Imperial quality, and floral scrolls one of the most frequent forms of decoration. Dia. 14″

104. In the 16th century Chinese porcelain sometimes found its way to England overland by way of the Levant or by sea around the Cape of Good Hope. As it was extremely rare the most skillful English silversmiths were often com-missioned to make mounts for it. The bowl is decorated with a design of peony and phoenix in underglaze blue.

105. The fullness of her face suggests a Late Ming date. Enameled on the biscuit and covered with a transparent colorless glaze. Bears the in-scription *Made as an offering of respect to Te Tse*. She holds in her right hand a ju-i scepter. Ht. 14½″

106. Under K'ang Hsi the principal polychrome enameling style is the so-called Famille Verte (green family). In a distinctive and favorite variant the Famille Verte enamels were applied as glazes on the biscuit, in colors limited prncipally to green, yellow and aubergine-purple, with draw-ing in black. To this variety belong the sumptuous Famille Noire wares with a rich black ground and the Famille Jaune with a yellow ground. Tall ornamental vases generally decorated with flowers are typical of this class. In this example the Famille Noire ground enhances the plum tree breaking into spring blossom painted in Famille Verte enamels on biscuit. Ht. 27½″

107. Ch'ing monochromes are among the most remarkable technical accomplishments of the Chinese potter. The interest in them rests not only in the beauty of color and texture of their glazes but also in their classic forms. Clair de Lune is one of the rarer glazes of the period. Ht. 6¼″

108. Perhaps the most important examples of Fukien porcelain are the porcelain figures, and of these the best known is Kuan Yin. The bold and sensitive modeling with an admirable sense of rhythm was enhanced by the rare quality of the material. The edges invariably remain sharp and the most delicate detail is never lost under the thick glaze. The peach is the symbol of im-mortality. Ht. 15″

109. Decorated in Famille Verte enamels applied on unglazed (biscuit) porcelain. Enamels painted on biscuit have a softer, richer quality than when painted on glaze. Each with a Chou character on forehead; base pierced at center in form of a Ju-i scepter head. Ht. 14¾″; 14½″

110. On a wood stand; a carved wood cover has been substituted for the original porcelain cover.

The entire surface is covered with delicate plum blossoms reserved in white on a pure sapphire underglaze blue ground broken by a network of lines resembling cracked ice. The design, one of the best known in Chinese ceramic art, symbolizes the approach of spring as the aged plum tree bursts once more into blossoms, which occurs about the time of the Chinese New Year, that is, earliest spring. Ht. 11$\frac{11}{16}$″

111. Stoneware teapots were the chief production at Yi Hsing, and were much exported along with tea to Europe. They were supposed to be the best ware for brewing tea and were imitated in Holland by Arij de Milde, in England by the Elers and in Germany by Böttger. Thus they were the original European teapots. Ht. 3$\frac{1}{4}$″

112. Under Yung Chêng the Famille Rose palette had largely supplanted the Famille Verte style of enameling. It derived its name from the dominant pink enamel newly introduced from Europe. Famille Rose colors were almost invariably opaque; an opaque white was freely used, permitting the blending of many shades not previously available.

113. Copper-red flambé glaze streaked with purple and opalescent blue. No doubt such glaze effects as occur in this vase inspired the work of a number of late 19th century artist-potters striving for vertical line effects, a feature of Art Nouveau ceramics. Potters of the 1900 era also made use of this form.

114. Five-piece garniture decorated in colored enamels; two raised medallions on either side reserved in a stippled ground with slightly raised stylized floral pattern. The larger medallion bears the arms, Rigby. Ht. 11$\frac{1}{2}$″ or less

115. Decorated in underglaze blue; the form was copied from a characteristic English silver punch bowl. Dia. 12$\frac{5}{8}$″

116. So-called States pattern, as the border contains the names of the States of the Union. One of a set given to Martha Washington by André Everard Van Braam Houckgeest, commercial director of the Dutch East India Company in Canton from 1788 to 1795. Bears monogram of Martha Washington.

117. Plate from George Washington's Cincinnati porcelain service with underglaze blue Fitzhugh border. In the center is a nymph bearing the insignia of the Order of the Cincinnati. Dia. 9$\frac{1}{2}$″

118. Decorated in the Fitzhugh pattern centering the American eagle and shield. L. 18$\frac{1}{2}$″

119. Inlaid celadon; with incised decoration inlaid in white and black slips under a celadon glaze showing a fine crazing. Inlaid designs are the most famous Korean decoration. They range from small-scale starlike flowers to the firm naturalism of flowering plants, cloud scrolls, cranes and other birds as seen on this gallipot. In material the Korai celadons form a single class, having a hard grey porcelaneous stoneware body.

120. Painted celadon with incised details under a thin transparent bluish-green glaze. This class of celadon wares painted in brownish-black began to be made toward the end of the Yi period when relations with China became closer. It is reputed that the introduction of painting on pottery was due to the example of Tz'u Chou wares. They are often called by the Japanese name e-gorai (painted Korean).

121. Painted in underglaze copper-red; admirable use was made of copper-red during the Yi dynasty.

122. Later in the Yi dynasty perhaps not before the 17the century, porcelain began to be made in Korea. The forms for this class of ware are characteristically Korean, possessing strength and elegant simplicity.

123. Greyish stoneware with incised decoration under a celadon glaze. Celadon wares made here at this time reveal in their forms a distinctive and typically Siamese combination of strength and elegance. Ht. 9$\frac{3}{4}$″

124. Celadon ware with confronted heads in relief on lids; incised details; rims of top and bottom mounted in silver gilt with scalloped edge; hinged at one side. Ht. 7$\frac{3}{8}$″

125. It is thought that the peculiar shape of this class of drinking vessel is of early Indian origin. This example, which has a light stoneware body, is decorated in underglaze brown on a greenish-grey ground. Ht. 6″

126. Greyish stoneware, painted and glazed; pierced top of head and through extended right hand. In lands where writing is done with a brush the water-dropper is a customary accessory of writing equipment. Ht. 4″

127. Coarse buff-red earthenware of rope and basket work pattern. Displays notable elaboration and refinement both in form and design. Ht. 15″

128. The Haniwa sculptural figures evolved from the clay cylinders which were erected above the enormous burial tumuli customary at this time. They represent men and women and also include models of animals and buildings. Swiftly worked in soft clay, their features are singularly impressionistic. Ht. 54″

129. One of Japan's two most celebrated tea bowls. Opaque white Shino glaze with design painted in iron-rust brown showing a bamboo trellis, in allusion to which the tea bowl's poetic name, U-no-hanagaki, literally The Flower Trellis of Utsugi Blossom, has been devised.

130. This very low-fired bowl covered with a thick, soft, black lead-glaze is attributed to Chojiro, 1515-1592. Raku ware is peculiarly Japanese, devised for use in the tea ceremony. No other pottery better exemplifies the fastidious taste of the tea masters than an original Raku tea bowl with its primitive simplicity of form, its crude uneven modeling, and its thick glaze which is pleasant to the lips.

131. Brownish-colored clay body covered with a thick yellow glaze in which are spots of copper-green. Seto ware has always been highly prized by the tea masters. The aesthetic qualities of the tea bowl rest in fulfilling its function. Its soft, coarse clay is a nonconductor of heat, so that although filled with hot tea, it may be grasped with comfort by the fingers. Its shape allows it to be passed from one person to another without fear of spilling, and its slightly rolled-in rim with thick glaze enhances the pleasure of tea drinking.

132. Square earthenware dish with a design of stripes.

133. One of Japan's two most celebrated tea bowls. So named in allusion to the glaze effect. Among the many amateur potters who produced Raku tea bowls, the most famous was Koetsu, a celebrated painter, calligrapher, lacquer artist and tea master.

134. Brownish-colored clay body covered with a greenish-brown lead glaze; decorated with a design of flowering grasses executed in swift brush strokes.

135. Chocolate-colored clay body covered with a pale greenish glaze.

136. Lustrous black, lacquer-like glaze and a design of round fans in red and light-green overglaze enamel colors with touches of silver and gold. The traditional Japanese characteristic of balancing motifs against bare, undecorated areas is exemplified in this tea bowl.

137. The painting in dark brown under a greyish cream-colored glaze has been executed in a masterly style of swift, economical brush strokes. This style was preferred by Kenzan; however, it was his brother, the famous painter Korin, who decorated this dish. It depicts Huang Shan-Ku, a Chinese legendary personage, observing birds in flight. Bears a stanza of poetry.

138. The plastic character of the fine clay used is supposed to account for the quality of the numerous excellent figures, produced principally in the 18th century.

139. Lotus leaf and textile design painted in underglaze blue and overglaze polychrome enamels, in which green, purple and yellow are prominent.

140. Design of peonies and lions in overglaze enamels.

141. Design of horse chestnuts in polychrome enamels.

142. Design copied from silk brocade patterns in underglaze blue, overglaze enamels and gilding. A fine example of the so-called brocaded Imari.

143. Painted in underglaze blue, overglaze polychrome enamels and gilding. Dishes of the brocaded Imari class were sometimes painted with ships of the Dutch East India Company and figures of Dutch traders in contemporary costumes.

144. Plum tree and deer design in overglaze polychrome enamels. In the Western world, Kakiemon is perhaps the most familiar of all Japanese porcelain. European factories copied it freely. At Chantilly it was much copied from examples in the collection of the Prince de Condé.

145. Plum and bamboo design in overglaze enamels.

146. Peonies and phoenix design in overglaze enamels.

147. Design of camellias and banded hedge in overglaze enamels.

148. This form of shallow dish or deep plate on a rather high foot rim was used to serve main courses at formal meals and was very typical of Nabishima production. Almost always the Nabishima potter decorated the foot rim with an underglaze blue comb-tooth pattern which became its most distinguishing characteristic.

149. Wisteria branches painted in underglaze blue.

150. Buddhist emblem within a circle of Ju-i

motifs, and wild orchids, painted in underglaze blue.

151. Design of cherry and maple trees in colored enamels.

152. Ming Three-Color ware was the inspiration for Kairaku-en porcelain. In this example the design of flowering grasses has been outlined with a slight ridge which effectively separates one colored glaze from the other.

153. Painted in underglaze blue in imitation of a distinctive class of 17th century Chinese porcelain, known as Shonsui ware.

ISLAMIC POTTERY

154. The Near Eastern potters were never able to make true porcelain because of the lack of suitable clays. For a time they imitated its whiteness by covering buff earthenware with an opaque glaze containing ashes of tin. This example was then decorated with a deep cobalt blue sparingly applied with a few quick brush strokes in small scale patterns. Dia. 8"

155. Under the Abbasid Caliphs in Mesopotamia the potters of the 9th and 10th centuries discovered and perfected the technique of painting in metallic "gold luster." The greenish-yellow luster decoration depicts three stylized peacocks. Ht. 6⅜"

156. Under the Samanid dynasty, 878-999, in the eastern Persian province of Khurasan, the potters discovered the "secret" of painting beneath a fluid lead glaze without the danger of having the design destroyed or dissolved in the firing. This technique has been aptly called slip-painting, as the metallic oxides used for the colors were combined with an earth medium that had a similar composition to the clay slip and so formed a bond strong enough not to be dissolved by the liquid glaze. In this example the slip-painted pattern is in reddish-brown on a yellow slip ground; the whole is covered with a shining translucent glaze. Dia. 13½"

157. Sari wares, a group of slip-painted wares related to the Nishapur pottery, derive their name from the small town of Sari in Mazanderan close to the southeast corner of the Caspian Sea. They are chiefly in the form of small conical bowls on

which are represented walking birds amidst flowers on long stalks and pseudo-Kufic inscriptions. In this example the white slip ground is slip-painted in yellow, brown and green under a transparent lead-glaze. Dia. 7¾" Ht. 3"

158. The "secret" for luster painting passed to Egypt under the Fatimid rulers, 969-1171. This example in greenish-yellow luster painted in a masterful style on a white glazed ground is signed by the artist Muslim, one of the two leading painters among the many artists known (S'ad being the other). Dia. 10"

159. In their attempt to emulate Sung Ting ware the Persian potters used a new composite paste of powdered quartz and alkaline frit. The glaze was also made of a similar alkaline frit thus guaranteeing that it would adhere. The decoration consisted chiefly of incised floral designs. These white wares were perhaps the pre-eminent achievement of the Persian potters. Essentially they were so fine that the overall effect is that of true porcelain. White wares are attributed to Rayy and Kashan and can be dated to the middle and second half of the 12th century. Dia. 7¾"

160. In the shape of a bird with a human face; body decorated with delicate reliefs. The application of the face to what appears to be the body of a bird recalls the mythological figure of the harpy which is frequently found in Islamic art. Ht. 3⅜" (See preceding)

161. Hard light-colored composite body. Bears on its hump an enclosed baldachin saddle of

the type used by Muslim women. Perhaps it was made for the particular pleasure of the nobles of the court. Through the centuries the turquoise blue alkaline glaze has changed to a silvery tone. Ht. 8"

162. With an openwork outer wall painted in blue and some black under a transparent turquoise blue glaze; inner wall covered with the same monochrome glaze. Neck with deer, body with two pair of confronted sphinxes and harpies, dogs coursing hares, amid arabesques of dark blue in slight relief. Persian inscriptions reserved on black bands above and below pierced design. (Trans. upper) *Your pride is freed entirely from the net! Alas! Your image be freed from my heart! If you hasten to be free for other bonds and if you fear a delay, Be freed from the net!* (Trans. lower) *My hand and my lips are accustomed to the lock of hair of my beloved; My heart is on the threshold of the house of love; I am quite intoxicated from one shining glance; My soul is attached to her feet. Written in the year 612 AH.* A rare luxury piece and technical masterpiece. Ht. 8"

163. In this class of ware the Persian potters painted the carved surfaces with polychrome glazes, the raised or incised lines keeping the different glazes from running together. The present example depicts a heavily drawn stag in slight relief painted in polychrome glazes on a cream slip ground under a transparent glaze with accidental crackle. Dia. 11⅞"

164. In this class of so-called black silhouette-painted slipware the potter carved out a design from the thick black slip right down to the body and then covered the entire surface with either a clear turquoise or crackled ivory glaze, achieving a pleasing effect. This example is decorated with a Kufic inscription which may be translated as a salutation to the owner. Dia. c. 5+"

165. The "secret" of painting in luster passed from Egypt to Syria and Persia. The earliest specimens of Rayy luster with their large human or animal figures still reveal Egyptian Fatimid taste. In this example the figure and floral motifs are reserved in a deep brown luster ground. The greatest difference between these luster wares and those of the early period is that on the early examples the decoration was painted in luster, while on these later wares the background was lustered, usually but not invariably, in dark brown or yellow, thus the space remained open for decoration in reserve. Dia. 7⁷⁄₁₆"

166. Mina'i ware is one of the most beautiful forms of pottery made in the Islamic world. This bowl has the distinction of being signed by an artist who added to his name the *Nisbah* (indication of place of origin) al-Kashani. The exterior bears the full signature of a painter called Abu Zayd and the date 4th Muharram of the year 582 After the Hegira (March 26, 1186 A.D.) and the inscription *Glory to the Owner of this Bowl*. The interior, covered with an opaque turquoise glaze and painted in enamel colors, depicts a court scene with enthroned rulers and attendants; with inscriptions. Made of a carefully prepared hard light body. Dia. 8½" Ht. 3½"

167. Probably Kashan, about 1200; carefully prepared hard light body; painted over the opaque white glaze in enamel colors fixed by a second firing at low temperature. Depicts a scene of Bahram Gur and his mistress Azada hunting. Kufic inscription around rim *Opulence*; behind neck of camel *Bahram Gur*. Exterior, Persian verses. The kind of painting on wares of the Mina'i type is closely related to miniature painting and probably the fine examples were painted by the same artists who illuminated manuscripts. Dia. 8⅜"

168. The production of finer Rusāfa and Raqqa wares date from 1171 (the fall of the Fatimids) and 1279 (when the Mongols sacked Raqqa). The two principal types, luster and underglaze-painted wares, both have a body of a white, very soft quartz material. The earliest examples of the underglaze-painted wares were painted only in black under a transparent turquoise glaze. This jar is a remarkable example of the class. Ht. 9"

169. The very dark brown luster immediately distinguishes Raqqa luster from other contemporary luster wares. (See preceding)

170. Under the Safavid dynasty, 1499-1736, there was a genuine renaissance not only in ceramics but in all the arts. Several new types appeared of which one was Kubachi ware. This example is painted in brown, green, blue and dull yellow under a clear colorless crackled glaze.

171. Gombroon ware, of which the true origin is unknown, is another new type. It has a very

thin, hard, white, almost translucent body, and, like the fine Persian "white ware," the decoration was incised under the glaze, and occasionally small holes were pierced in the body and filled with glaze so that light would penetrate and further heighten the impression of translucence. Dia. 7⅝"

172. Fine white body beautifully painted with a design of birds and clouds chiefly in bright blue and some soft pale yellow under a clear glaze. Ht. 12½"

173. Fine white body painted in cobalt-blue with black outlines on a white ground and covered with a clear glaze. Dia. 15¾" Ht. 7"

174. The following examples (174-180) were all made at Isnik between the late 15th and early 17th centuries. Their low-fired white body is a composition of white clay and glassy matter with a carefully prepared porcelain-like surface on which patterns were painted under a transparent alkaline glaze. In this example, painted in blue-green, the Turkish potters were inspired by contemporary blue and white Ming porcelain. Dia. 14¼"; Ht. 4⁷⁄₁₆"

175. This distinctive type of Ottoman ware decorated with finely drawn linear spirals painted in blue on a white ground was previously known as Golden Horn, as it was presumed to have been made at Istanbul in a district on the Golden Horn. Ht. 9¹¹⁄₁₆" (See 174)

176. Of the Golden Horn type. Mosque lamps made of pottery were almost certainly purely decorative objects given as commemorative tokens to mosques by the sultan or high officials of the court, since being made of pottery they could not well serve any practical purpose. This mosque lamp painted in two shades of blue and with

turquoise blue bands on a white ground illustrates the beauty of the written word which attracted Muslim artists of all periods. Ornamental inscriptions, in many varieties of beautiful Arabic script, recall that the art of writing had religious associations with the Koran. This Koranic inscription may be translated: *There is only one as brave as Ali and only one sword, the Zulfikar* (sword given by Mahomet to his son-in-law Ali). *Power belongs to God alone.* Ht. 6⅝" (See 174)

177. Floral stylized pattern; ground clouded blue; in center white reserve containing blossoms in mauve and blue; other colors include turquoise and grey. (See 174)

178. With a hollow bell-shaped base forming sides of drip pan supporting candleholder; painted in two shades of blue on a white ground. Bottom of base with wave and rock pattern. Bears Arabic inscription: (trans.) *Owned by* (or *made for*) *Hajji Mohammed Ibn Soliman.* Ht. 9⅜" (See 174)

179. Painted in high temperature colors, blue, copper-green and an intense scarlet (Armenian-bole) with black outlines on a white ground; rim is decorated with the so-called rock and wave pattern derived from Chinese models, which appears on most Isnik plates. A remarkably colorful plate revealing the Turkish love of garden flowers, carnations, tulips, hyacinths, roses and many others. (See 174)

180. Painted in underglaze colors white, blue and "tomato" red with black outlines on an emerald green ground. The Turks were great sailors and sails were always a part of the city's skyline along the Bosphorus. Ships with lateen-sails that dominate the decoration of this jug were imitated at a later time on European faïence but they were altered to conform more closely with European craft. Ht. 8⅜" (See 174)

BYZANTINE POTTERY

181. With sgraffiato decoration cut through the white slip over a red body, covered with a pale green lead glaze; exterior emerald green glaze, with six spiral patterns painted on white slip. The orientalizing features of the design suggest that it is probably from the Chersonese on the northern coast of the Black Sea or possibly the Caucasus. Dia. 31.7 cm; Ht. 3⅝"

182. Design of lioness incised through cream-colored slip ground; the emerald green and yellow-brown glazes which fill out the design have run in the clear covering glaze. Exterior Y-shaped bands incised through slip. Dia. 21 cm; Ht. 4 ¹¹⁄₁₆"

183. Body decorated with four horizontal zones; upper and lower ones covered with decorative

patterns; two middle ones with fantastic animals and half-human figures confronting each other, probably illustrate a fable. Colors are varied greens and brown against a yellow ground.

184. Painted with white slip, glazed pale green on inside and dark green on outside. The elaborate overall tendril design, brown in color, is made by scraping the slip away, leaving the pattern in sunken relief. Dia. 23.4 cm; Ht. 3$\frac{5}{16}$"

185. Incised in thick lines through the slip; green and brown-yellow glazes splashed alternately over the pattern. Exterior, vertical Y-shaped designs with alternating strips of green and brown glazes. Dia. 22 cm; Ht. 4$\frac{11}{16}$"

RENAISSANCE EUROPE: SALT-GLAZED STONEWARE

186. No doubt the most important contribution made by Germany to the art of ceramics apart from her discovery of hard paste porcelain was in the development of salt-glazed stoneware. From about 1400 Siegburg stoneware jugs are of marked slenderness. Of the earliest Siegburg productions the Jakobakanne type long remained a popular form. Ht. 10$\frac{3}{4}$"

187. Of baluster form with a hand-gadrooned foot; decorated with three molded and applied medallions; one with Renaissance motifs and two depicting the Temptation of Adam and Eve. This type of jug characterized by a flaring or funnel-shaped mouth was among the earliest Siegburg productions and retained its popularity for a long time. The flaring mouth of this example is not the original. Ht. 5$\frac{3}{8}$"

188. Bottoms-up drinking vessel, grey stoneware with touches of blue; in the form of a warrior carrying a pistol and powder horn; legs molded on side of cup, the flaring rim of which serves as base for the figure. Possibly by Anno Knütgen, working at Siegburg 1570-1590. A popular Sieburg type. Ht. 15$\frac{1}{2}$"

189. Spouted pear-shaped jug or ewer with relief decoration; mounted in silver. From the workshop of Christian Knütgen, working 1568-1605. Signed C. K. His later work shows a marked Renaissance feeling. Subjects adapted from Virgil Solis, Peter Flötner, Heinrich Aldegrever, and others, with commonly found on his characteristic richly decorated spouted jugs. Ht. 11"
graceful leafy scrolls, animals and birds are

190. With relief decoration of St. George and the Dragon and the Arms of England, each repeated three times; domed pewter cover. Signed and dated beneath the center coat-of-arms H.H.

1573; the monogrammist H.H. is presumed to be Hans Hilgers, or Heilgers, working c. 1569-1595. This type of tall slender gradually tapering tankard is perhaps the most characteristic early Siegburg type. It was produced in five sizes corresponding to the standard measures of Cologne. Ht. 15$\frac{5}{16}$"

191. Commemorating a marriage; frieze in low relief depicting a Peasants' Dance, which may be after a print by Bartel or Hans Sebald Beham. Signed and inscribed on frieze *IV/HE/ DIE/ HOCH/ Z/ EIT/ MA/ CH/ ET/ LV/ S/ TIGE/ L/ EVT/ HH (By the wedding makes gay people H.H.)* The monogrammist HH is presumably Hans Hilgers or Heilgers. Ht. 3$\frac{3}{4}$"

192. With a light-brown salt-glaze. This type of jug, probably of Roman Germanic derivation, was characteristic of Cologne. Great numbers of them were made at the Maximinenstrasse workshops. Ht. 8$\frac{1}{4}$"

193. This type of jug with a flaring mouth somewhat resembling a Siegburg Trichterbecher is a typical Dreihausen form. Originally the four small handles held stoneware rings which created a festive noise as the cup was passed around the table. The iron oxide in the clay gave a brownish color to the vessel after it was fired. Ht. 11$\frac{1}{8}$"

194. With a brown salt glaze; initialed and dated IE (Jan Emens Mennicken), 1576. About 1576 Jans Emens, perhaps the greatest figure in the history of Rhenish stoneware, began to produce some large jugs with important relief decoration in double friezes, which number among his masterpieces. The top frieze of this jug is decorated with the procession of the Wise Men of the East visiting the Queen of Sheba while the bottom frieze depicts the battle of the Centaurs and

Lapiths mentioned in the inscription in the band encircling the neck. Ht. 21¼"

195. Belongs to a class of tankards with roulette work at top and bottom and with decoration in relief of allegorical figures of Virtues and of a potter at his wheel, inscribed Hans Glier, sometimes appearing as a youth and sometimes as a greybeard. This example inscribed Hans Glier depicts him as a youth seated at a potter's wheel, with figures of Faith and Fortitude on one side, of Justice and Prudence on the other. These Glier tankards and many others related were probably made at Penig or Zeitz near Waldenburg. Ht. 8½"

196. Of pear shape, grey stoneware; belongs to a distinctive class decorated with carved bands of palmettes, rosettes and the like painted over in enamel colors, often restricted as in this example to black and white, hence the misleading name Trauerkrüge (mourning jug) applied to this group. Frequently they were enriched with embossed pewter mounts of notable quality by Samuel Günther, 1659-1682, and Gottfried Köhler, 1676-1697, both of Freiberg. Ht. 7"

197. Brownish stoneware with a dark brown salt glaze, painted in bright enamel colors, chiefly blue, green, yellow and brown, in the style of the German and Bohemian enameled glass of that period. Decorated with the portraits of the family of the potter Johannes Vogell (Vogel). Initialed and dated, J.V. 1675. Band around base bears the inscription in characteristic Roman lettering: *WER AUS MIR TRINCKT ZU JEDER ZEIT DEM GESEGNE ES DIE H. 3 FALTIKEIT. (Whoever drinks out of me will each time be blessed by the Holy Trinity.)* Tankards of squat cylindrical form with a pewter lid and foot rim were peculiar to Kreussen. The Family was one of the favorite themes for this class of tankard; other themes include the Apostles, the Electors of the Empire, and the Planets. Ht. 10¼"

198. Beauvais potters were the first in France to make stoneware. This example of "grès azurés de Beauvais" (blue stonewares of Beauvais) with a dark blue glaze is decorated in relief on one side with a stag hunt, on the other the arms of a bishop or abbot. Ht. 11¾"

199. Probably from the Bradwell Wood pottery of John and David Elers. The decorative technique of applying molded motifs to the surface of pottery continued to find favor with Staffordshire potters until well into the 18th century. Ht. 4"

RENAISSANCE EUROPE:
LEAD-GLAZED EARTHENWARE

200. Toward the end of the 15th century the technique of lead-glazed earthenware improved rapidly, achieving perfection in the 16th century. It flourished in a number of French provinces. This example, perhaps inspired by contemporary silversmiths' work, is handsomely enriched with Renaissance stamped motifs in green and yellow glazes on an aubergine ground. Ht. 14¼"

201. Nearly white ground inlaid with small repeating motifs in black and reddish brown arranged in zones. The simple form is derived from metal work. This example is representative of the first group of Saint-Porchaire pieces. Ht. 5"

202. Bears the crescents of Henri II and the Arms of France. This richly decorated salt cellar of architectural form and with a lavish use of applied and intricate inlaid decoration is characteristic of a second group of Saint-Porchaire pieces; colors purplish-brown, blue and green. In the medieval and Renaissance periods the salt cellar played an important part on the banquet table; hence the wealth of decoration. Ht. 6⅞"

203. Decorated in high relief, with colored lead glazes. Typical of Palissy's rustic wares or rustic grottoes which follow an Italian fashion and were perhaps inspired by the Italian DREAM OF POLYPHILUS, 1546, where a rustic grotto filled with lizards, frogs, fishes and the like made of pottery is described in detail. L. 12¾"

204. With polychrome and white lead glazes. Such wares as this dish decorated with Renaissance ornament in relief are in marked contrast to the typical Palissy rustic grottoes. Dia. 10"

205. With colored lead glazes, decorated with figures of Bacchus and Ceres, who holds a cornucopia in relief against green foliage and vine; blue ground. Exterior mottled blue, green, red-brown. Figures are often introduced into Palissy compositions; here, the classical figures are in the manner of the Fontainebleau School. L. 7¼″

206. Cast from a pewter original by François Briot, c. 1585-1590; decorated in yellow, cream, green and aubergine lead glazes on a blue granulated ground. Ovoid body with three bands of decoration separated by fillets; in the upper and lower bands, masks, winged horses, arabesques and satyrs; central band three cartouches with allegorical figures, Faith, Hope and Charity, surrounded with foliage. Originally these pewter ewers all had basins of which one by Briot had a medallion in the center with the subject inscribed *La Temperantia*, giving the basins their name. Other dishes and ewers of the same character are grouped around it. Ht. 11″

207. Decorated with colored lead glazes; from the workshop of Bartélémy de Blénod. Modeled with charming simplicity, this well-known figure, La Nourrice, was copied at Chelsea and elsewhere.

208. Le Joueur de Cornemuse decorated with colored lead glazes. This figure and its companion piece La Vielleur (The Hurdy-Gurdy Player) are considered principal pieces of the workshops of Avon.

209. With polychrome lead glazes, the elegant elongated figure is in the style of the classical School of Fontainebleau. Neptune holds a dolphin in one hand and in the other a trident.

210. Probably from the workshop of Paul Pre-

uning. A decorative pattern of raised threads of applied white clay prevents the blue, green, aubergine and yellow lead glazes from running into each other. Within a deep niche at the front of the jug are the figures of two men fighting with battle axes; behind them in low relief is an armor-clad figure between two amorini. On either side are half-draped figures of two women, one with sword and flail, the other with cross and chalice. On the lower part of body are scattered oak leaves (presumed to be the badge under which German peasants of the Reformation fought for their freedom). On the shoulder is an openwork gallery interrupted by three bird cotes. An especially rich example. Ht. 14″

211. Effigy beakers which the Dutch called Geuzenbekers, or Beggar beakers; a folk art. Both wear yellow robes, green stoles; on reddish-brown base. Behind head of each is a spoutlike opening in the form of a sack or hood. Ht. 6¹³⁄₁₆″

212. Companion to 211.

213. Four-handled cup with slip-trailed decoration and applied stamped pads of white clay. One of the pads bears the stamped initials JL (John Livermore, d. 1658, one of the earliest slipware potters working at Wrotham). It also bears the initials WSC of the couple ·for whom Livermore made it. Ht. 6¼″

214. By Thomas Toft; with trailed slip decoration in white and two tones of brown depicting a mermaid combing her hair. Perhaps intended for display on a court cupboard in the Great Hall. Dia. 17¼″

215. With incised decoration; the characteristic tall flaring collar or neck has been broken off.

EUROPE: TIN-GLAZED EARTHENWARE

216. Tableware glazed in the cuerda seca or dry cord technique made at Triana, the potters' district at Seville, was thick and clumsy. Across the surface of this plate a fantastic harpy spreads its wings, painted in enamel-like patches of color separated by dark unglazed outlines. Dia. 15½″

217. While the fronts of Valencian luster ware were superbly decorated the backs were given con-

siderable attention as well, indicative of the care the Valencian potters devoted to every piece they made. This example, the richly decorated reverse of an armorial deep dish, displays a heraldic eagle painted with great verve in gold luster on a ground of tangled plant forms. The obverse shows bands and medallions of pseudo-Arabic inscriptions in blue and gold luster encircling a shield bearing arms, perhaps those of the Despujol family of Catalonia. The purely Muslim motifs that decorate this plate are typical of Valencian luster decoration during the first several decades of the 15th century. Dia. 19″

218. Albarelli were abundant in Valencia throughout the 15th century. Of Near Eastern derivation where they were used for transporting spices and aromatic herbs, those produced by the potters of Manisses were used as storage jars for spices, herbs and medicinal compounds. The decorative pattern of this albarello with bands of blue and gold vine leaves intermingled with gold acacia leaves and small flowers was widely popular at Manisses from about 1430 to 1500. Ht. 12⅝″

219. Emblazoned with the arms of the Guasconi family of Florence, the pattern of this plate, which can best be described as acacia flowers and bryony leaves, became one of the most popular background patterns for heraldic devices of Valencian luster ware from 1430 well into the second half of the 15th century. The small six-petaled flowers and bryony leaves of rich blue glaze are arranged across a background of pliant stalks, dots and leaf-like designs in gold luster. Dia. 18½″

220. Painted in blue and gold; bears the arms of Joan Payo Coello, Abbot of Poblet, 1480-1499. The gadrooned background pattern filled in with a patchwork of stylized minute motifs was a favorite background pattern for armorial plates, and represents one of the last stylistic developments of the 15th century. Dia. 18⅛″

221. An unusual example of this kind of bowl, having four flat lugs to lift it. An informative document relating to Valencian luster ware is a letter dated November 26, 1454, to Don Pedro Buyl, Lord of Manisses, from Maria of Castile, consort of Alfonso V of Aragon, in which she orders a dinner service of luster ware: water ewers and large basins (for rinsing hands at the dining table), porringers, broth bowls, and other bowls of various sizes, meat dishes, two-handled flower vases, and mortars, all of which were to be lustered on both the inner and exterior surface. Dia. 12″

222. With painted luster decoration. Drawn in blue outline, the gold-luster lion rampant strides forth in a regal manner on a white ground covered with a pattern of lustered foliage. An interesting contrast to the typical meticulously drawn floral background patterns developed in the 15th century. Dia. 18¾″

223. Prudence, from the workshop of Luca Della Robbia. A two-faced figure of a woman in white against light blue background; originally decorated with rays painted in gold; she holds a mirror in one hand and a green serpent in the other; border of fruit and foliage. The snake is the symbol of wisdom, the mirror of reflection; the two faces may indicate that Prudence gives to youth the wisdom of old age, or that Prudence looks both forward and backward. A companion piece representing Temperance is in the Cluny Museum. Dia. 55½″

224. Plate with deep sunken center and narrow rim; painted in blue with portions in ochre, green and manganese-purple. In the center is represented a serpent swallowing a child, which is the armorial bearing of the Visconti Sforza family of Milan. The background is studded with clusters of dots and surrounded with peacock feathers. The rim is decorated with pointed leaves arranged diagonally. Dia. 15″

225. The entire surface, both exterior and interior, is covered with an elaborate pattern of very conventional small peacock feathers skillfully combined with spiral lines in cobalt-blue, ochre, copper-red and white. This distinctive motif, originally derived from earliest antiquity, was most successfully expressed in Italian majolica of the final quarter of the 15th century. It is said that at Faenza it was an allusion to the name of Cassandra Pavoni (pavone meaning peacock), mistress of Galeotto Manfredo, Lord of Faenza (d. 1488) to whom the majolica potters intended it as a sign of loyalty. At a later date the peacock pattern was used at Meissen, Chelsea and other porcelain factories. Dia. 12½″

226. Painted chiefly in blue and yellow with some orange, green and black. Around the bowl are six bright yellow oval bosses bordered in green on a "muddy" yellow ground alternating with scroll and water leaf motifs with details in blue and green. Dome-shaped foot is molded in eight peacock feather bosses on a molded eight-lobed base. The design permits an admirable distribution and presentation of the basic colors, creating an illusion of greater richness. Ht. 11⅛″

227. Painted in cobalt blue, ochre and touches of manganese. Pharmacy vases were made in the

form of albarelli for ointments and dry drugs and spouted drug pots or drug vases (French chevrettes) for the storage and dispensing of syrups and other liquid medicaments. Round the body on this spouted drug jar is inscribed in blue Gothic lettering on a white banderole *Sy. de Papavero* (Syrupum de Papavero), Syrup of Poppies, a favorite sleeping draught in medieval pharmacies. Ht. 11¼″

228. Painted in blue with portions in ochre and touches of pale green. Within a large oval wreath of stylized laurel leaves is figured a seated lion, to left. Round the center is a broad horizontal band with the inscription ⸅V.∴. Violato. Ht. 10½″ (See preceding)

229. With a scroll handle on each side; painted in green, blue, black, yellow and ochre. From about the middle of the 15th century it became the custom and by the end of the century the vogue to adorn the pharmacies, which were popular meeting places, with sumptuous services of drug vases, drug jars and pots. In this colorful example the body is covered with a diaper of fish scale imbrications, a pattern much favored by majolica potters. Ht. 12⁵⁄₁₆″

230. Painted in blue, green, opaque white, some yellow and brown. Flat handle on each side with a notched edge. Bears a shield with coat-of-arms. Ht. 9½″

231. From the workshop of Nicola Pellipario who was perhaps the greatest of all majolica painters. Portrait busts as a decorative style appeared on a class of majolica plates and albarelli. This specimen depicts a woman with red hair wearing a headdress, dress and necklace in ruby and gold luster. Bears the inscription *CASA/ ND/ RA/ BELL.* Dia. 9½″ Ht. 2″

232. Istoriato or Beautiful style. The story of Cephalus and Procris painted by Francesco Xanto Avelli of Rovigo, perhaps the greatest of Pellipario's followers. The painting on plates by a number of great artists vies in beauty with the contemporary Italian masterpieces in oil and fresco and has in addition the advantage of an imperishable medium. Dia. 11¼″

233. From the workshop of Orazio Fontana with Urbino Raphaelesque decoration and stories, painted in blue, orange, yellow, green and black n a white ground. Scenes from the Romance of

Amadis of Gaul with corresponding inscriptions in Spanish on the back of each scene. Scene at upper left shows the maid lowering into the river the child Amadis who was hidden in a chest. Upper right, a Scottish knight catches the chest, takes out the child and gives him to his wife to rear, etc. Accompanying the introduction of Urbino grotesques came an increasing use of plastic decoration. L. 26¼″

234. This rare wine cooler skillfully painted with Urbino Raphaelesque grotesques is attributed to the workshop of Orazio Fontana. In the bottom of the bowl is a scene representing a battle (perhaps Hannibal crossing the Alps). Predominant colors are a brilliant orange-yellow, blue and green. W. 23½″ Ht. 12⅞″ (See preceding)

235. From the workshop of Abaquesne, in the Italian majolica style with high-temperature polychrome decoration. Portrait busts were much favored by the Italian majolica potters for the decoration of albarelli. The nationality and realistic treatment·in this example is, however, unmistakably French.

236. Probably from the workshop of Antoine Syjalon. In the Italian majolica style with high-temperature polychrome decoration. Ht. 9½″

237. From the workshop of Antoine Syjalon, painted in high temperature colors; inscribed *Nismes, 1581.* On a blue ground, it bears the arms of John Casimir of Bavaria, Count Palatine of Simmern, 1543-1592, and his wife Elizabeth, daughter of Augustus I, Elector of Saxony. The treatment of the grotesques, reminiscent of the à candalieri style, strongly reflects the influence of Italian majolica. Ht. 15″

238. An example of the rare faïence made at Lyons; decorated with high temperature colors in the Italian majolica Istoriato style. The subject depicted, Joseph receiving his brethren in Egypt, is inscribed in French on the back: *Les frères de Joseph venus à lui en Egypte, au Genèse XLIII.* The subject has been taken from Salomon Bernard's illustrations in books edited by the Lyons printers, Jean de Tournes and Guillaume de Rouille. Dia. 16⅝″

239. Painted in high temperature blue and yellow on a white ground; pastoral scene in a medallion surrounded by a border of grotesques in the Urbino style, the grotesques deriving from Raph-

ael's decoration for the Loggia of the Vatican. At their best, Italian-inspired grotesques rank among the finest examples of the pottery painter's art. Dia. 9¾"

240. Belongs to the class of bleu de Nevers (also called bleu Persan) and displays the characteristic decoration of flowers and foliage with birds and insects among them, painted in high temperature opaque white and two shades of yellow in a style known as décor Persan (Persian decoration) on a deep blue (bleu de Nevers) tin-glazed ground. Because of certain associations with the East these wares have been erroneously described as bleu Persan and décor Persan. Regardless of their name they rank probably as the most important Nevers creation and were widely imitated.

241. A related and very rare class of bleu de Nevers with a solid strong-yellow tin-glazed ground; the decoration of the typical flowers and birds in the so-called décor Persan are in opaque white with some blue. Ht. 12¾"

242. Belongs to a small, related but distinctive class of bleu de Nevers. Decorated with flowers and foliage in green with touches of lavender and yellow on a white tin-glazed ground and with narrow bands of decoration in black on a yellow ground, in horizontal zones. Ht. 9¾"

243. Painted in opaque white (blanc fixe) on a bleu de Nevers ground. Dia. 9¾"

244. This plate with high temperature polychrome decoration belongs to a class of faïence decorated in a typically French style. Country scenes and pastorals mirror the spirit of fashionable novels as on this plate with a scene of Celadon and Astrée from the romance L'ASTRÉE by Honoré D'Urfé. It is thought that the name Celadon may have been given to a class of Chinese wares from the character Celadon in this novel who wore grey-green clothing.

245. With a detachable head forming a cup, painted in high temperature blue. Bears the arms of Joachim Friedrich, Elector of Brandenburg, c. 1598-1608. Perhaps by Lorenz Speckner who is likely to have served his apprenticeship at Nuremberg before settling at Kreussen where he worked occasionally for the Vests from about 1618 and later. Owl jugs appear to have been a favorite subject of European, especially German, faïence potters from the 16th century onward. Ht. 16½"

246. With a scene of St. George and the Dragon, painted in high temperature colors. Most of the surviving Hamburg specimens are of large jugs of rather peculiar form with a pear-shaped body, spreading foot and most frequently a straight-sided neck narrowing upward to the mouth. Ht. 13½"

247. From the workshop of Lorenz Speckner, with relief decoration, painted in underglaze blue. The form of this flask with either four or six sides and the corresponding number of panels is found only at Kreussen. Frequently religious inscriptions in beautiful Roman lettering and symbols are found in the panels. In this example the subjects in the six panels are: *MARIA/ INRI/ IHS/* Sacred Heart/ Crucifix/ Symbols of the Passion. Ht. 11¹¹⁄₁₆"

248. Painted in Schwarzlot (black enamel). Bears the signature of Johann Schäper, one of the most celebrated of German Hausmalerei. Landscapes with ruins were a favorite theme, often, as in this example, in an oval panel, enclosed in a wreathed border. Gold was sparingly employed. Jugs used by Schäper were chiefly of Hanau faïence and were either of Enghalskrug form or of pear shape with a wide neck; frequently richly mounted in gilt bronze. Ht. 10¾"

249. Of pear-shape form; the Adoration of the Magi painted by Wolf Rössler, a leading Nuremberg Hausmaler. His important pieces are notable for the richness of their enamel colors in which a vivid crimson and strong emerald green, as in this example, are outstanding. Their exceptional color is generally enhanced by a brilliant colorless glaze imparting an almost lacquer-like quality in the same way as Italian coperta or Dutch kwaart. The pictorial medallion was often enclosed in a vividly painted wreath of flowers. Rössler favored large roses, of which one was distinctively rendered at the top. Ht. 8⅝"

250. Painted in colors by Bartholomüs Seuter, well-known Hausmaler of Augsburg. Naturalistic flowers, birds and insects used together was one of Seuter's favorite decorative themes. This type of jug (Enghalskrug) with a narrow neck was a widely popular form for German faïence. Ht. 12"

251. The earliest pieces of Habaner ware were decorated only with flowering plants in high temperature colors like this example. The earliest

dated specimen appears to be an openwork dish, dated 1599. Small globular jugs with a short neck are a typical form. Ht. 6⅜"

252. Painted in high temperature colors, chiefly blue and yellow. Dia. 5"

253. Armorial shields were always popular as a decoration in Switzerland, often with the addition on the rim of flowers or fruits like this example, painted in strong and bright high temperature colors. Dia. 11¾"

254. In the form of three conjoined cups, entirely unpainted. Ht. 3¼"

255. With underglaze blue decoration reflecting Chinese influence, perhaps imitated from Dutch versions. It has a pierced neck and a rim with three spouts and a hollow handle. Puzzle cups frequently bear challenging inscriptions, such as, *Here Gentlemen come try your skill/ I'll hold a wager if you will/ That you don't drink the liquor all/ Without you spill or let some fall/.* This example is without inscription. Ht. 9"

256. Commemorates the birth of Ruth Twiss (identity unknown). Decorated with birds, flowers and insects inspired by Chinese porcelain and painted in high temperature colors, blue, green, yellow and iron-red. The inside of the bowl bears the inscription: *Ruth Twiss was borne December The Second Day in the year—1705,* enclosed in a wreath of flowers. Between the four arched handles of the cover are applied fleurs de lis in blue; a cup shaped like a crown fits on the top; inside the cover is depicted The Nativity in underglaze blue with the inscription *Christs Nativity.* Ht. 17¹¹⁄₁₆"

257. Copied from a well-known oval earthenware dish, La Fécundité, depicting a woman and her children, with vivid colored glazes and decoration in relief which had been made at the workshop of Bernard Palissy in the second half of the 16th century. Dia. 18⅛"

258. Painted with the equestrian figure of King William III, 1689-1701, in high temperature colors; inscribed K.W. This class of shallow dish, crudely, but vigorously, painted with a bold design that is chiefly variations on particular themes such as Kings and Queens of England, stylized figures of men in armor, Adam and Eve, tulips and other flowers in pots, generally having a narrow border

of slanting dashes in blue round the edge, became an important part of the English potter's output from about the middle of the 17th century. Dia. 13¼"

259. Depicting Adam and Eve with the Tree of Knowledge, painted in high temperature colors. Almost two hundred dishes with this widely popular subject, dating from about 1635 until the early years of the 18th century, are still extant. Dia. 13¾" (See preceding)

260. Made at the Greek A factory of Samuel van Eenhoorn, painted in underglaze blue and manganese purple. Pieces like this example marked SVE are earliest among the classic wares produced at Delft and are chiefly elaborate but accurate versions of Chinese original designs. Ht. 7¼"

261. This vase of traditional European form, painted in underglaze blue, was made at the Greek A factory of Adrianus Koeks for Hampton Court Palace just before 1695. Iike everything else made for the palace, its bold Baroque design originates in the work of the Dutch court architect, the Frenchman Daniel Marot. Ht. 12"

262. From a Coronation Service in underglaze blue with the insignia of Austria and the dates of the Double Coronation of Charles VI in 1711 and 1712 as Holy Roman Emperor, made at the Double Tankard factory of Louwys Victorsz. The back of the plate is decorated with Oriental flowers in blue. It is interesting to note that the Chinese Imperial Family always preferred to use white porcelain tablewares which were either painted in underglaze blue or unpainted. This taste for underglaze blue was cultivated by the European aristocracy. Dia. 15½"

263. Decorated in underglaze blue, the design deriving from Late Ming export ware. The deer drawing the flower cart is rendered in a fanciful and lively manner that is entirely captivating.

264. Molded mask on front with open mouth forming aperture. Intended to be hung above its basin on the wall. Made at The Three Cindertubs Factory (De Drie Astonne), decorated in underglaze blue with scenes selected from everyday home life depicting such fashionable social amenities as The Tea Hour.

265. Made at The Young Moor's Head factory of Rochus Hoppesteyn; with high temperature polychrome decoration in the Chinese taste. Ht. 4"

266. Made at The Metal Pot factory of Lambertus van Eenhoorn, with high temperature polychrome decoration in the Chinese style. This reeded form called cachemire was especially favored for vases and for the ambitious sets of garniture in the Chinese manner, usually comprising five vases, to go on the tops of cupboards. Ht. 19½"

267. Made at The Greek A factory of the Koeks family; with high temperature polychrome decoration enlivened with touches of gilt in the manner of Japanese Imari porcelain which began to reach Europe in quantity in the first years of the 18th century.

268. Made at The Rose factory, with the familiar Chinese flowers, rocks and birds painted in clear and strong high temperature colors. This type of tall-necked jug with a plaited or rope-twist handle and a body lobed and radially ribbed (not too pronounced in this example) is a characteristic Dutch faïence form. Ht. 12½"

269. The form of the jug reproduces that of silver which faïence was to supplant. The decoration in blue on a white ground and in reserve on a blue ground is a perfect example of the elaborate Baroque lambrequin style, a Rouen innovation in pottery. Lambrequins (lit. hanging draperies) were for the most part adapted from the contemporary ornamental designs of Bérain and other fashionable Maîtres Ornemanistes. Ht. 10⅝" (See 271)

270. Decorated in blue and enlivened with a rather dull Indian red characteristic of Rouen. A very typical example of the decorative scheme known as Style Rayonnant from the radial and symmetrical arrangement of the characteristic lambrequins.

271. Style Rayonnant painted in underglaze blue camaieu; bears the arms of Louis Poterat, Seigneur de St. Etienne, owner of the Rouen factory. The vogue for this kind of Rouen faïence reached its climax about 1709 when Louis XIV and his courtiers, in a national emergency due to the disastrous wars, sent their gold and silver table services to the mint to be melted down and substituted faïence for them. Some of the greatest French pottery frequently bearing the arms of princely families belongs to this period. The majestic quality of the form is no doubt accountable to its silver prototypes. (See 269)

272. Painted in blue camaieu and Rouen red, the latter sharing the decoration almost equally with the blue. Decorated with a deep border of radiating lambrequins combined with an exotic scene of figures in the garden in a style known as Sino-Dutch, though they were freely adapted from K'ang Hsi prototypes. Dia. 17¾"

273. An example of the Chinese style which achieved its acme in Rouen faïence between the years 1720 and 1750 when skillful versions of Chinese Famille Verte porcelain of the K'ang Hsi period were made concurrently with the elaborate lambrequin style. This "Famille Verte" plate with high temperature polychrome decoration touched with red was made at the Guillibaud factory and is signed in full Guillibeaux. It bears the arms of Charles-François-Frédéric de Montmorency, Duke of Montmorency-Luxemburg, and is one of a service reputed to have been made as a present from the town of Rouen on the occasion of his appointment as Governor of Normandy in 1728. Dia. 13¾"

274. Plateau de table in the Rococo style, painted in high temperature colors with touches of red. Decorated with birds, insects and flowers; rocaille cartouche framing a mythological subject, Venus Flogging Cupid With Roses, after the painter Nattier, with the inscription: Nul amour sans peine/ nul rose sans épine. At either side a smaller cartouche representing Venus and Cupid and Venus and Adonis. Painted by Pierre Chapelle. The considerable size indicates great technical ability. L. 25"

275. In the Rococo style which flourished at Rouen, 1745-1770. The fanciful theme of decoration known as à la corne or cornucopia, painted in high temperature colors and touches of red, was one of the most popular used at Rouen. Dia. 15"

276. The decorative style of the underglaze blue painting is known as Bérainesque as it derives from the work of Jean Bérain. Scrollwork and slight architectural motifs form a delicate web enclosing fanciful figures, singeries, birds and other devices painted in miniature. This extremely popular style ranks as the most fully original Moustiers creation, where it flourished from about 1710-1740. L. 12¼"

277. From a service ordered for Mme. de Pompadour, 1745. Made at the Olerys and Laugier fac-

tory, with garland and medallion decoration in high temperature colors, mostly blue, a peculiar orange-toned yellow and some muted green, touched with gilding. Floral festoons, swags and garlands enclose medallions which show Jupiter, Venus, Apollo and Diana; on the handles are amorini; on the flat knob of the cover a bust of Diana. The rim of the matching stand for the bowl is decorated with a festoon of flowers; the center depicts Apollo Slaying the Python in the Garden of the Hesperides, enclosed in a rocaille cartouche. Dia. 10⅛″

278. In blue camaieu. Belongs to a class of well-known plates, assiette à la Camargo, painted with a dancer and two musicians and a long inscription, so-called because the subject was inspired by a painting by Nicolas Lancret (1660-1743) of the celebrated dancer Marie-Anne de Cupis de Camargo (b. Brussels 1710-d. Paris 1760) after her triumphant return to L'Opéra in 1740. Portraits of Mme. Camargo are at the New Palace, Potsdam; The Hermitage, Nantes and the Wallace Collection, London. The plates are ascribed to Bordeaux, Marseilles (Leroy's factory) and also Moustiers. They were much copied by forgers. The long inscription relates this plate to the Faïence Parlante class. Dia. 9¼″

279. Made at Strasbourg during the Charles-François Hannong period, 1721-1739; with molded decoration. The chinoiserie decoration painted in high temperature colors is in a style ultimately derived from Rouen.

280. With molded decoration and polychrome enamel painting made during the Paul Hannong period at Strasbourg. In fanciful Rococo form; the rim and foot bordered by scrolls, shell motifs and foliage outlined and shaded in rich yellow, strong blue and deep violet red, sumptuous colors especially characteristic of Strasbourg; eagle-head handles in dark aubergine; the finial on the cover in the form of a rose with leaves in relief painted green. Some time in the late 1740's Paul Hannong introduced painted decoration in enamel colors at Strasbourg where his innovations in this medium set a fashion followed at most other French and German factories. L. 15″

281. Life-size duck in two parts, painted in polychrome enamels, made during the Paul Hannong period. Modeled by Johann Wilhelm Lanz who was chief modeler at Strasbourg, c. 1745-1754.

This delightful class, the so-called trompe-l'oeil wares, was much in fashion for the decoration of sideboard tables and long banqueting tables. Ht. 13″

282. Oval dish for fruit, reticulated in imitation of a wicker basket, with matching stand, painted in enamel colors, magenta predominating. The magnificent Strasbourg flowers inspired by Meissen Deutsche Blumen quickly acquired a great reputation and were widely copied at other French factories. During the Joseph Hannong period, c. 1762-1781, naturalistic flower painting was imbued with a new richness and freedom. Dish L. 13¼″; Stand L. 14″

283. In the Rococo style; decorated in relief and painted in petit-feu or low temperature colors. Jacques Chapelle who was originally chemist and sole proprietor, 1759-1763, intended that Sceaux faïence should rival porcelain in its thinness and refinement of potting and in its carefully executed painting. L. 10″

284. The gracefully elegant Rococo scrolls form a two-lobed body with a spout at each end, on a scrolled three-part base; the scroll handle at the back is surmounted with a crouching dog. The outlines of the Rocaille scrolls are shaded in soft rose-red and red-violet enamels. Ht. 5″

285. Attributed to the factory of Gaspard Robert, painted in overglazed enamel colors. The seaport view evocative of Marseilles, ultimately deriving from Meissen harbor scenes, has been rendered in the manner of a water color. Dia. 9½″

286. Made at the Veuve Perrin factory. Both the form and floral decoration painted in overglaze enamel colors on a solid yellow ground have an ease and spontaneity, a supple rhythm that is typically Rococo. Faïence with a yellow ground is peculiar to the south of France. The quality of color of Marseilles (Veuve Perrin and Fauchier) is highly esteemed. L. 10″

287. Made at the Veuve Perrin factory; with a pale turquoise ground color. The pattern of simple flowers painted in natural colors and large bows of knotted ribbon in a rich deep rose, with details in gold and insects in gold, is an exceptional type from this factory and like all fine Veuve Perrin painting shows the unlabored charm which is its chief claim to fame. Dia. 9⅞″

288. Some of the finest German faïence was made at Ansbach, particularly in the decade between 1730-1740, when a beautiful class painted in the colors of Chinese Famille Verte porcelain was made. This plate painted in green, yellow, blue, manganese-purple and dark iron-red is decorated with the so-called Carp pattern with birds, peonies and fish. The green of the Ansbach Famille Verte was very beautiful. Dia. 10³⁄₁₆″

289. Painted in overglaze enamels enlivened with gilding; on one side a harbor scene in the early Meissen porcelain style, on the other chrysanthemums. The painting of exceptional fineness bears the signature of Adam Friedrich von Löwenfinck who introduced the technique of painting in enamel colors on faïence, which affected most of the German and French faïence factories. Ht. 7½″

290. Painted in overglaze enamel colors with a view of the estate of Baron Küner near Memmingen. Inscribed on ribbon above view *Künersberg bey Memmingen.* L. 20¾″

291. Of inverted pear shape, painted in high temperature colors; a distinctive feature at Alcora is a beautiful style of flower painting. Ht. 13″

292. Many fantastic little beasts, presumably attempts to reproduce the faïence of Alcora ware, were made at Talavera in the closing decades of the 18th century. The simple and direct modeling of this toylike animal accented with color is especially striking.

293. In the form of a huge head of cabbage decorated in shaded and mottled tones of green with bluish-green edges and manganese stalks and veining; the cover with a frog finial, painted in tones of green and manganese. On a matching cabbage leaf stand. L. 15¼″

294. In the Rococo style; made at The Old Moor's Head factory when Geertruij Verstelle was proprietor; painted in muffle colors enlivened with gilding. Ht. 14″

295. This dish decorated in the Imari style in enamel colors enlivened with gilding is from a table service presented about 1776 by the Polish king Stanislaus Augustus Poniatowski "in proof of his most complete affection and utter devotion" to the Turkish Sultan Abdul Hamid I with whom Poniatowski was at that time allied in war against Russia. The oval cartouches bear Turkish inscriptions: (trans.) *These gifts are sent/ to the Tsar of the race of Osman/ by the king of the Lekhs.* The best known wares of the Belvedere factory comprise parts of this service. Dia. 11⅛″

296. Painted in enamel colors by Abraham Leihamer (d. 1774). He and the potter and modeler Johann Buchwald worked together at Stockelsdorf from about 1771 to 1774, where they achieved a high standard of artistic excellence. The form of this vase is peculiar to this factory. Ht. 17⅜″

297. Painted in blue, made at the Store Kongensgade factory. Bowls of this form were especially popular for drinking a type of punch called "Bishop" and were made in a number of the Northern factories. The inscription on this example may be translated: *Prosperity to King and Country.* Ht. 13¾″

EUROPE: PORCELAIN

298. Painted in blue; the form resembles ewers made at about this time by the majolica potters of Urbino, while the rhythm of the flower painting is not unlike that on contemporary Turkish Isnik wares. Ht. 8″

299. With a molded gadrooned band round the base, in blue camaieu, decorated with Louis XIV style Baroque compositions set alternately on a ground and in reserve. After the Italian experiments in soft-paste the first attempts were made at the French faïence factories of Rouen and Saint-Cloud. Ht. 7⅞″

300. It appears that the family of the faïence-maker Pierre Chicaneau (d. 1678) improved upon a process discovered by him for making porcelain and after 1693 made porcelain as "fine as the Chinese." This example is decorated in blue camaieu with Bérainesque lambrequins and arabesques in the manner of contemporary Rouen faïence. Ht. 17½″

301. In the form of a setting fowl, tail forming handle, tiny spout under neck, separate cover; bird's comb, feathers and wings molded in relief and incised. Vessels of this type were of stone-

hardness, resonant and entirely waterproof. To make them Böttger used a red clay found near Meissen and as flux an easily fusible red earth found near Dresden. Ht. 4½"

302. Squatting "pagoda" figure in Böttger stoneware which having been overfired has become more or less blackish-brown on the surface. In this condition it is often called eisenporzellan or iron porcelain. Probably Georg Fritzsche, active at Meissen 1712-1730, was the modeler. This class of figures with open mouths was no doubt copied from an original Chinese import. They were often adapted as pastille or incense burners, in which case they have a small round hole in the mouth or in the head. Ht. 3⅞"

303. Black-glazed reddish-brown Böttger stoneware with chinoiserie decoration painted in soft colors and gold. Böttger invented this brilliant black glaze, made from lead oxide with manganese or cobalt. Apparently it was unknown in China. Ht. 6¾"

304. Plastic work in Böttger porcelain includes an important series of small grotesque dwarfs known as "Callot" figures chiefly derived from engravings in IL CALLOTO RESUSCITATO (a popular collection of engravings first published in Amsterdam in 1716) and believed to be the work of the modeler Georg Fritzsche. The engraving "Mad Meg" from IL CALLOTO RESUSCITATO was the source used for this "Callot" figure. Flesh painted natural color, basket and contents green, with gilding. Ht. 3¼"

305. Decorated in enamel colors by J. G. Herold who introduced his fanciful chinoiseries about 1725; they were produced in the magnificent new colors which he perfected about 1722. Ht. 4½"

306. The king's desire that his porcelain should equal the Chinese in all respects led to many close copies of Chinese and Japanese designs from about 1725-1730. The Red Dragon pattern, entirely in iron-red and gold, dates from about 1730. The cover is decorated with two dragons, each chasing a pearl or *chu*, one of the Eight Precious Objects or Pa Pao, with two phoenixes coiled in the middle, while the bowl is decorated with two dragons chasing pearls. The Meissen mark on this example includes the letters KHC (Königliche Hof Conditorei or Royal Court Store Room or Pantry).

307. Fabled animal modeled by Johann Gottlob Kirchner. Belongs to the series of colossal figures of birds and animals for the king's Japanese palace in Dresden. Ht. 27"

308. Modeled by Kaendler and made at Meissen, February, 1733. The magpies face each other in a defiant pose and interpret "noisy talk." From 1733, for more than twenty years, Kaendler and several assistants continued without interruption to model the very numerous porcelain figures on which the fame of Meissen so largely depends. Ht. 21"; Ht. 21½"

309. Tea jug in the shape of a seated squirrel nibbling at three hazelnuts. One pierced to serve as spout, the scrolling tail as handle and the tail-end as mouth. Modeled by Kaendler and made at Meissen, May 1735. Ht. 5½"

310. Teapot in the form of a seated Mother Monkey with two young; the monkey in her arms serves as a spout, the second monkey climbing upon her back forms the handle, holding a fruit to form the pierced mouth of the pot (the missing top of the fruit designed as cover). Modeled by Kaendler and made at Meissen, July 1735. Ht. 7½"

311. Modeled by Kaendler and made at Meissen. The popularity of trompe l'oeil ware has not diminished through the years. Ht. 10½"

312. A large cluster of blue-grey grapes forming a box, with a cover having a finial in the form of a twig. Made at Meissen. Ht. 6¼"

313. Teapot formed as a smiling Chinese lady, riding sideways upon the back of a rooster and holding a vase with cover which serves as mouth; the rooster's open beak forms the spout. Modeled by Kaendler and made at Meissen, 1737. This teapot was part of the "Plat de Ménage" made by Kaendler for Count Brühl. Ht. 8¾"

314. The designing of table services with rich plastic decoration became the chief concern at Meissen from 1733, which marked the beginning of Count Brühl's administration. The finest and most beautiful service ever made was the Swan Service made for Count Brühl and his wife. Kaendler worked for four years, 1737-1741, with all his assistants but mostly with Eberlein in the preparation of this service. It was a dinner, tea, coffee and chocolate service of 2,200 pieces. Kaendler was aided by von Brühl's confectioner La Chapelle. Every piece bears the arms of von Brühl Kolowat. It was with the creation of this service that Kaendler first embraced the Rococo style. The motifs of

an aquatic theme are mainly inspired by French engravings but the motif of two swans came from a travel book published by Leonhard Buggels in 1700 at Nuremberg. The motifs are modeled in low relief on flat pieces and in the round on tureens, candleholders and the like. The candleholders are copies of silver ones by Meissonnier, 1735. Ht. 9$\frac{7}{16}$" Fruit dish, one of a pair. Ht. 6$\frac{9}{16}$"

315.   Modeled by Kaendler. When Kaendler introduced his first independent small figures toward 1736 it ranked as a creation of an entirely new type. The vogue for Meissen small figures reached its height 1740-1750. The idea of using them for display on the dinner table instead of those in sugar and wax belongs to this period. From medieval times it was customary in Germany to have at banquets an elaborate table centerpiece and around it many small figures made by Court confectioners. Ht. 6$\frac{1}{2}$"

316.   Figure, Tailor Riding Goat, was modeled by Kaendler and made at Meissen, November 1740. Figure, Tailor's Wife Riding Goat, was modeled by J. F. Eberlein and made at Meissen, 1740. Both figures enjoy enduring popularity. Ht. 9"; Ht. 7$\frac{1}{4}$"

317.   Modeled by Kaendler and made at Meissen June 1744. A fine example of the dramatic sense of movement and restless outline, the riotous vitality that mark Kaendler's creative genius in this branch of porcelain art. Ht. 8$\frac{1}{2}$"

318.   Figure of Madame de Pompadour from the opera "Acis and Galatea" in porcelain and painted in colored enamels, made at Meissen. On a Rococo base. After Kaendler's visit to Paris in 1750 with the wedding gift for the Dauphiness the ascendancy of the Rococo was established. Ht. 8$\frac{1}{4}$"

319.   The porcelain figure representing Spring was originally modeled by J. F. Eberlein at Meissen in 1745. The fashion for porcelain flowers painted in naturalistic enamel colors mounted on slender metallic stems and placed in vases or used to decorate chandeliers and candelabra was a great success at Meissen, and was widely copied. Ht. 15$\frac{1}{2}$" (See 352)

320.   The famous Schneeball (guelder-rose) vases were typical of Kaendler's style from the late 1740's onward, a period anticipating the change in style to French Rococo.

321.   Modeled by Franz Bustelli at Nymphenburg. Italian Comedy figures are characteristic of his best work. His figures possess an intense vitality and a supple stylized movement. When they are left unpainted as in this example the rhythmical play of line can be readily appreciated. Ht. 6$\frac{11}{16}$"

322.   Modeled by Franz Bustelli at Nymphenburg and painted in colored enamels. Ht. 7$\frac{3}{8}$" (See preceding)

323.   Modeled by Franz Bustelli and made at Nymphenburg. Ht. 6$\frac{1}{2}$" (See 321)

324.   Modeled by Karl Gottlieb Lück who was model master at Frankenthal from 1766-1775. His figures are noted for their exquisite workmanship. Painted in enamel colors. Ht. 6$\frac{3}{4}$"

325.   Modeled by Johann Peter Melchior and made at Höchst. Painted in enamel colors. Ht. 5$\frac{5}{8}$"

326.   With landscape framed in molded Rococo scrollwork. Potpourri vases, an important type of early German porcelain, were a fashionable form of garniture for chimney-pieces, and were made in three sizes. Höchst and Furstenberg are well known for their potpourri vases which were invariably carefully painted.

327.   On either side a large medallion with harbor scene in black framed by scrollwork in red-violet and gold; spout, scroll-handle and floral finial on cover gilded. This European miniature style with landscapes, notably harbor scenes, and small figures, was introduced at Meissen about 1740 and started a universal fashion. Ht. 6$\frac{3}{4}$"

328.   Modeled by Simon Feilner; his models at Fürstenburg where he was model master, 1753-1768, included important Italian Comedy figures and Miners. Ht. 8"

329.   This charming Venetian Fair was probably modeled by Jean-Jacob Louis who was a modeler at Ludwigsburg from 1762-1772. Shop Ht. 6"; Man 2$\frac{3}{4}$"; Woman 2$\frac{1}{2}$"

330.   A satirical miniature group painted in enamel colors, modeled by Jean-Jacob Louis and made at Ludwigsburg. In the second half of the 18th century women's headdresses reached an extravagance of folly, passing all that had come before it. Hair kneaded with pomatum and flour was drawn up over a cushion or pad of wool and twisted into curls and knots and decorated with

artificial flowers and bows of silk ribbon. All this required the aid of a skilled hairdresser. Engravers found the subject irresistible; inevitably their engravings charmed the ceramic modeler. Ht. 5″

331. A delightful example of the widely popular class of objects made of porcelain in fanciful form called "Toys" which were a Meissen creation. Ht. 3″

332. The second European factory producing hard paste porcelain was started here in 1719. This teapot in the style of J. G. Herold of Meissen with the beautiful Vienna iron-red as a ground color is decorated with white reserves on each side, two with chinoiseries and two with "Indian" flowers in polychrome enamels. Ht. 5 9/16″

333. The decoration of elaborate and fanciful Laub-und-Bandelwerk with a Chinese figure on either side under a suspended canopy is painted in Schwarzlot (black enamel) with touches of gilding by the Hausmaler Ignaz Preissler at Breslau. Two handles in form of lion masks. Ht. 6 3/8″

334. The chinoiserie decoration after Elias Baeck (1679-1747), painted in brownish-black enamel (Schwarzlot) enlivened with gilding was done by the Hausmaler Ignaz Preissler at Breslau. Ht. 6 1/4″

335. Bacchic scenes were one of the favorite types of decoration during the last 10 or 15 years of the Du Paquier period, 1719-1744. Painted in purple camaieu. Ht. 5 7/8″

336. The body is painted with sprays of Deutsche Blumen in natural colors beneath gilt relief decoration. Each of the four chamfered corners of the base is filled by the term figure of a man holding a mug in his right hand and a hat in his left. Ht. 15 1/4″

337. The resumption of producing porcelain in Italy was chiefly due to German and Austrian influence. One group of factories was in and around Venice, another at Doccia, near Florence, and a third, those of the Bourbon Kings in Naples and later in Spain. This vase made at the Vezzi factory is painted in polychrome enamels with plants and flowers of Oriental derivation, intermingled with birds and buildings in a loose and artless manner that is charming and effective.

338. Made at the Ginori factory. The relief decoration in enamel colors depicts Silenus, the foster father of Bacchus, returning from a Bacchanalian Feast, being carried by bacchantes and satyrs. On the opposite side is the Flaying of Marsyas.

339. Made at the Capo di Monte factory which used only a soft paste porcelain body. A class of figures comprising Neapolitan folk types and especially Italian Comedy figures, was made here that ranks among the best made in Europe. Ht. 8 5/8″

340. A remarkably fine example of modeling, graceful and animated, meticulously finished, from this factory where figures were the chief production. Ht. 8″

341. One of the two chief classes of figures in the Gricci period, 1760-1770, were naked boys frequently symbolical of Seasons or Continents or playing with goats or rams, bacchantes and the like, which reveal the hand of Gricci himself. All these small figures from Buen Retiro, as in this group, are graceful and vigorous with vivacity in their expressions.

342. Molded in relief; the scene depicts Christ beside a well conversing with the Woman of Samaria who holds a vase; enclosed in an oval Rocaille border developing a shell-form basin at the base. Ht. 23 1/4″

343. Saint-Cloud forms are of great interest and beauty; the heavy build of pieces, as in this example with polychrome enameled chinoiserie decoration, are typical. Ht. 4 1/4″

344. Belongs to an interesting small class decorated with applied gold leaf raised and tooled so that it has the appearance of creased foil. Generally seen only on pieces such as snuff boxes, small pots, jars and the like. Ht. 1 3/4″

345. Probably the most characteristic of all Chantilly wares are those in the Japanese "Kakiemon" style painted in colored enamels which owing to the quality of soft-paste acquired a new charm and softness. Ht. 4 1/8″

346. Magots were a popular subject of all the earliest European porcelain factories and were for the most part remarkably similar to the Chinese originals. Ht. 6 1/2″

347. Sprays of plum blossoms are characteristic of Saint-Cloud and Mennecy; they were also favored at Bow. Ht. 6 1/4″

348. The enamel painting is conspicuously cool and fresh in color, a distinctive feature of their best work. L. 8¼"

349. It appears that Mennecy made a specialty of fashionable trinkets. This small box painted in enamel colors with gold and enamel mounts and a rock crystal lid bears the inscription *MON PETIT SOULIER EST A VOUS/ JOLI PETIT NOEL Y SONGEZ-VOUS.* L. 3½"

350. Molded in the popular basketwork pattern and painted with flowers in the Deutsche Blumen manner. The forms of this factory, like this salt dish, were generally simple and graceful. Ht. 1⅛"

351. From the central interior of the bowl, depicting a view of the castle of Vincennes where the Dubois brothers obtained rooms for starting the manufacture of soft-paste porcelain in 1738. This event was of great importance in French ceramic history, as it was from here that stemmed the beginning of the great Sèvres factory which was to eclipse all the early French factories.

352. This celebrated bouquet of naturalistic flowers painted in colors was sent by Marie-Josèphe, Dauphiness of France, to her father Augustus III, Elector of Saxony. The flowers are arranged in a white enameled porcelain vase with a group on either side symbolizing the Arts by Dupierreux; mounted on a boldly scrolled Rococo gilt bronze base by Duplessis.

353. Made for Marie-Josèphe, Dauphiness of France. On a turquoise blue ground; on one side the scene La Chasse in enamel colors, on the opposite side a Rococo cartouche surmounted by a crown enclosing a trophy of the hunt. Ht. 6½"

354. The original model is attributed to Boucher and was destined to be one of the most popular models reproduced in later times. Ht. 9½"

355. E. M. Falconet made the original model in 1757. Of the works produced by E. M. Falconet during his period of directorship at Sèvres, 1757 to 1766, the group La Lanterne Magique may be mentioned as typical and one of the best known. Ht. 6⅛"

356. The form is called *vaisseau à mât* as it is shaped like a masted ship. Objects of this class are rare luxury pieces, *ouvrages de grand luxe,* each one being a masterpiece of technical skill because soft paste lacks plasticity. Ht. 17½"

357. The neck of each vase is embellished with a pair of adorsed elephants' heads in white porcelain touched with gold, with upturned trunks for the support of candle sockets. The modeling is attributed to Duplessis. It is often thought that many of the "important" vases were made for diplomatic presents to serve as centerpieces for elaborate table services. Ht. 15½"

358. Boldly molded reverse scroll bracket supporting two branching arms of curling oak leaves and berries. Deep blue-green enlivened with gilding. The modeling is ascribed to Duplessis. Such *bras de cheminée* are extremely rare among Sèvres products. Ht. 17"

359. Ice pail with cover and liner, part of a dinner service, in the style and period of Louis XVI. Ice pails for cooling drinks and foodstuffs were much in fashion in the closing decades of the 18th century. Ht. 7⅞"

360. The ambitious work was commissioned by Napoleon I and was taken from a design by Percier. It served as a prototype for countless 19th century variants.

361. The signing of the Treaty of Alliance between France and the United States, February 1778. Inscription (on treaty): *Indépendence/ de l'Amérique/ Liberté/ des Mers/* One of the three thought to be the work of the sculptor Charles-Gabriel Sauvage, known as Lemire. Ht. 12¾"

362. In the form of Pu T'ai Ho Shang, the Chinese God of Happiness; mushroom hat with floral finial serving as cover. This tea caddy forms part of a small group of the Triangle Period models copied from Chinese Blanc-de-Chine originals. Perhaps it was this taste for pure white which caused the rapid improvement of the paste and glaze at Chelsea. It was to be succeeded by a preference for colored decoration of the Raised and Red Anchor periods. Ht. 6¾"

363. In the form of a scallop shell with moss and coral markings, supported by a crayfish; rock base with seaweed and shells in applied relief. The form was probably taken from silver. Salt cellars of this class were included in Horace Walpole's famous collection at Strawberry Hill. Ht. 2¾"

364. Hob-in-the-Well painted in enamel colors in the Japanese Imari style. "Flora or Hob-in-the-Well" was the name of a farce by Colley Cibber which had been popular from 1715. Dia. 12¼"

365. Molded in the form of a cauliflower partially covered with its leaves and resting on its side, the leaves painted on the edge with graduated tones of bright yellow-green. An extremely popular model. Ht. 5¼″

366. A shepherd instructing a shepherdess to play the flute, both seated on a mound before a bocage of flowering hawthorn. Modeled after the engraving by R. Gaillard of François Boucher's painting L'Agréable Leçon. Versions of the painting were made at Vincennes about 1753 and at Frankenthal by J. F. Lück. The Chelsea Music Lesson is characteristic of the last phase of English Rococo with its exuberance of form and decoration. The use of a hawthorn bocage was also favored at Bow, Derby, and Plymouth, where Chelsea models were often adapted and sometimes copied. Ht. 15″

367. After a Meissen model by Kaendler representing Water from a famous set of four vases symbolical of the Four Elements first made for Count Brühl in 1747-1748 and much reproduced later. Two handles in the form of cattails growing up against the side; small rope handle at front and back; rock base with pair of water fowl; white basket with decoration in green, lavender and brown, gilded details. Ht. 10¼″

368. After one of Kaendler's most popular productions, the guelder-rose or schneeball vases closely covered with small white flowers of the most fragile description applied in full relief. This vase encrusted with tiny white blossoms with yellow centers, also described as checkerberry and snowdrop, is decorated with festoons of molded red berries and green leaves, the stems forming the handles; cover finial in the form of a bunch of red berries.

369. Shows the influence of Sèvres. The dark blue ground color intended to imitate the gros blue of Vincennes with painting in gold (in this example peacocks, exotic birds and flowering shrubbery) imparts an effect of subdued richness. Part of the cover has a white ground painted in gold. Ht. 5⁵⁄₁₆″

370. Painted in enamel colors with touches of gilt; molded with a basket pattern enclosing quatrefoil flowers touched with red-violet; two brown twig handles with flowers and foliage in natural colors and in relief applied at attachments; cover pierced, decorated in the same manner. With matching stand. Ht. 5½″

371. A fine example of the so-called Worcester-Japan patterns, which were chiefly free adaptations of Imari Nishiki. They were done almost from the very beginning at Worcester where they remained in vogue for a long time. The starlike treatment of the Japanese Kiku comprising sixteen petals and a central calyx was widely popular in this class of Worcester-Japan patterns.

372. This popular rose pattern painted in polychrome enamels was also used at Bow and Chelsea.

373. A widely popular pattern in the style of Sèvres; painted in gold and enamel colors, with garlands of green leaves and red berries hanging between vertical bands of trelliswork in crimson and gold.

374. Transfer-printed in black from an engraving by Robert Hancock; the technique of transfer printing was adopted quite early, about 1755-1757, at Worcester. This engraving of Milkmaids and Haymakers, one of Hancock's most popular compositions, is in keeping with the fashionable taste for rustic simplicity stemming from Marie Antoinette and her make-believe peasant life in the cottages she had built at the Petit Trianon. Ht. 4⅞″

375. In the flower-encrusted style of decoration, interspersed with songbirds, a cock and hen and the figure of a girl at the top of the cover. Ht. 16¼″

376. Vases, such as this model with applied decoration of leaves and flowers with Rococo frills and scrolls painted in enamel colors, were a delightful Bow creation; probably decorated in the London workshop of James Giles. Ht. 12⅝″

377. From an orchestra group inspired by a Meissen original, the Monkey Band, caricaturing the Saxon Court Orchestra. Ht. 6¾″

378. Probably intended for feeding a child or invalid. Decorated in underglaze blue. Soft-paste porcelain made at Lowestoft resembles that of Bow which contains bone ash as one of its ingredients. Ht. 3″

379. Made at the Royal Copenhagen Porcelain Manufactory; decorated with flowers in natural colors surrounded by Rococo cartouches in green, five knobs modeled as apples, one as a rosebud. Ht. of cup 3⅛″

380. The design, painted in underglaze blue, from the Immortelle pattern of Meissen, was one of the first patterns borrowed at the Royal Copenhagen Porcelain Manufactory where its appeal continues to the present. In fact, the blue fluted dinner service may be called Denmark's National Service. Ht. 11¾"

381. Perhaps the most famous work in Copenhagen porcelain made at the Royal Copenhagen Porcelain Manufactory. In heavy classical forms; the painting in fresh natural colors shows a pleasing arrangement of the flowers; with gilding.

382. Probably modeled by Johann Valentin Sonnenschein, previously of Ludwigsburg. His figures at Zurich were chiefly inspired by those of Ludwigsburg and include musicians, soldiers, peasants, vendors, fishermen and others in contemporary costume. The Bird Vendor is characteristic of this genre. Ht. 6½"

383. Painted in enamel colors and made at the St. Petersburg Imperial factory. Peasants in the different costumes of the Empire were a popular class of figure models at the Russian porcelain factories. As a rule they were derived from the Abbé J. G. Georgi's DESCRIPTION DE TOUTES LES NATIONS DE L'EMPIRE DE RUSSIE, a work first published in 1776-1777 and dedicated to the Empress Catherine II. Modeled in a simple and direct manner, these figures possess vitality and charm. Ht. 8"

384. From a dinner service ordered by the Empress Elizabeth I, 1741-1762, made at the Imperial factory; decorated with an expanding trellis pattern of raised gilt lines intersected by mauve flowers with yellow centers; gilt scalloped rim.

STAFFORDSHIRE: 18th CENTURY

385. This coffeepot belongs to a charming group of lead-glazed earthenwares made of a colored clay generally decorated with cream-colored stamped motifs in relief. The range of colors used for the body include various shades of ochre from pale buff to orange and brown and reds varying from light to very dark chestnut. These wares are attributed to John Astbury; however, present-day evidence does not substantiate the tradition that he was the originator of them. Astbury type wares were made by a number of potters, not only in Staffordshire, but elsewhere.

386. Of the Astbury type. (See preceding) It may also be called "Jackfield" because the body has the characteristic "shining black" finish. (See following) Then, too, because Whieldon made practically every kind of lead-glazed earthenware and stoneware of that era, except enamel-painted and transfer-printed wares, it may be attributed to Whieldon. Briefly, there is a choice. Ht. 4¾"

387. By adding manganese to both the red clay and lead glaze a black ware was produced which is occasionally called "shining black" or more frequently "Jackfield." The Staffordshire variety was often decorated with vine leaves and flowers in applied relief, which were sometimes oil-gilded as in this example or coated with a cream-colored slip.

388. Ascribed to Thomas Astbury. Apparently peculiar to Astbury are the very artless renderings of cavalrymen, generally quite small. Ht. 8"

389. There are two sorts of variegated wares; those which are colored throughout and those where the effect is confined to the surface only. In this example the color clay slips were trailed, combed and mingled on the surface. Dia. 13¾"

390. Marbled in two shades of brown and covered with cream-colored slip. The design is obtained by cutting through the slip to reveal the brown marbled body. Inscribed *John and Dorothy Cook 1766.* Ht. 9½"

391. In this type of variegated ware clays were kneaded together to imitate natural stone such as agate, marble, granite and onyx. Beautiful results were obtained, as in this example formed of blue and white clay.

392. Brownish-black and white. (See preceding)

393. The tortoiseshell effect was achieved by dusting metallic oxides onto the unfired lead-glazed surface. When the piece was fired the mingling of the oxides produced splashes or mottlings of color. This creamware oval stand of silver design with a molded border gadrooned at the edge, mottled with colored glazes in manganese-

brown, blue and green (and in manganese-brown on the underside) is ascribed to Thomas Whieldon. L. 16"

394. Tortoiseshell ware of the Whieldon type; teapot with crabstock handle and spout and upright flower knob, decorated with a vine and floral pattern in applied relief. Ht. 4½"

395. Milkmaid and Cow with dog under stylized tree; of the Whieldon type; predominantly mottled with leaf-green, greyish-blue and yellow glazes. The base bears the inscription *Remember Me Mary Chapman When This You See MB.* Ht. 7½"

396. Made by Wedgwood and Bentley. The surface color-glazed mottling of the body is much more controlled and successfully simulates the stone vases of the day which were being used as architectural themes. The original leaf gilding has been replaced by a solid cream glaze. The ewer illustrates the Neo-Classical taste in England brought into fashion by the Adam brothers. Ht. 11"

397. By Greatbatch and Wedgwood. In 1764, according to Wedgwood correspondence, William Greatbatch was supplying Josiah Wedgwood with "Colly flower" ware; one order included 20 dozen teapots. In this example the upper part is cream-color, the lower part, handle and spout a rich geen glaze. At Ivy House Wedgwood introduced his first distinctive and original ware with the invention of a brilliant clear green glaze which he used to decorate leaf and vegetable shapes well suited to the Rococo taste of the period. Ht. 4½"

398. Molded by Jean Voyez and made by Ralph Wood the Younger. A tree trunk with figures in high relief, on one side a standing youth and a dog and on the other a girl offering a nest full of eggs taken from a branch held in her right hand. On a paper fastened to the tree is inscribed *Fair Hebe* and on another *A bumper, a bumper.* Coated in colored glazes, chiefly blue and shades of green under a clear lead glaze. Wares by the Ralph Woods are notable for their distinctive colored glazes. Ht. 8¾"

399. Made by Ralph Wood the Younger and coated in colored glazes under a clear lead glaze; the figure holds in his left hand a plug of tobacco and in his right a small jug. Ht. 11½"

400. Made by Ralph Wood the Younger, body roughly incised to suggest fur; color-glazed with patches of pale brown, green, yellow and white, under a clear lead glaze; eyes touched with black. Ht. 7"

401. Made by Josiah Wedgwood. The finished service was enameled in sepia, while the trial pieces are in polychrome and are much more pleasing. Before enameling on creamware became popular, the painted decoration was entirely in colored glazes, of which Whieldon was a leading exponent.

402. One of six plates made at John Turner's factory and decorated in polychrome enamels in Holland. Each plate depicted a scene from the story of the Prodigal Son. This example plate 3 bears the inscription *Zyn Hoerery* (His Dissolute Life). Quantities of English creamware were exported to Holland in the "white" and then enameled there.

403. Made by Neale and Company; painted in colored enamels. Their figures were delicately finished and frequently, as in these two examples, show a foliated scroll pedestal above the rectangular base. Ht. 5½"

404. Much creamware of the finest quality was made at The Old Pottery, Leeds, from about 1764 to 1820. Pierced work usually over-elaborated was especially characteristic.

405. Made at Pont-aux-Choux; molded in relief in the Rococo style. The popularity of English creamware on the Continent resulted in the manufacture of pottery in the English style by many continental factories. Ht. 7⅞"; W. 9½"

406. Depicts a scene in the Neo-Classical taste painted in polychrome enamels. The mark includes the initials G.M.B. (Giovanni Maria Baccin who in 1774 became manager for the Widow Antonibon and in 1780 started a new factory in partnership with G. B. Viero of Bassano.) Ht. 10½"

407. With crabstock handle and spout and applied relief decoration. This class of red stonewares in imitation of Chinese Yi-hsing wares was made in Staffordshire from the late 17th century to about 1765, when the material was named Rosso Antico by Wedgwood. Ht. 9¼"

408. Between two narrow bands of fine roulette tooling one side is decorated with sharp reliefs representing Admiral Vernon's capture of Porto Bello, 1739; on the opposite side an inscription in five columns: *The British Glory Rev : V : D/ By Admiral Vernon/ He Took Porto Bello/ With Six Ships : : Only/ Nov : Ye: 22 1739*. Dia. 5″; Ht. 3″

409. The introduction of plaster of Paris intaglio molds about 1745 led to an outburst of fanciful modeling, like this slip-casted teapot and the following example. In this casting process slip was poured into the assembled plaster mold which absorbed the water quickly, leaving a thin lining of clay. This was repeated until the lining was sufficiently thick when, after it had dried, it was removed from the mold. The decoration was devised to disguise the joins in the mold. Ht. 7¾″

410. Ht. 5⅞″ (See preceding)

411. It appears that enameling on salt-glazed stoneware which preceded enameling on earthenware by at least a decade or more was first introduced at Cobridge about 1740. In early examples the enameled decoration was occasionally either entirely or partly in the form of applied reliefs as on this teapot with a crabstock handle and spout. Ht. 3⅝″

412. Molded in relief; two crouching goats at the base; bee in center of flower; spray painted in enamel colors. Chelsea made an all-white soft-paste porcelain goat-and-bee milk jug in 1745.

413. Molded in relief and painted in enamel colors.

414. Mottled crabstock spout, handle and handle cover. The charming chinoiserie decoration is effectively painted in polychrome enamels. Ht. 5⅞″

415. Probably by William Littler at Longton Hall. Entirely covered with a rich deep blue lead glaze and decorated in white enamels. This class of ware was made by a number of Staffordshire potters and was not confined only to Staffordshire. Ht. 3¼″

416. Probably by William Littler at Longton Hall. Molded in relief with overlapping leaves; enameled in green, yellow and pink. Ht. 4″

417. Certain details are picked out in a brownish-black enamel. Sometimes the suggestion has been made that these delightfully stylized seated figures known as Pew Groups were the work of the Staffordshire potter Aaron Wood. Ht. 7½″

418. Rattle in the form of a bear crushing a small dog (an allusion to the popular sport of bear baiting); certain details picked out in a brownish-black enamel. Ht. 2¾″

419. Greyish stoneware; brown eyes, tongues and colors; blue on noses, ears and forepart of bodies. These rare figures are a creditable attempt to copy Chinese models. Ht. 8⅝″; Ht. 8⅛″

420. Probably enameled by William Littler at Longton Hall. Count Charles de Ferriol's book of 100 engravings entitled LES DIFFÉRENTES NATIONS DU LÉVANT, first published in Paris in 1714, was a source for a series of Meissen porcelain figures first modeled in the 1740's. Two of these figures of a Turkish lady and gentleman (the latter copied from a model by Kaendler) seem to have had particular appeal in England for they were copied not only in porcelain at Bow, Derby and Longton Hall, but also in stoneware and earthenware in Staffordshire. Ht. 6½″

421. Black basalt was the first of the ornamental wares to be developed by Josiah Wedgwood. This vase of black basalt is decorated with a frieze of ten figures painted in red and white "encaustic" enamels after a design from a Greek hydria in the British Museum. A fine example of Wedgwood's so-called Etruscan ware. Ht. 18″

422. At Brick House where Wedgwood first produced his black basalt he also made his first unglazed red stoneware which he called Rosso Antico. Most of it was engine-turned but later it was often ornamented with applied decoration of either black or white. This example made by Wedgwood combines both decorative techniques. Ht. 7½″

423. Jasper ware was the last of the ceramic bodies developed by Josiah Wedgwood. This pale blue and white jasper plaque of Dancing Hours figures, probably the most famous of John Flaxman's models for Wedgwood, was designed in 1775. L. 18⅜″; Ht. 5⅝″

424. Pale blue and white jasper plaque of Apotheosis of Homer was designed and modeled by John Flaxman in 1784 for Josiah Wedgwood.

425. A jasper reproduction of the Portland vase was completed by Wedgwood 1790 after four years of experiment. This is one of the first issue which was sold to Thomas Hope of Amsterdam in 1793 and who appears in the original list of subscribers in Thomas Byerley's notebook.

AMERICA: 19th CENTURY

426. Painted in bright underglaze colors over a white slip. The inscription around the border reads *Shave me beautiful and fine that I will please the beloved one of mine.*

427. Decorated with the widely popular tulip motif in the slip-trailed technique. The traditions of country pottery have chiefly survived through the style of earthenware known as slipware. Slip may be used decoratively in several different ways, of which the two most prominent are trailing and sgraffiato.

428. The direct and simple carving in openwork complements the form of the bowl in a manner that is entirely pleasing. Dia. 10½″

429. With twin lids and handle. A delightful example of rural pottery as simple and substantial as its contents.

430. Glazed red earthenware with sgraffiato decoration made in Upper Hanover Township, Montgomery County. The decoration was obtained by cutting through the white slip to the red body beneath; the whole being covered with a lead glaze. Inscribed (in the center) *FG/B/Liberty for Polk;* (on the rim) *In the dish on the table/Merry is he who is yet single/Samuel Troxel Potter 1846* (See 427)

431. Bowl with cover in red earthenware with trailed slip decoration in green and cream under a lead glaze. Ht. 3⅝″ (See 427)

432. Red earthenware covered with a cream slip; sgraffiato decoration of fuchsias and leaves; finally given a lead glaze. Made at Tylersport, in Montgomery County, in the vicinity of Jacob Scholl who was working about 1830. Ht. 8½″ (See 427)

433. Underglaze blue decoration; made by Edmands and Company. Ht. 13″

434. Underglaze blue decoration; made by R. C. Remmey Pottery Company. Bears the name Anna Jamison. A bird or birds perched on top of a coin bank was a metaphor few potters could resist.

435. Decorated with Gothic panels in relief under a dark brown "Rockingham" glaze. Made by the American Pottery Company. Ht. 8⅞″

436. Underglaze black transfer-printed portrait of William Henry Harrison and inscription *W. H. Harrison* in each panel; log cabin and legend *The Ohio Farmer* above and the American eagle below. Made by the American Pottery Company. Ht. 10½″

437. With underglaze blue transfer-printed decoration; Civil War battle scene depicting Pickett's Charge at Gettysburg. Made by the Edwin Bennett Pottery Company. L. 18″

438. A popular class of Bennington wares. This example is mottled in brown and white. Ht. 10⅜″

439. Lion figure with "cole-slaw" mane. Modeled by Daniel Greatbach and made at the Fenton-directed United States Pottery. Ht. 9¼″

440. Pitcher with diamond pattern. Made at the United States Pottery of Christopher Webber Fenton. Perhaps the rarest kind of pottery made by Fenton is his little-known scroddled ware which is the same in principle as solid agate. Pitcher Ht. 11″; Bowl Dia. 13″

441. With hunting scene in relief, and covered with a dark brown "Rockingham" glaze. Made at the Fenton-directed United States Pottery. Ht. 11¼″

442. All white with smear glaze; low relief decoration simulating a waterfall. Made at the Fenton-directed United States Pottery. Ht. 8¼″

443. Made at the Fenton-directed United States Pottery. The most important production of the English style relief-decorated jugs and related wares in the 1850's came from the Fenton pottery. Many of the patterns were derived from English designs, but they were mainly produced in a type of parian porcelain either uncolored or, as in this

example, with a white relief pattern clearly defined against a blue pebbled or pitted ground. Ht. 10½" (See 444, 452, 469, 470)

444. Parian porcelain with a shiny glaze molded in relief with a design of cornstalks, showing cobs, leaves and long silky styles; the handle molded in the form of a cornstalk. Made by the Southern Porcelain Company. Ht. 9½" (See preceding)

445. From the original statue of the same title by the Vermont sculptor Hiram Powers. Made by the Trenton Pottery Company. The original purpose of parian porcelain had been to reproduce statuary items generally made in marble by costlier sculpture. Ht. 12⅞"

446. Modeled by Isaac Broome and made by Ott and Brewer for the Centennial Exhibition held in Philadelphia, 1876. In the same year the National League of Professional Baseball Clubs was organized, comprising eight clubs including the Athletics from the Centennial City of Philadelphia. Ht. 34"

447. White undecorated soft-paste porcelain vase with caryatid handles in the Neo-Classical taste; made by Dr. Henry Mead; earliest extant piece of porcelain made in the United States known at the present time.

448. Made by William Ellis Tucker and bought at his workshop by Burkett Webb, 1827-1828. Pitchers like this example with a white ground, floral decoration in bright enamel colors and gilt banding, were made in quantity at the Tucker factory. The shape and the reeding around the bottom reveal an interest in classical form. Ht. 9½"

449. Pedestal vase painted in enamel colors with gilding; in the Neo-Classical style. The gilt bronze handles terminating in winged griffins' heads were designed by Friedrich Sachse and cast by C. Cornelius and Son, a Philadelphia firm famous for lamps and chandeliers. This ambitious vase, made at the Tucker-Hemphill factory, shows that their products could also be elaborate. Ht. 22" (See preceding)

450. The scenes depicting the Philadelphia Water Works on the teapot and a rustic dwelling below, are transfer-printed under the glaze in sepia and black. Made by the Tucker-Hemphill factory, who no doubt copied the form and style of

decoration from a French prototype; the scenes, however, are characteristically American. Ht. 11¼"

451. In the Rococo taste; painted in enamel colors enlivened with gilt. Made by Kurlbaum and Schwartz. Ht. 9¾"

452. Relief-decorated jug made by William Boch and Brother at their Greenpoint factory which in time became the Union Porcelain Works. Vaguely classical scenes, like this jug depicting young Bacchus in the grape arbor, shared honors in the 1840's and 1850's with Gothic decoration on this widely popular class of relief-decorated jugs, the majority of which by far were made in England in stoneware. Ht. 9¾" (See 443)

453. The Century vase commemorates events in American history and was exhibited at the Centennial Exhibition held in Philadelphia in 1876. It was designed by Karl Müller and made by the Union Porcelain Works. Ht. 22¼"

454. In the classical taste, made by Hugh G. Robertson at the Chelsea Keramic Art Works. Dia. 8"

455. Plate in the form of a clam decorated in high relief; a scallop, mussel and four oyster shells against a ground of marine life including a snail, lobster claw, whelk and seaweed—a decorative arrangement reminiscent of Bernard Palissy's rustic ware. This style, first revived in France in the 1840's, appealed to countless Victorian potters. Patented by the Union Porcelain Works, January 4, 1881; also bears retailer's mark, Tiffany and Company, New York. W. 8⁹⁄₁₆"

456. Walter Scott Lenox, famous for founding the Trenton Pottery which has borne his name since 1896, designed this Belleek pitcher in 1887 when he was art director of Ott and Brewer. A pleasing expression of the Rococo as interpreted in late 19th century ceramic art. Ht. 9⅜"

457. Made by the Ceramic Art Company of Trenton, New Jersey, which later became Lenox. The Swan dish was one of their most widely known pieces. Ht. 4¾"

458. Sweetmeat dish in the form of a shell designed by Joshua Poole and made by Knowles, Taylor and Knowles. Dia. 4¾"

459. Painted in enamel colors and enlivened with touches of gilding. It appears that Coalport's

interpretation of the Revived Rococo style in their popular flower-encrusted vases was the principal inspiration for this vase in which the decoration has been successfully integrated into the design. Ht. 9½″

460. Underglaze painting in colored slips by Mary Louise McLaughlin, who had first seen this technique in wares by Haviland of Limoges shown at the Centennial Exhibition held at Philadelphia, 1876. Ht. 37¼″

EUROPE: 19th CENTURY

461. Painted under the lead glaze in high temperature colors of blue, green and yellow of the so-called Pratt-ware class. Made at Ferrybridge, south of Leeds, near Castleford. Dia. 5″

462. Single Rose pattern. Painted under the glaze in high temperature colors of red, blue and green, outlined in yellow in place of gilding, border in blue.

463. War Bonnet pattern. Painted under the glaze in high temperature colors of red, bright blue and touches of green, enlivened with gilding.

464. Peafowl pattern, perhaps the most popular pattern of this class of so-called Spatterware, made chiefly for the Pennsylvania German trade. Painted in high temperature colors; bird in blue, orange and yellow, leaves sponged in green; an attractive naïve style of decoration.

465. Peafowl pattern; background sponged in rose; bird in blue, yellow and green.

466. Rainbow pattern, two-color, alternately green and lavender stripes. The Rainbow pattern is commonly done in three to five colors in alternating stripes.

467. American historical view: New York from Heights near Brooklyn. Made in 1823-1829 in two variants by the Staffordshire potter Andrew Stevenson at Cobridge. In this method of decorating the print is taken on specially prepared tissue paper from a copper plate or roller on which the pattern is engraved. Then it is applied on the surface of the ware, vigorously rubbed on to insure firm adhesion. The paper is then washed away, leaving the printed pattern transferred. Finally given a lead glaze.

468. American historical: Pennsylvania State Arms printed in 1829 by Thomas Mayer of Stoke. His blue printed wares were extensively exported to the United States. (See preceding)

469. Belongs to that immensely popular class of Victorian relief-decorated jugs. This example, the most famous of the Gothic jugs and the one which established the style for most of the others, was registered in 1842 by Charles Meigh and bears a relief figure in each of the eight Gothic niches. Ht. 9¼″

470. Relief-decorated with "Silenus" group on a blue colored ground made by Mintons. Probably the most popular of the "Classical" jugs described as such only in so far as the decoration includes figures which are classical in origin or in spirit. Usually the figures are combined with loose vine patterns. In this example Silenus, the foster-father of Bacchus, a bit tipsy, is combined with a grapevine pattern. Ht. 7⅝″

471. In imitation of ancient Greek red-figure ware made by Dillwyn and Company. Inevitably in this age of stylistic eclecticism the 1840's saw a revival of interest in imitation Greek wares which were generally known at this time as Etruscan or Etrurian. In effect it carried on the tradition of Wedgwood's black basalt. Ht. 14⅜″

472. A delightful example of Victorian majolica made by Josiah Wedgwood. Ht. 9¼″

473. Lithophanes, also called lithophanies, with their predominantly sentimental pictures, were a great success and were intended for hanging as transparencies in windows. Made of unglazed porcelain, they are molded on the reverse side with a pictorial subject in intaglio so as to give the appearance of a low relief when light shines through. They were introduced at Meissen in 1828 and appeared about the same time at the Royal Porcelain Manufactory at Berlin, where this example was made. The process was also used for lamp shades. Ht. 5⅞″

474. Made at Coalport which was outstanding for its interpretation of the Revived Rococo. This

factory, often known as Coalbrookdale, probably made most use of "encrusted" decorations of applied flowers and leaves in the Revived Rococo style, supplemented by quite lavish painting in enamel colors and gilding.

475. Made by Minton and painted in enamel colors enlivened with gilding by Thomas Allen in 1848. This ambitious pedestal vase in the revived Neo-Classical taste was shown at the Great Exhibition of 1851.

476. Made by the Worcester Royal Porcelain Company. With bamboo handle and spout; painted in enamel colors, enlivened with gilding. In England double-walled objects both useful and ornamental, having the outer wall pierced in a honeycomb effect, were introduced at Worcester about 1845, and may be regarded as a Worcester innovation. The original inspiration for this model derived from Sèvres.

477. Made by the Royal Copenhagen Porcelain Manufactory, the figure is a small scale copy of a statue made in 1818 by Thorwaldsen, who was perhaps the most successful of all the imitators of classical sculpture. Many of his statues of pagan deities are modeled with much of the antique feeling for breadth and purity of design. Ht. 11½"

478. From the Belleek factory of D. McBirney and Company, probably designed by R. W. Armstrong. Modeled in the form of a shell and decorated with marine life in characteristic Belleek fashion.

479. Made by Minton with pâte-sur-pâte decoration in white on a blue ground by Marc Louis Solon, the Frenchman who brought this decorative technique to England where the parian porcelain body was found to be especially suitable.

480. Made by Doultons of Lambeth and purchased from the Centennial Exhibition at Philadelphia in 1876. The floral decoration shows Turkish influence and was painted by Mary Butterton, one of the most competent of the artists at Doultons. L. 14"

481. Made by Doultons of Lambeth and decorated by George Tinworth, the first of the student-artists from the Lambeth School of Art to be associated with Doultons. Perhaps the first English product which can be called artist-pottery

was the salt-glazed stoneware decorated at Doultons by these students. Ht. 10⅜"

482. With inicised decoration on a brown ground, inscribed *R. W. Martin & Bros., London & Southall, 9-1886*. The floral decoration shows the influence of Near Eastern pottery. Ht. 9⅜"

483. Made by William de Morgan in his Persian manner, at Sand's End Pottery, Fulham.

484. Pottery from Castle Hedingham in Essex is notably different from normal slipware country pottery. It is unmistakable both because of its markedly individual style and because it bears the initials of the potter Edward Bingham, son of a potter who came to Castle Hedingham in the 1830's, and the symbol of a castle. Much later, young Bingham with his son E. W. Bingham began to specialize in making individual ornamental pieces. This dish in the Palissy manner is inscribed respectively over each one of the six masks: *NOBILIS/ ACVTVS/ PLACIDA/ HONESTVS/ FIDELIS/ SPERVS/* with flowers above. Expressing decorative symbolism by means of an inscription is a medieval idea and was reintroduced by the Gothic revivalists.

485. With underglaze painting in blue by Arnold Krog, made by the Royal Copenhagen Porcelain Manufactory. Shows the growing interest in the use of Oriental forms and the influence of the Japanese concept of painted decoration.

486. Modeled by Arnold Krog and made by the Royal Copenhagen Porcelain Manufactory. Painted in pastel underglaze shades which relate successfuly to their medium of slip-cast porcelain with a smooth glazed surface. These owls in near abstraction are in contrast to the more realistic style to be continued at Copenhagen in later years. Ht. 12¾"

487. With underglaze painting by Bertha Nathanielsen made by the Royal Copenhagen Porcelain Manufactory. The sense of abstraction is reminiscent of a style of Japanese gold lacquer painting of the Muromachi period.

488. With black and cream-colored glazes. In Denmark the use of ceramics as a medium of expression for the individual artist was initiated with the work of Thorwald Bindesbøll in the 1880's, who used earthenware as a medium.

489. Massier's work decorated around the turn

of the century with luster glaze effects stood somewhat apart from the principal movement of artist-pottery centered in Paris which focused on the possibilities of Far-Eastern glazing techniques.

490. Chaplet was more instrumental than any other in developing the cult of glazing techniques among French artist-potters in the closing years of the 19th century. He made all his wares by hand and sometimes without even the aid of the wheel. His *grès* stonewares and porcelains of blues, violets, greys and copper-reds possessed great beauty.

491. The glaze of velvet-like richness enhances the strongly modeled form.

492. Slightly asymmetrical, this vase shows Dalpayrat's sense of form in relation to glaze effects.

493. Covered with a light golden brown flecked glaze with streaks of darker brown; a technically interesting example of Far Eastern glazing techniques.

TWENTIETH CENTURY WORLD: USEFUL WARES

494. With decoration in the Art Nouveau manner, painted in green, lavender and grey. Designed by Edward Colonna and made at Limoges.

495. From a service designed by Henry van de Velde for the Meissen Manufactory about 1905. The pattern of the border molded in relief with underglaze painting in blue and overglaze gilding combines the French curvilinear with the Austrian simple geometric, the square, as developed by Hoffmann.

496. Designed by Richard Riemerschmid and manufactured by Reinhold Merkelbach of Grenzhausen. The simple geometric ornament in the form of a circle reflects the influence of Hoffmann and Olbrich.

497. From the "Donatello" service designed by Philipp Rosenthal and made by the Rosenthal Porcelain Manufactory. The form reflects the influence of the Modern Movement; the original version was without the painted underglaze decoration.

498. From a service designed by the Lenox China Company as part of the first American-made dinnerware to be used at the White House in 1918 by President Wilson. Its rim is of cobalt blue with an outer border of etched gold. The 48 stars show on an inner etched rim. In the center of the plate is the President's seal executed in raised 24-carat gold.

499. Designed by Joseph Hoffmann for the Augarten factory at Vienna. Hoffmann, who was an important figure in the Modern Movement, reveals a fine sensitivity for the plastic character of the material.

500. Designed by Trude Petri-Raben for the Royal Berlin Porcelain Manufactory. The entire service is the prototype of the modern white porcelain dinnerware, most of which depends for its effect on precise geometric shapes whose finely finished surfaces are their sole decoration.

501. Designed by Ena Rottenberg for the Augarten factory, the service is an interesting exercise in the Modern style tempered somewhat exotically by the finials in the form of a Chinaman's head.

502. Designed by Eva Zeisel for the Castleton China Company in collaboration with the Museum of Modern Art in New York.

503. Designed by Friedel Kjellberg and made by Arabia. This ever-popular technique in which small holes of a desired shape are made in the moist porcelain and filled with a glazing material is believed to have been a Chinese innovation of the 15th century. It also occurred in the Persian Gombroon ware. The popularity of the Rice pattern in Japan continues.

504. Hand-thrown stoneware with brown and cream-colored slip glaze made by the designer-craftsman Lucie Rie.

505. Decorated with grey and gilt bands, designed by Giovanni Gariboldi and made by the Richard-Ginori factory. In this service the Modern style has been interpreted with admirable creativity.

506. Designed by Axel Salto and made by the Royal Copenhagen Porcelain Manufactory. It exemplifies the balance between form, function and material which is the governing thought in modern Danish design.

507. Designed by Robert Minkin and made by Josiah Wedgwood and Company. Tableware pieces of black basalt are glazed on the inside.

508. Pieces in white and plain colors from the "Kilta" service designed by Kaj Franck and made by the Arabia factory. This revolutionary service, which combines many of the functions of cooking, serving and table use, established a general style for this class of wares.

509. Designed by Magnus Stephensen and made by the Royal Copenhagen Porcelain Manufactory.

510. Designed by Ulla Procopé for Arabia, this deep brown Liekki (which means flame in Finnish) ware is suitable for direct use on a flame. Dishes are so made that they can be stacked and the lids of the cooking vessels can be used as serving dishes.

511. Designed by Heinz H. Engler and made by the Lorenz Hutschenreuther Porcelain Manufactory. The popular stacking feature is typically European contemporary.

ORNAMENTAL WARES

512. Decorated by Mary Shearer at the Newcomb College Pottery. The emphasis on the vertical reflects the coming influence of Art Nouveau. Ht. 12″

513. In the Art Nouveau style. Made at the Rörstrand factory and probably designed by Alf Wallander. Floral decoration modeled in slight relief forms the rim. Painted in muted underglaze colors in the manner initiated at Royal Copenhagen. Ht. 8⅜″

514. In brown and pale blue made by Alexandre Bigot, with mounts by Edward Colonna. Both of these French artist-craftsmen were influential friends of Art Nouveau.

515. The relief decoration reveals the linear rhythm of Art Nouveau.

516. This delightful manifestation of Art Nouveau, painted in green, lavender and grey, is the work of Georges de Feure; the potter was E. Gérard.

517. The form designed by J. Jurriaan Kok and painted by J. Schellink, from the Rozenberg pottery. In this example the theme of Art Nouveau is expressed not only in the decoration but also, and much more rare in ceramics, in the form. Ht. 10″

518. From the table setting *Le jeu de l'écharpe* modeled by Agathon Léonard for the Sèvres Manufactory, shown at the Paris Exhibition, 1900. A beautifully rendered expression of the swirling movement of Art Nouveau. Ht. 12⅜″

519. Made by Richard-Ginori. After the merger in 1896 with the Richard Company the earliest work was dominated artistically by the adoption of the Art Nouveau style. This example illustrates the Italian blend of Art Nouveau in which naturalism and the modern spirit are the principle ingredients. Ht. 15³⁄₁₆″

520. In the Art Nouveau style. With painted underglaze slip decoration, made by Artus van Briggle at the Rookwood pottery. Ht. 8¾″

521. Leaflike motifs modeled in relief in the Art Nouveau manner, soft blue and green mat glaze; made by Artus van Briggle at his Colorado Springs pottery. Ht. 5″

522. With vertical leaf-like motifs modeled in slight relief in the Art Nouveau style, covered with a yellow mat glaze; made at the Grueby Faïence Company. Ht. 10⅞″

523. Brown glaze and light decoration, made by the J. B. Owens Pottery Company and decorated by Albert Haubrich. The taste for light decoration on a brownish ground, introduced at Rookwood, established a general style for many other potteries. Ht. 22⁵⁄₁₆″

524. This ambitious and elaborately carved piece of work entitled "The Apotheosis of the Toiler" is popularly known as the Scarab Vase. Ht. 16½″

525. Made at Artel and designed by Vlastislav Hofman, this yellow glazed vase shows a Cubist approach in geometrical forms. Ht. 11½"

526. Modeled by Paul Scheurich for the Berlin State Porcelain Manufactory. An effective rhythmic expression of classicism with early 20th century intent. Ht. 15"

527. Figures and towers in polychrome, arches in gilding; made at Richard-Ginori and designed by Gio Ponti. The attenuated urn shape and cube plinth emphasize the concept of Art Moderne. Ht. 19½"

528. The great period of French artist-pottery, the period of stoneware with beautiful glazes, was continued after the First World War in the work of such artist-potters as Emile Decoeur and Emile Lenoble. This vase by Emile Decoeur is covered with a mat pale-green crackled glaze of great beauty; the form is in accordance with fine Chinese traditions.

529. Glazed stoneware with more insistent and incised motifs and with heavier forms was a development dating from the 1920's. (See preceding)

530. From the 1920's the scope of French artist-pottery began to widen. Such potters as René Buthaud were covering their stoneware with human figures in an Art Deco theatrical manner.

531. Silver chevron pattern on a mat-green glazed ground; designed by Wilhelm Käge for the Gustavsberg factory. The simple yet sophisticated treatment of pattern demonstrates an artistic assurance.

532. Made by the Herman A. Kaehler factory and painted in black by Jens Thirslund on a greyish-white mat glaze with bands at neck and foot in red luster. The bold linear outline of the figure establishes the contemporary mood of the cup.

533. Modeled by Arno Malinowsky and made by the Royal Copenhagen Porcelain Manufactory. Like all figures by Arno Malinowsky, this figure reflects a certain humor and grace of the artist's personality.

534. With a mottled glaze, from the Bing and Grøndahl factory, modeled by Knud Kyhn, who liked to work in stoneware which was in time to supplant porcelain as the favorite material for figure-making in Denmark.

535. Made by the Royal Copenhagen Porcelain Manufactory and modeled by Jais Nielsen, who also liked to work in stoneware. In forming his subjects he often drew his inspiration from the Bible.

536. Modeled by Kai Nielsen and made by Bing and Grøndahl. Potters through the centuries have found the subject of Silenus, the foster-father of Bacchus irresistible. See 338, 470.

537. The principal piece in the group The Sea, modeled by Kai Nielsen for Bing and Grøndahl. Nielsen frequently drew his inspiration for subjects from classical mythology. The allegory of Fecundity has always appealed to ceramists. (See 257)

538. Made by Bing and Grøndahl and modeled by Jean René Gauguin. His work is always dynamic and masterful.

539. Decorated with liquid clay slips under a lead glaze. The sturdiness of the form is in striking contrast to the lightness of the design. Ht. 11⅝"

540. Grey and brown glaze; the playful fantasy of the decoration is accentuated by the solid interpretation of form. Ht. 15"

541. Made by the Spanish potter José Llorens Artigas. A mature example of his work.

542. Made by the Spanish potter José Llorens Artigas and painted by his fellow Catalan Joan Miró. The jar is a demonstration of the consistency of Miró's expression in all media. Ht. 11⅜"

543. With brushwork decoration. A bold and assertive work.

544. Unglazed red-orange Bizen ware; an entirely satisfying expression of form. Ht. 9"

545. Brown and grey slip with incised designs under a grey glaze. A fine example of his art.

546. Made by Royal Worcester and modeled by Dorothy Doughty.

547. A ceramic narrative made by Bing and Grøndahl. Modeled by Mogens Bøggild, head of the Royal Academy of Art and noted for his famous bird sculptures executed in polychrome.

548. Made by the Lorenz Hutschenreuther Porcelain Manufactory and modeled by. Gunther Granget. The playful spirit of this ceramic work momentarily masks the miracle of potting.

549. Water vessels in unusual forms are occasionally found from Segorbe. Belongs to that category of "art without epoch."

550. "Cavalier sur sa Monture" designed and decorated by Picasso in the Madoura workshop of Suzanne and Georges Ramié. Painted in black and brown with incised detail. Ht. 15½"

551. Made by Axel Salto at the Royal Copenhagen Porcelain Manufactory. A rich play of color in the greenish-brown glaze is achieved by letting it flow down over the sculptural relief decoration, Salto's so-called "budding" style. Ht. 10½"

552. Salto's inspiration was Life and Nature. He expressed it in this way: "It is of far greater importance to an artist to create in accordance with Nature than to copy her exterior. The creative artist does not draw from what he sees but from what he knows and surmises." He called this vase "The Core of Nature's Force."

553. Incised geometrical design; light green with decoration in dark green; designed by Eva Staeher-Nielsen and glazed by Nathalie Krebs, made at the Saxbo pottery. Possesses an unsophisticated simplicity evocative of Japanese tea-ceremony wares.

554. A fine globular form with "Leopard spot" glaze, rust, tan and orange. Ht. 15"

555. With turquoise copper glaze. Solid of form and exceptionally stable of foot, this vase is further distinguished by the delicate shaping of the lip.

556. Squared and carved, interior green glaze flowing over the top, blending with exterior glaze of thinly applied white; speckled clay body showing through. The rhythmic flow of the design plays a counterpoint to the solidity of the silhouette. Ht. 10"

557. Formed by the coiling technique and glazed only on the inside. A successful interpretation of the primitive concept. Ht. 8¾"

558. A distinctive ruggedness characterizes much of Gádor's pottery. Ht. 11¾"

559. Fired clay, black, white and red. The checkers give the massive form an aura of whimsicality. Ht. 8"

560. White glazed stoneware of thrown and slab construction. A juxtaposition of crude materials with refined imagination. Ht. 37½"

561. With iron slip. Ht. 40" (See preceding)

562. Slab construction. The projections develop in an upward movement and grow out of the planes. Ht. 38"

BIBLIOGRAPHY

General: Histories

BURTON, WILLIAM. *A General History of Porcelain.* 2 vols., London, 1921.

CHARLESTON, ROBERT JR., ed. *World Ceramics.* New York, 1968.

COX, WARREN E. *The Book of Pottery and Porcelain.* 2 vols., New York, 1944.

HANNOVER, EMIL. *Pottery and Porcelain: A Handbook for Collectors.* Translated by W. W. Worster. Edited with notes and appendices by Bernard Rackham. *Europe and the Near East Earthenware and Stoneware,* vol. I; *The Far East,* vol. II; *European Porcelain,* vol. III. London, 1925.

HONEY, WILLIAM BOWYER. *European Ceramic Art: From the end of the Middle Ages to About 1815.* 2 vols., London 1952.

JACQUEMART, ALBERT. *History of the Ceramic Art.* Translated by Mrs. Bury Palliser. London, 1873.

LANE, ARTHUR. *Guide to the Collection of Tiles in the Victoria and Albert Museum.* London, 1960.

MARRYAT, JOSEPH. *History of Pottery and Porcelain: Medieval and Modern.* Third edition, London, 1868.

General: Repertories of Ornament and Ornemanistes

BERLINER, RUDOLF. *Ornamentale Vorlage-Blätter des. 15 bis 18 Jahrhunderts.* 4 vols., Leipzig, 1924–1926.

BOSSERT, HELMUTH THEODOR. *An Encyclopedia of Color Decoration: From the Earliest Times to the Middle of the Nineteenth Century.* New York, 1928.

———. *Ornament in Applied Art: Reproducing decorative motifs from the arts of Asia, primitive Europe, North, Central and South America, Africa, Oceania and from the peasant arts of Europe.* New York, 1924.

CHENAVARD, AIME. *Nouveau recueil des ornements.* Paris, 1833–1835.

GUILMARD, DESIRE. *Les maitres ornemanistes.* 2 vols., Paris, 1880.

JESSEN, DR. PETER. *Der Ornamentstich.* Berlin, 1920.

———. *Meister des Ornamentstichs.* Berlin, 1923.

MEYER, FRANZ SALES. *Handbook of Ornament.* Fifth edition, New York, n.d.

SPELTZ, ALEXANDER. *Styles of Ornament: from Prehistoric Times to the Middle of the Nineteenth Century.* Translated from the second German edition by David O'Conor. Revised and edited by R. Phene Spiers. London, 1910.

Marks

BARBER, EDWIN ATLEE. *Marks of American Potters.* Philadephia, 1904.

BURTON, W., and HOBSON, R. L. *Handbook of Marks on Pottery and Porcelain.* London, 1928.

CHAFFERS, WILLIAM. *Marks and Monograms on European and Oriental Pottery and Porcelain.* European and Oriental section edited by Frederick Litchfield and R. L. Hobson; British section edited by Geoffrey A. Godden. Fifteenth edition, 2 vols., London, 1965.

CUSHION, J. P. *Pocket Book of English Ceramic Marks.* London, 1965.

———. *Pocket Book of German Ceramic Marks.* London, 1961.

———. *Pocket Book of French and Italian Ceramic Marks.* London, 1965.

CUSHION, J. P., and HONEY, W. B. *Handbook of Pottery and Porcelain Marks.* London, 1956.

DANCKERT, LUDWIG. *Handbuch des Europäischen Porzellans.* Munich, 1954.

GODDEN, GEOFFREY. *Encyclopedia of British Pottery and Porcelain Marks.* New York, 1964.

———. *Handbook of British Pottery and Porcelain Marks.* London, 1968.

GRAESSE. DR. J. H. *Th. und E. Jaennicke. Fuhrer für Sammeler von Porzelan und Fayence.* Edited by Arthur Behse and Luise Behse. Twenty-first edition, Braunschweig, n.d.

HONEY, WILLIAM BOWERY. *European Ceramic Art: From the End of the Middle Ages to about 1815.* 2 vols., London, 1952.

JUSTICE, JEAN. *Dictionary of Marks and Monograms on Delft Pottery.* London, 1930.

PENKALA, MARIA. *European Pottery.* Rutland, Vt., 1968.

TILLEY, FRANK. *Principal Marks on Continental Porcelain of the Eighteenth Century.* Cambridge, 1955.

Technical, Aesthetic, Social and Related Subjects

BINNS, CHARLES F. *The Potter's Craft.* New York, 1947.

BURTON, WILLIAM. *Porcelain: A Sketch of Its Nature, Art and Manufacture.* London, 1906.

COLBECK, JOHN. *Pottery: the Technique of Throwing.* London, 1969.

COOPER, DOUGLAS, ed. *Great Family Collections.* New York, 1965.

DALTON, W. B. *Craftsmanship and Design in Pottery.* London, 1957.

GREEN, DAVID. *Pottery: Materials and Techniques.* London, 1967.

HETHERINGTON, ARTHUR LONSDALE. *Chinese Ceramic Glazes.* Cambridge, 1937.

HILLIER, BEVIS. *Pottery and Porcelain: 1700–1914.* London, 1968.

HONEY, WILLIAM BOWYER. *The Art of the Potter.* London, 1946.

LEACH, BERNARD. *A Potter's Book.* Second edition, London, 1945.

———. *A Potter's Portfolio: A Selection of Fine Pots.* London, 1951.

———. *A Potter in Japan: 1952–1954.* London, 1960.

LANE, ARTHUR. *Styles in Pottery.* London, 1948.

MORLEY-FLETCHER, HUGO. *Investing in Pottery and Porcelain.* London, 1968.

NELSON, GLENN C. *Ceramics: A Potter's Handbook.* Revised edition, New York, 1966.

NORTON, F. H. *Ceramics for the Artist Potter.* Reading, Mass., 1956.

PICCOLPASSO, CIPRIANO. *I tre libri dell' arte del vasia* [The three books of the potter's art]. Translated by Bernard Rackham and Albert Van de Put. London, 1934.

REICHWEIN, ADOLF. *China and Europe: Intellectual and Artistic Contacts in the Eighteenth Century.* Second edition, London, 1969.

REITLINGER, GERALD. *The Economics of Taste.* 2 vols., London, 1961–1963.

RHODES, DANIEL. *Clay and Glazes for the Potter.* Philadelphia, 1957.

———. *Stoneware and Porcelain: The Art of High-Fired Potery.* Arts and Crafts Series. Philadelphia, 1959.

———. *Kilns: Design, Construction and Operation.* Philadelphia, 1968.

SCHMIDT, R. *Porcelain as an Art and Mirror of Fashion.* Translated by W. A. Thorpe. London, 1932.

SEARLE, A. B. *The Glazer's Book.* London, 1948.

TILLEY, FRANK. *Teapots and Tea.* Newport, Monmouth, England, 1957.

WINTERBURN, MOLLIE. *The Technique of Handbuilt Pottery.* London, 1966.

Primitive World

Art of Oceania, Africa and the Americas from the Museum of Primitive Art. New York: Metropolitan Museum of Art, 1969.

BENNETT, W. C., and BIRD, J. B. *Andean Culture History.* Handbook Series, no. 15. New York: American Museum of Natural History, 1949.

BOSSERT, HELMUTH T. *Folk Art of Primitive Peoples: Africa, Asia, Australia and Oceania, North, Central and South America.* New York, 1955.

BUSHNELL, GEOFFREY HEXT SUTHERLAND. *The Archaeology of the Santa Elena Peninsula in South-West Ecuador.* Cambridge, 1951.

———. *Ancient Arts of the Americas.* London, 1965.

BUSHNELL, GEOFFREY HEXT SUTHERLAND, and DIGBY, ADRIAN. *Ancient American Pottery.* London, 1955.

COE, MICHAEL D. *Mexico.* London, 1962.

———. *The Jaguar's Children: Pre-classic Central Mexico.* New York, 1965.

CRANSTONE, B. A. L. *Melanesia: A Short Ethnography.* British Museum, 1961.

DOCKSTADER, FREDERICK J. *Indian Art in America.* Third edition, Greenwich, Conn., 1966.

DRUKER, PHILIP. *La Venta, Tabasco: A Study of Olmec Ceramics and Art.* Washington: Bureau of American Ethnology, 1952.

EMMERICH, ANDRE. *Art Before Columbus: The Art of Ancient Mexico.* New York, 1963.

FEWKES, JESSE WALTER. *Designs on Prehistoric Pottery from the Mimbres Valley, New Mexico.* Washington, 1924.

KELEMEN, PAL. *Medieval American Art.* New York, 1956.

LEHMANN, HENRI. *Pre-Columbian Ceramics.* Translated by Galway Kinnell. New York, 1962.

LINNE, SIGVALD. *Archaeological Researches at Teotihuacan, Mexico.* Publication no. 1. Stockholm; The Ethnographical Museum of Sweden, 1934.

————. *Zapotecan Antiquities.* Publication no. 4. Stockholm: The Ethnographical Museum of Sweden, 1938.

LOTHROP, SAMUEL KIRKLAND. *Treasures of Ancient America.* Cleveland, 1964.

————. *Pottery of Nicaragua and Costa Rica.* Heye Foundation, Contribution no. 8. New York: Museum of the American Indian, 1926.

MEGGERS, BETTY JANE. *Ecuador.* London, 1956.

MORLEY, SYLVANUS GRISWOLD. *The Ancient Maya.* Stanford, Calif., 1946.

REICHEL-DOLMATOFF, G. *Colombia.* London, 1965.

SAWYER, ALAN R. *Ancient Peruvian Ceramics in the Nathan Cummings Collection.* New York: Metropolitan Museum of Art, 1966.

UBBELOHDE-DOERING, HEINRICH. *The Art of Ancient Peru.* London, 1952.

VAILLANT, GEORGE C. *Excavations at Zacatenco. Excavations at El Arbolillo. Excavations at Gualupita. Early Cultures of the Valley of Mexico.* Papers in a series from the *American Museum of Natural History Anthropological Journal.* New York, 1930–1936.

WANCHOPE, R., ed. *Handbook of Middle American Indians.* Texas, 1964.

WORMINGTON, H. M. *Prehistoric Indians of the Southwest.* Denver Museum of Natural History, Popuar Series no. 7. Second edition, Denver, Colo., 1951.

Ancient World

AKURGAL, EKREM. *The Art of the Hittites.* New York, 1962.

ARIAS, P. E., and HIRMER, M. *A History of Greek Vase Painting.* London, 1962.

BEAZLEY, SIR JOHN D. *Attic Red-Figure Vase Painters.* Second edition, Oxford, 1963.

————. *The Development of Attic Black-Figure.* Oxford, 1951.

————. *Attic Black-Figure Vase Painters.* Oxford, 1956.

BOARDMAN, JOHN. *Pre-Classical: From Crete to Archaic Greece.* Harmondsworth, England, 1967.

CHARLESTON, ROBERT J. *Roman Pottery.* London, 1955.

COOK, ROBERT MANUEL. *Greek Painted Pottery.* London, 1955.

EVANS, SIR ARTHUR JOHN. *The Palace of Minos at Knossos.* London, 1921–1935.

FOLSOM, ROBERT S. *Handbook of Greek Pottery.* London, 1967.

FRYE, RICHARD N. *The Heritage of Persia.* New York, 1963.

HUTCHINSON, RICHARD WYATT. *Prehistoric Crete.* Harmondsworth, England, 1962.

LANE, ARTHUR. *Greek Pottery.* London, 1963.

LLOYD, SETON. *Early Anatolia.* Harmondsworth, England, 1956.

————. *Art of the Ancient Near East.* London, 1961.

MARINATOS, SPYRIDON. *Crete and Mycenae.* London, 1960.

MALLOWAN, MAX EDGAR LUCIEN. *Nimrud and Its Remains.* New York, 1966.

————. *Twenty-Five Years of Mesopotamian Discovery: 1932–1956.* London, 1959.

————. *Early Mesopotamia and Iran.* London, 1965.

MELLAART, JAMES. *The Chalcolithic and Early Bronze Ages in the Near East and Anatolia.* Beiruth, Lebanon, 1966.

NICHOLSON, FELICITY. *Greek, Etruscan and Roman Pottery and Small Terracottas.* London, 1965.

NOBLE, JOSEPH VEACH. *The Techniques of Painted Attic Pottery.* New York, 1965.

PARROT, ANDRE. *Sumer: The Dawn of Art.* Translated by Stuart Gilbert and James Emmons. New York, 1961.

————. *The Arts of Assyria.* Translated by Stuart Gilbert and James Emmons, New York, 1961.

PFUHL, ERNST. *Masterpieces of Greek Drawing and Painting.* Translated by J. D. Beazley. Second edition, London, 1955.

PORADA, EDITH. *The Art of Ancient Iran.* New York, 1965.

RICHTER, GISELA M. A. *Attic Red-Figured Vases.* Revised edition, New Haven, Conn., 1958.

————. *Greek Painting.* New York, 1952.

————. *Handbook of Greek Art.* London, 1959.

RICHTER, GISELA M. A., and MILNE, MARJORIE J. *Shapes and Names of Athenian Vases.* New York, 1935.

RICHARDSON, EMELINE HILL. *The Etruscans: Their Art and Civilization.* Chicago, 1964.

ROUX, GEORGES. *Ancient Iraq.* London, 1964.

STROMMENGER, EVA. *5000 Years of the Art of Mesopotamia.* Translated by Christina Haglund. New York, 1964.

WEBSTER, THOMAS BERTRAM LONSDALE. *Greek Terracottas.* London, 1950.

ZERVOS, CHRISTIAN. *L'art des Cyclades: au début à la fin l'âge du bronze, 2500–1100 avant notre ère.* Paris, 1957.

————. *L'art de la Crète: Néolithique et Minoenne.* Paris, 1956.

———. *L'art en Grèce: du troisième millénaire au IV siècle avant notre ère.* Paris, 1946.

Far Eastern World

AUDSLEY, G. A., and BOWES, JAMES L. *The Keramic Art of Japan.* London, 1881.

BEURDELEY, MICHEL. *Chinese Trade Porcelain.* Translated by Diana Imber. London, 1962.

BOSSERT, HELMUTH THEODOR. *Decorative Art of Asia and Egypt: Four hundred decorative motifs in color.* New York, 1956.

BRINKLEY, CAPTAIN FRANK. *Japan Ceramic Art.* Japan and China: Their History, Arts and Literature, vol. VIII. London, 1904.

———. *China Ceramic Art.* Japan and China: Their History, Arts and Literature, vol. IX. London, 1904.

BUSHELL, STEPHEN W. *Oriental Ceramic Art: Illustrated by examples from the collection of W. T. Walters.* New York, 1897–1899.

FITZGERALD, CHARLES PATRICK. *China: A Short Cultural History.* London, 1935.

GARNER, SIR HARRY. *Oriental Blue and White.* London, 1954.

GOLDSMITH, JOHN PHILLIPS. *China-Trade Porcelain.* Cambridge, Mass., 1956.

GOMPERTZ, GODFREY ST. G. M. *Chinese Celadon Wares.* London, 1958.

———. *Korean Celadon: And Other Wares of the Koryo Period.* London, 1963.

———. *Korean Pottery and Porcelain of the Yi Period.* New York, 1968.

———. *Celadon Wares.* London, 1969.

GRANDJEAN, BREDO L. *Dansk Ostindisk porcelaen: importen fra Kanton, c. 1700–1822.* Copenhagen, 1965.

GRAY, BASIL. *Early Chinese Pottery and Porcelain.* London, 1953.

JAPANESE CERAMICS SOCIETY. *Catalogue of the Exhibition of Kakiemon, Imari and Nabeshima Wares.* Tokyo, 1959.

———. *Catalogue of the Exhibition of Japanese Pottery and Porcelain Through the Ages.* Tokyo, 1957.

HOBSON, ROBERT LOCKHART. *Chinese Pottery and Porcelain: An Account of the Potter's Art in China from Primitive Times to the Present Day.* 2 vols., New York, 1915.

———. *Catalogue of Chinese Pottery and Porcelain in the Collection of Sir Percival Victor David* London, 1934.

———. *Handbook of the Pottery and Porcelain of the Far East.* Third edition, London, 1948.

———. *Chinese Art.* Revised by Soame Jenyns. Second edition, London, 1952.

———. *Catalogue of the Chinese, Corean and Persian Pottery and Porcelain in the George Eumorfopoulos Collection.* 6 vols., London, 1925–1928.

———. *The Later Ceramic Wares of China.* London, 1925.

———. *The Wares of the Ming Dynasty.* London, 1923.

HONEY, WILLIAM BOWYER. *Corean Pottery.* London, 1947.

———. *The Ceramic Art of China and Other Countries of the Far East.* London, 1945.

HYDE, JOHN ALDEN LLOYD. *Oriental Lowestoft.* New York, 1936.

JENYNS, SOAME. *Ming Pottery and Porcelain.* London, 1953.

———. *Later Chinese Porcelain.* London, 1965.

———. *Japanese Porcelain.* London, 1965.

———. *Japanese Pottery.* London, 1970.

JOLY, HENRI L. *Legend in Japanese Art.* London, 1908.

JOURDAIN, M., and JENYNS, R. S. *Chinese Export Art in the Eighteenth Century.* London, 1950.

KIM, CHAE-WON, and GOMPERTZ, G. ST. G. *The Ceramic Art of Korea.* New York, 1961.

KOYAMA, FUJIO, ed. *Japanese Ceramics: From Ancient to Modern Times.* California, 1961.

———. *One Hundred Selected Masterpieces of Japanese Ceramics.* Tokyo, 1962.

———. *Chinese Ceramics: One Hundred Selected Masterpieces from Collections in Japan, Engand, France and America.* Tokyo, 1960.

LEACH, BERNARD. *Kenzan and His Tradition.* London, 1964.

LEE, SHERMAN E. *Tea Taste in Japanese Art.* New York, 1963.

MILLER, ROY ANDREW. *Japanese Ceramics.* After the Japanese text by Okuda, Koyama, Hayashiya et al. Tokyo, 1960.

MUDGE, JEAN McCLURE. *Chinese Export Porcelain for American Trade: 1785–1835.* New York, 1962.

MUNSTERBERG, HUGO. *The Ceramic Art of Japan.* Tokyo, 1964.

NAGATAKE, TAKESHI. *Kyushu Ko-Toji* [Ancient Ceramics of Kyushu]. Tokyo, 1963.

NAGATAKE, TAKESHI et al. *Kakiemon.* Sponsored by the Society for the Investigation of Kakiemon. Saga, 1957.

————. *Ko Imari.* Sponsored by the Society for the Investigation of Imari. Saga, 1959.

NOMA, SEIROKU. *The Art of Clay: Primitive Japanese Clay Figurieres, Earthenware and Haniwa.* Tokyo, 1954.

OKUDA, HAYASHIYA, and OKUDA, KOYAMA, eds. *Japanese Ceramics.* Tokyo, 1954.

OKOCHI, MASATOSHI. *Kakiemon and Iro-Nabeshima.* Fourth edition, Tokyo, 1933.

SANSOM, G. B. *Japan: A Short Cultural History.* Revised edition, New York, 1943.

SEKAI TOJI ZENSHU. *Catalogue of World's Ceramics.* 14 vols., Tokyo (?), 1955–1958.

————. *Collection of World Ceramics.* Edited by Seiichi Mizuni. 16 vols., Tokyo, 1961.

TUDOR-CRAIG, SIR ALGERNON. *Armorial Porcelain of the Eighteenth Century.* London, 1925.

VOLKER, DR. T. *Porcelain and the Dutch East India Company: 1602–1682.* Leiden, 1954.

————. *The Japanese Porcelain Trade of the Dutch East India Company After 1863.* Leiden, 1959.

WERNER, EDWARD THEODORE CHALMERS. *A Dictionary of Chinese Mythology.* Shanghai, 1932.

————. *Myths and Legends of China.* New York, 1922.

WILLIAMSON, GEORGE C. *The Book of Famille Rose.* Rutland, Vt., 1970.

WU, CHIN-TING. *Prehistoric Pottery in China.* London, 1938.

Islamic

HOBSON, ROBERT LOCKHART. *A Guide to the Islamic Pottery of the Near and Far East.* London, 1932.

LANE, ARTHUR. *Early Islamic Pottery.* London, 1947.

————. *Islamic Pottery from the Ninth to Fourteenth Centuries, in the Eldred Hitchcock Collection.* London, 1956.

————. *Later Islamic Pottery: Persia, Syria and Turkey.* London, 1957.

RACKHAM, BERNARD. *Islamic Pottery and Italian Majolica: Ilustrated Catalogue of a Private Collector.* London, 1959.

RICE, DAVID TALBOT. *Islamic Art.* New York, 1965.

WILKINSON, CHARLES K. *Iranian Ceramics.* New York, 1963.

Byzantine

MORGAN, CHARLES HILL, II. *The Byzantine Pottery.* Cambridge, Mass., 1942.

RICE, DAVID TALBOT. *Byzantine Glazed Pottery.* Oxford, 1930.

————. *Byzantine Art.* Revised edition, London, 1954.

European Pottery and Porcelain

ALFASSA, PAUL, and GUERIN, JACQUES. *Porcelaine Française: du XVII au milieu du XIX siècle.* Paris, 1931.

ALFASSA, P.; BLOCK, J., and CHOMPRET, J. *Répertoire de la faïence Française.* Paris, 1935.

ANDRADE, CYRIL. *Astbury Figures.* London, 1924.

AUSCHER, ERNEST S. *History and Description of French Porcelain.* Translated by William Burton. London, 1905.

AVERY, C. LOUISE. *Catalogue of the Exhibition of Masterpieces of European Porcelain in the Metropolitan Museum of Art Collection.* New York, 1949.

BALLARDINI, GAETANO. *La maiolica Italiana: dalle origini alla fine del cinquecento.* Florence, 1938.

————. *L'eredità ceramistica dell' antico mondo Romano.* Rome, 1964.

BALLOT, MARIE JULIETTE. *La céramique Française.* 2 vols., Paris, 1925.

BALSTON, THOMAS. *Staffordshire Portrait Figures of the Victorian Age.* London, 1958.

BARBER, EDWIN A. *Hispano-Moresque Pottery in the Collection of the Hispanic Society of America.* 2 vols., New York, 1915.

BARRETT, FRANKLIN A. *Worcester Porcelain.* London, 1953.

————. *Caughley and Coalport Porcelain.* London, 1951.

BARNARD, HARRY. *Chats on Wedgwood Ware.* London, 1924.

BEMROSE, GEOFFREY. *Nineteenth Century English Pottery and Porcelain.* London, 1952.

BERLING, KARL. *Das Meissner Porzellan und seine Geschichte.* Leipzig, 1900.

————. *Festschrift zur 200 Jährigen Jubelfeier der Ältisten Europäischen Porzellanmanufaktur.* Meissen, 1910. English edition, Leipzig, 1911.

BLATTLER, UGO. *La ceramica in Italia.* Rome, 1958.

BLUNT, REGINALD, ed. *The Cheyne Book of Chelsea China and Pottery.* London, 1924.

BONEY, KNOWLES. *Liverpool Porcelain.* London, 1957.

BOSSERT, HELMUTH THEODOR. *Folk Art of Europe.* 1923. Translated by Sybil Mohoy-Nagy. New York,

BRYANT, GILBERT ERNEST. *The Chelsea Porcelain Toys.* London, 1925.

BURTON, WILLIAM. *History and Description of English Earthenware and Stoneware.* London, 1904.

————. *Josiah Wedgwood and His Pottery.* London, 1922.

———. *A History and Description of English Porcelain.* New York, 1902.

CHARLES, ROLLO. *Continental Porcelain of the Eighteenth Century.* London, 1964.

CHARLESTON, ROBERT J., ed. *English Porcelain 1745–1850.* London, 1965.

CHAVAGNAC, XAVIER-ROGER-MARIE, COMTE DE, and GROLLIER, GASTON-ANTOINE, MARQUIS DE. *Histoire des manufactures Françaises de porcelaine.* 2 vols., Paris, 1906.

CHOMPRET, DR. JOSEPH. *Répertoire de la majolica Italienne.* Paris, 1949.

CLARKE, HAROLD GEORGE. *Underglaze Color Picture Prints on Staffordshire Pottery.* London, 1949.

CONNAISSANCE DES ARTS. *Les porcelainiers du XVIIIe siècle Français.* Paris, 1964.

———. *L'oeuvre des faïenciers Français: du XVIe à la fin du XVIIIe siècle.* Paris, 1966.

CUSHION, JOHN P. *Animals in Pottery and Porcelain.* New York, 1966.

DANCKERT, LUDWIG. *Handbuch der Europäischen Porzellans.* Munich, 1954.

DAUTERMAN, CARL C. *Porcelain.* Wrightsman Collection, vol. IV. New York, 1970.

DE JONGE, DR. CAROLINE H. *Delft Ceramics.* Translated by Christine Kellin. Rotterdam, 1969.

DINGWALL, KENNETH. *The Derivation of Some Kakiemon Designs on Porcelain.* London, 1926.

DIXON, JOSEPH L. *English Porcelain of the Eighteenth Century.* London, 1952.

DUCRET, SIEGFRIED. *German Porcelain and Faïence.* Translated by Diana Imber. New York, 1962.

———. *Meissen Porcelain.* Translated by Marjorie Gibson Craig. Berne, 1964.

EISNER, EISENHOF, ANGELO, BARON VON. *Le porcellane di Capo-Di-Monte.* Milan, 1925.

ENGLISH CERAMIC CIRCLE. *Commemorative Catalogue of an Exhibition of English Pottery and Porcelain at the Victoria and Albert Museum, May 5–June 20, 1948.* London, 1949.

ERDBERG, JOAN PRENTICE VON, and ROSS, MARVIN C. *Catalogue of Italian Majolica in the Walters Art Gallery.* Baltimore, 1952.

EYLES, DESMOND. *Royal Doulton 1815–1965.* London, 1965.

FALKE, OTTO VON. *Das Rheinische Steinzeug.* 2 vols., Berlin, 1908.

FINER, ANN, and SAVAGE, GEORGE. *The Selected Letters of Josiah Wedgwood.* London, 1965.

FISHER, STANLEY W. *The Decoration of English Porcelain: A Description of the Painting and Printing on English Porcelain, 1750–1850.* London, 1954.

FONTAINE, GEORGES. *La céramique Française.* Paris, 1965.

FORTNUM, CHARLES DRURY EDWARD. *A Descriptive Catalogue of the Majolica, Hispano-Moresque, Persian, Damascus and Rhodian Ware in the South Kensington (Victoria and Albert) Museum.* London, 1873.

———. *A Descriptive Catalogue of the Majolica and Enamelled Earthenware of Italy . . . in the Ashmolean Museum.* Oxford, 1897.

FROTHINGTON, ALICE WILSON. *Catalogue of Hispano-Moresque Pottery in the Collection of the Hispanic Society of America.* New York, 1936.

———. *Capo di Monti and Buen Retiro Porcelains: Period of Charles III.* New York, 1955.

———. *Lusterware of Spain.* New York, 1951.

———. *Talavera Pottery.* New York, 1944.

GARNER, SIR HARRY. *English Delftware.* London, 1948.

GARNIER, EDOUARD. *The Soft Porcelain of Sèvres.* London, 1892.

GAUTHIER, JOSEPH. *Faïences et poteries rustiques.* Paris, 1929.

GIACOMOTTI, JEANNE. *French Faïence.* Translated by Diana Imber. New York, 1963.

GILHESPY, F. BRAYSHAW. *Derby Porcelain.* London, 1961.

GODDEN, GEOFFREY A. *Caughley and Worcester Porcelain, 1775–1800.* London, 1969.

———. *The Illustrated Guide to Lowestoft Porcelain.* London, 1969.

———. *Victorian Porcelain.* London, 1961.

———. *Coalport and Coalbrookdale Porcelains.* London, 1970.

———. *Minton Pottery and Porcelain of the First Period.* London, 1968.

———. *An Illustrated Encyclopedia of British Pottery and Porcelain.* London, 1966.

GRANDJEAN, BREDO. *Kongelig Dansk Porcelain.* Copenhagen, 1962.

HACKENBROCH, YVONNE. *Meissen and Other Continental Porcelain: Faïence and Enamel in the Irwin Untermyer Collection.* Cambridge, Mass., 1956.

———. *Chelsea and Other English Porcelain, Pottery, and Enamel in the Irwin Untermyer Collection.* Cambridge, Mass., 1956.

HAGGAR, REGINALD G. *The Concise Encyclopedia of Continental Pottery and Porcelain.* London, 1960.

———. *Staffordshire Chimney Ornaments.* New York, 1955.

———. *English Pottery Figures, 1660–1860.* London, 1947.

HAVARD, HENRY. *La céramique Hollandaise.* Amsterdam, 1909.

HAYDEN, ARTHUR. *Royal Copenhagen Porcelain.* London, 1911.

HARE, RICHARD. *The Arts and Artists of Russia.* London, 1965.

HAYWARD, JOHN FORREST. *Viennese Porcelain of the Du Paquier Period.* London, 1952.

HERNMARCK, CARL. *Marieberg.* Stockholm, 1946.

————. *Fajans och Porslin.* Stockholm, 1959.

————. *Orrefors.* Stockholm, 1951.

HOFMANN, FRIEDRICH HERMANN. *Das Porzellan der Europäischen Manufakturen im 18 Jahundert.* Berlin, 1932.

HONEY, WILLIAM BOWYER. *Dresden China.* New edition, London, 1954.

————. *English Pottery and Porcelain.* Revised by H. J. Charleston. Sixth edition, London, 1969.

————. *German Porcelain.* London, 1947.

————. *French Porcelain of the Eighteenth Century.* London, 1950.

————. *Wedgwood Ware.* London, 1948.

HOVEY, WALTER READ. *Potteries and Porcelains.* Frick Collection, An Illustrated Catalogue, vol. VIII. New York, 1949–1955.

HUDIG, FERRAND WHALEY. *Delftur Fayence.* Berlin, 1929.

HUGHES, G. BERNARD. *Victorian Pottery and Porcelain.* London, 1959.

HURLBUTT, FRANK. *Bow Porcelain.* London, 1926.

————. *Bristol Porcelain.* London, 1928.

————. *Chelsea China.* London, 1937.

HUSELER, KONRAD. *Deutsche Fayencen.* 3 vols., Stuttgart, 1956–1958.

IMBER, DIANA. *Collecting Delft.* London, 1968.

JEWITT, LLEWELLYN. *Ceramic Art of Great Britain 1877: From prehistoric times down to the present day.* Second edition, London, 1883.

KELLY, ALISON. *The Story of Wedgwood.* London, 1962.

KING, WILLIAM. *Chelsea Porcelain.* London, 1922.

————. *English Porcelain Figures of the Eighteenth Century.* London, 1925.

KOETSCHAU, KARL. *Rheinisches Steinzeug.* Munich, 1924.

KOLLMANN, ERICH. *Berliner Porzellan.* 2 vos., Braunschweig, 1966.

KORF, DINGEMAN. *Dutch Tiles.* London, 1963.

KRISZTINKOVICH, BELA. *Habaner Pottery.* Rotterdam, 1965.

LANE, ARTHUR. *English Porcelain Figures of the Eighteenth Century.* London, 1961.

————. *French Faïence.* London, 1948.

————. *Italian Porcelain.* London, 1954.

LAIDACKER, SAMUEL. *American Historical Views; Gaudy Dutch, Spatter, etc.* Anglo-American China, part I. Revised second edition, Bristol, Pa., 1954.

————. *Other than American Views.* Anglo-American China, part II. Bristol, Pa., 1951.

LARSEN, ELLOUISE BAKER. *American Historical Views on Staffordshire China.* Revised second edition, New York, 1950.

LECOMTE, GEORGES. *A. Delaherche.* Paris, 1922.

LIVERANI, GIUSEPPE. *Five Centuries of Italian Majolica.* London, 1960.

LUKOMIKI, GEORGE II. *Russisches Porzellan, 1744–1923.* Berlin, 1924.

MACKENNA, F. SEVERNE. *Chelsea Porcelain: The Gold Anchor Wares.* Leigh-on-Sea, England, 1952.

————. *Chelsea Porcelain: The Red Anchor Wares.* Leigh-on-Sea, England, 1951.

————. *Chelsea Porcelain: The Triangle and Raised Anchor Wares.* Leigh-on-Sea, England, 1948.

————. *Cookworthy's Plymouth and Bristol Porcelain.* Leigh-on-Sea, England, 1946.

————. *Champion's Bristol Porcelain.* Leigh-on-Sea, England, 1947.

MANKOWITZ, WOLF, and HAGGAR, REGINALD G. *The Concise Encyclopedia of English Pottery and Porcelain.* New York, 1957.

MARTI, MANUEL GONZALEZ. *Cerámica Española.* Barcelona, 1933.

MEAGER, KILDARE S. *Swansea and Nantgarw Potteries.* Swansea, 1949.

MORAZZONI, GIUSEPPE. *Le maioliche di Milano.* Milan, 1948.

————. *Le porcellane Italiane.* Milan, 1935.

MORLEY-FLETCHER, H. *Meissen.* London, 1970.

NANCE, E. MORTON. *The Pottery and Porcelain of Swansea and Nantgarw.* London, 1942.

NEURDENBURG, ELIZABETH. *Old Dutch Pottery and Tiles.* Translated by Bernard Rackham. London, 1923.

PAZAUREK, GUSTAVE E. *Deutsche Fayence und Porzellan Hausmaler.* 2 vols., Leipzig, 1925.

PENKALA, MARIA. *European Porcelain.* Rutland, Vt., 1969.

————. *European Pottery.* Rutland, Vt., 1968.

POCHE, EMANUEL. *Bohemian Porcelain.* Translated by Richard K. White. London, 1957.

PONCETTON, FRANCOIS, and SALLES, GEORGES. *Les poteries Françaises.* Paris, 1928.

RACKHAM, BERNARD. *Guide to the Italian Majolica in the Victoria and Albert Museum.* London, 1933.

————. *Dutch Tiles, the Van den Bergh gift: A Guide to the Collection, in the Victoria and Albert Museum.* London, 1931.

————. *Catalogue of Italian Majolica in the Victoria and Albert Museum.* 2 vols., London, 1940.

————. *Catalogue of the Herbert Allen Collection of English Porcelain.* London, 1917.

————. *Porcelain.* Catalogue of the Charles Schreiber Collection in the Victoria and Albert Museum, vol. I. London, 1929.

————. *Earthenware.* Catalogue of the Charles Collection in the Victoria and Albert Museum, vol. II. London, 1930.

————. *Medieval English Pottery.* New York, 1949.

————. *Italian Majolica.* London, 1952.

————. *Early Staffordshire Pottery.* London, 1951.

————. *Catalogue of the Glaisher Collection of Pottery and Porcelain in the Fitzwilliam Museum.* 2 vols., Cambridge, 1935.

————. *Animals in Staffordshire Pottery.* London, 1953.

————. *Early Netherlands Majolica.* London, 1926.

————. *Guide to the European Pottery and Porcelain in the Fitzwilliam Museum.* Cambridge, 1935.

RACKHAM, BERNARD, and READ, HERBERT. *English Pottery: Its Development from Early Times to the End of the Eighteenth Century.* London, 1924.

RAY, ANTHONY. *English Delftware Pottery in the Robert Hall Warren Collection, Ashmolean Museum, Oxford.* London, 1968.

RICCI, SEYMOUR DE. *Catalogue of Early Italian Majolica in the Collection of Mortimer L. Schiff.* New York, 1927.

RICE, D. G. *The Illustrated Guide to Rockingham Porcelain.* London, 1970.

ROSS, MARVIN C. *Russian Porcelains.* Norman, Okla., 1968.

RUCKERT, RAINER. *Meissener Porzellan, 1710–1810.* Munich, 1966.

SANDON, HENRY. *The Illustrated Guide to Worcester Porcelain.* London, 1969.

SCHMIDT, ROBERT. *Deutsche Hafnerarbeiten der Gotik und Renaissance.* Frankfurt-on-Main, 1919.

SHAW, SIMEON. *History of the Staffordshire Potteries.* Hanley, Stoke, 1829.

SITWELL, SACHEVERELL. *Theatrical Figures in Porcelain: German Eighteenth Century.* London, 1949.

SMITH, ALAN. *The Illustrated Guide to the Liverpool Herculaneum Pottery, 1796–1840.* London, 1970.

SOLON, LOUIS MARC EMANUEL. *A History and Description of Old French Faïence.* London, 1903.

————. *A Brief History of Old English Porcelain and Its Manufactories.* London, 1903.

STAEHELIN, WALTER S. *The Book of Porcelain.* Translated by Michael Bullock. Bern. 1965.

STRAUSS, KONRAD P. *Alte Deutsche Kunstöpferien.* Berlin, 1923.

STRINGER, GEORGE EYRE. *New Hall Porcelain.* London, 1949.

TILMANS, EMILE. *Porcelains de France.* Paris, 1953.

TOWNER, DONALD C. *Leeds Pottery.* London, 1963.

————. *English Cream-Coloured Earthenware.* London, 1957.

ULDALL, KAI. *Gammel Dansk Fajence.* Copenhagen, 1967.

VAN DE PUT, A. *Hispano-Moresque Ware of the Fifteenth Century.* London, 1904.

————. *The Valencian Styles of Hispano-Moresque Pottery, 1404–1454.* New York, 1938.

VERLET, PIERRE; GRANDJEAN, SERGE; and BRUNET, MARCELLE. *Sèvres.* Le XVIIIe Siècle par Verlet. Les XIX & XX Siècles par Grandjean. Les Marques de Sèvres par Brunet. 2 vols., Paris, 1953.

VYDRA, JOSEF, and KUNZ, LUDVIK. *Painting on Folk Ceramics.* Translated by Roberta Finlayson Samsour. London, 195-?

VYDROVA, JIRINA. *Italian Majolica.* Translated by Ota Vojtisek. London, 1960.

WAKEFIELD, HUGH. *Victorian Pottery.* London, 1962.

WALLIS, HENRY. *Italian Ceramic Art: The Albarello, a Study in Early Renaissance Maiolica.* London, 1904.

————. *The Oriental Influence on the Ceramic Art of the Italian Renaissance.* London, 1900.

————. *Egyptian Ceramic Art.* London, 1900.

WARE, GEORGE WHITAKER. *German and Austrian Porcelain.* Frankfurt-on-Main, 1951.

WATNEY, BERNARD. *English Blue and White Porcelain of the Eighteenth Century.* London, 1963.

————. *Longton Hall Porcelain.* London, 1957.

WEDGWOOD, HENSLEIGH C., and GRAHAM, JOHN M. I. *Wedgwood: A Living Tradition.* New York: Brooklyn Museum, 1948.

WHITER, LEONARD. *Spode: A History of the Family, Factory and Wares, 1733–1833.* London, 1970.

American

ALTMAN, SEYMOUR, and ALTMAN, VIOLET. *The Book of Buffalo Pottery.* New York, 1969.

BARBER, EDWIN ATLEE. *The Pottery and Porcelain of the United States.* Third edition, New York, 1909.

————. *Tulip Ware of the Pennsylvania-German Potters.* Second edition, New York, 1926.

BARRET, RICHARD CARTER. *Bennington Pottery and Porcelain.* New York, 1958.

CRAWFORD, JEAN. *Jugtown Pottery.* Winston-Salem, 1964.

GREASER, ARLENE, and GREASER, PAUL H. *Homespun Ceramics.* Allentown, Pa., 1964.

HENZKE, LUCILE. *American Art Pottery.* Camden, New Jersey, 1970.

KETCHUM, WILLIAM C., JR. *Early Potters and Potteries of New York State.* New York, 1970.

PECK, HERBERT. *The Book of Rookwood Pottery.* New York, 1968.

RAMSAY, JOHN. *American Potters and Pottery.* Clinton, Mass., 1939.

SCHWARTZ, MARVIN D., and WOLFE, RICHARD. *American Art Porcelain.* New York, 1967.

SPARGO, JOHN. *Early American Pottery and China.* New York, 1926.

————. *Potters and Potteries of Bennington.* Boston, 1926.

WATKINS, LURA WOODSIDE. *Early New England Potters and Their Wares.* Cambridge, Mass., 1950.

Twentieth Century

BEARD, GEOFFREY. *Modern Ceramics.* New York, 1969.

BILLINGTON, DORA. *The Technique of Pottery.* London, 1962.

BIRKS, T. *The Art of the Modern Potter.* London, 1967.

CASSON, MICHAEL. *Pottery in Britain Today.* London, 1967.

DIGBY, GEORGE WINGFIELD. *The Work of the Modern Potter in England.* London, 1952.

FARE, MICHEL. *La céramique contemporaine.* Paris, 1954.

FORSYTH, GORDON MITCHELL. *Twentieth Century Ceramics.* London, 1936.

HETTES, K., and RADA, P. *Modern Ceramics.* London, 1965.

HIORT, ESBJORN. *Modern Danish Ceramics.* Translated by Eve M. Wendt. Copenhagen, 1955.

KLEIN, A. *Moderne Deutsche Keramik.* Darmstadt, 1956.

LAGERCRANTZ, BO. *Modern Swedish Ceramics.* Translated by Burnett Anderson. Stockholm, 1950.

PATAKY-BRESTYANSZKY, I. *Modern Hungarian Ceramics.* Translated by Lili Halápy. Budapest, 1961.

POOR, HENRY VARNUM. *A Book of Pottery: From Mud into Immortaity.* Englewood Cliffs, N.J., 1958.

ROSE, MURIEL. *Artist Potters in England.* London, 1955.

ROSENTHAL, ERNST. *Pottery and Ceramics: From Common Brick to Fine China.* London, 1949.

SAVAGE, GEORGE. *The American Birds of Dorothy Doughty.* Worcester: Royal Porcelain Company, 1965.

————. *The British Birds of Dorothy Doughty.* Worcester: Worcester Royal Porcelain Company, 1967.

VALOTAIRE, MARCEL. *La céramique Française moderne.* Paris, 1930.

VAL BAKER, DENYS. *Pottery Today.* London, 1961.

WILDENHAIN, MARGUERITE. *Pottery: Form and Expression.* New York, 1959.